A Companion to *Under the Volcano*

A COMPANION TO
UNDER THE VOLCANO

Chris Ackerley and Lawrence J. Clipper

UNIVERSITY OF BRITISH COLUMBIA PRESS
Vancouver
1984

A COMPANION TO *UNDER THE VOLCANO*

© The University of British Columbia Press 1984

This book has been published with the help of a grant from the
Canadian Federation for the Humanities, using funds provided by the
Social Sciences and Humanities Research Council of Canada.

Canadian Cataloguing in Publication Data

Ackerley, Christopher John, 1947–
  A companion to Under the volcano

Includes index.
Bibliography: p.
ISBN 0-7748-0199-9

1. Lowry, Malcolm, 1909–1957. Under the volcano.
I. Clipper, Lawrence J. (Lawrence Jon), 1930–
II. Title.
PS8523.097U53 1984   C813'.52   C84-091112-2
PR9199.3.L68U53 1984

International Standard Book Number 0-7748-0199-9
Printed and bound in Canada
by John Deyell Company

To Pat and Deirdre
No se puede vivir sin amar.

Cuenta la tradición que un paraiso
de ensueño y maravilla
era esta tierra muy remotos
magnifica entidad donde fulgura
la antorcha del civismo
asiento del trabajo que asegura
el amor, la esperanza y la fe pura:
tres virtudes que salvan del abismo.
— José Urbán Aguirre,
Canto al estado de Morelos

"But as Shelley says, the cold world shall not know."
— Malcolm Lowry,
Under the Volcano

Contents

Preface

As Malcolm Lowry was only too well aware, an uncanny force of coincidence seems at times to rule our universe: *les dieux existent, c'est le diable.* This book began as two independent studies, each author working in ignorance of the "other," and each submitting his manuscript to the same publisher in the same month. Collaboration seemed the only sensible course, and this study, combining the best features of both manuscripts, is the outcome. There were, naturally, differences of opinion and emphasis, but goodwill prevailed, and the act of working on a joint endeavour has, we feel, resulted in our immeasurably better understanding of Lowry's masterpiece.

A joint study was possible only because both authors shared certain basic suppositions about the novel we were working with and the mind of the author behind it. It may or may not be accidental that the word "lowrie" is described in the *OED* as a "fox," with the secondary sense of a crafty person. How suitable for a person who was often described as having a foxy look about the eyes and who, all agreed, seemed to come and go in a sly, foxy manner. One is reminded of Isaiah Berlin's distinction between the fox and the hedgehog: the hedgehog is the great thinker with a single large idea which he nourishes, explores, exhausts; the fox is the great man who scouts the terrain, is unsatisfied with the single idea but rather explores a multitude, hurrying from one to the other. Lowry is a fox: *Under the Volcano* is not a novel with one big idea, but a book which is constantly shifting its ground, one which continually evades its reader. We have not in this study tried to reduce its mulifarious complexities to a single statement, or monomyth, but rather to provide the necessary information to help the reader pursue his quarry as far as he can.

Our aim has been twofold: firstly, to offer the beginning reader of *Under the Volcano* a commentary, page by page and point by point, in which he may find readily at hand the information necessary to clarify the many difficulties which the text presents; secondly, to offer the more sophisticated reader of the novel a challenging and detailed consideration of those very difficulties. In principle, then, each note is written to present the relevant facts clearly and concisely, before moving on to consider their wider application.

The note format seemed most suitable for a number of reasons. It is, above all, convenient, for the numbering system (combining the Penguin and standard hardback editions of the text) allows immediate access to the details under consideration, while the Index and inbuilt crossreferences should facilitate further investigation. It also allows interesting details to be discussed at length, without necessarily imputing to them an undue significance in terms of the book as a whole; one should be able to study each tree without becoming lost in the dark wood. Finally, it reconciles the difficulty of writing for neophyte and magus simultaneously, for the beginner should be able to get the essential facts at once and leave the hidden mysteries until later, while the hierophant can deal with the preliminaries in a cursory manner and move quickly to more esoteric matters. The novel is written this way; Lowry was concerned that a very faithful surface realism should conceal greater depths, and it is a mark of his genius that the book should cohere so well on so many levels.

Perhaps the greatest problem in writing these notes was knowing where to stop, for with a writer as introspective and discursive as Lowry there is no end to what may be brought out of the bottomless bag of allusions. This study offers some 1,700 notes in all, ranging from a few words to several pages in length, and covering (at a rough estimate) some five to six thousand separate points. There are a number of details that leave us still baffled, and we are morally certain (Lowry being so derivative a writer) that not all his obscure sources have yet been tracked down. Nevertheless, the major points have been noted in detail, and much that is new has emerged.

The philosophy behind our approach is largely that expressed in E. D. Hirsch's *Validity in Interpretation,* particularly as summed up in his statement that "each interpretative problem requires its own distinct context of relevant knowledge." We have no particular thesis to push, but broadly speaking (not wishing to become bogged down in metaphysical and metafictional complexities), we accept Hirsch's contention that validity in interpretation is a possible and desirable objective and that "meaning" is to be equated with the author's probable intention. Only occasionally has the "distinct context of relevant knowledge" been extended to include things obviously beyond Lowry's ken. A number of times, however, we present in detail the context of something that Lowry refers to only obliquely (and which in some instances he did not know, or has got wrong); any allusion or reference of necessity implies a context, and Lowry's intention must be measured against or in relation to such "relevant knowledge." And occasionally (like Lowry) we have been unable to resist including the odd *mot* which, strictly speaking, is not quite *juste* (the reference to Gerald Hanley's *The Consul at Sunset,* note **167.1,** is an example). In each instance, however, the guiding principle has been what Northrop Frye has called in his *Anatomy of Criticism* "a sense of tact": that of not imputing to the text at any point greater significance than it warrants and ensuring that the weight of criticism is roughly in proportion to what the text will bear.

We have tried to acknowledge, wherever possible, debts to other writers on Lowry, and like all who build on what has gone before are faced with the insoluble difficulty of distinguishing where our debt to others ends and our own contribution begins. There are many references in *Under the Volcano* to what may broadly be called the Common Heritage, and in such instances we have not felt it necessary to acknowledge other writers simply because they drank at the fountain first. There are also many aspects of Lowry's own writing which are common knowledge to all Lowry enthusiasts, and, again, even though certain critics have made some areas their own (Kilgallin on *Faust,* for instance), it would be pointlessly pedantic to cite every previous reference in Lowry criticism; one has only to read, for instance, Gladys Andersen's unpublished thesis to realize how many of the later published "discoveries" had already been anticipated in her early study. But whenever we have genuinely derived new insight from a particular writer or felt that an original point was clearly first established by him or her, we have endeavoured to acknowledge this scrupulously. The studies by Andersen, Day, Kilgallin, and Jakobsen have proved invaluable to our purposes, genuinely breaking new ground, while, to a lesser degree, those by Edmonds, Bradbrook, Cross, and Markson have proved useful for isolated details (despite an apparent similarity of intention, Markson's study and our own differ so radically at every point that one can almost believe in a doctrine of opposites). There will inevitably be times when our judgment and that of others will have overlapped, and there will be moments when we triumphantly proclaim as our own what others have thought of before; for these we can only apologize and hope that the rest of our study demonstrates our good faith.

Acknowledgments

We should like to acknowledge the assistance of many people throughout the world who have helped to make this work possible:

In New Zealand: the University of Otago and members of the Department of English, for having made possible a year of study leave and travel; Alan Horsman, for his quiet but consistent encouragement; Anaig Fenby and Penny Love for their assistance; Paul Armfelt for his map of Morelos.

In Canada: The University of British Columbia Special Collection of Lowry manuscripts and materials; Anne Yandle, Sherrill Grace, and Bill New, for their particular help; Robin Ramsey, for his generous hospitality.

In Mexico: Helen-Gate Cook of Tlaxcala, for some invaluable details; Frank Estano, for his many memories of Cuernavaca in the 1930's — gracias, buen amigo; "los amigos," Josef and Manuel, in Oaxaca, who offered an introduction to mescal and left the reckoning; to the lovely old lady in Guanajuato who knew about the names of the streets. But perhaps only mixed thanks to the Janitor Pansophus of *El Universal,* who allowed access to the English pages of 1937, but objected to 1938.

In South Bend: Donna Harlan, librarian at Indiana University in South Bend, and her staff, particularly Kathy Whitman and Beth Kenagy, for their patient and sometimes inspired help; D. Dean Willard and students in his library course. Lester M. Wolfson, chancellor, and members of his administration and faculty committees, who gave continued generous support in the form of sabbaticals and research grants; numerous faculty who assisted with specific information in their fields of expertise, particularly Ernie Brandewie, Rogelio de la Torre, David Barton, J. T. Chowattukunnel, Charles Harrington, Glenn Chesnut, and James Blodgett; to Alphonse Aguirre, who helped to untangle much of the Spanish and Mexican backgrounds. And to members of the staff who assisted with the preparation of manuscript — Lori Allriedge, Marie Fields, and Edith Petrie.

In Bloomington: Larry Furtado and his Interlibrary staff at the Main Library, and the administration and trustees of Indiana University for their distant but important support.

In England: Susan and Nigel Hooton, for their warm hospitality (and many trifles); David Carroll and the Department of English Literature at Lancaster University, for their generous provision of library and office facilities (with special thanks to Maureen Jex for her assistance); Deirdre Anstey, for her valuable insights into the novel and her invaluable hours at the typewriter (including the flaming sword at the gates of Eden to *warm* the profane, and the Strange Type which turned "Lowry could not resist the pun" into "Lowry could not resist the pub"). A special debt is owed to the university libraries and staff at Lancaster, Leeds, Manchester, and Cambridge; the Chester City Library; the library of the Foreign Office; the Victoria and Albert Museum; the Imperial War Museum. And, above all, that monument to civilization, the British Museum.

Finally, to all those individuals in Mexico, North America, New Zealand, and Great Britain who took the time and trouble to find out the answers to many questions that bedevilled us: Al Gleason (Toronto); Muriel Bradbrook (Cambridge); John O. West (University of Texas at El Paso); Russell Lowry; Stephen Rabson (*P & O*); Sir Peter Swinnerton-Dyer (St. Catharine's); Austin Whitaker (Winchester Archives); Mrs. Mae Heath (Oakville); Linda Wood (B.F. I); Mr. Thorne (*cartero* of Chagford); Mr. B. T. Bellis, Headmaster of The Leys School; Mr. Owen (Liverpool Mercantile Marine).

And to the many others who took the time to answer sometimes strange enquiries: without them, this study would be that much the less.

Note on the Text

References to *Under the Volcano* are tailored to both the Penguin edition and the standard hardback editions (Lippincott and Cape), available in both the U.S.A. and England. The references also match the first Reynal & Hitchcock U.S. edition and the Signet Plume paperback (the 1947 Cape edition had a different pagination). The figures given first refer to the Penguin volume; those in square brackets to the hardback editions. Where discrepancies exist in the citation of the text, preference has been given to the correct version of the text, usually the Reynal & Hitchcock edition (which Lowry proofread), and only the most significant mistakes in other editions have been pointed out. Crossreferences and Index listings are given in terms of the Penguin pagination, but since their prime purpose is to refer to our notes rather than the actual pages, difficulties should be minimal.

Introduction

I.1 [2] *Wonders are many, and none is more wonderful than man. . . . only against Death shall he call for aid in vain; but from baffling maladies he hath devised escape.* From *Antigone,* by the Attic tragedian Sophocles (496?–406 B.C.), in the translation of Sir Richard Jebb, C.U.P., 1900 (Jakobsen, p. 57). Antigone, daughter of Oedipus and Jocasta, disobeys the explicit orders of King Creon and buries the body of her brother Polyneices. Condemned for this to be buried alive, she takes her own life before Creon can change his mind. Lowry cites, with minor inaccuracies, ll. 332–61, the second long speech of the Chorus, immediately after the forbidden burial has been discovered. The words evoke not only the tragic inevitability of the Consul's death (like Polyneices he is to remain unburied, "dinner for birds and dogs"), but also the sense of wonder and loss felt at the destruction of such a piece of work as man.

I.2 [2] *Now I blessed the condition of the dog and toad. . . . that I could not find with all my soul that I did desire deliverance.* From *Grace Abounding to the Chief of Sinners, or a brief Relation of the exceeding Mercy of God in Christ, to his poor Servant, John Bunyan* (1666); a spiritual autobiography and homiletic narrative by John Bunyan (1628–88), relating his gradual awakening to religion. Lowry quotes from #104 of *Grace Abounding,* minor inaccuracies arising because his direct source is not Bunyan but William James, *The Varieties of Religious Experience,* p. 155, in a chapter appropriately entitled "The Sick Soul" (Lowry's copy of James has this precise quotation marked off in pencil). The passage, reflecting Bunyan's worst moments of doubt and torment, anticipates Lowry's recurring images of dog and horse and neatly sums up the Consul's Faustian dilemma: his inability to even desire the salvation offered to him.

I.3 [2] *Wer immer strebend sich bemüht. . . . him can we save.* From *Faust 2,* by Johann Wolfgang von Goethe (1749–1832). *Faust,* a dramatic poem in two parts (the first published in 1808, the second in 1832), deals with the attempt by Mephistopheles to effect the ruination of Faust's soul. Disillusioned by the world and philosophy, Faust enters into a compact with Mephistopheles to become the latter's servant should he ever admit to being satisfied, and Part I concerns the attempts to satisfy Faust, culminating in the seduction of Margarete, her death, and her salvation. Part II is complex and obscurely symbolic. The first portion concerns Faust's ardent pursuit of Helen of Troy and her final separation from him; the second portion shows the purified Faust pursuing the service of man and, with the aid of Mephistopheles, reclaiming from the sea a stretch of submerged land. Finally, conscious of good work done, the now blind Faust calls upon the fleeting moment to stay and falls down dead. Hell tries to seize his soul, but angels bear it away. These lines, 2.11936–37, uttered by an angel bearing the immortal part of Faust upwards, epitomize the striving associated with the Faustian figures created by Goethe and Marlowe and imply that Lowry's Consul is not unworthy of their company. Lowry mentions "the battering the human spirit takes (doubtless because it is overreaching itself) in its ascent towards its true purpose" ("LJC," p. 63) and suggests that there is "a hint of redemption for the poor old Consul at the end, who realizes that he is after all part of humanity" ("LJC," p. 85).

CHAPTER ONE

9.1 [3] *Two mountain chains traverse the republic.* The Sierra Madre Occidental and the Sierra Madre Oriental (the mother ranges of the west and east) run north to south in Mexico, coming closer near Mexico City to cradle between them the altiplano, or high central tableland, which is traversed by deep barrancas, or ravines, and surrounded by the highest peaks in the country, forming a formidable barrier between the coastal plains and the interior. Lowry's opening paragraph is strikingly similar to that of Domingo Díez, whose *Summa Morelense* (1934?) is a popular account of the history and geography of the state of Morelos. But as William Gass points out (*F & FL,* p. 57): "Lowry is constructing a place, not describing one; he is making a Mexico for the mind where, strictly speaking, there are no menacing volcanoes, only menacing phrases, where complex chains of concepts traverse our consciousness." The distinctive quality of Lowry's description, as many of the following notes will reveal, is his use of the physical details of landscape in such a way as to bring out their symbolic implications.

9.2 [3] *Quauhnahuac.* The Nahuatl or Tlahuican name for present-day Cuernavaca; the Indian word meaning, as Yvonne reflects, p. 49 [44], "near the wood" (from Nah. *cuáhuitl,* "a tree"). Unable to pronounce the Nahuatl name correctly, the Spaniards hispanicized it to Cuernavaca, or "Cow's horn" (see note **64.3**). A favourite summering place for the Aztec nobility and celebrated for its beautiful gardens, it became a favoured retreat of Hernán Cortés, as it was later to be for Maximilian and Carlota (see notes **16.10** and **18.3**). The state capital of Morelos, some fifty miles south of Mexico City, Cuernavaca is usually described by guide books as the attractive resort town it must have been in Lowry's time, but "the city of eternal spring" is now a bustling, dirty, and polluted city of almost half a million, in which, however, many of the important features of *UTV* may still be discerned: although much of his terrain is either imaginative or based on "Oaxaca and sus anexas" (*DATG,* p. 121), Lowry has by and large maintained a strict observance of actual place and distance.

In his autobiographical *Dark as the Grave wherein My Friend Is Laid,* Lowry identified Cuernavaca as the town of his novel. He lived there with his first wife Jan from December 1936 to December 1937 and visited it again with his second wife Margerie, in December 1945.

9.3 [3]   *the Tropic of Cancer.* An imaginary line around the earth, 23°28′ north of the equator (about 4° 30′ north of Cuernavaca). It is called a "Tropic" because it marks a "turning" and is the northernmost point of the sun's apparent movement in the sky; the detail anticipates the later allusion to the poor foundered soul "who once fled north" (p. 331 [331]). There may also be an allusion to Henry Miller's *Tropic of Cancer* (1934), which portrays modern society as being corrupted by various spiritual and physical malignancies. Cancer is also the fourth sign of the Zodiac, and the sign is sometimes interpreted as signifying the joining together of the male and female fertility powers, one of the main themes of the novel.

9.4 [3]   *the Revillagigedo Islands... Hawaii... Tzucox... Juggernaut.* The Revillagigedo Islands and Tzucox represent the western and eastern extremities of Mexico on the nineteenth parallel of latitude; the references to Hawaii and India anticipate respectively the childhood years of Yvonne and Geoffrey:
(a)   *the Revillagigedo Islands.* An archipelago of volcanic origin in the Pacific, some 500 miles from the Mexican coast, forming part of the state of Colima. They comprise the large island Socorro (San Tomás) and the three islets of San Benedicto, Roca Partida, and Clarión: the total area, 320 square miles. The islands were named after Francisco de Güemes y Horcasitas, subsequently Count Revillagigedo, viceroy of Mexico, 1746–55.
(b)   *the southernmost tip of Hawaii.* Ka Lae (or South Cape), latitude 18° 58′ N. It is near the town of Hilo, where Yvonne grew up.
(c)   *Tzucox.* This town is not to be found on any regular maps of Mexico (the town of Tzucacab is inland), but the name is genuinely Mayan, and the location near the nineteenth parallel and Atlantic seaboard of Yucatán, near the British Honduran border, fits Chetumal, the major town and port of that area. Hugh reflects, p. 107 [103], that his ship will head for Tzucox after it leaves Vera Cruz.
(d)   *Juggernaut.* From Skr. *Jagannātha,* "Lord of the World"; a title of Krishna, the eighth avatar or incarnation of the Hindu god Vishnu, whose idol is kept at Purī, in the state of Orissa on the Bay of Bengal. The idol is said to have so excited worshippers when hauled along on a large car during religious processions that they would throw themselves beneath the wheels and be crushed; hence the sense of the word in English as anything that requires blind devotion or total sacrifice or of a blind implacable force that crushes everything in its way. The name

anticipates the relentless blind destiny which will crush Geoffrey Firmin (and those in his way) or, alternatively, implies his determination to be so crushed.

9.5 [3] *the walls of the town...a hill....a goat track....eighteen churches...fifty-seven cantinas....four hundred swimming-pools.* These details anticipate important thematic concerns, some having a significance not readily apparent:

(a) *the walls of the town.* The walls of Cuernavaca in 1939 were not particularly obvious, but Lowry seems to be implying that his City of Eternal Spring is a *type* of the *hortus conclusus,* or walled Garden of Paradise, from which the Consul, like Adam, will be evicted.

(b) *built on a hill.* Though it slopes considerably north to south, Cuernavaca is not obviously "built on a hill"; the detail suggests "the city that is set on an hill" (Matthew 5:14), and anticipates the University City theme, both the Consul's ideal city in the snow, p. 72 [67], and Hugh's grimly realistic battle of the Spanish Civil War, p. 105 [101].

(c) *a goat track.* In fact, the Mexico City to Acapulco highway through Cuernavaca had been opened in 1927; local geography has again been shaped to the book's needs (see note **238.1**). Lowry comments (*SL,* p. 198) that Quauhnahuac's goat track has many meanings, among them suggestions of tragedy and cuckoldry (see note **70.1**). The fine American-style highway that loses itself in tortuous broken streets and comes out a goat track is emblematic of the Consul's promising beginnings, his increasing confusion in the byways of the Cabbala, and the tragedy of his personal life.

(d) *18 churches.* 1 + 8 = 9, a number which would not be of special significance had not Lowry changed, on p. 17 [11] his original, *366* churches (UBC 7-2, p. 9) to *306* (3 + 6 = 9), for esoteric reasons only partially clarified by Aleister Crowley's *The Sword of Song,* p. 10: "TRINITY OF TRIADS with MALKUTH pendant to them, manifesting their influence in the Material Universe" (that is, Nine is the number of Sephiroth, or emanations from the godhead, on the Cabbalistic tree of life above Malkuth, the kingdom or material universe).

(e) *57 cantinas.* 5 + 7 = 12, the number of chapters in the novel, but the number 57 is also a remnant of a cross-reference deleted from the final version: in the short story version (UBC 7-1, p. 19), the Consul was going to drown his remorse by having "fifty-seven drinks at the earliest opportunity." There is also the invincible Tomás Aguero (Sp. "omen of drink"?), who weighs 57 kilos and appears (by coincidence) on p. 57. In 1939, 57 would be an everyday reminder of the 57 varieties of Heinz, and Lowry undoubtedly intended a private allusion to Aiken's *Blue*

Voyage, p. 91, where this is cited in the context of one who is a dabbler in black arts and all known perversions: "the fifty-seven varieties were child's play to me."

(f) *four hundred swimming-pools.* The oppressive heat of Mexico and the undrinkable nature of Cuernavaca's water makes *thirst* a very real issue indeed. Throughout *UTV* swimming pools and fountains are associated with the slaking of thirst ("Might a soul bathe there," p. 84 [80]), and as Lowry would have known from Lewis Spence, the number 400, in the phrase "four hundred rabbits," was among the Aztecs a figure of total drunkenness, an offence punishable by death (see note **338.3**).

9.6 [3] *The Hotel Casino de la Selva.* In Cuernavaca today, an up-to-date 300-room hotel-restaurant, no longer near the wood and with no hint of the "desolate splendour" evoked here. Lowry points out ("LJC," p. 67) that "Selva means wood and this strikes the opening chord of the *Inferno*." His reference is to the first part of *The Divine Comedy* by Dante Alighieri (1265–1321). Dante's poem, comprising the *Inferno, Purgatorio,* and *Paradiso,* describes the journey taken by the poet through these regions, culminating with his vision of the eternal. The *Inferno* is Dante's description of hell, conceived as successive circles to which various categories of sinners are consigned and through which Dante is guided by Virgil. It begins:

> Nel mezzo del camin di nostra vita
> mi ritrovai per una selva oscura,
> che la diritta via era smarrita.

("In the middle of the road of our life / I found myself in a dark wood, / for the right way was lost.")

Lowry envisaged *UTV* as part of a greater whole, *The Voyage That Never Ends,* a kind of drunken *Divine Comedy* in which this novel was to be equivalent to the *Inferno.* His plan did not materialize, but the general analogies with the *Inferno* are important ("I am telling you something new about hell fire," "LJC," p. 80), and Lowry himself points out ("LJC," p. 67) the echoes here of the opening words of Ch. 6, the end of Ch. 7 (*El Bosque*), and the dark wood of Ch. 11.

9.7 [4] *jai-alai.* From the Basque words meaning "merry festival." A game like pelota, played with a hard rubber ball on a court called a frontón, comprising a back wall, a long sidewall, and a front wall of hard granite. The players, using a cesta (a crescent-shaped wicker basket attached to the arm to aid catching and throwing), try to win points by throwing the ball against the front wall (using the other walls if they wish) for an opponent to catch and return in one continuous motion; points being won when the opponent fails to return the ball. The side first reaching thirty is the winner.

9.8 [4] *the Day of the Dead.* In Mexico the Day of the Dead, "el Día de los Difuntos," is, strictly speaking, All Souls Day, 2 November, but because graveside vigils commonly begin the night before, the festival is usually considered to include 1 November, All Saints Day, "el Día de Todos los Santos." The Day of the Dead is the day on which the souls of those dead may communicate with the living. The coincidence of an Aztec festival of offerings to the spirits of the dead with the Roman Catholic All Souls Day, on which those living may communicate with and pray for the souls of those in purgatory, gave rise to a colourful festival. In Morelos and other parts of Mexico the day is celebrated by candle-lit processions and all-night vigils at cemeteries, offerings of food and flowers for the departed ones, parades and dances with death-masks and skeletons and skulls, and ingeniously wrought chocolate and candy animals, skulls, skeletons, and funeral wagons. The Day of the Dead is obviously appropriate for Lowry's purposes: not only is it the day in 1939 that Laruelle and Vigil remember the Consul, but it is also the day in 1938 that Yvonne, symbolically dead, came back for one day. However, as Edmonds has noted, p. 98, there are problems in Lowry's chronology, since 2 November 1938 fell upon a Wednesday, whereas the action of the novel is almost certainly set upon a Sunday. Lowry seems to have assumed that 1 November was in fact the Day of the Dead (Day, p. 214), and 1 November 1936, the date Lowry claimed to have arrived in Mexico, was a Sunday. The action of the novel was originally set in 1936, and in revising the novel Lowry seems to have overlooked the discrepancy. Nevertheless, the combination of the sunset, the Day of the Dead, and 1939 creates from the outset the atmosphere of a world about to plunge into darkness.

10.1 [4] *anís.* More properly, Sp. *anisado* or Fr. *anisette,* a clear licorice-flavoured liquor made by passing vapourized alcohol through a receptacle containing the seeds of the anís plant. "Anís del Mono" (Sp. "anis of the monkey") is made in Barcelona, by Vincente Bosch & Co., but neither the green (dry) nor the red (sweet) variety has a label showing a florid demon brandishing a pitchfork. The trademark of Anís del Mono since 1870 has been a diabolical greenish-brown monkey holding up a bottle in one hand and clasping in the other a scroll on which is written, "Es el mejor, la ciencia lo dijo, y yo no miento" ("It is the best, science says so, and I do not lie"). Lowry has changed the label, also seen by the Consul in the Farolito, p. 338 [338], to underline from the outset the relationship of drinking and damnation.

10.2 [4]   *the doctor's triangular, the other's quadrangular.* A typically unobtrusive instance of the number seven, reflecting the mystical union of the
triad with the tetrad. Lowry would have read in Frater Achad's *The Anatomy of the Body of God* (1925), p. 4, that this conjunction represents "a
perfectly proportioned Figure of the Tree of Life" (see note **198.1**).

10.3 [4]   *plangent.* Sad and melancholy (one of Lowry's favourite words).

10.4 [4]   *Dr Arturo Díaz Vigil.* The doctor's surname not only suggests
Virgil, Dante's guide through hell in the *Inferno,* but also echoes Walt
Whitman's "Vigil Strange I Kept on the Field One Night," in which the poet
keeps "vigil wondrous" over the body of a dead comrade. Kilgallin comments, p. 147: "The poem's narrator recounts how he cared for and buried
his comrade, just as Vigil does in the novel's opening pages...Doctor,
Laruelle and reader alike keep vigil for the remainder of the book's dark
night of the soul." Vigil's curiously attractive English is based on that of
Lowry's Zapotecan friend, Juan Fernando Márquez, who also served as the
model of Juan Cerillo (see note **109.5**); Lowry was unaware at the time of
writing that his friend had died.

10.5 [4]   *M. Jacques Laruelle.* A *ruelle* is a small street or lane, but also, in
the bedrooms of the French monarchs of the Golden Age, the narrow area
between the royal bed and wall, in which "attendant lords and ladies kept
all-night vigil over their sleeping monarchs" (Kilgallin, p. 147) and into
which the royal mistresses might be introduced. Strong sexual connotations
of the word are also present in Baudelaire's "Tu mettrais l'univers entier
dans ta ruelle / Femme impure!" ("You would put the entire universe into
your alley, / impure woman"—*Les Fleurs du Mal,* XXV). Lowry's short
story, "Hotel Room in Chartres," mentions the "Ruelle de la Demi-Lune"
and the "Café Jacques Restaurant Bar du Cinéma" (*P & S,* p. 20); a further
hint of the cuckold's horn, despite the happy ending of the story. Laruelle,
p. 18 [12], associates his "passion for Yvonne" with the sight of Chartres
Cathedral. Given the circular structure of *Under the Volcano* and its *de
casibus* theme, Laruelle's surname may evoke *La Roue,* the Wheel of Fortune (Kilgallin, p. 156), while his Christian name may hint at his better-
known compatriot, Jean-Jacques Rousseau (see note **312.10**), whose sexual
mores were no better than they should have been.

10.6 [4]   *the gigantic red evening...bled away in the deserted swimming
pools.* The sunset not only is identical to the "mercurochrome agony," p.
340 [339], of the evening that the Consul's life bleeds away, but it also suggests other aspects of his death: the "unbandaging of great giants in agony,"

p. 41 [35]; the apparition of the dead man beside the pool, p. 96 [91]; and the agony of Faustus, who sees Christ's blood stream in the firmament (see note **70.6**).

10.7 [4] *tintinnabulation.* An echo of Edgar Allan Poe's "The Bells," l. 11: "the tintinnabulation that so musically wells"; probably by way of Conrad Aiken, who used it often (as in "the tintinnabulation of the toads" — *Blue Voyage* p. 91). Hugh and Yvonne hear, p. 324 [324], "a ghostly tintinnabulation" like the sound of windbells.

10.8 [4] *the bangs and cries.* In a letter to Albert Erskine, Lowry claimed to have lifted this phrase "from a rather stupid story by J. C. Squire, chiefly about duck shooting, though also in relation to a fair" (*SL,* p. 115). The reference is to J. C. Squire's "The Alibi," in his collection of short stories *Outside Eden,* p. 180, shortly before Sir Richard Moorhouse discovers the body of his shooting companion, Henry Henderson: "A small foreboding gust of wind came over moor and marsh, and rattled the leaves of the forlorn trees on the high ridge behind him. It carried a sound with it, a dim sort of brazen music, faint bangs and cries. It was the fair."

10.9 [4] *the fiesta.* "Fiesta" was the proposed title of the first sequence (after the prologue) of Eisenstein's ill-fated *Que Viva Mexico!,* set in part on the Day of the Dead (see notes **57.2** and **77.1**). "Fiesta" tells how Boronito the picador steals from a bullfight to keep a clandestine rendezvous and is almost killed by a jealous husband. There may also be an echo of Ernest Hemingway's *Fiesta* (1927), a tale of tangled passions set against the background of the festival of San Fermin in Pamplona.

10.10 [4] *absinthe.* Another licorice-flavoured liquor, but derived from wormwood and other berries, and with a much higher alcoholic content than anís. It is often used, in Zola's novels and elsewhere, as a sign of physical and moral degeneration.

10.11 [4] *déalcoholisé.* Dealcoholized; that is, have his body cleansed of alcohol. The process of detoxification, sometimes called "drying out," is a long and painful one in which the system is gradually purified of its accumulation of alcohol. One technique is to have the patient drink a vomitive, which acts in such a way as to nauseate him whenever he subsequently drinks alcohol.

10.12 [4] *we doctors must comport ourselves like apostles.* An anticipation of Vigil's words, p. 142 [138]; "I must comport myself here like. . .like an apostle." Such anticipations abound in the opening chapter, forming a kind of overture to the following action, the consistency of thought and expression showing how closely the present for these men is tied up with the events of a year ago. Other such echoes are: "We played tennis that day," p. 238 [235]; "I lookèd the Consul in his garden" (ch. 5); and "when you telephoned, Arturo," p. 209 [206].

11.1 [5] *perfectamente borracho.* Sp. "totally drunk."

11.2 [5] *Sickness is not only in body, but in that part used to be call: soul. . . . Poor your friend, he spend his money on earth in such continuous tragedies.* Throughout *Dark as the Grave* (e.g., p. 141), these and similar sentiments are expressed by Sigbjørn's Zapotecan friend, Juan Fernando Martínez, whose real-life counterpart, Juan Fernando Márquez, gave Lowry the many picturesque phrases which characterize the speech of Dr. Vigil.

11.3 [5] *bastions.* Not a technical term used in jai-alai, but simply Lowry's figurative word for the three walls which constitute the jai-alai court.

11.4 [5] *the fountain. . . where a cactus farmer had reined up his horse to drink.* Cacti may be farmed for various reasons. Some are turned into tequila, mescal, or pulque; some, such as the prickly pear and the chollas, are cultivated for food; others are used in the preparation of medicinal drinks. Even the most innocent features of the surroundings reflect Geoffrey's tragedy: here, the opposition of fountain and cactus serves as a reminder of the Consul's constant thirst.

11.5 [5] *the horrors of the present would have swallowed it up like a drop of water.* Kilgallin suggests ("Faust," p. 27) that Geoffrey is here identified with Marlowe's Faustus through a related image. Right on the point of death, sc. xiv, Faustus pleads:

> O soul, be changed into little water-drops,
> And fall into the ocean, ne'er be found.
> My God! my God! look not so fierce on me!

Lowry's direct debt, however, appears to be to Rosa E. King, whose *Tempest Over Mexico,* p. 10, describes her feelings as she looks out over the Mexican volcanoes: "Looking that morning on those high and tragic peaks, a feeling of the great spans in which time was measured here came over me, and my own troubles seemed like a drop of water falling in the vastness of space."

11.6 [5] *the days when an individual life held some value. . . . He lit a cigarette.* The first of many examples in which the value of human life is equated with that of a cigarette (see note **52.4**).

11.7 [5] *the two volcanoes, Popocatepetl and Ixtaccihuatl.* Snow-capped volcanoes on the border of Puebla and Mexico states (Popocatepetl also bordering upon Morelos); respectively, the second and third highest peaks in Mexico and dominating the Valley of Mexico "like two colossal sentinels to guard the entrance to the enchanted region" (Prescott, III.vi, p. 264). Popocatepetl (from Nah. *popoca,* "that which smokes," and *tepetl,* "mountain"; hence "smoking mountain"), 17,887 feet, is still active; Ixtaccihuatl (from Nah. *iztac,* "white," and *cihuatl,* "woman"; hence "white woman"), 17,342 feet, is dead. Popocatepetl is the novel's dominating symbol, its snowy peak and burning heart epitomizing both man's aspiring and destructive capacities. At the moment of his death, the Consul imagines himself to be climbing towards its snows only to be tipped into the fiery furnace. Lowry had originally intended his volcanoes to be like Dante's Mount Purgatory (in early drafts the Consul calls them "Beatrice" and "Dante" respectively), but no direct traces of this crude parallelism remain. For a description of the tragic legend associated with the two volcanoes, see note **318.6:** the eternal vigilance of the princely Popocatepetl over the sleeping Ixtaccihuatl is here reflected in Laruelle's vigil over the dead Consul.

11.8 [5] *illegal smoke.* Possibly a sign of an illegal still. Carbon would be useful as a filter through which the crude mescal or tequila is passed in order to remove impurities. In order to obtain the carbon, wood would have to be burned, the resulting smoke serving as a tell-tale indication of an illegal liquor operation in the area.

11.9 [5] *river.* The Amacuzac River, a branch of the Río de las Balsas, which angles north towards Cuernavaca.

11.10 [5] *a prison.* The Penitenciaria del Gobierno del Estado, Atlacomulco. The official prison of the state of Morelos; it was built in 1934 on the outskirts of Cuernavaca, but as the city has expanded, its suburbs have come to engulf the penitentiary. There is a tower at each of the four corners, but that mentioned here is probably the central tower which overlooks the whole enclosed prison yard.

11.11 [6] *a Doré Paradise.* Paul Gustave Doré (1832–83), French illustrator, sculptor, and painter, whose works include a number of striking etchings of Dante's *Divine Comedy,* among them scenes from the *Paradiso* remarkable for their detailed effects of light and shade.

11.12 [6]   *No se puede vivir sin amar.* Sp. "One cannot live without loving" (not "without love"; the distinction is crucial). It is implied that the Consul, having discovered Yvonne's affair with Laruelle, painted these words in gold leaf and large letters on the wall of Laruelle's house (for the origin of the phrase, see note **199.2**). The words constantly remind Laruelle of his complicity in the Consul's death, but also epitomize Geoffrey Firmin's tragic inability to accept the love and salvation apparently offered by Yvonne.

12.1 [6]   *throw away your mind.* The philosophy of *La Vida Impersonal* (see note **17.6**). Vigil's advice to Laruelle is similar to that given by Sra. Gregorio to the Consul, pp. 230–31 [227]: "If your mind is occupied with all things, then you never lose your mind." Laruelle, like Geoffrey, is too much preoccupied with his own great battle and the uniqueness of his misery.

12.2 [6]   *Tehuacan mineral water.* Tehuacán, in the southeast of Puebla State, is renowned for its hot springs and mineral spas and has been since 1575 the town where most of the mineral water ("Agua mineral Peñafiel de Tehuacán") bottled in Mexico originates. The Consul tells Mr. Quincey, p. 136 [133], that he scarcely touched anything more than Tehuacan water the night before.

12.3 [6]   *Salud y pesetas.... Y tiempo para gastarlas.* Sp. "Health and wealth.... And time to enjoy them"; a conventional salutation, the irony being that Laruelle and Vigil do have the time (unlike Hugh and Yvonne, p. 328 [328], who use the same words). Edmonds argues, p. 94, that the omission of a third salutation "y amor" ("and love") is "of major significance." The toast "Health and wealth" is also used in Ben Jonson's *The Case Is Altered,* II.iii.54.

12.4 [6]   *Tehuantepec (that ideal spot where the women did the work).* Tehuantepec is the name of an area, town, and river in the southeast of Oaxaca state. Lowry may be being facetious, since the women of Tehuantepec are said to be the most beautiful in Mexico and the men the most henpecked (Fodor, p. 505). Lowry would have known of its reputation as a traditional matriarchy from Eisenstein's *The Film Sense,* p. 198: "Like the queen-bee, the mother rules in Tehuantepec. The female tribal system has been miraculously preserved here for hundreds of years till our time.... Activity is on the side of the woman in Tehuantepec." However, Lowry may be referring to a different tradition. In his *Mexico South* (1966), Miguel Covarrubias states:

Because superficial observers have noted that only women can be seen in the villages during the day, moving about and performing work at home in the market, they have failed to realize that the men have been out in the fields since sunrise and will not return until tired from a long day's work in the ferocious heat, with a desire to lounge and rest until supper time. . . . Each sex has clearly defined tasks to perform; the men engage in all agricultural work, the clearing of brush, the building and repairing of houses, of irrigation works and roads, the tending of cattle and horses, fishes, hunting, weaving on vertical looms, playing musical instruments, making salt, brown sugar, and fireworks. They work in wood, leather, iron, gold, silver, and so forth.

The author also explains that the people of Tehuantepec are fastidious about cleanliness and that "its picturesque river [is] filled at all hours of the day with nude bathers who splashed unselfconsciously in the brown waters." One may thus imagine how the legend arose.

12.5 [6] *the Virgin for those that have nobody with.* The Consul had gone to the church with Vigil (and the latter's revolver) on the night of the Red Cross ball, one year and a day ago, to pray for Yvonne's return, see p. 290 [289]. The Iglesia de la Soledad, the Church of the Solitary, has been transposed to Quauhnahuac from Oaxaca; Lowry's favourite church, it figures significantly in *DATG* as the place where Sigbjørn at last finds the peace and understanding which has eluded him (and, by implication, the Consul). Graham Greene captures its feeling perfectly (*The Lawless Roads,* pp. 252–53):

But the most human church to my mind in Oaxaca, unweighted with magnificence, is La Soledad; standing on a little terraced plaza, it contains perhaps the second holiest image in Mexico — that of the Virgin of Soledad (the Lonely), who appeared miraculously. She is the patroness of the state of Oaxaca and of all sailors; the size of a large doll, in a crown and elaborate robes, with a flower in her hand, she stands on the altar above the Host. She is Spanish of the Spanish, a Velasquez Virgin — and the loneliness she solaced, one imagines, was a Spanish loneliness of men heartsick for Castile.

12.6 [7] *and all the dogs to shark.* This, the hour of Geoffrey's death, is linked to Hugh's comment, p. 305 [304], about a Russian film he once saw in which a shark was netted with a shoal of other fish and killed. Hugh's point is that the shark, although dead, continued to swallow other living fish; the unspoken implication here is that those living are still entangled with the Consul's death. In *DATG,* p. 222, Sigbjørn at sunset recalls his friend Juan Fernando Martínez having said the same words.

13.1 [7] *Tomalín Zócalo.* The destination of the bus is the Zócalo, or central plaza, of Tomalín, that fictional town near Popocatepetl where the Consul, Yvonne, and Hugh go to the bull-throwing (the name was taken from the village of Tomellin in the north of Oaxaca, not far from Parián; there is also a Tomalín bar in the Hotel Casino de la Selva). The word *zócalo,* meaning "base" or "foundation" (as of a statue), was applied to an unfinished statue in the main square of Mexico City, La Plaza de la Constitución, then to the plaza itself, and thence to almost every town and village in Mexico. A zócalo is typically a paved central plaza with trees, benches, kiosks, and a bandstand. Yvonne says of the Tomalín bus, p. 119 [115], "It's the easiest way to get to Parián," and, like the stormy sky, the vultures, and the word "downhill," the bus serves as a reminder of the fatal journey taken one year ago (an early draft, UBC 10–2, p. 29, had Laruelle explicitly reflecting, "They must have taken that very bus").

14.1 [8] *Parián.* A fictional town, based upon a village of that name in Oaxaca state and possessing many attributes of the town of Oaxaca itself; the scene of the Consul's death in Ch. 12. For further details of the name, see notes **80.2, 119.2,** and **134.2.**

14.2 [8] *a professional indoor Marxman.* The pun mocks gun-runner Hugh's left-wing or Marxist sympathies. Laruelle may be echoing something that Geoffrey once said to him; the pun is otherwise somewhat out of character. In an early draft (UBC 10–14, p. 18) the phrase had been used in Ch. 10 by the Consul to Hugh to criticize the naivety of the latter's politics, and Conrad Aiken, in a letter to Lowry of 15 December 1939, had used it in the same way to criticize Lowry's style: "I think the influence of the Complex Boys, these adolescent audens spenders with all their pretty little dexterities, their negative safety, their indoor marxmanship, has not been too good for you" (Aiken, *Selected Letters,* p. 239; cited by Jakobsen, p. 58).

14.3 [8] *after the Consul had been 'discovered.'* The police had presumably "searched" for the body of the Consul, "found" it after a suitable length of time, and informed Hugh, who then telephoned Laruelle.

14.4 [8] *a British Consul.* There was not in 1938–39 a British consulate in Cuernavaca, but the British diplomatic service in Mexico City owned a property on the Calle Humboldt (Lowry's Calle Nicaragua), which was maintained as a weekend residence and acted as a point of contact for the not inconsiderable British community then living in Cuernavaca.

14.5 [9]   *Vera Cruz.* The town of Vera Cruz, in the state of the same name, is the leading port on Mexico's Gulf coast and hence the logical place for Hugh (or Laruelle) to join his ship. The name (literally, True Cross) indicates the religious purpose which the Spaniards attached to their mission in the New World, and it was from here that Cortés and his Spaniards set forth into the interior on their holy mission. Behind the high-sounding words, however, were men's ambitions to shape destiny and the desire to exploit the riches of New Spain, two themes touched on here through the conjunction of "case" and "providentially" and developed more fully in Ch. 10. Lowry may be hinting that the missions of both Hugh and Laruelle are similarly tainted by selfish concerns.

15.1 [9]   *he had made great films.* Lowry comments, "LJC," p. 71: "if we like, we can look at the rest of the book through Laruelle's eyes, as if it were his creation." Following up this hint, Kilgallin, pp. 131–47, explores Laruelle's role as film-maker, emphasizing his controlling consciousness and discussing the various cinematic techniques brought to the novel: the internal allusions to other films; the close but unobtrusive parallels between Laruelle and Sergei Eisenstein, whose *Que Viva Mexico!* (see note **77.1**) was to have been an epic representation of Mexico's history, with a trochal structure and an epilogue set on the Day of the Dead; and the particular relevance of the setting in the cinema, Ch. 1, where the luminous wheel turning backward is, among other things, that of camera and projector as Laruelle prepares to shoot the film of his life. Kilgallin's detailed analysis offers a structural justification for what many critics have seen as the novel's central weakness, that is, Lowry's "excessive" symbolism, whereby everything seems to relate obsessively to everything else. If, however, Chs. 2 to 12 are seen essentially as the product of Laruelle's controlling consciousness, as they must be, then the form of the novel contains its own justification of why it is as it is and not otherwise.

15.2 [9]   *The sun poured molten glass on the fields.* An anticipation of the Consul's vision, p. 281 [279], of the babel of broken bottles. The image is grounded in fact, since the volcanic rocks north of Cuernavaca often have a distinctly vitreous sheen.

15.3 [9]   *a wanderer on another planet.* Laruelle's "eccentric orbit," p. 29 [23], imitates that of various wanderers of ancient legends who journey over the earth, the moon, and the universe. The most celebrated of these is the

Wandering Jew, Ahasuerus, "Striker of Jesus" (*October Ferry,* p. 133), condemned for this to wander the universe without rest until Judgment Day. Laruelle was described in an early draft (UBC 7–2, p. 11) as desolately "wandering between two worlds," and the barrenness of the stony landscape testifies to the change in his world that has taken place since the Consul's death. Lowry also intends a reference to Julian Green's *Le Voyageur sur la terre* (1926): the account of the spiritual desolation of Daniel O'Donovan, to whom the world has become a place not quite in a dream, not quite in reality, and who, under the direction of his (self-created?) "other," puts an end to "une vie d'incertitude et de misère spirituelle" ("a life of incertitude and spiritual misery").

15.4 [9]   *one's own battle.* The words echo those of the Consul to Laruelle, pp. 220–21, and in terms of "la vida impersonal" (see note **17.6**) imply a similar limitation of consciousness. Lowry claimed (*SL,* p. 115) to have taken the phrase from somewhere in D.H. Lawrence's letters, where Lawrence was discussing World War I and saying that the "personal battle" should be carried into the soul of every man in England. The reference is perhaps to a letter to Katherine Mansfield, 12 December 1915 (*Letters,* p. 289), where Lawrence, "weary of personality," was seeking instead some new non-personal activity which was at the same time "a genuine vital activity"; alternatively, Lowry may have half-recalled Lawrence's words to Harriet Monroe, 17 November 1914 (*Letters,* p. 211): "The war is dreadful. It is the business of the artist to follow it home to the heart of the individual fighters." Laruelle, however, associates the phrase with World War II, which had broken out two months earlier.

15.5 [9]   *an abandoned plough.* The detail suggests Isaiah 2:4 "and they shall beat their swords into plowshares, and their spears into pruninghooks: nation shall not lift up sword against nation, neither shall they learn war any more." The suggestion of increasing belligerence in the world and the growing threat of war is also present in the later reference to ploughshares, p. 318 [317].

15.6 [10]   *the Tres Marías.* A small town to the north of Cuernavaca on the free road to Mexico City; also known as the Tres Cumbres, or Three Peaks. The three Marys were the three mourning women at the foot of the cross: the Virgin Mary, Mary Magdalen, and Mary the mother of James and John. The town is associated, p. 93 [88], with the Via Dolorosa (or Way of Sorrows; more commonly, the Way of the Cross), and its first mention here anticipates other instances of tragedy associated with the name María.

15.7 [10]   *the Cotswolds, Windermere, New Hampshire...the Eure-et-Loire...Cheshire.*
(a) *the Cotswolds.* An area of England northeast of Bath, extending about fifty miles to just northwest of Cheltenham and named after the low limestone hills. The area is known for its picturesque thatched houses, a breed of sheep, and its archetypically English rural life.
(b) *Windermere.* The largest lake in England, located in the Lake District area of northwestern England. Windermere is about ten miles long and one mile wide. The area is well-known in literature as the picturesque home of Wordsworth, Coleridge, and other Romantic writers.
(c) *New Hampshire.* A rural farming and mountain state in the northeastern United States.
(d) *Eure-et-Loire.* A department, or district, southwest of Paris. Its centre is Chartres, and its character is largely defined by large farms and country villages.
(e) *Cheshire.* A shire in the northwest of England, adjacent to Wales. Lowry and the fictional Firmin brothers spent their adolescent years in this area.

16.1 [10]   *in the twinkling of an eye.* The reference to I Corinthians 15:52 exemplifies Lowry's deft handling of common clichés: "In a moment, in the twinkling of an eye, at the last trump: for the trumpet shall sound, and the dead shall be raised incorruptible, and we shall be changed."

16.2 [10]   *three civilizations.* The Place of the Three Civilizations is to be found at the ruins of Monte Alban, near Oaxaca, in a stone edifice (Building L) which displays features of the three main civilizations of the Oaxaca Valley: the Olmecs, the Zapotecs, and the Mixtecs. There may also be a suggestion of La Plaza de las Tres Culturas ("The Place of the Three Cultures") at Tlatelolco in Mexico City (off Reforma at González), the site of the final battle between the Spaniards and Aztecs, 13 August 1521; it displays Aztec ruins, the Spanish colonial church of Santiago, and modern high-rise apartments. A monument near the church proclaims: "No fue triunfo ni derota fue el dolorosa nacimiento del pueblo mestizo que es el México de hoy" ("It was neither a triumph nor a defeat; it was the painful birth of the mixed nation which is the Mexico of today").

16.3 [10]   *the Earthly Paradise.* In general, the unfallen Eden of Genesis 1; in particular, the garden described in Dante's *Purgatorio,* XXVIII, where Dante enters the sacred wood (the antithesis of the *selva oscura,* or dark wood) and comes to a brook, on the banks of which a lady is gathering flowers. The lady answers the poet's questions about the earthly paradise, intimating that the golden age of which poets dream is a lingering memory of its innocence which they may hope to regain, as Geoffrey had hoped and Jacques now does, long after that innocence has been destroyed. For Lowry there is also a private reference to Ignatius Donnelly's *Atlantis: The Antediluvian World* (see note **91.1**). Donnelly begins his book, p. 2, by describing "a universal memory of a great land, where early mankind dwelt for ages in peace and happiness" and elsewhere comes to the "irresistible" conclusion that the earthly paradise, the Garden of Eden, and the lost Atlantis are one and the same.

16.4 [10]   *beautiful Mayan idols he would be unable to take out of the country.* The idols are described, p. 203 [199], as "cuneiform stone idols," squatting "like bulbous infants," in such a way as to represent the Consul's lost hopes. Laruelle will be unable to take them out of the country because Mexican law prohibits the exporting of such national treasures and artifacts.

16.5 [10]   *he had* —. The sudden breaking off may be Laruelle's way of evading the truth, if it is true that he has seduced his best friend's wife.

16.6 [10]   *A black storm breaking out of season!* The rainy season in Mexico lasts from May to October, but such unseasonable storms are not infrequent (as Laruelle has just noted, there was a similar storm at the hour of the Consul's death, one year ago). According to Prescott, VI.viii, pp. 608–9, there was a tremendous thunderstorm on the night of the destruction of Tenochtitlán (see note **33.1**). The black clouds suggest the darkness over all the earth at the hour of Christ's crucifixion, but also form a Swedenborgian image of a world denied God's love (see notes **18.4** and **42.9**).

16.7 [10]   *love which came too late.* In Shakespeare's *All's Well That Ends Well* (V.iii.57–60), the King of France castigates Bertram, count of Rousillon, for his reluctance in accepting Helena as his wife and for his belated admissions of love (Bertram believing her to be dead):

> But love that comes too late,
> Like a remorseful pardon slowly carried,
> To the great sender turns a sour offence,
> Crying, "That's good that's gone."

There may be a further allusion to St. Augustine's *Confessions,* X.xxvii:

> Sero te amavi, pulchritudo tam antiqua et tam nova, sero te amavi! Et ecce intus eras et ego foris et ibi te quaerebam.

("Too late I loved thee, beauty so ancient and so new, too late I loved thee! And behold thou wert in me and I without, and there I searched for thee.")

16.8 [10] *Tonnerre de dieu.* Fr. "Thunder of God"; a mild and common oath. Laruelle uses it because it is appropriate to the "black storm breaking," but Lowry would be aware of Part V of T. S. Eliot's *The Waste Land,* where the voice of thunder may promise relief for the parched land. Lowry's "warmth returned to the surprised land" closely echoes Eliot's "Summer surprised us" (*The Waste Land,* l. 8), and the passage as a whole foreshadows Geoffrey's wakening, p. 129 [125], from his thirsty vision of Himavat.

16.9 [10] *It slaked no thirst.* An echo of "Clorinda and Damon," a pastoral poem by Andrew Marvell (1621–78), in which Clorinda invites the reluctant Damon to her unfrequented cave, that they might "seize the short Joyes":

D. That den?   C. Loves Shrine.   D. But Virtue's Grave.
C. In whose cool bosome we may lye
   Safe from the Sun.   D. not Heaven's Eye.
C. Near this, a Fountaines liquid Bell
   Tinkles within the concave Shell.
D. Might a soul bath there and be clean,
   Or slake its Drought?   C. What is't you mean?
D. These once had been enticing things,
   Clorinda, Pastures, Caves, and Springs.
C. And what late change?   D. The other day
   Pan met me.

The lines are frequently alluded to by the Consul (See pp. 78, 84, and 211 [73, 80, and 207]; Damon's virtue in resisting Clorinda is so like yet unlike his own resistance to Yvonne. Marvell's poem touches on a number of matters central to the Consul's psyche: his fear of the sun, his thirst for salvation, his determination not to be enticed by Yvonne's vision of Paradise, and his allegiance to other powers.

16.10 [10] *the dark castled shape of Cortez Palace.* The Palacio de Cortés, or Cortez Palace (the Penguin "Cortex" is a misprint), is a solid but attractive stone stronghold in the centre of Cuernavaca, built for Hernán Cortés between 1526–29, and used by him to administer the vast domains granted him by the Spanish Crown. After the death of Cortés, the palace fell into decay, but in 1767 it was restored and used as the administrative centre of the town. In 1939 it acted as the municipal headquarters, and since 1965 it has been an archaelogical museum, ironically distinguished by Rivera's famous murals which depict the exploitation of the Indians by the Spaniards (see note **215.4**). There are strange legends of subterranean passages linking the castle to other parts of the city; although exaggerated, the stories have some basis in fact, as excavations had revealed by 1937 (de Davila, p. 53). Given Lowry's intense interest in the demonic realms below, his failure to even mention the legends suggests he did not know of their existence.

16.11 [10] *gondolas.* The cars or seat baskets of the Ferris wheel. The word is invariably associated with Venetian canalboats, but is technically correct as used here.

16.12 [11] *the St Louis Blues.* A well-known jazz piece published in 1914 by "Father of the Blues," W. C. Handy (1873–1958), its theme of loneliness expressed in the opening lines:

> I hate to see de evenin' sun go down,
> 'Cause my baby she done left this town.
> Feeling tomorrow like I feel today,
> Gonna pack my trunk and make my getaway.

17.1 [11] *the Alcapancingo road.* That taken by Hugh and Yvonne when they go riding in Ch. 4. Acapantzingo today is a small, tough district of Cuernavaca, a far cry from the "sort of struggling suburb" (*UTV*, p. 109) surrounded by open fields which it was in 1939. It lies directly opposite the Calle Humboldt (Lowry's Calle Nicaragua) but on the other side of the Amanalco barranca. The Acapantzingo road, which existed in the 1930's (de Davila, p. 66), has long been swallowed up by a growing Cuernavaca, but it was then the logical route south from town, past the prison, towards Maximilian's casa. To return, Laruelle takes the Calle Nicaragua (Humbolt), which in 1939 crossed the barranca but was subsequently redirected (*DATG*, p. 133).

17.2 [11] *the Mexican lake-bed, itself once the crater of a huge volcano.* The Valley of Mexico, at an elevation of 7,500 feet, is a large oval valley some sixty miles by forty in size, surrounded by high porphyritic and volcanic hills which indeed create the illusion of one gigantic crater (though this is not in fact the case). In Aztec times the valley contained extensive lakes, but these have been almost completely drained over the centuries,

Mexico City now spreading over the former lake-bed. Cholula is not within the Valley of Mexico, but the easiest (if not the most direct) route from Cuernavaca to Cholula would be via Mexico City and the valley whose tragic history so much reflects the Consul's own.

17.3 [11]   *Cholula... the ruined pyramid... the orginal tower of Babel.* Cholula, now on the outskirts of Puebla, was the holy city of the Toltecs and an important religious centre before and during the Aztec period. Tradition claims that 365 Christian chapels, one for each day of the year, were built upon the ruins of pagan temples; the actual number is about 70 (Lowry's 306 is unusual, especially when an earlier draft, UBC 7-2, p. 9, reads "366 churches, each to replace a pagan temple"; see, however, note **9.5.d**). The centre of Cholula is dominated by a massive pyramid, begun in pre-Classic times, but now stripped of its outer layers and considerably reduced in size. It is, nevertheless, the largest man-made monument in pre-Columbian America, being some 177 feet high, with a base 1,423 feet long and covering about 44 acres (Prescott, III.vi, p. 263). The original Tower of Babel is described in Genesis 11: 1–9: the descendants of Noah tried to build a tower that would reach heaven, but God punished their presumption by causing the builders to speak in different languages so that they could not understand one another (hence, by popular etymology, the derivation of "babble" from "Babel," which Laruelle assumes here and which the Consul notes, p. 367 [366]). The analogy between the pyramid at Cholula and the Tower of Babel is by no means original with the Consul. Prescott, Appendix I, p. 694, notes the coincidence of Hebrew and Indian legends about the building of these edifices, the subsequent dispersion, and the confusion of tongues but criticizes those who (like the Consul) would build up bold hypotheses on flimsy foundations. Donnelly, p. 203, is less critical; he compares the story of Babel with the Toltec account of the pyramid of Cholula built by the giant Xlehua as a means of escaping from a second flood, should it come (see note **35.2**) and concludes that "Both legends were probably derived from Atlantis."

17.4 [11]   *its two barber shops, the 'Toilet' and the 'Harem'.* Lowry seems to have noted the names of these *peluquerías* mainly for their incongruity, but the reference to the barber shops sounds the note of betrayal underlying memories of the visit to Cholula (which the Consul also recalls, p. 209 [205]). Cholula was the scene not only of countless human sacrifices, but also in 1519 of a barbaric massacre by Cortés of some 3,000 Cholulan Indians in pre-emptive retaliation for their planned betrayal of him. The reference to Cholula suggests the general theme of betrayal (see notes **288.6** and **304.2**), while that to the barber shops anticipates in particular the theme of "cuckold-shaven" (see notes **64.3** and **177.2**). Cholula is associated with the Tower of Babel, Tarot card 16, which is described by Ouspensky (*A New Model of the Universe*, p. 235) as an emblem of deceit.

17.5 [11]   *the Sorbonne.* The most prestigious college of the University of Paris, founded by Robert de Sorbon in 1257 A.D. and celebrated for medicine, theology, and law.

17.6 [12]   *perfectamente borracho. . . . completamente fantástico. . . . Si, hombre, la vida impersonal. . . . Claro, hombre. . . . ¡Positavamente! . . . Buenas noches. . . .* Sp. "Totally drunk . . . completely fanciful. . . . Yes, my friend, the impersonal life. . . . Positively! Good night. . . . Good night." Laruelle cannot but sense the relevance of these half-heard phrases to the Consul's life, and having previously responded to Vigil's "Come, *amigo,* throw away your mind," p. 12 [6], probably understands the reference to "la vida impersonal," glossed in *DATG,* p. 251 as: "the philosophy of La Vida Impersonal, that of the 'throwing away of the mind,' where every man was his own Garden of Eden. Personal responsibility is complete, though the life is all interior." Andersen, p. 438, suggests that the philosophy is almost a Western counterpoint of the Oriental view that the cause of suffering is action resulting from desire for a separate self. Her view is supported by Lowry's own discussion of it in "Garden of Etla," p. 46, where he recalls listening over mescal to his friend Fernando Atonalzin (Juan Cerillo in *UTV,* Fernando Martínez in *DATG*):

> Time merely repeated itself; history likewise. . . . Why boast about that which has been done before? You could try to do better, you could succeed; but best keep silent about it. Life itself should strive, so far as possible, to be impersonal.
>
> Man he likened to the valley of Etla. Perhaps I would understand this better if he said the Garden of Eden. Every man was, in a sense, his own Garden of Eden. To this extent others could be seen as spiritual modifications of oneself. This was evil, but not wholly an illusion.
>
> What was not an illusion at all was that you found yourself either within this symbolic garden or, mysteriously — and here I had to accept the paradox that this did not mean that you were exiled from your own soul — you were made aware that you had been exiled from it. If not, one of the surest ways to become evicted was by boastfulness, though this had a deeper meaning than was contained in the mere word. Be impersonal as you may, the moment you attibuted any formidable value to yourself for this, you went out.
>
> Then, one of the most certain ways never to return was by excessive remorse, or sorrow for what you had lost. This to a Zapotecan was

more of a sin than it was held to be by the Catholics of his upbringing; it was another form of boasting: the assumption of the uniqueness of your misery.

The Consul has violated this philosophy in many respects. He sees others as spiritual modifications of himself, he has placed a "formidable" value upon his sufferings and his own great battle, and he has shown excessive remorse for what he has lost. In terms of la vida impersonal, then, he is responsible for his eviction from his own Garden of Eden, and in his assumption of the uniqueness of his misery, he has little hope of regaining it.

18.1 [12] *pocket torch for scrip.* Laruelle's flashlight is likened to the bag or wallet of a medieval pilgrim, used to carry food and alms (as such, it is not particularly appropriate for a knight).

18.2 [12] *model farm.* After his election in 1934, President Lázaro Cárdenas of Mexico pushed through several revolutionary programmes, including the expropriation of lands from private owners and their conversion into communal co-operatives and model farms (see notes **108.5** and **111.4**).

18.3 [12] *the ruins of Maximilian's Palace.* For details of the tragic history of Maximilian and Carlota, see note **20.3**. During their brief reign in Mexico, 1864–67, the royal couple regarded Cuernavaca as a favourite summer retreat and spent much of their time there. They made their official residence at the Borda Gardens, but also acquired in the south of Acapantzingo a small casa named Olindo (Díez, p. 113). The casa (it could scarcely be called a palace) is today a botanical centre and herbal museum, in slow process of being rescued from decades of weeds and neglect; but even making allowance for the passage of years, it bears little resemblance (apart from its location and historical significance) to the ruins described on p. 20 [14]. Lowry has superimposed upon Maximilian's casa the features of Cuernavaca's Borda Gardens, which he otherwise inexplicably ignores: these gardens, built in the late eighteenth century from the fortune of José de la Borda, silver king of Taxco (see note **308.7**), have most of the features described on p. 20 [14] — the broken pillars, the pool, the crumbling walls — and in *DATG,* pp. 132–33, Lowry clearly distinguishes the Borda Gardens from Maximilian's palace, describing the former as if they were part of *UTV:*

> the blackened dead branches and empty dead fountains of the gardens where the doomed Maximilian and Carlotta, pale royal ghosts of the Consul and Yvonne, had wandered, began to weave a pattern of

mournful music through his consciousness... the Borda Gardens appeared to him much as the House of Usher had appeared to Poe: gloomy, no flowers, grassless, even the trees were dark.

Now an attractive tourist centre (as indeed they were in 1939), the Borda Gardens still convey the sense of a place "where love had once brooded" (*UTV*, p. 20 [14]). For Laruelle, however, the dream has turned into the nightmare of history and a tragedy of blighted love.

18.4 [12] *an immense archangel, black as thunder.* The black archangel represents what Éliphas Lévi calls "that black phantom which presents itself when you do not look to God" (*Transcendental Magic*, p. 98). This is an image also present in Swedenborg's *Heaven and Hell* #549, which deals with spirits (both men and angels) who have chosen to cast themselves down to hell:

Evils and their falsities are like black clouds interposed between the sun and the human eye, which take away the brightness and serenity of its light.... In proportion as any one in that spiritual world is in falsities from evil, he is encompassed by such a cloud, and this is black and dense according to the degree of his evil.

The immediate reference is to Milton's Satan of *Paradise Lost,* 1.600, but fallen angels, evil angels, and the dark Angel of Death have been part of Christian and Hebraic traditions for centuries, and Lowry may be thinking also of the Evil Angel of *Doctor Faustus;* the Angel of the Abyss in Baudelaire's *Les Fleurs del Mal;* the Terrible Angel of Rilke's *Duino Elegies,* and Donnelly's "Archangel of the Abyss" (spoken of in the Chaldean tradition and hinting at floods about to be unleashed).

18.5 [12] *Saint Près.* More accurately, Saint Prèst. A small village of about one thousand inhabitants lying to the northeast of Chartres.

18.6 [12] *the twin spires of Chartres Cathedral.* One of the finest examples of Gothic architecture in the world, the famous cathedral is some sixty miles southwest of Paris and dates from the early thirteenth century. It is celebrated for its splendid stained glass, its magnificent sculpture, and its lofty spires (which, built at different times, are not at all identical). The approach to the cathedral which Laruelle recalls is particularly spectacular: as pilgrims approach across a totally flat rural landscape, they see the spires of the cathedral rising into the heavens long before the village of Chartres is in sight. The towers symbolize man's lofty aspirations, but in the crypt of the church there is also a deep well into which heretics were formerly hurled to their deaths.

19.1 [13]   *secret mines of silver.* In a letter to Albert Erskine (*SL,* p. 115), Lowry admits to the influence of D. H. Lawrence at this point. In a letter to Witter Bynner, 5 October 1923, from Navojoa, Sonora (*Letters,* p. 581), Lawrence writes of the wild hopeless landscape pressing upon him, the "little towns that seem to slipping down an abyss" and "In the mountains, lost, motionless silver-mines." He even mentions a dead dog in the market place. There may also be a hint of Joseph Conrad's *Nostromo* (1904): in an early draft (UBC 8–13, p. 10) Lowry described Laruelle as having "found the Consul here and stayed on and like him played the silver market": Nostromo, too, felt the secret burden of silver pressing upon his soul.

19.2 [13]   *a faded blue Ford.* Quite possibly the Consul's Plymouth, mentioned in his letter, p. 42 [36], and described to Yvonne as "lost," p. 57 [52]: certainly, for Laruelle, an emblem of his lost blue-eyed friend, and hence the immediate transition of his thoughts to the long-belated postcard, delivered p. 197 [193], and slipped beneath his pillow, p. 205 [201], to be discovered at almost exactly the moment of Geoffrey's death.

19.3 [13]   *small, black, ugly birds. . . . within the fresno trees.* The birds are known locally as urracas: slim, torpedo-shaped magpies or small crows, with long fan-like tails, and a loud raucous cry ("apparently practicing to be vultures," *DATG,* p. 130). Fresnos (from L. *fraxinus,* "an ash") are tall, stately trees with grey trunks and small light-green leaves. Commonly found in Mexican zócalos, they were a feature of Cuernavaca in 1939, but have since been removed. Nevertheless, the "unbelievable screeching" (*DATG,* p. 131) of the urracas has continued to shatter the evening peace in Cuernavaca.

20.1 [14]   *wrecked entablature, sad archivolt.* An entablature is the upper section of a wall or temple, often decorative, supported by columns or pillars; an archivolt is the ornamental moulding around an arch.

20.2 [14]   *where love had once brooded.* A deliberately incongruous echo of the final lines of the sentimental song by Hermann Löhr, "Little Grey Home in the West" (see note **354.1**):

> It's a corner of heaven itself
>   Though it's only a tumble-down nest —
> But with love brooding there, why, no place can compare
>   With my little grey home in the west.

20.3 [14]   *France, even in Austrian guise, should not transfer itself to Mexico.* After fifty years of independence from 1810, Mexico's internal politics and economics were in sufficient confusion to give Louis Napoleon Bonaparte, emperor of France, a pretext for invasion. The French military achieved mixed success, but anti-democratic forces within Mexico pressed for a monarchy, and, with the backing of the French, invited the Austrian Archduke Ferdinand Maximilian Joseph of Hapsburg to accept the throne. Genuinely believing he had the support of the Mexican people, Maximilian arrived in the New World in 1864 with his young wife Marie Charlotte (Carlota). They found Mexico idyllic at first, but the liberal forces led by Juárez continued guerrilla warfare, and with the withdrawal of French troops in late 1866, Maximilian found himself in an impossible position. Carlota returned to Europe to seek aid, but Maximilian stayed on and was obliged to surrender to the liberal forces on 15 May 1867. Despite international pleas for clemency, Juárez had Maximilian shot (see note **127.3**); Carlota remained in Europe, where she later died insane at an advanced age. Like Maximilian, Laruelle may now be regretting his time in Mexico and his lost love there.

20.4 [14]   *the Miramar.* The imperial castle belonging to Maximilian, built between 1854–56, on the Adriatic coast about four miles from Trieste; Carlota lived there for a long time after Maximilian's execution, until her death in 1927.

20.5 [14]   *everyone who ever lived there.* The Hapsburg family was indeed plagued with what might be called bad luck: Maximilian was shot by the Mexicans in 1867; his brother Franz Joseph lived long enough (1916) to see the Austro-Hungarian Empire fall apart during World War I; Franz Joseph's eldest son Rudolph shot himself and his mistress, the Baroness Marie Vetsera, at the hunting lodge "Mayerling" on the outskirts of Vienna in 1889; and Rudolph's cousin, the Archduke Francis Ferdinand, was assassinated at Sarajevo.

20.6 [14]   *the Empress Elizabeth of Austria.* Elizabeth of Austria (1837–98), the beautiful, popular, and unconventional wife of Franz Joseph I, who was stabbed to death by an Italian anarchist on a steamer on Lake Geneva, 10 September 1898.

20.7 [14]   *the Archduke Ferdinand.* Archduke Franz Ferdinand (1863–1914), nephew of Franz Joseph I and heir presumptive to the Austro-Hungarian throne, whose assassination by the young Serbian revolutionary Gavrilo Princip on 28 June 1914 in Sarajevo precipitated World War I.

20.8 [14] *two lonely empurpled exiles.* The word "purple," from its first appearance, p. 11 [6] ("the purple hills of a Doré Paradise"), to its last, p. 318 [317] ("low hills . . . purple and sad"), is associated with the sense of a lost paradise, an innocence which cannot be regained. Lowry's authority for this appears to be W. H. Hudson's *The Purple Land,* originally titled *The Purple Land That England Lost* (1885), the theme of which is less England's loss of the *Banda Orientál* (Uruguay), than the narrator's memories of a girl he rendered unhappy and the happy days long gone.

20.9 [14] *Eden.* The Garden of Eden, described in the first book of Genesis and in Bk. IV of Milton's *Paradise Lost,* symbolizes the world of innocence before the Fall of Man. Lowry comments, "LJC," p. 66: "The allegory is that of the Garden of Eden, the Garden representing the world." See also note **132.3.**

20.10 [14] *beginning to turn . . . into a prison and smell like a brewery.* The Alcapancingo Prison and the Cervercería Quauhnahuac (see p. 116 [12]) are both on the lands that were once part of Maximilian's gardens.

20.11 [14] *'It is our destiny to come here, Carlotta. . . . Let us be good and constructive and make ourselves worthy of it.'* These words are probably not meant to be taken as historically accurate, but the sentiment was typical of Maximilian in his more idealistic, more naive moods. For example:

> Yet I do not regret the present; it is devoted to action, effort and creation. The peaceful joy of life may be lacking, but there is a deep satisfaction in the thought that one is serving humanity and that I can now contribute a few drops of oil to the great lamp of enlightenment; that it is granted to me to take part in that work of improvement at which men of goodwill have been working for hundreds, nay, thousands of years. (Egon Corti, *Maximilian and Charlotte of Mexico,* II, p. 466)

20.12 [14] *there were ghosts quarrelling.* Although the quarrelling voices materialize as those of the Consul and Yvonne, they begin as Maximilian and Carlota, whose life together, despite a public veneer of well-bred civility, was not one of emotional tranquillity: it was rumoured that something had gone wrong on the young couple's honeymoon and that thereafter and throughout their time in Mexico they lived together without physical intimacy, Maximilian taking a mistress in Cuernavaca (one Concepción Sedano y Leguizano, a married woman of Spanish descent, by whom he had a natural son). The casa at Acapantzingo was built in part to facilitate discreet rendezvous (de Davila, pp. 60–65). Lowry probably knew these rumours (see note **64.4**), but he may have suppressed them in order not to spoil his picture of tragic romance.

21.1 [15]   *High Life.* A department store at Madero and Gante streets in Mexico City; Laruelle exaggerates the Mexican pronunciation of the words.

21.2 [15]   *getting too fat . . . for taking up arms.* A combination of *Hamlet,* V.ii.301: "He's fat, and scant of breath," and III.i.59: "Or to take arms against a sea of troubles"; the two allusions underlining Laruelle's tragic inability to act.

21.3 [15]   *the barranca.* The town of Cuernavaca is flanked on either side by enormous *barrancas,* or deep steep ravines, which run for miles through the countryside, as if a giant Prometheus had unzipped his fly. The fearful drop is described in Conrad Aiken's *A Heart for the Gods of Mexico,* pp. 463–64, as he stands in precisely the spot Laruelle is standing:

> Twice he had stumbled down to the bridge . . . which crossed that incredible tree-filled gorge. The fern-like trees were so interlaced across it that one thought of course it must be very shallow, only when one looked a second time did one glimpse — far below — and with a sudden contraction of the heart — tiny rocks and ripples in the filtered sunshine, knotted roots on the dark side of the narrow little canyon, and the sinister suckers of the creepers, venomous and dark, hanging down hundreds of feet in search of a foothold. The *barranca.*

Generally assumed to be the product of huge cataclysmic and volcanic forces in bygone ages, or attributed in legend to the black magician Tezcatlipoca (also the inventor of pulque), the barrancas have an origin which is more prosaic: underground rivers once ran through the largely limestone underlying rock, eroding it until it collapsed along long fault lines (Díez, p. 3). Now partially filled in and choked with rubbish, they nevertheless remain fearsome chasms, a perfect symbol of the demonic realm of Lowry's tripartite universe (heaven and hell, with the world precariously between), and of the abyss within the heart of man. For further significance of the abyss, see note **26.2**.

21.4 [15]   *Dormitory for vultures.* Laruelle's speculation anticipates that of the Consul, p. 134 [131], who looks down into the barranca and thinks of "the cloacal Prometheus who doubtless inhabited it."

21.5 [15] *City Moloch.* Moloch, god of the Ammonites (I Kings 11.7), a man with the face of a bull, whose bowels were a furnace into which children were cast as burnt offerings, is described in Milton's *Paradise Lost,* I.392–93: "First Moloch, horrid King besmear'd with blood / Of human sacrifice, and parents tears." The "city Moloch" is Rabbah in the land of Gad (Jeremiah 49.1–3). More generally, Moloch represents any power or driving passion to which appalling sacrifices of great treasures are made. In Nordahl Greig's *The Ship Sails On,* p. 2, the ship is described as "A Moloch that crushes the lives of men between its iron jaws"; an image also used in Lowry's early poem, "For Nordahl Grieg's Ship's Firemen," published in the *St. Catharine's College Magazine,* December 1929, pp. 26–27: "They see an iron Moloch / Securely waiting to swallow the lives of men."

21.6 [15] *the sea-borne, hieratic legend.* Prescott, VI.iii, p. 533 describes the barranca near Cuernavaca as "one of those frightful rents not unfrequent in the Mexican Andes, the result, no doubt, of some terrible convulsion in earlier ages," while Matthew 27:51, describing the crucifixion, reads: "And, behold, the veil of the temple was rent in twain from the top to the bottom; and the earth did quake, and the rocks rent." Lowry's "legend" of the earth opening throughout the country probably derives from these two sources imaginatively combined, since there is no well-known legend of this kind in Cuernavaca (legends of Morelos mention the black magician Tezcatlipoca as opening the ravines, but offer no hint of a Christianized version). Lowry's precise sense of "sea-borne" and "hieratic" (that is, "pertaining to the priestly office") is obscure; it is likely that he is anticipating the Consul's "intercourse between opposite sides of the Atlantic," p. 22 [16], in a suitably Atlantean manner, but he may simply mean that the legend arrived with the Spanish.

21.7 [16] *a film about Atlantis.* Atlantis, the fabled island and civilization described in the *Timaeus* and *Critias* of Plato, is generally reputed to have been somewhere west of the Pillars of Hercules in the Atlantic (though some Atlantologists equate it with Thera in the Aegean, destroyed by an immense volcanic eruption about 1500 B.C. and others with the Atlas Mountains in North Africa). In Plato's account, its once virtuous and powerful inhabitants, having become degenerate, were defeated by the Athenians, and the island sank beneath the ocean as the result of a terrible cataclysm. The "science" of Atlantology was given a great boost in 1882 by Ignatius Donnelly's *Atlantis: The Antediluvian World* (see note **91.1**), a book which the Consul is trying to outdo, with the result that images of the destruction of Atlantis by fire and flood are ever-present in the patterns of his thought. Laruelle, however, probably has in mind the film *Women of Atlantis,* or

L'Atlantide, produced by Jacques Feyder in 1921 (Kilgallin, p. 136); the successful silent movie was based upon the story by P. Benoît, and a sound-track version was made by G. W. Pabst in 1932. The story tells how two sol-diers serving in Africa discover the lost city of Atlantis, whose queen, Antinea, has the power to make all men fall in love with her; one of the sol-diers resists, with disastrous consequences.

22.1 [16]   *'huracán'. . . intercourse between opposite sides of the Atlantic.* As noted by Andersen, p. 36, and Kilgallin, p. 136, the Consul's cryptic remark is almost a direct quotation from Ignatius Donnelly's *Atlantis: The Antediluvian World* (see note **91.1**). In Pt. II.iii, p. 103, discussing "The Deluge Legends of the Americas" (essentially a comparison of the American versions of the flood with the Hebrew and Chaldean ones), Donnelly comments: "And here may I quote that this word *hurakan* — the spirit of the abyss, and god of storm, the hurricane — is very suggestive, and testifies to an early intercourse between the opposite shores of the Atlantic." Hurakán was a powerful god of the Quiche Mayas, who presided over the whirlwind and thunderstorm (hence our word "hurricane") and who vented the anger of the gods upon the first human beings by causing a deluge and thick resin-ous rain to complete their destruction. Donnelly finds the similarities between this legend and those of Noah and Deucalion "very suggestive," but the Consul goes further by identifying Huracán with the Vedic storm god Vindra (see note **259.2**).

22.2 [16]   *some obscure relation.* Laruelle's stumbling upon the Consul and Yvonne embracing in the ruins of Maximilian's palace, p. 21 [15], bears an "obscure relation" to the Hell Bunker episode, pp. 26–27 [20], in that it ex-emplifies the eternal return, the recurrence at a different time and place of something that has already happened and will always happen. Just as Laru-elle's earlier chance sighting of Geoffrey with a girl in the Hell Bunker had created a sexual tension and sense of guilt between himself and the Consul, so too does this later duplication of the incident contain within itself the seeds of destruction. Lowry's use of words like "obscure," "odd," or "strange" seems deliberately designed to provoke this kind of speculation.

22.3 [16]   *meaningless correspondences. . . 'favourite trick of the gods'.* Lowry would have read in Swedenborg's *Heaven and Hell* #303 the doctrine that "there is a connection of the natural world with the spiritual world, and that hence there is a correspondence of all things which are in the natural world with all things which are in the spiritual world." To Lowry, such cor-respondences were not meaningless but indicative of a powerful a-causal force of coincidence operative in a serial universe (Jung called it synchronicity), often malignant, bringing together individuals and configurations in time and space and correlating by affinity and analogy. The "favourite trick of the gods" echoes Cocteau's statement, "The gods exist, they are the devil," which Geoffrey wrongly attributes to Baudelaire (see note **212.6**), while the word "correspondences" itself suggests Baudelaire's "Correspondances," one of Lowry's favourite poems, which is an emphatic statement that such apparent coincidence is not meaningless:

> La Nature est un temple où les vivants piliers
> Laissant parfois sortir de confuses paroles;
> L'homme y passe à travers des forêts de symboles
> Qui l'observent avec des regards familiers.

("Nature is a temple where living pillars / sometimes allow confused words to escape; / man passes there through forests of symbols / that watch him with familiar glances.")

22.4 [16] *Languion. . . . Courseulles . . . Calvados.* Towns and districts of northern France:
(a) *Langion.* Also Longuyon. A small town in the Meurthe-et-Moselle Département in northeastern France, near the western border of Luxembourg; an area famous for its wines.
(b) *Courseulles.* Courseulles-sur-Mer. A village resort on the English Channel at the mouth of the Seulles River; about ten miles north of Caen and fifteen miles east of Bayeux.
(c) *Calvados.* A department of France in Normandy on the English Channel; it includes Caen and Courseulles and is noted for its farming and for its calvados (apple brandy).

22.5 [16] *Abraham Taskerson.* A tasker is one who works, or is paid, by the task or piece; in particular, one who threshes corn with a flail (a not unsuitable description of the poet's efforts). Abraham, in Genesis 17:1–6 was made "exceedingly fruitful" by God; hence "at least six" young Taskersons. Day comments, p. 336, that Taskerson was "very loosely modelled on Conrad Aiken," and the Taskerson-Firmin relationship encapsulates a number of elements of the Aiken-Lowry symbiosis. Conrad Knickerbocker earlier suggested that the Taskerson family was based upon a family named Hepburn. Although Russell Lowry (*The Art of Malcolm Lowry* by Anne Smith, p. 22) objects to this identification (suggesting instead the Furness family of Liverpool), Patrick Hepburn's death is not dissimilar to that of the Consul's father: in the Late Country, December 1927, he disregarded warnings of darkness and foul weather and was caught and drowned in a flash flood. The suggestion of suicide hangs over his death, as it does over that of Geoffrey's father.

22.6 [17]   *collateral relatives.* Of the same ancestral stock but not in the same line of descent.

22.7 [17]   *Geoffrey Firmin.* Geoffrey, "God's peace," or "beloved of God" (the etymology is debated); Firmin, an obvious inversion of "infirm," but also (Kilgallin, p. 147) with a suggestion of St. Firminus, martyred at Amiens, or St. Fermin, patron saint of Pamplona, the Spanish bullfighting town celebrated by Hemingway (the two saints are in fact one and the same). The name Firmin is related to "fireman," and to that extent it is a constant reminder to Geoffrey of the unfortunate incident with the furnaces of the S.S. *Samaritan.* There is also a hint of "firmament," beneath which the abyss is ever-present. The name was first used by Lowry of an old prospector and veteran of World War I in his short story, "June the 30th, 1934" (*P & S,* pp. 36–48).

23.1 [17]   *cleeks.* From Du. *cleek,* "a hook"; antiquated wooden golf clubs, iron headed with narrow, slightly sloping faces (as used in *The Clicking of Cuthbert*—see note **178.17**). The gutta-percha golf balls, made of a single lump of moulded rubber latex, are equally antiquated; they were introduced to the game in the 1840's, replacing the "featheries" (leather spheres stuffed with feathers), but were in turn replaced by the rubber cored ball (a narrow rubber thread wound tightly about a solid core) about 1902.

23.2 [17]   *'Old Bean'.* Though the sobriquet is common enough, it is used in the opening pages of P. C. Wren's *Beau Geste* (1924) by the Frenchman Henri de Beaujolais ("Jolly") of his English friend George Lawrence.

23.3 [17]   *the erect manly carriage of the Taskersons.* At moments of total inebriation, or particularly at such moments, the Consul will be conscious of the need to maintain this admirable carriage. Lowry admits that the Taskerson episode may be unsound "if considered seriously in the light of a psychological etiology for the Consul's drinking or downfall" ("LJC," p. 68), but he points out the number of times that the episode is alluded to in the novel and how, at the end, the Consul is still trying to walk in the same erect manly manner.

23.4 [17]   *Leasowe.* In the early 1900's, a tiny village and railway station on the Wirral peninsula, North Cheshire, between Hoylake and Birkenhead.

Lowry has retained its name but shifted its location closer to Hoylake, which has a golf course (the Royal Liverpool Links) and is situated on the very wide estuary of the River Dee. The Taskerson home is modelled on the Lowry one at Inglewood, Caldy (a few miles south of Hoylake), where Lowry's wealthy father had built a small golf course on the family estate.

23.5 [17] *white horses. . . . Welsh mountains.* The golf course is adjacent to the estuary of the River Dee, and from it may be seen the white caps of the waves where the river meets the sea and the Clwydian range of mountains in northern Wales, on the other side of the estuary.

23.6 [17] *an antediluvian forest. . . an old stubby lighthouse. . . a windmill. . . . a curious black flower. . . a donkey.* Carefully unobtrusive intimations of the Atlantis theme (**91.1**); the Farolito (**203.6**); Don Quixote (**45.1** and **250.3**); the song "Black Flowers" and its theme of betrayal (**307.1**); and the final Christ-like sacrifice (**374.1**). Although the description of the scene is "literally precise" (Bradbrook, p. 153), the Consul's future is presaged even in his childhood years.

23.7 [17] *hydropathic hotels.* "Hydropathic" normally implies the treatment of disease by the use of water; here used, with mild irony, of the kind of seaside hotel still found on the Wirral.

24.1 [18] *Pierrot shows.* A popular form of seaside entertainment, particularly in the early years of the century. The character of Pierrot derives through French pantomime from the Pedrolino of the Italian *commedia dell'arte,* a booby in an ill-fitted suit and large soft-brimmed hat, with a whitened face, a ruff, loose white pantaloons, and a jacket with large buttons.

24.2 [18] *unprecedented, portentous walkers.* The adjectives are unusual (one might expect "prodigious") and may anticipate the Consul's walk in Ch. 6.

24.3 [18] *a strict Wesleyan school.* One run by the Methodist Church, which was founded by John Wesley (1703–91) as a non-conformist and de-ritualized breakaway from the Anglican Church. The connotations are of joyless discipline and fear of God, which account in part for the sense of guilt the Consul feels, p. 79 [73], when he hears the church bell and imagines its "hellish Wesleyan breath." It is ironic that Geoffrey received his education from Methodist teachers, strongly opposed to alcohol. "The Leys," Lowry's public school, was also Methodist (Day, p. 78).

25.1 [19]   *Srinagar.* Srinagar, on Lake Dal in the Vale of Kashmir, is the chief city of Kashmir and celebrated for the beauty of its waterways and surrounding mountains. The Valley of Kashmir itself is in the basin of the upper Jhelum river, surrounded by some of the world's highest peaks. It is described in Francis Younghusband's *Kashmir,* p. 2, as: "the world-re-nowned Vale of Kashmir, a saucer-shaped valley with a length of 84 miles, a breadth of 20 to 25 miles, and a mean height of 5600 feet above sea-level, set in the very heart of the Himalaya." Often called "'the Happy Valley" or "Paradise on Earth," it was a favourite resort for the Mogul emperors (as Cuernavaca was for Maximilian and Carlota) and has inspired countless songs and tales of romance, among them Thomas Moore's *Lalla Rookh* (see note **87.7**). Srinagar acts as a point of departure for many Himalayan expe-ditions, and the disappearance of Geoffrey's father into the mountains in search of the sacred mountain Himivat (see note **129.2**) anticipates the William Blackstone theme (see note **56.1**) and the Consul's desire, however adequate its psychological motivation, for similar oblivion. The Kashmiri element of *UTV,* despite its very late appearance in the manuscripts, is of considerable importance in defining not only the Consul's metaphysical aspirations but also his desire to complete the circle of his existence by going back to its beginnings.

26.1 [20]   *ze wibberlee wobberlee walk.* A copy of the "Wibberlee-Wob-berlee Song," with lyrics by Lowry and music by Bernhard Rooenstrunck and dating from Lowry's Cambridge days is to be found in the Lowry Col-lection in Special Collections, the University of British Columbia Library (UBC 6–55). As Muriel Bradbrook notes, p. 153, Malcolm had learnt the song from his brothers, who had in turn picked it up from a minstrel troupe, and the Lowry boys used it at The Leys school when obliged as new boys to entertain their fellows with a song.

26.2 [20]   *The Abyss yawned.* The Hell Bunker is "a well known hazard" (Bradbrook, p. 153) of the short, par 5 eighth hole of the Royal Liverpool Links at Hoylake, though the name does not seem to be in general usage now and time has filled or imagination deepened the actual hole; the delib-erate hyperbole here links it to the barranca, p. 21 [15], and the dark bunkers of the Farolito in Ch. 12. The choice of "yawned" is not accidental: as Eric Partridge says (*Origins,* p. 91): "Intimately akin to Gr *khaos* is Gr *khasma,* a gaping abyss, a vast cleft in the earth: whence L *chasma,* adopted by Med for excessive yawning: whence E *chasm.*" The word "abyss" has numerous connotations, of which the following would seem to be most directly rele-vant to Lowry:
(a) *the Bible.* In Genesis 1:2, the darkness is said to be upon the face of the

deep (in the *Vulgate,* "super faciem abyssi"); in Genesis 7:11, all the fountains of the great deep are broken up ("rupti sunt omnes fontes abyssi magnae"), and the waters of the abyss cover the entire face of the earth.

(b) *St Augustine.* In the Confessions there are frequent allusions to the human heart as an abyss or in an abyss. Bks. XII and XIII in particular form a sustained meditation upon the meanings, both corporal and spiritual, of the opening verses of Genesis, and St. Augustine explicitly likens the "tenebrae super abyssum" ("the darkness over the abyss") to the human heart which lacks the light of God.

(c) *Dante.* Markson comments, pp. 20–21:

> Hell in quotation marks, an abyss that yawns in the middle of a field, the field numbered as the eighth of a sequence. Whereas in Dante's description of the eighth circle of his own hell: "Right in the middle of the malignant field yawns a well." Some few lines later, as Dante peers into that other "bunker," we discover what Laruelle saw: "In the bottom," Dante writes, "the sinners were naked."

The precise reference is to the *Inferno,* XVIII.1–25; the "well" is the Malbolge, into which Hugh and Yvonne peer, p. 104 [100].

(d) *Milton.* Throughout *Paradise Lost,* in accordance with the opening verses of Genesis, Milton consistently differentiates the "dark unbottom'd infinite Abyss" (l. 405) from the pit or gulf in which the fallen angels lie, but unlike Burnet he does not equate the abyss or deep specifically with the waters beneath the firmament.

(e) *Thomas Burnet.* In his *Sacred Theory of the Earth* (see note **193.7**), Burnet uses the word "abyss" consistently to mean the waters of the deep within the orb of the earth; when the shell of the earth cracked open, those waters were released upon the earth, causing thereby the universal deluge and the end of our first world.

(f) *Edgar Allan Poe.* In that catalogue of horrors, *The Narrative of Arthur Gordon Pym,* the abyss (as a pit) figures prominently in the final pages, and in Ch. 24 the narrator feels an almost irresistible urge to lean over and fall in.

(g) *Henry James.* As Cross has noted, p. 131, the 1940 version of *UTV* had for one of its epigraphs a quotation from Henry James, written within a day of Britain's entry into World War I (*The Letters of Henry James,* ed. Percy Lubbock, 2:384):

> The plunge of civilisation into this abyss of blood and darkness

... is a thing that so gives away the whole long age during which we have supposed the world to be, with whatever abatement, gradually bettering, that to have to take it all now for what the treacherous years were all the while really making for and *meaning* is too tragic for any words.

Other references noted by the Consul include: the "awful unbridgeable void" between Chesed and Binah, p. 44 [39]; Marston's "mighty gulf," p. 134 [130]; Coleridge's deep romantic chasm, p. 204 [200]; and the crag "in Shelley or Calderón or both," p. 339 [338]. Lowry, however, ignored all the above and pointed instead to Julian Green, where a thought like "there was always the abyss" occurred (*SL,* p. 116). The reference is to Green's *Journal,* 26 May 1934; "Horreur de l'abîme qui peut s'ouvrir à tout moment" ("Horror of the abyss which can open at any moment"), a phrase used directly in response to Green's reading of Donnelly's *Atlantis* (see note **91.1**).

27.1 [21] *Peeping Tom.* When Lady Godiva, wife of Leofric, the cruel lord of Coventry, rode naked through the town to gain relief for the citizens from the burdensome taxes imposed by her husband, the citizens kept closely indoors, but one wretch, known thereafter as "Peeping Tom," looked out and was stricken blind for his curiosity. The story is an ancient one, but the Peeping Tom detail dates from only the seventeenth century.

27.2 [21] *the bizarre scene.* Jennifer Webb contends, p. 85, that this is *the* crucial psychological moment of the novel, the impact of which largely determines what happens thereafter. For the first time in Geoffrey's experience, he is made to see his self from the outside, observing it through Laruelle's eyes; his unity of self is shattered, and the guilt which is freed becomes a dominant part of his consciousness. Nor does Laruelle remain unaffected by the scene; from this moment on he is linked to the Consul in a defined role which combines voyeurism with shared sexual guilt (a moment repeated when he sees the Consul and Yvonne embracing in the ruins of Maximilian's casa). For both men the case is indeed altered.

27.3 [21] *The Case is Altered.* This is the title of a play by Ben Jonson, not unfairly dismissed by Markson, p. 109, as "a forgettable Jonson play, based on changed identities, disguises, etc.," whose relevance to the novel seems only peripheral: a general named Maximilian, a moderately villainous beggar named Jaques, and the refrain "The Case Is Altered" reiterated each time a turgid complexity unfolds. The name of the tavern is not as queer as it seems, since a number of public houses by this name exist. Its origin is explained on p. 125 of *The Case Is Altered* (1932), a novel by William

Plomer (by curious coincidence, the reader for Cape who rejected *Under the Volcano*):

> The pub had a funny name when you came to think of it. It was called "The Case is Altered" though everyone simply called it "The Case." Inside the bar there was a framed notice which told the story of how the place had got its name. It was originally called "The Three Cranes," but in the eighteenth century a famous highwayman was caught there unawares by a young lord whom he had robbed. "Now, sir," cried the peer as soon as he had made sure of his capture, "it seems the case is altered!"

Plomer's novel is a badly written account of a jealous husband, who, suspecting his wife of numerous infidelities, finally murders her, after which life for the other tenants of the boarding house can never be quite the same.

27.4 [21] *Johnny Walkers.* Whiskies, anticipating the Consul's beloved bottle, pp. 73 and 95 [68 and 91], just as the "providential" eviction from the tavern anticipates that from the garden (see note **132.3**).

27.5 [21] *equinoctial.* About the time of the autumn equinox (22 September).

27.6 [22] *Darkness had fallen like the House of Usher.* "The House of Usher" (1839) is a short story by Edgar Allan Poe (1809–49) about a night of Gothic horrors in an isolated mansion at the end of which the House of Usher suddenly splits asunder and sinks into the dank tarn. Poe's story was the basis for the 1928 film by Jean Epstein (1897–1953), *La chute de la maison Usher,* which Laruelle probably has in mind (Kilgallin, p. 138), and which, unexpectedly, has a happy and hopeful ending imposed on it. Lowry comments in *DATG,* p. 260:

> What was the theme of *The House of Usher?* It was, or so it seemed to him at the moment, of the degradation of the idea of resurrection. But in the film, when the entombed was Usher's wife and not his sister, she came back in time, as it were with the doctor's help, to save him: they went out into the thunderstorm, but into new life.

The complexity of Lowry's allusion resides in the fact that having set up a possible reference to Epstein's film, Usher reconciled with his wife in this life, he belies its significance by reverting to Poe's ending.

28.1 [22]   *The horse reared wildly.* This horse foreshadows the frequent appearances throughout the novel of the horse with No. 7 branded on its rump, while its drunken rider epitomizes Geoffrey Firmin: "this too, obscurely, was the Consul." The horse has many meanings: it suggests the Four Horsemen of the Apocalypse, especially the pale horse of Death (Revelation 6:8); the equestrian statue of the turbulent Huerta, p. 49 [44], that turns into the giant horse of the screen, p. 268 [266], to pursue Yvonne Griffaton down the dark streets; and, in an almost Lawrentian sense, the psychological forces of destruction within the soul of man that unleashed lead to his death (hence the trampling of Yvonne in Ch. 11). The general Cabbalistic significance of the horse is stated in Éliphas Lévi's *Transcendental Magic,* p. 98 (also cited by Kilgallin, p. 187): "Jehovah is He Who dominates Nature like a magnificent horse and makes it go where He wills; but CHAVAJOH—otherwise, the demon—is an unbridled horse which overthrows its rider and precipitates him into the abyss."

28.2 [22]   *for long after Adam had left the garden the light in Adam's house burned on.* The first identification of the Consul as Adam, now evicted from the Garden of Eden (see note **132.3**), but whose light, like a votive candle brought to the graveside on the Day of the Dead, is a constant reminder of his past presence there.

29.1 [23]   *he had taken a cut to the left.* Like Don Quixote avoiding a town invested with his abhorrence because of his excesses there (*UTV*, p. 84 [79]), Laruelle, "a knight of old" (p. 18 [12]), still armed with his tennis racket, avoids his own house by taking the same sideroad that Yvonne was so anxious to take, p. 193 [190], to avoid him on that day one year earlier.

29.2 [23]   *the Avenida de la Revolución.* This is described, p. 235 [232], as "the main highway," when the Tomalín bus takes the same route, but there is no street by this name leading out of the zócalo in Cuernavaca: Lowry has in mind the Avenida Guerrero (*DATG,* p. 208, and *UTV,* p. 227), which goes north from the zócalo, but he has invested the street with features such as the barracks and cinema that more properly belong to Morelos, the main street of Cuernavaca. The name of the street forms a pun on Laruelle's circular route, completed by the camión in Ch. 8.

29.3 [23]   *Dr Arturo Díaz Vigil, Médico Cirujano y Partero, Facultad de México, de la Escuela Médico Militar, Enfermedades de Niños, Indisposiciones nerviosas... consultas de 12 a 2 y 4 a 7.* Sp. "Dr. Arthur Díaz Vigil, Physician, Surgeon and Obstetrician, Faculty of Mexico [and] of the Military Medical School, Childhood Illnesses, Nervous Complaints... Consultations from 12 to 2 and 4 to 7." Such signs are a common feature of Mexican streets and windows.

29.4 [23] *the notices one encountered in the mingitorios.* Dr. Vigil also treats venereal diseases, as is indicated by his notices in the public toilets, one of which the Consul reads in the mingitorio of the Farolito, p. 352 [352].

29.5 [23] *Quauhnahuac Nuevo.* Unidentified (Lowry has almost certainly invented the name), but in context a small broadsheet put out by the paramilitary and fascist *Unión Militar* (see note **187.3**). The paper is pro-Almazán, that is, supporting Juan Andreu Almazán, conservative candidate for the 1940 presidential election (see note **35.7**); and pro-Axis, that is, supporting the Axis alliance of Germany, Italy, and Japan (and by implication Franco's Spain). Mexico at this stage had by no means committed itself to entering the war, as it eventually did, on the side of the Allies, particularly since relations with the U.S.A. and Britain were still strained as a result of Cárdenas's policies of nationalization (see note **36.1**).

29.6 [23] *Un avión de combate Francés derribado por un caza Alemán. Los trabajadores de Australia abogan por la paz. ¿Quiere Vd?... vestirse con elegancia y a la última moda de Europa y los Estados Unidos?* Sp. "A French combat plane brought down by a German fighter. The workers of Australia plead for peace. Do you wish . . . to dress with elegance and in the latest style of Europe and the United States?" The hardback edition "Lost" is undoubtedly a typographical error.

29.7 [23] *French army helmets and grey faded purple uniforms.* Although this is not an inexact description of the Mexican military uniform at the time, Lowry's choice of words ("French," "faded," "purple") seems deliberately contrived to evoke the ghost of Maximilian (see notes **18.3** and **20.3**).

29.8 [23] *Approaching the cinema.* In the fictional world, the location of "Quauhnahuac's one cinema" (*UTV,* p. 11 [6]) is distinct: it stands out on an incline some distance up the main street, the Avenida de la Revolución, which leads directly north from the zócalo, and it is opposite the Borda Gardens (*UTV,* p. 308 [307]). A difficulty arises when one tries to relate the fictional world of Quauhnahuac to the real world of Cuernavaca: the Ciné Morelos (at Morelos and Rayón) is roughly opposite the Borda Gardens, but not on a street leading out of the zócalo, nor sufficiently far north to allow Jacques (or the bus in Ch. 8) to cover the distance. This is one of the few instances of Lowry violating the actual topography of Cuernavaca.

30.1 [24]   *the arcature.* A small arcade or arched passageway; very often a covered passageway in front of a row of shops.

30.2 [24]   *the Washington Post March.* A stirring march, hopelessly out of place here, by the American bandmaster and composer, John Philip Sousa (1854–1932), originally written for a celebration marking the fiftieth anniversary of the newspaper, *The Washington Post,* in 1889.

30.3 [24]   *tortilla stands.* Curb-side hot-plates on which tortillas (large thin corn-meal pancakes) are cooked to be filled with chicken, meat, and vegetables for a tasty if not always hygienic snack. *Naptha* is a derivative from coal that has been used for lighting purposes since the late eighteenth century.

30.4 [24]   *Las Manos de Orlac... 6 y 8.30. Las Manos de Orlac, con Peter Lorre.* Sp. "*The Hands of Orlac... 6* and *8.30. The Hands of Orlac,* with Peter Lorre." This is the same film coincidentally, that was playing this day one year earlier. Originally *Orlacs Hände,* Austria, 1925, directed by Robert Weine, with Conrad Veidt in the title role; remade 1935 with Peter Lorre as Orlac (entitled *Mad Love* in the U.S.A.). As Hugh says, p. 114 [110], "He's a great actor but it's a lousy picture.... It's all about a pianist who has a sense of guilt because he thinks his hands are a murderer's or something and keeps washing the blood off them. Perhaps they really are a murderer's, but I forget."

In the 1935 Hollywood version Colin Clive (who had played the scientist in the classic *Frankenstein* of 1931) was cast as Steve Orlac, a famous concert pianist. Peter Lorre plays Dr. Gogol, who is in love with Orlac's wife Yvonne, an actress in Grand Guignol theatre (Lowry may have taken his heroine's name from this movie). Dr. Gogol forces his attentions on the young wife, who not only rejects him but at one point faints at his grotesque attentions. Orlac loses his hands in a railroad accident, and Yvonne reluctantly turns to Gogol, the world's greatest surgeon in such cases, for assistance. He hears that a murderer named Rollo has been guillotined that same day, and he grafts Rollo's hands onto Orlac. Gogol then embarks on a plan by which Orlac, Yvonne, and the police will come to believe that Orlac — or Rollo's hands — is guilty of a series of crimes. At the least, he hopes that Orlac will be driven mad and that he then will be able to win Yvonne. Eventually, Gogol is revealed to be the murderer. Stephen kills him in a struggle, and the couple are reunited. There is a remote parallel between this version and Lowry's novel since the main characters are in love with a heroine named Yvonne, but more relevant are the bloody hands which, like those of the pelado, p. 253 [250], symbolize the collective guilt of mankind ("LJC," p. 69).

Peter Lorre (1904–64) was a Hungarian-born actor introduced to Hollywood audiences with *The Hands of Orlac*. Among his other major films were *Spring Awakening* (1928); Fritz Lang's *M* (1931); Hitchcock's *The Man Who Knew Too Much* (1934); and Sternberg's *Crime and Punishment* (1935). While many reviewers thought that Lorre's performance was on a level above the quality of the film, current critical opinion does not agree with Hugh's low estimate; it has been ranked among the best fantasy films ever made (its director, Karl Freund, had also done the classic *Dracula* of 1931). For Lowry and Laruelle, *The Hands of Orlac* was a powerful symbol of the horrors of the 1930's and the oncoming violence in Europe.

30.5 [24] *the Student of Prague.* The film, *Der Student von Prag,* of which there were three versions: 1913, directed by Stellan Rye, with Paul Wegener; 1926, directed by Henrik Galeen, with Conrad Veidt and Werner Krauss (the one Laruelle has in mind); and 1936, directed by Arthur Robison. Based on the Faust legend and Poe's "William Wilson," the film concerns a student named Baldwin, who has sold his reflection to a sorcerer, Scapinelli, and who becomes a social outcast when his mirror image slays in a duel a man whose life Baldwin had promised to spare. Baldwin buys back his soul at the cost of his own life and shoots his mirror image, thereby killing himself in a displaced form of suicide.

30.6 [24] *Wiene.* Robert Wiene (1881–1938), a German film director who achieved international recognition with *Das Cabinett der Dr. Caligari* (1919). His other films include *Raskolnikov* (1923), based on Dostoievsky's *Crime and Punishment; Orlacs Hände* (1925); and *Ultimatum* (1938).

30.7 [24] *Werner Krauss.* Werner Krauss (1884–1959), a German actor whose major roles include the insane doctor in *Das Cabinett der Dr. Caligari* (1919); Pontius Pilate in *INRI* (1924); Jack the Ripper in *Waxworks* (1924); and the butcher in *Joyless Street* (1925). Unfortunately, he is remembered more for his support of Hitler and his starring role in the viciously anti-Semitic film *Jud Suss* in the war years.

30.8 [24] *Karl Grüne.* Karl Grüne (1885–1962), a minor German film director of Czech-Austrian origin, who "dealt with pacifist and patriotic themes and experimented with naturalism and other new forms" (Andersen, p. 206). His major film was *Die Strasse* (1923), but minor ones include *Arabella* (1925); *Königin Louisa* (1928); and *Waterloo* (1929).

30.9 [24]   *the Ufa days.* "Ufa" stands for *Universum Film Aktiengesellschaft,* a German production company founded in 1917 to promote German culture and improve Germany's image abroad. The Ufa *Film Palast am Zoo* was a big cinema in Berlin, opened in 1919. The Ufa in effect controlled the German film industry and produced most of the important expressionist films in the 1920's, but later it lost most of its best actors and directors to Hollywood. With the rise of Nazism, the Ufa was brought increasingly under state control, and it ceased to exist by the end of World War II.

30.10 [24]   *Conrad Veidt.* Conrad Veidt (1893–1943), a famous German character actor, equally impressive as hero or villain. His major roles were in such early German films as *Das Cabinett der Dr. Caligari* (1919); *Der Janus Kopf* (1920); *Waxworks* (1924); *Orlacs Hände* (1925); and *Der Student von Prag* (1926), but he went on to make films in Britain: *The Wandering Jew* (1933); *King of the Damned* (1935); *Dark Journey* (1937), and in the U.S.A.: *A Woman's Face* (1941); and *Casablanca* (1942).

30.11 [24]   *that particular film.* The 1925 version of *The Hands of Orlac;* this earlier version was slightly more subtle than the 1935 one, stressing the pianist's sense of guilt rather than the melodrama.

31.1 [25]   *the hieroglyphic of the times.*   In an early draft (UBC 7-13, p. 7), Laruelle "remembered Sir Thomas Browne having said of tavern music, a hieroglyphical and shadowed lesson of the whole world." The reference is ironic, since Sir Thomas Browne (*Religio Medici,* Pt. 2, #9) sees in even such vulgar music a sign of the greater harmony which perfectly orders all things, whereas Laruelle sees only a world plummeting to its bloody destruction.

31.2 [25]   *Cervecería XX.* Sp. "Brewery *Dos Equis,*" that is, two X's (Andersen, p. 85). Dos Equis, a dark beer, is offered by Cervantes in the *Salón Ofélia,* p. 293 [291], but the name of the cantina also suggests the Cervecería Quauhnahuac of Ch. 4, visited by Hugh and Yvonne, mounted on two horses.

31.3 [25]   *Chingar . . . chingado.* The verb *chingar* means "to fuck" or "to rape," and its various forms can be used in a variety of ways as expletives or terms of abuse. Sr. Bustamente's use of the words anticipates that of one part of the crowd about the dying Indian, p. 247 [244].

31.4 [25]   *the wires have decomposed.* Sr. Bustamente's peculiar anglicization of the Sp. *descompuesto,* "out of order," anticipates Dr. Vigil's comment, p. 148 [144], "But after much tequila the eclectic systemë is perhaps *un poco descompuesto, comprenez,* as sometimes in the *cine: claro?"*

32.1 [26] *'Tequila. . . . No, anís—anís, por favor, señor. . . . Y una—ah—gaseosa.'* Sp. "*Tequila. . . .* No, *anís—anís,* please. . . . And a—ah—soda water." A gaseosa is not any fizzy soft-drink, but rather Tehuacán water (see note **12.1**) "con gas," that is, unsugared and carbonated, its salts and carbonates supposedly beneficial in a way that tequila and anís are not. M. Laruelle hesitates, possibly because he subconsciously recalls his words of one year ago: "If I ever start to drink that stuff, Geoffrey, you'll know I'm done for" (see note **219.3**).

32.2 [26] *compañero.* Sp. "companion"; the word is that uttered by the dying Indian (see note **250.1**) and by the old fiddler to the dying Consul (see note **374.2**). All three instances of this highly significant word were surprisingly late additions to the manuscripts.

32.3 [26] *we have not revived it. It has only returned.* In an earlier draft (UBC 10-2, p. 7), Sr. Bustamente was even more philosophical: "they return, they begin all over again. It is the return eternal." Lowry had found in Ouspensky and Dunne a philosophical confirmation of his own feelings about the unreality of time and its possible displacement in a serial universe and in Nietzsche the idea of the eternal return (which Dunne explicitly dismisses, *An Experiment with Time,* p. 214). All these ideas for Lowry were exemplified by the cinema, as Paul Tiessen suggests (Woodcock, p. 140):

> That the present cannot escape the past, that the impotence of man's present merges with the guilt of his past, is symbolically best expressed in a cinematic style where the circularity of the form, imitating the circular motion of the reel, can manipulate the overlapping and merging of time.

32.4 [26] *the Spanish War.* The Spanish Civil War, which officially began with the landing of Foreign Legion troops in Spain on 19 July 1936 and the ensuing revolts of sympathy by army garrisons in Seville and Andalusia. It had ended early in 1939. Thus the newsreels which Sr. Bustamente is showing are well out of date.

32.5 [26] *autoridades box.* A box seat reserved for the theatre manager.

32.6 [26] *a garish threesheet*. A one-sheet is a single advertising poster, 28 inches by 42 inches; a three-sheet is a poster equivalent in size to three one-sheets and is so-called because it is folded twice, dividing the sheet into three parts.

32.7 [26] *La simpatiquísima y encantadora María Landrock, notable artista alemana que pronto habremos de ver en sensacional Film*. Maria Landrock was a minor German actress, born 1922, who became well known as a young skater (taking part in the 1936 Olympics) before turning to the theatre. Her brief film career lasted from 1940 to 1944 (her first film was *Aus erster Ehe,* 1940), which makes the mention of her here slightly anachronistic. Her presence, Lowry suggests ("LJC," p. 70), sounds an ominous political note, being one more reminder of the constant German presence, while the "garish" display of her features suggests the sexual temptation embodied in the other María, p. 348 [348].

32.8 [26] *frijoles*. Beans, usually of the pinto variety, dried or boiled with onion, pepper, garlic and chili; a very basic dish.

32.9 [26] *three cigarettes were lit on one match*. An allusion to the old belief that this is bad luck; Laruelle is sensitive to the sinister qualities of the scene. See also note **308.1**.

32.10 [26] *It was already seven o'clock*. The precise hour of the Consul's death, one year earlier. Ominous hints of that event are present in the shape of pariah dogs; the procession of torch-lit shadows hinting at a spiritually inverted world; the reference to *autoridades,* or officials; and the *salida,* or exit, sign at the rear.

32.11 [27] *the Gambrinus or Charley's Place*. Restaurants in Cuernavaca. The Gambrinus (named after the mighty German brewery, itself named for the patron saint of brewers) at Morelos 405 has long disappeared (the building now houses the Bellas Artes Institute). Charley's Place (now flourishing as "Pepe's Moustache" beside "Malinche's Grill and Bar") was in 1938 "unmistakable — you could see the sign a mile off, a little corner café with open stone arches and red-covered tables, facing the palace square" (Conrad Aiken, *A Heart for the Gods of Mexico,* p. 464). It was once the scene of a violent quarrel between Lowry and Aiken, described in the latter's *Ushant,* p. 352, concerning the son's need to devour his spiritual father.

33.1 [27] *the meeting of Cortez and Moctezuma in Tenochtitlán*. Perhaps the most significant single moment in Mexico's history:

(a) *Cortez*. Hernando, or Hernán Cortés (1485–1547), Spanish conquistador and conqueror of Mexico, who set sail in 1519 from Cuba with a
small band of adventurers, landing at and founding the city of Vera
Cruz before marching the two hundred miles inland to the Aztec capital
of Tenochtitlán. After initial skirmishing with the Tlaxcalans, traditional enemies of the Aztecs, Cortés won them to his cause and advanced via Cholula (see note **17.3**) towards the capital. Moctezuma, the
Aztec emperor, half believing that Cortés was the god Quetzalcóatl (see
note **301.4**), received the Spaniards with guarded but generous hospitality, but Cortés, seeing how precarious his position was, resolved to
take the emperor hostage. Eventually, the Aztecs rose up against the
Spaniards, and, on the "Noche Triste," or Sad Night, 1 July 1520,
Cortés lost most of his men trying to break out of the city (see note
289.6.c). Cortés immediately made plans to return, and with the help of
Spanish and Indian reinforcements, a fleet of ships (see note **301.6**),
and a smallpox plague which carried off tens of thousands of Aztecs, he
laid seige to Tenochtitlán. After some months of fierce fighting, the city
fell on 21 August 1521. Cortés consolidated his success so well that
within twenty years Mexico was completely controlled by Spain. He
was rewarded with the title of Marquis of the Valley of Oaxaca, but not
with that of viceroy, which he believed he deserved, and after an abortive expedition to Honduras, he returned to his palace and hacienda in
Cuernavaca, spending his last two decades in Mexico and Spain in
largely frustrating and disappointing civil disputes.

(b) *Moctezuma*. Moctezuma II (1466–1520), was Aztec emperor from 1502
and undisputed ruler over wide territories in Central Mexico and some
thirty million subjects. He was venerated as semi-divine and respected
for his proven prowess, but he lived in the shadow of historical inevitability since he knew that Quetzalcóatl would return to reclaim his
rightful throne. Unable to resist the apparent invincibility of the
Spaniards, Moctezuma welcomed them to Tenochtitlán, but he was
taken hostage and later killed, probably by a stone thrown by the
Aztecs as he was urging them not to resist the Spaniards. His death
signalled the beginning of outright hostilities between the Spaniards
and the Aztecs, culminating in the total destruction of the latter's
civilization.

(c) *Tenochtitlán*. The Aztec capital on an island in Lake Texcoco, founded
about 1325 (see note **49.5**). From humble beginnings among the
swamps and reeds it rose to become a magnificent and impressive city
of some sixty thousand houses, with gleaming white stucco buildings,

canals and dikes, clean wide streets, busy market places, fountains, palaces, pyramids and temples, floating gardens (chinampas) to sustain a population of perhaps three hundred thousand, and long causeways and aqueducts linking the island to the mainland: a city and a civilization easily the equal of anything in Europe at the time, despite its emphasis upon militarism and human sacrifice. The final Spanish assault upon the city reduced it literally to rubble, and after the Aztec defeat the Spaniards completed the work of destruction, creating the new Mexico City from its ruins.

(d) *The Meeting of Cortez and Moctezuma.* On 8 November 1519 — a Spanish force of about four hundred, with six thousand Tlaxcalan allies, crossed the causeway and drawbridge from the south to enter Tenochtitlán where they were met by a splendid retinue of Aztec warriors and the royal palanquin of Moctezuma, who descended in gorgeous finery to greet Cortés, who was dressed in shining armour and mounted on his great war horse. The two saluted each other, gifts were exchanged, and Moctezuma welcomed the Spaniards into his capital, which they were to destroy within two years. The place of the meeting (the corner of Salvador and Pino Suarez) is now marked by the sixteenth-century Hospital of Jesus of Nazareth.

33.2 [27] *El último Emperador Azteca... Moctezuma y Hernán Cortés representativo de la raza hispana, quedan frente a frente: dos razas y dos civilizaciones que habían llegado a un alto grado de perfección se mezclan para integrar el núcleo de nuestra nacionalidad actual.* Sp. "The last Aztec Emperor... Moctezuma and Hernán Cortés, representative of the Spanish race, meet face to face: two races and two civilizations which had attained a high degree of perfection unite to form the nucleus of our present national character." Apart from the generally misleading hyperbole, the calendar makes at least one error of fact: Moctezuma was not the last Aztec emperor, since he was followed by Cuitláhuac and Cuauhtémoc before the fall of Tenochtitlán. As Walker suggests, p. 250, the "relatively innocuous bit of nationalistic bravado" becomes in relation to the farreaching Conquest motif of *UTV* "an ironic portent of considerable magnitude." In some of the earlier manuscripts there is evidence that Lowry was also trying to draw parallels between the meeting of Cortés and Moctezuma and that of Hitler and Chamberlain (and even Franco and Sir Samuel Hoare), but the obvious attempt to do so was dropped.

33.3 [27] *the thumbed maroon volume of Elizabethan plays.* Geoffrey's copy of *Eight Famous Elizabethan Plays,* edited by E. C. Dunn (New York, Random House, Modern Library College Edition, 1932). The book had been lent to Laruelle some eighteen months earlier to help him research a possible film based on the Faustus story and never returned. The eight plays are *The Tragical History of Doctor Faustus,* by Christopher Marlowe; *The Shoemaker's Holiday,* by Thomas Dekker; *A Woman Killed with Kindness,* by Thomas Heywood; *Volpone, or The Fox, A Comedy,* by Ben Jonson; *The Maid's Tragedy,* by Francis Beaumont and John Fletcher; *A New Way to Pay Old Debts,* by Philip Massinger; and *'Tis Pity She's a Whore,* by John Ford. Lowry had a copy of the book, a gift from his second wife; it is addressed on the flyleaf "To my husband—Christmas, 1940, with all my love. Margie."

33.4 [27] *the roses and the plumbago and the waxplants 'like dilapidated préservatifs.'* The plants seem innocent in themselves, but, as the Consul's "diabolical look" implies, each possesses additional alchemical or mystical significance:
(a) *roses.* The flower of Venus, but with the cross (the rose upon the rood of time) the most important symbol of the Rosicrucians, the mystical order founded in the fifteenth century by Christian Rosenkreuz and introduced to England by Robert Fludd and Thomas Vaughan. W. B. Yeats's "Rosa Alchemica" (1897) tells of the initiation into the Order of the Alchemical Rose, whose secrets are revealed in "The Tables of the Law" (1897) to be "not of this earth."
(b) *plumbago.* Pliny's *molybdaena,* or leadwort; so-called because of the bluish lead-like colour of its spikes of flowers. Lead is the metal of Saturn, the softest and most lowly of metals, which might act as the base metal for attempted transmutations to a higher form.
(c) *waxplants.* Otherwise *Hoya,* a genus of tropical climbing plants of the milkweed family, with shiny green leaves and a large waxy white flower (which the Consul rather unfairly describes in terms of a used condom). Ceration (from Gk. *keros,* "wax") is one of the standard processes in alchemy, implying the changing of a substance into a soft wax-like condition as a prelude to further activity.
The Consul's comment about "dilapidated *préservatifs*" underlines the alchemical references noted above, since dilapidated (from L. *lapis,* "a stone") hints at the philosopher's stone and préservatif (despite its basic meaning of "condom") at the elixir of life.

33.5 [27] *an emblem of what even now it is impossible to return.* A reference to his wife's lost virtue, taken by Laruelle.

33.6 [28] *A modern film version of the Faustus story.* The original Faust seems to have been a wandering conjurer living in Germany about 1488–1541, who has come to symbolize man's aspiring quest for forbidden knowledge. *The Tragical History of Doctor Faustus* (1691), by Christopher Marlowe (1564–93), is a drama in blank verse and prose taking the legend for its subject matter. Faustus, weary of the sciences and master of permitted knowledge, turns to magic and summons up the figure of Mephistophilis with whom he makes a pact to sell his soul in return for twenty-four years of unlimited pleasure and power. This is granted him, and Faustus indulges himself, but as time runs out, he begins to despair. Torn between good and evil, his familiars offering the choice of salvation or despair, Faustus agonizes, unable to turn to the salvation apparently held out to him. At the crucial moment, Mephistophilis sends him a vision of Helen of Troy ("the face that launched a thousand ships"), and Faustus succumbs to his fate. In a final hour of intense despair, he contemplates his fate before being dragged off, screaming, to hell. *Doctor Faustus* is Lowry's single most important source for *Under the Volcano*. Parallels between Faustus and the Consul are frequently iterated; the action of the novel closely imitates that of the play in many ways; the dilemma of the choice between salvation and despair is central to both dramas; and both work within the bounds of a tightly moralistic structure only to penetrate disturbingly into the complexities of human motivation. For the suggestion that Chs. 2 to 10 represent Laruelle's "modern film version of the Faustus story," see note **15.1**; in the first novel version (UBC 7–2, p. 4) Laruelle was much more explicit about his intentions:

> "My God," said Laruelle, "If only I had time to put a character like the Consul on film! Yes, supposing Doctor, that all the suffering and the chaos and conflict of the present were to take human form. And to become conscious of itself! That is the impression I would want to give of my man: a man whom, too, like Jesus, a great betrayal of the human spirit would appear in the guise of a private anguishing betrayal. And you would realize somehow too that this character of mine was yet aware of all the agonies with which the human lot would become involved. And my word, now that I think of it, Doctor, it almost does seem possible that it already happened! Supposing that all these horrors of today before they became a part of our lives suddenly convulsed upon themselves to create a soul, and then the soul sought a body, and the only body it had found sufficiently photophobic for its purposes was the Consul's!" He was looking intently at Vigil, his eyes excited. "Yes, if I could only convey the effect of a man who was the very shape and motion of the world's doom," he went on, "But at the same time the living prophecy of its hope!"

"You would need a screen as big as the world to show it in," said the doctor.

33.7 [28] *Trotsky.* Leon Trotsky (1879–1940), the name assumed by Lev Davidovich Bronstein, the Russian politician of Jewish origin second only to Lenin as the outstanding architect of the Russian Revolution. He had early joined the Social Democrat Party, but despite some differences of opinion with Lenin joined the Bolsheviks in 1917, taking an active part in the Revolution and then as commissar for war directing the Red Army in the ensuing civil war. After Lenin's death in 1924, Trotsky was defeated in the struggle for leadership by Stalin, dismissed from office in 1925, and expelled from the Soviet Union in 1929, finally entering Mexico in 1937 and taking up residence at Coyoacán in Mexico City. He remained in Mexico until 20 August 1940, when he was assassinated with a pick-axe by a Stalinist agent, Ramón Mercader, whom he knew and trusted. This murder, which Lowry would have been aware of when writing but which had not in 1939 yet come to pass, casts a shadow of tragic inevitability over the novel, particularly on p. 358 [358], when the Consul is "identified" as Trotsky.

34.1 [28] *the one jalousie door.* A typical cantina might have a heavy metal door which can be rolled up when the cantina is open and which affords security when it is shut and within that a much lighter and shorter door to screen drinkers from the street. A jalousie door is one made of overlapping slats which keep out the sun while letting in light and air (rather like a Venetian blind) or, as seems likely in the Cervecería XX, a wooden door into which such slats are set.

34.2 [28] *an appoggiatura.* From It. *appoggiare,* "to lean"; in music, an embellishing note or tone preceding the key melodic tone or note and usually written as a note of smaller size.

34.3 [28] *the bicho.* Sr. Bustamente means *bicho viviente,* literally, "living soul"; a common cliché, but one particularly relevant on this Day of the Dead. In Mexican Spanish the phrase has the connotation of one who is a little odd, a screwball.

34.4 [28] *The Americano.* There is a widespread penchant among Mexicans to identify all non-natives, including Canadians and Europeans, as Americans.

34.5 [28] *a solid frieze carved into the wall.* The waiting men resemble the

Tlahuican warriors of the Rivera murals on the Cortés Palace (see note **215.6**), while the reference to "the murderer's hands" suggests the bloody hands of the conquistador (see note **237.1**). There may also be a suggestion of Arthur Robison's 1922 film, *Warning Shadows,* subtitled "A Nocturnal Hallucination." A film remarkable for its use of light and shadows, it depicts six persons in a state of trance, watching their shadows act out their passions, before they awake from their collective nightmare (Kracauer, p. 113).

34.6 [29] *the poor guy, he have no socks.* Nor does the Consul have socks on, p. 50 [45], when Yvonne first sees him. Although there are physical and medical reasons for the Consul's painfully swollen feet, this disorder in his dress reflects his psychic state, as Kilgallin makes clear, p. 185, quoting from W. J. Turner's *The Duchess of Popocatepetl* (1939), p. 114: "Education . . . is entirely a matter of adjusting the proper expression and repression of the human psyche according to circumstances and needs. In other words it is simply a question of when to take off and put on your socks."

35.1 [29] *it was only during the last year that he had been drinking so heavily.* The Consul comments, p. 67 [62], on Jacques's weak stomach for drink; this change in his drinking habits is one small indication that Laruelle is being depicted as a miniature Consul figure, as one who shares Geoffrey's guilt as he too becomes aware of a love that has come too late. On p. 213 [210] this identification between the two is made by the Consul himself in such a way as to suggest that something of himself "for obscure purposes of his own" is passing into Jacques. This suggestion is here reinforced by Laruelle's vision of himself lying in the bath; an intimation very similar to the Consul's recurrent hallucination, p. 96 [91], of the dead man beside the swimming-pool, the "other" who is in part himself.

35.2 [29] *his own zacuali . . . his useless tower against the coming of the second flood.* The coming storm reminds Laruelle not only of his own zacuali, the strange tower on his house in the Calle Nicaragua (see note **198.3**), but also of the Aztec creation myth about the Deluge. The myth exists in many variants, but Lowry's direct source is Donnelly's *Atlantis,* pp. 103–4:

It is found in the histories of the Toltecs that this age and *first world,* as they call it, lasted 1716 years; that men were destroyed by tremendous rains and lightning from the sky, and even all the land, without the exception of anything, and the highest mountains, were covered up and

submerged in water *fifteen cubits* (caxtolmolati); and here they added
other fables of how men came to multiply from the few who escaped
from this destruction in a "toplipetlocali;" that this word nearly signifies a close chest; and how, after men had multiplied, they erected a
very high "zacuali," which is today a tower of great height, in order to
take refuge in it should the second world (age) be destroyed. Presently
their languages were confused, and, not being able to understand each
other, they went to different parts of the earth.

According to Prescott, Appendix I, p. 693, two persons survived this
deluge: Coxcox and his wife (see note **91.3**), who built a boat. Their many
children remained dumb until a dove gave them the gift of languages, but
these differed so much that the children could not understand one another
(hence the associations not only with Noah and Deucalion, but also with the
Tower of Babel—see note **17.3**). Lewis Spence casts doubts upon the
validity of interpretations of the Codices giving exactly what the Christian
interpreters wanted to find and recounts an alternative tradition of the giant
Xlehua building the pyramid at Cholula as a tower to escape the second
deluge should it come (*M of M & P*, pp. 120–21). Even so, this is remarkably like the widespread vulgar error, "That the Tower of Babel was erected
against a second deluge" (Sir Thomas Browne, *Pseudodoxia Epidemica*,
Bk. VII, Ch. 6). In an earlier draft (UBC 7–2, pp. 10–11), Laruelle was
more explicit about the zacuali, which he claimed was built after the Deluge
to prevent the destruction of the "second world"; he linked the tower
explicitly to his own house, expressing more clearly his fears that with the
outbreak of war the world might be on its way to destruction and his house,
an inadequate refuge.

35.3 [29] *Night of the Culmination of the Pleiades!* The Pleiades were the
seven daughters of Atlas and Pleione, who were turned into doves after
their deaths, then placed by Zeus among the stars, where they form part of
the constellation of Taurus. There is a traditional association of the
Pleiades with beneficent spring showers and autumn storms (in Mexico,
more or less coinciding with the beginning and end of the rainy season), but,
in addition, as R. H. Allen notes, the Pleiades "are intimately connected
with the tradition of the flood found among so many and widely separated
nations" (*Stars and Their Names*, p. 398). The culmination of a constellation is simply the moment at which it reaches its highest point in the sky, but
Lowry's capitals and the general sense of threat which Laruelle expresses
point to something more than a vague fear of flooding. Lewis Spence notes
that the movement of the Pleiades was closely associated among the Aztecs
with the fear of the world coming to an end every fifty-two years (*M of M & P*,

p. 41), and his meaning is further clarified by Prescott, I.iv, p. 73, who discusses the Aztec tradition of the destruction of the world and describes how they would sacrifice a victim and kindle a new fire by the friction of sticks placed in his wounded breast to ensure the beginning of a new cycle at the end of every fifty-two year "century" (see note **86.7**). Prescott says that this was done when the Pleiades approached the zenith, that is, in late December during the five unlucky days of Uayeb (the month the Consul likes best—see note **86.9**), but he also quotes two previous authorities (Sagahun and Torquemada) who say that such sacrifices took place at the actual moment of the culmination of the Pleiades, at midnight in mid-November. This latter notion seems to be what Laruelle is referring to, yet Lowry has used Prescott to get the best of both worlds: to suggest the "sacrifice" of Geoffrey during the unlucky month of *Uayeb*, while yet retaining the consistency of his action in November. Above all, he is anticipating the death of Yvonne, p. 337 [336], who senses herself like one of the daughters of Atlas being gathered up towards the Pleiades.

35.4 [29] *What, after all, was a Consul that one was mindful of him?* An allusion to Psalm 8:3-5:

> When I consider thy heavens, the work of thy fingers,
> the moon and the stars, which thou hast ordained;
> What is man, that thou art mindful of him? and the
> son of man, that thou visitest him?
> For thou hast made him a little lower than the angels,
> and hast crowned him with glory and honour.

The psalm is one of total faith, jubilation, and exaltation, praising the excellence of the Lord, who has set his glory above the heavens; the reference here is magnificently ironic in the context of the second flood and the night of the culmination of the Pleiades.

35.5 [29] *the days of Porfirio Díaz.* Díaz was the president of Mexico, 1877-80 and 1884-1911. His regime is commonly considered one of total corruption even though it brought Mexico forcibly into the twentieth century as well as to the point of revolution (see note **112.4**). Lowry's next sentences are an almost direct quotation from John Kenneth Turner's bitter indictment of that era, *Barbarous Mexico,* p. 240:

> Nearly every small town along the Mexican border harbors a personage
> who enjoys the title of Mexican consul. Consuls are found in villages
> hundreds of miles from the Mexican border. Consuls are supposed to

be for the purpose of looking after the interests of trade between countries, but towns in California, Arizona, New Mexico and Texas which
do not do a hundred dollars worth of trade a year with Mexico have
consuls who are maintained by Diaz at the expense of tens of thousands
of dollars a year.

Such consuls are not consuls at all. They are spies, persecutors,
bribers.

Turner also notes, p. 237, that Douglas, Arizona, was a major centre for
Mexican liberals living in the United States and tells how in 1906 the
machinations of such "consuls" resulted in large groups of Mexican liberals
being arrested and many being returned to Mexico on the flimsiest of
pretexts.

35.6 [29] *the Ponciano Arriaga.* A liberal political organization formed in
San Luis Potosí in the early 1900's. On 24 January 1902 it was bold enough
to hold a public meeting, but the audience was infiltrated by soldiers and
police, who, on a given signal, rose up in protest, disrupted the meeting,
and arrested the organizers for disturbing the peace (Turner, *Barbarous
Mexico,* pp. 140–41).

The club is named after Ponciano Arriaga (1811–63), an orator and
liberal idealist from San Luis Potosí, whose opposition to Santa Anna had
led to his own removal from office and imprisonment. In the war against
the United States, 1847, he distinguished himself, bitterly opposing the
peace treaty and the ceding of territory, but when Santa Anna was restored,
he went to New Orleans, where he was closely associated with liberal groups
led by Juárez and Melchor Ocampo. For his work in the reform movement
and his ideas upon federation, Arriaga is known as "the Father of the Constitution." He is sometimes confused with another of the same name, a
general who had supported Juárez against Maximilian and died in 1892.

35.7 [29] *Almazán.* Juan Andreu Almazán (1891–1965), general and politician, who was the right-wing conservative candidate (representing the
PRUN, or *Partido Revolucionarío de Unificación Nacional*) for the 1940
presidential elections and who was destined to lose to Avila Camacho. His
career up to 1939 had been a mixture of brilliance and opportunism; he had
supported in turn Madero, Huerta, Zapata, and Carranza, switching sides
at precisely the right moment to save his skin and further his career. He was
reputedly one of the richest men in Mexico.

36.1 [30] *England had severed diplomatic relations with Mexico.* Perhaps
the most significant event of the presidency of Lázaro Cárdenas (1934–40)

took place on 18 March 1938, when the Mexican government signed a de-cree nationalizing the holdings of seventeen foreign oil companies, including a number of British interests and resisted demands for compen-sation on the grounds that the original investments had been regained many times. The nationalization decree became something of an international cause célèbre, evoking the patriotic support of other Latin American heads of state and the majority of Mexicans, but American and British retaliation caused serious political and economic difficulties: embargos were imposed upon Mexican oil, production fell, the value of the peso dropped, and Cárdenas, though a committed socialist, was forced to turn to the Axis powers for sales and machinery. Compromise was eventually achieved, but one immediate effect was that diplomatic relationships between Mexico and England worsened until in April 1938 they were severed, remaining so for three years. Geoffrey Firmin's consulate is therefore closed (see p. 223 [220]), and he has been technically out of a job for some months, which raises the question of why he has stayed on in Quauhnahuac. Given the con-fused political situation existing in Mexico at the end of 1938, the charges of spying made against him are not altogether ridiculous, and even if they are unfounded, a deliberate ambiguity clouds the Consul's motives for staying on in Mexico (for Lowry's original intentions in this matter, see note **81.1**). In an important sense, the severing of relations is also a metaphor for the Consul's broken marriage; as Geoffrey makes clear in his letter, p. 42 [36], both publicly and privately he is adrift.

36.2 [30] *a sort of spy, or, as he put it, spider.* The pun arises from the similarity of Sp. *espía,* "spy," and English *spider* (though Lowry apparently believed that the Spanish word for spy was really *espidero*). How real the Consul's fears of being "around the town pursued by other spiders" are is an open question (see note **56.4**), but the man in dark glasses makes a number of appearances throughout the novel, and the bald boy with earrings is seen swinging madly on his hammock, p. 243 [240].

36.3 [30] *desconsolado.* Sp. "disconsolate"; with possibly a pun on "dis-Consulate," since the Consul (like a peri outside the gates of Paradise — see note **322.1**) has just been described as "dispossessed."

36.4 [30] *could not cross the border in a cattle truck.* As Hugh had done, p. 101 [96], for the kind of dubious political reasons which would be of great interest to right-wing sympathizers.

36.5 [30] *the cantina El Bosque.* The "terminal cantina," which the Consul visits before leaving for Tomalín; see pp. 228-33 [225-30]. The Spanish word *bosque* means "wood" or "forest," thereby echoing the dark wood theme sounded by *Selva* on p. 9 [3]. In *DATG,* p. 247, Lowry states that the original cantina El Bosque was in Oaxaca, by 1946 converted into "an innocent lonchería of some kind."

36.6 [31] *Sanctuario.* More correctly, Sp. *Santuario,* "sanctuary." In fleeing to Señora Gregorio this way, the Consul is observing the old tradition of seeking a place of refuge in order to escape punishment for his offences; in the Middle Ages such protection was afforded by the Church to those evading the law. The word is an important motif throughout the novel, the Consul ultimately finding the paradise of his despair in the dark sanctuary of the Farolito, p. 339 [338].

37.1 [31] *simpatico.* Sp. "sympathetic"; but possessing a much deeper sense of empathy and understanding than the English word implies. It is the quality displayed on p. 342 [341] by the one-legged beggar who puts a coin into the legless beggar's hand and by the potter, the old woman, and the fiddler, pp. 368 and 374 [367 and 374], to the poor Consul when he in his turn is taken by the police.

37.2 [32] *Guillaume Apollinaire.* The name assumed by Wilhelm Apollinaris Kostrowitzky (1880–1918), French poet of Polish extraction born in Rome, who joined up in 1914 and fought bravely at the Front, revelling in the military life. His best work is contained in the two volumes *Alcools* (1913) and *Calligrammes* (1918), the cubist and surrealist qualities of which placed him at the head of the avant-garde movement. Laruelle has in mind, however, poems such as "L'adieu du Cavalier" ("The Horseman's Farewell"), with lines such as "Ah Dieu! que la guerre est jolie" ("Ah God! how beautiful war is"), which glorify war as a marvellous adventure — a fact belied by Apollinaire's own war wounds and death shortly before the armistice.

38.1 [32] *the S.S. Samaritan.* The ship's name (grimly incongruous, considering its mission) brings to mind the parable of the good Samaritan (see note **67.1**) and anticipates the dying Indian of Ch. 8, the Consul's guilt about his involvement or lack thereof being an important psychological force driving him to his destruction. It has been argued (Dodson, p. 25) that the Consul is of "an impossibly tender age to have been commander of a gunboat" (on p. 22 [16] he is described as aged fifteen in 1911, which would make him about twenty-one at the presumed time of the incident). Manuscript notes (TM, VI, p. 45) show that Lowry was aware of the problem, which he seems to have resolved by deliberately creating a mystery: on the one hand, with the accelerated promotion and appointment possible by privilege in the British wartime navy (to say nothing of Geoffrey's undoubted abilities), Geoffrey's rank is not impossible; on the other, especially since the incident is seen only from the point of view of Laruelle, whose knowledge is equally limited, there remains a strong possibility that the Consul has fabricated or exaggerated the extent of his involvement or responsibility. We can never know, but the natural curiosity aroused by the desire to find out gives the incident great emotional intensity and ensures the reader's engagement with the Consul's guilt from the outset.

Ronald Binns (*MLN* 8) has tracked down the probable historical source of the Samaritan incident: the so-called "*Baralong* incident" of 19 August 1915, after the capture of the British ship, the *Nicosian,* by the German submarine U-27. A British Q-ship, the *Baralong,* appeared flying the American flag, let fall its false sides, and sank the submarine. The master, Lieutenant-Commander Godfrey Herbert (whose name and rank is similar to Geoffrey's), ordered his crew to give no quarter, and twelve German sailors were shot. There was no court-martial nor any suggestion of officers being put in the furnace, but the incident aroused great resentment among the Germans.

38.2 [32] *steering a rather odd course.* The S.S. *Samaritan* obviously has some inkling of a German U-boat off the southern coast of Japan. The location is historically impossible, since German U-boats did not operate so far afield and since the range of British Q-ships was restricted to a circle from Archangel to New York to Gibralter (Gordon Campbell, *My Mystery Ships,* p. 5). The Bungo Strait separates Kyushu from Shikoku, and the "various interesting islands" are to be found scattered over an area directly south of Japan, their interest for Lowry as much a function of their names as their locations:

(a) *Lot's Wife.* Also known as Sofu-gan, or Rica de Oro, or Black Rock; in the Izu-shichito group; a remarkable pillar of black rock sticking some 326 feet out of the water and said to resemble from a distance a ship in full sail. In Genesis 19:26, as Lot and his wife flee Sodom and Gomorrah, the wife disobeys God's instructions not to look back and is turned into a pillar of salt.

(b) *Arzobispo.* Sp. "archbishop"; the name given by early Spanish explorers to Chichijima, the largest of the Bonin Islands (also known as the Ogasawara Gunto), some 550 miles south of Tokyo. The name Arzobispo was sometimes applied to the group as a whole.

(c) *Rosario.* Sp. "Rosary"; also known as Nishino Shima and Disappointment Island; a rocky barren island in dangerous waters, about one hundred miles west of the Bonin group.

(d) *Sulphur Island.* A former name of Iwo-jima, the largest and most

important of the Volcano Islands, known for its large volcano and
extensive sulphur mines. In March 1945 it was the scene of a bloody and
decisive battle between American marines and Japanese forces.

(e) *Volcano Island.* The Volcano Islands (Kazan-retto) are an eighty-six-
mile chain of volcanic islands some two hundred miles southwest of the
Bonin Islands, named by Bernard de Torres in 1543 for the large volcano on the central island. Lowry seems to have used the name of the
group for one island, but he may have been aware (from descriptions in
the *Admiralty Pilots*) that between 1872 and 1906 many ships had reported sighting a mysterious Volcano Island. Though it is not located
precisely, evidence suggests that an island or islands had emerged as a
result of volcanic activity, only to disappear again.

(f) *St Augustine.* More correctly, San Augustino, now known as Minami
Iwo Jima; south of Sulphur Island and San Alessandro; a mile in extent,
with a conical peak some 3,000 feet high. The name suggests St. Augustine of Hippo (354–430 A.D.), whose *Confessions, De Trinitate,* and
City of God made him the greatest thinker of Christian antiquity.

(g) *Guy Rock.* Otherwise, Farallon de Pajaros. A small island at 20° 32′ N,
144° 54′ E. The name suggests Guy Fawkes (1570–1606), the English
gunpowder plot conspirator, whose abortive attempt to blow up the
House of Lords in 1605 led to his torture and execution.

(h) *the Euphrosyne Reef.* Not located; the Geographical Survey Institute of
Japan suggests an area north of Farallon de Parajos. Euphrosyne was
one of the Charites, the Three Graces of Greek mythology.

Two things are significant about Lowry's place names. First, the course
steered by the *Samaritan* is not direct, but rather the kind of zigzag taken by
a vessel on a search mission (the general direction is east then south of
Japan, past the Bonin and Volcano Islands). Second, the names are paired
as divine contraries: Lot's Wife and Arzobispo; Rosario and Sulphur
Island; Volcano Island and St. Augustine; Guy Rock and Euphrosyne. This
opposition perhaps reflects the ambiguity of the Consul's involvement in the
Samaritan incident, being heroic and hellish at the same time.

The cargo carried by the S.S. *Samaritan,* though valuable to the British
wartime economy, possesses undefined alchemical significance: quicksilver,
or mercury, is a vital element in all alchemical practice; wolfram, or tung-
sten, is linked with antimony through the well-known *Currus Triumphalis
Antimonii* of Basil Valentine (Leipzig, 1604), in which antimony is described as the *lupus metallorum,* the wolf of metals (also known as the grey
wolf), because of the way it "devours" (that is, unites with) all metals except
gold. The unstated emphasis on mercury, sulphur, and salt suggests what
the *Triumphal Chariot of Antimony* calls the three great principles of
health, corresponding to the Three Principles of Paracelsus, whose secret
purpose "was to analyse, rectify, integrate, the human spirit; and to

produce the perfect man" (A. E. Waite, *The Secret Tradition in Alchemy,* p. 3).

38.3 [32] *British Distinguished Service Order or Cross.* The *D.S.C.* is a cross of silver awarded to officers in the Royal Navy below the rank of lieutenant-commander for distinguished combat performance. The *D.S.O.* is also awarded for distinguished wartime service. Laruelle's uncertainty on the point may suggest something of the unreliability of all this information.

39.1 [33] *Lord Jim.* A novel, published in 1900, by Joseph Conrad (1857–1924), telling the story of a young Englishman, Jim, who signs on as a chief mate of the *Patna,* an old steamer "eaten up with rust worse than a condemned water-tank" carrying a load of pilgrims to Mecca. In mid-ocean, on a still night, the *Patna* hits something, and in the ensuing moment of crisis Jim jumps overboard and abandons ship along with two or three others. The *Patna* somehow staggers into port, and in the following enquiry Jim loses both his certificate and his personal sense of honour. From then on he wanders the ports of the East trying to escape both his past and his guilt. He finally settles in Patusan, a remote district of Malaya, where his courage and integrity earn him the title of *Tuan Jim,* or Lord Jim. There at last he finds the chance to die bravely and possibly expiate his guilt and sense of shame. Although the Consul denies that any stigma is attached to him over the Samaritan affair, his sense of guilt is remarkably like Jim's; the mystery at the beginning of each novel is similar (what did the *Patna* hit, what really happened to the German officers?), deliberately enigmatic, and a source of brooding concern for both characters; and the manner of their deaths, by an almost willed shooting, suggests that Lowry had Conrad's novel in mind at many points of his own.

39.2 [33] *the Paris-Soir.* Founded in 1923 as a daily, the *Paris-Soir* was in the 1930's the leading evening paper of Paris, with a circulation of some two million. It was rather brash and sensationalistic, thriving on the kind of scandal implied in the Consul's alleged court-martial. The paper was to be suppressed by the Vichy government in 1943 following its refusal to submit to censorship.

39.3 [33] *People simply did not go round . . . putting Germans in furnaces.* Lowry's oblique way of reminding the reader, Markson suggests, pp. 16–17, that the Germans were shortly to go round doing precisely that to others.

39.4 [33] *mescal.* An alcoholic liquor distilled from the juice of the argave cactus (see note **219.3**).

40.1 [34]   *Then will I headlong fly into the earth: / Earth, gape! it will not harbour me!* From Marlowe's *Doctor Faustus,* sc. xiv, during Faustus's long last speech before the clock strikes twelve. Laruelle, shaken, senses the immediate relation of the lines to Geoffrey's fatal descent into the barranca. As he realizes, the text should read "run" rather than "fly," but the mistake serves to foreground a number of subsequent references to flying and running, culminating at the end of Ch. 10 when the Consul, having chosen hell, goes running from the Salón Ofélia towards the Farolito and his own death.

40.2 [34]   *a golden faceless figurine.* The figure of Prometheus, bringer of light, which is the emblem set into the cover of such Modern Library editions as the *Eight Famous Elizabethan Plays* which Laruelle is holding. Intaglio is the process in printing (as in die stamping and gravure) in which a plate is used to incise an image below the surface.

40.3 [34]   *the sacred ibis.* The Egyptian god Thoth, the god of learning, inventor of hieroglyphics and scribe of the gods, who was often depicted with the head of an ibis: he was the universal demiurge, "the divine ibis who hatched the world-egg at Hermopolis Magna" (*Larousse Mythology,* p. 27). In Cabbalistic and hermetic tradition he was regarded as the first of magicians. Donnelly, p. 125, equates him with Hermes, whose books of magic and sacred writings (the meaning of "hieroglyphics") commanded all the forces of nature and gave power over even the gods themselves. In *UTV* he is further manifested in the figure of the public scribe, p. 58 [53], and the corporal inscribing something in copperplate handwriting, p. 340 [340].

40.4 [34]   *some correspondence... between the subnormal world and the abnormally suspicious.* This very phrase is used by Geoffrey at a moment of crisis, p. 355 [355], when the world about him seems very much a projection of his abnormal inner self. Like his creator, the Consul fully accepts the Swedenborgian notion that every phenomenon in the natural world has its counterpart in the spiritual one and that "the rhyming of the natural with the spiritual enables man to communicate with the heavenly mysteries, the celestial machinery" (Kilgallin, p. 46); or, as here, the infernal machinery. See also note **22.3.**

40.5 [34]   *sortes Shakespeareanae. Sortes* (pl. of L. *sors,* "lot") is the art of divination or prophecy by chance selection from the writings of a book or author. The words of Shakespeare, like the books of the Bible, are commonly used in such prediction. The game was a favourite with Aiken and Lowry, and the phrase *sortes Shakespeareanae* appears in *Blue Voyage,* p. 86.

40.6 [34]   *And what wonders I have done all Germany can witness. Enter Wagner, solus.* Laruelle is opening the book at random, but his first two selections are from *Doctor Faustus:* the first from the beginning of sc. xiv, where Faustus is despairing that his offence can never be pardoned and that he must remain in hell forever; the second from the end of sc. vi, where Wagner, Faustus's servant and magician manqué, is envying (as Laruelle envies Geoffrey) what Faustus has achieved while he has done nothing.

40.7 [34]   *Ick sal you wat suggen. . . . towsand, towsand ding.* Quoted a little inaccurately from *The Shoemaker's Holiday,* III.i.1–4, by Thomas Dekker (1572–1632). The Dutch-English pidgin may be translated: "I'll tell you what, Hans; this ship that is come from Candia, is quite full, by God's sacrament, of sugar, civet, almonds, cambric, and all things, a thousand, thousand, things." Candia was and is a major port in Crete. The speech is that of a Dutch skipper who plays a very minor role in the play, and it may act as a kind of metaphorical comment on Laruelle's crowded memory and the novel that is to follow.

40.8 [34]   *Cut is the branch. . . . regard his hellish fall.* Laruelle could not have chosen a more resonant passage. The lines form part of the Epilogue to *Doctor Faustus,* spoken by the Chorus after Faustus has been dragged off to hell. They shake Laruelle because they seem so directly appropriate to the Consul: another cruelly cut down before his great gifts have been realized and who had dared to practise "more than heavenly power permits," that is, one who had travelled beyond the realms of most men, but whose knowledge and learning had been directed ultimately towards self-destruction. The moral is clear — "regard his hellish fall" — but in both Marlowe's play and Lowry's novel this is a patently inadequate response to the hero's aspirations.

41.1 [35]   *Hotel Bella Vista.* Sp. "Belle View Hotel"; ironically, the place where Yvonne sees the dishevelled figure of the Consul in Ch. 2. No longer a hotel but a sophisticated commercial complex on the north of the zócalo, it was in 1938–39 the best-known hotel of Cuernavaca. The name has a private irony for Lowry, since it has the same name as Bellevue Hospital in New York City, where Lowry underwent extensive treatment for alcoholism in 1935, his experiences there giving him the substance of his short novel, *Lunar Caustic.*

41.2 [35]   *the t's like the lonely wayside crosses.* The Consul's handwriting forms an image of his very soul, while his t's foreshadow the encounter at the lonely wayside cross with the dying Indian in Ch. 8, which begins with the word "downhill" and marks the beginning of the final descent which he will be unable to resist.

41.3 [35]   *the dark's spinets.* A spinet (from Giovanni Spinetti, its inventor) is a small variety of harpsicord with a single keyboard. The Consul thinks, p. 343 [342], of a similar dreadful night awaiting him, again with demonic orchestras, snatches of fearful sleep, imaginary parties arriving, and the terrible music of the dark's spinets.

41.4 [35]   *the unbandaging of great giants in agony.* Lowry points out (*SL,* p. 116) a possible echo of Virginia Woolf's *To the Lighthouse,* which he said he had not then read, but whose central symbol, the Lighthouse, seems closely related to his own Farolito. The lines in question, from the poetic "Time Passes" section of *To the Lighthouse,* describe the noises at night in a deserted house: "Now and again some glass tinkled in the cupboard as if a giant voice had shrieked so loud in its agony that tumblers stood inside a cupboard vibrated too."

41.5 [35]   *howling pariah dogs, the cocks . . . the drumming, the moaning . . . . sad faced potters and legless beggars.* This letter, written in the Farolito, is full of anticipations of the final scene: the pariah dog, p. 376 [375]; the cock, p. 372 [372]; the ceaseless drumming from Parián (see note **80.2**); the groans of love so like those of dying, p. 350 [349]; the sympathetic potter, p. 368 [367]; and the legless beggar, p. 342 [341]. The effect of such echoes is to bind the first chapter tightly to the last, asserting not only the continuity of the experience but also the cyclic form of the novel.

41.6 [35]   *the misericordes of unimaginable cantinas.* The basic sense of the word is that of compassion or pity, but as Markson has pointed out, p. 63, it also refers to the medieval dagger used to apply the so-called "mercy-stroke."

41.7 [35]   *the cocks that herald dawn all night.* In *Hamlet,* I.i.150, "the cock, that is the trumpet to the morn" puts an end to the ghostly wanderings of Hamlet's father, and Marcellus says (I.i.60–64), as if in deliberate contradiction to the Consul, that:

> The bird of dawning singeth all night long:
> And then, they say, no spirit can walk abroad;
> The nights are wholesome; then no planets strike,
> No fairy takes, nor witch hath power to charm;
> So hallow'd and so gracious is the time.

41.8 [35] *I went to Oaxaca.* Oaxaca, capital of the state of the same name, some three hundred miles south of Cuernavaca, was Lowry's private City of Dreadful Night, to which he went after his first wife had left him. His experiences there imbued it with a sense of horror, as he indicated to James Stern in 1940 (*SL,* p. 29):

> I was thrown, for a time, in Mexico, as a spy, into durance vile, by some fascistas in Oaxaca (by mistake; they were after another man. How it arose was: he was a friend of mine, very sober and a communist, and they could not believe, because he was sober, that he was an agitator and therefore thought he must be me, who was not sober, but, nevertheless, not an agitator, not a communist). I subsequently found it difficult to explain why I had absolutely had to be drawing a map of the Sierra Madre in tequila on the bar counter (sole reason was, I liked the shape of them). Jan left me some months before, so I had no alibi. On Christmas Day they let out all the prisoners except me. Myself, I had the Oaxaquenian third degree for turkey. Hissed they (as *Time* would say), "You say you a wrider but we read all your wridings and dey don't make sense. You no wrider, you an espider and we shoota de espiders in Mejico." But it was an improving experience.

Many of Lowry's personal experiences were transferred from Oaxaca to Parián, as is clear from *DATG* where such details as the vulture in the washbasin, the fawns being slaughtered, and the Farolito itself are discussed in graphic particularity. It was in one sense a relief but in another a disappointment when Lowry returned in 1946 to find that Oaxaca had lost all its sinister horror.

41.9 [36] *the child whose life its mother and I saved.* Ramsey suggests, p. 46, that this incident shows the beneficial effects of alcohol, which if rightly directed rather than abused may possess the power to save life. Lowry may have derived the incident from a similar one involving an asphyxiated baby in Aiken's *Blue Voyage,* p. 49, where a dream suddenly turns into a nightmare.

41.10 [36] *the hotel where we were once happy.* The Hotel Francia, Calle 20 de Noviembre, Oaxaca (thinly disguised as El Infierno, pp. 350–51). D. H. Lawrence had spent much of his time in Mexico here ("excoriating Murry," Lowry claimed, *SL,* p. 116). In *DATG* the Francia is called La Luna, as if to underline the mutability of such happiness.

42.1 [36] *some extraordinary land from which he can never return.* The obvious echo here is of *Hamlet,* III.i.79-80, as Hamlet contemplates the consequences of suicide: "The undiscover'd country from whose bourn / No traveller returns," but the Consul's further comment that the name of this land is hell also suggests the opening of T. S. Eliot's "The Love Song of J. Alfred Prufrock," which cites the passage from Dante's *Inferno,* XXVII. 61-66, where Dante is addressed by one who assumes that the poet can never return to the world:

> S'io credessi che mia risposta fosse
> a persona che mai tornasse al mondo,
> questa fiamma staria senza più scosse.
> Ma per ciò che giammai di questo fondo
> non tornò vivo alcun, s'i'odo il vero,
> Senza tema d'infamia ti respondo.

("If I thought that my answer were / to one who might ever return to the world, / this flame would shake no more; / but since from this depth / none ever returned alive, if what I hear is true, / I answer you without fear of infamy.")

42.2 [36] *England is breaking off diplomatic relations.* This detail dates the letter as having been written in March 1938 (see note **36.1**).

42.3 [36] *my Tlaxcaltecan friend Cervantes... at the Salón Ofélia.* Cervantes, innkeeper and cockfighter, whose name incongruously echoes that of the author of *Don Quixote,* comes from Tlaxcala, Mexico's smallest state (see note **297.2**); and his restaurant-cantina in Tomalín, the Salón Ofélia, suggests the tragic heroine of Shakespeare's *Hamlet* (see note **283.2**). There was once a Salón Ofélia in Cuernavaca, near the Portel Morelos, but Lowry notes in *DATG* p. 237 that "Cervantes' old joint, The Salón Ofélia" in Oaxaca had been "turned into a drugstore called the *Farmacia de la Soledad*"; it still exists as such, at Independencia and Díaz Ordaz, just two blocks from the Church of the Virgin for those that have nobody with.

42.4 [36] *the Farolito in Parián.* The cantina (Sp. "the Little Lighthouse") which acts as a beacon to the Consul throughout the novel (see note **203.6**), and which, like El Infierno, p. 350 [350], opens at four in the morning. The Consul's journey to Parián in the latter chapters of the novel duplicates almost exactly that described here.

42.5 [36] *ochas.* Described, p. 368 [368], as "raw alcohol in steaming herb tea." Lowry comments in *DATG,* p. 76: "Ochas is boiled orange leaves and should be drunk hot with raw alcohol put into it. But mescal put into it is still more exciting."

42.6 [36]   *through hell there is a path, as Blake well knew.* William Blake (1757–1827), poet, engraver, artist, and mystic, best known for his *Songs of Innocence* (1789) and *Songs of Experience* (1794), but also writer of a number of more obscure prophetic books, the best known of which is *The Marriage of Heaven and Hell* (1793), to which the Consul is alluding. In the opening "Argument" Blake writes:

> Once meek, and in a perilous path,
> The just man kept his course along
> The vale of death.

The path is also that taken by Dante through hell, as described in the *Inferno* (for which Blake made several illustrations). For both Dante and Blake the path to a higher innocence lay through hell.

42.7 [36]   *some northern country.* The northern paradise, a direct antithesis of and possible alternative to the inferno of Mexico, is based directly upon Lowry's life at Dollarton, British Columbia, where most of the novel was written. The Consul's longing anticipates Yvonne's hopes for a new life in Canada, pp. 123 and 271 [119 and 269], and is important as a dream which they once shared, an innocence they both wish to regain. Even the train rolling eastward is the direct antithesis of the Freudian death-train which roars on its metalled ways through the opening pages of Chs. 2 and 10, transporting the Consul to hell.

42.8 [37]   *Venus burning hard in daylight.* In northern latitudes, the planet Venus is sometimes conspicuous in daylight hours, but its presence here in the Consul's mind is an emphatic reminder of Yvonne's absence (Yvonne is constantly to be identified with Venus).

42.9 [37]   *like Swedenborg's angels.* Emanuel Swedenborg (1689–1772), Swedish scientist, philosopher, and mystic, who claimed divine authority to explain natural and spiritual evidences after a mystical revelation in 1745 and said that his soul had been permitted to travel into hell, purgatory, and heaven. His visions and communications with spirits and angels, proclaimed in his *Heaven and Hell* (1758), set forth the teachings and scriptures of what he called the New Church, summarized in the *OCEL:*

According to his theosophic system God, as Divine Man, is infinite love and infinite wisdom, from whom emanate the two worlds of nature and spirit, distinct but closely related. The end of creation is the approximation of man to God. This end having been endangered by evil spirits, Jehovah descended into nature, restored the connexion between God and man, and left the Scriptures as His testimony, of which Swedenborg was the appointed interpreter.

In the very first paragraph of *Heaven and Hell,* Swedenborg claimed emphatically "it has been permitted me to associate with angels, and to talk with them as man with man," and later in the treatise he discusses the various ranks and attributes of angels in great detail. They are here described as facing east, because in Swedenborgian terms east is the source of God's love and light:

> Thus in heaven it is the east which determines all the other quarters. That quarter where the Lord appears as the Sun is called the east or orient because all life has its origin from Him as the Sun; and also because in proportion as heat and light, or love and intelligence, are received from Him by the angels, the Lord is said to arise upon them. Hence also it is that the Lord in the Word is called the East. (# 141)

Swedenborg influenced, in particular, William Blake, whose *Marriage of Heaven and Hell* drew heavily (though sometimes satirically) upon Swedenborg's *Heaven and Hell,* the work which most influenced Lowry, who assumes with enthusiasm its tripartite universe—heaven, earth, and hell—and who is constantly trying to sense the interpenetration of the natural and the spiritual worlds. Swedenborg's other major works (which Lowry seems not to have used) are *Arcana Coelestia* (1749-58); *Four Preliminary Doctrines* (1763); *The Apocalypse Revealed* (1766); and *The True Christian Religion* (1771).

43.1 [37]   *reboant.* Rebellowing, echoing loudly.

43.2 [38]   *a great wheel.* Although the wheel is perhaps the most common motif in *UTV,* this reference to the unseen ship seems deliberately to anticipate Hugh's similar sense of himself standing at the wheel, pp. 107-8 [104], steering the world out of the western ocean of its misery.

43.3 [38]   *Wells Fargo.* The orginal Wells Fargo Company was organized in 1852 as a shipping and banking company for miners, and by 1856 it was the leading express company in California. As a mail service, it lasted in California only till 1895, but it was still operating in Mexico in 1938, and its offices (Avenida Madero 14, México D.F.) were commonly used for post restante purposes.

43.4 [38]   *sent me a postcard even.* Ironically, she has done so. It will arrive / has arrived on 2 November 1938.

44.1 [38]   *these letters. . . . I have some of them on me.* The Consul will leave them behind in the Farolito, where he is writing, but will pick them up and read them six months later, in Ch. 12. Although he claims not to have read the letters, he has obviously glanced over them, since phrases from them emerge accusingly from time to time.

44.2 [39]   *the Compañía Telegráfica Mexicana.* The Mexican Telegraph Company, in 1938 at San Juan de Letrán and Independencia in Mexico City, from whence Hugh sends the fatally incriminating telegram, p. 98 [94].

44.3 [39]   *between Mercy and Understanding, between Chesed and Binah.* Although the Consul frequently sees the universe in Cabbalistic terms, the degree to which *Under the Volcano* is informed by the Cabbala is much debated. Lowry was evasive on the matter. In "LJC" he stressed Cabbalistic elements and hinted at others, as if to prove "there are depths," but in a letter to David Markson, 20 June 1951 (Woodcock, p. 114), he admitted to going on about the Cabbala in a way "quite misleading and probably not a little juvenile." Nevertheless, he also stated quite definitely that he met a Cabbalist at a "critical and coincidental moment in the writing of the book." While it can be shown that the novel existed in substantially its present form before Lowry met Charles Stansfeld-Jones (Frater Achad) and before Cabbalistic details were inserted, it can equally be argued that such details are not superficial and that this element of the book (like the sign in the garden and the Spanish Civil War references), though late, retrospectively focused and clarified many previous details of Lowry's design.

As Frater Achad admits (*QBL,* p. xi), "Philosophically speaking a great deal of rubbish has accumulated around the roots of The Tree of Life," and it is not always easy to see the tree for the wood. The roots of the Cabbala go back to Old Testament times: Cabbalists claim that the word "Cabbala" derives from the Hebrew root *QBL,* "to receive," and that its mysteries were first taught by God to a select company of angels; after the Fall it was graciously communicated to Adam, to furnish the means of his posterity returning to their pristine nobility and felicity; and thence imparted to Noah and to Abraham, who revealed some of the mysterious doctrine to other

men (MacGregor-Mathers, *The Kabbalah Unveiled,* p. 5). The written Cabbala has two main sources:
(a) the *Sephor Yetzirah,* the "Book of Formation," probably written in Babylonia between the third and fourth centuries A.D.
(b) the *Zohar,* or "Book of Splendour," written about 1280 in Spain and attributed to Moses de León. In addition, there are many commentaries and explications, as well as esoteric matters rumoured to be too secret to be committed to print.

Andersen, pp. 64–66, describes the basic principles of the Cabbala which seem to have most influenced Lowry:

> The Cabala posits a universe unified and organized into a complex pattern of correspondences culminating in the idea that man is a microcosm of the universe and of God. The basic correspondences are expressed by a system of symbols based on the twenty-two letters of the Hebrew alphabet and the numbers from one to ten. In addition, there are, at each stage of the basic system, a corresponding color, divine name, angel, virtue, vice, Tarot card, body organ, heavenly body, jewel, and so on. Many cabalistic symbols are shared with the Tarot and alchemy, as well as with various forms of magic, Jungian psychology, and oriental religions and philosophies.
>
> The cabalistic universe is expressed visually by a diagram ... called the Tree of Life. This diagram consists of ten spheres (Sephiroth) connected by twenty-two lines (paths). The Sephiroth are arranged in three vertical rows (pillars), the two outside ones consisting of pairs of opposites which are "reconciled," given balance or equilibrium, by the spheres in the middle column. At the top of the diagram is the sphere named Kether (light), which represents God (Ain Soph), the sum of all things, limitless, infinite, eternal, by definition unknowable. God makes himself known and in fact makes man and the universe possible by a succession of ten emanations, of which the spheres are the symbols. In one sense, these symbols are God and therefore constitute his sacred Name. The emanations progress in succession down the Tree of Life in a zigzag path resembling lightning. The Tree of Life is simultaneously visualized as a series of three triangles, arranged vertically, with a single sphere, Malkuth, at the bottom.
>
> The aim of the serious cabalist is to develop from a spiritual neophyte into an adept by proceeding from Malkuth to Kether, retracing the "Path of God's Lightning". . . . The first step is to tread the twenty-second path, to project his astral body into the lower of the three triangles, which has Yesod as its base. . . . Once the initial projection has been achieved, the signs and symbols of each sphere are mystically projected upward as the aspirant threads the paths by means of thoughts of

wisdom, deeds of kindness, and meditation on the infinite. To a special
few may be granted the ultimate, the crossing of the great Abyss which
separates the two bottom triangles from the supernal triangle. "To walk
in light" . . . is, in effect, to achieve union with God, an achievement
equal in rarity and importance to achieving the Philosopher's Stone by
an alchemist or to the breaking from the Cycle of Necessity by an oriental mystic. Those who fail even to start the journey or who backslide
too far are said to be in the realm of evil, of "husks" and "shells," called
the Qliphoth, which some say, is ruled by Beelzebub.

(a) *between Chesed and Binah.* Chesed and Binah (Mercy and Understanding) are respectively the fourth and third emanations (Sephiroth) from
Kether on the tree of life, and the movement from the fourth to the
third Sephira as one progresses towards the light is fraught with spiritual danger, as Frater Achad makes clear in *QBL,* pp. 66–67 (noted by
Kilgallin, p. 155):

> for there is indeed a great Gulf fixed between Chesed and Binah
> and this is called THE ABYSS. Strange as it may seem, he must
> give up all he has attained, including himself, before he can pass
> this Abyss and be reborn of the Spirit into BINAH where he be-
> comes known as NEMO or No-Man. He is now MASTER of THE
> TEMPLE for having given up "self" he is able to comprehend and
> understand ALL.

In his *Anatomy of the Body of God,* p. 42, Frater Achad talks of the
"Horrors of 'the Abyss' between Chesed and Binah," but he states quite
definitely that it is bridgeable by wisdom and understanding. As Kilgallin
notes, pp. 155–56, citing Frater Achad's *The Chalice of Ecstasy,* man is
given freedom of will to ally himself with the divine will, and should he
make the mistake (as the Consul seems to have done) of attempting to
turn the divine will to merely personal ends, he must fail, cut himself
off from the universal current, and slowly and surely be lost in the
abyss.

(b) *equilibrium is all.* The principle of equilibrium is absolutely central to
Cabbalistic thinking. It is defined by MacGregor-Mathers (*The Kabbalah Unveiled,* p. 16) as "that harmony which results from the analogy
of contraries" and by Swedenborg (*Heaven and Hell,* #293) as the
precarious freedom man must hold between the influence of good and
evil forces acting upon him. It is the great law of nature, which, if
abused, may react terribly and inevitably against man: as Captain
Nemo says in *Twenty Thousand Leagues under the Sea,* Pt.II, Ch.15,

"we cannot prevent equilibrium from producing its effects. We may brave human laws, but we cannot resist natural ones." Having offended against the principle of equilibrium by abusing the mystical powers of alcohol, the Consul must pay the penalty; the Cabbalistic statement of precarious balance which is reflected in Yvonne's death, losing her balance, falling from a tree (Markson, p. 23), is closely related to the way that the Consul here sees himself falling from the tree of life into the abyss. As Andersen notes, p. 385, the Consul's phrase "equilibrium is all" echoes King Lear's "ripeness is all" (V.ii.11) and Hamlet's "the readiness is all" (V.ii.236), both phrases uttered shortly before their deaths.

(c) *the all-but-unretraceable path of God's lightning.* As Frater Achad notes (*QBL,* Appendix p. 5), "The Qabalists tell us that the SEPHI-ROTH were emanated by means of the FLAMING SWORD, or LIGHTNING FLASH, which descended from Kether unto Malkuth." The lightning flash which connects the ten Sephiroth thus marks the path which the adept must seek to retrace to achieve his spiritual ends. At the moment of his death, p. 373 [373], the Consul senses the presence of this lightning.

(d) *the Qliphoth.* This term is not to be found in Frater Achad's writings, nor is it commonly used by other Cabbalistic writers, but Lowry discovered this word for "the world of shells and demons" ("LJC," p. 65) in MacGregor-Mathers's *The Kabbalah Unveiled,* p. 30, where the world of matter, made up from the grosser elements of the other three worlds, is said to be the abode of evil spirits called Shells, Qliphoth. As Epstein says, p. 25: "the world of rinds and shells, being farthest from the creative force, is subject to the grossest impurities of matter. For matter is the utmost limit of spirit."

44.4 [39] *the Triumph of Humpty Dumpty.* The Triumph of Humpty Dumpty, like that of the Consul, would be to put his shattered self together again. In a letter to Conrad Aiken (*SL,* p. 50), Lowry refers to the story of his life being "almost as poignant as the 'Triumph of the Egg,'" and, as Doyen notes, p. 196, this reference is to Sherwood Anderson's short story "The Egg" in *The Triumph of the Egg* (1921), pp. 47–48:

> One unversed in such matters can have no notion of the many and tragic things that can happen to a chicken. It is born out of an egg, lives for a few weeks as a tiny fluffy thing such as you will see pictured on Easter cards, then becomes hideously naked, eats quantities of corn and meal brought by the sweat of your father's brow, gets diseases called pip, cholera, and other names, stands looking with stupid eyes at the

sun, becomes sick and dies. A few hens and now and then a rooster, intended to serve God's mysterious ends, struggle through to maturity. The hens lay eggs out of which come other chickens and the dreadful cycle is thus made complete. It is all unbelievably complex.

Although there is no beautiful place without chicken farms, where life can be a happy eggless affair, the triumph of the egg is to persist in fultility, creating hens to lay more eggs.

44.5 [39]   *the Nose with the Luminous Dong.* A mildly obscene inversion of "The Dong with the Luminous Nose," from the nonsense poem of that name by Edward Lear (1812–88). It has been suggested (the author may remain anonymous) that the shattered Humpty Dumpty (the Consul) can only be made whole again in successful union with the archetypal woman through the agency of the luminous dong.

44.6 [39]   *like Clare, 'weaving fearful vision'.* John Clare (1793–1864), poet and madman, who suffered throughout his life from fits of melancholy and who was declared insane and committed to Northampton County Asylum in 1837. He is best known as a poet of rural and pastoral verse, with volumes such as *Poems Descriptive of Rural Life* (1820); *The Village Minstrel* (1821); *The Shepherd's Calender* (1827); and *The Rural Muse* (1835). The phrase "weaving fearful vision" is from "Summer Images," one of the *Poems Written at Helpstone* (1824–32), ll. 106–12:

> And note on hedgerow baulks, in moisture sprent,
>   The jetty snail creep from the mossy thorn,
> With earnest heed and tremulous intent,
>   Frail brother of the morn,
> That from the tiny bents and misted leaves
>   Withdraws his timid horn,
> And fearful vision weaves.

The phrase was a favourite of Lowry's, who used it in his poem "Autopsy" — a poor piece of verse, wildly exaggerating the traumas of his childhood, but concluding effectively: "But turned, to discover Clare in the poor snail, / And weave a fearful vision of his own."

45.1 [39]   *the Knight of Sorry Aspect.* A reference to *Don Quixote de la Mancha* (1605–15), the great satirical romance by Miguel Saavedra Cervantes (1547–1616): the story of the ingenious gentleman of La Mancha whose wits are turned by his compulsive devotion to works of chivalry and who roams the country as knight-errant, dressed in rusty armour, mounted on his sorry steed Rosinante and accompanied by his squire, Sancho Panza, on a donkey. To his disordered imagination commonplace objects assume fearful proportions (see note **250.3**), and he is consequently involved in absurd adventures with distressing consequences to himself. He is finally prevailed upon to abstain from chivalrous exploits, resolves to turn shepherd, and, returning to his village, recovers his sanity before dying. The title "Knight of Sorry Aspect" is a translation of the Spanish "El Caballero de la Triste Figura" (more commonly, "Knight of the Sorrowful Countenance"), the appellation given to himself by Don Quixote after an adventure which costs him several teeth (Pt.I, III.xix). Because the knights of old assumed such names as "the Knight of the Burning Sword" or "the Knight of the Griffin" by which they would be known throughout the world, Don Quixote resolves to have a sorrowful figure painted on his shield and to be known henceforth by that title.

45.2 [39] *the Strauss song we used to sing.* "Allerseelen" ("All-Souls"), 1882; the eighth and final song of Opus 10 by Richard Strauss (1864–1949), German composer and writer of Lieder. The song, set to the words of the Austrian poet Hermann von Gilm (1812–64), makes reference to the belief that on All Souls Day (2 November) the souls of the dead will communicate with the living and depicts one trying to use this to revive an old love affair, which, it seems, has died:

> Stell' auf den Tisch die duftenden Reseden,
> die letzten roten Astern trag' herbei,
> und lass uns wieder von der Liebe reden,
> wie einst im Mai.
>
> Gib mir die Hand, dass ich sie heimlich drücke,
> und wenn man's sieht, mir ist es einerlei,
> gib mir nur einen deiner süssen Blicke,
> wie einst im Mai.
>
> Es bluht und duftet heut' auf jedem Grabe,
> ein Tag im Jahr ist ja den Toten frei,
> komm an mein Herz, dass ich dich wieder habe
> wie einst im Mai.

("Set on the table the fragrant mignonettes, / bring in the last red asters, / and let us talk of love again, / as once in May.

Give me your hand, so I may secretly press it, / and if anybody sees, it's all one to me; / give me just one of your sweet glances, / as once in May.

Flowers bloom and spread their fragrance today on every grave. / One day in the year is sacred to the dead. / Come to my heart, that I may have you again, / as once in May.")

45.3 [39] *The Generalife Gardens and the Alhambra Gardens.* Gardens of two Moorish palaces in Granada, the last stronghold of the Moors in the south of Spain:

(a) *the Alhambra.* An ancient fortress on a hill to the north of Granada, overlooking the city, and residence of the Moorish monarchs. It is described in Washington Irving's *Tales of the Alhambra,* p. 29:

> It was the royal abode of the Moorish kings, where, surrounded with the splendours and refinements of Asiatic luxury, they held dominion over what they vaunted as a terrestial paradise, and made their last stand for the empire in Spain.

Most of the Alhambra was built between 1248 and 1354, though Charles V extended it in the mid-sixteenth century. The name signifies in Arabic "the Red," from the *tapia* or red bricks of which its outer walls were built. Although some of its architecture and decoration was destroyed after the expulsion of the Moors in 1492, the Alhambra is celebrated for the intricate splendour of its architecture: towers, galleries, courts, rooms, fountains, and a magnificent wooded garden. Lowry had first met Jan near the Alhambra in June 1933; later that year he met her again at the Alhambra Palace, a music hall in Leicester Square, London (Day, p. 182).

(b) *the Generalife.* From Ar. *Gennat-al-Arif,* "the Place of the Builders"; separated from the Alhambra by a ravine and slightly above it, the Generalife was originally an outwork of the fortress and afterwards the summer palace of the sultans of Granada: "a fairy palace full of storied recollections" (*Tales of the Alhambra,* p. 123).

45.4 [39] *Shadows of our fate at our meeting in Spain.* Although Hollywood and Los Angeles suggest Yvonne's past life as a starlet, and the Pensión México their present existence, the intimations of fate implicit in these names seem more applicable to Lowry's own life than that of his characters. Mexico was where he separated from his first wife, Jan; Los Angeles, where he met his second wife, Margerie. Both women contribute to the character of Yvonne: Jan, without whom Lowry could not have got into his creative mess; and Margerie, without whom he could not have got out of it (*TLS,* 26 January 1967, p. 57).

45.5. [40]   *In Paris—before Hugh came.* A reference to Hugh's "betrayal" of Geoffrey with Yvonne, which the Consul cannot quite forgive and which during the day increasingly gives him an excuse for refusing to take the positive steps necessary to be reconciled with Yvonne. It has been argued (Dodson, p. 33), that the betrayal was never quite a physical one, but this seems unlikely; the reticence each displays about the affair is more naturally to be seen as a reluctance to admit it really happened, despite the darkening presence of its shadow.

45.6 [40]   *several mescalitos later.* In the Oaxaca region, mescalito differs from mescal (see note **219.3**) in being the straight distillation from the juice of the agave cactus without the addition of the more usual sugars. It is a potent, colourless liquid, usually drunk straight. The Consul sometimes (though probably not here) uses the word as a diminutive, as if to convince himself that he is drinking only little mescals.

45.7 [40]   *we cannot allow what we created to sink down to oblivion in this dingy fashion.* A foreshadowing of the Consul's last words, p. 374 [373]: "Christ . . . this is a dingy way to die," as he at last discovers the love that comes too late.

45.8 [40]   *Lift up your eyes unto the hills.* From Psalm 121, which expresses confidence in the power of the Lord to preserve men from all evil and preserve the soul. The psalm begins:

> I will lift up mine eyes unto the hills, from
> whence cometh my help.
> My help cometh from the Lord, which made heaven
> and earth.

Ironically, the little red plane flying in over the hills from Acapulco is described, p. 49 [44], as a "winged emissary of Lucifer."

46.1 [41]   *come back to me, Yvonne, if only for a day.* This plea, so poignantly echoing Richard Strauss's "Allerseelen" (see note **45.2**), is answered, to the letter, by Yvonne's return in Ch. 2, on the day the dead come back to life.

47.1 [41]   *he held it into the candle flame.* Lowry comments, "LJC," p. 70, that Laruelle's action is poetically balanced by the flight of vultures ("like burnt papers floating from a fire") at the end of Ch. 3 and by the burning of the Consul's manuscript in Yvonne's dying dream, Ch. 9. The description culminates in images of demonic flames and husks, suggestive of the ending of *Doctor Faustus* as hell opens to reveal the awaiting fires, but its essence is the intense elegaic beauty of the transition from life to death.

47.2 [42]   *crepitant.* From L. *crepitare,* "to crackle"; to make a crackling sound.

47.3 [42]   *a bell spoke out, then ceased abruptly: dolente . . . dolore!* A distinct echo of the bell that rings out at the moment of the Consul's death, p. 374 [373]. On the one hand, it asserts damnation, for as Kilgallin has noted ("Faust," p. 28), the Consul, like Faustus, has been cursed by bell, book, and candle; on the other hand, it rings out for all mankind as does the passing bell in John Donne's *Devotions upon Emergent Occasions: Meditation XVII* (1623):

> No Man is an *Iland,* intire of it selfe; every man is a peece of the *Continent,* a part of the *maine;* if a *Clod* bee washed away by the *Sea, Europe* is the lesse, as well as if a *Promontorie* were. . . . Any Mans *death* diminishes *me,* because I am involved in *Mankinde;* And therefore never send to know for whom the *bell* tolls; It tolls for *thee.*

The words *dolente . . . dolore* are taken from the inscription above the entrance into Hell, in Dante's *Inferno,* III.1-2: "Per me si va nella città dolente / Per me si va nell'etterna dolore" ("Through me you enter the woeful city, / through me you enter eternal grief.")
     By a curious coincidence which would have intrigued Lowry, Father Hidalgo, who first rang the bell for Mexican independence in 1810, came from the parish of Dolores in the state of Querétaro; the famous "Grito de Dolores" is repeated every 16 September, and the bell is ceremoniously rung. Another coincidence saw Maximilian shot in 1867 outside the town of Querétaro, on the Cerro de las Campañas, or "Hill of the Bells" (see note **127.3**). The Consul's death truly involves all mankind.

47.4 [42]   *backwards revolved the luminous wheel.* Literally, the big wheel in the zócalo; symbolically, many other things, as Lowry points out, "LJC," pp. 70-71:

> it is Buddha's wheel of the law (see VII), it is eternity, it is the instru-

ment of eternal recurrence, the eternal return, and it is the form of the book; or superficially it can be seen simply in an obvious movie sense as the wheel of time whirling backwards until we have reached the year before and Chapter II and in this sense, if we like, we can look at the rest of the book through Laruelle's eyes, as if it were his creation.

The image of the wheel thus integrates the novel's thematic concerns and its trochal structure within the mind of Laruelle, as once again he turns back to relive the events of the past.

CHAPTER TWO

48.1 [43] *A corpse will be transported by express.* These ominous words, predictive of his own headlong rush to oblivion, are uttered by Geoffrey Firmin; they are reinforced by Fernando's reply, *"absolutemente necesario"* and by the "mysterious contrapuntal dialogue" ("LJC," p. 72) supplied by Weber, the smuggler who flew Hugh down to Mexico and who is mixed up with the local thugs and sinarquistas ultimately responsible for the Consul's death. The Consul's words are not as strange as might appear: he is studying a blue and red Mexican National Railways timetable, see p. 51 [46], and, as Geneviève Bonnefoi has noted in her "Souvenir de Quauhnahuac," pp. 97–98, it was formally stipulated on p. 5 of that document, under the rules concerning *Transportation of Corpses,* that this was to be done only by express and that someone responsible for tending the corpse and provided with his own ticket must travel in the same train.

48.2 [43] *the Bella Vista.* In 1938 the most prominent hotel of Cuernavaca; once the manor house of a great hacienda, it was remodelled into a hotel in 1910 by an Englishwoman, Rosa King, who tells her story and that of the hotel during the Mexican Revolution in *Tempest Over Mexico* (1935). The hotel acted as the pick-up point for first-class cabs and carriages (which is why the taxi "insisted" on taking her there). The drop-off point at the Bella Vista was the Portel del Aguila del Oro, or "Gateway of the Golden Eagle" (de Davila, p. 91), which may account in part for Yvonne's confusion about the etymology of Quauhnahuac, p. 49 [44].

48.3 [43] *the tiny Quauhnahuac airfield.* There is no airfield in the immediate vicinity of Cuernavaca. Lowry may have in mind the tiny strip at Tequesquitengo (twenty-five miles south) which serves the region generally, but more probably he wanted Yvonne to fly in so as to underline the almost ethereal quality of her presence. In the 1940 draft (UBC 7-3, p. 20) Yvonne and Hugh arrived together from Acapulco in Weber's plane, landing in a field just outside Quauhnahuac.

48.4 [44] *a hurricane of immense and beautiful butterflies.* Despite the clear sky and the beautiful day, Yvonne's arrival in Acapulco is not without intimations of Hurakán (see note **22.1**) and her own death (figured in the relationship of butterflies to the burnt letter, p. 47 [42], and the ascending soul, p. 337 [336]). The most important underlying reference, however, is the story of Psyche and Cupid, as told by Apuleius in his *Metamorphoses,* Bks. 4-6. Psyche was a maiden so beautiful that she aroused the envy of Venus, who sent her son Cupid to inspire her with love for the meanest of men. Cupid fell in love with Psyche, visited her by night, and warned of dire consequences should she look upon him. Psyche's curiosity prevailed; she lit a lamp and saw the god of love at her side, but a drop of oil fell upon him, and he awoke, reproached her, and flew away. Psyche set out to look for him, and after long wanderings and a set of almost impossible tasks imposed by Venus, she was united with her lover and made immortal. Psyche is commonly regarded as the personification of the human soul and is often depicted as a butterfly. The story is usually interpreted as an allegory of the human soul guided by love eventually attaining complete happiness by purification through sorrow, as in Thomas Taylor's explanation of the fable (cited by Frater Achad, *Psychomagia* p. 6), "designed to represent the lapse of the human soul from the intelligible world to the earth." Yvonne is often to be identified with Psyche, wandering in search of her lost love, but her dream of reunification and complete happiness seems unlikely to be attained.

48.5 [44]   *the Pennsylvania.* A passenger ship of 18,000 tons, the *S.S. Pennsylvania* was in service running between various west coast ports in the 1930's, after a period of running between San Francisco and New York. Like Yvonne, Lowry and his first wife Jan arrived at Acapulco from San Diego on the *Pennsylvania* (later sunk off Vancouver — *SL,* p. 288). Lowry claimed to have arrived on 1 November 1936, which he called the Day of the Dead (Day, p. 214), an error apparently maintained in this chapter (see note **9.8**).

49.1 [44]   *a taxi strike that afternoon.* In early versions of the novel, this detail had a significance not readily apparent in the final version. Because the taxis were on strike, the projected trip to Guanajuato (see p. 150 [146]) could not take place (the Consul's car had broken down, and Vigil's offer did not then exist), which left open the bus trip to Parián — yet one more instance of how all elements inform against the Consul on this his last day.

49.2 [44]   *its air of slumbering Harlequin.* In pantomime, Harlequin is a masked clownish figure, usually dressed in a diamond-spangled costume and carrying a wooden sword or bat. The figure had its origins in the *commedia dell'arte,* and first appeared in England in a 1685 adaptation by William Mountford of Marlowe's *Doctor Faustus* (David Mayer III, *Harlequin in His Element,* p. 4). Harlequinades reached the height of their popularity on the English stage between 1806 and 1836, combining burlesque and clowning with a tangled tale of romance between Harlequin and Columbine, harried by Pantaloon and the Clown. The "air of slumbering Harlequin" refers to the scene in a typical Harlequinade before the transformation of the lovers into Harlequin and Columbine and the subsequent scenes of frenzied activity. The etymology of "harlequin" is the clue to Lowry's meaning: he would have found in Donnelly, p. 210, the comment, "the Hellequin of France becomes the Harlequin of our pantomimes," and hence, as Kilgallin notes, p. 157, the word "suggests not only Faustian drama but also the old French Hellequin, one of a troop of demon horsemen riding by night." There is thus an immediate association with the equestrian statue of the turbulent Huerta and the demonic horse that rides Yvonne down.

49.3 [44] *the equestrian statue of the turbulent Huerta.* Victoriano Huerta (1854–1916), Mexican general and president, who came into power in 1913 by leading a military coup and almost certainly murdering his predecessor, Francisco I. Madero. He resigned in July 1914 under American pressure and fled to Europe where he drank himself to death. His seventeen-month presidency was marked by corruption and violence and by personal criminality and drunkenness. His equestrian statue is thus a demonic parody or inversion of the Consul, who has similarly abnegated responsibility. At the moment of her death, Yvonne confuses the horse about to trample her with the statue: "the horse, rearing, poised over her, it was the statue of Huerta, the drunkard, the murderer, it was the Consul," p. 336 [336]. There is not, nor has there ever been, a statue to Huerta in the zócalo of Cuernavaca, but at the northern entrance to the town (at Zapata and Univeisidad), there is a magnificent stone statue of Emiliano Zapata on a wild-eyed galloping horse: the plaque is dated 1879–1979, the centenary of Zapata's birth, but the statue had been in Cuernavaca for many years (at Zapata and Tetela) and is almost surely the force behind Lowry's inspiration.

49.4 [44] *nutant.* From L. *nutare,* "to nod"; drooping, nodding.

49.5 [44] *where the eagle stops.* Yvonne is confusing the origin of Quauhnahuac, meaning "near the wood," with that of Tenochtitlán, the Aztec capital and site of present day Mexico City. Her confusion is understandable, given that the terminal at the Bella Vista was named the Portel del Aguila del Oro (see note **48.2**), but perhaps arises because the Nahuatl *quauhtli,* "eagle," is very similar to *cuáhuitl,* "wood," and may have suggested to her the legend of the founding of Tenochtitlán. In the year 1325 the wandering Aztecs halted near the lake of Texcoco and saw a magnificent royal eagle perched on a nopáli cactus with a serpent in his talons and his wings open to the rising sun; they hailed the auspicious omen as a sign from their god Huitzilopotchli that here was to be their future city. The emblem of eagle, cactus, and serpent is that depicted on the present-day Mexican flag and coat of arms. The glyph representing Quauhnahuac in the Aztec codices, depicting a talking tree (Bonnefoi, p. 95), confirms that "Louis" rather than Yvonne is correct, but the manuscripts of *UTV* reveal that up to the very last drafts Lowry too was in error: there was no mention of "near the wood" at this point, but another comment, subsequently deleted from Ch. 11, described the eagle as "of the kind for which the Aztecs had named Quauhnahuac itself" (UBC 8–23, p. 5), showing how deliberately Lowry had wanted the earlier reference to anticipate Yvonne's later freeing of the eagle.

49.6 [44] *Louis.* For the probable identification of this mysterious figure, see note **53.2**.

49.7 [44] *a river of lapis.* From L. *lapis,* "a stone"; probably *lapis lazuli,* the semi-precious stone whose azure colouring fits the heraldic setting (see also p. 43 [37]): "this scrolled silver rim of wash striking the shore"); perhaps also *lapis infernalis* or lunar caustic (fused nitrate of silver), with a hint of the coming of Lucifer.

49.8 [44] *the horn of Venus.* Venus, second planet from the sun and brightest star in the sky, as the morning star (Sp., "el lucero del alba") is also called Lucifer, "light-bearer," and is considered in Toltec mythology to be the stellification of Quetzalcóatl, star of the morning. Yvonne sees the planet in its crescent phase, partly darkened on the side away from the rising sun, so that its illuminated part appears as a crescent, which thins out into two "horns," suggesting not only the horns of Lucifer but those of cuckoldry: Aphrodite (Venus), given in marriage to Hephestus (Vulcan), the lame smith, betrayed her husband with Ares (Mars) and was exposed to the ridicule of the gods. The entire background of Yvonne's betrayal of Geoffrey with Hugh is thus implied in the identification of Yvonne with Venus.

49.9 [44] *Compañia Mexicana de Aviación.* Known throughout Central America as the CMA, this airline was begun by two Americans in 1924 and quickly established itself as the leading airline of Latin America by 1940. It continues as a relatively independent airline to this day.

49.10 [44] *winged emissary of Lucifer.* Lucifer, son of the morning (Isaiah 14:12), the brightest of the angels before his fall, is commonly identified with Satan, but in occult literature he is usually considered one of the four chief spirits (with Leviathan, Satan, and Belial); A. E. Waite, in fact, would deny any connection between Satan and Lucifer on the grounds that the Zoharic prince of demons is never compared to the morning star or any other luminary of heaven (*The Holy Kabbalah,* VII.ii, p. 276). One derivation of the name Lucifer is given in MacGregor-Mathers's *The Sacred Magic,* p. 110, where a long list of "emissaries" can be found: "Lucifer: − From Latin, *Lux,* Light, and *Fero,* to bear = A Light Bearer. There is a name "Lucifuge" also employed occasionally, from *Lux,* Light, and *Fugio,* to fly from = He who shuns the Light." Ironically, the plane bearing Yvonne to her husband and supposedly carrying the promise of a rebirth of their love and marriage is transformed into an instrument of evil.

49.11 [45] *the Servicio de Ambulancia within Cortez Palace.* Up until 1965 the Cortés Palace was used as the *ayuntamiento,* or civic administration centre (now relocated in the *Palacio Municipal*). In early drafts of the novel Lowry had emphasized that the ambulance drivers were on strike in order to increase the Consul's guilt by his knowing that the dying Indian was even less likely to receive aid.

49.12 [45] *Hotel Bella Vista Gran Baile Noviembre 1938 a Beneficio de la Cruz Roja. Los Mejores Artistas del radio en acción. No falte Vd.* Sp. "Hotel Bella Vista Grand Ball November 1938 for the benefit of the Red Cross. The best radio stars in action. Don't miss it." The Consul's attendance at this ball is in marked contrast with his later inability to render the dying Indian first aid.

50.1 [45] *the Spanish Main.* The words, with their connotations of piracy and romance, are used rather loosely by Yvonne, since they are normally restricted to the Atlantic seaboard and waters plied by the Spanish merchantmen sailing between Spain and the New World.

50.2 [45] *like young Tritons.* Triton, a sea deity, the son of Poseidon and Amphritrite, is usually depicted with the head and upper body of a man and the tail of a fish and as carrying a conch shell trumpet to raise or quieten the waves. He gave his name to other strange creatures, half man, half fish, which played lasciviously among the waves, blowing noisily upon their conches.

50.3 [45]   *the little towns... their humped churches.... cobalt swimming pools.* Hints of a malformed or demonic mode of existence corresponding with the normal one are present even at this moment as Yvonne flies towards the volcanoes: the word "cobalt," from Ger. *kobold,* "a goblin," the demon of a mine, picks out what is suggested only obliquely by the other adjectives (though "humped" churches may have for Lowry a private connotation of the Hunchback of Notre Dame).

50.4 [46]   *wearing no socks.* Because his feet and ankles are swollen from excessive drinking, but also (see note **34.6**) a sign of psychic disorder. The name Oedipus means "swell-foot," and the Consul's affliction (like his limp) suggests the identification.

51.1 [46]   *Cafeaspirina.* In Mexico, Cafiaspirina (Lowry spells it correctly in most of the drafts, but probably could not resist the pun) is a common variety of aspirin that has caffein as one of its active ingredients. In the manuscripts Lowry toyed with the idea of doing something with the Bayer company's German origins, but the idea was dropped. Cafeaspirina is important thematically because, among other things, it claims to give relief from "dolores."

51.2 [46]   *tequila añejo.* Sp. "old Tequila"; presumably Tequila Añejo de Jalisco (see note **131.2**), a bottle of which the Consul has secreted in his garden.

51.3 [46]   *absolutamente necesario.* Sp. "absolutely necessary," or, in one of Lowry's deft translations (UBC 11–13, p. 12), "indispensable." The advertisement for Cafeaspirina is next to that for *Las Manos de Orlac,* now playing (as it will be one year later) at the local cinema, and the juxtaposition of the two signs arouses in Yvonne's mind a sense of inevitable guilt.

51.4 [46]   *her scarlet bag.* The oblique reference to the Whore of Babylon (Revelation 17:4) suggested by the woman wearing a scarlet brassiere is here reinforced and then further asserted by Weber's, "We came through with heels flying," which had for Lowry the force of a private allusion to his first wife Jan's numerous and flagrant infidelities. The association is brought out in Conrad Aiken's *Ushant,* p. 349: "the faithless little heels were all too faithlessly and obviously going away... a flat declaration that the heels were damned well going to be unfaithful"; but it is also manifest in *UTV:* on p. 191 [187], Yvonne's heels are described as red, and on p. 144 [140], there is an oblique reference to "whore's shoes" (the antithesis of the good luck symbols on a wedding cake). In the Consul's mind at least,

Yvonne is coloured as a scarlet woman, and his resentment of her infidelity triggers off the following sexual puns.

52.1 [47]   *From Acapulco, Hornos.* The Hotel Mirador in which Yvonne stayed overnight is not in fact near the Playa Hornos in Acapulco, the beach celebrated for its afternoon swimming. The word *hornos* means in Spanish "furnace" or "oven," but the Consul underlines the themes of hell and cuckoldry by referring to Cape Horn (Sp. Cabo de Hornos), on Horn Island, just south of Tierra del Fuego, that tip of the tail to the scorpion-shaped south of the American continent and thereby anticipates his own favourite story, p. 339 [338], of the scorpion surrounded by flames stinging itself to death.

52.2 [47]   *San Pedro — Panama Pacific.* San Pedro is a port in the extreme south of Los Angeles harbour; there may be an allusion to St. Peter, hinting at Yvonne's mission to save her husband. Panama Pacific was a steamship line operating along the west coast of Mexico and the U.S.A.; one of its ships was the *Pennsylvania*.

52.3 [47]   *bull-headed Dutchmen.* Andersen suggests, p. 135, that this phrase and Webster's previous "with heels flying" constitutes a reference to the legend of the flying dutchman, who, having challenged heaven and hell, was condemned to sail the seas until Judgment Day, unless, on one day every seven years, he can find the woman who will redeem him by her faithful love. The "bull-headed" Consul, unlike Wagner's dutchman, refuses the chance of such redemption.

52.4 [47]   *Alas!* Sp. "wings"; Wings was a brand of American cigarette whose dolorous name recurs to the Consul throughout the day. Andersen points out, pp. 89–90, that cigarettes are used consistently throughout the novel as "a symbol of the small value a human life seems to have" and cites such instances as the submarine burning helplessly, "a smoking cigar aglow on the vast surface of the Pacific," p. 38 [32]; the Consul's cigarette "consuming itself in an ashtray," p. 51 [46]; Hugh's cigarette "that seemed bent, like humanity, on consuming itself as quickly as possible," p. 105 [101]; and the "ravaged cigarette" dropped down the ravine, p. 106 [102]. The symbolism is explicit in Lowry's poem "Men with Coats Thrashing" (*SP,* p. 57).

52.5 [47]   *Calle Nicaragua, cinquenta dos.* Sp. "Nicaragua Street, 52"; in Cuernavaca, the Calle Humboldt (named after Baron Alexander von Humboldt, explorer and man of science and letters). A certain mystery surrounds the location of Lowry's house in Cuernavaca, clearly the model for that of the Consul: Day, p. 215, locates it as No. 15, at the intersection of Calle de

Humboldt and Calle de Salazar, but this does not tally with either the description in the novel or with letters written by Conrad Aiken from Cuernavaca, where Lowry's address is given as 62. In *DATG,* pp. 123 and 153, the numbers are given as 65, by 1945 changed to 55. In the novel, the Consul's house is located well down the Calle Humboldt, in a most desirable residential area where several embassies, including the British, maintained weekend houses. Lowry probably had a specific place in mind, but frequent changes of numbering since 1938 and the demolition of many houses in the area make a precise identification of either Lowry's or the Consul's house very difficult. In the novel, however, the number 52 seems to have been chosen as an oblique reference to the night of the culmination of the Pleiades (see note **35.3**).

52.6 [47] *Yvonne pressed a tostón on a dark god.* In Mexico, a *tostón* is a silver coin worth 50 centavos. The dark god is possibly an ironic allusion to D. H. Lawrence's *The Plumed Serpent* (1926) and its strange cult of primitivism; Lowry had read the novel and found it "pretty dreadful" (Kilgallin, p. 160), and references to it in *Under the Volcano* are conspicuously absent (see, however, notes **59.5** and **256.1**).

52.7 [47] *'Have a drink?'...'—'.* Costa comments, p. 71, that the dash is all Yvonne can answer in response to the Consul's brazen invitation to drink, since, after all, she left him because of his drinking.

53.1 [48] *Fort Sale..... shoeshot..... Brownings:* Fort Sale is probably Lowry's phonetic version of Fort Sill, a U.S. Army reservation at Lawton, Oklahoma, and the home of the Army's Field Artillery School; the name is mildly ironic in the context of gun-running. Shoeshot is probably Shurshot, a kind of Winchester repeating rifle, and Brownings are BAR's (Browning Automatic Rifles).

53.2 [48] *Louis.* Lowry may have in mind Louis Fischer (1896–1970), the journalist with *The Nation* who was the first American to enlist with the International Brigades and who was later very active on behalf of the Republicans in the purchasing of arms. Hugh's career and politics are very similar to those of Fischer, whose *Men and Politics* (1941) Lowry may have read. Fischer made frequent short visits to the United States, one at the end of 1938 (just one month too soon for Yvonne to have run into him). The name Louis was a late change to the manuscripts, earlier versions reading "Tom Taylor" (the "Tom" who rings from America, p. 81 [76]).

53.3 [48] *To Oaxaca.* Despite the fact that Yvonne and Geoffrey "had found each other once" in Oaxaca, the Consul's experiences there since

Yvonne's departure (see note **41.8**) render his toast more than slightly ambivalent.

53.4 [48]   *the great tree.* A giant ahuehuetl or cypress, now dying despite the best efforts to save it, at the village of Santa María de Tule a few miles from Oaxaca on the road to the ruins at Mitla. The tree, some 135 feet high and impressively wide with an immense bole, towers above the nearby church. It is said to be the oldest living thing in Mexico, at least 3,000 years old. Cortés is reputed to have dined beneath its branches on his way to Honduras in 1524.

53.5 [48]   *Etla and Nochitlán.* The village of San Pedró y San Pablo Etla and the town of Ascunsión Nochixtlán, respectively some twenty and eighty miles from Oaxaca on the road north towards Cuernavaca.

53.6 [49]   *damas accompañadas de un caballero, gratis!* Sp. "ladies accompanied by a gentleman, free!"

53.7 [49]   *the ancient fragrant Mayan air.* In trying to evoke the splendour and magic of a long-gone civilization, Yvonne is in error: the Mayans, whose magnificent civilization reached its height between 300 and 900 A.D. before inexplicably declining, built their cities throughout Central America and the Yucatán but did not really extend their rule as far north as Oaxaca, the centre in turn of the Olmec, Zapotec, and Mixtec civilizations; Lowry probably felt that the magnificence of the Mayan civilization more powerfully expressed the loss of what once had been.

54.1 [49]   *cluster-lamps.* On cargo ships, a cluster-lamp was a large lamp some eighteen inches in diameter attached to the end of a long rope so that it could be lowered into hatches to facilitate unloading at night. The "curious familiar glare" in Geoffrey's eyes seems to indicate that the ship of his soul is very much under the control of some other malignant force.

55.1 [50]   *Ras Algethi.* Ar. "Head of the Kneeler": a giant red star (one of the largest known) of variable brightness in the constellation Hercules; also known as Alpha Herculis.

55.2 [50]   *Antares.* In popular etymology, *anti Ares,* "the rival of Mars"; also known as "the Scorpion's Heart" (Ar. *Kalbal 'Akrab*). A star of the first magnitude in the centre of the constellation Scorpio, described on p. 323 [322] as "raging to its end — a smouldering ember yet five hundred times greater than the earth's sun." These intimations of disaster are borne out by the fact of the novel's action being set in Scorpio.

55.3 [50] *An old woman from Tarasco who plays dominoes at seven o'clock in the morning.* The Tarascans (or Purépechas) were an Indian tribe who resisted Aztec rule and attained a considerable level of culture in pre-Columbian times, but they declined in both numbers and importance after their subjugation by the Spaniards in 1533. The Tarascan language is still spoken, and the name Tarasco (not be be confused with the gulf state of Tabasco) is applied in a general way to an area of lagoons and mountains in the northeast of Michoacán State. There was also a cantina, El Tarasco, near the old market place in Cuernavaca.

The old woman is clearly a figure of fate, for the chill Yvonne feels is the presentiment of death. The word "domino," originally signifying a cloak or half-mask, suggests the black death-mask invariably worn by Mixcóatl, the Aztec god of death, and by various Mayan deities whose presence boded ill. The dominoes themselves, Epstein suggests, p. 80, are for "reading fate by means of *gematria*," that is, using numerical values to interpret the secret mystery of words; while the chicken, pecking among the dominoes, suggests the Roman *tripudium* or the art of divination according to the way food fell from the mouths of the sacred chickens (Cicero, *De Divinatione,* II.xxxiv). The prophecy of death is clearly present, would the Consul but heed it.

56.1 [51] *William Blackstone.... 'The man who went to live among the Indians.'* William Blackstone (1595–1675), graduate of Cambridge and minister of the Church of England, left England in 1623, several years before the main body of Puritans. Solitary by nature, he moved across the Charles River to what is now Boston, but in 1635, after a dispute with the Puritans, he moved off to what is now Rhode Island ("away from the people with ideas," *UTV,* p. 96 [92]), to spend most of the next forty years on his farm at Study Hill on the river later named after him. He was said to have a large library, to have grown apple trees, to have ridden a bull instead of a horse, and to have been a friend to the Indians (who nevertheless fired his house after he died). Blackstone was Conrad Aiken's literary discovery and was used by him in a 1937 essay, "Literature and Massachusetts," as the figure of the man who wished to be alone. As the prototype of solitary American individualism, William Blackstone also figured in Aiken's 1947 poem, "The Kid":

> Where now he roves, by wood or swamp whatever,
> the always restless, always moving on,
> his books burned, and his own book lost forever,
> under the cold stars of New England, gone.

In his autobiographical novel *Ushant,* p. 291, Aiken suggests that Lowry felt a "mystic identification" with the figure of William Blackstone. Certainly, he was much taken with the theme, announced to Aiken that Blackstone was henceforth *his* property (Day, p. 223), and romanticized Blackstone's life into the legend of "the man who went to live among the Indians" —a myth which, like the story of his father's disappearance, caters to the Consul's desire for oblivion and his hatred of interference.

56.2 [51]   *tabid.* From L. *tabere,* "to waste away"; progressively thinning, wasting away. The word, with its overtones of neuritis and atrophy, would seem more applicable to the Consul than to the music.

56.3 [51]   *army and navy.* Like the word "consular," the phrase has a ring of spruce efficiency. The Army and Navy stores headquarters in Victoria Street, London, offer a dazzling range of quality merchandise. As their name implies, the stores began as suppliers to the armed forces.

56.4 [52]   *the ragged Mexican with the dark glasses.* Apparent confirmation of the Consul's fears, expressed by Laruelle, p. 36 [30], of being "around the town pursued by other spiders"; the question as to whether these supposed followers are real or "figments of a paranoid brain" (Jakobsen, p. 10) admits no easy answer, since Yvonne too is aware of them. Their presence, real or imagined, suggests a correspondence, as the Consul would put it, between the subnormal world and the abnormally suspicious (*UTV,* p. 40 [34]).

57.1 [52]   *what a card he is.* The "joke" is that the Consul has deliberately wished the ragged young Mexican "Buenas tardes" ("Good afternoon") when it is still early in the morning ("buenas días" is the correct greeting). The notion of the Consul as a joker, and the word "card" suggests the likelihood, in terms of the Tarot, of the Consul as the Fool, one for whom the abyss lies waiting (Ouspensky, *A New Model of the Universe,* p. 227).

57.2 [52]   *The fiesta.... The bright banners, the paper streamers... the great wheel.* A marginal note in the manuscripts (UBC 10-8, p. 8) makes specific reference to Eisenstein's *Que Viva Mexico!,* one part of which was to be called "Fiesta." Eisenstein's more important contribution, however, is the technique of montage which Lowry uses in the following scene, juxtaposing shots of the background against those of the characters.

57.3 [52]   *Box!.... ARENA TOMALÍN, Frente al Jardín Xicotancatl. Domingo 8 de Noviembre de 1938. 4 Emocionantes Peleas.... ¡BOX! Pre-*

*liminar a 4 Rounds. EL TURCO (Gonzalo Calderón de Par. de 52 kilos) vs.
EL OSO (de Par. de 53 kilos)... ¡BOX! Evento Especial a 5 Rounds, en
los que el vencedor pasará al grupo de Semi-Finales. TOMÁS AGUERO (el
Invencible Indio de Quauhnahuac de 57 kilos, que acaba de llegar de la
Capital de la República). ARENA TOMALÍN. Frente al Jardín Xicotan-
catl.* Sp. "Boxing!...Tomalín Arena. Front of the Xicotancatl Gardens.
Sunday November 8 1938. 4 thrilling contests.... Boxing! Preliminary of 4
Rounds. *The Turk* (Gonzalo Calderón weighing 52 kilos) vs. *The Bear*
(weighing 53 kilos).... Boxing! Special event of 5 Rounds, from which the
winner will pass into the Semi-final group. *Tomás Aguero* (the Invincible
Indian from Quauhnahuac of 57 kilos, who has just returned from the
Capital of the Republic). *Tomalín Arena.* Front of the Xicotancatl Gardens." Boxing was a Saturday night tradition in Cuernavaca during the
1920's and 1930's. Lowry comments that "the recurring notices for the
boxing match symbolize the conflict between Yvonne and the Consul"
("LJC," p. 72). Other hints of conflict are also present: the name Tomás
Aguero (suggesting Sp. *tomar,* "to drink," plus *aguero,* "omen"); the reference to the warrior Xicotancatl (see note **303.2**); and the phrase "el
vencedor pasará" with its echo of the Republican Civil War cry, "no
pasarán" (see note **303.3**). 8 November 1938 was not a Sunday, but a Tuesday; the day holds true for 1936 when Lowry arrived in Mexico and when
the action of the novel was originally set (see note **9.8**).

57.4 [52] *Or is it the sprue?* Psilosis, a chronic disease of the digestive system caused by poor absorption of fats and vitamins from the small intes-
tine. It is characterized by a sore throat, raw tongue, and digestive disturbance and occurs particularly in tropic countries. The word "sprue" is of
Dutch origin. The Penguin "O" is a misprint.

58.1 [53] *mescalito!* The word appears to be used in the sense of "sot" or
"drunk" (one who has had too much mescal), but this meaning is unusual,
and its oddity may account for the Consul's remembering it, p. 215 [211]. It
is also possible that the Consul, erroneously assuming a connection between
mescal and mescaline, understands a reference to Mescalito, the god who
guides those who take peyote (as in Carlos Castaneda, *The Teachings of
Don Juan*).

58.2 [53] *the little public scribe.* A person who fills out forms, types up
documents, and writes letters for the numerous illiterate citizens in the
town. In Mexico, such scribes may carry on their business in the public
square.

58.3 [53] *change of worlds.* Despite Lowry's claim (*SL,* p. 144) that he had
not then read *Ulysses* through, there is almost certainly "direct influence" at
this point. In Ch. 5 of Joyce's novel Martha Clifford mistakenly writes, "I
do not like that other world," and two hours later in the cemetery (Hades),
her words come back to Leopold Bloom: "There is another world after
death named hell. I do not like that other world she wrote. No more do I."
On a different level, the little public scribe is an embodiment of Thoth,
inventor of hieroglyphics and scribe of the gods (see note **40.3** and Webb,
p. 101), recording the last hours of the Consul's existence before his final
"change of worlds."

58.4 [53] *La China Poblana.* The name of the shop is derived from the
china poblana dress, originally the costume of Puebla village girls (*poblana,*
the adjective from *puebla,* "village" or "town"; *china,* an Indian or Mestizo
servant girl). The china poblana, now almost a national costume, consists
of a red and green sequin-embroidered dress worn over many petticoats, a
white blouse, and a *rebozo,* or shawl, worn crossed at the front (Fodor,
p. 200). The shop is still to be found in Cuernavaca, in a small arcade just
off the zócalo, selling handicrafts and souvenirs to tourists at prices
unheard of in the villages.

58.5 [53] *Baños de la Libertad, Los mejores de la Capital y los únicos en
donde nunca falta el agua, Estufas especiales para Damas y Caballeros.* Sp.
"Liberty Baths, the best from the Capital, and the only ones where water is
never lacking: special Stoves for Ladies and Gentlemen" (that is, heating
appliances for Turkish baths or saunas). Lowry has taken his Liberty Baths
from those in Mexico City, once famous not only as public steam baths but
also as a training centre for Mexico's best boxers.

58.6 [53] *Sr Panadero: Si quiere hacer buen pan exija las harinas 'Princess
Donaji'.* Sp. "Mr. Baker: if you want to have good bread, ask for 'Princess
Donaji' flour."

58.7 [54] *Peegly Weegly.* Piggly Wiggly Southern is a supermarket chain
based in Georgia and Florida. The chain never operated in Mexico, but its
success in the United States, and the cleverness of the name, encouraged
independent operators in Mexico to use it without authorization. There was
in 1938 a celebrated one, the first of its kind in Mexico City (on Independencia), with a small branch in Cuernavaca, on Guerrero, one block north
of the zócalo. Both have long since disappeared. Yvonne's grief and the
Consul's sudden contrition is something of a mystery (even more accentuated in the manuscripts, UBC 10–7, p. 10). There appears to be a reference

to the nursery rhyme, "This little piggy went to market," and one can only speculate that the Consul has somehow tactlessly reminded Yvonne of her own dead child or of the children she has denied him.

59.1 [54]   *desperate as a winze.* A winze in a mine is "a shaft or inclined passage sunk from one level to another, but not rising to the surface" (*OED*). Lowry seems to have in mind passages such as Swedenborg's *Heaven and Hell,* #588: "There are also hells beneath hells. There are communications between some of the hells by passages." Lowry notes in *DATG,* p. 121, that the steep narrow street adjacent to the palace had gone when he returned in 1945.

59.2 [54]   *an ocean creature. . . . coppered. . . . charioting the surf.* Yvonne, already identified with Venus, is now described in the terms of the birth of Aphrodite (the Greek Venus), who rose from the foam on the island of Cyprus (in some accounts, Cythera). She is described as "coppered" because copper is the alchemical metal associated with Venus. The chariot of Venus is usually pulled by doves, but Lowry may have in mind the sea-shell depicted in Botticelli's *Birth of Venus* (1485).

59.3 [54]   *windrows.* A row in which mowed hay or corn is laid before being piled up and tied into sheaves. The Penguin "windows" is an error.

59.4 [54]   *the already spinning flywheel of the presses.* A flywheel is a heavy metal wheel attached to a machine to regulate its speed and uniformity of motion. Lowry draws attention ("LJC," p. 72) to this wheel as one of his wheels; that is, as an unobtrusive reminder of the infernal machine and the forces inexorably drawing the Consul to his fate.

59.5 [54]   *La Despedida.* Sp. "The Parting." The split rock, incongruously placed among the wedding invitations and prints of "extravagantly floriferous brides," symbolizes for Yvonne the inevitable disintegration of her life with Geoffrey and the impossibility of their becoming one again. Kilgallin suggests, p. 160, that Lowry may have taken the word from D. H. Lawrence: the words "Despedida, despedida Eran fuentes de dolores" ("Parting, parting They were fountains of sorrows") occur in a letter of 3 October 1924 to J. M. Murry (*Letters,* p. 615), and the word despedida is to be found in *The Plumed Serpent,* Ch. 18, in the hymn "Jesus' Farewell": "Farewell, Farewell, *Despedida! /* The last of my days is gone." Certainly the split rock is a favourite Lawrentian image (though Lawrence tends to use it very differently), but Kilgallin, p. 160, is probably right to suggest that Lowry's immediate source was Conrad Aiken's *Great Circle* (1933), where the rock as a symbol of suffering is used to convey Andrew Cather's sense of separation from his adulterous wife. The episode as a whole, Sherrill Grace argues, may have been suggested by a scene in Murnau's film *Sunrise* (see note **204.5**), where the man and his previously unwanted wife, reconciled after near disaster, gaze at wedding photographs in a window ("Expressionist Vision," p. 106).

59.6 [54]   *detritus.* Misused here: detritus is the material left after disintegration rather than the force of disintegration itself.

59.7 [55]   *It was inevitable.* The phrase reinforces the "absolutemente necesario" of p. 48 [43] and anticipates the end of Ch. 7: "Es inevitable la muerte del Papa."

60.1 [55]   *some fanciful geologic thaumaturgy. . . . a superlapidary effort.* Deliberate hyperbole to emphasize the immensity of Yvonne's task; a task as difficult, ultimately as impossible, as the alchemist's search for the philosopher's stone:
(a) *thaumaturgy.* Gk. *thaumatourgia,* from *thauma,* "a wonder," and *ergon,* "work"; a working of miracles or magic. In Éliphas Lévi's *Transcendental Magic,* pp. 360 ff., the thaumaturge is described as a physician, one who makes things whole, but this particular thaumaturgy is beyond the powers of Geoffrey Firmin, magician manqué.
(b) *superlapidary.* A supreme effort in stone; from L. *lapis,* "a stone," and *supra,* "above"; a neologism which suggests the philosopher's stone of the alchemists, by the agency of which base metals might be transmuted into gold and imperfect man made spiritually whole. If the word is Lowry's pun on "superlapsarian" (that is, pertaining to the doctrine that predestination was antecedent to the Creation and Fall), then the sense of inevitability is underlined.

60.2 [55]   *Calle Tierra del Fuego.* Sp. "Street of the Land of Fire." In Cuernavaca, the Calle de Las Casas (named for the early Spanish missionary, Fr. Bartolomé de las Casas, famous for his charity to the Indians), leading from the centre of town past the Cortés Palace towards the Calle Humbolt (Nicaragua); Lowry has exaggerated its length and steepness (even though the street runs differently today). Tierra del Fuego, the "Land of Fire," is the cold inhospitable island at the south tip of South America; Yvonne relates the name to the fires that have split the rock and to what the Consul has earlier said about Cape Horn (see note **52.1**).

60.3 [55]   *Molino para Nixtamal, Morelense.* Sp. "Milled by *Nixtamal,* of

Morelos." *Nixtamal* (from Nah. *nextli,* "ash" or "lime," and *tamalli,* "tortilla") refers to the process whereby cornmeal is boiled with lime to soften it, then cooled and ground, the unleavened saltless flour thus formed being ready-mixed for tortillas. *Morelense* is the adjective from Morelos, the state; the slightly odd syntax is explained not by the vagaries of advertising but by Lowry's misreading of a sign still extant on the Calle de Las Casas: "Molino para Nixtamal, El Morelense"; the latter being the name of the shop.

60.4 [55] *Lechería.* Sp. "milk-shop" or "dairy" (with a pun on "lechery").

60.5 [56] *chorizos.* Small spicy sausages, made of pork ground up with spices and peppers and usually served chopped up in egg, bean, or mixed meat dishes.

61.1 [56] *the abarrotes.* Roughly translatable as "grocery store," but the typical abarrotes sells wines, spirits, beers, and alcholic drinks, with other products an almost secondary concern.

61.2 [56] **Eggs.** As Jakobsen notes, p. 66, the Spanish word *huevos,* "eggs," also means testicles; the ruffianly male laughter hence implies that those in the shop think the Consul is trying to buy virility, to cope with "the beautiful *layee.*" In fact, he is probably having a hair-of-the-dog prairie oyster or a similar egg-based drink to steady himself.

61.3 [56] *Tortu... the ideal University.* The Consul is referring to Tartu University, in Tartu (or Yuryev) in Estonia. Founded by Gustavus Adolphus II of Sweden in 1632, it was suppressed from 1656 to 1802 and was at its best during the brief period of Estonian independence, 1918–40. The university is built around an old fortified hill topped by a restored thirteenth-century cathedral (the site of the university library). In the 1940 version of the novel the Consul had gained a degree in languages at Liverpool, was a lecturer in Zoology at Helsingfors, spoke Finnish and Hungarian, was an expert on Tolstoy, and "Then he was at Tortu, Lithuania, for a time" (UBC 7–5, p. 25); the references to Tortu and *War and Peace* are now the only traces of this background. The "ideal university" of the Consul's aspirations is in marked contrast to University City, Madrid (also with a library built on a hill), the scene of a violent pitched battle during the Spanish Civil War (see note **105.3**).

61.4 [57] *La Cucaracha.* Sp. "The Cockroach"; a jaunty song of obscure origin which became particularly popular during the Revolution, with its verses full of satirical jabs at revolutionary leaders and events. The song begins:

> La cucaracha, la cucaracha,
> ya no puede caminar,
> porque le falta, porque le falta
> mariguana que fumar.

("The cockroach, the cockroach, / can't walk any more, / because it lacks, because it lacks, / marijuana to smoke").

Even on the Day of the Dead, the song is hopelessly inappropriate for a child's funeral.

62.1 [57] *the bizarre house.* That belonging to Jacques Laruelle, with its crazy towers and its inscription "No se puede vivir sin amar" ("one cannot live without loving"), which Yvonne does not wish to see because it reminds her of her past infidelity. The house still stands in Cuernavaca, on the Calle Humboldt directly opposite the Calle Las Casas, but it is by now almost unrecognizable as the house of the book: the towers, one of which had disappeared by 1945 (*DATG*, p. 153), have gone completely, and the shabby façade (half-hidden by an enormous Pepsi sign) gives no hint of its former impressive stature. Lowry, superstitious at the best of times, became almost mesmerized by coincidence when he revisited Cuernavaca in 1945 and was able to rent an apartment in this very house, which he had previously observed only from the outside (*DATG*, p. 124).

62.2 [58] *lunar potholes... state of frozen eruption.* An anticipation of the Valley of the Moon and "freezing of culture" themes so central to Ch. 4 (see notes **99.1** and **105.9**).

63.1 [58] *She saw the mountains again in the distance.* In 1938, Popocatepetl and Ixtaccihuatl could be seen distinctly from Cuernavaca, though Lowry has greatly exaggerated their dominance of the landscape (in *DATG*, p. 121, Sigbjørn tries to show them to Primrose, but they look in vain). Today, with increased atmospheric pollution, the truly magnificent volcanoes can be observed only with some difficulty even under favourable conditions.

63.2 [58] *Mauna Loa, Mokuaweoweo.* Mauna Loa (13,675 feet), on the island of Hawaii, is the largest single volcano in the world (though not the highest). There had been a large lava flow from it in 1935–36.

Mokuaweoweo, on the summit of Mauna Loa, is the second largest of its numerous craters and one of the largest active craters in the world. The sight of the Mexican volcanoes and their tragic romantic story (see note **318.6**), remind Yvonne, in the words on p. 58 [53], that "she'd had volcanoes in her life before."

63.3 [58] *Bishop Berkeley.* George Berkeley (1685–1753), bishop of Cloyne, whose *esse est percipi* summarizes his philosophical contention that material things exist only insofar as they are perceived and that the mind, being conscious of subjective impressions only, cannot therefore know external things.

63.4 [58] *the four o'clock mirabilis jalapa.* The "mirabilis jalapa" (from L. *mirabilis,* "wonderful" and Jalapa, the state capital of Vera Cruz) is a plant of the four o'clock family: an ornamental plant with spikes of various coloured flowers, which open about four o'clock in the afternoon but remain closed in the morning.

64.1 [59] *the White Russian Embassy in Zagreb in 1922.* In the civil war which followed the Russian Revolution of 1917, the White Russian armies under General Deniken and later General Wrangel were beaten back from all Russian soil in the southwest by the spring of 1920. They were forced to retreat from the Crimea to Istanbul and thence dispersed through the various kingdoms of the Balkans and Eastern Europe, the army attempting to maintain itself in the kingdom of the Serbs, Croats, and Slovenes (Yugoslavia), even though most of its troops were fading away. As an effective force and entity White Russia was dead by the summer of 1921, but a number of Western nations, including Britain, were reluctant to recognize the Reds and retained nominal recognition of Wrangel's White Army as the provisional ruler of Russia (though the British had in fact made a *de facto* recognition of and entered into a trade treaty with the Bolsheviks by April of 1921; hence, perhaps the "sublime, dishonest detachment"). A group of White-guard emigrés which called itself a Russian Consulate operated in Zagreb up to the beginning of 1924. Although the British had maintained consular offices in Sarajevo, Belgrade, and Zagreb, Lowry's reference to the last is rather puzzling, since the capital and diplomatic centre of Yugoslavia was Belgrade; in an earlier draft (UBC 7–3, p. 8) the Consul, talking to Yvonne, who was then his daughter, had said that her mother "was never attaché to the White Russian Embassy in Belgrade in 1922."

64.2 [59] *a British Q-ship.* A "mystery ship"; that is, a naval gunboat (such as the S.S. *Samaritan,* p. 38 [32]), disguised as a merchantman, with false bulkheads and concealed guns, used to lure enemy submarines into easy range before opening fire (see note **135.5**). The Consul's reference to Tottenham Court Road in the middle of London deliberately mocks Yvonne's inexperience and, by implication, her limited understanding of his guilt and responsibility.

64.3 [59] *Cuckoldshaven.* Through its etymology, the town of Cuernavaca (from Sp. *cuerna,* "a horn") is associated in the Consul's mind with his recent cuckoldry and linked to Cuckoldshaven, on the Surrey side of the Thames, a mile or so below London Bridge: so-called, according to tradition, because in King John's reign a miller living there had a beautiful wife who attracted the King's favour, the miller being compensated by a grant of as much land on that side as he could see from his house (*OCEL*). The location was formerly distinguished by a tall pole topped by a pair of horns. Kilgallin, p. 159, senses an allusion to the Jacobean play *Eastward Ho!* (1605), by Chapman, Jonson, and Marston and links it to the motif of "cuckold-shaven" (see notes **17.4** and **177.2**).

64.4 [59] *the lost love of Maximilian and Carlota.* For the tragic history of Maximilian and Carlota, see notes **20.3** and **20.12:** given the context of cuckoldry, it is at least possible that Lowry is here hinting at the fascinating but little-known story of Maximilian's secret love life, though it is ironic that Yvonne should be the guilty party.

64.5 [59] *¡BOX! ARENA TOMALÍN. EL BALÓN vs EL REDON-DILLO.* Sp. "Boxing! Tomalín Arena. The Balloon vs. the Bouncing Ball" (as the Consul translates the names, p. 192 [188]).

65.1 [60] *¡BOX! ARENA TOMALÍN. FRENTE AL JARDÍN XICO-TANCATL. Domingo 8 de Noviembre de 1938. 4 Emocionantes Peleas. EL BALÓN vs EL REDONDILLO. . . . Las Manos de Orlac. Con Peter Lorre.* Sp. "Boxing! Tomalín Arena. Front of the Xicotancatl Gardens. Sunday 8 November 1938. 4 thrilling contests. The Balloon vs. the Bouncing Ball. . . . The hands of Orlac. With Peter Lorre." The cinematic juxtaposition of the boxing against the film further underlines the guilty tension between Yvonne and the Consul (see notes **57.3** and **30.4**).

65.2 [60] *unpukka.* "Pukka" is a Hindi word meaning "first class" or "genuine." It was often used by the English military and colonial officers living in India during the heyday of the Victorian Empire. "Unpukka" thus implies a shabbiness or falseness about Hugh's costume.

65.3 [60] *Hoot S. Hart in the Riders to the Purple Sage.* The Consul probably means William S. Hart (1870–1946), the leading screen cowboy of innumerable silent westerns between 1914 and 1925, but there is also a suggestion of Edward "Hoot" Gibson, another popular cowboy star. The Consul's carelessness with detail may lightly mock Yvonne's brief cinematic career. There are a number of film versions of *Riders of the Purple Sage* (1918, 1925, 1931, and 1941), based on the 1911 novel by Zane Grey, but none has the kind of poker-faced hero typically played by Hart. The story concerns a crooked lawyer, run out of town, who takes a woman and her daughter with him as hostages. Jim Lassiter, the woman's brother, sets out to find them, falls in love on the way, finds and kills his man (now a judge), and flees the posse to a canyon, where he rolls down a boulder to seal off the only entrance, leaving the lovers together but doomed.

65.4 [60] *Weber. . . . I didn't meet him. . . . The Consul knocked out his pipe on his heel. . . . everyone comes flying to see me.* A complex and ominous nexus of verbal motifs: the Consul will meet Weber in Ch. 12; his life, like his pipe, will be "knocked out" (see note **368.4**); the combination of "heel" and "flying" is a reminder of Yvonne's infidelity (see note **51.4**); and "flying" suggests not only Yvonne's arrival but also the Consul's departure, like Faustus, headlong into the earth (see note **40.1**).

65.5 [61] *the London Globe.* A fictitious name. *The Globe,* founded in 1803, was an evening paper, at first espousing Whig principles but by 1866 supporting Tory policies. It folded in 1921. Hugh's *London Globe* is perhaps modelled on the *Daily Herald* (see note **98.1**), founded in 1912, taken over officially by the Labour Party in 1923, and which had by 1939 a circulation of about two million.

66.1 [61] *The Consul decapitated a dusty coquelicot poppy.* The Consul's decapitation of the scarlet coquelicot or corn-poppy (whose name suggests "coquette") effectively underlines his willed separation from Yvonne. The poppy itself is a symbol of sleep, forgetfulness, and death.

66.2 [61] *I gather he had some idea we might let.* Hugh's idea remains a mystery but may involve Geoffrey's connivance in his now-limited consular capacity with some aspect of his gun-running plans (which the Consul seems to suspect, but refrains from telling Yvonne). To the extent that the Consul is aware of Hugh's plans he is guilty by association (at least in his own mind) of the crime for which he is condemned in Ch. 12.

66.3 [61] *his fine Italian hand.* The words usually apply to calligraphy (perhaps Italics) but here suggest poisoning, associated above all with the infamous Borgia family of Renaissance Italy.

66.4 [61] *to play Theodore Watts Dunton. To my Swinburne.* Theodore Watts-Dunton (1832–1914), a serious and well-meaning man, took care of Algernon Swinburne (1837–1909) during the last nine years of the poet's life, restoring him to physical health mainly by stopping his drinking (weaning him gradually from brandy to port to burgundy to claret to beer). This "progresión a ratos" was "successful" in that Swinburne's health improved, but tragic and disastrous in that, it is commonly believed, the poet's genius was stifled. (Modern criticism, however, has suggested that Watts-Dunton's ministrations in fact permitted Swinburne to finish many of his best works.) The Consul's repeated rejection of Hugh's interference is in large part a reaction against being brought back to such well-intentioned normality, though, as Andersen observes somewhat cynically, p. 403, "it is the loss of the pleasure of dissipation rather than the loss of the creative voice that most distresses the Consul at this stage."

66.5 [61] *mute Swinburne.* The Consul's allusion is not so much to Thomas Gray's "Elegy in a Country Churchyard," l. 59: "Some mute inglorious Milton here may rest"; as to the comment sometimes made about that line: there are no "mute inglorious Miltons"; if they are mute, they are not Miltons. Swinburne, after Watts-Dunton's treatment, was not Swinburne.

66.6 [61] *like a red rag after a bull.* The story Hugh has got wind of is outlined in his cable, p. 98 [94]: that the German Legation in Mexico City is actively behind a campaign to expel small Jewish manufacturers from Mexico. Lowry's source for his image is D. H. Lawrence's *Fantasia of the Unconscious,* Ch. 2: "And you may be sure that a red rag is, to a bull, something far more mysterious and complicated than a socialist's necktie."

66.7 [62] *¿Quien sabe?* Sp. "Who knows?" As Yvonne's confusion reveals, the Consul's reply has brought out the ambiguity of "we" and indirectly gives an answer to Laruelle's question on p. 37 [31]: "But why had all this happened? *¿Quien sabe?*"

66.8 [62] *a very popular front.* The idea of the Popular Front (essentially the solidarity of all anti-capitalist and anti-bourgeois elements of society) was advocated by the Seventh Congress of the Communist International in Moscow in August 1935 and was taken up quickly and enthusiastically by a number of countries. In Spain, the Popular Front consisted of a number of anti-fascist parties that gained the day in the elections of February 1936, though, by the quirks of the Spanish electoral law, their majority in the Cortes was much greater than their share of the total votes (Thomas, p. 6); this discrepancy, plus the Front's dubious support by the Anarchists opposed even to it, afforded the Nationalists an opportunity to exploit its weaknesses and reassert themselves. In Mexico, a Popular Front was called for by the C.T.M. (see note **98.3**) and consisted of the principal worker organizations, the peasants, government employees, the army, and small businessmen; that is, a general front rather than a homogenous organization with a concerted policy or aim. The Front received the qualified support of the Cárdenas administration, which did not, however, lose control of it, and in collaboration with the government it pressed for a number of socialist reforms. The Consul is mocking the widespread and often uncritical support that English liberals and intellectuals offered to such movements in the 1930's, and in so doing he expresses his fundamental reservations about "people with ideas."

67.1 [62]   *the Good Samaritan*. In Luke 10:30–36, Jesus replies indirectly to the question, "And who is my neighbour?":

> And Jesus answering said, A certain man went down from Jerusalem to Jericho, and fell among thieves, which stripped him of his raiment, and wounded him, and departed, leaving him half dead.
>
> And by chance there came down a certain priest that way: and when he saw him, he passed by on the other side.
>
> And likewise a Levite, when he was at the place, came and looked on him, and passed by on the other side.
>
> But a certain Samaritan, as he journeyed, came where he was: and when he saw him, he had compassion on him,
>
> And went to him, and bound up his wounds, pouring in oil and wine, and set him on his own beast, and brought him to an inn, and took care of him.
>
> And on the morrow when he departed, he took out two pence, and gave them to the host, and said unto him, Take care of him; and whatsoever thou spendest more, when I come again, I will repay thee.
>
> Which now of these three, thinkest thou, was neighbour unto him that fell among the thieves?

Christ's parable is at the heart of Lowry's novel and brings together the three key scenes of the S.S. *Samaritan,* the dying Indian, and the Consul's death (see notes **38.1, 250.1,** and **374.2**). The Consul may or may not see himself as a priest (but one who has betrayed the mysteries, p. 291 [289]), or as a Levite (a disciple of Éliphas Lévi—see note **178.2**); but he knows with certainty that he has not been a neighbour. He may also be uncomfortably aware of Jacob Boehme's admonition in *Signatura Rerum,* VII, #36 (cited by Grace, p. 52): "Now wilt thou be a Magus? Then thou must become the Samaritan, otherwise thou canst not heal the wounded and decayed; for the body which thou must heal, is half-dead, and sorely wounded."

67.2 [63]   *bougainvillea.* A tropical vine with red and/or purple leaves used consistently throughout the novel as an emblem of deceit (see note **146.1**).

67.3 [63]   *a watchtower, the eternal mirador of Parián state.* A *mirador* (from Sp. *mirar,* "to see," "to behold") is a balcony or observation point commanding an extensive view. Like the *mirador* of Laruelle's house, p. 198 [194], this watchtower surveys the town of Parián, an ever-visible temptation to the Consul (there are hints, perhaps, of the watchman of Ezekiel 33). The state of Parián is fictitious. Walker comments, p. 263: "Parián itself is an apocryphal state located in the northeastern corner of the actual state of Morelos. It is clearly very close to Popocatepetl and Ixtaccihuatl, on the other side of which lies the state of Tlaxcala." More simply, it can be assumed that Lowry has equated his fictional Parián with the actual state of Morelos without having closely defined his borders. For more details about the name "Parián," see notes **80.2** and **134.2**.

68.1 [63]   *less Mexico than a Spaniard's dream of home.* An apparent allusion to Graham Greene's *The Lawless Roads,* p. 253, where Greene evokes the Virgin of La Soledad (see note **12.5**): "Spanish of the Spanish, a Velasquez Virgin—and the loneliness she solaced, one imagines, was a Spanish loneliness of men heartsick for Castile."

68.2 [63]   *dark open sinister bunkers.* The bunkers where the carbon (coal or charcoal) is kept have been anticipated on pp. 62 and 63 [57 and 58], but only now do they reveal their ominous implications. The reminder of the Hell Bunker, p. 26 [21], not only evokes the furnace room of the S.S. *Samaritan* and the sinister fate of the German officers, but it also anticipates the "numerous little rooms, each smaller and darker than the last," p. 204 [200], of the Farolito. To that last dark bunker, which opens out upon the abyss, the Consul (as cabrón) is fetched by a different María. The subterranean geography is full of demonic insinuations, expressed in the imagery of Coleridge's "Kubla Khan" but opening out into Swedenborg's hell: the high walls concealing the houses are similar to those girdling round Coleridge's "gardens bright"; the gutters running underground before tumbling out into the sunlight demonically invert the sacred river and mighty fountain; and the "dark entrance in the ditch," which opens up to the abandoned iron mine running beneath the Consul's garden, not only suggests "caverns measureless to man," but also forms a gate to Swedenborg's hells, as described in *Heaven and Hell,* #583–84:

> The hells too are not seen, because they are closed, except the entrances, which are called gates. . . . The hells are everywhere, under the mountains, hills, and rocks, also under the plains and valleys. The openings or gates to the hells, which are under the mountains, hills, and rocks, appear to the sight like holes and clefts of the rocks. . . . They all appear dark and dusty when looked into, but the infernal spirits in them are in a light such as arises from burning charcoal.

68.3 [63] *the rising waters of possible catastrophe.* The gushing gutters intimate disaster: in general, the threat of the Deluge or Second Flood (see note **35.2**); in particular, Thomas Burnet's sense of "the rising world" perched precariously over the troubled waters of the abyss beneath (see notes **26.2.e** and **193.7**). The fountains of the deep seem likely to break open at any moment.

68.4 [64] *the little church that had been turned into a school.* On the Calle Humboldt there is a little church in this area, still functioning as a church, with a school for small children right behind it. It seems likely that Lowry has given the facts a small twist to suggest the political tension between church and state, this in turn underlining that between the Consul and Yvonne.

68.5 [64] *the abandoned iron mine.* Although Cuernavaca was never a mining centre, iron ore in minable quantities had once been found there, but the mines were quickly worked out and abandoned (Díez, p. 29).

69.1 [64] *To and fro from school. . . /Popocatepetl / It was your shining day.* This "poem the Consul liked" (p. 318) is "Romance," by W. J. Turner, which (the author claims in *The Duchess of Popocatepetl,* p. 208) "is included in nearly every anthology of English poetry published since it was first printed in 1916":

> When I was but thirteen or so
> I went into a golden land,
> Chimborazo, Cotopaxi
> Took me by the hand.

My father died, my brother too,
    They passed like fleeting dreams,
I stood where Popocatepetl
    In the sunlight gleams.

I dimly heard the Master's voice
    And boys far-off at play,
Chimborazo, Cotopaxi
    Had stolen me away.

I walked in a great golden dream
    To and fro to school —
Shining Popocatepetl
    The dusty streets did rule.

I walked home with a gold dark boy
    And never a word I'd say
Chimborazo, Cotopaxi
    Had taken my speech away:

I gazed entranced upon his face
    Fairer than any flower —
O shining Popocatepetl
    It was thy magic hour:

The houses, people, traffic seemed
    Thin fading dreams by day,
Chimborazo, Cotopaxi
    They had stolen my soul away!

The happy song hints ominously at the Consul's coming fate; by the end of the day Popocatepetl will have indeed stolen his soul away (see note **318.5**).

69.2 [64]   *strange.* As Jakobsen notes, p. 27, an illusory and momentary sense of peace is disturbed by the fact of this word also being the Consul's reaction to *La Despedida,* p. 59 [54], (this former reference being a much later addition to the manuscripts). On p. 70 [65], the comment is made: "alas, that that which you have known in the blood should ever seem so strange," and on p. 76 [71], the Consul replies to Yvonne's half-assertive "Here I am, aren't I?" with the word "strange"; once more betraying his deliberate distancing and willed estrangement of her.

69.3 [64] *A hideous pariah dog followed them in.* A pariah (from Tamil *paraiyan,* "outcast" — but see also note **80.2**) is typically "a yellow vagabond dog of hideous aspect and low breed which frequents towns and villages of India and South East Asia" (*OED*). As Hugh remarks, p. 110 [106], such dogs seem to shadow his brother everywhere. The dog is a familiar, or accompanying evil spirit, representing essentially the state of the Consul's soul and corresponding to the black poodle of Goethe's *Faust,* in which guise Mephistophilis first appears. Lowry may have derived the image in part from Conrad's *Lord Jim:* at the enquiry into the *Patna* affair (see note **39.1**), a yellow dog is present, and Jim takes the remark "Look at that wretched cur" as a reference to himself. Marlow comments, Ch. 5:

> I am willing to believe each of us has a guardian angel, if you fellows will concede to me that each of us has a familiar devil as well. I want you to own up, because I don't like to feel exceptional in any way, and I know I have him — the devil, I mean. I haven't seen him, of course, but I go upon circumstantial evidence. He is there right enough, and, being malicious, he lets me in for that kind of thing. What kind of thing, you ask? Why, the inquiry thing, the yellow-dog thing . . . the kind of thing that by devious, unexpected, truly diabolical ways causes me to run up against men with soft spots, with hard spots, with hidden plague spots.

CHAPTER THREE

70.1 [65] *The tragedy.* The word tragedy is derived from the Gk. *tragōdia,* "the song of a goat" (from *tragos,* "a goat" and *oīde,* "a song") and is variously explained as referring to a goat offered as a prize at the early dramatic contests, the goatskin dress of the performers, or the vellum on which the plays might have been written. For Lowry, however, the key association is with the Sp. *cabrón,* "a goat," which has emphatic overtones of "cuckold": "The goat means tragedy (tragedy—goat song) but goat—*cabrón*—cuckold (the horns)" (*SL,* p. 198). In this opening phrase exists prepotentially all the anguish and disaster of the coming sexual problems of infidelity and impotence which will form the emotional core of the chapter.

70.2 [65] *crepuscular.* From L. *crepusculum,* "twilight." The Consul's world, as seen through his dark glasses, is a shadowy one.

70.3 [65] *perishing on every hand of unnecessary thirst.* As in T. S. Eliot's *The Waste Land,* the tragedy of the ruined garden and the dry land is a reflection or projection of the sexual and psychological desolation of the central character. The emphasis upon thirst, sterility, and staggering suggests in particular Pt. V of Eliot's poem, ll. 335–38:

> If there were water we should stop and drink
> Amongst the rock one cannot stop or think
> Sweat is dry and feet are in the sand
> If there were only water amongst the rock

The person walking by the Consul's side, "suffering for him," directly echoes Eliot's "Who is the third who walks always beside you?" (l. 359). For both Eliot and Lowry the allusion is to the risen Christ, who, having suffered, appears to two disciples on the road to Emmaus (Luke 24) but is at this point unrecognized.

70.4 [65] *like dying voluptuaries.* A voluptuary is one whose life is spent in the gratification of his senses and the pursuit of physical pleasure.

70.5 [65]   *Touch this tree, once your friend.* In Canto XIII of the *Inferno,* Dante and Virgil enter a pathless wood full of withered trees. Hearing a mournful wailing but seeing no one, the poet stops and is advised by Virgil to break off a little branch from one of the trees. Dante does so; the tree becomes dark with blood and begins to cry: "Perché mi scerpi? / non hai tu spirto di pietade alcuno?" ("Why do you tear me? / Have you no spirit of pity?"). The trees are the suicides, those who have wantonly destroyed their lives and poisoned their souls and are therefore fixed for eternity in barren sterility.

Lowry may have found a similar story in Lewis Spence's *The Magic and Mysteries of Mexico,* p. 62: the butterfly-god, Itzpapalotl, "being in a garden of great delight, he pulled some roses, but . . . suddenly the tree broke and blood streamed from it"; as a consequence, his followers were cast out of the garden and into the world.

70.6 [65]   *Look up at that niche . . . where Christ is still, suffering, who would help you if you asked him: you cannot ask him.* In Mexico, figures of Christ or the Virgin Mary are common features of house or garden walls and are intended to be reminders of the suffering Christ assumed on behalf of mankind. Here, the words also evoke the suffering figure of Faustus: the earlier "Regard" recalls his hellish fall, but the emphasis here, as with the echoes of Eliot and Dante above, is on blood and sorrow and compassion. Faustus, in distress and anguish, cannot look up to heaven for the mercy which is there; one drop of Christ's blood would save his soul, but he cannot avoid despair. Like Faustus, the Consul is unable to ask for relief, even though it is so immediately at hand.

70.7 [65]   *Consider the agony of the roses.* If there is a precise source for this phrase, it remains obscure, but among Lowry's familiar sources there are three references that seem pertinent:
(a) *the Bible.* The cadence of the sentence closely imitates that of "Consider the lilies of the field" (Matthew 6:28), but the more appropriate reference is to the sorrows of the Virgin, whose emblem is the rose: like Mary, Yvonne must watch in agony the sufferings of her loved one.
(b) *Lewis Spence.* On p. 190 of *The Gods of Mexico,* Spence discusses the Aztec myth of the expulsion from Paradise: Xochiquetzal, the Mexican Eve (see note **145.1**), sinned by plucking roses and was unable to look up to heaven.
(c) *Conrad Aiken.* "The Charnel Rose," the first section of the longer work, *The Divine Pilgrim* (1919–25), is described by Aiken as being about "nympholepsy . . . that impulse which sends man from one dream, or ideal, to another, always disillusioned, always creating for

adoration some new and subtler fiction." The poem abounds in images of roses and pain, for example, Pt.I. 2:

> He saw red roses fall again:
> Rose-wreathed skeletons advanced
> And clumsily lifted foot and danced:
> And he saw the roses drop apart
> Each to disclose a charnel heart.

Other images of blood and the suffering Christ are also present to demonstrate Aiken's theme "That man's salvation rose through pain."

70.8 [65] *the plantains with their queer familiar blooms.* The plantain, whose botanical name, ironically, is *Musa paradisiaca,* closely resembles the banana and is extensively cultivated throughout Mexico. In his autobiographical essay *Ushant,* p. 75, Conrad Aiken recalls being:

> at Cuernavaca with Hambo [Lowry], watching the lightning-flash flirtation of the hummingbird and the banana blossom, the flight-and-return vigil, with its ultimate reward, when at last the great voluptuous and fleshy blossom had disclosed its secret, its hidden honey, to be probed with bliss.

In the Consul's mind, however, any sense of beauty or bliss has been replaced by the image of the "hideously elongated cucumiform bundle" of the almost obscenely phallic purple flower.

70.9 [65] *poison has become your daily food.* An ostensible reference to the strychnine routine which Hugh has imposed but indirectly reflecting the Consul's realization that drinking is slowly poisoning his will to live. As Robert Heilman comments in "The Possessed Artist and the Ailing Soul" (Woodcock, p. 23):

> How present the central conception—that of the ailing soul? There are endless symbols for ill-being, from having cancer to taking dope. But Geoffrey's tremendous drinking is exactly the right one, or by art is made to seem the right one. In greater or lesser extent it is widely shared, or at least is related to widely practised habits; it is known to be a pathological state; it may be fatal, but also it can be cured. It lacks the sinisterness of dope, the irresistibility of cancer; hence it is more flexible, more translatable. And Lowry slowly makes us feel, behind the brilliantly presented facts of the alcoholic life, a set of meanings

that make the events profoundly revelatory: drinking as an escape, an evasion of responsibility, a separation from life, a self-worship, a denial of love, a hatred of the living with a faith.

70.10 [66]   *Perro!* Sp. "dog"; here used as a mild expletive (roughly equivalent to an amiable "son of a bitch"). The dog appears "familiarly" because he is in one sense the Consul's "familiar," that is, as Charles Fort might say, an elementary spirit which follows the Consul around.

70.11 [66]   *the garden's a rajah mess.* The Anglo-Indian slang acknowledges (without in the least assuming responsibility for) the dereliction of the garden and, by implication, of the Consul's own person, both of which, despite the efforts of the unpukkah Hugh, p. 65 [60], remain a mess.

71.1 [66]   *debouched.* From Fr. *bouche,* "mouth." The word usually has the sense of "emerged," or "issued forth," but here seems to be used in the sense of "narrowed into."

71.2 [66]   *imbricated.* From L. *imbricare,* "to cover with roof tiles." Lapped over each other.

71.3 [66]   *leaf-cutter ants.* Also known as "umbrella ants" or cuatalatas, these voracious creatures can destroy entire fields by cutting and carrying away portions of leaves to form their nests (de Davila, p. 95).

71.4 [66]   *the Cosmic Egg.* In many creation myths that have water or chaos as a primary condition of reality, there is found the legend of a cosmic egg as the potential source of life: a symbol of fecundity, of the earth, of order arising from chaos. Egyptian, Babylonian, Orphic, Indian, and many other *ab ovo* creation stories exist, but Lowry has in mind primarily Thomas Burnet's *Sacred Theory of the Earth* (1680–89), which was central to his own cosmology (see note **193.7**). Burnet maintained, as literal truth, that the earth was once a giant egg, but, the action of the sun making volatile the waters of the deep within, the shell cracked and the waters rushed forth (the Deluge), fragments of the shell now forming the mountains and continents of our present world. The Consul's cosmic egg is decidedly addled, the drains of Quauhnahuac being quite unlike the life-renewing annual visitations of the waters of the Nile.

71.5 [66]   *trumpet vine.* One of the *Bignoniaceae* family of vines and shrubs that flourish in Latin America. The trumpet is the instrument of the

Angel Gabriel, who, according to Milton, was placed as a guard in the Garden of Eden:

> Gabriel, to thee thy cours by Lot hath givn
> Charge and strict watch that to this happie place
> No evil thing approach or enter in.
>
> *Paradise Lost,* IV.560-2

71.6 [66]   *runnel.* From O. E. *rinnan,* "to run," "to flow"; a small stream or rivulet, or the bed of such. The Consul will later discover a dead scorpion in the runnel of the mingitorio, p. 353 [352].

71.7 [66]   *floribundia.* More accurately, *floribunda.* A kind of rose derived from crossing polyantha and tea roses; they grow in clusters and have no fragrance.

71.8 [66]   *tyrant flycatchers.* A large family (over 360 species) of songbirds that catch insects in flight; they range from South America to Canada.

71.9 [66]   *mistress to some gnarled guardian of the mine beneath the garden.* Another reminder of the existence, within the Consul's consciousness at least, of the demonic mode of existence which runs in correspondence with the natural one. Gnomes are listed (with sylphs, undines, and salamanders) among Éliphas Lévi's "elementary daimons" (*Transcendental Magic,* p. 62) and are associated particularly with the element earth.

71.10 [66]   *the trapeador or American husband.* A trapeador is simply a floormop, but the word also possesses the slang meaning of something worthless or contemptible, thus reflecting the common Mexican opinion of the American male as dominated by his wife.

71.11 [66]   *Concepta.* The name of the maid, with its implications of "conception" and "conceiving," is possibly an ironic contrast to the childlessness of Yvonne. In the drafts, she was originally named Josephina.

72.1 [67]   *Here is your history.* The bespangled luggage bespeaks a mode of life both nomadic and meaningless, revealing that Yvonne's return to Geoffrey is something she needs as much as he does. The labels range from Honolulu, before she met Geoffrey; to Spain, where they met and married; to various consular appointments at Galilee (the first stage of the Via Dolorosa), Paris (where Hugh entered the story), London, and finally

Mexico. The Regis Hotel (Avenida Juárez) is the quality hotel where they first stayed in Mexico City; the Canada Hotel (Cinco de Mayo 47), the shabby scene of their parting (the Penguin punctuation is confused). Yvonne recalls the Hotel Astor, N.Y., and Town House, L.A., on pp. 266–67. In Acapulco she stayed in the Hotel Mirador, the "Lookout Hotel" (Quebrada 74), the oldest in Acapulco, before catching the small red plane of the Mexican Aviation Company, which is responsible for internal flights within Mexico.

72.2 [67]   *the S.S. Ile de France.* The pride of the French line, Transatlantique compagnie générale, built in France in 1926, and at 43,500 tons one of the largest liners of her time, running a regular mail and passenger route between Le Havre and New York. Lowry's first wife Jan travelled to New York on the *Ile de France* alone in 1934, shortly after their marriage, a parting which formed the basis for Lowry's short story, "In Le Havre" (Day, pp. 183 and 188).

72.3 [67]   —*por qué no, agua caliente.* Sp. ["And] why not, hot water."

72.4 [67]   *a University City in the snow.* Ixtaccihuatl is a twin volcano with an irregular jagged cone; it is here associated with the Consul's ideal university of Tortu (see note **61.3**) in a vision of whiteness later to merge with his vision of Granada, p. 303 [302]. The word "jagged" is appropriate to the hostility between the Consul and Yvonne (who is to be identified with the "white woman"), but it also suggests the ruins of University City, Madrid (see note **105.3**).

72.5 [68]   *from which the Consul averted his eyes.* Because he is aware of the temptation offered by the bottle of tequila which he has hidden among that "indescribable confusion of briars."

73.1 [68]   *uncomfortable stuffed Quixotes.* Straw figures of Don Quixote mounted on his sorry nag Rosinante, the discomfort being more in the Consul's mind than the knight-errant's body. The presence of these figures on the wall affords a constant critique of the Consul's inadequate romantic performance.

73.2 [68]   *claret.* A dry red table wine. At one time only red Bordeaux wine was called "claret," but now the term is applied to almost any similar wine.

73.3 [68]   *strychnine.* Strychnine is the principal alkaloid obtained from the seeds of the Indian tree, *strychnos nux vomica.* It is colourless, odourless, bitter, and highly poisonous and is commonly used as a rat poison, but taken in small doses it can be a tonic or stimulant to the central nervous system. Its efficacy in Geoffrey's case seems somewhat dubious, but Hugh may intend it as a kind of aversion therapy. Lowry himself had been subjected to this treatment in Cuernavaca (Day, p. 228).

73.4 [68]   *wormwood.* Specifically, *Artemisia absinthium,* a bitter tasting oil used in making absinthe; more generally, any bitter liquid, hence the strychnine. In Lamentations 3:15 wormwood forms part of the tribulations inflicted upon the Children of Israel, but the usual reference is to Revelation 8:10–11:

> And the third angel sounded, and there fell a great star from heaven, burning as it were a lamp, and it fell upon the third part of the rivers, and upon the fountains of the waters;
> And the name of the star is called Wormwood: and the third part of the waters became wormwood; and many men died of the waters, because they were made bitter.

73.5 [68]   *a voice said in the Consul's ear.* The first of many appearances of Geoffrey's "voices" or "familiars" which, like the good and evil angels in Marlowe's *Doctor Faustus,* do battle for his soul. The challenge they make to the Consul's sense of moral duty is unequivocal: is he the man to drink at this critical and longed-for hour of Yvonne's return, thereby evading his responsibility, or will he be able to resist the temptation? His answer to the challenge is implicit in the words "five hundred drinks" (see note **288.6**). Like Helen, like Malinche, like the traitorous Tlaxcalans, the Consul will betray himself and Yvonne. At this moment, however, as his "Not even a straight wormwood?" has implied, he seems to feel that she has betrayed him, for the third time, by refusing to drink with him.

73.6 [69]   *casuistry.* Originally, the application of principles to cases, but the word has come to mean devious thinking; in particular, the application of doctrine (such as church dogma) falsely to problems of morality or law.

74.1 [69]   *cassis.* Fr. "black-currant"; a syrup flavoured with black currants and often mixed with liquors.

74.2 [69]   *cabrón.* Sp. "goat"; but as the Consul is only too well aware, the word also means "cuckold" (see note **70.1**).

74.3 [69]   *that would be the beginning of the end.* The tequila, hidden in the garden, is a temptation to be resisted because it would lead to mescal, and mescal, as the Consul says on p. 219 [216], "would be the end." See also notes **283.1** and **338.1**.

74.4 [70] *nació 1820 y siguiendo tan campante.* The Spanish equivalent of the slogan on a bottle of Johnny Walker Scotch whiskey: "Born 1820 still going strong." Johnny Walker established his "spirits business" in Kilmarnock, Scotland, in that year.

75.1 [70] *I said three times . . . for Pete's sake have a decent drink.* Whereas Peter denied his master three times, Yvonne urges the Consul to have a drink, but the sense of denial implicit in the allusion, and the repetition of "I'll just sit here and cheer," see p. 52 [48], shows that her heart is not in the words. The allusion, together with the "dead calm in the garden," suggests a parody of Christ's agony in the Garden of Gethsemane.

75.2 [70] *somewhere, out of the heavens, a swan, transfixed, plummeted to earth.* The immediate allusion to Richard Wagner's opera *Parsifal* in turn suggests the wider applications of the legends of the Holy Grail, the Waste Land, and the impotence of the Fisher King to Geoffrey's physical and spiritual condition. Act I of Wagner's opera opens with the knights of the Holy Grail guarding the vessel used at the Last Supper and the Spear which pierced Christ's side at the crucifixion. The ruler of the knights, Titurel, has appointed his son Amfortas to succeed him, but Amfortas has yielded to the enchantress Kundry (in "LJC," p. 81, Lowry identifies Kundry with Yvonne), has been wounded with the sacred spear, and awaits relief from his wound. Parsifal enters, having in innocence killed a wild swan, but failing to understand what is required of him, he is thrust roughly forth. In Act II, in a scene set in the magic garden, Kundry tries to entrap Parsifal with a kiss, but Parsifal's mission is suddenly revealed to him, and in Act III it is accomplished: the wound of Amfortas is healed, the Holy Grail revealed, and Kundry, her long pilgrimage accomplished, sinks lifeless before it.

Kilgallin notes, p. 167, that Geoffrey's mental and sexual impotence is implied through the symbol of the swan and that Lowry has in mind Charles Stansfeld-Jones's *The Chalice of Ecstasy,* a magical and Cabbalistic Interpretation of the drama of Parzival, in which the swan shot down "represents Ecstasy brought down to earth." Yvonne is further identified with the swan, p. 89 [84], when the Consul's impotence brings him down to earth with a thump, and the scene turns into something reminiscent of the beginning of Aldous Huxley's 1936 novel, *Eyeless in Gaza* (set partially in Mexico). Having made unsatisfactory love, Antony Beavis and his mistress Helen Amberley are sunbathing naked; suddenly, out of a clear blue sky, from an aeroplane passing overhead, a dog falls, splattering them with blood from head to foot and ending the affair.

75.3 [70]   *El Puerto del Sol.* Sp. "The Door of the Sun"; the cantina whose warmth is alluded to a few lines later. Independencia is the main street of Oaxaca and the location of many of Lowry's favourite cantinas, but Lowry has based the name on the small abarrotes of this name in Mexico City, on Avenida 16 Septiembre (the name is interchangeable with Independencia), only a block or two from the Hotel Canada. Lowry would also have been aware that El Puerto del Sol was the central square of Madrid, the scene of much conflict in the Spanish Civil War (hence the reference to doomed men and a crash of trumpets).

75.4 [70]   *doomed men . . . crowding into the warmth of the sun.* Underlying this passage and that dealing with Consul's dislike of the sun, p. 76 [71], is the song from Shakespeare's *Cymbeline,* IV.ii.258–63:

> Fear no more the heat o' the sun,
>   Nor the furious winter's rages;
> Thou thy worldly task has done,
>   Home art gone, and ta'en thy wages:
> Golden lads and girls all must,
> As chimney sweepers, come to dust.

The Consul, always hiding behind his dark glasses, expresses on the next page his fear of the sun: "There's been plenty of sun here. . . . Too much of it. . . . I don't like it." His reluctance to get out in the sun is in the Swedenborgian sense a turning away from the love of God towards the darkness within himself.

75.5 [70]   *the ursa horribilis of the night.* The *ursus horribilis* is the Grizzly Bear; with a pun on the Great Bear, on constellation of Ursa Major. Significantly, the Consul has altered the gender to the feminine. There is a celebrated statue of a bear in El Puerto del Sol, Madrid.

75.6 [71]   *Arturo Díaz Vigil, Médico Cirujano y Partero, Enfermedades de Niños, Indisposiciones Nerviosas, Consultas de 12 a 2 y de 4 a 7, Av. Revolución Numero 8.* Sp. "Arturo Díaz Vigil, Physician, Surgeon and Obstetrician, Childhood Illnesses, Nervous Complaints, Consultations from 12 to 2 and 4 to 7, No. 8 Revolution Avenue"; a card very similar to the sign in Dr. Vigil's window, p. 29 [23].

76.1 [71]   *'Strange,' the Consul commented.* At a moment of possible reconciliation the Consul insists, wilfully or not, upon estrangement (see note **69.2**) and further alienates his affections by reaching for the drink that he has just refused.

76.2 [71] *to dispute with Lucretius.* Titus Lucretius Carus (99–55 B.C.), Roman poet, whose life work *De Rerum Natura* ("Concerning the Nature of Things") is a philosophical poem in hexameters, in six books, arguing that the course of the world can be explained without resorting to divine intervention and seeking to free mankind from terror of the gods. Lucretius argues that there need be no fear of God or death since man is "Lord of himself." Everything, he claims, is made up of atoms and the laws of nature control all. Thus it follows that the soul is also material and so closely associated with the body that whatever affects one will affect the other: the mind is begotten with the body, grows with it, and with it grows old; consciousness ends with death, and there is no immortality of the soul. These ideas are summed up in Bk. III.455–58:

> ergo dissolui quoque convenit omnem animai
> naturam, ceu fumus, in altas aeris auras;
> quandoquidem gigni pariter pariterque videmus
> crescere et, [ut] docui, simul aevo fessa fatisci.

("Therefore it follows that the entire nature of the soul is dissolved, / like smoke, into the high winds of the air; / since we see it born with the body, / and growing with it, and, as I have shown, at the same time becoming weary and worn out with age.")

76.3 [72] *Cliff. . . . Geoffrey.* Yvonne's first husband and dead child. Yvonne had married Cliff (described on p. 264 [263] as "six foot three of gristle and bristle") and had a son, Geoffrey, in 1932. The boy lived only six months and died the same year. They divorced in 1934 (the first ticket to Reno). Yvonne met the Consul in 1935 and, at the age of twenty-seven, married him in Granada (having lost the child, she may have turned to a man of the same name).

77.1 [72] *Eisenstein.* Sergei Mikhailovich Eisenstein (1898–1948), celebrated Russian film director, whose completed works were *Strike* (1924); *The Battleship Potemkin* (1925); *October* (1928); *Old and New* (1929); *Alexander Nevsky* (1938); and *Ivan the Terrible Pt. 1* (1944). Of most relevance to *Under the Volcano,* however, is the unfinished *Que Viva Mexico!,* one episode of which came out in 1933 as *Thunder Over Mexico,* while other footage was incorporated into *Death Day, Eisenstein in Mexico,* and

Time in the Sun. Que Viva Mexico! was to have been an epic representation
of Mexico's history, a celebration of the nation's peculiar spirit, placing particular emphasis upon the clashes of life and death, beauty and corruption,
freedom and oppression. There were to have been six episodes in all: a prologue, four novels or cameos, and an epilogue set on the Day of the Dead in
which the "multi-threads of the preceding parts would be synthesized in a
philosophical climax" (Kilgallin, p. 141). Eisenstein himself drew attention
to such aspects of his film as the eternal circle, Death Day in Mexico as the
day of greatest fun and merriment, and the unmovable law of death and
said his film was to be "held together by the unity of the weave — a rhythmic
and musical construction and an unrolling of the Mexican spirit and
character" (*The Film Sense,* p. 197). Spender, p. xiii, is largely correct in
seeing Eisenstein as "the most direct influence on this extraordinary book"
and its technique as "essentially cinematic"; for a detailed consideration of
Lowry-Laruelle's debt to Eisenstein, see Kilgallin, pp. 139–46. It is difficult
to believe that a director like Eisenstein could have been influenced by the
cheap westerns in which Yvonne acted.

77.2 [72] *the demoted skipper's lost command.* The image, with its suggestion of Lord Jim's failure of nerve and loss of ticket, has its origins in the
Consul's own court-martial over the *Samaritan* affair (see p. 38 [32]). The
"someone" who approved Yvonne's outfit was possibly Louis (see p. 49
[44]).

78.1 [73] *Goethe's famous church bell.* As the town bells chime, and
Yvonne twists her wedding ring, the Consul is reminded of Goethe's poem,
"Die Wandelnde Glocke," ("The Wandering Bell") and its call to duty:

> Es war ein kind, das wollte nie
> Zur Kirche sich bequemen,
> Und Sonntags fand es stets ein Wie,
> Den Weg ins Feld zu nehmen.
>
> Die Mutter sprach: "Die Glocke tönt,
> Und so ist dirs befohlen,
> Und hast du dich nicht hingewöhnt,
> Sie kommt und wird dich holen."
>
> Das Kind, es denkt: die Glocke hängt
> Da droben auf dem Stuhle.
> Schon hats den Weg ins Feld gelenkt,
> Als lief' es aus der Schule.

Die Glocke, Glocke tönt nicht mehr,
Die Mutter hat gefackelt.
Doch welch ein Schrecken! hinterher
Die Glocke kommt gewackelt.

Sie wackelt schnell, man glaubt es kaum;
Das arme Kind im Schrecken,
Es läuft, es kommt als wie im Traum;
Die Glocke wird es decken.

Doch nimmt es richtig seinen Husch,
Und mit gewandter Schnelle
Eilt es durch Anger, Feld und Busch
Zur Kirche, zur Kapelle.

Und jeden Sonn- und Feiertag
Gedenkt es an den Schaden,
Lässt durch den ersten Glockenschlag,
Nicht in Person sich laden.

("There was a child who would never / agree to go to church, /and on Sundays he would always find a way / to go into the fields.

His mother said, "The bell is ringing, / and that's an order for you, / and if you don't go / it will come and fetch you,"

The child thinks: the bell is hanging / up there in the belfry. / Already he is off to the fields, / as if he were running out of school.

The bell, the bell rings no longer. / Mother was talking nonsense. / But what a terrible thing! / The bell is coming waddling after him.

It waddles quickly, it's almost unbelievable. / The poor child runs in terror, as in a dream. / The bell will smother him.

But he scuttles off directly, / and with great speed / hurries through meadow, field and bush, / towards the church, towards the chapel.

And every Sunday and holiday / he thinks of this misadventure, / and on the first stroke of the bell / doesn't wait to be invited in person.")

The "hellish Wesleyan breath" of the bell has, in effect, followed

Geoffrey all his life, but its call to duty cannot simply be blamed on the rigours of his Methodist schooling; the Consul's evasion is one of human responsibilities, as the bell continues to remind him, echoing the stern compassion of the *dolente... dolore* at the end of Ch. 1 and the passing bell which rings out at his death, p. 374 [373]. There is a parallel to this incident in Melville's *Redburn,* Ch. 36, where the bells of the church of St. Nicholas "seemed to carry an admonition" as they ring to remind the young hero not to forget to go to church.

78.2 [73]   *the swimming pool ticked on. Might a soul bathe there and be clean or slake its drought.* The association between the noise of the water trickling into the swimming pool and the passing of time, first made on p. 75 [70], is recalled by the church bell and evokes Marvell's lines from "Clorinda and Damon" (see note **16.9**), with the implication that the time for such salvation is fast running out.

78.3 [73]   *a touch of the goujeers.* A spurious form of "goodyears" (from Du. *goedtjaar,* "good year"), usually taken to mean "the French disease" (as in Johnson's *Dictionary*); but elsewhere "used in imprecatory phrases as denoting some undefined malefic power or agency" (*OED*). In an early version (UBC 10–13, p. 8), the Consul's troubles were identified as meningitis, which would explain the glare in his eyes and the need for dark glasses without reference to undefined malefic power (Yvonne's child, Geoffrey, died of meningitis).

78.4 [73]   *Die Glocke Glocke tönt nicht mehr.* Ger. "The bell, the bell rings no longer." Goethe's bell is on its way; the moment of confrontation cannot be put off much longer.

78.5 [73]   *neuritic.* Neuritis is any inflammatory or degenerative condition of the nerves; it is accompanied by pain, the loss of reflexes, disturbances of the senses (such as hallucinations), and, in extreme cases, paralysis. One form of neuritis is caused by alcoholism and may result in a severe swelling of the muscles of the arms and legs.

78.6 [74]   *Mariana and the moated grange.* The clear reference is to Shakespeare's *Measure for Measure,* IV.i.1–8: "The moated Grange at St. Luke's," is the home of Mariana, who sings:

> Take, O take those lips away,
>   That so sweetly were forsworn;
> And those eyes, the break of day,

> Lights that do mislead the morn:
> But my kisses bring again,
> > bring again;
> Seals of love, but seal'd in vain,
> > seal'd in vain.

More directly appropriate, however, is Tennyson's poem "Mariana," which uses "Mariana in the moated grange" as its epigraph. The desolate garden setting, the sense of blighted love, and Mariana's wish for death all explain the Consul's allusion. The poem concludes, ll. 81-84:

> Then, said she, "I am very dreary,
> > He will not come," she said;
> She wept, "I am aweary, aweary,
> > O God, that I were dead!"

78.7 [74]   *suppose ... you abandoned a besieged town to the enemy.* In John Donne's "Batter my heart, three person'd God" (*Divine Poems,* XIV), the poet likens himself to "an usurpt towne, to another due." The analogy of the soul as city is a commonplace of Christian symbolism from St. Augustine's *De Civitate Dei* (413-27 A.D.) to Bunyan's *Pilgrim's Progress* (1679-84); the Consul presumably dislikes it because it suggests that he has lost faith and abandoned Yvonne and not vice-versa.

79.1 [74]   *the same green graces.* In theology, grace means the unmerited favour extended by God to man. In his *Grace Abounding,* #108, Bunyan speaks of "those Graces of God that now were green on me." Yvonne had earlier noted, p. 63 [58], that the grass was not as green as it should be. There may also be a further allusion to Marvell's "The Garden," which evokes the images of "a green thought in a green shade" and the flight of a bird as the Platonic form of the soul, and which continues: "Two paradises 'twere in one, / To be in Paradise alone."

79.2 [74]   *the awful bell ... giant protruding tongue ... hellish Wesleyan breath. . . . the hibiscus.* The Consul, watching Yvonne twisting her wedding ring, is reminded of the sexual duty owed by the husband to the wife in marriage. The large bell-shaped flower of the hibiscus, with its phallus-like stamen, fuses in his mind with Goethe's bell (the poem makes no mention of the bell's tongue) and with the childhood memories of sexual guilt and joyless discipline to form a composite image of inevitable doom.

79.3 [74]   *the Canyon of the Wolves.* The Cañon de Lobos is in El Cerro de Barriga de Plata y las Tetillas, the low range of mountains dividing the cañada of Cuernavaca from Yautepec Valley; it is about fifteen miles west of Cuernavaca, a little beyond the (hopelessly misnamed) town of El Progreso, on the road to Yautepec and Cuautla. A winding steep valley of scrub and grass and, incongruously, a rich source of marine fossils, the canyon is physically unprepossessing, and Lowry seems attracted more by its name than its physical appearance. In Lowry's poetry the wolf is frequently used as a figure of the self-reliant solitary wanderer (a *Steppenwolf*), an image perfectly in keeping with the William Blackstone theme sounded here.

79.4 [75]   *Trogon ambiguus ambiguus.* As the Consul says, this is the scientific name of the coppery-tailed trogon, described in Peterson's *Field Guide,* p. 102, as about 11½ inches long, with head and upper parts a dark glossy green and underparts bright rose-red; tail square-tipped and moderately long; bill stout and pale; with a slightly Parrot-like profile and a cry consisting of a rapid series of low coarse notes. There are over thirty species, ranging from North America to Argentina, but the *trogon ambiguus ambiguus* seems rather out of its natural habitat, being usually confined to the mountains of south Arizona. The most important member of the trogon family is the quetzal, also known as the "paradise trogon," and the fact that the trogon in the Consul's garden is the ambiguous bird rather than the quetzal may be a sign of how far that garden has been corrupted. The Consul identifies with the trogon's solitary nature and, imagining it living in the Canyon of the Wolves, away from the people with ideas, associates it with his private myth of William Blackstone.

80.1 [75]   *completely obliterated in spinach.* Yvonne's feeble jest likens Popo to Popeye the Sailor, the popular cartoon figure (created 1929 by Elzie Crisler Segar) whose favourite spinach always gives him the strength to deal with his immediate problems.

80.2 [75]   *Pariah: that meant drums too. Parián.* The word pariah is derived from the Tamil *paraiyar,* plural of *paraiyan,* and is the name of the largest of the lower castes in India; hence commonly used in the sense of "untouchable." The word *paraiyan* in fact means "drummer" and derives from Tamil *parai,* a large drum beaten at certain festivals. The words "pariah" and "Parian" are to be found side by side in the *OED,* from which Lowry has taken their etymologies (see also note **134.2**). Lowry would also be aware, from W. H. Prescott and Lewis Spence, of the Aztec *huehue,* the large sacred drum in the temple of Huitzilopotchli, which would be sounded at times of danger or sacrifice, and he might also have read in Spence (*M of M & P,* p. 16) of the Toltec legend of Huemac:

Tovego, a cunning sorcerer, collected a great concourse of people near Tollan, and by dint of beating upon a magic drum until the darkest hours of the night, forced them to dance to its sound until, exhausted by their efforts, they fell headlong over a dizzy precipice into a deep ravine.

80.3 [75]   *not only the garden . . . with horror, the horror of an intolerable reality.* A strong echo of T. S. Eliot's *The Waste Land,* to which Eliot had originally intended to affix as epigraph Conrad's "The horror! The horror!" from *Heart of Darkness.* In Eliot's poem, the remembered ecstasy of the Hyacinth Garden has become in the present of the poem an unrelieved horror, and the so-called "real world" has taken on the illusory quality which Conrad's Marlow experiences on his return from Africa.

80.4 [75]   *what some insane person suffers.* Behind the Consul's fearful vision is the image of John Clare (1793–1864), poet and madman, whose last twenty years were spent in Northampton County Asylum and who in such poems as "The Dream" and "The Nightmare" (1821) spoke of the horrific mystery of his existence. Kilgallin (1965), p. 18, suggests that the particular reference is to Clare's "Written in a Thunderstorm July 15th, 1841," which begins:

> The heavens are wroth—the thunder's rattling peal
> Rolls like a vast volcano in the sky;
> Yet nothing starts the apathy I feel,
> Nor chills with fear eternal destiny.

80.5 [76]   *the timber line of Popocatepetl . . . like a gigantic surfacing whale.* Popocatepetl is to the Consul what Moby Dick is to Captain Ahab. Although in the final version of *Under the Volcano* this relationship between the smoking mountain and the white whale is never insisted on, throughout the drafts it is often explicit, and in earlier versions of this passage Moby Dick is mentioned by name. The allusion is to the final words of Ch. 1 of *Moby Dick:* "one grand hooded phantom, like a snow hill in the air" (an image repeated in Ch. 133). A note in Prescott suggests the very devious route by which this terrestrial whale may have grounded itself on the volcano. Discussing the shape of Ixtaccihuatl from a similar vantage point, he writes: "This mountain . . . with its neighbour Popocatepetl . . . has been fancifully likened, from its long dorsal swell, to the back of a dromedary" (Prescott, V.vii, p. 495). Lowry knew his *Conquest of Mexico,* and probably appreciated Prescott's tendency to use latinate words in their original etymological sense, but the word dorsal would here seem incongruously inappropriate: very like a whale, in fact.

80.6 [76] *the gardener... contained a horrible threat against him.* The gardener, slashing his way through the tall grasses, is a figure of both the head gardener and Death the Reaper, who will garner the Consul in Ch. 12. The Tarot card XIII, Death, the card which rules over Scorpio and the end of the year, depicts such a figure.

81.1 [76] *Tom's muted voice.* The background to the call remains deliberately mysterious. "Tom" is ringing from America, and his call concerns some property (we learn from p. 87 [82]), which has been confiscated, presumably under President Cárdenas's reforms. The call has something to do with silver, and part of the mystery surrounding the Consul's staying on in Quauhnahuac is clarified by earlier versions of the novel which indicate his involvement in a get-rich deal with silver. The United States stopped buying Mexican silver in March, 1938, in reprisal for Mexico's appropriation of oil holdings; wild speculation in silver continued throughout the year; and the Consul may well be involved in such shady activities. Lowry originally made a more emphatic analogy between the Consul and the conquistadors and attributed much of the Consul's later guilt to the knowledge that he too was exploiting the Indians for his own gain. In the final version, Lowry seems to have downplayed this background to increase the mystery about the Consul's reasons for staying on and to relate his guilt more specifically to his feelings for Yvonne.

Throughout the novel, telephone calls are used as a mode of communication between the natural and spiritual worlds, and it seems likely (see note **53.2**) that Lowry associates in his own mind the name "Tom" with Thomas Taylor the Platonist (1758–1835), author of *The Hymns of Orpheus* and commentator upon the Eleusinian and Bacchic mysteries (see note **319.1**). The Consul's act of hanging the receiver the wrong way seems to be an involuntary attempt to frustrate such communication.

81.2 [76] *Erikson 43.* A telephone number on the Erikson (more correctly, Ericsson) exchange. As Jakobsen notes, p. 70, the Swedish firm L. M. Ericsson built one of Mexico's early telephone systems; since there were two systems (mutually incompatible), the name of the system would be listed with the number. Lowry commented in a draft of *DATG* (UBC 14–24, p. 331), "Half the telephone numbers in Mexico are Erikson something or other. It's a Swedish company that owns the telephone exchange. So there's nothing very mysterious about that."

For Lowry, the mystery began when he originally gave a hero of his lost

In Ballast to the White Sea the name of Erikson, then arrived in Cuernavaca to find that his own number was Erikson 34 (UBC 14–24, p. 331). The mystery deepened when he read about an American shot in Taxco and thrown down a barranca, the murdered man's name just happening to be William Erikson (UBC 14–24, pp. 336–39: the Consul's name at this point was William Ames). In *DATG* Lowry uses the name Erikson for a character based on Nordahl Grieg; "Erikson," like Grieg, died in a bomber raid over Berlin in 1943, and Lowry's Erikson 43, an inversion of his own 34, commemorates that death: they got his number.

81.3 [77] *Never had it seemed such a long way to the top of this hill.* Though there is a distinct hill at this point on the Calle Humboldt in Cuernavaca, the road stretching on "like a life of agony" seems to have derived its physical qualities from a steep rocky hill in Yautepec (*DATG,* p. 183) and its symbolic implications from Christ's walk to Calvary and his death.

81.4 [77] *900 pesos.* The silver peso was worth, officially, about 22 cents in 1938. Hence 900 pesos would equal $198.00, and each bottle of whiskey would cost $1.98, and each bottle of tequila about $0.22.

81.5 [77] *Argal.* A corruption of L. *ergo,* "therefore": often used, as here, as a self-conscious admission of specious logic. As Jakobsen says, p. 70, "Well-known from the graveyard scene in *Hamlet* and associated with clownish reasoning."

81.6 [77] *Away! Away!* From "Ode to a Nightingale," ll. 31–34, by John Keats (1795–1821):

> Away! away! for I will fly to thee,
>   Not charioted by Bacchus and his pards,
> But on the viewless wings of Poesy,
>   Though the dull brain perplexes and retards:

The allusion is magnificently incongruous: the Consul, head aching and a drowsy numbness paining his sense, even half in love with easeful death, is seeking to "drink, and leave the world unseen" or, like William Blackstone, "fade away into the forest dim." However, he cannot escape the shakes, the sorrows, the leaden-eyed despair, and instead of "flying," crashes face-down on the deserted street.

82.1 [77] *a whiskerando.* A rough, bewhiskered, but picturesque character; the word modelled on *desperando* (but in context of the cantina, perhaps with a suggestion of "whiskey" about it). A character named Don Ferolo Whiskerandos appeared in Sheridan's 1779 play *The Critic,* but Lowry would have found the word in Melville's *Redburn,* Ch. 1: "Two of these were sea-pieces. One represented a fat-looking, smoky fishing-boat, with three whiskerandoes in red caps, and their trowsers legs rolled up, hauling in a seine."

82.2 [77]   *a dog guarding it.* An innocuous detail, but nevertheless a suggestion of Cerberus, guardian of the gates of Hades, who was to prevent the living from entering the infernal regions and the dead from escaping.

82.3 [77]   *carte d'identité.* Fr: "identity card." Before World War I, the passport was generally sufficient identification for the traveller, but after the war many nations began to require more elaborate documents.

82.4 [77]   *the passport . . . whose number I remember to this day is 21312.* In earlier drafts, the number of Hugh's passport was C 35671 (UBC 10–13, p. 9); its later palindromic form hints at Hugh's being a mirror image of the Consul, who later in the day will find himself "in a fix" because he is without his passport; but it is probably not coincidental, given Lowry's later interest in the Cabbala, that the number was changed to 21312 since by gematria (the equating of numerical values for letters of the Hebrew alphabet) its total of nine equals the letter T, teth, or the serpent (MacGregor-Mathers, *The Kabbalah Unveiled,* p. 3); thereby anticipating the "snake in the grass" reference, p. 145 [141].

82.5 [78]   *since Father went up into the White Alps alone.* In an earlier draft (UBC 10–17, B), Hugh was drawing parallels between his Socotra and Geoffrey's Kashmir and commented: "All this must be like Kashmir must have been. Now I understand why Geoff — though it was before he came here — kept quoting that line of Webster's or somebody's, about Father: Nurse I am sick, oh my love is slain, I saw him go up into the White Alps alone." The precise reference remains obscure; the lines do not seem to be in any of John Webster's plays.

82.6 [78]   *this valley . . . the Valley of the Indus.* The Consul's analogy is somewhat forced. Although the Valley of Cuernavaca is surrounded by hills, it is not dominated by mountains the way that the Vale of Kashmir is by the Himalayas. Either the Consul is likening Popocatepetl and Ixtaccihuatl to Nanga Parbat (see note **87.10**), or he is implying that his fictional state of Parián falls somewhere within the Valley of Mexico, which is ringed with mountains. Either way, they are mountains of the mind.

82.7 [78]   *Taxco... Srinigar.* The "turbaned trees" of Taxco are royal palms (*palmas reals*), whose leafy upper boles can resemble turbans, but apart from this rather tenuous analogy, and the attractive appearance of both towns, there is little in common between the Mexican silver-mining centre with its quaint cobbled streets, in the hills of Guerrero, and the Kashmiri capital (here misspelt by Lowry) with its waterways, in the Vale of Kashmir.

82.8 [78]   *Xochimilco... the Shalimar.* Two celebrated gardens:
(a) *Xochimilco.* The floating gardens of Xochimilco, now an impressive tourist trap in the southeast of Mexico City, are all that remain of a unique system of agriculture that once was the basis of Aztec self-sufficiency in food. With much of the Valley of Mexico a vast lake (now mostly drained) and land at a premium, intensive gardening was carried out on the chinampas; not, strictly speaking, artificial islands, but rafts made of stakes and excavated mud which eventually became rooted to the shallow lake bottom and on which up to seven crops per year might be produced.
(b) *the Shalimar.* The Shalimar Gardens, on the hill-slope of the east bank of the Dal Lake, were laid out in 1619 by Mogul Emperor Jehangir and extended in 1633 by Shah Jehan. They are arranged in four terraces, through which a stream flows in beautiful stone chutes, creating fountains and reservoirs on its way to the lake. Although celebrated for their exquisite pavilions, cascades, fountains, lawns and shady walks, the gardens are by no means floating ones; the Consul seems to have associated the Shalimar with other floating gardens of the Dal Lake and with the houseboats that are a feature of Srinagar.

83.1 [78]   *Damchok.* More usually, *Demchok* (though both spellings are found), a town marked on the map accompanying Francis Younghusband's *Kashmir* as being on the Tibetan side of the Tibet-Kashmir border, on an ancient trade route up the Indus between Ladakh and Tibet. Since Ladakh is commonly taken as the back of beyond in northern India and Demchok is beyond that, it perfectly suits the Consul's vision of nowhere.

83.2 [78]   *the P. and O., the old erratic Cocanada.* The Peninsular and Oriental, the shipping line of the East India Company, established 1837 and travelling between England, Gibraltar, and the East. The name Cocanada (more usually Kakanada) refers to the once-important port on the coast of Andhra Pradesh, near the delta of the Godavari river. The S.S. *Cocanada* would not have been very old when Hugh and Geoffrey travelled on her, for she was built in 1910 (her use of staysails made her seem as if from an earlier era). She was owned by the British India Steam Navigation Co. (a subsidiary of P & O, but jealous of its independence) and acted as a troop-ship in World War I. She was used on the Rangoon-Coromandel run during the 1920's, and her career came to an unheroic end in January 1947 when she overturned in dock at Bombay.

83.3 [78]   *too many surrogates in Harrogate.* A surrogate is a legal term for one who acts for another; here, a guardian. Like the Firmin brothers, Lowry was controlled by surrogate parents for much of his life since trustees were responsible for administering his allowance each month. Harrogate, in West Yorkshire, is known for its mineral springs with supposedly medicinal properties, but the Consul seems more interested in the rhyme than the location. The phrase was a late addition to the manuscripts but develops the significance of "I continue in a bottle": there is probably an allusion to Huxley's *Brave New World,* Ch. 1, where the embryos in their bottles in the decanting room are given a rich surrogate; as Webb notes, p. 115, the subsitute mother theme ("Bottle of mine, it's you I've always wanted") is reinforced, p. 95 [91], when the Consul murmurs "I love you" to his bottle of whiskey.

83.4 [79]   *it is not yet over.* Some historians see the Second World War as a continuation of the First, but the Consul is also implying, as Laruelle does on p. 15 [9] that in either case "one's own battle would go on."

83.5 [79]   *God has little patience with remorse.* Because, as Geoffrey is only too well aware, it differs from penitence in being still oriented towards the self and therefore still stresses the importance of that self. In "Garden of Etla" (see note **17.6**), Lowry suggested that every man was, in a sense, his own Garden of Eden, but:

> the moment you attributed any formidable value to yourself for this you went out . . . one of the most certain ways never to return was by excessive remorse, or sorrow for what you had lost. This to a Zapotecan was more of a sin than it was held to be by the Catholics . . . it was another form of boasting: the assumption of the uniqueness of your misery.

84.1 [79]   *the inevitable bladder on the brain.* Lowry may be using "bladder" in the obsolete sense of "a morbid vesicle containing liquid of putrid matter; a boil, blister, pustule" (*OED*) to suggest a build-up of pressure that can be relieved only by sudden release; but he is also referring to the pig's bladder attached to a stick with which clowns used to hit each other. The "sawdust" that follows is that found in a circus ring.

84.2 [79]   *my Elizabethan plays.* When the Consul gave Jacques the volume, p. 33 [27], he did so with the implication that the book would become an emblem of something that could not be returned. In like manner, the Consul's "gift" of Yvonne to Laruelle and Hugh has altered the case by creating a condition that cannot be reversed.

84.3 [79]   *seven hundred and seventy-seven and a half.* The Penguin "seven hundred and seventy-five and a half" is an error. The phrase echoes Genesis 5:31: "And all the days of Lamech were seven hundred seventy and seven years: and he died." The Consul may also be recalling the question put to Christ by Peter (Matthew 18:21–22): "Then came Peter to him, and said, Lord, how oft shall my brother sin against me and I forgive him? till seven times? Jesus saith unto him, I say not unto thee, Until seven times: but, Until seventy times seven." 777 was also the occult signature of Frater Achad, just as 666 was of Aleister Crowley.

84.4 [79]   *like Don Quixote avoiding a town.* Don Quixote is often depicted as refusing to enter a town on the grounds that knights-errant should rather sleep in the fields and forest (for example, Pt. 2, II.xix), but the only reference to his avoiding a town "invested with his abhorrence because of his excesses there" can be to Pt. 2, IV. lix, where the Sorrowful Knight decides to avoid the town of Saragossa because of false rumours (those recounted in the spurious continuation of the first part by Alonso Fernandez de Avellaneda) of his previous exploits there. One year from now, Jacques Laruelle, "a knight of old," will take a cut to the left to avoid his own house (see note **29.1**).

84.5 [79]   *the English 'King's Parade' voice.* King's Parade is a main street in Cambridge, England, and the spruce Oxbridge tones of the good Samaritan remind Geoffrey how badly he is letting down the old school; he springs to his feet instantly, "sober as a judge."

84.6 [79]   *an M.G. Magna.* A British sportscar made by Morris, of 1929 vintage, which like its owner is incongruously out of place; according to Day, p. 133, "the only car Lowry ever drove, let alone owned." In *October Ferry,* p. 117, Ethan Llewelyn recalls being caught drunk at the wheel of a 1932 model (the date presumably forming a reference to Lowry's term of ownership).

84.7 [79]   *the English striped tie, mnemonic of a fountain in a great court.*
The tie, which the Consul recognizes as being that of Trinity College, Cambridge (dark blue, with thin diagonal red and yellow stripes), immediately brings to his mind an image of Trinity's Great Court (the largest of any in the Oxbridge Colleges), and its fountain, commissioned by Sir Thomas Nevile in 1602 and famous as an outstanding piece of English renaissance work. The image of the fountain in turn evokes the lines of an old Trinitarian, Andrew Marvell, whose "Clorinda and Damon" (see note **16.9**) sums up so well the Consul's inability to slake his thirst.

85.1 [80]   *Trinity. . . . Caius.* Colleges of Cambridge University:
(a) *Trinity.* Trinity College was founded by Henry VIII in 1546, absorbing King's Hall (founded by Edward III in 1336) and Michaelhouse (founded by Harvey de Stanton in 1323), as well as some minor hostels. The most celebrated of all Cambridge colleges, it is remarkable for its Great Court, its Great Gate, and its library (designed by Sir Christopher Wren), which contains such rare treasures as the first sketch of *Paradise Lost.* Through its portals have passed such illustrious figures as Herbert, Newton, Byron, Thackeray, Macaulay, and Russell, as well as writers like John Donne, Andrew Marvell, and John Cornford, who contribute so much to *Under the Volcano* that one can almost talk of a Trinity motif.
(b) *Caius.* The College of Gonville and Caius (pronounced "keys") was founded by Edmond Gonville in 1348 and enlarged by Dr. Caius in 1557. It is a minor Cambridge College, which accounts for the Englishman's merry face becoming a shade redder as he is caught out unexpectedly in a minor breach of decorum.

85.2 [80]   *Burke's Irish.* Burke's Three Star Irish Whiskey, incongruously offered by the English samaritan, is that made by Edward and John Burke Ltd., Export Bottlers, 57 Upper O'Connell St., Dublin.

85.3 [81]   *Bungho.* An expression of farewell, with faintly ludicrous connotations.

86.1 [81]   *the Ministerio de Relaciones Exteriores.* Sp. "The Ministry of Foreign Affairs." The passage was one that Lowry was prepared to omit ("LJC," p. 72), but the unexpected presence of the card prefigures the discovery of the telegram in the other jacket, p. 370 [369]. In earlier drafts Lowry had considered using the Columbian government to assert a parallel with British Columbia; Caracas (as the Consul's "Why not?" seems to indicate) now forms an anagram of Sp. *cáscara,* "husk" or "shell" (see note **193.9**): the possibility of Eden is replaced by a touch of hell.

86.2 [81] *A gaily coloured Oaxaqueñan serape.* A serape is a woollen blanket or shawl, often brightly coloured, frequently worn as an outer garment. Those of Oaxaca are particularly renowned. For Eisenstein, the serape was a symbol of his film *Que Viva Mexico!* (see notes **77.1** and **256.4**), the different themes and motifs "held together by the unity of the weave." For the Consul at this moment, however, the underweave of the blanket is the suggestion of Oaxaca (see note **41.8**).

86.3 [81] *ranchero eggs.* Fried eggs with a hot chile sauce, served on a tortilla and usually accompanied by frijoles (beans). The name is derived from the fact that this is the common breakfast of the ranches of the north.

86.4 [81] *The magazine was the amateur astronomy one she subscribed to.* This magazine is *The Sky,* a monthly magazine published by the Hayden Planetarium in New York. The issue is specifically that of June 1939, which features on its cover the three domes of the Yerkes Observatory (likened by the Consul to Roman helmets), silhouetted against a cloudy night sky illuminated by lightning. It contains an article entitled "The Astronomy of the Mayas" by Clifford N. Anderson of the Bell Telephone Laboratories, which concludes on p. 21: "Although their Venus tables are very accurate and the Mayas were in general far advanced in observational astronomy, it is doubtful if they had any insight as to the mechanism or ever suspected a Copernican system." There is an anomaly of Yvonne's reading on the morning of 2 November 1938 a magazine not to be issued until the following June, but the relevance of cover and content to the characters and events of Lowry's novel justifies the anachronism.

86.5 [81] *The Mayas . . . were far advanced in observational astronomy.* With the simplest of instruments (they had no telescopes), the Mayans were able to predict with amazing accuracy the synodical revolutions of the major heavenly bodies, the likelihood of eclipses, and the heliacal risings and settings of the morning and evening stars. Their lunar and Venus tables were astonishingly detailed and accurate and formed the basis of an extremely sophisticated calendrical system (see note **86.7**). As Prescott says, I.iv, p. 72:

> that they should be capable of accurately adjusting their festivals by the movements of the heavenly bodies, and should fix the true length of the tropical year with a precision unknown to the great philosophers of antiquity, could be the result only of a long series of nice and patient observations, evincing no slight progress in civilization.

86.6 [81]   *a Copernican system.* Nicholas Copernicus (1473–1543), Polish astronomer and mathematician, is often regarded as the father of modern astronomy on the basis of his *De revolutionibus orbium coelestium,* which, published after his death, proved that the planets, including the earth, revolved about the sun.

86.7 [82]   *the "vague" years of the old Mayans. And their "pseudo years" . . . . And their delicious names for the months.* Although the Mayans strictly speaking had only one calendar, their astronomers kept both Venus and lunar tables, and their calendar thus comprises two distinct cycles: one, a Venus cycle of 260 days; the other, a cycle of 365 days (the "vague year"). A complete calendar round, whereby the first day of the first cycle again matched that of the second cycle took place only after fifty-two vague years (see also note **35.3**).

An understanding of why this should be involves a basic comprehension of the Mayan calendrical system. The Mayans had twenty names for the days, arranged in an unvarying series: *Ik, Akbal, Kan, Chicchan, Cimi, Manik, Lamat, Muluc, Oc, Chuen, Eb, Ben, Ix, Men, Cib, Caban, Eznab, Cauac, Ahau,* and *Imix.* In addition, the numbers 1 to 13 were applied to the day names in regular sequence. Since each day had both a number and a name, there would be no exact repetition for 13 x 20 = 260 days. This 260-day period (the *tzolkin*) formed one cycle.

The other cycle was a 365-day year, divided into eighteen months of twenty days each, plus a final month, *Uayeb,* of five days. The months in order were: *Pop, Uo, Zip, Zotz, Tzec, Xul, Yaxkin, Mol, Chen, Yax, Zac, Ceh, Mac, Kankin, Muan, Pax, Kayab, Cumhu,* and *Uayeb.* The positions in each month were numbered 0 to 19 (*Uayeb* 0 to 4); thus, 0 *Pop,* the beginning of the year, occurred every 365 days. This second cycle is called the "vague year" because it does not reproduce the seasons on the same date each year. Clifford N. Anderson, p. 20, also calls this cycle a pseudo-year and does not make the distinction which the Consul implies (see note **86.4**).

There is a basic mathematical incompatibility of the first cycle (based on 20 x 13) with the second (based on 18 x 20, plus 5). The table on page 127 shows how a year might be tabulated, beginning with 0 *Pop* falling on 1 *Ik.* The second year, however, would not be identical, because 0 *Pop* would fall on 2 *Manik;* the third year would begin with 3 *Eb,* the fourth with 4 *Caban,* the fifth with 5 *Ik . . .* the fifty-second with 13 *Cabab*—which would end a calendar round, since the next year would again see 0 *Pop* fall on 1 *Ik.* A complete calendar round thus consists of a day number (1 to 13), a day name (one of 20), a month position (0 to 19), and a month name (one of 19); for example, *1 Ik 0 Pop,* or *12 Ben 16 Pax.* Such dates can repeat only once in fifty-two vague years (seventy-three *tzolkins*) or 18,890 days (18,890 being the lowest common multiple of 13 day numbers, 20 day names, and 365 positions in the year). The above notes are indebted to John E. Teeple, "Maya Astronomy," *Contributions to American Archaeology* 1 (August 1930): 36–38.

Names of Months

Names of Days	Pop	Uo	Zip	Zotz	Tzec	Xul	Yaxkin	Mol	Chen	Yax	Zac	Ceh	Mac	Kankin	Muan	Pax	Kayab	Cumhu	Uayeb
0 Ik	1	8	2	9	3	10	4	11	5	12	6	13	7	1	8	2	9	3	10
1 Akbal. . . .	2	9	3	10	4	11	5	12	6	13	7	1	8	2	9	3	10	4	11
2 Kan	3	10	4	11	5	12	6	13	7	1	8	2	9	3	10	4	11	5	12
3 Chicchan .	4	11	5	12	6	13	7	1	8	2	9	3	10	4	11	5	12	6	13
4 Cimi	5	12	6	13	7	1	8	2	9	3	10	4	11	5	12	6	13	7	1
5 Manik . . .	6	13	7	1	8	2	9	3	10	4	11	5	12	6	13	7	1	8	
6 Lamat . . .	7	1	8	2	9	3	10	4	11	5	12	6	13	7	1	8	2	9	
7 Muluc . . .	8	2	9	3	10	4	11	5	12	6	13	7	1	8	2	9	3	10	
8 Oc.	9	3	10	4	11	5	12	6	13	7	1	8	2	9	3	10	4	11	
9 Chuen . . .	10	4	11	5	12	6	13	7	1	8	2	9	3	10	4	11	5	12	
10 Eb.	11	5	12	6	13	7	1	8	2	9	3	10	4	11	5	12	6	13	
11 Ben.	12	6	13	7	1	8	2	9	3	10	4	11	5	12	6	13	7	1	
12 Ix	13	7	1	8	2	9	3	10	4	11	5	12	6	13	7	1	8	2	
13 Men	1	8	2	9	3	10	4	11	5	12	6	13	7	1	8	2	9	3	
14 Cib	2	9	3	10	4	11	5	12	6	13	7	1	8	2	9	3	10	4	
15 Caban . . .	3	10	4	11	5	12	6	13	7	1	8	2	9	3	10	4	11	5	
16 Eznab . . .	4	11	5	12	6	13	7	1	8	2	9	3	10	4	11	5	12	6	
17 Cauac. . . .	5	12	6	13	7	1	8	2	9	3	10	4	11	5	12	6	13	7	
18 Ahau	6	13	7	1	8	2	9	3	10	4	11	5	12	6	13	7	1	8	
19 Imix	7	1	8	2	9	3	10	4	11	5	12	6	13	7	1	8	2	9	

←——— 'Tzolkin' ————→

←————————— 'Vague Year' ————————→

86.8 [82] *Mac.* The month of fertility for the Mayans; the subject is especially relevant to Yvonne (Baxter, p. 79).

86.9 [82] *And Uayeb: I like that one most of all.* Uayeb is the last, short month of the Mayan year, its five days being considered particularly unlucky. Lewis Spence comments (*M & M of M,* p. 226):

> During the five days at the end of the year people in Mexico were careful not to fall asleep during the day, nor to quarrel or trip in walking. . . . On these days men left the house as seldom as possible, did

not wash or comb themselves, and took special care not to undertake any menial or difficult task.

It is noticeable that the Consul almost deliberately violates each of the above conditions during his final day, thereby inviting the divine retribution which these precautions were specifically designed to ward off.

87.1 [82] *the philosophical section of War and Peace. War and Peace* (1865–72), by Count Leo Nikolaevich Tolstoy (1828–1910), is an epic tale of the Napoleonic Wars, counterpointing the fortunes of individual members of the Rostóv and Bolonski families against the wider sweep of historical destiny. The novel concludes with two epilogues, the second of which is a long philosophical section called "The Forces That Move Nations," in which Tolstoy attempts to assess the relationship between individual freedom and historical necessity, concluding (in a passage of direct relevance to the Consul's "choice" of destiny) that history teaches us that we must renounce a freedom that does not exist and recognize a dependence of which we are not conscious.

87.2 [82] *before I could dodge about in the rigging of the Cabbala like a St Jago's monkey.* For the Cabbala, see note **44.3.** Likening its intricacies to those of a ship's rigging is not inappropriate (both aspire to the heavens). Ch. 24 of Melville's *Redburn* is subtitled "He Begins to Hop about in the Rigging Like a Saint Jago's Monkey" and deals with Redburn's growing confidence aloft, "hovering like a judgement angel between heaven and earth." As Harold Beaver notes (*Redburn,* Penguin edition, p. 425), a St. Jago's monkey is "a deft and nimble Portuguese sailor from São Thiago, the largest and most populous of the Cape Verde Islands."

87.3 [82] *that Napoleon's leg twitched.* From *War and Peace,* IX.vi. When General Balashev visits Napoleon to bring him a letter from Czar Alexander, insisting that the French withdraw beyond the Nieman as a condition of peace negotiations, Napoleon becomes angry and excited and his left leg begins to twitch increasingly. Despite the Consul's claim to have remembered only this small vulgar detail, he is able to recall much of the "philosophical section" later in the day (at the end of Ch. 10). The reference to Napoleon is linked to the immediately preceding reference to the Cabbala through a passage a little further on in *War and Peace,* IX.xix, where, by gematria, the words L'Empereur Napoléon are shown to possess the numerical significance 666, thereby revealing him to the Beast of Revelation (see Kilgallin, p. 185, and note **192.1**).

87.4 [82] *They haven't my number yet.* The Consul is referring to his mysterious interests in silver (see note **81.1**), but the words have ominous overtones of death and anticipate the extensive telephoning in Ch. 12, when his fate is decided.

87.5 [82] *But for one's habit of making money.* As Lowry would have been aware, William Spratling of Taxco, author of *Little Mexico* (1932), had the reputation among the civilized British and American community of Cuernavaca of being "the American gone native" (de Davila, p. 174), but he had nevertheless made a fortune in silver and built up a superb collection of pre-Columbian art. It is at least arguable that the local example of this other William plays some small part in the Consul's dramatization of William Blackstone. In an earlier draft (UBC 10–13, p. 14) "Tom" had previously been "Bill," and the Consul (then named William Ames) had said to him "we no longer need a consul in Quauhnahuac, yet we still do make money enough, God knows how, in the midst of disaster." The Consul's reasons for staying on in Quauhnahuac, and for thinking of becoming a Mexican subject, are intricately bound up with his speculation in the silver market. See also notes **81.1** and **215.6**.

87.6 [83] *the pictures on the wall.* These pictures by the Consul's mother are (to phrase it politely) excellent imitations of those by Major Edward Molyneux, collaborator with Francis Younghusband on the book *Kashmir* (London: A. & C. Black, 1909). The book contains a set of seventy watercolour illustrations, thin and rather charming, but which have no relation whatsoever to the accompanying text. Two are instantly recognizable from the Consul's description: "Lalla Rookh's Tomb, Hassan Abdal," plate 50, opposite p. 162; and "Gorge of the Sind Valley at Guggangir [sic]," plate 37, opposite p. 108.

87.7 [83] *Lalla Rookh's tomb. Lalla Rookh,* by Thomas Moore (1779–1852), is a series of four oriental verse tales connected by a story in prose published in 1817. The story tells of the journey of Lalla Rookh, daughter of the Emperor Aurungzebe, from Delhi to the Vale of Kashmir, where she is to be given in marriage to the young king of Bucharia. On the way she is entertained by and falls in love with Feramorz, a young poet of Kashmir, who, on her arrival at the Shalimar Palace, reveals himself to be the young king. The four tales, presenting a variety of verse forms and subjects of a romantic "oriental" kind, are: "The Veiled Prophet of Khorassan," "Paradise and the Peri," "The Fire-Worshippers," and "The Light of the Haram."

87.8 [83]   *the ravine at Gugganvir.* More precisely, "Gorge of the Sind Valley at Guggangir," a watercolour by Edward Molyneux in Francis Younghusband's *Kashmir* (see note **87.6**). Guggangir, more commonly Gagangir, is a small village in the Sind Valley ten miles west of Sonamarg, on what was reputed to be the roughest part of the route between India and Turkestan.

87.9 [83]   *the Shalimar looked more like the Cam than ever.* For the Shalimar Gardens, see note **82.7**; the emphasis here is on their romantic associations, perhaps as described in Thomas Moore's own notes to *Lalla Rookh:*

> In the centre of the plain, as it approaches the lake, one of the Delhi Emperors, I believe Shah Jehan, constructed a spacious garden called the Shalimar, which is abundantly stored with fruit-trees and flowering shrubs. Some of the rivulets which intersect the plain are led into a canal at the back of the garden, and, flowing through its centre, or occasionally thrown into a variety of waterworks, compose the chief beauty of the Shalimar.

In his mother's painting, the "magnificent Shalimar" has become the gentle Cam, the river running through Cambridge, which is associated above all with the pleasures of punting.

87.10 [83]   *a distant view of Nanga Parbat from the Sind. Nanga Parbat* (Kashmiri "naked mountain"), is at 26,660 feet the seventh largest mountain in the world and is in the West Punjab Himalayas to the northwest of Srinagar. The Sind Valley mentioned here is not that of the lower Indus, but a side valley extending from the Vale of Kashmir, perhaps forty miles northeast of Srinagar. Although there is no painting by Edward Molyneux with precisely this title, there is, opposite p. 246 of *Kashmir,* one called "Distant View of Nanga Parbat from the Kamir Pass," and another, opposite p. 254, called "In the Sind Valley." Nanga Parbat has been the goal of a number of disastrous climbing expeditions, for example, in 1934 and 1937, when several climbers were killed, and in 1895, when the noted climber A. F. Mummery disappeared in a way not altogether dissimilar to Geoffrey's father.

87.11 [83]   *speculation . . . seigniorage.* Two words that suggest that the Consul may be involved in speculation in the silver market. Seigniorage is a technical term that means the tax collected by a government from a manufacturer of coins, equal to the difference between the face value of the coin and the metal value of its composition.

88.1 [83] *to tighten, if almost imperceptibly, a screw.* The infernal machine is operative (see note **212.3**); here, perhaps, with a hint of Henry James's *The Turn of the Screw* (1898), a mysterious tale of ghastly apparitions and psychic terrors, provoked by a neurotic governess, which increasingly close about two unhappy and apparently haunted children and lead to inevitable tragedy and death.

88.2 [83] *Goethe's church bell was looking him straight between the eyes.* "Die Wandelnde Glocke" (see note **78.1**) has now caught up with the truant child, who has nowhere further to run and must turn to face his responsibilities.

88.3 [84] *a Bleecker Street mummer.* Bleecker Street, in downtown Manhattan, forms part of the jazz area associated with Greenwich Village; if Lowry means to imply that Bleecker Street is in Philadelphia, he is in error, but it is Philadelphia rather than New York which is famous for its mummers' clubs and elaborate parades.

88.4 [84] *Newcastle. . . . Charleston.* New Castle is a small town on the Delaware River; its cobbled streets are carefully maintained. Charleston, South Carolina, is one of the oldest and most charming cities of the American South, noted for its old homes and gracious living. In the manuscripts (UBC 7–3, p. 10) these towns were described as "a bit of heaven."

89.1 [84] *the paths and spheres of the Holy Cabbala.* The aim of the Cabbalist is to develop from a spiritual neophyte into an adept by retracing the paths of God's lightning which lead from Malkuth to Kether (see note **44.3**). These paths are considered to constitute thirty-two in all, comprising the ten Sephiroth (usually depicted on diagrams of the tree of life by spheres) and the twenty-two paths, each associated with a letter of the Hebrew alphabet and allegedly corresponding with one of the Major Arcana cards of the Tarot pack, connecting the spheres. As Frater Achad notes, *QBL* p. 20: "We are clearly told that the Paths of Wisdom are thirty-two in all, that is to say, the Ten Numerical Emanations and their connecting links formed by the Twenty-two Letters."

89.2 [85] *yes, the importance of a drunkard's life.* In terms of la vida impersonal (see note **17.6**), the Consul's error at this point is the attribution of "formidable value" to his own sufferings; an error which precludes his regaining the lost intimacy with Yvonne.

90.1 [85]   *Bloodthirsty, did I hear you say bloodthirsty, Commander Firmin.* Memories of German friends (see note **292.3.e**) rise relentlessly to the surface of the Consul's mind.

90.2 [85]   *nux vomica or belladonna.* Poisons: *nux vomica* is the tree from whose seeds strychnine is derived (see note **73.3**); *belladonna* (It. "beautiful lady") is the deadly nightshade, *atropa belladonna,* from which is made the potion so beloved of Renaissance poisoners.

91.1 [86]   *new data on Atlantis! The most extraordinary thing of its kind since Donnelly.* Ignatius J. Donnelly (1831–1901), lawyer, politician, and writer, is described by his editor Egerton Sykes (p. xi) as: "a great liberal mind, an impassioned champion of the eternal verities, and the founder of the modern science of Atlantology." Donnelly's *Atlantis: The Antediluvian World* (1882) tried to demonstrate that Plato's fabled island of Atlantis actually existed; that it was the original Garden of Eden and Garden of the Hesperides; that it was the cradle of all civilization; that the Atlanteans colonized Egypt and America, invented the alphabet (Mayan and Phoenician), first smelted iron and worked precious metals; and that as a result of a terrible convulsion of nature the island was submerged by the ocean, a few people escaping to pass down to the different nations related legends of the golden age and deluge. Donnelly's main proof of the existence of Atlantis was based upon the notion of "intercourse between the opposite sides of the Atlantic" (see note **22.1**): that is, the existence of relations and resemblances of plant and animal life; geological similarities; linguistic, religious and cultural correspondences; and common mythologies. His approach to his evidence has been described as legalistic rather than scientific since he chose what suited his case without scrupulous regard to the facts which might argue against it; as a result, his conclusions are a mixture of the strangely pertinent and the totally fanciful. Despite its uncritical acceptance of dubious authorities, Donnelly's book quickly achieved a remarkable air of authority itself and stimulated an interest in Atlantology that has far outlasted his own time.

As Andersen notes, p. 35, the Consul's interest in Atlantis (and also alchemy) is an occult and mystical one. He dreams of assembling from the ruins of a rediscovered Atlantis the secret knowledge which can lead to spiritual perfection; in practice, he finds only disaster.

91.2 [86]   *the Bishop of Tasmania.* In all probability, Henry Hutchinson

Montgomery (1847–1932), father of Viscount Montgomery of Alamein. Born in India, educated at Cambridge, and ordained in 1872, he was appointed Anglican bishop of Tasmania in 1889 and remained there until recalled in 1901. He was an excellent administrator and zealous in his work, often walking long distances to remote parts of the country (see note **280.2**). He was known in his later years as a visionary and mystic, publishing in 1909, 1913, and 1915 his three books entitled *Visions,* which argue that personal mystical experience is of crucial importance in the human soul's finding direct communication with God and which occasionally draw on the imagery of alchemy to describe the transmutation of the human soul that turns to God; these probably form the basis for the Consul's regarding him as an alchemist.

91.3 [86]   *Coxcox and Noah.* The Consul is alluding to the chapter in Donnelly's *Atlantis* entitled "The Deluge Legends of the Americas," where Donnelly points out in great detail the similarities between the Biblical accounts of the Flood (the story of Noah, Genesis 6–8) and the various deluge legends of Central America. Donnelly, p. 99, cites the story of Coxcox, "the Noah of the Mexican cataclysm," who saved himself and his wife Xochiquetzal on a raft. Prescott, Appendix I, p. 693, tells the story in even greater detail, and both he and Donnelly give another version of the Michoacán Tezpi, who escaped the deluge in a boat full of various kinds of animals and birds. After the god Tezcatlipoca decreed the waters should retreat, Tezpi sent forth a vulture, which did not return (it remained to feed on the bodies of dead giants that were in the earth in those days); then a dove (or hummingbird), which came back with a leafy branch in its beak.

It were to be wished, says Prescott, "that the authority for the Michuacan version were more satisfactory." Lewis Spence, in *The Gods of Mexico,* pp. 53–54, discusses what he calls "the Coxcox fallacy," showing that attempts to prove such parallels between Coxcox and Noah are based on mistaken interpretations of the codices; the glyph assumed to be Coxcox floating simply represents the wanderings of the Aztecs in the Valley of Mexico. There are deluge myths in the Americas (see note **35.2**), but in the light of Spence's conclusive rebuttal of the theories advanced by Prescott and Donnelly, it is difficult to imagine what more the Consul might "work in" to his own book.

91.4 [86]   *a publisher interested too; in Chicago.* Almost certainly the New Aeon Publishing Co., acting for the *Collegium ad Spiritum Sanctum* (Chicago, Ill.), a group of theosophists led in the 1920's by Lowry's subsequent friend and neighbour Charles Stansfeld-Jones (Frater Achad), who himself had a number of Cabbalistic books and tracts published by the

Collegium (Epstein, p. 92). There is a neat irony here, as the Consul is aware, since Chicago is better know as the major centre of stockyards and abbatoirs in the United States.

91.5 [86]   *how the human spirit seems to blossom in the shadow of the abattoir.* This idea, so central to *UTV,* is presented again on p. 318 [317], in the image of vultures defiling themselves with blood and filth, yet capable of rising above it to the heights. The idea is also central to Baudelaire's *Les Fleurs du Mal,* for example, "Réversibilité," the very title of which suggests the possibility of the poet's anguish, shame, remorse, and terror finding its essential opposition in the "angel" which incarnates the feminine ideal (see note **283.4**).

91.6 [86]   *the old alchemists of Prague.*   Under the Holy Roman Emperors Maximilian II (1564–76) and Rudolf II (1576–1612), the court at Prague supported and entertained many of the leading alchemists of Europe. The *Zlatá Ulička,* or Golden Alley, where the alchemists had their dens, was the leading centre of such activity. Rudolf in particular became obsessed by alchemy and astrology, increasingly withdrawing from public affairs and shutting himself in his castle at Prague to devote more time to his experiments. The court servants were in effect laboratory assistants, and the court poet was charged with the composition of laudatory odes to successful adepts and the versification of alchemical treatises. All alchemists could be sure of a welcome, and those who showed proof of a striking experiment were amply rewarded. Rudolf himself was reputedly credited with the achievement of the philosopher's stone (Holmyard, pp. 231–32).

91.7 [86]   *the cohabations Faust himself. Cohabation* (more usually, cohobation) in alchemy is the operation of repeated distillation by pouring the distillate back upon the residue in the retort (using a vessel called a pelican) in the attempt to obtain greater purity. Kilgallin suggests, pp. 164–65, that Lowry took the word from Ben Jonson's *The Alchemist,* II.v.26–28:

> Subtle: What's cohobation?
> Face: 'Tis the pouring on
> Your *aqua regis,* then drawing him off,
> To the trine circle of the seven spheres.

In reply to his publisher's emendation, Lowry noted on the galley proofs (UBC 9-15) "Cohabations is correct"; the Penguin "cohabitations" reverts to the error, but the pun is certainly intended, an earlier version reading: "in the cellar among the alchemists and the cohabitations—sorry, *cohabations!* of Faust" (UBC 10–14, p. 12).

91.8 [86] *litharge and agate and hyacinth and pearls.* Substances with alchemical properties:
(a) *litharge.* From Gk. *lithargyros,* "foam of silver"; yellow or red prot-oxide of lead partially fused; used in the manufacturing of glass, enamels, paints, and insecticides. Alchemically significant in the making of the white elixir.
(b) *agate.* From Gk. *achates,* "an agate" (named after the river Achates); a hard semi-precious variety of chalcedony with various tints in the one specimen. According to Pliny's *Natural History,* XXXVII.liv.139, it is used to counteract the bites of spiders and scorpions, to increase the strength of the eyes, and to allay thirst.
(c) *hyacinth.* From Gk. *hyakinthos,* "a hyacinth"; a gem, such as the sapphire, zircon, garnet, or topaz. The name is of the youth beloved of Apollo, whose transformation into the flower was regarded by alchemists as an image of transmutation (Pernety, p. 203). It has the virtue, Kilgallin suggests, p. 165, of promoting sleep.
(d) *pearl.* The New Testament "pearl of great price" (Matthew 13:46), or spiritual immortality, was often regarded by alchemists as analogous to the achievement of the philosopher's stone, as in the *Pretiosa Margarita Novella,* the *New Pearl of Great Price,* by Petrus Bonus (c. 1330; published in Venice, 1546).
   The conjunction of hyacinth and pearl, however, suggests a transformation which is less happy; in Pt. II of *The Waste Land,* the ecstasy of the Hyacinth Garden has gone, only to be recalled painfully in the line "those are pearls that were his eyes." Eliot's note to l. 126 explicitly links the two scenes; the text originally reading: "I remember the hyacinth garden / Those are pearls that were his eyes."

91.9 [87] *A life which is amorphous, plastic and crystalline.* The Consul perhaps means the transmutation of his life from its present shapeless form into the nobler spiritual state, the process imitating that typically undergone by metals. This is in line with the teachings of Paracelsus (1493–1541), who saw the goal of alchemy not so much as the physical transmutation of base metals into gold, but as the psychological transmutation of the soul into a higher, one might say crystalline, form. Lowry, however, may have been thinking of Jack London's *The Jacket* (see note **161.7.c**), the final paragraph of which reads (p. 333):

There is no death. Life is spirit, and spirit cannot die. Only the flesh dies and passes, ever a-crawl with the chemic ferment that informs it, ever plastic, ever crystallizing, only to melt into the flux and to crystallize into flesh and diverse forms that are ephemeral and that melt back into the flux. Spirit alone endures and continues to build upon itself through successive and endless incarnations as it works upward toward the light.

91.10 [87]   *Copula Maritalis.* The potential puns on "cope," p. 89 [84], and "cohabitation" are realized in this term for sexual intercourse or the "rights of marriage." Lowry took the phrase directly from a list of similar words and symbols in Frater Achad's *QBL,* p. 83, but it was originally a mediaeval theological term, deriving from two basic religious axioms: the worthiness of the propagation of children and the necessity of preserving the state of marriage. Saint Thomas Aquinas sums up the mediaeval position in the *Summa Theologica,* Part II-ii, questions 88, 154, and 186; and in the supplement, questions 41, 49, 55, and 65.

91.11 [87]   *from alcohol to alkahest.* The Consul forsees his own dissolution as one spirit leads to the other:
(a) *alcohol.* From Ar. *al-kohl,* referring to a kind of black eye-paint; the name transferred quite arbitrarily by Paracelsus to the spirit of wine.
(b) *alkahest.* A term invented by Paracelsus, probably modelled on Ger. *allgeist,* "all-spirit"; originally applied to a spirit acting efficiently upon the liver, but soon coming to designate an imagined universal solvent; hence, perhaps, the immediate reference to *El Universal* and the corpse travelling eastward.

92.1 [87]   *a sudden peculiar sense of embarrassment.* The Consul's unease is not simply caused by his sense that Yvonne is a stranger, but also hints at the various Oedipal problems arising from his neglected childhood.

92.2 [87]   *La Fontaine's duck had loved the white hen.* There is no story of this kind in La Fontaine's *Fables,* nor in the fables of Aesop; it seems likely that Lowry has made up the story, perhaps basing it on something read or heard elsewhere, and attributed it to La Fontaine.

92.3 [87]   *In November 1895, in convict dress . . . Oscar Wilde stood on the centre platform at Clapham Junction.* From Oscar Wilde's *De Profundis* (1905), the prose apologia based upon his experiences in prison after having been sentenced to two years' imprisonment with hard labour for homosexual practices; in it Wilde recounts his efforts, finally unavailing, to rise "out of the depths." Halfway through the work he writes:

> Everything about my tragedy has been hideous, mean, repellent, lacking in style; our very dress makes us grotesque. We are the zanies of sorrow. We are clowns whose hearts are broken. We are specially designed to appeal to the sense of humour. On November 13th, 1895, I was brought down here from London. From two o'clock till half-past two on that day I had to stand on the centre platform of Clapham Junction in convict dress, and handcuffed, for the world to look at. I had been taken out of the hospital ward without a moment's notice being given to me. Of all possible objects I was the most grotesque. When people saw me they laughed. Each train as it came up swelled the audience. Nothing could exceed their amusement. That was, of course, before they knew who I was. As soon as they had been informed they laughed still more. For half an hour I stood there in the grey November rain surrounded by a jeering mob.

92.4 [88] *the Via Dolorosa.* L. "Street of Sorrows." More usually, "The Way of the Cross," the route taken by Christ on his way to Golgotha. There is no street by this name in Mexico City, but Lowry may have in mind the Calle Dolores, running off Juárez from the Alameda Park, which fits perfectly the description in *DATG,* p. 104, of "a transverse street" close to the Hotel Canada.

92.5 [88] *the Hotel Canada.* In Mexico City, on the Calle Cinco de Mayo 47, close to the zócalo. In *DATG* it is called the Cornada and described, p. 90, as "a nasty little hotel" with bad plumbing (it has since been extensively renovated). The hotel was the scene of Lowry's final break with Jan, December 1937; a parting here attributed to the Consul and Yvonne. The Regis is a better-class hotel (see note **72.1**).

93.1 [89] *Oedipuss... Pathos.* The fate of poor Oedipuss (Geoffrey has already been identified with the cat's Greek namesake) anticipates that of the Consul.

94.1 [89] *No work has been done by the little cat.* Not identified; perhaps (like "Peegly Weegly," p. 58 [54]), intended to be a completely private allusion.

94.2 [89] *the prelude.* In music, typically a short story played as a preliminary to a longer piece, but Lowry may have in mind the sexual encounter anticipated in Conrad Aiken's *Blue Voyage,* p. 133: "This is the prelude, thought Demarest. This is merely the announcement of that perfect communion of which I have often dreamed."

94.3 [89] *like that jewelled gate the desperate neophyte, Yesod-bound, projects for the thousandth time on the heavens to permit passage of his astral body.* The Consul's attempt at lovemaking is described in Cabbalistic terms of a neophyte, or beginner, trying in vain to initiate the first stage of his spiritual journey:

(a) *his astral body.* The essential spiritual body which may survive the death of the physical body and, for those of heightened spiritual consciousness, which may leave the body during life; when this separation takes place, the astral body is said to have entered the astral plane. The Consul's inability to "project" (that is, to externalize) his astral body means that he is unable to initiate the mystical process by which his spiritual being may enter into a higher reality.

(b) *the desperate neophyte.* The term neophyte indicates a distinct stage in the hierarchy of Cabbalistic enlightenment, as Frater Achad makes clear, *QBL,* p. 65:

> I will now tell you something of the Order whereby one may learn the Path to the Highest. First one becomes a PROBATIONER, that is, one who is outside the Order but who is OBLIGATED to "Obtain a Scientific Knowledge of the Nature and Powers of his own being." When he has accomplished this task he becomes a NEOPHYTE and enters the sphere of MALKUTH. There he learns to CONTROL the Nature and Powers of his own being. He finds these much wider than he expected and his task before reaching YESOD is to control the ASTRAL PLANE which he accomplishes by use of the Pentegram which makes it possible either to Invoke or Banish all the Elements and to control them.

(c) *Yesod.* Yesod is the ninth Sephira of the Cabbalistic tree of life (see note **44.3**), the foundation which typifies reproductive power, and the Sephira which corresponds to the genitals of the microcosmic man. An aspirant beginning his spiritual journey upward from Malkuth to Kether must first attain Yesod, the bottom sphere of the lowest astral triangle. As Epstein remarks, p. 93, the Consul's attempted lovemaking is described "in accurate cabbalistic terms which equate the sex act with the symbolic entry of the soul into Yesod" (the "jewelled gate" having the Cabbalistic significance of a crowned or blessed path, as well as obvious phallic implications). The Consul's neophytic inability to "project" or initiate the sexual act is thus, in Cabbalistic terms (which is how *he* sees it), a failure to celebrate the mystery of sex and therefore a barrier to his further spiritual progress.

94.4 [90]   *A brigand with an iron scorpion.* In Mexico, the typical cantina or abarrote uses iceboxes to keep drinks cool. The ice is usually delivered from a refrigerating plant and dumped outside on the pavement, from where it is dragged inside with the aid of large metal pincers curved exactly like the front pincers of a scorpion. The metaphor is not common currency in Spanish, but it reflects perfectly the Consul's state of mind.

95.1 [90]   *eructating, exploding:* "Eructating" derives from L. *eructare,* "to belch"; "exploding" from L. *explodere,* "to drive off with clapping." Lowry is using the latter word partially in its original sense of "to decry or reject with noise," but also as a pun on flatulence.

95.2 [90]   *La Prensa and El Universal.* Newspapers of Mexico City: *La Prensa* is a popular tabloid, with large headlines and plenty of pictures; *El Universal,* established 1916, was in 1938 the leading daily, slightly conservative, offering (particularly on its English page) a comprehensive news coverage.

95.3 [90]   *a small rain of plaster showered on his head.* An intimation of Atlantis, Pompeii, and disaster that will soon be overwhelming.

95.4 [90]   *A Don Quixote fell from the wall.* As Lowry says, "LJC," p. 73: "The scene between the Consul and Yvonne where he is impotent is balanced by a scene between Consul and María in the last chapter: meanings of the Consul's impotence are practically inexhaustible." Here the ineffectiveness of the Consul's "lance" is to the fore as his romantic quest becomes a sorry failure.

95.5 [90]   *Strychnine is an aphrodisiac.* The Consul is probably deluding himself, but as late as 1945 a Philadelphia laboratory was making sexual stimulants using *nux vomica,* the source of strychnine.

95.6 [91]   *Parkinson's disease.* Named after James Parkinson (1755–1824), the English physician who first diagnosed it: a degenerative disease, *paralysis agitans,* usually confined to later life, caused by the deterioration of part of the brain and characterized by muscular rigidity and a continual shaking of the hands.

95.7 [91]   *quartern*. A fourth of any measure; here, a quarter of a pint.

95.8 [91]   *Nació 1820 y siguiendo tan campante*. The slogan on the Johnny Walker whisky bottle is here ironically contrasted with the Consul's degeneration and his inability to say "I love you" to Yvonne.

96.1 [91]   *Have you forgotten the letters Geoffrey Firmin*. The tone and style of this paragraph is consciously Faulknerian, and the internal dialogue and eternal questioning very similar to that of Quentin Compson in *The Sound and the Fury* (1929). The voices will haunt the Consul all day, growing in intensity before his "suicide" in the Farolito, where the lost letters will be found. There may also be an echo of the song "Have You Forgotten Yvonne," recorded 18 March 1926 by Henry Leoni, French musical comedy star and cabaret entertainer very popular in England after the war (Rust, p. 417).

96.2 [91]   *the object shaped like a dead man*. The "other" is a hallucination, yet, like the mysterious "other" in Julian Green's *Le Voyageur sur la terre* (see note **15.3**), corresponds in a way that the Consul does not fully understand "to some fraction of his being," p. 362 [362]: it is both himself as a dead man and the dying Indian he will meet later in the day. Lowry comments ("LJC," p. 73): "The dead man with hat over head the Consul sees in the garden is man by the wayside in Chapter VIII. This can happen in really super D.T.'s. Paracelsus will bear me out."
    Ramsey suggests, pp. 26–28, that Dunne's understanding of serial time underlies this kind of experience: insofar as man exists within absolute time, which contains all moments of "past," "present," and "future," he may possess the power to experience a "pre-presentation" of the future, yet retain the freedom to act responsibly *in time* and influence the course of events (the Consul does not).

97.1 [92]   *I can still carry the eighth green in three*. The "eighth green" is that behind the Hell Bunker, p. 26 [21]: the abyss which "yawned in such a position as to engulf the third shot of a golfer like Geoffrey," who is no longer, alas, such a naturally beautiful and graceful player.

97.2 [92]   *alcohol is an aphrodisiac. . . . alcohol is a food*. The Consul is deluding himself again, since these statements are at best only half truths. Alcohol may suppress inhibitions, but it reduces the co-ordination and nervous control which directs sexual performance; it has calories that can be turned to work and heat, but lacks essential nutriments.

97.3 [92] *and I smashed the electric-light bulb.* At a climactic moment of Joyce's *Ulysses,* Stephen Dedalus raises his ashplant and smashes the chandelier before rushing out of the brothel, his act symbolically freeing him from the bondage of his past; the Consul's action seems almost a parody of this act of independence. Lowry may also have in mind a paragraph in Lawrence's *Fantasia of the Unconscious,* Ch. 12: even "if the servant smashes three electric-light bulbs in three minutes," the individual must say: "Alone. Alone. Be alone, my soul."

97.4 [93] *The will of man is unconquerable.* An echo of Milton's lines (*Paradise Lost,* I.105–8):

> What though the field be lost?
> All is not lost — th'unconquerable will,
> And study of revenge, immortal hate,
> And courage never to submit or yield.

Satan's words undercut the Consul's "fatuous self-congratulation" (Jakobsen, p. 29) in many ways: by the transparent inadequacy of his statements of well-being and the sober virtuous life; by excuses for his failure ("a sign of my fidelity, my loyalty"); by his viewing the volcanoes as an "image of the perfect marriage"; by his seeing the waiting vultures as "more graceful than eagles"; and by his falling asleep with a crash. Above all, he is violating the basic Cabbalistic principle of the law of will, which permits man's domination over the elements (*Transcendental Magic,* p. 67), but must be cultivated, disciplined, and controlled if man is to move closer to Ain Soph, the source of light (which the Consul seems so wilfully to have smashed).

97.5 [93] *a pale gibbous moon.* "Gibbous" is a term applied to the moon between three-quarters and full, when more than half the visible surface is sunlit (the opposite to "crescent"), but applied to persons or animals the word has connotations of "hump-backed" or "misshapen" (see note **211.8**).

97.6 [93] *like burnt papers floating from a fire.* The hovering vultures, associates of the bringer of fire (see note **225.1**), are harbingers of disaster for the Consul. They anticipate the burning of his manuscript, p. 336 [336]; Laruelle's burning of his letter, p. 47 [42]; Yvonne's death, p. 337 [336] (when her soul like an eagle is released); and his own death. Underlying the identification of the vultures as eagles is the disputed King James translation of Matthew 24:28, where the Gk. *aetos* clearly means "vulture": "For wheresoever the carcase is, there will the eagles be gathered together."

CHAPTER FOUR

98.1 [94] *Daily Globe intelube.* In a letter to Albert Erskine (Woodcock, p. 111) Lowry wrote: "significance of 'interlube' has passed from my mind. But it might have something to do with the London Daily Herald or the United Press, if that matters. Cable is based on a real one and used by permission of the reporter who sent it I having sat in at the concoction thereof. Cable was, until lately, in my possession." The original cable is in the Templeton collection (1–1) at the University of British Columbia.

98.2 [94] *head-coming antisemitic campaign.* The story Hugh has "got wind of," p. 66 [61], has complex political implications, given the ambiguous feelings of Mexico towards Britain and Germany. The C.T.M., or Confederation of Mexican Workers, has issued a petition objecting "to certain Teutonic huggermugger," p. 100 [96], behind the threatened expulsion from Mexico of "small Jewish textile manufacturers"; Hugh has discovered through a "reliable source" that the German legation in Mexico City has been actively behind the campaign, to the extent of sending anti-Semitic propaganda to the Mexican Department of Internal Affairs. Shops and businesses of the small Jewish community in Mexico City were frequently the target of such fascist vigilante groups as the "goldshirts" (a widespread paramilitary organization that also attacked the unions and striking workers), and Nazi organizations within Mexico tried to whip up racial hatred and industrial tension before World War II in an effort to bring down the Cárdenas government and keep Mexico out of the war. The campaign had started in 1937 and gathered momentum during 1938, when Mexico's economic situation became increasingly precarious. The textile industry, allegedly operated by small Jewish firms, was a particular target of the labour unions as well as fascist agitators (hence their peculiar collusion implied in Hugh's "propetition" and "proexpulsion" in the telegram). On 24 June the C.T.M. (see below) petitioned the secretary of the interior to take advantage of the constitution, which, they argued, allowed him to expel any "alien" from Mexico. On 23 June, embarrassed by the curious alliance apparently developing between left and right, the general secretary of the C.T.M. explained to the foreign press that Mexico was not anti-

Semitic and went on to accuse the German legation of espionage activities in Mexico and of giving money to certain "conservative newpapers" which continued an anti-Jewish press campaign. The fascist influence continued to grow: trade relations were established with Germany and Japan; Jewish refugees were sent back (2 November 1938); laws were passed limiting their entry into Mexico; and in 1939 there were anti-Jewish riots in Mexico City. Hugh's telegram thus reflects accurately much of the confused political background of the period.

98.3 [94] *see tee emma.* C.T.M., the "Confederación de Trabajadores de México" ("Confederation of Mexican Workers"), whose support of and by the government of Lázaro Cárdenas was the most crucial factor behind the fulfilment of many of the reforms set out in law after the 1910–20 Revolution. The C.T.M., formed in 1936, was the most important of all Mexican unions and represented the vast majority of organized workers. Ashby comments, pp. 274–75:

> a Congress for the Unification of the Labor Movement was held in Mexico City, and the outcome was the formation of the C.T.M., a central federation composed of independent national trade unions, primarily industrial in structure. . . . Although the organization was composed of unions of diverse strengths, philosophies, and tactics, it reflected, in general, the qualities of its head, Lombardo Toledano. The organization claimed to embrace no single socio-economic philosophy but to be merely a popular front of labor unions designed to strengthen labor's condition through both collective bargaining and the support of "revolutionary" political leaders. The C.T.M., containing perhaps a million workers, became the dominant labor central of the Cárdenas era.

Cárdenas refused to let the C.T.M. absorb the unions representing peasants and government workers and thus kept control of it, but from the outset the collaboration of his government with the C.T.M. permitted the effective implementation not only of labour but also of wider social and political reforms.

98.4 [94] *the Oficinia Principal of the Compañía Telegráfica Mexicana Esq., San Juan de Letrán e Independencia, México, D.F.* The main office of the Mexican Telegraph Company was in 1938 on the corner (despite Lowry's confusing punctuation, "Esq." must mean *esquina*) of San Juan de Letrán (now Lázaro Cárdenas) and Independencia, in the Federal District of Mexico. It has since been relocated at Balderas 93.

98.5 [94]   *gladstone bag.* A travelling bag with flexible sides on a rigid frame that opens flat into two compartments. It is named for William Ewart Gladstone, English prime minister during much of the late nineteenth century.

98.6 [94]   *eyes in my feet . . . as well as straw.* The conjunction of eyes and straw forms an allusion to T. S. Eliot's "The Hollow Men," and the image of Guy Fawkes in that poem may hint at the probable fate of Hugh's quixotic enterprise.

98.7 [95]   *clothed entirely in sunlight.* A hint of Revelation 12:1, "And there appeared a great wonder in heaven; a woman clothed with the sun, and the moon under her feet, and upon her head a crown of twelve stars." This woman, who gives birth to a child who kills the great dragon, is usually identified with Mary and is the antithesis of the Whore of Babylon, with whom the Consul has previously identified Yvonne (see note **51.4**).

99.1 [95]   *Jack London's Valley of the Moon.* A novel published in 1913 by Jack London, who is clearly a favourite of Hugh's (see note **161.7**). The novel's hero is Billy Roberts, brawny teamster and part-time prizefighter, and its heroine, Saxon Brown, who works in an Oakland laundry (her name symbolizing the purity and strength of the Anglo-Saxon race—the irony of "Brown" escaped the author). The first part of the novel explores the proletarian life of Oakland and the labour strife of the 1890's, but after Bill loses his job and Saxon her child, they quit the city and seek a purer air and life, looking for their own "Valley of the Moon," which, after meeting a thinly disguised version of the author, they find in the Sonoma Valley of northern California. Jack London's Valley of the Moon was a 129-acre area of volcanic rock out of which he envisaged creating an agricultural Eden of happy workers and beautiful fields (now the *Jack London State Historical Park* near Glen Ellen), but which was in reality a monument to the vast wealth he earned by writing. Hugh, in this chapter a *Sailor on Horseback* (the title of Irving Stone's 1938 biography of Jack London), considers himself a figure in the Jack London heroic mould, but his socialism is equally fraught with contradictions.

99.2 [95]   *the German bookstore opposite Sandborns* [sic]. Sanborns' House of Tiles (between Madero and Cinco de Mayo in downtown Mexico City), a seventeenth-century building completely covered with blue-and-white Puebla tiles, is one of the city's best known landmarks. Originally a private mansion, it later housed the exclusive Jockey Club; then, for a short time after the Revolution, it served as headquarters for what was to become the first national labour union in Mexico before being bought by the brothers Sanborn, who turned it into the restaurant-tea room that quickly became the city's smartest meeting-place. The German bookstore, long gone, is yet another reminder of the ubiquitous German presence, and there is considerable irony in Hugh's following up his telegram by buying, in a German bookstore, a novel which advocates blatantly prejudiced views of racial purity (see note **99.1**).

99.3 [95] *on the Ebro they were retreating.* The Ebro is the second largest river of the Iberian peninsula, flowing in the north of Spain some five hundred miles southeast between the Pyrenees and the Iberian Mountains to the Mediterranean. The area around Gandesa, about seventy miles from the delta, was the scene of one of the most decisive battles in the Spanish Civil War from August to November, 1938. At this stage of the war the Republican forces were under great pressure, the Nationalists controlling the area along the Ebro and cutting off the Republican forces in Barcelona from those in Valencia. On 25 July, therefore, the Republicans under Modesto embarked on an offensive, crossing the Ebro, capturing the strategic high places about Gandesa, and taking four thousand Nationalist prisoners. In early August the major battle took place at Gandesa, but while the Republican advance was contained, the Nationalists could not at first regain the captured territory. After six weeks of heavy fighting and bombing, however, the Republicans were forced to retreat though they held most of their ground. On 30 October a long-awaited Nationalist counter-offensive began (Hugh could have heard the news in Mexico City, though the timing is fine), and on the night of 1–2 November, after heavy assaults and bombing, the Republicans became convinced that all was lost. They began to retreat with heavy losses, and by the eighteenth no Republicans remained west of the Ebro. Casualties were high, much material had to be abandoned, and in effect the battle marked the beginning of the end for the Republicans.

The phrase echoes in Hugh's mind throughout the novel, as a sign of the guilt he feels about dallying with Yvonne; his "betrayal" of the Republicans thus acting as a correlative for his betrayal of Geoffrey.

99.4 [95] *Bill Hodson.* Bill Hodson is the cowboy star whose leading lady Yvonne had been in three pictures when she was fifteen (see p. 263 [262]); the name is fictional, but in a letter to Albert Erskine (Woodcock, p. 111), Lowry writes "For Bill H. — substitute Bill Hod." It is possible that he has in mind William S. Hart (see note **65.3**), suggesting an even greater amount of theatricality about Hugh's get-up.

100.1 [96]   *the new message from Garcia.* A mocking allusion to the heroic deed of army Lieutenant Andrew S. Rowan, who carried a message in April 1898 into the hills of Cuba for General Calixto Garcia, the leader of rebel guerrillas in the Spanish-American War. Rowan was to determine what kind of help was needed by Garcia and by heroic persistence got the message through. The incident stirred Elbert Hubbard (1856–1915) into writing his best-selling "preachment" or inspirational tract, "A Message to Garcia" (1899), a highly wrought eulogy of Andrew S. Rowan as a man of action, the man who does what is needed, the man for whom the world cries out. Hubbard's tract was the basis for the 1936 Fox photoplay, *Message to Garcia.*

100.2 [96]   *Teutonic huggermugger.* German secrecy and interference in Mexican politics (see note **98.2**).

100.3 [96]   *Hugh slipped it into the pocket of his jacket.* An unthinking action with disastrous consequences, for that jacket will be worn by Geoffrey when he is later searched by the militia and found with the telegram as his only "identification."

100.4 [96]   *head tax.* There used to be a flat $10 duty on cattle brought in from Mexico to the United States, but never on U.S. cattle taken to Mexico. Hugh's jest, "disguised as a cow," is probably a reference to wild Texans (*patones,* or "big-hooves") indistinguishable from their beasts: "I'm wild and woolly and full of fleas, / And never been curried below the knees."

100.5 [96]   *England being persona non grata here.* The expropriation of British oil interests by President Cárdenas in 1938 (see note **36.1**) and the subsequent British retaliation rendered British subjects in Mexico open to abuse or even danger, as Graham Greene reports in *The Lawless Roads,* pp. 226–27:

> All that happened was that the atmosphere of hostility thickened — and directed itself against me. A drunken group passed and repassed, throwing out gibes; they had revolvers under their waistcoats, so there was nothing to be done but sit, like a prudish maiden lady, pretending not to hear. I was suffering for the ancient wrongdoing of the oil pioneers, the tiresome legal rectitude of the English Government.

101.1 [97]   *Isn't the garden a wreck.* Yvonne's words to Hugh are almost identical to those she used to Geoffrey, p. 78 [74], and thus evoke something of the desolate garden scene and lost love of Tennyson's "Mariana." Her sudden change of topic barely conceals her unease, while Hugh's unspoken comment, "They are losing the Battle of the Ebro," also reveals his underlying guilt. Despite its beauty, the unweeded garden is a wreck: the *bougainvillea* is an emblem of deceit (see note **146.1**); the fragrant pink and white flowers of the oleander are highly poisonous; and the flowerbed, p. 102 [98], is strangled by "a coarse green vine" — convolvulus — used consistently as a symbol of something that chokes proper growth.

In *The Holy Kabbalah,* VIII.i, p. 261, in a section entitled "The Myth of the Earthly Paradise," A. E. Waite states that the Garden of Eden is in one sense the mystery of sex (embodied in womanhood) and that this garden was ravished. Yvonne comments, p. 102 [98], that her garden was "like Paradise," but it is now in all senses a fallen landscape, and she must take some responsibility for that Fall, rather than simply "get the hell out of it" with Hugh.

101.2 [97]   *El Paso ... Chihuahua ... Cusihuriachic* [*sic*]. El Paso, in southwest Texas near the Mexican border, is the largest of border cities and a major railroad and cattle centre; Chihuahua, capital of the state of the same name, is some 220 miles south of El Paso and is a road and rail centre in the heart of the Mexican cattle country (hence a most likely destination for a cattle truck); Cusihuiriachic, a small town some 55 miles southeast of Chihuahua, at the eastern foot of the Sierra Madre Occidental, is a rail terminus and mining centre which has a small airport.

101.3 [97]   *the Foreign Legion.* La Légion Étrangère, the French military force formed in 1831 to protect the regime of Louis Philippe and to serve in North Africa. The officers and N.C.O.'s were predominantly French, but the men came from all corners of the globe, often serving under false names to escape their pasts. The conditions of enlistment are stated by a weary recruiting sergeant in P. C. Wren's *Beau Geste,* p. 170:

> The engagement volontaire for La Légion Étrangère is for five years, in Algiers, or any other French colony, and the pay is a *sou* a day. A *legionnaire* can re-enlist at the end of the five years, and again at the end of ten years. At the end of fifteen years he is eligible for a pension according to his rank. A foreigner, on completion of five years' service, can claim to be naturalized as a French subject.

The legion was basically infantry, though cavalry and paratroop battalions were added later. It operated in French territories throughout the world, particularly in North Africa, but also in Mexico 1863–67, and later in Syria and Indochina. The legion had a deserved reputation for toughness and attracted many "semi-fascist blokes" because of its discipline and ruthlessness.

101.4 [97]   *birds and flowers and pyramids.* The blouse has been bought "for Geoff's benefit" in that the birds and pyramids have vague neo-Platonic and occult implications, while the Empress, Tarot card 3, is dressed in flowers as a symbol of Venus, goddess of love (Ouspensky, *A New Model of the Universe,* p. 230).

101.5 [97]   *bastardo.* Sp. "bastard." In Spanish, however, the word is without a pejorative sense and simply designates the fact of illegitimacy.

102.1 [98]   *the muted voice of England long asleep.* The Consul's snoring can be interpreted as a reference to England's failure to intervene in the Spanish Civil War; a point made explicitly in the manuscripts (UBC 7–7, p. 8), where England is likened to Ralph Hodgson's old bull waiting for death (see note **275.1**), liable to wake up and find itself in the same position as Spain. George Orwell's *Homage to Catalonia* (1938) concludes with a vision of Englishmen "all sleeping the deep, deep sleep of England, from which I sometimes fear we shall never wake till we are jerked out of it by the roar of bombs." Though England was generally sympathetic to the Republican cause and did not at first discourage volunteers for Spain, she did not commit herself to aiding the Republicans either politically or materially; in fact, Chamberlain's policy of appeasement, the passive acceptance of Franco's blockade (see note **107.2**), and the withdrawal of the brigades in September 1938, let the Republicans down badly at the crucial moment. Hugh's reproach of his "ruddy monarch" implies a like criticism of Geoffrey's neglect of Yvonne.

102.2 [98]   *Robinson.* The ambiguous bird leads the thoughts of Hugh and Yvonne to Robinson, a district in the southwest of Paris (coincidentally, next to the *Vallee-aux-Loups* — see note **79.3**). The area was so called when in 1848 an enterprising cafe owner, cashing in on the popularity of Johann Wyss's *The Swiss Family Robinson* (1812), built a restaurant in the branches of a hugh chestnut tree and turned the area beneath into a place for dancing and entertainment. The thoughts of Hugh and Yvonne remain "unspoken" because neither wishes to recall what is presumably the day of their affair and hence their "betrayal" of the Consul. The unknown fate of the bicycles (one is meant to wonder what on earth *could* have happened, both to them and to Hugh and Yvonne) is paralleled by the unknown fate of the Consul's blue Plymouth, p. 57 [52].

102.3 [98] *Okies.* A general term for migratory agricultural workers, particularly those forced in the 1930's to migrate from Oklahoma and other parts of the Dust Bowl area because of drought, soil erosion, and farm foreclosure. Thousands set out west in search of better opportunities, but their presence in Texas and California was often resented by the established settlers, who not only denied them land and work but sometimes (as Hugh has discovered) actively sought to turn them back. The classic treatment of the Okies and their plight is John Steinbeck's *The Grapes of Wrath* (1940), an epic account of an emigrant family trying to leave the Dust Bowl and reach the promised land of California.

103.1 [99] *Nosey Parker.* An inquisitive person. Probably an allusion to Matthew Parker (1504–75), archbishop of Canterbury, who was not so much an inquisitive man as one who introduced many unpopular reforms into the management of the Anglican Church. The expression became part of navy slang whereby a particular adjective was associated with a given surname ("Dusty" Miller, "Pincher" Martin, "Nosey" Parker, etc.).

103.2 [99] *Munich.* The capital of Bavaria, southern Germany; the scene of talks between Hitler and the British prime minister, Neville Chamberlain, which resulted in the ill-fated Munich agreement of 30 September 1938, by which the British government, seeking to delay the outbreak of war or even to avoid it altogether, acceded to Hitler's demands that the Sudetenland, the German-speaking part of Czechoslovakia, be included without plebiscite within the German Reich. The policy of appeasement, which Chamberlain considered to have brought "peace with honour," was regarded by Hitler as diplomatic weakness and encouraged him to continue his policies of territorial annexation. Like most British socialists, Hugh sees Munich as a betrayal, not only of the Sudetenland and Czechoslovakia but of Republican hopes in Spain, for Chamberlain, delighted with his "success" over Czechoslovakia, had suggested a similar conference to solve the Spanish problem. News of the proposal leaked out and caused the Republicans to fear that they were to share the same fate as Dr. Beneš's Czechoslovakia (Thomas, p. 849).

103.3 [99] *the pinch-bottle of habanero.* Habanero (the name deriving from Havana, where it originated) is a strong rum-like aguardiente now made in Tabasco; a pinch-bottle is defined by *Webster's* as "a bottle with pinched or indented sides."

103.4 [99] *the old bull-ring. . . . That's where they crucified the women in the bull-rings during the revolution and set the bulls at them.* Weber's details, applied to Cuernavaca, are not historically true, yet are not altogether unrealistic. There is no bull-ring in Cuernavaca (though there used to be one a few miles to the south), and there is no record of the events Weber describes having taken place. Lowry seems to have taken an incident in Puebla, 13 July 1911, when fifty people, including women and children, were killed in a bull-ring that was being used as a revolutionary headquarters (Womack, p. 105) and embroidered it with details from Eisenstein's *Que Viva Mexico!*, one scene of which depicted a crucifixion.

The historical truth, however, is grim enough. Morelos was a centre of Zapatista revolution 1910–20, and Cuernavaca came under siege several times from both revolutionary and governmental forces. Local historians (Aguirre and Díez) trace the ebb and flow of battle in detail up to the beginning of May 1916, when the government forces of General Pablo González took Cuernavaca, then simply say, in effect, without giving details of atrocities, that here began the era of blood, the most shameful days in the history of Morelos. The plunder, rape, torture, and execution that followed apparently made the previous six years of confusion and slow starvation seem a fiesta in comparison.

103.5 [99] *the purple slopes . . . of paradise.* Although the scene murmurs of peace, the conjunction of purple with paradise suggests an Eden already lost (see note **20.8**); a suggestion further supported by the phallic image of lizards darting into the bougainvillea; the half-shored-in hole (a Swedenborgian gate to hell); the precipitous fields leading to the abyss; the presence of the prison watchtower and old bull-ring; and the current ravishing of China by Japanese armies astride all roads to Shanghai, (p. 184 [180]).

103.6 [99] *China.* Hugh's trip to China may have been modelled on Jack London's equally futile assignment in Asia in 1904 as war correspondent for the *San Francisco Examiner,* covering the Russo-Japanese conflict, or, possibly, on the trip to China by Auden and Isherwood (*Journey to a War,* 1938). Hugh's role in China is not very clear, and given how recent his visit was, it seems strangely suppressed in his mind. He could not have been (unlike Edgar Snow, author of *Red Star Over China,* 1937) with the communist forces in the isolated northwest, so, like many Western pressmen, he must have been with the Nationalist forces under Chiang-Kai-Shek in the south, who were in 1938 the main opposition to the invading Japanese (by October 1938, astride all roads to Canton). Given this possible ideological conflict, as well as the very real physical danger, it might indeed have seemed healthier to go to California. The reference to "China" is also a private allusion to Lowry's short story of that title, written in 1934 and based on the theme that every man lies imprisoned in his own consciousness: "And you carry your horizon in your pocket wherever you are," (*P & S,* p. 54).

103.7 [99] *I fell out of an ambulance.* The general context suggests an oblique reference to Ernest Hemingway, who was an ambulance driver in World War I and a newspaper correspondent in Spain during the Spanish Civil War and whose novel *For Whom the Bell Tolls* (1940) is set against the latter background. Hugh's will to action, to say nothing of his later role in the bull-throwing, is almost a parody of what Vladimir Nabokov has called "bells, balls and bulls" (*Strong Opinions,* p. 80).

103.8 [99] *a billy goat.* The goat is a materialization of the Consul, who has already called himself a cabrón, p. 74 [69]. The sudden change, the patriarchal contempt, the destructive urge, p. 104 [100], and the Machiavellian eye, p. 110 [106], embody the Consul's malevolent feelings, which, as here, too often have the effect of driving Yvonne closer to Hugh. Lowry may also have intended a reference to *Moby Dick,* Ch. 99: "stand aside! Here's the battering-ram, Capricornus, or the Goat; full tilt he comes rushing, and headlong we are tossed."

104.1 [100] *the Malebolge.* It. "evil ditches." In Dante's *Inferno,* the name given to the eighth circle of hell, consisting of ten circular trenches, or *bolge,* in which are placed seducers, panderers, flatterers, simoniacs, sorcerers, barrators, hypocrites, thieves, sowers of discord, and falsifiers (likened by Hugh to journalists), to each of whom is meted out an appropriate affliction.

104.2 [100] *prescinded.* From L. *praescindere,* "to cut off in front"; hence, to withdraw attention from.

104.3 [100] *Bernal Díaz and his Tlaxcalans.* Bernal Díaz del Castillo (c. 1492–1581), conquistador with Cortés and author of the *Historia verdadera de la conquista de la Nueva España* (finished in 1568, but not published until 1632). Although its objectivity is severely limited by the unhesitating pride that Díaz took in the Spanish triumphs and by a sense of complete justification in all that was done, the *True History* is nevertheless an account which has all the colour and immediacy of first-hand experience. It is doubtful, however, that Lowry had read this history before writing *Under the Volcano,* since all his references to Díaz could have been taken equally from Prescott (see note **104.4**).

The Tlaxcalans were Indians from the independent republic of Tlaxcala (see note **297.1**), some six thousand of whom accompanied Cortés on his first visit to Tenochtitlán (see note **33.1**). Many of them also accompanied Cortés on his march south in April 1521 to capture Quauhnahuac. Without the assistance of these Indian allies, Cortés could not have contemplated the subjugation of either city.

104.4 [100]   *Prescott.* William H. Prescott (1796–1859), American historian, whose *History of the Conquest of Mexico* (1843), despite obvious errors of fact and a sometimes uncritical use of previous sources, still remains the classic account in English of the Spanish conquest of Mexico. Prescott's account is sometimes prejudiced by his assumptions of the natural superiority of European religious and social institutions over those of the "rude Indians" (often in defiance of the obvious facts), but it is a comprehensive and exciting account of an almost unbelievable set of exploits. The episode Hugh refers to is discussed in Prescott, VI.iii, pp. 532–34, when Cortés, in the course of subduing some of the outlying cities before his attack on Tenochtitlán, arrived before Quauhnahuac, a town "singularly situated, on a projecting piece of land, encompassed by *barrancas,* or formidable ravines," to find his progress arrested by a vast barranca whose bridges had been broken in anticipation of the coming of the Spaniards. Prescott describes the chasm, then how the Spaniards managed to cross it to subdue the city:

> From the cliffs on the opposite sides of the barranca two huge trees shot up to an enormous height, and, inclining towards each other, interlaced their boughs so as to form a sort of natural bridge. Across this avenue, in mid air, a Tlascalan conceived it would not be difficult to pass to the opposite bank. The bold mountaineer succeeded in the attempt, and was soon followed by several others of his countrymen, trained to feats of agility and strength among their native hills. The Spaniards imitated their example. It was a perilous effort for an armed man to make his way over this aerial causeway, swayed to and fro by the wind, where the brain might become giddy, and where a single false movement of hand or foot would plunge him into the abyss below. Three of the soldiers lost their hold and fell. The rest, consisting of some twenty or thirty Spaniards, and a considerable number of Tlascalans, alighted in safety on the other bank.

Hugh's comment about it making even old Díaz's head swim is based on Prescott's footnote, quoting from the *Historia verdadera,* that "his head swam so . . . that he scarcely knew how he got on." The tendency towards exaggeration in Prescott is exemplified in the above passage by the detail about three soldiers falling; they do in Díaz too, but the cost is one broken leg. The precise location of the crossing is unknown, but it is generally accepted that it was over the Amanalco Ravine (de Davila, p. 53), more or less where Hugh and Yvonne are standing.

104.5 [100]   *Spengler.* Oswald Spengler (1880–1936), German philosopher whose *Der Untergang des Abendlandes* (*The Decline of the West*), 1918–22, was widely read between the wars. Spengler argues that civilizations, of which he counted eight so far, pass in a life-cycle from youth through maturity and old age to death, with that of Western Europe being in its last stages. Lowry was attracted not only by Spengler's cyclic view of history, but also by his use of Faustian imagery to define the condition of Western man, "a condition which pictured man as ageing and wasted, but still hoping to comprehend and achieve everything, including the impossible" (Kilgallin, "Faust," p. 29). Spengler's belief that human endeavours cannot prevent the decay of civilizations is very similar to the Consul's belief, p. 311 [309], that "there's a sort of determinism about the fate of nations," and, as Monbet notes, p. 20, there is irony in Hugh citing Spengler, whose cyclic view of history is completely opposed to the communist philosophy of dialectic evolution.

Spengler often criticizes the press (for example, Vol.II, XII.iv, pp. 460–65), arguing that there should be freedom *from* rather than *of* the press. The passage Hugh alludes to (also noted by Jakobsen, p. 73) is from Vol.I, X.vii, p. 360:

> Diatribe belongs necessarily to the "religion of the irreligious" and is the characteristic form that the "cure of souls" takes therein. It appears as the Indian preaching, the Classical rhetoric, and the Western journalism. It appeals not to the best but the most, and it values its means according to the number of successes obtained by them. It substitutes for the old thoughtfulness an *intellectual male-prostitution* by speech and writing, which fills and dominates the halls and market-places of the megalopolis.

105.1 [101] *an English friend fighting in Spain.* In a letter to Albert Erskine (Woodcock, pp. 111–12), Lowry identifies this friend as "John 'Volunteer in Spain' Summerfield [*sic*], who survived after all." John Sommerfield, author of *Volunteer in Spain* (1937), had served with the International Brigade at the battle for University City, where the De Quincey episode took place (see note **105.4**).

105.2 [101] *Franco.* Generalissimo Franciso Franco y Bahamonde (1892–1975), Spanish commander of the fascist forces during the Spanish Civil War and thereafter dictator of Spain until his death. He had commanded the Spanish Foreign Legion in Morocco and became chief of staff in 1935. Considered dangerous, he was sent to govern the Canaries in 1936, but with the growth of dissent upon the mainland, he flew to Morocco, landed troops in Spain, and with the aid of Hitler and Mussolini overthrew the Republican forces in the Civil War, establishing a right-wing dictatorship. Politically astute, he kept Spain neutral in World War II, though he displayed marked pro-Axis sympathies and consolidated his power in the peninsula. On his death, Spain reverted to the monarchy which Franco had intimated he would restore as early as 1947.

105.3 [101]   *University City.* The grim reality of this University City is in marked contrast with the Consul's "ideal University" in Tortu, p. 61 [56]. In November 1936 *Ciudad Universitaria,* the university area on a hilltop in the northwest of Madrid, was the centre of fierce fighting in the Battle of Madrid between the attacking Nationalist forces led by General Mola and the entrenched Republican populace. Thanks largely to the support and experience of the International Brigades fighting alongside them, the poorly armed Republicans were able to hold out against a vastly superior force with the result that there was no decisive outcome. Madrid remained for some time under siege, and the Republicans denied the Nationalists the important victory they sought.

105.4 [101]   *De Quincey.* Thomas De Quincey (1785–1859), English essayist, critic, and opium addict. He is best known for his *Confessions of an Opium Eater* (1822), an account of his early years and gradual addiction to opium and of the tumultuous dreams and dreadful nights for eight years before he largely broke the habit. John Sommerfield, however, was reading De Quincey's *Recollections of the Lakes and Lake Poets,* which is even more incongruous in the given situation. In *Volunteer in Spain,* p. 150, Sommerfield describes how he and a number of others (including John Cornford) were holed up in Philosophy and Letters, behind bullet-proof barricades of Indian metaphysics and early nineteenth-century German philosophy, and how he found a set of Everyman classics left behind:

> On a cold morning I found De Quincey's Lake Poets and rolled myself up in a carpet and read voraciously; the day passed in a stupor, I was with Wordsworth and Coleridge, in another place, another time. Twice we had shelled the buildings opposite and twice I had to leave my book to shoot at the Falangists who popped out like rabbits when the shells burst.

In his letter to Albert Erskine (Woodcock, pp. 111–12), Lowry says that the De Quincey episode is mentioned in *Volunteer in Spain* as well as in a letter to himself, but that "De Quincey comes in also because of Mr Quincey and knocking on the gate bit" (see note **140.1**).

105.5 [101] *a dog named Harpo.* After Harpo Marx (1888–1964), with Chico and Groucho, one of the three celebrated Marx brothers, zany comedians and stars of such inspired nonsense as *Animal Crackers* (1930), *Monkey Business* (1931), *Duck Soup* (1933), *A Night at the Opera* (1935), and *A Day at the Races* (1937). Chico played the piano eccentrically and spoke with an impossible Italian accent; Groucho had a painted moustache and a cigar and made most of the wisecracks; Harpo (real name Arthur) was the child-like mute who played the harp. Harpo had visited the Soviet Union in 1935, where he had given a most successful performance, prefaced by a long speech by a Soviet producer on the role of humour in society, the social significance of Hollywood, and the real meaning of Marx (Fischer, p. 300).

105.6 [101] *another friend who went to China.* The reference to China is a reminder that a similar civil war was being fought there between nationalist and communist forces, but Lowry's allusion is specifically to a Cambridge contemporary, Julian Bell, nephew of Virginia Woolf and son of Clive Bell, who had been teaching English at Wu Han University in Central China on the outbreak of civil war, but who, "harassed as much by amorous complications in China as by what he thought was his conscience" (*The Last Great Cause,* p. 50), had returned to England in March 1937. Although his family tried to dissuade him from joining up and finally prevailed upon him to take on a noncombatant role, he nevertheless insisted on going to Spain with the medical aid detachment. He drove an ambulance until it was smashed by a bomb, upon which he went as a stretcher-bearer to the front, where he was killed by an artillery shell, 18 July 1937, aged twenty-nine, having been in Spain only one month.

105.7 [101] *about a year before it started.* The Spanish Civil War broke out on 16 July 1936 when army garrisons arose throughout Spain to support Franco. It drew to its close early in 1939, with the complete triumph of Franco's Nationalist forces.

105.8 [101] *the Loyalists.* Another name for the Republicans, that is, those loyal to the elected government of the Republic, as opposed to the Fascists or Nationalists under Franco; neither side had much time for the Monarchists supporting the exiled King Alfonso XIII, the Separatists wanting home rule in Catalonia and the Basque country, or the Anarchists, who rejected everybody else.

105.9 [101] *a sort of "freezing" of culture.* The Consul has also been reading Spengler (see note **104.5**). Though the metaphor itself is not used by

Spengler, he defines culture as an organism, blooming and dying when its
soul has actualized the sum of its possibilities, and "hardening," "mortify-
ing," or "congealing" (the words are Spengler's) at a certain level of civilization (Vol.I, I.III.vii, p. 106). Spengler talks of the "irreversibility" of history
(Vol.I, IV.i, p. 119), implying that each great cycle of history has its destiny
that cannot be altered.

A revealing passage in Conrad Aiken's *Ushant,* p. 351, not only reveals
what Geoffrey means by a "freezing" of culture, but also suggests that
Lowry took his argument (as he did the political views expressed by the
Consul at the end of Ch. 10) from Aiken rather than directly from Spengler.
Aiken recalls a political argument with Lowry and reflects:

> Revolutions were a waste both of time and human material; — you lost a
> hundred or more years only to find yourself just where you'd begun. A
> revolution was an attempt to freeze society on a particular level, and
> this was itself stultifying, no matter what the level might be. If the Nazis
> had frozen theirs on a slightly higher level than the Russians, with a
> shade less destruction of its living inheritance of culture, well, that
> made it a trifle less wasteful, but that was the best that could be said
> for it.

106.1 [102]   *the Madrid show.* In general terms, the Siege of Madrid,
which lasted from October 1936 until virtually the end of the war in March
1939, when the Republican populace, half-starved and completely out of
supplies and munitions, was forced to surrender to the Nationalist forces;
specifically, the early part of that siege, towards the end of 1936, when a
well-equipped Nationalist army of some twenty thousand, supported by
German and Italian tanks and aircraft, tried to take Madrid by force, but in
the Battles of Madrid and University City (see note **105.3**), an enormous but
ill-armed urban mass, supported by some Russian weaponry and by the
International Brigades, held out against them.

106.2 [102]   *Brihuega.* Brihuega is the village in Guadalajara Province,
central Spain, some fifty miles northeast of Madrid, in the vicinity of which
the Battle of Guadalajara took place in March 1937. Italian forces on the
Nationalist side, trying to capture the town of Guadalajara to facilitate the
advance on Madrid, met with stiff Republican opposition, particularly
from the International Brigades (which also included an Italian division),
were crushingly defeated, and lost some two thousand men. The battle, a
morale booster for the Republicans, effectively held up the advance on
Madrid for some months, and much of the area remained in Loyalist hands

until the close of hostilities. As Yvonne seems to sense, Hugh feels somewhat guilty about not having been there at the time, the word "heel" again expressing a sense of betrayal (see note **51.4**).

106.3 [102] *he meticulously dropped his ravaged cigarette down the ravine.* An action summing up the futility of the war, which consigns so many men to the abyss (see note **52.4**).

106.4 [102] *¿Cui bono?* L. "To whom the good" or, more commonly (as Hugh translates the words, p. 121 [117]), "What's the good?" The words were made famous by Cicero, quoting in his *Second Philippic* from Lucius Cassius, who in a trial for murder had instructed a jury to enquire who would benefit by the crime. Hugh's cynicism ("the noble army of pimps and experts") is designed to throw Yvonne off the scent.

106.5 [102] *since they got the Internationals out.* In September 1936, the Russian ambassador in Madrid suggested that aid be given to the Republicans in the form of volunteers raised internationally by foreign communist parties (though also including non-communists), who would be organized by the Comintern (the Communist International) to form an international Red Army giving direct military assistance to the Spanish Republicans. Thousands of volunteers were raised in many different countries; they travelled to Albacete in Murcia, where they were organized into battalions along roughly national lines, given basic training, and armed. The International Brigades bore a heavy part of the fighting at Brihuega, Madrid, and the Ebro, but by 1938, with the Nationalist forces clearly in the ascendancy and horrific tales emerging from Spain, the flow of volunteers dried up. Following the Munich agreement of September 1938 (see note **103.2**) and Stalin's growing understanding with Hitler, it was decided that all foreign volunteers should be pulled out, and in September–October 1938, with the Battle of the Ebro still unresolved, the brigades were officially withdrawn. Despite Hugh's bitterness, it is unlikely that the Munich agreement in fact "crimped" the Ebro offensive.

106.6 [102] *before Chamberlain went to Godesburg.* Bad Gödesberg, a spa outside Bonn in West Germany, was the scene of a preliminary conference between Chamberlain and Hitler on 22 September 1938, leading to the Munich pact of 30 September (see note **103.2**). As Jakobsen notes, p. 74, Hugh has confused the date of the meeting at Gödesberg with that of Munich, but what he says is true in substance: at Gödesberg effective agreement, ratified at Munich, was reached on the fate of Czechoslovakia, and Chamberlain also agreed that despite the withdrawal of the International

Brigades from Spain, Italian forces on the Fascist side could stay on.

106.7 [102]   *with half the last bunch of volunteers still rotting in gaol* [*sic*] *in Perpignan.* Perpignan, in southern France near the Spanish border, was the logical point of entry into Republican Spain, and most of the volunteers arriving overland were funnelled through it. Because of its proximity to Spain and its large Spanish population, it was an important centre for refugees, intrigue, and arms smuggling. On 7 August 1936 a declaration of non-intervention was made by a number of countries, including Britain, and on 8 August France closed the frontier to the export of war materials. By February 1937 it was illegal to volunteer for Spain in all of the non-intervention countries, and many who tried were arrested and imprisoned in France on their way to the front. Perpignan was also an internment centre for the retreating Loyalist forces in the latter stages of the war; many former Loyalists were in fact interned for years.

106.8 [102]   *an A.B.'s ticket.* An A.B. is an able bodied seaman, that is, one whose service record and demonstrable skills have raised him above the rank of ordinary seaman. Although the rank of A.B. is so documented on a seaman's card, Hugh's use of "ticket" is slightly unusual, since that usually implies the certificate of an officer, or even master. It would not automatically entitle him to act as a "quartermaster," whose duties involve steering, signalling, and the keeping of logs.

106.9 [102]   *Galveston. . . . Vera Cruz. . . . Havana . . . Nassau . . . the West Indies . . . São Paulo. . . . Trinidad.* Having missed getting a berth in Galveston, the deep-water port of southern Texas some forty-five miles from Houston, Hugh anticipates leaving Vera Cruz, Mexico's major port of the gulf, and travelling to Havana, the capital of Cuba and a major deep-water port; then on to Nassau, the capital of the Bahamas; and from there southwards past the West Indies to Venezuela, calling by Trinidad, the southernmost and largest of the Lesser Antilles; and from there perhaps going as far south as São Paulo, in southeast Brazil. The "real fun" he anticipates coming out of Trinidad may be a reference to the island's volatile racial situation, but it is probably just a pun on the word "Trinity" (unless, as seems horribly likely, Lowry intends a very private allusion to Charles Fort's *Wild Talents,* p. 931, which mentions an epidemic of insidious hydrophobia, "caused by mad vampire bats," as taking place in Trinidad).

107.1 [103]   *the S.S. Noemijolea.* Presumably the British ship, the *Noemi-Julia,* which was registered with the Republican Agency in England to deliver merchandise to several ports in the Republican zone. Between July

1936 and February 1939 she was engaged in transferring weapons and ammunition between Marseilles and Spain, often coming under heavy Nationalist attack (on 23 August 1937 she was bombed by Nationalist aeroplanes but managed to reach Barcelona). Details of the *Noemi-Julia* may be found in J. L. A. Nassaes's *La marina Italiana en la Guerra de Espana*.

The S.S. *Noemijolea* is ostensibly bound for Freetown, Sierra Leone, her declared cargo of antimony and coffee concealing her true purpose. She is in fact bringing munitions to the Loyalist forces in Spain (who were indeed hard-pressed and were almost on the point of final surrender). Many of the arms bought in the United States were carried in this kind of devious way to avoid flagrant breaches of official policies of non-intervention, and after the French had closed the frontier (see note **106.7**), access by sea was the most practical way. Hugh's voyage was probably suggested by that of the unfortunate *Mar Cantábrico* (see note **301.7**), which was captured in Franco's blockade, and to that extent his chances seem grim.

The *Noemijolea* is to proceed to Tzucox, that mysterious port on the Yucatán coast (see note **9.4.c**: this second allusion was a very late addition to the manuscripts, pencilled in on UBC 10–18, p. 12). She will presumably pick up more arms; after which she will sail from the Caribbean to the Atlantic via the Windward (separating Cuba from Haiti) and Crooked Passages (a deep channel in the Bahama Islands). Her first landfall on the east side of the Atlantic will be the Madeira Islands, a volcanic archipelago belonging to Portugal, some six hundred miles south of Spain; then, avoiding Port Lyautey in the Rabat area of northwest Morocco (a Nationalist stronghold), she will pass through the Straits of Gibraltar into the Mediterranean Sea. The Capes de Gata, de Palos, and de la Nao are the three most conspicuous promontories of the Spanish mainland on the port side as the ship proceeds northwards past the Pityusa Isles (Iviza and Formentara, both held by the Nationalists), along the Gulf of Valencia, past the town of San Carlos de la Rápita on the delta of the Ebro River, and along the rocky Costa de Garraf, southwest of Barcelona (an area which affords few natural harbours). Her cargo will be discharged while still at sea near Vallcarca (the Penguin spelling is wrong), part of the municipality of Sitges on the Garraf coast some twenty miles south of Barcelona (which was by November 1938 one of the last strongholds of Republican resistance).

107.2 [103] *Franco's blockade.* As part of the policy of non-intervention, Britain, France, Germany, and Italy agreed in January 1938 to initiate a blockade of Spanish waters, and patrols became effective from April 1937. The blockade was not directed in principle on behalf of the Nationalists, but as the Republicans were most in need of food and arms, Franco was determined to make it effective, and there were a number of incidents in which Nationalist gunboats forcibly took over or fired upon ships trying to run the blockade.

107.3 [103]   *Potato Firmin or Columbus in reverse.* Since huge profits could be made by shipowners willing to run the blockade, many were prepared to take the risk, but the British blockade of the northern Spanish coast and its rather dubious standing in both international law of the sea and public opinion made attempts to bring supplies to the Republicans a complex issue. As Thomas notes, p. 622, merchantmen, their cargoes paid for and rotting, became impatient:

> Three vessels, all commanded by Welsh captains named Jones (therefore differentiated from their cargoes as "Potato Jones," "Corn Cob Jones," and "Ham and Eggs Jones"), gained notoriety by pretended attempts to set out from port. "Potato Jones," whose potatoes concealed weapons and whose motives were material, gained a sudden, if unmerited reputation, from a series of breezy answers to a reporter of the *Evening News,* as a rough salt in the Conradian tradition.

Hugh imagines himself at the wheel of the *Noemijolea* like Potato Jones of the *Marie Llewellyn* running the blockade and, like Jones, possibly being turned back (Jones eventually delivered his cargo in Valencia). The reference to Columbus, who sailed the other way from Palos, suggests Joshua Slocum's *Sailing Alone around the World* (1900), Ch. 5: "Columbus, in the Santa Maria, sailing these seas more than four hundred years before, was not so happy as I, nor so sure of success in what he had undertaken."

107.4 [104]   *the lee scuppers . . . the forecastle head . . . one bell . . . white to blue.* Nautical terminology:
(a) *lee scuppers.* Scuppers, or vents, in the side of the ship, on the lee or downwind side, to drain waters from the deck.
(b) *chipping a winch.* Removing old paint from the winch used for hauling up the anchor or hoisting cargo.
(c) *the forecastle heads.* Pronounced "fo'c'sle," the forecastle is the forward part of a ship, traditionally the location of the sailors' quarters; so called from the foremost of the two castle-like structures set on the decks of medieval vessels to command enemy decks. Being raised and forward, the head or upper portion of the forecastle is a usual place for a look-out.
(d) *one bell.* Various bells are struck at half-hour intervals to mark off the passage of the watches on spells of duty; one bell signals the end of the

first half hour of a new watch, eight bells the end of the watch. Thus, the one bell here means either 8:30 A.M., 12:30 P.M., or 4:30 P.M.

(e) *white to blue.* The change from white to blue uniform, here signifying a change from summer to winter, also indicates the transition from "foreign" to "home" waters. The choice of colours goes back to George II (who admired them upon a mistress), but white uniform for the tropics became regulation only in 1885.

108.1 [104] *there ain't no brigade no mo'.* Hugh's words casually adopt the lilt of the Negro spiritual, "I ain't gonna dream my Lord no mo'," which begins:

> Oh, you cain't get to heaven on roller skates
> 'Cause you'll roll right past dem pearly gates,
> I ain't gonna dream my Lord no mo'.

The dream which was once embodied in the International Brigades has been shattered by their forced withdrawal a few weeks earlier (see note **106.5**).

108.2 [104] *the Western Ocean.* Since the time of Plato, a traditional name for the Atlantic Ocean beyond the pillars of Hercules.

108.3 [104] *the paths of glory lead but to the grave.* From "Elegy in a Country Churchyard" (1750), by Thomas Gray (1716–71). The poem is a melancholy reflection upon thoughts called up in the poet's mind as he looks at the graves of those whose humble lot was so different from that of the great, but whose final fate is identical (ll. 33–36):

> The boast of heraldry, the pomp of power,
>   And all that beauty, all that wealth e'er gave,
> Awaits alike the inevitable hour.
>   The paths of glory lead but to the grave.

108.4 [104] *his full mental height of six feet two (he was five feet eleven).* Joseph Conrad's *Lord Jim* begins with a description of Jim: "He was an inch, perhaps two, under six feet." Both Jim and Hugh fall that slight bit short of heroic stature (according to tradition, Christ alone was exactly six feet tall).

108.5 [104] *a model dairy farm.* Cuernavaca's growth has swallowed up areas of open countryside such as those described here, and if there was once a model farm in Acapantzingo (as seems highly likely), all traces of it have long disappeared. The agrarian reforms initiated in Cárdenas's presidency (see note **111.**4) included provisions for the establishment of a number of agricultural colleges and model farms on which workers from the ejidos could learn the skills to benefit their communities. For Yvonne, however, the farm remains as a model of what could be possible on Geoffrey's island in British Columbia: "A real farm, you know, with cows and pigs and chickens—and a red barn and silos and fields of corn and wheat," p. 122 [118]. However, the idyllic picture of the dairy, and the sweet smell of milk and vanilla, is immediately ruined by the unwitting images of cuckoldry in Hugh's references to Texas longhorns, stags, and greater kudus.

109.1 [105]   *the Paseo de la Reforma . . . the statue of Pasteur.* The Paseo de la Reforma, the best known avenue in Mexico City, runs from the western limits of ˋthe city, through the fashionable Lomas district and Chapultepec Park, into the heart of town. Although the street was designed and built for Maximilian as a royal carriageway, it was later named for the Reform Movement led by Juárez in the 1850's. The street is lined with statues; that of Pasteur is located at Reforma and Insurgentes (near Paris), one of the busiest intersections in the city. It commemorates Louis Pasteur (1822–95), the French chemist whose research into fermentation and infectious disease led to the science of immunology (Hugh's mind has leapt from the model dairy farm to the statue by way of "pasteurization"). The statue was donated by the French community of Mexico City to commemorate the centenary of Mexican independence, 1810–1910.

109.2 [105]   *Muy incorrecto.* Yvonne may be criticizing Hugh's boots, her own slacks (women in Mexico do not dress this way), or the fact of their riding together without her husband's knowledge.

109.3 [105]   *an affectionate scrubbed woolly white dog.* As Hugh reflects, p. 110 [106], this dog is very different from "those dreadful creatures that seemed to shadow his brother everywhere." The dog, trained to detect snakes, is part of the earthly paradise through which Hugh and Yvonne will soon be riding, an innocent and idyllic landscape which, despite the ominous shadow of the Alcapancingo Prison, is a reminder of what has been lost.

109.4 [105]   *the high prison walls.* The State Penitentiary of Morelos was fairly recent in 1938 (the old prison had been in the Cortés Palace); it is an ominous looking building on the Atlacomulco Road, surrounded by barbed wire and high towers which would be visible from the Consul's house on the other side of the ravine.

109.5 [106] *Juan Cerillo.* Hugh's Mexican friend who has been with him in Spain. His close resemblance to the dying Indian, p. 245 [243], and the value Hugh places upon such a friendship, underlines the compañero theme (see note **250.1**), but the rather shadowy mode of Juan Cerillo's existence scarcely makes him into a figure of sufficient magnitude to set against the Consul. Juan Cerillo is based upon Lowry's close friendship with a Zapotecan Indian, named in *DATG* as Juan Fernando Martínez (in real life, Juan Fernando Márquez, and in Lowry's essay "Garden of Etla," Fernando Atonalzin), who came to represent for Lowry an ideal of manhood, exemplifying in his personal life "la vida impersonal" which Lowry found so attractive (see note **17.6**).

109.6 [106] *as in gardens.* That is, sidesaddle; the kind of ladylike riding position which one might see in city parks or on horsetrails.

109.7 [106] *Guapa.... Ah, muy hermosa.* Sp. "Dashing.... Ah, very pretty."

110.1 [106] *Wh-wh-wh-wh-wh-wh-wh-wh-wheeee-u.* Juan Cerillo, from whom Hugh has learnt to whistle, is a Zapotecan Indian from the highlands of Oaxaca, and the Zapotecan Indians of the Sierra, like some of the Canary Islanders, have a whistling language known as "chiflío" which enables them to communicate over great distances.

110.2 [106] *withers.* The ridge between the shoulder bones of a horse.

110.3 [106] *the dying fall.* From Shakespeare's *Twelfth Night,* I.i.1–8, when the love-sick Orsino speaks of the pangs of unrequited love:

> If music be the food of love, play on;
> Give me excess of it, that, surfeiting,
> The appetite may sicken and so die.
> That strain again; it had a dying fall;
> O! it came o'er my ear like the sweet south,
> That breathes upon a bank of violets,
> Stealing and giving odour. Enough! no more:
> 'Tis not so sweet now as it was before.

The words are used in T. S. Eliot's "Prufrock," l. 52, and in his "Portrait of a Lady," l. 122, but Lowry more probably has in mind Conrad Aiken's "the dying fall of a ukelele" (*Blue Voyage,* p. 28).

110.4 [106] *two fierce cornucopias.* From L. *cornu copiae,* "horn of plenty," in classical mythology the horn of the goat that suckled Zeus; hence, a horn overflowing with abundant fruits, flowers, and grains. Here, following the implied reference to "the food of love," the horns of the cabrón are an ever-present reminder of how the horn of plenty was undone.

110.5 [106] *a Machiavellian eye.* A look of calculated malevolence. From Nicolo Machiavelli (1469–1527), Florentine diplomat and political theorist, whose famous book *Il Principe* (*The Prince*), which argued that for the establishment and maintenance of authority expediency was more important than morality, gained him a not altogether warranted reputation of one who believed that the ends justify the means. The goat's "words" are very much in the tone of Geoffrey's father, and Hugh's sense of Papa watching his every action does not put him in the least at his ease.

111.1 [107] *allowed for one hour a glimpse of what never was.* A strong suggestion of the earthly paradise (see note **16.3**): a lingering memory of the innocence which cannot be regained since "brotherhood was betrayed" by Hugh's earlier affair with Yvonne.

111.2 [107] *Hugh pictured Juan Cerillo distinctly now, tall.* Zapotecan Indians are rarely taller than 5'6", so Juan Cerillo's height raises him literally as well as figuratively above his fellows; Hugh, it is noted on p. 108 [104], is some inches below "his full mental height of six feet two."

111.3 [107] *the generous help Mexico had actually given.* The Mexican government sent some two million dollars worth of military aid to the Republicans in Spain, but more importantly it was the only Western nation to officially declare itself in support of the Loyalists, to send arms and supplies to Spain, and to welcome Republican refugees when the fighting was over. There was no Mexican battalion among the International Brigades, but a number of Mexican liberals and socialists fought in Spain the way that Juan Cerillo is here described as having done.

111.4 [107] *the Ejido.* Mexico historically had been a land of huge haciendas, or estates, which had combined land monopoly by the few with blatant exploitation of the landless many. Over the centuries, the haciendas frequently had encroached upon or swallowed up the ejidos, or communal lands, of the villages. One of the aims of the Mexican revolution 1910–20 had been agrarian reform, which had been embodied in Article 27 of the 1917 Constitution, but in a rather loose manner, so that in the years before the presidency of Lázaro Cárdenas, 1934–40, token efforts only had been made at redistributing hacienda land to communities and in regulating and financing the ejidos. Under Cárdenas, the process was speeded up and extended considerably: in all, some fifty million acres were reallocated to the villages and to those who actually worked the land. The principle behind the ejido was socialistic (hence the often direct action taken by opposing right-wing groups): the lands were to be held and worked in common, with economic and social control in the hands of ejido administrative committees elected by the ejidatarios themselves. The programme could not have been successfully instituted without the National Bank of Ejidal Credit, which was created by Cárdenas expressly for the purpose of financing loans to enable communities to become self-sufficient and to improve the quality of such things as crops, seeds, fruit trees, farm machinery, water supplies, power, housing, and education. Loans were advanced to some 3,500 ejidos with minimal security (money being advanced on the basis of crop expectations). There were naturally many economic failures, since the success of the venture depended upon the sound functioning of the ejidos, and as well as problems of organization, there was often resistance from suspicious peons as well as from local authorities who saw their power being eroded. Overall, however, the project was a huge success. Farm income and production rose measurably, and the quality of life and habits of eating improved greatly, but above all material improvements was "the change in the people's psychology from servility to independent worker" (Ashby, p. 176). Hugh's admiration for Juan Cerillo and his dissatisfaction with himself stem largely from the other's having engaged himself totally with a "human cause" of demonstrable worth while he is frittering away his time and talents on a doomed enterprise.

111.5 [107] *Zapotecan.* An Indian tribe whose descendants are located in the state of Oaxaca and on the isthmus of Tehuantepec. The Zapotecan civilization reached its height in the fifteenth century, before being subjugated by the Aztecs.

111.6 [107] *Viva el Cristo Rey.* Sp. "Long live Christ the King"; the rallying cry of the pro-church revolutionary forces who had opposed attempts by the state government to subordinate church to state during the nineteenth century; specifically, the cry of the Cristeros, a militant Catholic guerrilla force centred in Jalisco but also active further south (there were three bands in Morelos, but no serious sympathy for the movement). Their rebellion was mainly in support of the church's strike in protest of the enforcement of anti-clerical articles in the constitution, but the activities of some of the bands continued long after that strike was resolved and into the Cárdenas era. Between 1926 and 1929 they attacked many government-run schools and institutions, killing a schoolteacher for every priest shot by the socialists. Their most notorious attack took place on 20 April 1927 when a train was attacked, captured, and set afire with its passengers still on board. Over one hundred men, women, and children died in the blaze. Rumours spread that some of the attackers were dressed in the garb of Catholic priests; the government responded by banishing the highest members of the church hierarchy and forbidding church services. By the end of the month the country was without either priests or services. Graham Greene's *The Power and the Glory* gives one account of this bizarre period in Mexican history.

111.7 [107] *Cárdenas.* Lázaro Cárdenas (1895–1970), president of Mexico from 1934 to 1940, whose term of office saw the introduction of some of the most important legislation in modern Mexican history. He came to the presidency via the military, but unlike his immediate predecessors he refused to be the puppet of strongman Plutarco Elías Calles, who had dominated the previous decade. Instead, Cárdenas removed Calles's supporters from privileged posts and inaugurated a new regime based on socialistic principles of reform. He reorganized the railways, nationalized Mexico's oil wealth (see note **36.1**), initiated wide-ranging agrarian reforms (see note **111.4**), and did much to give the labour movement greater strength, making it abundantly clear that the policy of his administration would be to support organized labour in its efforts to improve the living conditions of the Mexican masses (Ashby, p. 273). His presidency gave Mexico and Mexicans a new self-respect both at home and abroad, but by his opposition to clerical privilege and the entrenched rights of landowners he also created many enemies.

111.8 [107] *the stamps showed archers shooting at the sun.* The 10¢ violet of 1934 (Express Delivery), commemorating Cárdenas's assumption of office (though the 10¢ violet of 1938 is just possible). The stamp depicts an Indian archer shooting upwards, possibly Moctezuma Ilhuicamina, Aztec emperor, 1446–68, whose name means "Angry Lord Who Shoots the Sky." Insofar as the scene depicts an attempt to arrest the progress of the sun across the sky, it points to the futility of Hugh's efforts to stop the Consul from destroying himself.

There may also be an impenetrable mystical significance behind this message. In Frater Achad's *QBL,* p. 111, is the comment: "Stamped with an archer: Q.B.L." (*Q.B.L.* being the Hebrew root "to receive"); and in the Appendix, p. 34, is a further obscure reference: "For had the ARROW = Sagittarius (Ruled by Jupiter) been put on the plane of Jupiter, and the Spirit, Shin, been included in the CENTRE of the TRIAD we should have obtained . . . UNITY."

111.9 [108] *Cuicatlán.* A town in the north of Oaxaca state, in the Sierra some thirty miles northeast of Nochixtlán; a centre of considerable activity in the Revolution. Lowry's friend, Juan Fernando Márquez, had been transferred there from Oaxaca.

112.1 [108] *Juarez.* Benito Juárez (1806–72), president of Mexico, 1857–63 and 1867–72, his terms of office being interrupted by the French intervention of 1864–67 which set the ill-fated Maximilian on the throne. A Zapotec Indian from the state of Oaxaca, Juárez was orphaned at three and set to work as a shepherd boy, but he was rescued by Don Antonio Salaneuva, a Franciscan priest who saw the boy's potential and taught him to read and write (Juárez did not speak Spanish until he was thirteen). Initially trained for the priesthood, Juárez was to become its bitterest foe; after dropping out of the seminary, he worked and educated himself to become a lawyer, then turned to politics to implement his liberal ideals. As president, he relentlessly opposed the conservative policies of the church and, after winning the War of the Reform, 1858–61, initiated a far-reaching series of industrial, legal, and educational reforms that set Mexico well on the way towards economic recovery (the Ley Juárez, abolishing entrenched privilege, has been the basis in principle of most subsequent reforms). Hugh's respect for Juan Cerillo is very similar to that most Mexicans have for Juárez, commonly considered the greatest Mexican president, and the rough similarity between the backgrounds and ideals of the two Zapotecans suggests that the parallel is intended.

112.2 [108] *the Yaquis, the Papagos, the Tomasachics.* Indian tribes of northern Mexico, whose treatment by the Mexican government indeed constitutes a sorry record and whose numbers have declined drastically:
(a) *the Yaquis.* An Indian tribe of the Sonora desertlands, feared in Aztec times as vicious fighters. Their numbers in 1903 were calculated at only twenty thousand after uprisings in the late nineteenth century led to wholesale deportations to the Yucatán as a means of eliminating the troubles permanently. The horrors of the deportations and enforced slavery are described at length in John Kenneth Turner's *Barbarous Mexico,* a book that Lowry has used often. Ch. 2, entitled "The Extermination of the Yaquis" tells how the Yaquis were goaded into war to fight for their lands, of the mass killings and brutalities against the tribe, and of the "final solution" of the Yucatán slave camps and the henequen plantations.
(b) *the Papagos.* A once important tribe of Sonora and Arizona, now confined to a small area at the top of the Gulf of California, their best lands and waters having been expropriated for European haciendas.

Their numbers were fewer than five thousand at the turn of the century. As Turner notes, p. 106: "In like manner have the Mayos of Sonora, the Papagos, the Tomosachics — in fact, practically all the native peoples of Mexico — been reduced to peonage, if not to slavery."

(c) *the Tomasachics.* Despite the above, the Tomosachics were not a tribe but rather the natives of the village of Tomosachic in Chihuahua. Turner notes, p. 109, that following the refusal by the villagers to hand over the paintings of their church to General Lauro Carrillo, an exorbitant tax was levied upon the town, and when the Indians could not pay it, Carrillo took hostages and then attacked, massacring between eight hundred and two thousand Indians.

112.3 [108] *the terrible Valle Nacional.* The details of Juan Cerillo's life are drawn directly from Turner's *Barbarous Mexico,* pp. 53–57. Turner describes Valle Nacional, p. 56, as:

a deep gorge from two to five miles wide and twenty miles long tucked away among almost impassible mountains in the extreme northwestern corner of the state of Oaxaca. Its mouth is fifty miles up the Papaloapan river from El Hule, the nearest railway station, yet it is through El Hule that every human being passes in going to or coming from the Valley.

That is, the valley forms a natural prison, and in the early years of the century it was used as such. Turner states categorically, p. 54, that "Valle Nacional is undoubtedly the worst slave hole in Mexico. Probably it is the worst in the world." Theoretically, it was a plantation centre where peons were employed on a contract labour basis; in practice it was a brutal slave camp, based upon kidnapping, child labour, and ruthless exploitation. Ninety-five per cent of those taken there died in seven months, some fifteen thousand per year — a figure Turner would have found unbelievable had he not been told so by the masters themselves. In a passage directly used by Lowry, Turner comments, p. 67:

The Valle Nacional slave holder has discovered that it is cheaper to buy a slave for $45 [pesos] and work and starve him to death in seven months, and then spend $45 for a fresh slave, than it is to give the first slave better food, work him less sorely and stretch out his life and his toiling hours over a longer period of time.

112.4 [108] *Porfirio Díaz.* Porfirio Díaz (1830–1915), president of Mexico, 1877–80 and 1884–1911. An Indian from Oaxaca, he distinguished himself fighting against the French, 1864–67, and assumed the presidency by overthrowing Lerdo in 1867. For the next thirty-four years he controlled the destiny of Mexico, bringing it forcibly into the modern world by inviting industrialization and overseas investment. He gave Mexico law and order, political stability, and, for the first time since independence, a solvent economy. Railways and roads were built, drainage and sewerage schemes initiated, and oil fields brought into production. Yet the name of Díaz is widely detested because progress was made at such cost to humanity: corruption and bribery throughout the civil service, exploitation of Mexican resources by foreign powers, no freedom of the press, virtual slavery for the uneducated classes, and extravagant displays of luxury and wealth among the rich. The gap between rich and poor had never been wider, and because the costs of modernization had been so great and had caused such widespread discontent, the seeds of insurrection were sown, culminating in the bloody Revolution of 1910–20.

112.5 [108]   *rurales*. A rural police force established under Juárez before the French intervention, 1864–67, when they played a major peacekeeping role. Under Díaz, however, the corps was strengthened considerably, and in addition to its original patrolling function, it was used to guard ore shipments, escort prisoners, support local police forces, and enforce unpopular court decisions. Turner notes that rurales were used to transport and guard slaves in the Valle Nacional (*Barbarous Mexico,* p. 59). Because of their cruelty and ruthless excesses, the rurales were feared and detested by villagers who saw many of their activities as a form of legalized brigandage. The offshoots of that system are still present in *UTV:* with regular police on strike, much of the real power is in the hands of such vigilantes as those who turn up on p. 250 [247].

112.6 [108]   *jefes políticos*. Sp. "political bosses," most of whom, under Díaz, were military men given civic offices in return for services rendered. Turner comments, pp. 58–59:

> A *jefe politico* is a civil officer who rules political districts corresponding to our counties. He is appointed by the president or by the governor of his state and is also mayor, or *presidente,* of the principal town or city in his district. In turn he usually appoints the mayors of the towns under him, as well as all other officers of importance. He has no one to answer to except his governor — unless the national president feels like interfering — and altogether is quite a little Czar in his domain.

The system of appointment encouraged graft and corruption and a capricious administration of justice, but the system of dependent loyalty among the jefes politicos was the basis of Díaz's firmly entrenched position.

112.7 [108] *Huerta.* Victoriano Huerta (1854-1916), president, 1913-14 (see note **49.3**). Although Huerta ousted Madero from power, his authority was resisted in the provinces, and he failed to pacify the country. One of the troubled areas had been the state of Morelos, where Emiliano Zapata (1879-1919) had earlier linked himself with Madero's cause and raised an insurgent army which scored some victories over the federal troops. When relations between Madero and Zapata soured because of Madero's unwillingness to accede immediately to Zapata's call for land reform, the Zapatistas promulgated their Plan de Ayala calling for immediate agrarian and social reform, and armed revolution spread widely through the neighbouring states. After Huerta had taken over from Madero, Zapata angrily rejected Huerta's call for solidarity and scored impressive victories against the federal troops, but when Venustiano Carranza assumed office in March 1917, thousands of federal troops were sent into Morelos, and in some of the bloodiest fighting in the entire civil war, the Zapatistas were beaten back. With Zapata's betrayal and assassination on 10 April 1919, the Morelos insurrection more or less came to an end. Juan Cerillo has almost certainly been fighting with Zapata, whose views on social and land reform were similar to his own, and although the incident of his killing his father seems rather ineptly contrived by Lowry, it epitomizes the sordid conflicts of honour and idealism which characterized that period.

112.8 [108] *must ceaselessly struggle upwards.* An echo of the citation from Goethe's *Faust* placed at the beginning of the novel: "Wer immer strebend sich bemüht, den können wir erlösen." The positive values implicit in this epigraph and embodied in the person of Juan Cerillo (and to a lesser degree in Hugh) are set in deliberate opposition to the Consul's downward fall.

112.9 [108] *What was life but a warfare and a stranger's sojourn?* From the *Meditations* of Marcus Aurelius, Bk. II.17 (translated by A. S. L. Farquarson, vol.I, p. 33):

> Of man's life, his time is a point, his existence a flux, his sensation clouded, his body's entire composition corruptible, his vital spirit an eddy of breath, his fortune hard to predict, his fame uncertain. Briefly, all things of the body, a river; all things of the spirit, dream and delirium; his life a warfare and a sojourn in a strange land, his after-fame oblivion.

Marcus Aurelius Antoninus (121-180 A.D.), Roman emperor 161-180, was the author of *Meditations,* twelve books in Greek expressing the stoic ideal. Man's duty, he argued, is to obey the divine law that resides in his reason, be superior to pains and pleasures, forgive injuries, regard all men as brothers, and await death with equanimity (*OCEL*). The only consolation for man's sojourn in a strange land, his only companion, is philosophy.

112.10 [108] *the tierra caliente of each human soul.* The tierra caliente (Sp. "hot land") is the broad lowland tract along the gulf coast of Mexico associated with high temperatures and malarial fevers (as in Prescott, I.i, p. 10), but the phrase seems to be used here as equivalent to the volcano within each individual.

113.1 [109] *with the divine surety of a Cristoferus.* St. Christopher, the patron saint of travellers, was a man of gigantic stature. He wished to serve the mightiest of masters and sought Christ. He lived alone by a ford where many travellers passed, and one night when he was carrying a child across the river, his burden became so heavy that he could barely get across. The child then told Christopher (whose name means "bearer of Christ") that he had been carrying the weight of the whole world and revealed himself as the Christ. A St. Christopher's medal (sometimes called a "Christoferus") is often worn by travellers.

113.2 [109] *immelmaning.* An Immelman turn, named after Max Immelman, German air ace of World War I, is a manoeuvre in which an aeroplane half-loops to an inside-down position, then half-rolls back to a normal upright flight. It was used by Immelman and other ace fighters to make turns which would gain altitude and take following aeroplanes unexpectedly from behind.

113.3 [109] *a pulquería.* A cantina which sells pulque, the fermented beer-like drink made from the aguamiel or juice of the maguey cactus. Its taste has been variously described as like a sweet and foaming mead or a stale, sweaty sock. Pulque is manufactured and drunk almost exclusively in the Central Highland area of Mexico from Guadalajara to Oaxaca since the pulque maguey does not thrive outside this area and since the complex fermentation process complicates wider distribution. Pulque (Nah. *octli poliuhqui,* from *octli,* "wine," and *poliuhqui,* "decomposed"; misunderstood and simplified by the Spaniards to pulque) was the only alcoholic drink known to the Aztecs, who imposed rigorous strictures against drunkenness but also used the alchohol in religious rites (this possibly accentuates Geoffrey's sense of his drinking as an abuse of his mystic powers). Lowry points out that "Revelations such as that Pulquería, which is a kind of Mexican pub, is also the name of Raskolnikov's mother should doubtless not be taken too seriously" ("LJC," p. 82); meaning, no doubt, that one should be at least aware of the suggestion of crime and punishment.

113.4 [109]   *La Sepultura.* Sp. "the Sepulchre": the underlying association of drinking and death is reinforced by the presence of the horse with number 7 on its rump, the advertisement for *Las Manos de Orlac* (see note **30.4**), and the quixotic windmill on the roof (see note **250.3**). The name alludes to Matthew 23:27: "Woe unto you, scribes and Pharisees, hypocrites! for ye are like unto whited sepulchres, which indeed appear beautiful outward, but are within full of dead men's bones, and of all uncleanness." The pulquería was originally named (UBC 10–18, p. 12), in bad Spanish, "Los Muerte de las Dolorosas" ("The Death of Sorrows"), but the "humorous connotation" of the name La Sepultura is, doubtless, the reference in Turner's *Barbarous Mexico,* pp. 82–83, to the Valle Nacional slave-farm of that name.

113.5 [109]   *your horse doesn't want to drink, Yvonne.* Hugh's words, repeated on p. 114 [110], are an example of Lowry's deft use of the cliché: the proverbial expression "You can lead a horse to water but you cannot make him drink" has ironic reference to the Consul, who, p. 76 [71], had flexed his muscles and announced, "Still strong as a horse, so to speak, strong as a horse!" (a phrase repeated by Hugh, p. 126 [122]). That Yvonne senses the aptness of the cliché is perhaps revealed by her ironic little smile and by her secret amusement, p. 263 [261], when she recalls the incident.

114.1 [110]   *Cimarron.* A 1931 western, produced by William Le Baron and directed by Wesley Ruggles, starring Richard Dix and Irene Dunne, based on the novel by Edna Ferber about the opening of the Cimarron Strip in Oklahoma. The most celebrated western of the early sound era, earning two million dollars and three Academy Awards, it is the sweeping saga of Sabra, a young Kansas girl who weds a wandering poet and gunfighter named Yancey Cravat and moves to Oklahoma during the land rush of 1889. She is deserted by her husband and left to manage the newspaper office they have established. Years later, in 1911, they meet again; she is now a distinguished congresswoman, and he a dying nobody.

114.2 [110]   *Gold Diggers of 1930.* More correctly, *Gold Diggers of 1933,* a remake of the 1929 musical, *Gold Diggers of Broadway,* based on Avery Hopwood's play *The Gold Diggers* about a group of chorus girls in search of rich husbands. There were others in the series (*Gold Diggers of 1935. . . . 1937. . . . in Paris*), "their lethargic plots being more or less compensated for by Busby Berkeley's kaleidoscopic dance ensembles" (Halliwell, p. 298).

114.3 [110]   *Come to Sunny Andalusia.* Particularly ironic in the context of the Spanish Civil War: Andalusia, which embraces eight provinces of the south and southeast of Spain, is renowned for its glorious sunshine and resort towns, but it was the scene of heavy fighting during the early part of the war when most of the area fell to the Nationalists. The name of the travelogue (not listed in the B.F.I. catalogue) is probably based on the "Come to sunny Spain" poster put up in the university library, Madrid, as described in John Sommerfield's *Volunteer in Spain,* pp. 150–51: at the end of the afternoon, there was an appalling crash and the room was thick with dust and smoke, a hole appearing where the "sunny Spain" poster had been.

114.4 [110]   *the Peter Lorre movie. Las Manos de Orlac* ("The Hands of Orlac"), currently showing at Sr. Bustamente's cinema (see note **30.4**).

114.5 [110]   *convolvulus.* The *convolvulaceae* are known to have intoxicating semi-narcotic powers and may have been used in the religious rituals of some Mexican Indian tribes. The seeds of two species, *rivea corymbosa* and *ipomoea violacea,* are sources of hallucinogenic drugs. It is the serpentine plant on p. 102 [98]: "a flower bed that was completely strangled by a coarse green vine." Because it is a climbing plant that grows parasite-like and lives on other trees, it is also the symbol of Hugh, a "serpent" in the garden.

115.1 [111]   *Judas . . . that Madrugada . . . thirty pieces of silver.* The Spanish word *madrugada* simply means "dawn," but Hugh is using it in the sense "the hour before dawn, the last hours of the condemned" (*DATG,* p. 172); in the Spanish Civil War the word was invariably associated with the shooting of prisoners of war at dawn. Here the reference is to the first Good Friday in the Garden of Gethsemane. Judas betrayed Christ for thirty pieces of silver and then hanged himself; Hugh imagines his feelings of guilt for having betrayed Geoffrey are very similar to those of Judas. Although Lowry claimed that "Any resemblance is purely coincidental" (Woodcock, p. 112), he may have got the idea for this passage from Dorothy Wellesley's "The Morning After," which concludes:

> Judas Iscariot, sun half arisen,
> Went out in the gloom.
> Beautiful Judas Tree,
> April in bloom.

115.2 [111]   *what is that to us, see thou to that.* From Matthew 27:3–5, where Judas returns to the chief priests and elders ("the bastardos") repenting too late:

Then Judas, which had betrayed him, when he saw that he was condemned, repented himself, and brought again the thirty pieces of silver to the chief priests and elders.

Saying, I have sinned in that I have betrayed the innocent blood. And they said, What is that to us? see thou to that.

And he cast down the pieces of silver in the temple, and departed, and went and hanged himself.

115.3 [111]   *the future-corruptive serpent.* In an obvious sense, a reference to the serpent of the Garden of Eden, whose presence prefigured the corruption and fall of man; here, the temptation Hugh feels to re-enact his previous betrayal of Geoffrey with Yvonne (whose very name suggests Eve); in a wider sense, man's capacity to corrupt his future by almost wilfully choosing the path which leads to his own destruction.

In earlier drafts the snake had been a twig on the pathway, and Lowry had used the phrase "this little twig of suspicion," noting on the manuscript that it was "a pinch from a poem in Poetry" (Pottinger, p. 77). The reference appears to be to a poem by M. Jean Prussing called "September 2, 1939" in *Poetry* 55 (1939–40): 67.

> What we have feared
> assumes dimension and a name;
> the long shadow emerges from the wall;
> the smoke is flame.
>
> So wind we heard in elm tree branches
> is a voice after all;
> so corners wake,
> and stairways speak,
> and the twisted stick becomes the snake.

On p. 131 [127], the Consul sees a little snake and thinks it is a twig (his mistake anticipating his later reference to Hugh as a snake in the grass).

115.4 [111]   *Be Mexico.* Mexico is summed up, in Hugh's mind, by the national emblem depicting the eagle whose talons grasp the serpent (see note **49.5**). The infernal paradise of Mexico, Lowry rightly thought, was ideally suited to the "drama of man's struggle between the powers of darkness and light"; it is "a kind of timeless symbol of the world on which we can place the Garden of Eden" ("LJC," p. 67). Hugh's struggle is to resist the temptation represented by the serpent, the urge to betray his brother with Yvonne.

115.5 [111]   *Have you not passed through the river?* Hugh's sense of the irrevocability of the past compresses a number of allusions: the dictum of Heraclitus (c. 540–480 B.C.), who said "It is not possible to step twice into the same river" (*Fragment* 91); the river of Lethe, whose waters were drunk by departing spirits that they might forget their past; and the Rubicon, the small river in northern Italy forming the boundary of Gaul, across which Julius Caesar took the irrevocable step in 49 B.C. to begin civil war with Pompey.

115.6 [111]   *a Gila monster.* From Gila, a river in Arizona: a stout sluggish poisonous lizard with a short stumpy tail and a body covered with beadlike scales arranged in rings of black and orange found in the desert regions of the southwestern U.S.A. and Mexico.

116.1 [112]   *what might have been a French château.* The Cervecería Quauhnahuac, like the prison, is on lands that were once part of the estate of Maximilian and Carlota and which, had fate decreed otherwise, "might have been" still part of that lost Eden. It is very likely that Lowry intends a punning allusion to the Château d'If off the coast of Marseilles. In Ch. 8 of Alexandre Dumas's *The Count of Monte Cristo,* the prisoner Dantès is brought to the "black and frowning rock" and consigned to the castle's dungeons. The Château d'If is mentioned twice in Lowry's letters (*SL,* pp. 15 and 29), and Hugh hears the noise of the brewery, p. 118 [115], as *"dungeons: dungeons: dungeons."*

116.2 [113]   *an ostiole.* More correctly an *ostiolo,* from L. *ostiolum,* "a little hole"; hence, simply, a hole or opening into the brewery through its wall.

117.1 [113]   *some engine of destruction.* The armadillo (of the order *Edentata*), is a lower order of mammal, but it is not, despite its armour and reptilian aspect, an evolutionary anachronism. Lowry's concern here is to make a general comparison between his infernal machine (see note **212.3**) and the entire process of evolution, which after countless eons of struggle, mutation, and survival seems to have culminated in this machine-like animal.

117.2 [113]   *General Winfield Scott . . . the ravines of the Cerro Gordo.* Winfield Scott (1786–1866) was the American general and leader of the U.S. Army of Occupation in the Spanish-American war of 1847, which confirmed the United States's title to Texas and cost Mexico huge Californian and New Mexican territories as well. Scott was renowned as a bold fighter and daring strategist, but his attack on Vera Cruz, 9 March 1847, took the lives of innocent civilians, and his name is despised in Mexico (this tends to de-

flate Hugh's posturing a little). The Cerro Gordo is a mountain pass
between Jalapa and Vera Cruz where Mexican troops under Santa Anna
were firmly entrenched to halt Scott's advance from Vera Cruz to the capital. Scott noted the possibility of bypassing the Mexicans on the left flank,
and while a small force feigned attack from the front, the bulk of the
Americans fell upon the Mexicans from the rear with devastating results.
Hugh may be confusing Scott with another general of the Mexican-
American war, Zachary Taylor, who was more likely to have ridden in the
distinctive manner described, leg athwart the pommel. Scott ("Old Fuss and
Feathers") was an older, fatter general, who could not have adopted such a
position in the saddle.

117.3 [113] *W. H. Hudson . . . found out to his cost.* William Henry
Hudson (1841–1922), English naturalist and writer, whose early years spent
in South America left an indelible mark on his life and writing. His works
include *The Purple Land* (1885); *British Birds* (1895); *Green Mansions*
(1904); *Afoot in England* (1909); and *Far Away and Long Ago* (1918). He
also wrote many pamphlets and monographs on behalf of the Society for
the Protection of Birds, and Hyde Park Bird Sanctuary was established in
1925 in his memory. Hugh is referring to Ch. 4 of *Far Away and Long Ago:
A History of My Early Life* where Hudson describes how an armadillo,
seeking to escape the fumes which plantation workers were pumping down
holes to kill rats, bolted from its earth and began digging vigorously to
escape by burying itself in the soil:

> Neither men nor dogs had seen him, and I at once determined to cap-
> ture him unaided by any one and imagined it would prove a very easy
> task. Accordingly I laid hold of his black bone-cased tail with both
> hands and began tugging to get him off the ground, but couldn't move
> him. He went on digging furiously, getting deeper and deeper into the
> earth, and I soon found that instead of my pulling him out he was pull-
> ing me in after him. It hurt my small-boy pride to think that an animal
> no bigger than a cat was going to beat me in a trial of strength, and this
> made me hold on more tenaciously than ever and tug and strain more
> violently, until not to lose him I had to go flat down on the ground. But
> it was all for nothing: first my hands, then my aching arms were carried
> down into the earth, and I was forced to release my hold and get up to
> rid myself of the mould he had been throwing up into my face and all
> over my head, neck, and shoulders.

As Jakobsen notes, p. 76 (also citing this passage), "The armadillo's determination to disappear into the ground is as absolute as the Consul's pursuit

of self-destruction. If their purposes are crossed, both will pull another person with them."

119.1 [115] *Tepalzanco.* Probably Teopanzolco, an area of Cuernavaca near the railway station and the site of an ancient Tlahuican pyramid. The Tomalín bus described here and in Ch. 8 would pass just south of the area, but an alternative route to Cuautla via Tepotzlán would pass to the north of the station and pyramid.

119.2 [115] *Parián. . . . the old capital of the state. . . . a huge monastery there . . . rather like Oaxaca in that respect.* Although Lowry's Parián is a fictional place, it has the attributes of a number of distinctly recognizable places:
(a) *Chapultepec.* In *DATG,* p. 164, Lowry describes a journey to the bull-throwing at Chapultepec, the waterfall that used to be there, and the incident of the dying Indian which was to form the core of *UTV;* the route taken by the Tomalín bus is recognizably that to Chapultepec.
(b) *Cuautla.* Not only is Cuautla the right kind of distance from Cuernavaca to fit the bus journey undertaken in Ch. 8, on a continuation of the route beyond Chapultepec, but it was also, from 11 May 1874 until 1 January 1876, the state capital of Morelos (de Davila, p. 141).
(c) *Amecameca.* The town of Amecameca is *under* the volcanoes and near the state line (see p. 325 [324]) in a way that Cuernavaca, Cuautla, and Oaxaca are not.
(d) *Tepotzlán.* An ancient ruined Dominican convent at Tepotzlán may well be in part the origin of that in Parián.
(e) *Oaxaca.* In *DATG,* p. 121, Lowry tells of his fears of critics trying to pin down his geography: "They would suppose too that he had got the geography wrong due to his lack of observation, whereas in truth this was because that part of his terrain that was not wholly imaginative was equally based upon the city of Oaxaca and sus anexas." There is in Oaxaca, right beside the state museum and the Church of Santo Domingo, a large ex-monastery, once part of the church, but now (as in Lowry's day) the headquarters for the Oaxaqueñan military forces. In Parián a ruined monastery forms the headquarters for the Unión Militar (*UTV,* p. 340 [339]).

120.1 [116] *It was built by you English.* The Mexico City to Cuernavaca line is, strictly speaking, part of the Mexican Central system, a standard gauge line built by the cheaper American methods rather than by the British. Lowry has in mind the Mexican Southern Railway, 228 miles long, running between the cities of Puebla and Oaxaca. It had been originally contracted in 1881 to an American firm, but on their failing to meet the demands was reallocated in 1886 to the British firm of Read, Campbell & Co., who, despite an outcry about governmental patronage of foreigners, used British capital and British materials to complete by 1892 an excellent job through country that was an engineering nightmare. Telegraph lines from Mexico to Oaxaca had been put through by 1868, but after the line was built they were replaced with others following the tracks (Lowry's details seem to imply an ominous contrast of the leftward sweep of the railway against the direct route of the telegraph lines). The story about the British engineers taking the roundabout route because they were paid by the kilometre is probably apocryphal. Lowry alludes to it again in *DATG*, p. 76, in relation to the Oaxaca line, and in a letter to Conrad Aiken (*SL*, p. 18), he tells the same story of the railroad north from Mexico City.

120.2 [116]   *Punch*. The well-known English satirical magazine, established 1841, which would relish a story of the above kind. The magazine was named from the clownish figure of the Punch and Judy shows, hence the echo of Pierrot, p. 24 [20], and Harlequin, p. 49 [44]. Punch, or Poonch, in Kashmir, is a city and district in Jammu province to the southwest of Srinagar between the Jhelum river and West Pakistan. With a large Moslem population but a tradition of Hindu rule, it has long been a troubled land.

121.1 [117]   *Dr Guzmán*. The name was originally Gomez (UBC 7–1, p. 17). Although Guzmán is a common enough name in Mexico, Lowry's change designates one of the more infamous figures of the conquest — Nuño Beltrán de Guzmán, conqueror of New Galicia and founder of Guadalajara, whose treatment of the Indians made his name a byword for cruelty. The allusion may constitute Lowry's private revenge upon the Cuernavaca doctor who had prescribed a like routine for him.

121.2 [117]   *Papa*. Sp. "Pope" or "potato"; the first instance of Hugh's nickname for Geoffrey, suggesting not only the Consul's role *in loco parentis* (a role not unlike that of the older Haydn to Mozart, or Aiken to Lowry), but also anticipating the inevitable death of the pope (see note **233.4**). Papa was also the name given by some chroniclers, including Díaz, to the Aztec and other Indian priests.

122.1 [118]   *Maybe he's a black magician*. Black magic (as opposed to white) is defined in MacGregor-Mathers's *The Sacred Magic*, p. xxv:

In Magic, that is to say, the Science of the Control of the Secret forces of Nature, there have always been two great schools, the one great in

Good, the other in Evil; the former the Magic of Light, the latter that of Darkness; the former usually depending on the knowledge and invocation of the Angelic natures, the latter on the method of evocation of the Demonic races. Usually the former is termed White Magic, as opposed to the latter, or Black Magic.

The Sacred Magic also points out, p. 56, that the great point of black magic is "generally the forming of a Pact with an Evil Spirit." Though the entire business of black magic was a late addition to the manuscripts of *UTV,* the Consul's interest in such matters aligns him with necromancers such as Faust and Faustus. The question of how much the Consul actually knows about "all this alchemy and cabbala business" remains, however, an open one.

122.2 [118]   *white sculpturings of clouds, like billowing concepts in the brain of Michelangelo.* Michelangelo Buonarroti (1475-1564), often considered the greatest of renaissance painters and sculptors, whose most celebrated works include the paintings on the ceilings of the Sistine Chapel; the *Last Judgment* behind the altar of the same chapel; the *Pieta* in St. Peter's; the statue of David in the Florentine Academy; the figure of Moses in the church of San Pietro in Vincoli, Rome; and the tomb of Pope Julius II. Hugh seems to have in mind the story of how Michelangelo received confirmation of his destiny as a sculptor while gazing at the clouds billowing over the Apennines.

123.1 [119]   *Tristan da Cunha. . . . an admirable place for one's teeth.* Tristan da Cunha (named after the Portuguese admiral who discovered it in 1506) is the principal island of an isolated group in the South Atlantic, roughly halfway between South Africa and South America, and some 1,200 miles southwest of St. Helena, of which it has been a dependency since 1938. The island is some forty square miles, rising 7,640 feet to a volcanic crater (thought to be extinct, the volcano erupted in 1962). The group also includes Gough Island (Diego Alvarez), which is uninhabited, some 250 miles southeast of Tristan, as well as Inaccessible Island, Nightingale, Middle and Stoltenhoff Islands, and a few isolated rocks. The group is mentioned in Donnelly, p. 43, as forming a remnant of the lost continent of Atlantis. Hugh's reference to teeth is based on fact; the small community has no dentist, but there is little necessity for one since the lack of sugar in the diet and the presence of natural fluorides in the drinking water mean that the islanders invariably possess perfect teeth.

123.2 [119]   *Sokotra.* From Skr. *Dvīpa-Sakhādhāra,* "the island abode of bliss"; an island in the Arabian Sea, some 150 miles from Cape Guardafui and 200 miles from the Arabian coast. Discovered by Tristan da Cunha in 1507, it remained uncolonized until it was occupied by the East India Company in 1834, and in 1886 it became part of the British East Aden Protectorate. It is now part of South Yemen. The island is mountainous, dry, and attractive. Its five thousand inhabitants survive by fishing and trade, and the island is known for its ghee, dragon's blood, aloes, dates, and pearls.

Hugh is more fascinated by Socotra's ancient history, which is shrouded in legend. The island is mentioned in the first century *Periplus Maris Erythraei* (the unknown Greek trader calls it *Dioscorida*); in Pliny's *Natural History,* VI.xxxii, p. 153; and, above all, in the *Travels of Marco Polo* of the late thirteenth century. For a long time Marco Polo's island remained undiscovered by the West and legends accrued about it; it was known to the West as an island of spices (frankincense, myrrh, and ambergris); a Christian land whose converts had degenerated to savagery; a place guarded by fearsome scorpion men; and (as Marco Polo himself claimed), an island where "there are the best enchanters in the world" (*Travels of Marco Polo,* ed. Henry Yule, 1875, vol. 2, p. 399). There is no mention, however, of camels that climb like chamois, and the statement is categorically at odds with Charles Doughty's description of the "lumpish brutes" (*Arabia Deserta,* Ch. 3); Lowry's indirect source is perhaps Lieutenant J. R. Wellsted's "Memoir on the Island of Socotra" (*Journal of the Royal Geographical Society* 5 [1835]: 129–229), in which the history, geography, and commerce of the island is outlined and where the camels are described, p. 201, as being (unusually) "as sure-footed as mules."

124.1 [120] *Pineaus Lake.* Pinaus Lake, thirty miles from Vernon, B.C. (where Geoffrey was once Consul, p. 353 [353]). Kilgallin comments, p. 169, "Ironically, Pinaus Lake is famous for its agate, the alchemical antidote to thirst," and in his 1965 thesis, p. 26, he suggested a connection between Geoffrey's return to health on Pineaus Lake and Watts-Dunton's cure of Swinburne at his house called *The Pines* (see note **66.4**).

124.2 [120] *hardpan.* A hard layer of earth beneath the soil, composed mainly of clay and impervious to water.

124.3 [120] *Oh take me back to Poor Fish River.... Aneroid or Gravelburg.... Product.... Dumble.* Mostly tiny remote towns, rivers, and lakes of Canada:
(a) *Poor Fish River.* A small river draining Poorfish Lake in the Northwest Territories, close to the Manitoba and Saskatchewan borders.

(b) *Onion Lake.* A small lake in northern Ontario, north of Thunder Bay. Ethan Llewelyn, in *October Ferry,* p. 15, once had a poultry farm there.

(c) *the Guadalquivir.* The major river of southern Spain, draining the Andalusian plains and flowing through Cordoba and Seville before reaching the Atlantic.

(d) *Como.* A lake in Lombardy in northern Italy, twenty-five miles north of Milan, famed for its beauty and its handsome villas and resorts.

(e) *Horsefly.* Horsefly Lake, 28 miles long, in British Columbia's Chilcotins 120 miles southeast of Prince George, draining eventually into the Fraser River.

(f) *Aneroid.* A tiny village in Saskatchewan, a wheat centre about forty-five miles southeast of Swift Current.

(g) *Gravelburg.* More accurately, Gravelbourg. A small town in southern Saskatchewan.

(h) *Product.* A small town in Saskatchewan, east-southeast of Saskatoon.

(i) *Dumble.* Not located, but in *October Ferry,* p. 15, Angus McCandless mentions once having taken up a homestead "sixty miles from Dumble, Alberta."

124.4 [120] *I've been to Niagara Falls.* The predictable honeymoon trip, on the occasion of Yvonne's first marriage, to be followed by the equally predictable first ticket to Reno, p. 76 [72].

125.1 [121] *the Macs-Paps.* The Mackenzie-Papineau Battalion, which, with the Lincoln-Washington Battalion, formed the third unit of the 15th International Brigade in the Spanish Civil War. Named after two leaders of the 1837 rebellions against Britain, it was made up of Canadians, most of whom had previously been fighting with the Americans, and took an active part in the fighting in the north.

125.2 [121] *a Pict.* The Picts were an ancient people of Scotland who fought furiously against Roman rule. By referring to McGoff's Scots ancestry, Hugh implies his opposition to the British way of life (Romans and Britons sharing a common colonialist mentality). McGoff is the name of one of the sailors on the *Oedipus Tyrranus* in *Ultramarine.*

125.3 [121] *a sort of Pango-Pango quality.* Pago Pago, the largest town of American Samoa, represents for Hugh as Vancouver does for McGoff a kind of second-rate seediness.

125.4 [121] *Burrard Inlet.* An arm of the Strait of Georgia extending inland some twenty-three miles and separating Vancouver city from North Vancouver. Lowry's shack at Dollarton was on the north shore of this inlet at the point where Indian Arm breaks off from the main inlet.

125.5 [121]   *New Spain.* "Nueva España," the name given by Hernán Cortés and the early Spanish settlers to the Spanish-American territories in the Central Americas. Used loosely, it embraced all the land on the mainland north of Panama, the islands of the Caribbean, and even the Philippines; more precisely, it was restricted to present-day Mexico, plus the territories of California, Arizona, New Mexico, and Texas (lost to the U.S.A. in 1848), with perhaps the islands of Cuba and Hispaniola. The term fell into disuse after the independence of Mexico was proclaimed in 1821, so Hugh's use of it is deliberately archaic.

125.6 [121]   *Joe Venuti.* A celebrated jazz violinist and one of Hugh's heroes (see note **158.1**).

126.1 [122]   *the seine fishermen.* A seine net is large, buoyed at the top by corks and weighted at the bottom so it floats perpendicularly. The net is usually anchored at one point, and the fishermen inscribe a large circle to entrap the fish within it. The whiskerandoes in the opening chapter of *Redburn* are "hauling the seine" (see note **82.1**).

126.2 [122]   *jack-in-the pulpits.* An American plant of the lily family, which has a spike of flowers partly arched over by a hood-like covering.

127.1 [123]   *the Malebolge . . . the serpentine barranca.* The Malebolge is the eighth circle of Dante's hell (see note **104.1**), here applied to the barranca, whose other attribute, "serpentine," is a reminder that even in this apparent Eden the serpent is ever present. The Serpentine is a long, winding, artificial lake in Hyde Park, London, into which Shelley's first wife Harriet, pregnant and deserted, flung herself and drowned in 1816.

127.2 [123]   *Yvonne looked suddenly ill at ease.* Yvonne's sudden depression is caused by memories associated with the mouldering ruins; in part the lost love of Maximilian and Carlota, to which the Consul referred, p. 64 [59], but in particular the sudden recollection that it was here, while she and Geoffrey were embracing in the ruins, that Jacques Laruelle had first stumbled across them, a meeting recapitulating the earlier incident in the Hell Bunker. A pencilled note in the manuscripts (UBC 10–18, p. 35) indicated that Yvonne was to feel "a presage of her own death"; the intimation was to be underlined by her immediately asking for a cigarette.

127.3 [123] *Should Juarez have had the man shot or not?* After Maximilian surrendered to the Liberal forces on 15 May 1867, Juárez decided that the emperor should be tried by court-martial and that the state should seek the death penalty. Despite pleas for clemency from all over the world and a split decision in the six-man tribunal, the death penalty was pronounced. At dawn on 19 June 1867, on the Cerro de las Campañas, or "Hill of the Bells" outside Querétara, Maximilian and two of his officers were shot by firing squad.

128.1 [124] *He should have had old thingmetight, Díaz, shot at the same time.* Since Porfirio Díaz, later to become the oppressive and unpopular president who undid many of the liberal reforms initiated by Juárez (see note **112.1**), was a victorious general under Juárez, he could hardly have been shot in 1867. However, in 1871 Díaz ran against Juárez in the presidential elections and following the latter's victory proclaimed himself in revolt. His army was defeated by the federalists of Juárez, but before effective retaliation could be taken, Juárez had suffered a coronary seizure and died.

128.2 [124] *those wonderful names . . . the old astronomers gave the places on the moon.* When Galileo first turned his tiny telescope towards the moon in 1609, he was able to distinguish mountains and large dark areas which looked like great bodies of water, to which he gave the name *maria,* "seas." Other astronomers and mapmakers (Langrenus, 1645; Hevelius, *Selenographia,* 1647; Riccioli, *Almagestumnovum,* 1651) continued a tradition of fanciful names, and hence the still-current terms Oceans, Seas, Lakes, and Marshes to describe what are in fact huge, barren, dry plains. The Sea of Tranquillity is the *Mare Tranquillitatus* on the near side (close to the *Mare Crisium,* or "Sea of Crises"); the Marsh of Corruption is presumably the *Palus Putredinis,* or "Marsh of Decay," in the *Mare Imbrium,* or "Sea of Rains"; but the Sea of Darkness is either an ancient term no longer current (most of those coined by Hevelius were swept away by Riccioli, but no *Tenebris* appears to be among them), or, as seems most probable, Lowry has made his own contribution to selenography (there is, however, a *Taenarium Promontory,* named after the fabled entrance to the infernal regions).

Hugh's mention of the Marsh of Corruption perhaps reflects his feelings of guilt, while Yvonne's mentioning the Sea of Darkness and the Sea of Tranquillity may suggest something of her deepest longings. As an earlier draft made clear (UBC 7-5, p. 31), Yvonne remains for Hugh the other side of the moon, the side turned away.

128.3 [124]   *Sokotra... where the frankincense and myrrh used to come from, and no one has ever been.* For Socotra, see note **123.2.** Behind the romantic details about the mysterious island "where no one has ever been" is a more prosaic story, told by Hugh in an earlier draft (UBC 7-3, p. 15):

> "I've never known anybody who's ever set foot on Sokotra," he said. "But one ship I was on they kidded me into believing that the ship was actually bound there to get frankincense and myrrh. And it really is the island where the frankincense and myrrh used to come from, by the way. And the camels climb up the mountains like chamois."

CHAPTER FIVE

129.1 [125] *Behind them walked the only living thing that shared their pilgrimage.* Behind the first five lines of the Consul's nightmare is a specific reference to the great Hindu epic, the *Mahābhārata* (see note **178.6**). The *Mahāprasthānika Parva* and the *Svargārohana Parva,* the short seventeenth and eighteenth books of the *Mahābhārata,* tell of the journey of Yudhishthira, eldest of the Pāndavas, beyond Himavat towards the light of heaven, a journey in which he is accompanied at the outset by his four brothers, Draupadī their wife, and a dog. The story reads in part:

> When the Pandavas received the news, they lost all remaining attachment to life on earth. They crowned Parikshit, son of Abhimanyu, as emperor and the five brothers left the city with Draupadi. They went out on a pilgrimage, visiting holy places and finally reached the Himalayas. A dog joined them somewhere and kept them company all along, and the seven of them climbed the mountain on their last pilgrimage. As they toiled up the mountain path one by one they fell exhausted and died. . . . Yudhishthira saw these dear ones fall and die yet, serenely he went on not giving way to grief, for the light of Truth burned bright before him and he knew what was shadow and what was substance. The dog still followed Yudhishthira. The lesson enforced by the poet in this episode of the dog is that dharma is the only constant companion in life's journey. It was dharma who, in the shape of the dog, followed Yudhishthira up the wearisome mountain path, when his brothers and wife had gone leaving him alone.

The Consul's spiritual journey bears ironic similarities to Yudhishthira's; he has abdicated responsibility, he has shared his wife with others, and he has embarked upon a journey that will take him beyond death (Jakobsen, p. 15). At the moment of his death, however, he will not climb his holy mountain but rather plunge into its bowels, and instead of his virtuously refusing to abandon the dog, his constant companion, it will be thrown after him, contemptuously, to the bottom of the abyss.

129.2 [125]   *Himavat*. In Hindu mythology, Himavat is the personification of the Himalaya Mountains, and throughout the *Mahābhārata* it is invariably distinguished from Meru, the abode of the gods and centre of the universe, from whence the sacred Ganges flows. In the *Mahāprasthānika Parva,* or seventeenth book of the *Mahābhārata,* Yudhishthira and his companions, leaving behind the salt sea, proceed northwards and behold the mighty Himavat, which they must cross on their way to Mount Meru and heaven.

129.3 [125]   *chenars*. The *Plantanus orientalis* or oriental plane tree, the "Royal Tree" of the Mogul emperors, characterized by its great height and girth and the massiveness of its branches and foliage. Francis Younghusband comments (*Kashmir,* p. 208): "Of the trees which grow in the level portions of the valley the chenar is by far the most striking. As it grows in Kashmir it is a king among trees, and in its autumn foliage is one of the many attractions which go to make Kashmir one of the supremely beautiful spots in the world."

129.4 [125]   *and he was still thirsty*. Pt.V of T. S. Eliot's *The Waste Land* sets images of the parched land, thirst, and spiritual questing against a background largely derived from Indian epic, the Voice of Thunder proceeding from "over Himavant" (l. 397).

129.5 [125]   *But this rain, that fell only on the mountains. . . . standing, among cattle. . . . ponies, knee-deep beside him the cool marshes. . . . a village nestling among the mulberries*. The Consul's vision has its source in Francis Younghusband's *Kashmir,* p. 35:

> But early in September the valley renews its charms and visitors return. The atmosphere has been freshened and cooled by the rains which, though they fall lightly in the valley itself, are often heavy on the surrounding mountains. The ripe rice-fields show an expanse of green and yellow often two or three miles in extent. The villages, dirty and untidy at close quarters, it is true, but nestling among the chenars, willows, poplars, walnuts, and mulberries, show as entrancing islands amidst the sea of emerald rice. Ponies browse among the marshes up to their knees in water; and groups of cattle graze along the grassy edge of the stream.

129.6 [126]   *light, light, light, light, light*. In the *Mahābhārata,* Yudhishthira's quest for the heavenly light is crowned with success (he is the first to reach heaven with his human body); here, the Consul's search for the heart of light becomes a rude awakening into the light of earthly day. There may also be an echo of "Lights, lights, lights!" (*Hamlet,* III.ii.286), when Claudius, "Frighted with false fire," rises from the play and rushes away.

129.7 [126]   *horripilating.* From L. *horripilare,* "to bristle with hairs"; used in the popular sense of "bristling with horror." One of Conrad Aiken's favourite words, "horripilation" is defined in *Blue Voyage,* p. 121, as "when your hair walks backward on cold feet."

130.1 [126]   *gnattering.* Chattering; or gnashing of teeth. See p. 222 [218] ("like gnats") for the sense of baleful influence (*meteora*) behind the lights and flashes in the Consul's mind and ears.

130.2 [126]   *the impatient buskin of a William Blackstone.* A buskin is a half-boot or high shoe worn by the Indians as a protection against mud and thorns; the Consul's "more dramatic purpose," however, suggests the buskin of tragic actors (as opposed to the socks of comedy).

130.3 [126]   *the desperate mien of his friend Wilson.* The Consul's friend Wilson, who so magnificently disappears into the jungles of darkest Oceania, corresponds, as the Consul obscurely recognizes, "to some fraction of his being," p. 362 [362]. An earlier draft (UBC 7-6, p. 1) shows Lowry more consciously setting up the parallel between this mysterious disappearance, that of the Consul's father, the William Blackstone myth, and the Consul's projected death: "there was always his poor, but magnificent, ornithologist friend who had once strolled off, and in his dress trousers too, into the wilds of New Guinea. What of the books he had lent him, before he had set out upon the fateful expedition." The Consul's Christian name was at this point William, and underlying the mystery is Edgar Allen Poe's short story, "William Wilson" (1839), the classic treatment of the *doppelgänger* effect (Lowry alludes to the story, "LJC," p. 75): William Wilson, student at Eton and Oxford, has a double of the same name and nativity, whose moral superiority and persistent interference (noticed only by Wilson) finally infuriates the narrator to the point where he murders him, only to realize how utterly he has murdered himself.

The "University Expedition" is probably based upon that of the 1932 Oxford expedition to Sarawak, which included (as ornithologist) Lowry's Cambridge friend, Tom Harrisson, whose record of the trip (*Borneo Jungle*) was published in 1938. Harrisson was also a member of the university expedition to the New Hebrides in 1933–34.

130.4 [126]   *like a man who does not know he has been shot from behind.*

An image which Lowry may have derived from J. W. Dunne's *An Experiment with Time* (5th ed., p. 205), where Dunne suggests that the soldier in battle often does not know he has been wounded because his intensity of bodily feeling depends very largely upon the degree of his concentration of attention.

131.1 [127] *It was a real snake all right.* Whatever its reality, the snake is a reminder of the serpent in the Garden of Eden and a serpent that will insinuate itself into the Consul's mind throughout the rest of the chapter. Like the sailor in Ch. 5 of Conrad's *Lord Jim,* who traditionally "ought to see snakes" but does not, the Consul is obscurely proud of the fact that he is not much bothered "by anything so simple as snakes."

131.2 [127] *Tequila Añejo de Jalisco.* Sp. "old Tequila of Jalisco." Jalisco, northwest of Mexico City, is the state celebrated for its production of tequila (the town of Tequila is in this state). There are various grades of tequila añejo, depending upon how long the tequila has been aged in casks before bottling (the time varies from a few months to seven years, the varieties being proportionately more expensive). Regardless of its quality, the presence of the bottle in his garden offers the Consul a choice directly corresponding to that of Adam.

131.3 [127] *it did not strike him as being nearly so 'ruined' as it had earlier appeared.* Again, the Consul is deluding himself, for were he aware of Nature's correspondences, he might be more apprehensive. The "superb plantains" (see note **70.6**) and the "splendid trumpet vines" would appear obtrusively phallic; the "brave and stubborn pear trees" might hide a snake, as on p. 144 [140]; the papayas might seem grotesque (as in earlier drafts); and the treacherous bougainvillea could conceal, as on p. 144 [140], spikes and spiders. The garden also has a "murderous machete" and an "oddly shaped fork," the latter undoubtedly similar to the one on the bottle of anís (see note **10.1**).

132.1 [128] *a little vision of order... blended... into a strangely subaqueous view.* Joseph Conrad's favourite image of the ordered life is a well-found ship, controlled and directed on a voyage of discovery; in the Consul's mind such a vision of order is swamped by the rising waters of catastrophe, which, as in Thomas Burnet's *Sacred Theory of the Earth* (see note **193.7**), threaten to engulf his world.

132.2 [128] *multitudinously blazing south-south-east. Or was it north-north-west.* Two Shakespearean references blend to suggest a state of mind

that is not quite normal:
(a) *multitudinously*. Incongruously used of the indigo sun, the word suggests the equally extreme image in *Macbeth,* II.ii.61–64:

> Will all great Neptune's ocean wash this blood
> Clean from my hand? No, this my hand will rather
> The multitudinous seas incarnadine,
> Making the green one red.

(b) *north-north-west*. In *Hamlet,* II.ii.405–7, Hamlet, feigning madness, cryptically comments to Rosencrantz and Guildenstern: "I am but mad north-north-west: when the wind is southerly I know a hawk from a handsaw."

132.3 [128] *¿LE GUSTA ESTE JARDÍN? ¿QUE ES SUYO? ¡EVITE QUE SUS HIJOS LO DESTRUYAN!* Translated by the Consul as "You like this garden? Why is it yours? We evict those who destroy!" but, as he appreciates, p. 133 [128], the words on the sign seem to have more question marks than they should have. The correct version is given on p. 235 [232]: *¿Le gusta este jardín, que es suyo? ¡Evite que sus hijos lo destruyan!* — "Do you like this garden that is yours? See to it that your children do not destroy it!" As Lowry says, "LJC," p. 74, "the real translation can be in a certain sense even more horrifying." Lowry was concerned not only that the reader should be aware of the correct version of the sign (see note **235.9**), but also that he should have some hint of the occult implications of eviction, as outlined in his preface to the French translation of his novel (Woodcock, p. 13):

> In the Jewish Cabbala the abuse of magic powers is compared to drunkenness or the abuse of wine, and is expressed, if I remember rightly, by the Hebrew word *sod*. Another attribution of the word *sod* signifies garden, or neglected garden, and the Cabbala itself is sometimes considered a garden (naturally similar to that where grew the tree of forbidden fruit which gave us the Knowledge of Good and Evil), with the Tree of Life planted in the middle.

The novel, Lowry claimed, is concerned primarily with the forces in man which cause him to be terrified of himself; its allegory "that of the Garden of Eden, the Garden representing the world, from which we ourselves run perhaps slightly more danger of being evicted than when I wrote the book" ("LJC," p. 66). The theme of eviction is implicit in all its manifestations: the expulsion of Adam and Eve from Paradise; exclusion from one's personal

Garden of Etla (see note **17.6**); the failure to attain Yudhishthira's heaven
(see note **129.1**); the fall from the Cabbalistic tree of life (see note **44.3**); the
betrayal and loss of the mysteries (see note **291.1**); the failure to observe
Voltaire's final dictum in *Candide,* "il faut cultiver notre jardin"; the lost
innocence of William Blake; even *Peter Rabbit* ("everything is to be found
in *Peter Rabbit,*" *UTV,* p. 178 [175]). In the Garden of Eden were both the
tree of life and the tree of forbidden fruit, with the contingent responsibility
on man to exercise his choice freely and to act responsibly or else to suffer
for his abuse of that freedom. Nobody was more aware than Lowry of the
terrible forces within man that force him to choose, freely, his own
destruction.

132.4 [129]   *the subtle bouquet of pitch and teredos.* Although pitch can be
used in the treatment and flavouring of wine, the Consul associates the taste
of tequila with the hulls of sailing ships, caulked with pitch yet infested with
teredos or "shipworms" — a kind of worm-like mollusc that bores into and
infests submerged wood. The connection arises because the Consul has just
been thinking of mescal, closely akin to tequila, and the best bottles of
mescal invariably include "Gusano," the worm from the maguey plant, considered by regular drinkers of mescal to be an essential ingredient of each
bottle.

   The words "pitch and teredos" also have connotations of death and damnation. In Dante's *Inferno,* XXI, pitch is used to punish sinners in hell.
Teredos are like the worms that devour the body and soul. The *OED* offers
an early instance of teredos: "the body's infirmities . . . are few and scant, if
compared to the soul's which being a better piece of timber, hath the more
teredines breeding in it" (T. Adams, *Soul's Sickness,* 1616). There is a further allusion to the devil's pitchfork (see note **10.1**), again pointing to the
Consul's choice of hell: as he drinks the tequila, he enjoys the "subtle
bouquet" of hell, towards which he imagines he is being dragged.

132.5 [129]   *Mr Quincey.* The Consul's American neighbour, a retired wal-
nut grower, whose name most inappropriately evokes that of Thomas de
Quincey, English essayist and opium eater (see note **105.4**).

133.1 [129]   *by some Aztec.* The Aztec civilization dominated central
Mexico before the invasion by Spaniards led by Cortés reduced their city of
Tenochtitlán to rubble (see note **33.1**). The Jefe de Jardineros, or head gardener, who condemns the Consul in Ch. 12, embodies on one level the
demands of the old Aztec gods for human sacrifice as retribution for the
agonies inflicted upon the native peoples by the conquistadors and those of
European blood (see also notes **81.1** and **215.6**).

133.2 [130] *my old and good friend, Abraham Taskerson.* Since Abraham Taskerson is clearly modelled on Conrad Aiken (see note **22.5**) and since many details of the following pages were borrowed quite shamelessly by Lowry from Aiken, this tribute perhaps forms an acceptable *appoggiatura* for what is to follow.

134.1 [130] *a figure... in some kind of mourning.* The figure is both that of Christ in the Garden of Gethsemane on the night before the Crucifixion and the recurrence of that "other" (see note **96.2**) whose presence the Consul has by now begun to take almost for granted.

134.2 [130] *Parián!... a name suggestive of old marble and the gale-swept Cyclades.* The *OED* (which Lowry has clearly used) defines "parian" as "Belonging to the island of Paros, one of the Cyclades, famed for a white marble highly valued among the ancients for statuary." Previous notes so far have indicated: **14.1,** that the frequent mention of Parián in Ch. 1 looks ahead ominously to the Consul's death in Ch. 12; **80.2,** that the name "Parián" is closely associated with the Tamil *paraiyan,* "a drummer," and with the word "pariah" (hence there are ominous associations between the recurrent sound of drumming and the frequent apparition of the pariah dog throughout the day); **119.2,** that Lowry has built up his fictional Parián from recognizable elements of other places—Chapultepec, Cuautla, Amecameca, Tepotzlán, and (above all) Oaxaca.

The "real" town of Parián is in Oaxaca State, some twenty miles northeast of Nochixtlán, a village so tiny as to be non-existent on most maps, though during the Revolution of 1910–20 it had some strategic significance as a railway centre. Parián was personally significant to Lowry because it was at that railway station he waved farewell, for the last time, to Juan Fernando Márquez (*DATG,* p. 208). The name thus unwittingly commemorates his dead Zapotecan friend, who, like the Consul, was shot in a drunken barroom quarrel.

The meaning of "Parián," more correctly, El Parián, is "the marketplace." The name was associated with a market in the Philippines (from whence an annual galleon was sent to Mexico) and adopted in the eighteenth century by the wealthy Mexican Philippine traders as the name of their palacio or headquarters in Mexico City. The Parián was sacked in an uprising in 1828 and finally destroyed by orders of Santa Anna in 1843 (*Diccionario Porrua,* p. 1578), but Lowry would have known of its existence because in the lobby of the Hotel Canada, Mexico City, there was, and still is, a huge enlarged picture of the city centre at the end of the eighteenth century, inscribed underneath as being "del Palacio Nacional; de la Cathedral, del Parian, y estatua de Carlos IV" ("of the National Palace, the Cathedral, the Parián, and statue of Charles IV").

134.3 [130]   *a tiny fifth side to his estate.* Markson suggests, p. 76, that in much early architecture the apex of a four-faced pyramid or spire was considered a fifth "side," the one closest to God.

134.4 [130]   *the eternal horror of opposites.* The Consul's reflection encapsulates such notions as: the Taoist Yin and Yang (when these are properly balanced, tranquillity prevails); Ouspensky's world as the world of the unity of opposites (*Tertium Organum,* Ch. 21, p. 242); Blake's contraries, without which there is no progression (particularly his marriage of heaven and hell); the eternal opposition of the male and female principles; Coleridge's reconciliation of opposites in the *Biographia Literaria;* and, above all, Jakob Boehme's assumption of antithesis as the basic law of being, as summed up in the *OCEL:* "that all manifestation involves opposition, notably of God and Nature, that existence emerges from a process of conflict between pairs of contrasted principles (light and darkness, love and anger, good and evil, and so forth) and that in this way the universe is to be seen as the revelation of God." In occult thought generally, a theory of opposites is required to account for such matters as suffering, chaos, and evil, and the "eternal horror" is in large part the agony caused by the attempt to reconcile opposites. In *Lunar Caustic,* p. 11, Bill Plantagenet agonizes: "I am sent to find my father, to find my son, to heal the eternal horror of three, to resolve the immedicable horror of opposites." As Andersen notes, p. 150, "the inability to reconcile opposites prevents the Consul's salvation through love."

The principle of opposites is essential to the Cabbalistic notion of equilibrium (see note **44.3.b**), here demonstrated by the Consul's almost falling into the barranca. As Epstein notes, p. 12, it is a basic premise of occultism that "the world of opposites merges into equilibrium," but that equilibrium is so delicately balanced that a slight tilt may invert the tree of life and send one plunging into the abyss; this also constitutes the "eternal horror." Sherrill Grace comments, pp. 36–37: "If the tree were telescoped, Kether (the spiritual world) would coincide with Malkuth (the material world), thereby symbolizing the mystical unity of the two. The doctrine that Heaven and Hell are the same place or that the way up is the way down, ideas that tormented and fascinated Lowry, are basic to Achad's organic Tree."

134.5 [130]   *Thou mighty gulf, insatiate cormorant, deride me not, though I seem petulant to fall into thy chops.* The Consul is quoting from John Marston's "To euerlasting Obliuion," the final poem appended to *The Scourge of Villanie* (1598), a set of eleven satirical satires (dedicated "To his most esteemed, and best beloved Selfe") in which Marston sets out to castigate the follies and vices of his age. Having done so, he concludes with a wish for peace:

> Thou mighty gulfe, insatiate cormorant,
> Deride me not, though I seeme petulant
> To fall into thy chops. Let others pray
> For euer their faire Poems flourish may.
> But as for mee, hungry *Obliuion*
> Deuoure me quick, accept my orizon:

Marston's image is itself derived from Shakespeare's *Richard II,* II.i.38–39: "Light vanity, insatiate cormorant, / Consuming means, soon preys upon itself." The speech, by John of Gaunt, ends with the line: "How happy then were my ensuing death."

134.6 [130] *this immense intricate donga.* A *donga* is a native South African word meaning "a channel or gully formed by the action of water; a ravine or watercourse with steep sides" (*OED*). Lowry seems to be using "intricate" with an awareness of the L. *intricare,* "to entangle," "to intrigue."

134.7 [131] *general Tartarus and gigantic jakes.* Tartarus is often loosely equated with Hades but may refer specifically to the infernal abyss beneath Hades, home of the monster Typhoes (see note **340.2**), into which Zeus threw the rebel Titans who had revolted against his authority. The barrancas surrounding Cuernavaca are used all the time for rubbish disposal and are hence full of unsightly and unsanitary piles of waste which receive an inadequate flushing only in the rainy season. "Jakes" is common Elizabethan slang for "toilets." The word is also used by Conrad Aiken (Kilgallin, p. 147, detects a privy pun on Aiken's home, Jeakes House) in his *Ushant,* p. 296, where he describes "the vipers and dead dogs, and the human corpses, and human filth, or jakes, of the hideous barranca that cleft the town of Cuernavaca like a hairy and festering wound."

134.8 [131] *cloacal.* Referring to toilets or sewers. The word may be traced to the *Cloaca Maxima,* the great sewer of Rome, supposedly presided over by the goddess Cloacina.

134.9 [131] *Prometheus.* One of the Titans, who benefited mankind by stealing fire from Olympus and giving it to men. By so doing he incurred the wrath of Zeus, who chained him to a rock in the Caucasus, where all day long an eagle (or vulture) tore at his liver, which grew whole again during the night. Only after many generations did Hercules, with the consent of Zeus, shoot the eagle and free the heroic rebel. As the Consul is surely aware, the role of Prometheus as bringer of light and as saviour (he is imagined, p. 206 [202], as retrieving lost golf balls from the ravine) is at odds with his description here as "cloacal."

135.1 [131]   *Chester-le-Street.* A coal and iron-mining centre in north Durham, in the heart of the northern industrial region; described in the 1976 *Shell Guide to England,* p. 793, as "very old, and not much to show for it."

135.2 [131]   *that mighty Johnsonian prospect.* The allusion is to Boswell's *Life of Johnson,* Wednesday, 6 July 1763, when, among the guests dining with Boswell and Johnson at the Mitre, was the Reverend Mr. John Ogilvie, who was unlucky enough to choose for the topic of his conversation the praises of his native country, and made the unfortunate observation that Scotland had "a great many noble wild prospects": "JOHNSON. 'I believe, Sir, you have a great many. Norway, too, has noble wild prospects; and Lapland is remarkable for prodigious noble wild prospects. But, Sir, let me tell you, the noblest prospect which a Scotchman ever sees, is the high road that leads him to England!'"

135.3 [131]   *Liverpool, the Liver building.* Liverpool, the great port on the north bank of the Mersey, with seven miles of docks and countless shipping offices, was the outward destination of Melville's Redburn and the home port of Lowry's Dana Hilliot in *Ultramarine.* The waterfront is dominated by the Royal Liver Building, the offices of an insurance company; a seventeen-story building designed by Walter Thomas and built in 1908. The etymology of "liver" is obscure — it supposedly referred to the bulrushes growing along the river bank — but the citizens of Liverpool invented a legendary "liver bird" to explain the name of their city. The 295-foot towers of the Royal Liver Building are topped by these birds, and one is placed in the city's coat of arms.

135.4 [131]   *Caegwyrle Ale.* More correctly, Caergwyrle Ale; until 1948 brewed by the firm of Lassal & Sharman in the town of Caergwyrle, Flint County, North Wales (the brewery became a paint factory and then a graphite plant). The ale was popular in Flint and Cheshire (rather than Liverpool) between the wars, and in Lowry's short story "Enter One in Sumptuous Armour" (*P & S,* p. 232), the schoolboy hero thinks longingly of it.

135.5 [131]   *Q-boats.* More usually, "Q-Ships"; also known as "Mystery Ships" or "Hush-hush Ships." These were gunboats disguised as merchantmen used by the Royal Navy in World War I to tempt submarines to the attack in an effort to curb the increasingly heavy losses sustained at the hands of German U-boats. Guns were concealed beneath false hatches, and when a U-boat signalled the ship to stop, a boat with a "panic party" would leave the Q-ship and row off to a safe distance, leaving a gun crew on board, waiting for the submarine to present a suitable target. In 1918 (perhaps a little later) Lowry was taken by his brother Wilfrid to see a Q-Ship in the Liverpool Docks (Bradbrook, p. xi).

135.6 [131]   *Dr Livingstone, I presume.* The phrase made famous by Henry Morton Stanley on meeting David Livingstone at Ujiji, Central Africa, 10 November 1871. David Livingstone (1813–73) was a Scottish minister and explorer in darkest Africa whose long disappearance had caused concern. An expedition led by Stanley and financed by the *New York Herald* set out to find him, and on 2 July 1872 the *Herald* printed a "special from Central Africa" describing the crucial moment (Stevenson's *Quotations,* p. 2283):

> Preserving a calmness of exterior before the Arabs which was hard to simulate as he reached the group, Mr Stanley said: —
> "Doctor Livingstone, I presume?"
> A smile lit up the features of the hale white man as he answered: —
> "Yes, that is my name."

The incident is also described in Ch. 11 of Stanley's *How I Found Livingstone* (1872).

135.7 [132]   *Soda Springs.* A small town in southeast Idaho, named for its carbonic acid-charged springs. The town, like Mr. Quincey, epitomizes the values of Middle America, by which the Consul is found distinctly wanting.

136.1 [132]   *I expect Rousseau to come riding out of it at any moment on a tiger.* The reference is to Henri Rousseau (1844–1910), the French painter known as *le douanier,* "the customs officer" (though his rank in that service was in fact much lower). He is particularly known for his "jungle" scenes, at least two of which ("Tropical Storm with Tiger," 1891; and "Tiger Attacking a Buffalo," 1908) feature tigers. Rousseau's style, dismissed by his contemporaries as "le style concièrge," is deliberately childlike and artless. A legend developed, quite without foundation, that Rousseau as a young man had gone to Mexico and served under Maximilian to get the background for his jungles.

136.2 [133]   *Tehuacan water. . . . And a little gaseosa.* Mineral waters with supposedly beneficial effects (see notes **12.1** and **32.1**). The Consul's nervous giggle, "tee-hee" (deriving directly from Aiken's *Blue Voyage,* p. 78), suggests nevertheless a cross-reference to p. 309 [307] and that later invocation of intoxicating libations of soma.

137.1 [133]   *the sinister carapace of a seven-year locust.* The "seven-year locust" is also mentioned in *Blue Voyage,* p. 65; more correctly, it should be the "seventeen-years' locust," the *cicada septemdecim,* a North American species of locust so called because it is said to appear only at intervals of seventeen years in any given locality.

A carapace is literally the upper shell of a tortoise, "extended to the hard case investing the body in some other animals" (*OED*), though not usually applied to insects. Given the blatant insincerity of what the Consul is saying, Lowry may well be alluding to Ogden and Richards, *The Meaning of Meaning* (Ch. 2, p. 42), where the process of the word completely taking the place of the thought is likened to the shedding of the carapace.

137.2 [133]   *What if Adam wasn't really banished from the place at all?* In the Biblical account of the Garden of Eden, Genesis 3, Adam's sin of disobedience is punished by his eviction from the Garden. The Consul suggests that this is to be understood metaphorically, that the loss of Eden is equivalent to the loss of God's grace and that Adam's real punishment was to have to go on living in the Garden, which he loathed (an idea, Kilgallin suggests, p. 171, which Lowry may have found in Shaw's *Back to Methuselah*). Walker, p. 256, sees a parallel here with Graham Greene's *The Power and the Glory* (1940), where the whisky-priest is convinced that his punishment is having to stay on in Tabasco.

137.3 [133]   *God, the first agrarian, a kind of Cárdenas.* The presidency of Lázaro Cárdenas (1934–40) was notable above all for his policy of agrarian reform, by which many large estates and haciendas were broken up and the land redistributed to those who worked it (see note **111.4**). The "existing historical circumstances" reinforce the parallel between the Consul and Adam previously made by Laruelle, p. 28 [22]; as an owner of property and a foreigner, the Consul is now in constant danger of being evicted from Mexico.

137.4 [134]   *realpolitik.* Ger. "real politics"; politics based on practical and material realities, as distinguished from those based on theoretical, ethical, or moralistic considerations; in practice, a euphemism for power politics.

137.5 [134]   *licentia vatum.* More correctly, *licentia vatium,* "poetic licence"; the right of an author to manipulate his materials without strict regard for the literal truth.

137.6 [134]   *j'adoube.* Fr. "I adjust"; in chess, said by a player who wishes to adjust the position of a piece on the board without committing himself to moving it as the laws of the game normally require (the open fly here "verifying" the Consul's failure to make a move towards Yvonne an hour ago).

138.1 [134]   *the Old Man.* Naval slang for the captain of a ship; here applied to God, with overtones of an Old Testament Nobodaddy figure. Lowry and Conrad Aiken usually referred to Malcolm's father in this way.

138.2 [134]   *scorpions and leafcutter ants.* Traditional conceptions of Paradise would preclude such pests, but Mr. Quincey's patient questioning about the Consul's wife has quickly turned heaven into hell.

138.3 [134]   *my little-snake-in-the-grass-my-little-anguish-in-herba.* A reference to Virgil's *Eclogue* III, ll. 92–93, words spoken by the Shepherd Damoetas in contention with Menalcas: "Qui legitis flores et humi nascentia fraga, / frigidus, o pueri, fugite hinc, latet anguis in herba." ("Ye who cull flowers and low-growing strawberries, away from here, lads; a chill snake lurks in the grass.") The Consul's words are a direct response to Mr. Quincey's "I think he went out with your wife" and account for his greeting Hugh on p. 145 [141]: "Hi there, Hugh, you old snake in the grass."

138.4 [134]   *Mr Quincey's cat.* The Consul's playful puns have a slight edge to them:
(a) *Priapusspuss.* Priapus, son of Dionysus and Aphrodite and god of procreation, was usually depicted with an enormous phallus (the reference thus extending the latent sexual connotations of "snake in the grass").
(b) *Oedipusspusspuss.* Oedipus, who killed his father and married his mother and blinded himself when he saw what he had done; also the cat whose fate has already anticipated that of the Consul (see note **93.1**).
(c) *Xicotancatl.* Xicohtencatl the Younger, commander of the Tlaxcalans who opposed Cortés as the Spaniards passed through Tlaxcala (see note **303.2**); the hint of Tlaxcala inevitably suggests betrayal.

Lowry's cat puns are a tribute to Conrad Aiken, who liked both cats and puns. In *Blue Voyage,* p. 83, Demarest reflects: "The cat's prayer. Give us this day our daily mouse. And forgive us our trespusses as we forgive those who trespuss against us. . . . I really ought to give up this awful habit of punning."

138.5 [134]   *She thinks I'm a tree with a bird in it.* An observation originally made in Cuernavaca by Conrad Aiken, but claimed by Lowry for his own, as Aiken notes in *Ushant,* pp. 356–57:

And after all, in that so-long-elaborated symbiosis, who was to say just what was whose, and just which properties, of perception or invention, belonged to either? "He thinks I'm a bird in a tree"—so D. [Aiken] had observed of the little cat, at his feet, in the garden, who, hearing D.'s low whistle, had looked up at him with startled inquiry; and Hambo [Lowry], chuckling at the empathy, and empathizing with it himself (at one remove), could already be seen in the very act of entering that note, that bird-note, amongst the pile of other notes, in that creative nest of his on the verandah, where the new book was taking shape.

139.1 [135]   *Or was that another William Blackstone?* The "other" William Blackstone is Sir William Blackstone (1723–80), English jurist, king's counsel, and M.P., best known for his *Commentaries on the Laws of England* (1765–69) in which (II.25, p. 393) "On the Rights of Things," is considered the status of animals *ferae naturae:*

> For if the pheasants escape from the mew, or the fishes from the trunk, and are seen wandering at large in their proper element, they become *ferae naturae* again; and are free and open to the first occupant that has ability to seize them. But while they thus continue my qualified or defeasible property, they are as much under the protection of the law, as if they were absolutely and indefeasibly mine: and an action will lie against any man that detains them from me, or unlawfully destroys them. It is also as much felony by common law to steal such of them as are fit for food, as it is to steal tame animals: but not so, if they are only kept for pleasure, curiosity, or whim, as dogs, bears, cats, apes, parrots, and singing birds; because their value is not intrinsic, but depending only on the caprice of the owner.

The 1940 draft of Ch. 5 (UBC 7-6, p. 8) foregrounded the comment about cats being animals not fit for food by having Mr. Quincey reply, "Right here, in this town, during the Revolution, they barbecued 'em in the market place." As Mr. Quincey became more morose and taciturn in subsequent versions, that remark was deleted from the drafts.

139.2 [135]   *Or so Abraham.* The reference to Abraham half-acknowledges Lowry's indebtedness to Conrad Aiken for the William Blackstone story (see note **56.1**), if not for such details as Rousseau riding out of the jungle on a tiger, or the cat thinking of the Consul as a tree with a bird in it. There is another acknowledgment of Aiken's influence further down the page: the Consul's decisiveness is "borrowed on this occasion from the same source as the genius and his interest in cats."

139.3 [135] *the Indians are in here.* An image extended, p. 289 [287], by that of the soul with her savage and traitorous Tlaxcalans, her noches tristes, her pale Moctezuma; and deriving, Markson suggests, p. 82, from William Blake's "All deities reside in the human breast" (*The Marriage of Heaven and Hell*).

139.4 [136] *a clock was striking.* As we learn a little later, it is really 11:00 A.M., and not 10:45 as the Consul's watch suggests. Throughout the day, the Consul's sense of time is out of joint, but there is already a suggestion here of the fears of Faustus, who has "but one bare hour to live" (sc. xiv).

140.1 [136] *Old De Quincey; the knocking on the gate in Macbeth.* The paragraph combines a number of references to Thomas De Quincey's essay, "On the Knocking on the Gate in Macbeth" (1823), one of the first important critical articles on English literature. De Quincey tries to analyse why this particular passage of *Macbeth* (II.iii) should create such "a peculiar awfulness and a depth of solemnity" and concludes that it is the moment when the goings on of human life suddenly resume that makes us so intensely aware "of the awful parenthesis that had suspended them." Or, in the words cited by the Consul, from near the end of the essay:

> Here, as I have said, the retiring of the human heart, and the entrance of the fiendish heart was to be expressed and made sensible. Another world has stept in; and the murderers are taken out of the region of human things, human purposes, human desires. They are transfigured: Lady Macbeth is "unsexed"; Macbeth has forgot that he was born of woman; both are conformed to the image of devils; and the world of devils is suddenly revealed. But how shall this be conveyed and made palpable? In order that a new world may step in, this world must for a time disappear. The murderers, and the murder must be insulated—cut off by an immeasurable gulf from the ordinary tide and succession of human affairs—locked up and sequestered in some deep recess; we must be made sensible that the world of ordinary life is suddenly arrested—laid asleep—tranced—racked into a dread armistice; time must be annihilated; relations to things without abolished; and all must pass self-withdrawn into a deep syncope and suspension of earthly passion.

With the world of devils suddenly revealed to him by the striking clock and whispering wings, the Consul stands between the two realms of human and fiendish nature; he too experiences the feeling of vertigo as he steps back into the world of human affairs, made sensible that the world of ordinary life has been suddenly arrested.

140.2 [136] *knock, knock, knock: who's there?* The childish game (popular on radio music-hall shows during the 1930's) initiates a complex of inter-related puns:

(a) *Catastrophe.* From Gk. *katastrephein,* "to overturn"; a sudden denouement or violent change, especially a disastrous one. The term has particular reference to Greek tragedy.

(b) *Catastrophysicist.* One who believes in catastrophism, the theory that geological changes are the result of sudden and violent physical causes rather than continuous and uniform processes (a forerunner of modern catastrophe theory); also, one who believes that the millenium will be initiated by a sudden catastrophic event.

(c) *Katabasis to cat abysses.* Katabasis, from Gk. *katabainein,* "to go down," is literally a going down; in particular, a military retreat such as that of the Greeks described in Xenephon's *Anabasis.* The word leads naturally to "cat abysses," recapitulating the fate of poor Oedipuss, p. 93 [89], and anticipating that of the Consul, p. 376 [375].

(d) *Cathartes atratus.* A kind of vulture (the Penguin "cat hartes" is an error). From Gk. *kathairein,* "to clean," and L. *atratus;* "clothed in black." The *Cathartidae* are a New World sub-order of *Falconiformes* (or vulture). Strictly speaking, there is no *Cathartes atratus;* there is, however, the *Coragyps atratus,* or American Black Vulture, of a different sub-order. Lowry's term is obviously derived from W. H. Hudson's *Idle Days in Patagonia,* p. 47: "on the higher branches innumerable black vultures (*Cathartes atratus*) were perched, waiting all the dreary day long for fair weather to fly abroad in search of food."

140.3 [136] *murdering sleep.* From *Macbeth,* II.i.36–41, where Macbeth, having murdered Duncan, is tormented by thoughts of guilt:

> Methought I heard a voice cry "Sleep no more!
> Macbeth does murder sleep," the innocent sleep,
> Sleep that knits up the ravell'd sleave of care,
> The death of each day's life, sore labour's bath,
> Balm of hurt minds, great nature's second course,
> Chief nourisher in life's feast.

140.4 [136] *where the breath of the hoses had suddenly failed as if by magic.* Doctor Vigil exemplifies to the Consul what a white magician should be: one who uses his magical powers over nature for the betterment of humanity and life. (The long tradition of the poet Virgil as a white magician is based mainly on his *Eclogue* IV which seems to predict the coming of

Christ.) Nevertheless, the Consul is instinctively suspicious of the doctor's "secretive prowling," and his sense of a conspiracy leads the Consul, p. 150 [147], to reject the proposed journey to Guanajuato and "life."

141.1 [137] *Firmin innocent, but bears guilt of world on shoulders.* Recalling his guilt over the *Samaritan* affair (see note **38.**1), the Consul aligns himself with Christ, who carried the cross as an emblem of the sins of the world, and Atlas, who shouldered its weight. The further headline, "Body of Firmin found drunk in bunker," is a magnificently Freudian compression of all the Consul's subconscious fears of drink, death, the Hell Bunker, and the abyss.

141.2 [137] *ectoplasm.* In spiritualism, a vaporous luminous substance supposedly emanating from a medium's body during a trance. The scene itself suggests Rembrandt's painting "The Anatomy Lesson of Dr. Tulp" (1632).

141.3 [137] *Qué t-.... Por favor.* Sp. "Hello . . . Please." Qué tal is a common form of greeting, and Vigil's hoarse request, as the Consul loudly and loyally acknowledges, is that there be no indication to Mr. Quincey that the doctor is in no fit shape himself (hence the irony of Vigil magnificently giving away the Consul's "whole show," p. 146 [143]).

142.1 [138] *katzenjammer.* Headaches and nausea after drinking, sometimes used in the sense of "caterwauling"; from Ger. *Katz,* "cat" and *Jammer,* "noise." The word was popularized in English by the successful comic strip *The Katzenjammer Kids,* created by Rudolph Dirks in 1897 and starring Hans and Fritz, whose attacks upon authority and the English language ("Society iss nix") were nothing short of devastating.

142.2 [138] *I must comport myself here like . . . like an apostle.* A phrase used one year later by Dr. Vigil, p. 10 [4], as he reflects upon his failure to save the Consul. The unidiomatic nature of the expression derives from Vigil's use of the Spanish *comportarse,* "to behave."

142.3 [138] *maguey.* A general name for the argave cactus, from which pulque, tequila, and mescal are derived (see notes **113.3** and **219.3**). There are several varieties of maguey, not all of which produce alcohol, but each is characterized by spiky, splaying greyish-green leaves. The maguey is common throughout the Mexican highlands, increasing acres being devoted to its production. It is sometimes known in English as the century plant, because of its infrequent blooming (eight to twenty-five years).

142.4 [138]   *delirium tremens.* The D.T.'s. From L. *delirare,* "to rave," and *tremare,* "to tremble"; an affliction of the brain induced by excessive use of alcohol and characterized by sweating, anxiety, and hallucinations. A classic case of D.T.'s "of the worst kind" is described in *Lord Jim,* ch. 5, except that the patient sees millions of huge pink toads instead of snakes.

142.5 [138]   *the Pope's illness.* See note **233.4.**

142.6 [138]   *progresión.... a ratos.* Sp. "progression... from time to time," that is, intermittently, with a pun on Sp. *ratas,* "rats" (made explicit in the manuscripts, UBC 10-21, pp. 10-12: "You mean, not cats... but rather rats"). The pun anticipates the Consul's great question, p. 222 [218]: "Why do people see rats?"

143.1 [139]   *the Great Brotherhood of Alcohol.* A parody of the kind of title used by adepts of Masonic or Cabbalistic societies, yet not altogether facetious, since Lowry genuinely believed the agonies of the alcoholic were very similar to those of the mystic ("LJC," p. 71), and since Vigil, insofar as he is a white magician, is an "adept." The parody was further marked in an earlier draft (UBC 10-24, p. A): "the Giant Institutional Brotherhood of Alcohol."

143.2 [140]   *huge butterflies... blouses.* Yvonne, p. 101 [97], was described as wearing such a blouse (for Geoff) when Hugh saw her and felt in his heart a pain conspicuously absent from the Consul's present image of torn-up multi-coloured love letters.

144.1 [140]   *Hiding up a pear tree.* Although the Tree of the Knowledge of Good and Evil in the Garden of Eden is popularly supposed to be an apple tree (because of the similarity of L. *malum,* "evil," and *mālum,* "apple"), there is a tradition in English, dating from at least Chaucer's *Merchant's Tale,* associating pear trees with sexual infidelity and deception. The age gap between the Consul and Yvonne is hinted at in Chaucer's figures of Januarie and May.

144.2 [140]   *whore's shoes.* The Consul's mind moves from the image of a snake up a tree dropping rings round its prey to the ancient game of horseshoe-pitching, to the good-luck symbols on a wedding cake that are thrown after newly-weds, to the Horsehoe Falls at Niagara, and finally to his wife's infidelities ("with heels flying"—see note **51.4**).

144.3 [140]   *local horticultural college.* An Escuela de Agricultura had been established in Cuernavaca in 1913, but it no longer exists. Projects of this kind were also part of President Cárdenas's plans for ejido reform (see note **111.4**).

144.4 [140]   *the insect . . . flew out as might indeed the human soul from the jaws of death.* In the earlier drafts of this passage (UBC 7-6, p. 15, and UBC 10-21, p. 14), the insect's miraculous escape gave the Consul curious speculations: "Her lips suck forth my soul, see where it flies." . . . "Perhaps he thought it was a flying mouse." . . . "Perhaps the soul does leave the body behind when we die, like a locust leaves the carapace. Or do you think perhaps . . . that the body is like the cat, and wants to devour us, soul and all." In medieval and renaissance art the human soul was often painted as a butterfly or bird leaving the corpse through the mouth and winging its way to heaven. In a letter to the *TLS,* 16 February 1967, p. 127, Conrad Aiken discussed the background to this passage:

> It was not an *insect* the little cat had caught, but a wide-winged dragonfly, and it was not Malcolm who observed this astonishing scene, or drew the conclusion from it, but my wife and myself. My report to Malcolm is again repeated almost word for word. Except that some of the humour has escaped. For it was exceedingly funny: I've never in my life seen a cat look so utterly astounded — clearly, it thought it was flying. And then, when it opened its mouth, nonplussed by the whirring of the wings against its whiskers, and saw the lovely creature whizz into the sky, never was there such humiliation. The little cat — a stray whom we had befriended — slunk off round the villa as if it had been guilty of the ultimate of crimes, or uncatliness, and quite obviously still wondering.

144.5 [141]   *but suppose he's absolutely adamant.* This snatch of overheard conversation reinforces all the Consul's paranoid fears of a web being spun around him and makes him the more determined not to be a party to any plot requiring him to leave Mexico. He too expects to see "spiders" everywhere.

145.1 [141]   *Suchiquetal.* More usually, Xochiquetzal, the Aztec goddess of flowers, whose name means, "flower-feather"; the wife of Cintcotl, god of Maize, and companion of Piltzintecutl, the sun-god. She is often considered the first woman, from whom all mankind descended, but at some later stage she was translated into the patron goddess of prostitutes. In an earlier draft (UBC 7-6, p. 17) Lowry was more explicit about his reference: in reply to Yvonne's question, "Who was she," the Consul said, "The Mexican Eve.

Only she disgraced her posterity by gathering roses with spikes on them."
Lowry would have found this story in Donnelly, pp. 199–200, where
Donnelly, trying to point out parallels to the story of Eve in Indian legend,
claims that there was "a legend of Suchiquecal, who disobediently gathered
roses from a tree, and thereby disgraced and injured herself and all her posterity." The story is discussed in Lewis Spence, *The Gods of Mexico* p. 190,
where the goddess is named "Suchiquezal," and the further detail is given
that, having sinned by plucking the roses (Yvonne's arms are full of bougainvillea) she was unable to look up to heaven (see note **70.7.b**).

145.2 [141] *you old snake in the grass.* Underlying the cheerful familiarity
is considerable venom: the Consul cannot forget or forgive Hugh's betrayal
of him, a betrayal which even now he feels might have been repeated (see
note **138.3**). It may even be that the apparently coincidental arrival of Hugh
and Yvonne is part of a wider plot to get him out of the way, or at least out
of the country.

145.3 [141] *Why then should he be sitting in the bathroom?* From this
point on to the end of the chapter, scenes alternate between the specious
present of 12:15, when the Consul awakes with a glass of flat beer in his
hand, to various moments of the past hour when he has been virtually a
somnambulist. Lowry comments, "LJC," p. 74: "It should be clear that the
Consul has a blackout and that the second part in the bathroom is concerned with what he remembers half deliriously of the missing hour." The
episode as a whole illustrates Dunne's "concussion" of the brain which
"appears to destroy all memory of the events which immediately *preceded*
the accident" and may parody his notion of "large blocks of otherwise perfectly normal personal experience displaced from their proper positions in
Time" (*An Experiment with Time,* pp. 20 and 55).

145.4 [141] *12:15.* It is actually 12:30, since the Consul's watch is fifteen
minutes slow.

145.5 [141] *A procession of thought like little elderly animals filed
through the Consul's mind.* An image perhaps suggested by Claude Houghton's *Julian Grant Loses His Way,* p. 41: "A succession of dreary thoughts
began to lumber across his mind like a train of camels crossing a desert."

145.6 [141] *the new moon with the old one in its arms.* This is a phenomenon sometimes seen just after the New Moon, when not only is the crescent
visible but so too, in faint outline, is the rest of the moon's disc; this is because of "earthshine" or "earthlight", that is, sunlight reflected from the
earth back onto the moon.

The literary reference is to the anonymous thirteenth century ballad of "Sir Patrick Spens," who, dispatched to sea, has justified forebodings of disaster:

> Late, late yestreen I saw the new moone,
> Wi'the auld moone in hir arme;
> And I feir, I feir, my deir master,
> That we will com to harme.

These lines, slightly changed, were used by Coleridge to preface his "Dejection: An Ode" (1802), a poem mourning the loss of the visionary gleam. As Jakobsen notes, p. 35, they herald the gathering storm in the Consul's mind, a storm that breaks out, p. 149 [145].

145.7 [142] *Tarsius spectres.* The *Tarsius spectrum,* or *malmag,* is a small mammal of nocturnal habits, which resembles a lemur. They are described in Tom Harrisson's *Borneo Jungle,* p. 7:

> Tarsiers have huge round eyes and tiny heads, long prehensile toes and tail, move like an aged negus or a foetus that has never been born. No one knows if the queer querulous squeakings heard at night are made by tarsiers: it is very difficult to find one at all. No one had so far succeeded in keeping one alive in captivity. They simply stare out and slowly die.

In the margin of the galley proofs (UBC 9–17) an interesting exchange took place between Albert Erskine and Lowry:

> Qu: Is this reference to Tarsus? Saint Paul etc. Or is it right? See copy p. 196
>   AE.
> No ref. to St Paul: Some kind of nocturnal E. Indian mammal related to the lemurs.

145.8 [142] *Carta Blanca beer.* The number one selling beer in Mexico; a light, clear, moderate-strength beer, brewed (for "el momento dorado") by the Cervecería Cuauhtémoc of Monterrey. The name suggests "carte blanche," the freedom to do whatsoever one wishes.

146.1 [142] *Bougainville.* Louis-Antoine de Bougainville (1729–1811), French navigator and explorer and author of *Voyage autour du monde* (1771); after whom is named Bougainville Island in the Solomons, Cape

Bougainville in North Australia, and *Bougainvillea,* of the family *Nycta-ginaceae,* a genus of tropical climbing shrub whose small bright flowers are seen everywhere in Cuernavaca, but which is now associated in the Consul's mind with the spikes and spiders of betrayal. Yvonne's arms, p. 144 [141], were full of bougainvillea, which, as Baxter has noted, p. 24, acts throughout the novel as an emblem of deceit.

146.2 [142]   *the botica . . . favor de servir una toma de vino quinado o en su defecto una toma de nuez vómica, pero—.* Sp. "the chemist's shop. . . please be so kind as to give a glass of medicinal wine [quinine] or failing that a glass of strychnine, but—."

147.1 [143]   *Thou art the grave where buried love doth live.* From Shakespeare's *Sonnet* 31:

> Thy bosome is endeared with all hearts,
> Which I by lacking have supposed dead,
> And there reignes Love and all Love's loving parts.
> And all those friends which I thought buried.
>
> How many a holy and obsequious tear
> Hath dear religious love stol'n from mine eye,
> As interest of the dead, which now appear,
> But things remov'd that hidden in thee lie.
>
> Thou art the grave where buried love doth lie,
> Hung with the trophies of my lovers gone,
> Who all their parts of me to thee did give,
> That due of many, now is thine alone.
>
> > Their images I lov'd, I view in thee,
> > And thou—all they—hast all the all of me.

The Consul seems to have entirely ignored the force of the final couplet and to be looking upon Yvonne only as the graveyard (hung with trophies of *her* lovers) of all his hopes of love.

148.1 [144]   *another enemy. . . . a sunflower.* The sunflower, a heliotrope, turns to follow the sun, and in both Christian and occult symbolism it is an emblem of the way all created things should turn to the divine light (on Tarot card 19, it represents the sun). On p. 183 [179], the Consul tells Hugh that the sunflower "stares into my room all day. . . . Like God." The sunflower is the Consul's enemy because, having given his allegiance to darker powers, he is ever reminded by its presence that he too can turn to the light.

148.2 [144]   *unless we contain with ourselves never to drink no more.* The Sp. *se contender,* "to fight with oneself," "to struggle," suggests a pun in English upon the notion of continence.

148.3 [144]   *un poco descompuesto, comprenez, as sometimes in the cine: claro?* A mélange of Spanish, French, and English: "A little out of order, you understand, as sometimes in the cinema, you see." A year later, in the cinema, Sr. Bustamente will remark that "the wires have decomposed," p. 31 [25]. Lowry's brilliantly sustained metaphor of man's soul as a town and the nervous system as its electrical wiring leads naturally into the Swedenborgian notion of the ruined city as a metaphor for hell (Markson, p. 83), which may explain a cryptic marginal note in the manuscript (UBC 10–22, p. 24), "Why couldn't it have been a white path?" (that is, one, like God's lightning, leading back to God).

148.4 [144]   *eclampsia.* From Gk. *eklampein,* "to shine forth." Usually an attack of convulsions caused by any of the toxic conditions of the body and associated particularly with the later stages of pregnancy and miscarriage; thereby suggesting Yvonne's childlessness. The word is here used primarily in the rarer sense of an imaginary perception of light flashing in front of the eyes (in which sense it is particularly associated with epilepsy, an electric storm of the mind).

148.5 [145]   *a town ravaged and stricken.* Lowry's magnificently sustained image may derive in part from Ouspensky's *Tertium Organum,* Ch. 17:

> the mind of man has often been compared to a dark sleeping city in the midst of which watchmen's lanterns slowly move about, each throwing light on a small circle round itself. . . . At each moment there comes into focus a few of these circles illumined by the flickering light while the rest is plunged into darkness.

149.1 [145]   *cataplasms.* Simply poultices, but in the context of the coming storm within the soul, most evocative of the previous wordplay upon "catastrophe" and "katabasis."

149.2 [145]   *hierophants.* From Gk. *hieros,* "sacred," and *phaiein,* "to show"; in ancient Greece, priests who expounded the Elusinian mysteries (see note **319.1**); hence, more generally, interpreters of sacred mysteries and esoteric principles. The word is a commonplace of occult discussion, and the figure of the great master, "speaking in a voice only for those who have ears to hear" is represented on Tarot card 5, the Hierophant (Ouspensky, *A New Model of the Universe,* p. 232).

149.3 [145]   *a mene-Tekel-Peres for the world.* Behind the common expression, "the writing on the wall," with the implications of nemesis, is the sudden appearance on the wall at Belshazzar's Feast of the mysterious words *MENE, MENE, TEKEL UPHARSIN,* which, being interpreted, meant thus (Daniel 5:25–28):

> And this is the writing that was written, MENE, MENE, TEKEL, UPHARSIN. This is the interpretation of the thing: MENE; God hath numbered thy kingdom and finished it. TEKEL; Thou art weighed in the balances, and art found wanting. PERES; Thy kingdom is divided, and given to the Medes and Persians.

The Consul may have in mind ("for the world") a specific reference to Mac-Gregor-Mathers's *The Sacred Magic,* p. xxi: "The writing on the wall at Belshazzar's feast, their manifestation in the political and historical arena is like the warning of a *Mene, Mene Tekel, Upharsin,* to a foolish and undiscerning world."

150.1 [146]   *a child innocent as that infant sleeping in the coffin.* Lowry comments "LJC," p. 74, that the Consul at one point in this chapter identifies himself with the infant Horus, "about which or whom the less said the better." Andersen suggests, p. 220, that the key to this obscure reference is the Consul's identification of himself with the dead child seen earlier that morning, there being an analogy between the death of Horus, stung to death by a scorpion, and the funeral of the child, to the accompaniment of "La Cucaracha" ("The Cockroach").

150.2 [146]   *The uncontrollable mystery on the bathroom floor.* A reference to W. B. Yeats's "The Magi":

> Now as at all times I can see in the mind's eye,
> In their stiff, painted clothes, the pale unsatisfied ones
> Appear and disappear in the blue depth of the sky
> With all their ancient faces like rain-beaten stones,
> And all their helms of silver hovering side by side,
> And all their eyes still fixed, hoping to find once more,
> Being by Calvary's turbulence unsatisfied,
> The uncontrollable mystery on the bestial floor.

Whereas Yeats is speaking of the Christ-child in the manger, the Consul's mind may once more be running to Yvonne's douches and possible abortions. The allusion also anticipates the Taylor Holmes song, "The Face on the Barroom Floor (see note **371.1**).

150.3 [146] *circus of steepy hills.* Guanajuato is indeed ringed with attractive rounded hills perfectly described by Dr. Vigil's adjective "steepy," which, however, Lowry had found in Marlowe's "The Passionate Shepherd," ll. 1–4:

> Come live with me and be my Love,
> And we will all the pleasures prove
> That Valleys, groves, hills, and fields
> Woods, or steepy mountain yields.

150.4 [147] *Guanajuato . . . the streets.* Guanajuato, capital of the state of the same name, is perhaps the most attractive city in Mexico. Its corkscrew streets, beautiful plazas, flower-pot balconies, and attractive buildings are a sheer delight. The opposition of Guanajuato-Parián is an opposition of life and death, and though there are practical reasons for not going there (Cuernavaca to Guanajuato is a two-hundred-mile drive which neither the Consul nor Yvonne is up to), the Consul's rejection of Guanajuato in favour of Parián is a clear preference for death ("LJC," p. 74). The names of the twisting streets, inscribed on ceramic tiles, are strikingly unusual (Dr. Vigil's examples are typical of many), yet behind their enchantment there are hints of tragedy:

(a) *Street of Kisses.* The Callejon del Beso, a tiny narrow street of steps a block or two south up the hill from the centre of town. Characterized by overhanging balconies which almost touch, it was the scene many years ago of Guanajuato's version of *Romeo and Juliet:* Carlos loved Anna, and Anna loved Carlos, but Carlos was poor and Anna's family was rich. Her father did not approve and arranged another match. However, the closeness of the balconies separating the two lovers allowed the exchanging of kisses and other intimacies, until Anna's father, discovering the affair, brought it to an end by stabbing his daughter in the spine with a dagger.

(b) *Street of Singing Frogs.* The Calle de Cantarranas, running east to west off the Plaza de Baratillo. An enchanting name, but one given in derision by the Spaniards to describe the speech of the Indians they despised.

(c) *Street of the Little Head.* The Callejon de la Cabesita, a tiny stone-

paved lane twisting north uphill from the Plaza de Baratillo. Many
years ago, the story goes, two amigos quarrelled, and one killed and decapitated the other. The Callejon de la Cabesita traces the route down
which the head rolled.

As Dr. Vigil says, it is revolting, yet the awareness of the background to
the street names does not so much detract from the quaint charm and
appeal which the streets possess as add to them an element of romance and
fancy. Guanajuato remains, for both Lowry and the Consul, a symbol of
life and beauty.

150.5 [147]   *the place they bury everybody standing up.* One of the unique
tourist attractions of Guanajuato is its collection of mummies ("Las
Momias") from the local cemetery. Fodor comments, pp. 395–96:

> In Guanajuato, as in many other Mexican cities, the dead are buried for
> a minimum of five years. Unless a perpetual resting place has been pur-
> chased, the remains are then dug up to make room for fresher corpses.
> In the case of Guanajuato, coffins often are entombed in the walls sur-
> rounding the cemetery. For some reason, the dead in the walls some-
> times do not decompose ("There are no worms," explains one guide).
> They bloat and shrivel into leathery statues—mummies.
>
> A rather thriving business has resulted. The naked corpses stand free,
> lining the walls of a rather narrow passageway, mouths agape, dead
> eyes looking nowhere. A guide will point out the oldest mummy (dead
> over a century), the body of a woman who died in childbirth, her baby
> at her side, and the remains of an epileptic who was buried alive. For
> sheer ghoulishness, the exhibit is unsurpassed.

151.1 [147]   *Wheee, es un infierno.* Sp. "Whee, it's an inferno"; Vigil inadvertently punning on El Infierno, "that other Farolito" (p. 349 [349]). In an
earlier draft (UBC 10-21, p. 23) Lowry had originally written "Es un paraiso" ("It's a paradise").

151.2 [147]   *a bullthrowing.* A favourite sport in some parts of Mexico;
first played on large estates. Its earlier Mexican name was *jaripeo,* a term
which is now used to indicate "rodeo" or "bronco busting" as well. In its
original form, the cowboys would do tricks with a cow or bull, throw it on
the ground in order to mount it, get on its back singly or in pairs, ride the
animal as long as they could, and avoid being thrown off. In all of these,
one may see the origin of some of the events of the American rodeo. The
Consul, of course, wants to go to Tomalín because it is close to Parián.

151.3 [147] *a clock was striking nineteen: Twelve o'clock.* The time, so far out of joint, reconciles the hour of death for Faustus (12) with that of the Consul (7).

151.4 [147] *the dream of dark magician in his visioned cave.* From Shelley's "Alastor; or The Spirit of Solitude" (1816), ll. 681–88.

> O, that the dream
> Of dark magician in his visioned cave,
> Raking the cinders of a crucible
> For life and power, even when his feeble hand
> Shakes in its last decay, were the true law
> Of this so lovely world! But thou art fled
> Like some frail exhalation; which the dawn
> Robes in its golden beams, – ah! thou hast fled.

The poem, Shelley's first important work, is based on the poet's contemplation of his own certain death. It shows the idealist, happy in his pursuit of beauty, but seeking in reality the counterpart of his dreams; meeting with frustration, he plunges into despair and dies; his final sentiments epitomized in the lines cited by the Consul. The motto of "Alastor" is striking: "I loved not yet – I loved to love – I sought something to love – for I loved to love." See also notes **206.1** and **206.7**.

151.5 [147] *compañero.* Throughout the novel, the key word of human companionship and Samaritan charity (see note **250.1**).

151.6 [148] *Down, down to the frightful "poulps". Meropis of Theopompus... And the ignivome mountains.* As a manuscript note to his publishers explicitly acknowledges (UBC 9–18, p. 204), Lowry's "scholarly source" is Jules Verne's scientific romance, *Twenty Thousand Leagues under the Sea.* In Pt.II, Ch. 9, "A Vanished Continent," Captain Nemo invites M. Aronnax, the narrator, to accompany him on "a curious excursion," which turns out to be a visit to the lost continent of Atlantis, "the ancient Meropis of Theopompus, the Atlantis of Plato." En route they encounter "frightful looking poulps" and "a large crater... vomiting forth torrents of lava." The "frightful poulps" are enormous devil-fish or octopi, some of which later attack the *Nautilus* and impede her progress. The theory of Theopompus of Chios (376?–305 B.C.), Greek historian and writer of the *Meropidae,* was that the Atlanteans were descendants of the Meropes, inhabitants of a region called Merou (itself named after the hero of a deluge). The theory was enthusiastically taken up in Donnelly's *Atlantis.*

The *ignivome* mountains (from L. *ignis,* "fire," and *vomere,* "to vomit") are the volcanoes reputedly responsible for the destruction of Atlantis; the little shower of plaster that rains down, p. 152 [148], is another intimation that similar destruction for the Consul is not far off.

151.7 [148]   *hombre, un poco de cerveza, un poco de vino.* Sp. "My friend, a little beer, a little wine." As on p. 219 [216], the dichotomy is clear: tequila and mescal will be the beginning of the end.

152.1 [148]   *watching the insects.* As Jakobsen notes, p. 36, the Consul, having vainly awaited beneath the shower the coming of the second flood, now experiences amidst the booming buzzing confusion a presentiment of his own death as he sees the insect world closing in upon him (a hallucination recalled on p. 232 [228]).

153.1 [149]   *the persistent rolling of drums.* This, with the recurrent image of the dead man (see note **96.2**), is Parián calling, the drums demanding sacrifice (see note **80.2**). In Conrad Aiken's *Blue Voyage,* p. 90, Demarest reflects that *redrum* is an anagram of *murder.*

153.2 [149]   *a half-recognizable voice.* The voices can be identified as: the Consul's Good Angel; Dr. Vigil; Abraham Taskerson; the Bad Angel (adopting the tone of Weber); the Consul's father, calling from beyond Himavat (in the voice of David lamenting Absalom — II Samuel 18:33 and 19:4); and Yvonne, calling her lover in the words of the Strauss song they used to sing (see note **45.2**).

CHAPTER SIX

154.1 [150] *Nel mezzo del bloody cammin di nostra vita mi ritrovai in.* It. "In the middle of the bloody road of our life I found myself in": the opening lines of Dante's *Inferno* (see note **9.6**). Lowry invariably quoted this line with "in" rather than the correct *per,* though *cammin* may well be Hugh's error. Though Hugh is only twenty-nine (the phrase normally indicates thirty-five, Dante's age at the time of writing, and the average age of the Consul and Hugh), he finds himself very much at the mid-point of his life, seeking the path that will give him meaning and direction.

154.2 [150] *his thirtieth year.* An echo of François Villon's "Testament" (1461), in which the poet reviews his life, his mistakes, his tragedies of love, and his sufferings; expressing his horror of sickness, old age, the jail, poverty and death; and making a number of "bequests," many ironic or facetious, to those in his life. The poem begins:

> En l'an de mon trentiesme eage,
> Que toutes mes hontes j'eus beues,
> Ne du tout fol, ne du tout sage.

("In the thirtieth year of my life, having drunk all my shames, being neither quite foolish nor quite wise.")

154.3 [150] *A. E. Housman.* Alfred Edward Housman (1859–1936), poet and classical scholar, best known for his *A Shropshire Lad* (1896) and *Last Poems* (1922). His poems are characterized by an economy of diction and simplicity of style and treat the sadness of passing youth and the inevitability of death, as in poem xlix of *A Shropshire Lad:*

> Think no more, lad; laugh, be jolly:
>   Why should men make haste to die?
> Empty heads and tongues a-talking
> Make the rough road easy walking,

> And the feather pate of folly
> Bears the falling sky.
>
> Oh, 'tis jesting, dancing, drinking
> Spins the heavy world around.
> If young hearts were not so clever,
> Oh, they would be young for ever:
> Think no more; 'tis only thinking
> Lays lads underground.

154.4 [150]   *in the twinkling of an eye.* From I Corinthians 15:52; like Jacques Laruelle, p. 16 [10], Hugh feels intensely the passing of time. The "four years" he adds to his present twenty-nine as a basis for his calculations brings him to thirty-three, the age at which Christ died, having accomplished his mission.

155.1 [151]   *Old Compton Street.* A short street in Soho, London, running off Charing Cross Road, and lying to the west of Tottenham Court Road.

155.2 [151]   *prepared to lead the whole Jewish race out of Babylon itself.* The Babylonian Captivity is that period of exile for the Jewish nation after the destruction of Jerusalem in 586 B.C. by Nebuchadnezzar, king of Babylon (as described in II Kings 24 and 25); lasting until the conquest of Babylon by the Persians in 538 B.C., when Cyrus the Great gave the Jews permission to return to Palestine. Psalm CXXXVII begins with a recollection of this time of bondage: "By the rivers of Babylon, there we sat down, / yea we wept, when we remembered Zion."

155.3 [151]   *The seagull.* The idea of the seagull testifying to Hugh's future may derive from Ch. 15 of Joyce's *Ulysses,* where seagulls fly to Bloom's rescue during his imagined trial, reminding him of the corporeal work of mercy he had earlier performed. The episode anticipates the suggestion of Chekov's *The Seagull* in the Consul's "little white birds" (see note **232.2**), and Yvonne's releasing of the eagle, p. 321 [320]. The "edible stars" are, literally, starfish.

156.1 [152]   *Oxford Street.* Perhaps the most important shopping street in central London.

156.2 [152]   *on his uppers.* In total poverty (the soles of his shoes are worn through).

156.3 [152] *Shades of Charles Dickens!* In Charles Dickens's *A Christmas Carol* (1843), Bob Cratchit, the ill-used clerk of Ebenezer Scrooge (see note **227.1**), leads a life of misery and penury until the unexpected generosity of the repentant Scrooge safeguards his family's happiness.

156.4 [152] *Is it nothing to you all ye who pass by?* From Lamentations 1:12, where Jeremiah bewails the destruction of Jerusalem and the Babylonian captivity: "Is it nothing to you, all ye that pass by? behold, and see if there be any sorrow like unto my sorrow, which is done unto me, wherewith the Lord hath afflicted me in the day of his fierce anger." The removal of the figure of Christ (see also note **70.6**) contrasts glaringly with the "monstrous deceptions" of the electric signs.

156.5 [152] *the Fitzroy Tavern in Charlotte Street.* The Fitzroy Tavern, at 16 Charlotte Street, just north of the Soho area of London, was, in the 1930's, a well known bohemian pub and one of Lowry's favourite haunts. George Orwell, a committed socialist, avoided the Fitzroy once it became "overbourgeoisified" (*The Last Great Cause,* p. 89).

157.1 [153] *when even the Russians had given up.* By October 1938, the Russians, who had initiated the idea of the International Brigades and who had contributed substantially towards them, agreed to their withdrawal, and by the end of November the last volunteers had left Spain. Stalin's motivation was twofold: the writing was on the wall for the Republicans, and he was already contemplating an alliance with Hitler which was to form the ultimate betrayal of international socialism (see note **329.5**).

157.2 [153] *the City of Destruction.* In John Bunyan's *Pilgrim's Progress* (1678), Christian flees from the City of Destruction (Isaiah 19:18), leaving his wife and children, his friends and comforts, and makes his way through the Slough of Despond and the Valley of Humiliation towards the Celestial City. The "old dodge" is that employed by Christian's neighbours, who accuse him of deserting his family and responsibilities, while the phrase "to shake the dust from one's feet" derives from Matthew 10:14, where Jesus says to his disciples: "And whosoever shall not receive you, nor hear your words, when ye depart out of that house or city, shake off the dust of your feet."

157.3 [153] *an untouchable.* In India, a member of the lowest caste, who numbered millions, contact with whom was considered to defile those of higher status, especially Brahmins. Gandhi, calling them *Harijans,* "Children of God," did much to remove discrimination against them.

157.4 [153]   *The Andaman Islands.* A group of islands in the Bay of Bengal, forming part of the Indian state of the Andaman and Nicobar Islands. Port Blair, the only real town, was established as a penal colony in 1858, following the Indian Mutiny, and gained an unenviable reputation as a settlement rife with disease and brutality, from which few returned. At one point, the British insultingly announced that they were considering sending Gandhi there.

157.5 [153]   *until England gives India her freedom.* Under the political leadership of Nehru's Congress Party and with the moral guidance of Gandhi, the Indian nationalist movement made dramatic gains in popular support during the 1920's and 1930's. By 1938 it was clear that Indian independence was only a matter of time, and despite huge political and religious problems (including the status of Kashmir), independence and the partition of the sub-continent was finally realized on 15 August 1947.

157.6 [153]   *Mahatma Gandhi.* Mohandas Karamchand Gandhi (1869–1948), Indian politician, social reformer, and moral leader, whose policies of active non-violent resistance and civil disobedience were largely responsible for forcing the British government eventually to grant Indian independence. The title *Mahatma,* "Great Soul," was given him by the poet Rabindranath Tagore, in recognition of the outstanding moral and practical qualities that led him to denounce imperialism as a satanic system, to work for the rights of the untouchables, and to improve both social and spiritual conditions for millions. Gandhi opposed Indian involvement in World War II, even in return for independence, and he viewed the partition of the sub-continent in 1947 as a spiritual tragedy and a personal disaster. On 30 January 1948, at a prayer-meeting in Delhi, he was assassinated by a Hindu fanatic.

157.7 [153]   *Stalin.* Joseph Vissarionovich Djugashvili (1879–1953), Soviet statesman and leader of Russia for almost thirty years. Born in Georgia, he studied for the priesthood (like Juárez), but became an active revolutionary and took part in the civil war of 1917. After the death of Lenin he took power, beating off the challenge from Trotsky, and by a series of five-year plans and sweeping legislative changes he made Russia into a giant industrial state. Stalin's name today, however, is associated above all with the ruthless purges and forced labour camps which he used to eliminate all opposition. Hugh's respect for Stalin, so apparently odd when set alongside that for Gandhi, Cárdenas, and Nehru, would not have been shared by Lowry, but it was not untypical of many English socialists and liberals in the 1930's, when the full extent of Stalin's oppressive measures was unknown and before Stalin had made his unholy alliance with Hitler.

157.8 [153] *Cárdenas.* Lázaro Cárdenas (1895–1970), Mexican president, 1934–40, admired by Hugh for his policies of socialist and agrarian reform (see note **111.7**).

157.9 [153] *Jawaharlal Nehru.* Pandit Jawaharlal Nehru (1889–1964), Indian statesman and prime minister upon independence from 1947 to 1964. Educated in science and law at Harrow and Cambridge, he played a vital role in the negotiations over India's independence, and under the relatively enlightened leadership of his Congress Party, India made dramatic social and industrial progress. Hugh's respect for Nehru in 1938, some time before Indian independence, shows that he is closely in touch with world politics.

157.10 [154] *poltergeists of the ether, claquers of the idiotic.* Poltergeists (from Ger. *poltern* "to make a great noise," and *Geist* "spirit") are ghosts responsible for otherwise inexplicable noisy occurrences; claquers (from Fr. *claquer,* "to applaud") are applauding fawning admirers. In a crazy parody of Geoffrey's familiars and the demonic realm of existence, the voices tell of the deluge ("news of a flood"), misery, and disaster. Epstein comments, p. 120: "All occultists consider the ether to be a fifth element. More refined than the others, it contains all events of our world, past, present, future. It can be 'tuned in' only by those who are sensitive to its presence."

158.1 [154] *Joe Venuti.* "Joe" Guiseppe Venuti (1898–1978), violinist. The son of immigrant Italian workers, he was raised in Philadelphia where he met Eddie Lang (see note **158.2**), who was to be a consistent member of his celebrated "Blue Four" and with whom he made countless recordings and Broadway shows. After Lang's death, Venuti brought a group to London, where he recorded on violin and guitar, and thereafter, back in the States, regularly led his own band.

158.2 [154] *Ed Lang.* Eddie Lang, real name Salvatore Massaro (1902?–33), guitarist. While still at school he became a friend of Joe Venuti, and for most of his career worked alongside him. When Lang died in 1933 (from complications following a tonsillectomy) they had made over seventy recordings together, including many of Lowry's favourites.

158.3 [154] *poetical names like Little Buttercup or Apple Blossom* [*sic*]. Recordings made by Joe Venuti's Blue Four (details given by James Doyle, *MLN* 7, pp. 12–13):
(a) *Little Buttercup.* Also known as "I'll Never be the Same"; recorded in

New York, 10 June 1931; with Venuti (violin), Jimmy Dorsey (clarinet),
Frank Signorelli (piano), and Eddie Lang (guitar); Parlophone R 1252.
(b) *Apple Blossoms*. Recorded in New York, 18 October 1929; with Venuti
(violin), Eddie Lang (guitar), Frankie Trumbauer (C-melody sax),
Lennie Hayton (piano); Parlophone R 647.

158.4 [154]   *bacon scrubber.* Quite literally, one who removes (with hot
water) the bristles from the carcass of a pig before it is cut up for pork.
Hugh's summation of his life is similar in tone to that given by Tom Harrisson in his "Letter to Oxford," p. 13.

158.5 [154]   *Newcastle-under-Lyme.* An industrial town in north Staf-
fordshire, in the heart of the Arnold Bennett country, "quite another thing"
from Newcastle, Delaware (see p. 88 [84]).

158.6 [155]   *Wardour Street... the Marquis of Granby... the old Astoria
in Greek Street.* Hotels and streets in the Soho area of central London, off
Tottenham Court Road. The Marquis of Granby, at 2 Rathbone Street, was
an occasional haunt of Lowry's (Day, p. 149). Tithebarn Street, however, is
in downtown Liverpool, not too far from the Liver building.

159.1 [155]   *Like a nightmare in the soul of George Frederic Watts.* George
Frederick Watts (1817–1904), English painter and sculptor, whose first and
lasting renown was for his portraits, though in his later years he turned
increasingly to sculpture, fresco, and allegory. Remaining untouched by
Pre-Raphaelitism and impressionism alike, he regarded his art as the expression of a moral idealism which would capture the essence of the human
soul. As the phrase "giving up hope" suggests, Hugh has in mind here
Watt's best known painting, "Hope" (1886), now in the Tate Gallery: a
figure, seen at first as a picture of Despair but exemplifying the hopelessness
out of which Hope arises, sits on a globe, her eyes covered, clutching a
"songless lyre" which has but one string left.

159.2 [155]   *steamflies.* An unknown species; perhaps stoneflies, a species
similar to mayflies, but probably intended to anticipate the spiders of the
bath-house, p. 296 [294].

159.3 [155]   *Segovia.* Andres Segovia (b.1893), self-taught Spanish master
of the classical guitar whose excellence forced classical audiences to recognize the guitar as a serious musical instrument. He extended the possibilities
of the guitar by developing new techniques, particularly for the right hand,
to create a wider range of tone and volume and, to increase the quality of

the repertory, transcribed works by other composers and encouraged other players to do the same. Exiled he was, in that he was forced to leave his home in Spain by the Civil War; dying he was not, since he was still giving concerts in the early 1980's.

159.4 [155] *Django Reinhardt.* Jean Baptiste Reinhardt (1910–53), Belgian jazz guitarist who grew up in a gypsy camp, was burned in a caravan fire, and had to devise new fingering techniques to overcome the handicap of a mutilated left hand. He worked with Stephane Grappelli and became an international celebrity, living in France, but recording with top American jazz musicians who visited the Continent. He was a gifted composer and teacher, but above all an outstanding soloist with a magnificent sense of harmony, great melodic resourcefulness, and a flair for spontaneous variety.

159.5 [155] *Frank Crumit.* Frank Crumit (1889–1943) was an American singer and composer of popular songs, with a repertoire of over ten thousand tunes. He appeared in music hall, on the radio, and on Broadway, usually accompanying himself on a ukelele or, less frequently, a guitar or banjo. Hugh's "God help him" may imply some lofty contempt for Crumit's popular success with songs like "Abdul Abulbul Ameer" and "Down on a Bamboo Isle," in contrast with suffering idealists like Reinhardt and Venuti.

159.6 [155] *the Scotch Express.* The 4472 "Flying Scotsman," the non-stop overnight train on the 392-mile Edinburgh to London route (then the longest non-stop journey in the world). The non-stop service was inaugurated 1 May 1928 and aroused great public interest as successive journeys chipped minutes off the previous records. The date is not necessarily incompatible with Hugh's youthful success, since the possibility of such a service had been much in the news for quite some time before 1928. An oblique reference to Geoffrey's drinking and death-train is probably intentional (one would expect "Scots").

159.7 [156] *Parlophone.* In both New York and London, the label of the firm who recorded all kinds of music, but were leaders in the field of popular song and jazz during the 1920's and 1930's. The title of Hugh's "rhythm classic" picks up the theme of "Juggernaut" in the opening paragraph of the novel (see note **9.3.d**); the title is surely fictitious, but like the Scotch Express, suggests the cacophony of Hugh's music.

159.8 [156] *New Compton Street, London.* An address inconsistent with that given on p. 155 [151]: "Old Compton Street." New Compton Street was a continuation (now blocked off) of Old Compton Street, on the other side of Charing Cross Road. "Three Little Dog-gone Mice," by Lowry and Ronald Hill, was published in 1927 by Worton David Ltd., 6 New Compton Street, London (Day, p. 89).

160.1 [156]   *another frustrated artist, Adolf Hitler.* Adolph Hitler (1889–1945), German demagogue and führer of a Germany which in 1938 was only too obviously set on war. In his early years, Hitler had seriously entertained the thought of becoming an artist. At the age of eighteen he applied for entrance into the Vienna Academy of Art, but he failed the entrance examination. During his next few years, before the outbreak of war in 1914, he eked out a precarious living, partly by selling his drawings (some through a Jewish dealer), by drawing posters and advertisements for small shops, and by various poorly paid labouring jobs including, at least once, painting houses.

160.2 [156]   *the tin-pan alleys.* The original Tin Pan Alley, on 28th Street between Fifth Avenue and Broadway, was the hub of America's popular song and music publishing industry in the 1890's and 1900's. As pianos, guitars, and ukeleles became cheaper and more popular, music publishers became aware of a huge popular market which had suddenly emerged. Eventually the nickname of the street came to be used for the typically melodic and sentimental songs brought out by publishers there and for the whole world of popular music.

160.3 [156]   *at some crammer's.* From O.E. *crammian,* "to squeeze"; one who prepares students for an examination by force-feeding facts.

160.4 [156]   *the Public Trustees.* Functionaries appointed by the courts to act as controllers of wills or settlements; they are in charge of money or property left to others, and pay out such moneys according to the directions left in the will. See also note **83.3.**

160.5 [157]   *he had other songs.* As Hugh is well aware, the pseudo-southern titles of these "other songs" are a likely measure of their originality ("Dismal Swamp" may even be an echo of Melville's *Redburn,* Ch. 11, or *Moby Dick,* Ch. 96). Hugh's "I'm Homesick for Being Homesick" may be equivalent to the vocal fox-trot, "I've Said Good-bye to Shanghai" ("with ukelele accompt."), by Malcolm Lowry and Ronald Hill, published in 1927, but not featured with great success by anybody (Day, p. 90).

160.6 [157]   *profound, if not positively Wordsworthian.* Hugh uses

"Wordsworthian" in the pejorative sense of empty banality, the immediate context of homesickness perhaps mocking "The Solitary Reaper," ll. 5–8:

> Alone she cuts and binds the grain,
> And sings a melancholy strain;
> O listen! for the Vale profound
> Is overflowing with the sound.

161.1 [157] *the Marine Superintendent's office.* Mercantile marine offices were established by the Mercantile Marine Act of 1850 to act on behalf of merchant seamen and to see that the requirements of the Mercantile Shipping Acts and the Board of Trade were complied with (the marine superintendent was the official title of the head of such an office). For the purposes of administration, the United Kingdom was divided into five districts (though each port had its office), and seamen engaged on British ships trading outside home waters were required to sign an agreement at a mercantile marine office.

161.2 [157] *Garston . . . Oswaldtwistle.* Garston is a dockside suburb of Liverpool, hence much closer than London to the small east Lancashire town of Oswaldtwistle. Lowry's early novel *Ultramarine* opens with such a process of "signing on" at a similar Liverpool office.

161.3 [157] *the S.S. Philoctetes.* An S.S. *Philoctetes,* a cargo steamer built in 1922, was registered with the Blue Funnel Line, Alfred Holt and Company, Liverpool. For details of the name, see note **163.3**. H.M.S. *Philoctetes,* popularly known as the "Flock of Fleas," was the shore base in Freetown, Sierra Leone, during World War II.

161.4 [157] *Bix Beiderbecke.* Leon Bix Beiderbecke (1903–31), cornet and jazz trumpeter, who joined up with Frankie Trumbauer in 1925 and died an alcoholic at twenty-eight; in both his life and death he exemplified the ultimate of what the total jazz musician stood for, and after his death he became a cult figure. His 1927 "Singin' the Blues," recorded with Trumbauer, is a jazz classic and one which expressed to Lowry "a moment of the most pure spontaneous happiness" (see note **168.2**).

161.5 [157] *the infant Mozart.* Wolfgang Amadeus Mozart (1756–91) was a child prodigy and musical genius whose early works displayed unbelievable talent. He learned to play various instruments at four, to compose at five, and gave public performances at six, when he began with his father

Leopold a long series of tours through the courts of Europe. There are stories of him picking up a violin and playing without previous training, of improvisation at will; and of being able to remember on a single hearing and writing out in full a miserere which was the jealous preserve of the Sistine Chapel choir. Despite his precocity, Mozart seems to have been a happy child, but his early genius did not preserve him from later neglect and penury.

161.6 [158]   *the childhood of Raleigh.* Sir Walter Raleigh (1552?–1618), Elizabethan courtier, poet, historian, and adventurer; the founder of Virginia and explorer of Guiana. A personal favourite of the Queen, he incurred her displeasure by marrying her maid and under both Elizabeth and James I spent long periods in the Tower before being executed for treason on a rather dubious charge. Almost nothing is known of Raleigh's boyhood (even the year of his birth is uncertain), but Hugh seems to have in mind the painting by Sir John Everett Millais, "The Boyhood of Raleigh" (1870), now at the Tate, which depicts a small boy sitting at the foot of a sailor, listening spellbound to tales of the sea. A similar scene is described in *October Ferry,* p. 152, and the painting is mentioned by name.

161.7 [157]   *he had been reading too much Jack London.* Jack London (1876–1916), American novelist, socialist, and adventurer; in turn an oyster-pirate, hobo, sealer, gold-miner, war correspondent, writer, alcoholic, and suicide, who cast himself in the role of rugged individualist and Nietzschean superman and whose life Hugh seems at times almost consciously to imitate. London's life and socialism was fraught with contradiction (see note **99.1**), and he is at his best when depicting the ferocious individual struggle rather than the collective human dream. His best known works are *The Call of the Wild* (1903), *The People of the Abyss* (1903), *White Fang* (1906), *Martin Eden* (1909), as well as those which Hugh mentions:
(a) *The Sea-Wolf (1904).* The story of Humphrey van Weyden, dilettante writer and critic who, following a collision in San Francisco Bay, is picked up by Wolf Larsen, captain of the *Ghost,* and taken to the sealing grounds in Japan. A struggle for supremacy ensues, at the centre of which is the poetess Maude Brewster (somewhat improbably also rescued by the *Ghost*). Van Weyden and Maude escape to an island, where Larsen, deserted by his crew, also ends up, and after Larsen's death the lovers escape in the schooner. There may be some parallels to the triangle presented in *Under the Volcano* in the contrast of the older and younger man; the younger man's supposed sensitivity; the contrast of contemplative and active personalities; and the desire for a chaste life on some northern island.
(b) *The Valley of the Moon (1913).* See note **99.1**: Lowry's adjective "virile"

implies a judgment upon the "maturity" of Hugh's imagined advancement, the essence of which is the transition from the kind of fiercely individualist struggle depicted in *The Sea-Wolf* towards a socialist theory of return to the land as a next step in human evolution.

(c) *The Jacket (1915).* Better known as *The Star Rover* and published by Macmillan in the U.S.A. under that title in October 1915, but previously published in London (Mills & Boon, August 1915) under the former title. The novel, perhaps Jack London's best, is about a condemned man, Darrell Standing, an ex-professor of agronomics, who is in San Quentin for murder. He is placed in solitary confinement and is forced to undergo long spells inside the "jacket", a straitjacket into which he is tightly laced for up to ten days in a row. His method of surviving is to go "star-roving"; that is, to force his mind to eliminate all thoughts of the body and to take off into its own astral world, transcending the limitations of time and space and getting in touch with its previous existences. The novel thus celebrates "man's unconquerable will," which even Standing's final death cannot denigrate, but it is also relevant to Hugh, who is very much the prisoner of his own weaknesses and seeks achievement elsewhere. The chief irony for Lowry, however, is the relevance of the title to the Consul's fate.

161.8 [157] *Seamen and Firemen mutually to assist each other.* A direct quotation from the 1894 Seamen's *Articles,* the official contract between the owner or ship-master and his seaman, setting out the conditions and obligations of service. The words (also recalled by Dana Hilliot in *Ultramarine,* p. 19) read in full:

(a.) Should any of the crew fail to join at the time specified or fail to be on board at any time or times appointed by the Master he may ship substitutes at once.
(b.) The seamen and firemen shall mutually assist each other in the general duties of the ship.
(c.) The firemen shall keep the galley supplied with coal.

The clause is not part of the standard agreement, but part of a set of extra conditions, printed on gummed paper, and usually (but not invariably) added to the general agreement before it is signed. The phrase "without conscience or consideration" does not appear in the articles, but is lifted directly from the German anti-Semitic propaganda quoted in Hugh's telegram, p. 98 [94].

162.1 [158] *Rabat.* The capital of Morocco, where Geoffrey, not yet kicked downstairs, is in consular service. Given the political tension in nearby Spain and Spanish Morocco (see note **237.3**), the position is one of some delicacy.

162.2 [159] *Friday the thirteenth of May.* An ominous date of departure, since ships traditionally avoid sailing on any Friday, let alone the thirteenth. Thirteen May 1927 was in fact a Friday, but Lowry's own departure from Liverpool on board the *Pyrrhus* of the Blue Funnel Line was scheduled for Tuesday 17 May 1927, at 6 P.M.

162.3 [159] *Frankie Trumbauer ... For No Reason at All in C.* Frankie Trumbauer (1900–56), C-melody saxophonist and vocalist. Raised in St. Louis, he played piano, trombone, flute, and violin before turning to the C-melody saxophone. At the age of seventeen he formed his own band and worked with many lead jazz musicians, including Bix Beiderbecke. Lowry's date is correct: "For No Reason at All in C" was recorded in New York, 13 May 1927, by "Trum, Bix and Eddie": Frankie Trumbauer (C-melody sax), Bix Beiderbecke (piano), Eddie Lang (guitar); Parlophone R 3419, Columbia LP CL845 (James Doyle, *MLN* 7 p. 13).

163.1 [159] *to be a Conrad.* The phrasing suggests the well-known hymn "To be a Pilgrim" (words by John Bunyan, *Pilgrim's Progress,* Pt. 2). The allusion is rather apt, given the cargo of pilgrims on the *Patna* in Conrad's *Lord Jim.*

163.2 [159] *No silk cushions for Hugh, says Aunt.* Lowry's real-life version of this episode was an even greater cause for writhing: he was quoted in the *London Evening News* (14 May 1927, p. 5) as having himself said: "No silk-cushion youth for me. I want to see the world, and rub shoulders with its oddities, and get some experience of life before I go back to Cambridge University" (Day, p. 91).

163.3 [159] *Philoctetes.* Philoctetes was the most celebrated archer among the Greek forces attacking Troy, but also very much a victim of misfortune. The son of Poeas, he received from his father the famous bow and arrows of Heracles (see note **163.5**), but wounded in the foot (in some versions by his own arrows; in Sophocles's *Philoctetes* by a snake), he was left behind on Lemnos when the Greeks went to Troy. Because the Greeks needed his skills, he was tricked into returning to Troy, where he mortally wounded Paris in an archery contest.

The analogy between Philoctetes's bow and Hugh's guitar suggests that Lowry is deliberately alluding to Edmund Wilson's essay, "The Wound and the Bow" (1941), where Wilson, making use of Freudian psychology, sees the bow as the blessing given to the artist, the creative gift, which is necessarily accompanied by the wound, or neurosis: suffering is thus seen as a necessary accompaniment of creativity and as something that necessitates the artist's alienation from his society.

163.4 [159] *Poeas.* The father of Philoctetes, to whom he gave the mighty bow and arrows which Heracles had given to him, Poeas, when he set fire to the pines that formed the hero's pyre (see note **163.5**).

163.5 [159] *Heracles.* Heracles, or Hercules, son of Zeus and Alcmena, was the greatest of Greek heroes and one whose exploits seem to mock Hugh's paltry opinion of himself. While still in his cradle, Heracles strangled two snakes which Hera had sent to destroy him, and throughout his youth and early manhood, he performed prodigious feats of strength, the best known of which are the twelve labours imposed on him as penance for having killed his children in a fit of madness. After inadvertently putting on the poisoned shirt of Nessus, Heracles made and ascended his funeral pyre, gave his bow and arrows to Poeas, who kindled the pines, and was then carried off to Olympus among the immortals.

163.6 [159] *cross-bow.* Since Philoctetes would not have had a cross-bow, Lowry's reference is undoubtedly to Coleridge's "The Rime of the Ancient Mariner" (1798), ll. 79–82:

> "God save thee, ancient Mariner,
> From the fiends, that plague thee thus! –
> Why look'st thou so?" – "With my cross-bow
> I shot the Albatross."

For this gratuitous act a curse falls on the ship and the mariner is condemned by his fellows to wear the bird hung round his neck, until he is able to feel pity and pray, at which moment the albatross falls from his neck and into the sea.

163.7 [159] *Cathay and the brothels of Palambang.* The romanticized Orient:
(a) *Cathay.* The ancient name for China, the use of which hints at a kind of Marco Polo image in Hugh's mind.
(b) *Palambang.* More correctly, *Palembang* (as Lowry in fact spelled it in the manuscripts), the largest city of Sumatra, in 1938 part of the Dutch East Indies, but in the eighth century A.D. the centre of the flourishing Hindu-Sumatran kingdom of Sri Vijaya.

163.8 [159] *Jesus, Cock.* "Cock" is a less sacrilegious version of the word 'God', and was commonly used in swearing oaths and execrations. Lowry, however, would not be insensitive to the hints of betrayal associated with the oath.

163.9 [159] *he was on a false footing with his shipmates.* Although many of the following details are based upon Lowry's personal experiences and miseries when he went to sea (as described in *Ultramarine*), literary precedents for Hugh's humiliations exist in Nordahl Grieg's *The Ship Sails On* and, in particular, in Melville's *Redburn,* where the hero is resented by the common sailors because of his supposedly rich background and his only going to sea "for the humour of it." In Chs. 9 and 10, Redburn "converses with the sailors," but they abuse him relentlessly: "They asked me what business I, a boy like me, had to go to sea, and take the bread out of the mouth of honest sailors, and fill a good seaman's place." Even though Hugh is not quite as insufferable as Wellingborough Redburn, the sustained hostility of his fellows hurts him as much and lasts as long.

163.10 [160] *chipping hammers.* Small hammers with triangular-shaped heads used for chipping rust from the decks and metal fittings of a ship.

164.1 [160] *red lead.* Red oxide of lead (also called *minium*), used as the basis of a heavy anti-corrosive red paint; hence the paint itself. Red lead is also naval slang for tinned herrings in tomato sauce.

164.2 [160] *fagging.* In British public schools, the menial work which the younger boys are required to do for their seniors, such as running errands or shining shoes.

164.3 [160] *the forecastle... the poop.* The forecastle is the raised forward part of a ship, where the common sailors' quarters are traditionally located (see note **107.4.b**); the poop is the stern section of the ship, particularly the raised deck at that end. Hugh's version of what life should be on board seems to have been derived almost entirely from his reading, in particular of R. H. Dana's *Two Years Before the Mast* (1840), the story of a Harvard undergraduate who decides to go to sea and describes with grim romantic realism his forecastle quarters and the life at sea.

164.4 [160] *the Isle of Man boat.* A ferryboat plying between Liverpool and Douglas, on the Isle of Man.

164.5 [161] *six and eight bells.* "Eight bells" signals the end of a four-hour watch; "six bells" marks the end of the third hour; here, six bells indicates 3 P.M. and eight bells indicate 4 P.M.

165.1 [161] *bosun's mess.* The dining room for the bosun's mates. A bosun (or boatswain) is a petty officer on a ship, usually in charge of deck work.

165.2 [161] *tabnabs.* Normally buns, pastries, and confectionery reserved for first-class passengers and not for the crew; hence, pieces to be nabbed from the table.

165.3 [161] *the Sea Wolf.* The sadistic captain of Jack London's novel (see note **161.7.a**).

165.4 [161] *the P.O.'s mess.* The designated eating area of the petty officers (the lowest rating among non-commissioned naval officers). It was popularly known as "the Virgin," since it was screened off from the general mess area.

165.5 [161] *kippers.* Salted, dried, and smoked herrings, often served for breakfast.

165.6 [161] *tiddley.* Precisely ordered or arranged.

165.7 [162] *a fantastic mobile football field.* The twin masts of a turreted merchant ship, linked with a crosspiece, were commonly known as "goal posts." The S.S. *Pyrrhus,* on which Lowry sailed, was such a "goal-post ship."

166.1 [162] *Chips.* The invariable name of the ship's carpenter. On most merchant ships, the bosun is usually the more senior petty officer.

166.2 [162] *a tramp.* A freight ship that has no regular schedule, but picks up passengers and cargo wherever it can. The word has connotations of something makeshift or shabby, hence the captain's fury. The *Pyrrhus* was not a tramp.

166.3 [162] *Typhoons were to be expected.* The action of Joseph Conrad's "Typhoon" (1902) takes place off the China coast in the monsoon season. Captain McWhirr, of the steamer *Nan-Shan,* is an unimaginative, dour man who, nevertheless, when the barometer falls "during the season of typhoons" and the ship is smashed by winds and waves, proves to be the man to face the hurricane and bring her through.

166.4 [163]   *the Bitter Lakes.* Two lakes (Great Bitter, fourteen miles long, and Little Bitter, eight miles) in the isthmus of Suez, Egypt, linked and utilized by the Suez Canal. A "bitter lake" is one whose waters contain certain unusually large amounts of sodium sulphate and various carbonates and chlorides.

166.5 [163]   *in the roads at Yokohama.* Yokohama is the port for Tokyo and the major harbour of Japan. To avoid the heavy fees charged at such a port, a ship might lie "in the roads," that is, at anchor awaiting unloading in a protected place near the shore, but not tied up at the wharves.

166.6 [163]   *going through the Suez... sphinxes, Ismalia... Mt. Sinai.* Passengers passing through the Suez Canal might normally get off the ship at Giza, to visit the huge statue of the Sphinx; then rejoin it at Ismailia, on Lake Timsah at the midpoint of the canal; to pass by Gebel Musa (Ar. "Mount of Moses"), which is usually identified with Mt. Sinai where Moses received the Tablets of the Law (Exodus 34:28–29) and where may be found the Greek Orthodox Monastery of Saint Katherine, founded in 250 A.D.

166.7 [163]   *through the Red Sea... Hejaz, Asir, Yemen.* After leaving the Suez Canal, an outward bound ship would enter the Red Sea, pass by the region of Hejaz (inland of which are the holy cities of Medina and Mecca), then travel along the southwest Arabian coast region of Asir to reach Yemen, on the southwest coast of Arabia (past Doughty's *Arabia Deserta,* Felix Arabia, and the lands of T. E. Lawrence), before leaving the Red Sea and entering the Gulf of Arabia.

166.8 [163]   *Perim.* Perim is a rocky, barren, volcanic island of some five square miles in the Straits of Bab-el-Mandeb (Ar. "Gate of Tears"), at the southern entrance to the Red Sea. It was acquired by Britain in 1857 as part of the colony of Aden and was used as a coaling station until 1936. It now forms part of South Yemen. The island is mentioned in the anonymous Greek *Periplus Maris Erythraei* of the first century A.D., but Hugh's statement that it once "belonged to India" seems dubious: the island was known to Egyptian, Greek, Arabian, and, quite possibly, Indian traders of antiquity, but despite its important strategic location on the spice route, its total lack of water precluded settlement, and there is in fact little record of it "belonging" to anyone until it was explored by the Portuguese in 1513 and garrisoned briefly by Britain in 1799.

167.1 [163]   *An Italian Somaliland stamp with wild herdsmen on it.* Italian Somaliland, now part of the Somali Republic, was the coastal strip on the

African side of the Red Sea, then under Italian domination. It forms the setting for Gerald Hanley's 1951 novel, *The Consul at Sunset.* The stamp which Hugh is thinking of cannot be readily identified, as no Italian Somaliland stamp of this description exists, certainly not before 1927; the only possible stamp that fits this description is a 1932 design depicting a herdsman standing next to a prominent termite nest.

167.2 [163]   *Guardafui.* Cape Guardafui (the Cape of Spices in the ancient *Periplus Maris Erythraei*), on the horn of Africa south of the Gulf of Aden, forms the easternmost point of the African continent.

167.3 [163]   *Cape Comorin.* The rocky headland which forms the southernmost point of India.

167.4 [163]   *Nicobar.* A group of nineteen islands, 185 square miles in all, in the Bay of Bengal one hundred miles south of the Andamans, forming part of the Indian state of the Andaman and Nicobar Islands.

167.5 [163]   *the Gulf of Siam . . . Pnom-Penh.* The Gulf of Siam lies between the Malay Peninsula and what was in 1927 Indochina; Pnom Penh (now in Cambodia), on the Mekong River which flows into the Gulf of Siam, was in 1927 the capital of French Indochina, and the gateway to the fabulous ruins of Angkor Wat, the remnants of once-mighty Khmer temples dedicated to Vishnu.

167.6 [163]   *thrummed.* A conscious allusion to the word used by Conrad Aiken throughout *Blue Voyage* for the noise of the ship's engines; as on the last page, p. 166, where it is heightened with sexual anticipation:

> *Te-thrum te-thrum: te-thrum te-thrum.* . . . One became aware of it —
> one heard the engines: the beating of its lonely heart. One felt the frame
> quiver, saw it change its shape even, became startlingly conscious of the
> fact that one was all at sea; alone with the infinite; alone with God.

167.7 [163]   *videre; videre.* L. "to see; to see." The sound of the engines echoes Nordahl Grieg's *Skibet gaar videre* (1924), translated into English by A. G. Chater as *The Ship Sails On* (1927). The novel tells of the *Mignon,* "A Moloch that crushes the lives of men between its iron jaws," on her journey from Norway to the cape. When young Benjamin Hall joins her, he finds the forecastle full of whores, and despite being accepted by his fellows, he finds the trip a miserable experience and finally contracts V.D.

At the end of the voyage, holding the diseased ship's dog in his arms, Benjamin climbs over the rail to end it all (see note **232.3**), but he changes his mind and climbs back to face whatever lies ahead. Hugh's thoughts here are perhaps derived from *The Ship Sails On,* p. 57, where Benjamin contemplates the sea and the sky: "The boundless space around became so intimately small, since infinity has no scale. All was sky and sea. A little strip of wake bubbled behind the ship, and round about gleamed a few friendly miles of water."

Lowry's short story *"Punctum Indifferens Skibet Gaar Videre"* ("Pointless Point the Ship Sails On"), was strongly influenced by Grieg (it was published as *"Seductio ad Absurdam"* in *Best British Short Stories of 1931,* edited by E. O'Brien, and later incorporated as Ch. 4 of *Ultramarine*). Told in broken snatches of dialogue by the ship's crew, it leads up to the moment that Dana Hilliot, baited by the men, finally confronts his chief antagonist, Andy Bredahl. Sherrill Grace comments on Lowry's title, p. 4: "The point is pointless because individual existence and reality are never still but always moving on into the future; temporal flow cannot be broken down into static points of past, present, and future."

The words "to see, to see" ("to sea, to sea") suggest that, despite Hugh's not having then read a word of Conrad, Lowry has in mind the description of the artist's role in Conrad's Preface to *The Nigger of the "Narcissus"* (1898): "My task which I am trying to achieve is, by the power of the written word to make you hear, to make you feel—it is, before all, to make you *see.*"

167.8 [163] *the Pharisaism of his English elders.* The Pharisees were a dominant Jewish sect at the beginning of the Christian era, but their arrogance and their rigid adherence to the letter rather than the spirit of the law and to the traditions of the elders aroused Christ's censure (see Luke 18:10–14); hence Phariseeism, hypocrisy or self-righteousness in matters of religion (the pun on "elders" in the Presbyterian sense perhaps also being intentional).

167.9 [163] *the lamptrimmer.* The officer whose responsibility it is to tend and trim the oil-fuelled lamps (port, starboard, and masthead) and to report every half-hour at night all navigational lights as correctly burning.

167.10 [163] *the Forsyte Saga.* A series of novels written by John Galsworthy (1867–1933) between 1906 and 1929, the main theme of which is the possessive instinct embodied to an exaggerated degree in the figure of Soames Forsyte, a man with a passion for collecting all things desirable (*OCEL*), and extending from the late Victorian age to the depiction of a society shattered by the Great War, a suitable study in bourgeois decay for any budding communist.

167.11 [163]   *Peer Gynt.* A lyrical drama by Henrik Ibsen (1828–1906), published in 1867. The central character, Peer, though having the capacity for good, is essentially a boaster and a dreamer who flees his home to wander through the world. At one point his life is likened to an onion, with no centre, and when he finally returns home, he meets at the crossroads the button-moulder who will melt him down for having been neither actively good or bad, but simply worthless (see note **359.3**).

167.12 [164]   *the Red Hand.* Apparently the Ulster magazine which appeared briefly (four issues only) in 1920, publicizing left-wing views on Irish sovereignty, Irish unity, and a general pro-Labour policy. The red hand is the badge of Ulster—a heraldic hand, erect, open, and couped at the wrist. Lowry may also intend an allusion to Milton's *Paradise Lost,* II.174, where the "red right hand" of God is raised to smite the fallen angels (this is the sense in which he uses it in *Lunar Caustic,* p. 14).

167.13 [164]   *'Murder of Brother-in-Law's Concubine.'* The headline in the *Singapore Free Press* (since 1835, the best known of British weeklies then circulating in the Far East) is identical to that seen by Dana Hill in "On Board the West Hardaway" (*P & S,* p. 34) and by Dana Hilliot several times in *Ultramarine;* but as seen by Hugh in *Under the Volcano* perhaps possesses ominous implications previously lacking.

167.14 [164]   *Penang.* An island in the Strait of Malacca, ceded by Kedah to Britain in 1786 to be the first British Straits settlement and to form the most important port and anchorage of the Malayan mainland.

168.1 [164]   *breaks.* In jazz, a "break" is a section of a song between the initial statement of the melody and its reprise. It is an opportunity for the jazz soloists to improvise, improvisation being one of the major purposes and strengths of jazz music. During these sunset periods in Yokohama harbour, Hugh, freed from the mechanical routines of the day, is able to daydream, or "improvise," on his own.

168.2 [164]   *Singing the Blues.* Either Hugh is right up with the latest jazz or Lowry was not bothered about the slight implausibility, for, as James Doyle points out (*MLN* 7, pp. 13–14):

Lowry undoubtedly had in mind the Trumbauer-Beiderbecke version of

"Singin' the Blues," recorded New York, February 4, 1927, with Beiderbecke, cornet; Trumbauer, C-melody sax; Miff Mole, trombone; Jimmy Dorsey, clarinet; Doc Ryker, alto sax; Itzy Riskin, piano; Eddie Lang, guitar; Chauncey Morehouse, drums (Parlophone R 3323; Columbia LP CL845).

Lowry comments in "Forest Path", p. 257:

> One evening on the way back from the spring for some reason I suddenly thought of a break by Bix in Frankie Trumbauer's record of Singing the Blues that had always seemed to me to express a moment of the most pure spontaneous happiness. I could never hear this break without feeling happy myself and wanting to do something good. Could one translate this kind of happiness into one's life?

168.3 [164]   *Birkenhead Hippodrome.* The New Birkenhead Hippodrome was opened in December 1908 in opposition to the famous Argyle as a music-hall and variety venue, but it was soon given over to films exclusively (it seems likely that Hugh is equally thinking of the Argyle, whose "twice nightly" shows were a feature). The Hippodrome is several times nostalgically recalled by the homesick Dana Hilliot in *Ultramarine.* Like the Argyle, it was destroyed by German bombs in September 1940.

168.4 [165]   *the Oedipus Tyrannus.* The Greek form of the more usual *Oedipus Rex,* but unlike the *Philoctetes* (see note **161.3**), neither name is recorded among the vessels of the Blue Funnel Line (whose ships were invariably named after classical figures). The *Oedipus Tyrannus* is Dana Hilliot's ship in *Ultramarine,* the name revised by Lowry from the *Nawab* for the second edition, in order to conform to *Under the Volcano.* The name alludes to Oedipus, the son of Laius and Jocasta, king and queen of Thebes. Because of a prophecy that he would slay his father, he was abandoned at birth, but he was rescued by a shepherd and raised by the king of Corinth. Learning from an oracle that he must slay his father and marry his mother, Oedipus abandoned his supposed parents and eventually returned to Thebes, meeting and killing on the way Laius, his father. Thebes was then plagued by the Sphinx, but Oedipus, solving its riddle, obtained the kingdom and Jocasta as wife. Discovering the results of his actions, Oedipus blinded himself in horror and, led by his daughter Antigone, retired to Colonus in Attica, where he died.

169.1 [165]   *a foul berth.* Literally, a poor anchorage; more generally, a rough deal.

169.2 [165] *more days are more dollars.* Though a common enough expression, the words were originally used sarcastically by British seamen of their better paid American counterparts.

169.3 [165] *fourteen months (Hugh had not yet read Melville either) is an eternity.* Hugh is still romanticizing the life of a seaman: Melville's *White Jacket* is a brutally frank account of a fourteen-month tour which Melville spent on a United States Navy ship in 1843.

169.4 [166] *quarter.* The quarter of a circle to the rear of the beam of a ship, that is, beginning amidships and circling to the stern. There are two after quarters then, one to starboard and one to port. Observation of other ships or navigational aids is described in terms of their location on the quarters.

169.5 [166] *trankums.* Hugh presumably means *transoms,* the transverse timbers or beams secured to the sternpost of a boat; hence, any kind of horizontal bar. The *Oedipus Tyrannus* was described, p. 165 [162], as "a fantastic mobile football field"; a transom is also the crossbar of a rugby goal post. A *trankum* is described by the *OED* as "A personal ornament, a trinket," but the cross-reference to *trangam* is the clue to Lowry's meaning: "Applied to anything which the speaker views with contempt."

170.1 [166] *hull-down.* A ship at a certain distance may be hidden below the horizon except for her masts; she is then said to be "hull-down."

170.2 [166] *seven knots.* Seven sea-miles an hour; a very poor speed, but one which Hugh finds appealingly unmodern.

170.3 [166] *Colón.* Panama's second city, named after Christopher Columbus. It is an important port at the Atlantic end of the Panama Canal, within the Canal Zone, but forming part of Panama.

170.4 [167] *the dirty 'og.* A hog (from "'og wash," the sea) is naval slang for a poorly paid seaman from the dockyard slums.

170.5 [167] *Lord Jim, about to pick up pilgrims going to Mecca.* In Ch. 2 of Conrad's *Lord Jim,* Jim gives up the idea of going home and signs on board the *Patna,* "a local steamer as old as the hills, lean like a greyhound and eaten up with rust worse than a condemned water-tank," and, after the ship has been painted, eight hundred pilgrims bound for Mecca are driven on board. When Hugh feels he had "nothing in his mind of Lord Jim," he simply means he was not tempted to abandon ship (see note **39.1**).

171.1 [167]   *Miki.* There is a river port called Miki in southern Honshu, Japan, but Lowry's coaling port (with its ominous bunkers) is based on Port Swettenham, Selangor. In *Ultramarine* there is frequent mention of the Miki Bar and Dancing Saloon (little short of a brothel) in Tsjang-Tsjang (Yokohama), and Lowry seems to have transferred the name with a sense of deliberate incongruity.

171.2 [167]   *a trimmer.* A coal-passer; probably the least prestigious job in a ship's crew. The trimmer's duties include bringing coal to the furnaces; hauling and dumping ashes; cleaning the bilges; and, in port, chipping the scale which has accumulated on the inside of the boilers.

171.3 [167]   *through the hawsehole into the bourgeois upper air.* The hawsehole is a hole in the bows of the ship through which cables pass. To emerge from the hawsehole is to win promotion from the ranks of ordinary seaman or fireman (as opposed to joining as an officer-cadet); the deliberately socialistic phrasing reflects the ship's class structure and the opposition of those working the decks and bridges to the firemen and stokers of the lower depths.

172.1 [168]   *They lay at Gravesend waiting for the tide.* Gravesend, the outermost port of the Thames, is a pilot station for vessels using the port of London and lies on the Thames estuary, opposite Tilbury, about twenty miles east of London. The phrasing deliberately evokes the opening of Conrad's *Heart of Darkness* (1902), where the cruising yawl *Nellie* awaits the turning of the tide.

172.2 [168]   *the Yangtze-Kiang.* Commonly referred to by British seamen of the 1930's simply as "the River," the Yangtze is the longest river of Asia and China, flowing 3,430 miles from the Tibetan highlands to the Pacific near Shanghai and passing through many of China's greatest cities. It forms a major trading artery and can be used for many miles by ocean-going vessels. The river was soon to become famous in British naval history because of the 1949 "Yangtze Incident," in which the gunboat H.M.S. *Amethyst,* attacked by the communists, held off and made her way 140 miles downstream.

172.3 [168]   *someone knocked his pipe on a garden wall.* That is, the ship had pulled in so close to land that this seemed possible.

172.4 [168]   *Silvertown.* A docking area of the Port of London, near Woolwich, some miles up the estuary but before the city proper.

174.1 [170] *Izzy Smigalkin and his orchestra.* The fictional name may be modelled on that of "Izzy" (Irving) Friedman, who recorded frequently (though in New York) with Bix Beiderbecke, Ed Lang, and Frankie Trumbauer. Lowry's "Three Little Dog-gone Mice" (see note **159.8**) was in like manner "Featured with Great Success by Alfredo and his Band" (Day, p. 89), as Lowry too became wise in the ways of the world.

174.2 [170] *the Astoria. . . . the Elephant and Castle . . . the Kilburn Empire.* Hugh would have discovered at the Astoria (in Greek Street, Soho) that Izzy Smigalkin was playing at the Elephant and Castle (the well-known hotel, now replaced, in the middle of the square of the same name, Southwark), rather than at the Kilburn Empire (not the celebrated Empire Theatre on Leicester Square, but rather a little dive in the Kilburn area of northwest London).

174.3 [170] *Wapping Old Stairs.* A narrow lane off the Wapping High Street in Wapping, a run-down dockside area of East London. The lane ends in a set of stairs (no longer in commercial use), leading down to the beach. The area close by was where pirates were hanged, to await three turnings of the tide.

174.4 [171] *a certain resemblance to Adolf Hitler's.* That is, anti-Semitism. Hitler is said to have developed his anti-Jewish feelings during his early years as a struggling artist in Vienna.

175.1 [171] *the British Mercantile Marine.* The British Merchant Navy, flying under the Red Ensign (or "Red Rag"); the term "Merchant Navy" was used from World War I on, but for legislative purposes "Mercantile Marine" is preferred. Until 1850, legislation for merchant seamen conformed to that of the Royal Navy, but the Mercantile Marine Act of 1850, and other acts later, differentiated the two services and did much to improve the rights and conditions of merchant seamen.

175.2 [171] *pogroms.* From R. *gromit',* "to batter"; an organized massacre, particularly one directed against the Jews.

175.3 [171] *Rabat or Timbuctoo.* Rabat, in Morocco, from where Geoffrey sportingly sent his telegram, p. 162 [158]; Timbuktu, in the middle of the Sahara Desert and French West Africa (now the Mali Republic), is commonly used, as on p. 312 [310], as the equivalent of "the middle of nowhere."

175.4 [171]   *sheet anchor.* Probably from M.E. *shote,* a cable of two ropes spliced together; a large anchor, kept amidships, and used only in emergencies. Hence, a person to be relied upon.

175.5 [171]   *the Bolshevists.* From R. *bolshoi,* "big." That part of the Russian Social-Democratic party who took Lenin's side in the split within the party following its Second Congress in 1903; who gained control (at the expense of the more moderate Menshevists) of the party; and who seized power after the October Revolution of 1917. The word was commonly used in some circles of English society as equivalent to "Bogeyman."

175.6 [171]   *the Daily Mail.* A popular daily, the first halfpenny morning paper, launched in 1896 by Alfred Harmsworth (later Lord Northcliffe). Though it set new standards in popular journalism, it soon became known for its jingoism and entrenched middlebrow attitudes.

175.7 [172]   *Pangbourne Garden City.* Pangbourne was in the 1920's a Thameside town in Berkshire, about six miles from Reading, and well-known for its delightful woods and gardens. The politics of most of the community would have been conservative in the extreme.

175.8 [172]   *to do his good turn... to be prepared.* A boy scout (Dr. Gotelby had been a scoutmaster) is expected to do a good turn every day, and the motto of the boy scouts is "Be Prepared" — a phrase which less innocently implies carrying round a condom.

176.1 [172]   *Blackheath... Lewisham, Catford, New Cross, down the Old Kent Road, past, ah, the Elephant and Castle.* For a time in 1928 Lowry was living in Blackheath, southeast London (his address, 5 Woodville Road, is no longer identifiable), whence it is perhaps five miles or so into the City. Hugh's fifteen miles may be explained by his choice of route: Catford does not lie between Lewisham and New Cross, but is quite some way south (the directions are otherwise in a logical straight sequence). The Elephant and Castle is a large intersection in Southwark at the end of the New Kent Road (a continuation of the Old), directly south of Blackfriars Bridge which leads into the heart of London; Hugh catches his breath as he is reminded of the embarrassing failure of his songs.

176.2 [172]   *districts romanticized by Longfellow.* A reference to Henry W. Longfellow's review essay, "The Great Metropolis," which gives a romanticized view of the boroughs "in and below London" with no attention given at all to the squalor which was, and is, still visible there. A typical passage reads:

Then, close at hand, the great bell of St. Paul's, with a heavy, solemn sound, — one, two. It is answered from Southwark; then at a distance like an echo; and then all around you, with various and intermingling clang, like a chime of bells, the clocks from a hundred belfries strike the hour. But the moon is already sinking, large and fiery, through the vapors of morning. It is just in the range of the chimneys and house-tops, and seems to follow you with speed as you float down the river between the unbroken ranks of ships. Day is dawning in the east, not with a pale streak in the horizon but with a silver light spread through the sky to the zenith. It is the mingling of moonlight and daylight.

177.1 [173] *have calmly gone up to—*. Cambridge: though one quite normally "goes up" (from London) to Cambridge there is in Hugh's mind a conscious relief that he will not be "sent down" in disgrace.

177.2 [173] *asses'-milk soap*. Asses' milk is popularly supposed to have a rejuvenating effect on the skin (Cleopatra is reputed to have bathed in it each day). The name may be a brand name, but asses' milk itself contains no fat and is therefore unsuitable as a basis for soap. Hugh's act of shaving the Consul finally realizes the potential pun of "Cuckold-shaven" which has been earlier hinted at (see notes **17.4** and **64.3**).

177.3 [174] *the wheels*. The "shakes" are the D.T.'s, but as Hugh said in an earlier draft (UBC 7-7, p. 14), "At sea we used to call 'em the wheels" (presumably because the head spins round). Lowry, however, intends a ref-erence to Ezekiel's vision of the chariot of God, with its four wheels, each of which was "as it were a wheel in the middle of a wheel" (Ezekiel 1:16). These wheels within wheels traditionally symbolize God's freedom to move as and where he wishes, and the Chariot of Ezekiel (Tarot card 7) is used in occult and alchemical thought as an image of successful projection. The Consul, however, has abused his mystical powers by too much drinking and instead of seeing Ezekiel's glory of God experiences the horrific tremors of an inverted vision; he is unable to stand on his feet, and he dwells among scorpions (Ezekiel 2:1-6).

177.4 [174] *bay rum*. A liquid used for cosmetic and medicinal purposes, mainly as a hair tonic; originally prepared by distilling the leaves of the West Indian bayberry tree with rum.

177.5 [174] *pernod*. A French liqueur drunk as an apéritif and having the flavour of anisette. It is described in Ernest Hemingway's *Fiesta*, pp. 20–21: "Pernod is greenish imitation absinthe. When you add water it turns milky.

It tastes like licorice and it has a good uplift, but it drops you just as far."

178.1 [174] *the polygonous proustian stare of imaginary scorpions.* Although scorpions have eyes, these are not polygonous or compound, and their sight is very poor. These are rather scorpions of the mind, the Consul's vivid image conveying his paranoia as he imagines himself surrounded by swarms of them. The scorpions are proustian because they remind the Consul of a particular passage in Marcel Proust's *A la recherche du temps perdu,* in the section called "A l'ombre des jeunes filles en fleurs," p. 751, or, in Scott Moncrief's translation, "Within a Budding Grove," Pt. II, pp. 68–69. As the narrator returns to the hotel, he has the sudden sensation of being watched by somebody not far off. He turns his head, and sees a man looking intently at him, the eyes "dilated with observation . . . shot through by a look of intense activity such as the sight of a person whom they do not know excites only in men to whom, for whatever reason, it suggests thoughts that would not occur to anyone else — madmen, for instance, or spies." Proust's great work is a long, complex meditation upon many matters of interest to the Consul: the unreality and reversibility of time; the power of memory to recover the past; and the subject's consequent power over life and death. Proust explores the power of involuntary memory, and shows how phases of experience forgotten and deadened by the years can be jerked back into consciousness by an apparently trivial association just as the Consul's image "like being in a tank" has reminded him, sickeningly, of the furnaces of the S.S. *Samaritan.*

178.2 [175] *Dogme et Ritual de la Haute Magie.* By Éliphas Lévi, baptised Alphonse Louis Constant (1810–75), French occultist whose writings were very influential upon later students of magic. The son of a shoemaker, Lévi studied for the seminary but was obliged to leave because of his sexual permissiveness and his questioning of orthodox dogma. His writings include *Dogme et Rituel de la Haute Magie* (1855–56), *La Clef des Grands Mystères* (1861), and *La Science des Esprits* (1865); these gave him a reputation as a great authority upon occult matters. *Dogme et Rituel* was originally published in two parts: the first, *Dogme* (1855), dealing with the symbolism of numbers and the principles of occult thought; the second, *Rituel* (1856), dealing with the forms and rituals of magical invocation. The two were translated by A. E. Waite in 1896 as *Transcendental Magic: Its Doctrine and Ritual,* Waite admitting Lévi's influence and importance as a magus who had opened the doors of the occult to many but criticizing "his slipshod criticism, his careless reading and his malpractices in historical matters" as not making "for a proper understanding of occult reveries" and as initiating "a new and gratuitous phase in the study of the Kabbalah" (*The Holy Kabbalah,* X.xvi, pp. 490–95).

178.3 [175] *Serpent and Siva Worship in Central America.* Identified by Andersen, p. 381, and Jakobsen, p. 81, as "Serpent and Siva Worship and Mythology in Central America, Africa, and Asia," by Hyde Clarke (London: Trübner & Co., 1876), a fourteen-page tract from the *Journal of the Anthropological Institute.* The major concern of the article, despite its title, is comparative philology, Clarke arguing that the languages of the various Central American Indians have relations with those of the Old World and that, in particular, the worship of the Hindu God Śiva is the survival of a prehistoric legend also found in Central America. The underlying connection, and the reason for the tract's interest to the Consul, is explained by another work by Clarke: "The Legend of Atlantis in reference to protohistoric communication with America" (1886).

178.4 [175] *the Goetia of the Lemegaton of Solomon the King.* A book listed by Kilgallin, Appendix A, as forming part of the magical library of Charles Stansfeld-Jones:

> Crowley, Aleister, ed. *The Book of the Goetia of Solomon The King,* Translated into the English Tongue By a Dead Hand and Adorned With Diverse Other Matters Germane Delightful to the Wise. Society for the Propagation of Religious Truth, Bokeskine, Foyers, Inverness 1904.

Goëtic art is that which deals with incantations, sorcery, witchcraft, and black magic, this particular Goetia being the Lemegaton (or lesser key) which offers formulae to invoke demons. The book, dating from the seventeenth century, concerns the "Initiated Interpretation of Ceremonial Magic" (with a diatribe added by Crowley against A. E. Waite); its first part is "a Book of Evil Spirits, called Goetia" (p. 7). Later sections deal with different aspects of spirits, prayers, and orations, "which Solomon the Wise did use upon the Altar of the Temple" (p. 9), Solomon being reputedly one of the first and greatest of all Cabbalists. Since the edition which the Consul has on his shelf is "fairly new," it may be the small, bluebound edition printed in Chicago in 1916.

178.5 [175] *Gogol.* Nikolai Vasilievich Gogol (1809–52), Russian novelist and satirist, whose comic masterpiece *Dead Souls* (1846) was one of Lowry's favourite books and a model for his own novel ("Preface to a Novel,"

Woodcock, p. 11). The hero, Tchitchikov, forms the plan of buying up on paper serfs who have died since the last census and who are therefore officially alive in the records, gaining thereby the backing to raise money and acquire land. The book's lasting delight is its humorous and often savage portrait of all grades of Russian society, but Lowry's chief point is the significance of its title.

178.6 [175]   *the Mahabharata.* One of the two great epic poems of the Hindus, probably the longest of the world's epics, telling in some 220,000 lines and eighteen *parvans* or sections the story of the descendants of Bharata, the founder of the great Indian families of yore, culminating in the war of succession between the Kauravas and Pāndavas. Originally a short ballad composed in Prākrit, it is now preserved in Sanskrit and expanded to many times its original size with a considerable increment of digressive material — cosmology, theogony, statecraft, the science of war, ethics, legendary history, mythology, fairy tales, and philosophical interludes (the best known of which is the *Bhagavadgītā*). The battle of Kurukshetra, round which the epic is centred, is tentatively fixed between 850 and 650 B.C., but parts of the work are as late as A.D. 500 (*Hindu World,* II, pp. 8–9).

The Consul's dream in Ch. 5 (see note **129.1**) arises directly from the *Mahābhārata,* and many of the details, pp. 308–9, about *soma, bhang,* and the sacrifice of horses are discussed in detail in the Hindu epic. The edition on the Consul's shelf is probably the abbreviated poetic version by Romesh Dutt, published as no. 36 in the Temple Classics (Gollancz), 1898.

178.7 [175]   *Blake.* William Blake (1757–1827), English poet, painter, and mystic, better known for such early works as "Songs of Innocence" (1789), "The Marriage of Heaven and Hell" (1790–93), and "Songs of Experience" (1795), rather than for his later more obscure prophetic writings. References to Blake's works in *UTV* are surprisingly few, considering the importance of the "path through hell," p. 42 [36].

178.8 [175]   *Tolstoy.* Count Leo Nikolaevich Tolstoy (1828–1910), Russian novelist best known for his *War and Peace* (1865–72) and *Anna Karenina* (1875–76), novels which afford the substance of an argument between Hugh and the Consul at the end of Ch. 10. Tolstoy's tremendous command of detail, his strength of moral conviction, and his immense visionary powers made him a supreme novelist, though he later turned to religious mysticism and a way of life fraught with contradictions. In earlier versions of the novel, the Consul had been an expert on Tolstoy, but as he sadly admits, p. 87 [82], the only thing he can remember about *War and Peace* is that Napoleon's leg twitched.

178.9 [175] *Pontoppidan.* Erich Pontoppidan (1698–1764), Danish theologian and professor of theology at Copenhagen in 1738, bishop of Bergen in 1747, and author of such works as *Annales Ecclesiae Danicae Diplomatici* (1741–47), a Danish topography, a Norwegian glossary, and *Norges Naturlige Historie* (1752–53). This latter is the book which has probably attracted the Consul's interest; it was translated into English in 1755 and later published with a memoir on the Kraken signed by one Philalethes in 1775. Pontoppidan is mentioned twice in Jules Verne's *Twenty Thousand Leagues under the Sea:* once in relation to the Kraken (Pt. I, Ch. 1) and once in relation to the frightful poulps and other monsters of the deep (Pt. 2, Ch. 18).

Jakobsen, p. 81, and Andersen, p. 342, suggest that the reference is to Henrik Pontoppidan (1858–1943), Danish author of *The Promised Land* (1896) and *The Kingdom of the Dead* (1900), but the later author's naturalistic style and emphasis upon social criticism is at odds with everything else on the shelf.

178.10 [175] *the Upanishads.* From Hindi *upa-nishad,* "a near-sitting"; denoting works which embody mystical and esoteric doctrines of ancient Hindu philosophy, composed between 400 and 200 B.C. and so called because they were discourses given to chosen pupils permitted to sit at the feet of gurus and hear the sacred teaching. They now form the philosophical and speculative portions of the *Vedas* (the four ancient and sacred books of the Hindus) and have been the fountainhead of every school of Hindu philosophy. Their emphasis is upon metaphysical speculation, identifying the individual soul with the universal soul, and enquiring into the nature of Brahma. There are about 150 in all, though 108 are traditionally recognized, varying greatly in length. For the Consul they embody the essence of that mystical doctrine which drew his father beyond Himavat.

178.11 [175] *a Mermaid Marston.* John Marston (1575?–1634), English dramatist, poet, and satirist, best known for *The History of Antonio and Mellida* and *Antonio's Revenge* (1602), *The Malcontent* (1604), and the satiric poem "The Scourge of Villanie" (1598), from which the Consul has quoted (see note **134.5**). The Mermaid Series of *The Best Plays of the Old Dramatists* was published by T. Fisher Unwin in London between 1903 and 1909 (and by Charles Scribner's Sons in New York), but, as Jakobsen has noted, do not include a Marston. However, in the Mermaid Middleton, edited by Havelock Ellis, a note of volumes in preparation includes a Marston to be edited by J. A. Symonds, a promise apparently never fulfilled.

178.12 [175] *Bishop Berkeley.* George Berkeley (1685–1753), bishop of Cloyne, 1734–52, a philosopher of Irish birth whose work culminated in his *Theory of Vision* (1733). Berkeley's idealist philosophy, summed up in his famous dictum *esse est percipi,* "to be is to be perceived," is primarily an attack upon Locke's assertion of an external and material reality. Berkeley contended that material things and sensations can exist only insofar as they are perceived; that the mind cannot know external things but only the process of its own perception; that reality is essentially spiritual; and that man and this world exist, necessarily, as a perception in the mind of God. In his later years Berkeley was attracted to less rigorous and more metaphysical systems of thought, but his name is above all associated with a philosophical idealism that represented a total break from Cartesian dualism and Lockean materialism.

178.13 [175]   *Duns Scotus.* Joannes Duns Scotus (1265?–1308?), known as the *Doctor Subtilis,* a Franciscan who lectured at Oxford and Paris. An extreme realist in philosophy, he attacked the validity of natural theology, thereby being one of the first to undermine the harmony of faith and reason so essential to the doctrine of Thomas Aquinas. His followers, the Scotists, were a dominating scholastic sect until the sixteenth century, when their learning was attacked by humanists and reformers as a farrago of needless entities and useless distinctions, and the name Duns or Dunce, then synonymous with sophist, took on its present meaning of ignoramus.

178.14 [175]   *Spinoza.* Benedict (Baruch) de Spinoza (1632–77), a Jew of Portuguese origin who lived in the Netherlands. Expelled from the Jewish community because of his criticism of the Scriptures, he steeped himself in the doctrine of Descartes but rejected the Cartesian dualism of spirit and matter, affirming instead one infinite substance of which finite existences are modes or limitations. The universe was to be viewed *sub specie aeternitatis,* and God as the immanent cause of the universe, not a force outside it. Spinoza's pantheistic system led to a denial of any transcendental distinction between good and evil and of personal immortality. Morality he saw as founded upon the intellectual love of God, which moves man to develop and perfect himself, so that by goodness and piety he reaches perfect happiness (*OCEL*).

178.15 [175]   *Vice Versa. Vice Versa, or A Lesson for Fathers,* by F. Anstey (a pseudonym of Thomas Anstey Guthrie, 1856–1934). The novel, originally published in 1882, tells how Paul Bultitude, a rich but unfeeling merchant, is suddenly transformed into a schoolboy when he tells his son Dick, who does not want to go to school, "I only wish, at this very moment, I could be a boy again, like you." Through the agency of a Garudâ stone, brought from India by his brother-in-law, that wish is granted, and the two swap roles, each however retaining his own mind. Predictable complications follow before the charm is finally reversed, and Mr. Bultitude, a changed man, regains his former shape. The story is described by the young narrator of "Enter One in Sumptuous Armour" as "a favourite with the dormitory" (*P & S,* p. 245), and Hugh, p. 180 [176], sees his time at Cambridge as similar to that "the ill-fated Mr Bultitude" spent at Crichton House. The reversal of roles within the novel may suggest that Hugh and Geoffrey (the latter once a substitute father to the former) are two parts of one personality.

178.16 [175] *All Quiet on the Western Front.* A best-selling novel of 1929 by the German novelist Erich Maria Remarque (1897–1970). It affirms the brotherhood of men while telling simply and directly of the ugliness and squalor of war from the point of view of one who dies in October 1918, on a day so quiet that the army report confines itself to the single sentence—"All Quiet on the Western Front."

178.17 [175] *The Clicking of Cuthbert.* A volume of ten rather feeble stories put out in 1922 by P. G. Wodehouse (1881–1975); also known as *Golf without Tears.* The stories, told in the clubhouse by the Oldest Member, concern the ironies of golf and love, and the first of them, which gives the volume its title, recounts the stirring tale of how young Cuthbert Banks wins Adeline Smethurst from Raymond Parsloe Devine and the Wood Hills Literary Society by impressing the visiting Vladimir Brusiloff (who "specialised in grey studies of hopeless misery where nothing happened till page three hundred and eighty, when the moujik decided to commit suicide") with his greater knowledge of the literature of golf. "Clicking," from M.E. *cleek,* "a hook" (see note **23.1**), seems to be a rough pun linking golf and marriage.

178.18 [175] *the Rig Veda.* The most important of the four *Vedas,* or ancient and sacred texts of the Hindus, probably composed between 1500 and 900 B.C., the text fixed by 300 B.C. It is a collection of miscellaneous fragments of old legends, chants, and hymns, many of great beauty. It is divided into ten books or *mandalas* ("circles"), some of which are concerned with praises of and invocations to the various deities; others of which celebrate the great families. *Mandala* IX is a unique book, being devoted to the single deity *Soma* (see note **308.4**).

178.19 [175] *Peter Rabbit.* The much loved children's story by Beatrix Potter, about the disobedient little rabbit who disregards his mother's warnings and sneaks into Mr. McGregor's garden. As the Consul says, "Everything is to be found in Peter Rabbit": the garden, the gardener, the eviction from Paradise, the fate of Peter's father, the jacket, even an oblique reference to MacGregor-Mathers, Cabbalist and occult writer. The book's presence on the shelf is explained in the manuscripts (UBC 10–26, p. 26): it had been stolen by the Consul, "once when tight on board the *Aquitania*."

179.1 [175]   *the buttery. . . . gyps. . . . a supervision. . . . praelector.* University idiom:
(a) *the buttery.* Originally a storeroom for liquor, but extended to provisions generally. The residence of college members was recorded by the appearance of their names in the buttery-books.
(b) *gyps.* College servants, particularly those tending to undergraduates. The name is popularly attributed to Gk. *gyp,* "a vulture," but is short for either "gypsy" or "gippo" (the short tunic worn by such men).
(c) *a supervision.* A meeting between a student and his tutor, who will have "supervised" or looked over work prepared.
(d) *praelector.* From L. *praelegere,* "to announce"; a public reader, or one who comments on what is about to be read. At Cambridge the praelector is responsible for tending to the matriculation and graduation of the members of his college.

179.2 [176]   *Siegebert of East Anglia.* Siegebert became king of East Anglia, succeeding his half-brother Eorpwald in 631 A.D. and converted his people to Christianity. After reigning a short time, he abdicated to enter a monastery but was forced out reluctantly to lead his people against the invading Mercians led by Penda, and, not carrying any weapons, was slain in battle (between 637 and 644 A.D.). The monastery was near Cambridge, and since Siegebert was reputed to have founded a school in East Anglia, it was hotly debated among the champions of Oxford and Cambridge, vying to prove the antiquity of their institutions, whether he was thus the founder of Cambridge.

179.3 [176]   *John Cornford.* Rupert John Cornford (1915–36), poet and communist, who graduated from Trinity College in 1934 with first class honours in history and became in 1935 a full member of the Communist Party. Following the outbreak of the war in Spain, he threw in his scholarship, and in August 1936 (the first Englishman to enlist) he went to Barcelona and joined the P.O.U.M. (the Partido Obrera de Unificación Marxista), a semi-Trotskyist movement fighting for the Republicans. He returned to England in September to recruit volunteers for the International Brigades, then returned to Spain, where on 15 November he was wounded at the battle of University City (see note **105.3**). He was killed in battle at Lopera on the night of 27–28 December, the day of or after his twenty-first birthday (not, *pace* Kilgallin, Lowry's natal day). John Sommerfield's

Volunteer in Spain (see note **105.4**) is dedicated to John Cornford. There is a strong element of John Cornford in the characterization of Hugh: the communist leanings; the romanticism of Rupert Brooke (Cornford's namesake); and the desire to rush off to Spain in defence of a dubious freedom. Unlike Brooke and Cornford, however, Hugh has lived long enough to question for the first time the implications of his idealism.

179.4 [176]   *Bill Plantagenet.* The mockingly resonant name of the failed musician in Lowry's *Lunar Caustic,* who has lost his wife, whose hands shake and will not stretch an octave, but whose real problems are diagnosed by the doctor, p. 19: "Perhaps it was your heart you couldn't make stretch an octave." Bradbrook suggests, p. 156, that the name reflects Lowry's own first name, Clarence (the Plantagenet drowned in a butt of wine). Hugh's fear is shared by Melville's Redburn (see note **185.6**).

179.5 [176]   *Sherlock Court... the wheel of St Catherine.* St. Catharine's College, Cambridge University, was founded in 1475 by Dr. Robert Wodelarke, third provost of King's College, and was Lowry's college while he was at Cambridge, 1929–32. The college was named for St. Katherine of Alexandria, whose refusal to deny her faith and marry the Emperor Maxentius led to her being broken on a spiked wheel; her body was taken to Mt. Sinai, to the famous Greek Orthodox monastery now known as St. Katherine's. The college gates depict a small golden spiked Catherine's wheel, the arms of the college. Sherlock Court is a small inner court within the college, named for Thomas Sherlock, an eighteenth-century master and distinguished polemicist, who went on to be bishop of London.

179.6 [176]   *like Melville, the world hurling from all havens astern.* As the wheel of St. Catherine's turns into that of the *Pequod,* Hugh recalls *Moby Dick,* Ch. 96, "The Try-Works," where Ishmael, "starting from a brief standing sleep," becomes horribly conscious of something wrong:

> Uppermost was the impression, that whatever swift, rushing thing I stood on was not so much bound to any haven ahead as rushing from all havens astern. A stark bewildered feeling, as of death, came over me. Convulsively my hands grasped the tiller, but with the crazy conceit that the tiller was, somehow, in some enchanted way, inverted. My God! what is the matter with me? thought I. Lo! in my brief sleep I had turned myself about, and was fronting the ship's stern, with my back to her prow and the compass.

180.1 [176]   *Eight hundred years dead.* If the reference is to Siegebert of

East Anglia (see note **179.2**), then Hugh is out by some five hundred years, but his date better suits the founding of the university: although the first college, Peterhouse, was formally founded in 1284, Cambridge had been for some time before that a centre of learning, and many of the colleges were founded upon or absorbed previous hospitals or monastic centres.

180.2 [176] *fens.* Marshes. Cambridge is located in "the Fen Country" of England, and much of the nearby farmland was once swampy marsh.

180.3 [176] *Keep off the Grass.* It is a tradition jealously guarded in the various colleges of Cambridge that only members or fellows of a college may walk upon its lawns.

180.4 [176] *the ill-fated Mr Bultitude in Vice Versa.* See note **178.15**: Mr. Bultitude discovers, when he goes to Dr. Grimstone's school at Crichton House, that his aptitude for business is not the least bit useful when it comes to preparing his lessons. He is not so much confronted by the torments of puberty himself, but his son and Dulcie Grimstone were sweet on one another, and he finds himself unable to cope with the situation.

180.5 [176] *Digs. . . . debagged . . . pepper-and-salt.* University slang:
(a) *Digs.* Lodgings away from the college; usually a small room in a boarding house.
(b) *debagged.* Having one's trousers forcibly removed.
(c) *pepper-and-salt.* Jackets and trousers made of a cloth whose fine weave of black and white thread gives the suit a speckled appearance.

180.6 [177] *A.D. 1106.* Hugh's date has no particular significance (the first Jewish settlement in Cambridge is dated at 1073), but his general point is valid: after William of Normandy had conquered England in 1066, he invited (or at least allowed) the Jews of Normandy to cross the Channel, and for the next hundred years or so the Jews were favourably received in England. Henry I issued a charter regulating their status and insisting upon their allegiance and subservience to the Crown, but protecting their rights concerning property, religious expression, and other matters (including moneylending), and the favourable treatment thus accorded encouraged many European Jews to come to England. Conditions later worsened and persecutions began, and in 1290 there was a general expulsion of all Jews from England.

181.1 [177] *I bought a University weekly.* Lowry probably has in mind the magazine *Experiment,* edited by his friend Gerald Noxon, to which he was a contributor; but as Muriel Bradbrook notes, p. 124, the rather outstanding literary circle of Lowry's time at Cambridge "kept up a flow of publications, ran exhibitions and even some private printing presses."

181.2 [177]   *Zionism.* Named after Mt. Zion, the hill and citadel in Jerusalem, Zionism was the term popularised by Nathan Birnbaum and Theodor Herzl in the 1890's to denote the movement whose goal was the establishing of a Jewish national state in Palestine; a dream that came into being after World War II. Less precisely (some would say, inaccurately), it means the support of all things Jewish. Albert Einstein, whom Hugh is soon to recall having met, p. 186 [182], was a passionate Zionist.

181. 3 [177]   *Like Philoctetes's bow or Oedipus's daughter it was my guide and prop.*
(a) While Philoctetes lay wounded on the island of Lemnos, he depended absolutely upon his bow for survival, and when deprived of it through the deceit of Odysseus, he begged to be put out of his misery quickly.
(b) After Oedipus had blinded himself (see note **168.4**), his daughter Antigone led her father to Colonus in Attica, where at last purified of his abominable crimes, Oedipus was received by the gods.

181.4 [177]   *to represent me, in a rival paper, as an immense guitar.* Muriel Bradbrook states, p. 7, that Lowry was depicted this way by a student magazine in his undergraduate days, but neither artist nor magazine has been identified. The "cruel truth" that Hugh belatedly comes to see, as Bradbrook suggests, is the picture's "striking elements of infantilism," his absorption in his music preventing his proper development beyond that stage.

181.5 [179]   *the jugular vein and the carotid artery.* Two of the major blood supply channels to and from the head, lying side by side in the neck. Hugh's role as potential killer of his brother has been hinted at ever since the razor was called "cut-throat" on p. 179 [175].

181.6 [179]   *John Donne.* English poet (1573–1631). Among the few poems published in Donne's lifetime was *An Anatomy of the World* (1611), the same year as his prose work *Ignatius his Conclave.* The first collected poems appeared in 1633, two years after his death. The Consul seems to have picked the date out accidentally without having attempted to achieve factual accuracy.

181.7 [177]   *the Prince of Wales.* David Edward (1894–1972), later Duke of Windsor, was Prince of Wales from 1911 to 1936 and succeeded to the throne as Edward VIII on 20 January 1936 following the death of George V, but with intense pressure upon him because of his wish to marry Mrs. Simpson, an American divorcée, he abdicated on 10 December of the same year. Hugh's reflections may echo the popular song, "I danced with the man who danced with the girl who danced with the Prince of Wales."

181.8 [177] *Armistice Day.* Eleven November, anniversary of the day in 1918 on which a general armistice was declared between the Allies and the Central Powers preliminary to the signing of the Treaty of Versailles which concluded World War I.

181.9 [179] *the Amundsen society.* There is no record of such a society, and Hugh's audience seems to be a composite of the Royal Geographic Society, before which Amundsen read some of his papers, and the Oxford University Exploration Club, of which Tom Harrisson was a member (see note **130.3**). Captain Roald Engebregt Amundsen (1872–1928), Norwegian explorer, navigated the Northwest Passage in 1903; was the first to reach the South Pole in December 1911 (one month ahead of Scott) and the first to fly over the North Pole, from Spitzbergen to Alaska, in 1926. He was lost at sea trying to rescue a fellow explorer.

181.10 [178] *the French Chamber of Deputies.* During the Third Republic, 1871–1940, the French parliament, as provided for by the constitution of 1875, was a bicameral one, consisting of a senate, or upper house, and a chamber of deputies, whose members were elected directly (approximately equivalent to the British House of Commons). Hugh is being sarcastic about the optimism which reigned in European circles despite the unmistakable signs of coming war.

181.11 [178] *Metronome.* An influential New York magazine, begun in 1885 and, during the 1920's and 1930's dedicated to "Modern Music and its Makers." From January 1925 to January 1932 there were two editions, one for orchestras and the other for bands. *Metronome* became something of a sounding board for musicians, composers, and jazz fanatics, and its reviews of records and dance bands could make or break careers. A London periodical of the same name (*Metronome: Mainly about Music*) began in October 1924 but lasted only eight issues.

181.12 [178] *Nevertheless one dreamed frequently of dying, bitten by lions, in the desert, at the last calling for the guitar, strumming to the end.* The dream is reminiscent of the painting "The Sleeping Gypsy" (1897) by Henri "Le Douanier" Rousseau (see note **136.1**). The painting depicts a gypsy asleep in a moonlit desert expanse, his guitar lying beside him, while a curious lion stands brooding over him.

182.1 [178]   *Thalavethiparothiam*. A term derived from Sir James Frazer's monumental study *The Golden Bough* (1912), originally published in twelve volumes but more commonly (as in Lowry's personal copy) in a more readable condensed version. Ch. 24 is entitled "The Killing of the Divine King," #3 of which discusses kings killed at the end of a fixed term and describes an expedient resorted to in Malabar:

> When Kings were bound to suffer death, whether at their own hands or at the hands of others, on the expiration of a fixed term of years, it was natural that they should seek to delegate the painful duty, along with some of the privileges of sovereignty, by a substitute who should suffer vicariously in their stead. This expedient appears to have been resorted to by some of the princes of Malabar. Thus we are informed by a native authority on that country that "in some places all powers both executive and judicial were delegated for a fixed period to natives by the sovereign. This institution was styled *Thalvettiparothiam* or authority obtained by decapitation.... It was an office tenable for five years during which its bearer was invested with supreme despotic powers within his jurisdiction. On the expiring of the five years the man's head was cut off and thrown up in the air amongst a large concourse of villagers, each of whom vied with the other in trying to catch it in its course down. He who succeeded was nominated to the post for the next five years."

The Golden Bough begins with the dramatic image of the king of the sacred grove of Nemi, restlessly prowling about his domain, awaiting the inevitable appearance of the one who is to supplant him:

> In this sacred grove there grew a certain tree round which at any time of the day, and probably far into the night, a grim figure might be seen to prowl. In his hand he carried a drawn sword, and he kept peering warily about him as if at every instant he expected to be set upon by an enemy. He was a priest and a murderer; and the man for whom he looked was sooner or later to murder him and hold the priesthood in his stead. Such was the rule of the sanctuary. A candidate for the priesthood could only succeed to office by slaying the priest, and having slain him, he retained office till he was himself slain by a stronger or craftier.

That the Consul understands Hugh's allusion was revealed in an early draft of this passage (UBC 7–7, p. 16), when the Consul mutters, "The Golden Bough, eh?" and immediately draws attention to the maple tree outside.

182.2 [178]   *Now then, don't be careful, as the Mexicans say.* Hugh, unwittingly or otherwise, accentuates the hidden menace of his previous allusion to *The Golden Bough:* the Mexican proverb "Qué no te dé cuidado" literally means "don't be careful"; that is, "don't worry," but it can be used in the sense of "Look out." In *DATG,* p. 223, the phrase is attributed to a certain Oaxaqueñan named Coco, an unreliable drinking companion, very quick with the knife. The threat was accentuated in some of the early drafts (UBC 10–25, p. 13 and 7–7, p. 18) by the Consul and Hugh uttering such pleasantries as: "Well, I think you've made a very fine job of preparing the corpse," "The embalment seems complete. All that remains is the laying out," and (referring to some French hair-cream) "I think we might finish you off with some of this."

182.3 [178]   *abaft the beam.* On one of the quarters, that is, toward the rear (see note **169.4**).

182.4 [179]   *the News of the World.* An English Sunday newspaper, founded in 1843 and widely circulated throughout Britain; notorious for its muck-raking sensationalism and blatant sexual exploitation (it was known at sea as the *Red Lamp Gazette*). Its particular specialty was divorce scandals, which gives added irony to the fact of Hugh's writing for it.

182.5 [179]   *eternal troubadour, jongleur, interested only in married women.* The essence of troubadour poetry was the theme of constant but unrequited love for an inaccessible lady. Although Hugh's wandering life has much in common with that of the troubadour, his casual affairs with married women form a travesty of the medieval ideal.

182.6 [179]   *Bloody little man.* The implication is that Hugh should be thrown in the river (see note **329.2**).

182.7 [179]   *a childish thing to be put away.* From St. Paul's advice in I Corinthians 13:11: "When I was a child, I spake as a child, I understood as a child, I thought as a child: but when I became a man, I put away childish things." It is both ironic and irresponsible, then, that Hugh in Ch. 11 should pick up the guitar again.

183.1 [179]   *that poor exiled maple tree.* Exiled from its Canadian homeland, the Consul's paradise, the maple tree is like the Consul in danger of collapsing. In an earlier manuscript version of the passage (UBC 7-7, p. 16) the Consul drew an explicit parallel between the maple and the tree in the opening chapter of Sir James Frazer's *The Golden Bough* (see note **182.1**) and elsewhere imagined himself (UBC 7-10, p. 25): "hanging head downward from the crippled maple tree in the front garden, upside down like the clown in the tarot pack, in the branches condors brooding like bishops."

183.2 [179]   *that sunflower. . . . stares. Fiercely. All day. Like God.* For the image of one turning away from the divine light, see note **148.1**. As the Consul admits of the sun, p. 208 [205], "Like the truth, it was well-nigh impossible to face."

183.3 [179]   *the King of Bohemia.* A pub in Hampstead, London. Benskin's Ales and Stouts are popular in the south, and a group of Cambridge topers of the 1930's called themselves the Benskin Club.

183.4 [179]   *John.* John Sommerfield, Hugh's "English friend fighting in Spain" (see note **105.1**); rather than John Cornford, mentioned by Hugh a little earlier (see note **179.3**).

183.5 [179]   *the balgine run.* More correctly, the bulgine run, from the words of an old Navy song, "Clear the track and let the bulgines run." Bulgines are naval slang for engines.

183.6 [179]   *I Ain't Got Nobody.* A plaintive blues melody, first recorded in New York, 9 August 1916 by Marion Harris, a popular vaudeville and night club singer. Another version of the song, December 1922, featured the "St. Louis Blues" on the same record (Rust, pp. 333 and 335).

183.7 [179]   *The One That I Love Loves Me.* More probably, *The One I Love Belongs to Somebody Else,* recorded by Joe Schenk, 28 February 1924, and made popular by Al Jolson, March 1924 (Rust, pp. 649 and 375).

184.1 [180]   *the English page.* The Consul is reading from *El Universal,* in 1938 the foremost newspaper of Mexico City, which then featured a page in English called "News of the World": a mixture of news, personal items, golf hints, and social gossip, frequently interspersed (especially when hard news was short) with short whimsical paragraphs of useless information under snappy incongruous headings ("Meat-eating Moose," "Dog Stages Sit-down," "Thief chases Policeman," "Husband eats raw meat, wife wins divorce suit"). The following is typical:

> *Town count dog noses*
>   Independence, Mo. August 7
> Declaring that an "emergency exists" Mayor Roger T. Serman ordered a
> dog census here when it was estimated there were more canine noses
> than human noses to be counted.

This instance, from *El Universal* 8 August 1937, shows that Lowry took his
examples from a variety of sources rather than one specific newspaper and
that he was prepared to improve upon his source (the apostrophe, with its
faint hint of Cerberus, is not in the original). The other examples cited by the
Consul have not yet been found (they are not necessarily all from *El
Universal*). One can only guess, unfortunately, why the clink of coins
irritates in Fort Worth (a city in west Texas, thirty miles from Dallas); why
Alfonso XIII was unhappy in his exile; or what was significant about the
eggs found in the tree at the lumbering town of Klamanth Falls, Oregon.

184.2 [180]   *Japanese astride all roads from Shanghai. Americans evac-
uate.* A pun was intended, as the manuscripts make clear (UBC 7-7, p. 23):
"It sounds vaguely cloacal to me," remarked the Consul. Though Lowry
was able to resist the obvious crudity, he could not omit it altogether, and as
a result a distinct anachronism remains in the text: the Japanese armies had
taken Shanghai by November 1937, and by November 1938 they were
consolidating their hold on Canton. That Lowry was conscious of the
anachronism is revealed by other manuscript jottings (UBC 10-25, p. 15),
where the paper is described as "Nearly two years old," with this crossed out
and "a year" pencilled in. Finally unable to resist the privy pun, he left the
headline in without comment.

184.3 [180]   *One had not, however, played it.* Hugh's decision to quit playing the guitar had coincided with his development of a social conscience.

184.4 [180]   *A little self-knowledge is a dangerous thing.* Hugh is echoing
Alexander Pope's "Essay on Criticism" (1711), ll. 215-19:

> A *little Learning* is a dang'rous Thing;
> Drink deep, or taste not the *Pierian* Spring.
> There *shallow Draughts* intoxicate the Brain,
> And drinking *largely* sobers us again.

184.5 [180]   *the British Coasting Trade.* Before World War I the coast-
guard was a reserve for the British Navy, entirely controlled by the Admi-

ralty and conducted on naval lines (under the White Ensign); their duties consisted of preventing smuggling, assisting at wrecks, and generally keeping an eye on the coastline. After the war, the force became controlled by the Board of Trade, and with the demand for economy, stations were closed and the service substantially reduced in numbers of both men and ships (*Ships and the Sea*, p. 338). The implications of this policy probably form the substance of Hugh's article.

184.6 [180] *Saltcaked smoke-stacks.* From John Masefield's "Cargoes," a poem comparing the glories of the past with the sordid realities of the present:

> Quinquireme of Nineveh from distant Ophir
> Rowing home to haven in sunny Palestine,
> With a cargo of ivory,
> And apes and peacocks,
> Sandalwood, cedarwood, and sweet white wine.
>
> Stately Spanish galleon coming from the Isthmus,
> Dipping through the Tropics by the palm-green shores,
> With a cargo of diamonds,
> Emeralds, amethysts,
> Topazes, and cinammon, and gold moidores.
>
> Dirty British coaster with a salt-caked smoke stack
> Butting through the Channel in the mad March days,
> With a cargo of Tyne coal,
> Road-rail, pig-lead,
> Firewood, iron-ware, and cheap tin trays.

184.7 [180] *Britannia rules the waves.* A popular jingoist anthem, words by James Thompson (1710–78) to an air by Thomas Arne, orginally composed for the masque *Alfred* (1840), by Thompson and David Mallet. The refrain goes: "O rule Britannia! Britannia rule the waves! / Britons never never never will be slaves!"

184.8 [181] *"at modest sacrifice" . . . a Cadillac for 500 pesos . . . a white horse . . . anti-alcoholic fish . . . a centricle apartment . . . the remains of Juan Ramírez . . . the immodest behaviour of certain police chiefs.* More details from the English page of *El Universal* (see note **184.1**); the first five details from the regular personal column, "What you ought to know"; the other two more general snippets of news. The actual details have not been found. The list was originally much longer (UBC 7-7, pp. 12–13), including such details as "for 3 pesos 3 yards of well-rotted cow" (used in *October Ferry*, p. 34). As the Consul's "Strange" suggests, he senses the ominous implications of the white horse: the number 7, the Seventh Seal, the pale horse of Revelation 6:8, and the white horse used in Hindu sacrifice (see note **309.2.d**). The anti-alcoholic fish is, presumably, a fiche or pamphlet, but the mystery of Juan Ramírez is not clarified by knowing that in the manuscripts (UBC 14-25, p. 10) he was said to be Angelo Peralto, presumably Angela Peralta (1845–83), a popular singer and composer.

185.1 [181]   *the Parson's Nose.* A prominent spur on one of the approaches to Mount Snowdon, the highest mountain in Wales; its Welsh name *Clogwyn-y-person* literally meaning "Parson's Crag." The parson's nose, like the pope's nose, is the inelegant end of a chicken or goose, traditionally offered to the reverend visitor by those of the other persuasion.

185.2 [181]   *one had written, in the visitors' book.* The visitors' note was a favourite story of Lowry's according to William McConnell, who says that Lowry had seen the exchange in the visitors' book when he was a youth. The story evidently should be attributed to the Crazy Pinnacle, a needle-like crag on a different approach to Snowdon. Ashley P. Abraham warns that the reader should "Bear in mind the entry in a certain hotel visitor's book — 'So and so ascended the Pinnacle in 5½ minutes and found the rocks very easy' — and the subsequent entry by an indignant climber, 'The above party *descended* the Pinnacle in 5½ *seconds* and found the rocks very hard!'" (*Beautiful North Wales*, p. 49).

185.3 [181]   *the actor in the Passion Play.* Hugh is referring to the Oberammergau Passion Play, given once every ten years in the upper Bavarian village of Oberammergau, forty-five miles southwest of Munich. The play was first performed in 1634, to fulfil a vow made by the villagers during an outbreak of plague the previous year. The format has been revised many times (in recent years, to eliminate the notorious anti-Semitic references), but in eighteen acts, with numerous tableaux and musical embellishments, it tells the story from Christ's triumphant entry into Jerusalem until the Resurrection. The image occurs in *DATG*, p. 94:

> There was his youth. No wonder he did not want to go down in the lift! It was like a station of the cross, in the unfinished Oberammergau of his life, shadowy understudy even in that, it was much if he'd left his cross here, while he went off and got drunk on Pilsener one night and then had done something else, and forgotten the part he was playing.

185.4 [182]   *a Pilsener.* A light Bohemian beer with a distinctive flavour of hops; named after the Czechoslovakian town of Pilsen.

185.5 [182]   *the slippery belay.* In mountain climbing, a belay is the anchorage gained by securing a rope to a rock or crag.

185.6 [182]   *a simple gate, and climbing wind masts in port.* Hugh recalls his unseamanlike aversion to climbing over the gates of St. Catharine's, p. 179 [176]. The immediate reference to "the first voyage" suggests *Redburn,* Ch. 24; Redburn, having been afraid of climbing the masts in port, discovers to his amazement:

> that running up the rigging at sea, especially during a squall, was much easier than while lying in port. For as you always go up on the windward side, and the ship leans over, it makes more of a *stairs* of the rigging; whereas, in harbor, it is almost straight up and down.

186.1 [182]   *the pure Norwegian sea.* If Hugh intends a reference here to Nordahl Grieg's *The Ship Sails On* (see note **167.7**), it is undercut completely by Benjamin Hall's intense loathing of that element.

186.2 [182]   *Tufthunter.* In University slang, "tuft" has the sense of a titled undergraduate (one who formerly wore a tuft or tassel at Oxford or Cambridge); hence, a tufthunter is one who deliberately tries to become acquainted with such people, a social climber or snob.

186.3 [182]   *that pub.* The King of Bohemia, mentioned on p. 183 [179], where Hugh's leftist friends were singing songs which Hugh had then considered "bogus bolshy." His friends subsequently acted out their beliefs in Spain, leaving Hugh to now regret his failure to enter into the spirit of the moment.

186.4 [182]   *Einstein.* Albert Einstein (1879–1955), Jewish physicist and Nobel Prize winner (1921), whose *Special Theory of Relativity* (1905) and *General Theory of Relativity* (1916) were his outstanding achievements in a life of genius and whose work on time and space makes it especially incongruous that he should be asking Hugh the hour. Throughout the 1920's and until 1933 Einstein was in Berlin, as a member of the Prussian Academy of Sciences and director of the Kaiser Wilhelm Institute of Physics (he left Germany forever when Hitler came to power). Even though the incident described here is probably apocryphal, the timing is possible, since Einstein visited Cambridge for a week to receive an honorary degree early in 1930.

186.5 [182]   *the tumultuous kitchen of St. John's.* St. John's College, founded by Lady Margaret Beaufort, mother of Henry VII, in 1511. Inside its famous noisy kitchens, in the upper window on the left of the south wall, is a memorial inscription to the poet Wordsworth, who wrote of the rooms he occupied while an undergraduate in *The Prelude,* III.46–52:

> The Evangelist St. John my patron was:
> Three Gothic courts are his, and in the first
> Was my abiding-place, a nook obscure;
> Right underneath, the College kitchens made
> A humming sound, less tuneable than bees,
> But hardly less industrious; with shrill notes
> Of sharp command and scolding intermixed.

There is not, incidentally, any college clock visible from within the gothic courts of St. John's, but the next three lines of *The Prelude* contributed to Hugh's story:

> Near me hung Trinity's loquacious clock,
> Who never let the quarters, night or day,
> Slip by him unproclaimed.

186.6 [182]   *his hammock strung between Aries and the Circlet of the Western Fish.* An image used by Lowry in a letter to Seymour Lawrence (*SL,* p. 275) to symbolize the "transcendent beauty" of the great mind; there Conrad Aiken, here Einstein. Aries, the ram, is the first of the constellations; Pisces, the fish, is the last. Pisces is divided up into northern, southern, and western fish, the latter being the circle of stars at the end of the longer "leg" of the V-shaped constellation. The hammock strung between Aries and the Circlet of Western Fish, linking the last to the first, symbolizes the continuity, stability, and beauty of the old order that was to be so violently upset by Einstein's ideas of relativity, time, and space.

187.1 [183]   *the Jefe de Jardineros.* Sp. "The Chief of Gardeners"; in Ch. 12 to be associated in the Consul's mind with God (and perhaps Mr. McGregor) and responsible for the final irrevocable decision about the Consul's fate. His name, almost improbably, is Fructuoso Sanabria.

187.2 [183]   *a new statue to Díaz in Oaxaca.* Although Oaxaca was the natal state of Porfirio Díaz (see note **112.4**), there is not in Oaxaca, let alone the rest of Mexico, a public statue to his memory, so widely is it detested (though one unimportant street in Oaxaca is named after him). However, statues of Benito Juárez, also a native of Oaxaca (see note **112.1**), are to be found everywhere in Mexico. Hugh reads the possibility as a gloomy indication that fascism is on the rise in Mexico and elsewhere.

187.3 [183]   *this Union Militar, sinarquistas, whatever they're called.* The name Unión Militar, as Hugh's "prewar thingmetight, in Spain" suggests, was taken by Lowry from the Unión Militar Española, a group of young officers under Colonel Bartolomé Barba who plotted within the army against the republic, 1931–32, and who became closely associated with the fascist Falange when the Civil War broke out. In early drafts of the novel Lowry simply called them "vigilantes," but as Spanish Civil War references became important, the Unión Militar also found its way into the text. Edmonds notes, p. 71:

> Among the extreme rightist groups that came into existence in the late 1930's was the *Unión Nacional Sinarquista,* which received encouragement from the Spanish Falange and probably from Nazi Germany. The *Unión Militar* of *Under the Volcano* seems to be the arm of such an organisation.

The sinarquistas grew out of the Cristero movement (see note **111.6**). From 1934 on, groups of young extremists (Catholic fanatics, sons of hacienda owners, businessmen) met secretly, and on 23 May 1937 was born la Unión Nacional Sinarquista, a paramilitary organization whose numbers quickly grew into an effective force of many thousands, who adopted fascist uniforms and salutes and who opposed to the utmost the anti-catholic and pro-agrarian reforms of Cárdenas. Their aim was counter-revolution, summed up in the slogan "¡Abajo el agarismo!" ("Down with land-reform"). Though the movement faded after the 1940 elections, it generated great feeling while it lasted, its impetus being likened by Benítez, p. 109, to "una página arrancada de la serpiente enplumada de Lawrence" ("a page torn from Lawrence's *Plumed Serpent* ").

187.4 [183]   *the policía de Séguridad.* Sp. "the security-police (headquarters)." *El policía* means "the policeman"; *la policía,* "the police force."

187.5 [183]   *his socks. . . . the jacket.* Because of his neuritic condition, the Consul has to avoid irritation when putting on his socks. The reference to the jacket Hugh had borrowed, apparently so casual, ultimately determines the Consul's fate in Ch. 12, since Hugh's telegram is still in the pocket.

187.6 [183]   *he was only twelve years older than Hugh.* The Consul was born in 1896, so Hugh was presumably born in 1908.

188.1 [184]   *anti-aircraft gun.* A highly unlikely detail. The science of anti-aircraft weaponry was virtually non-existent, at best primitive, during World War I, and certainly did not exist on ships in the Pacific, where German air forces were not deployed.

188.2 [184]   *Coclogenus paca Mexico.* The very mundane meaning of this apparent grimoire has been sensed by Andersen, p. 94: "Probably either a punning or erroneous reference to *Coelgenus paca,* a tailless rodent found in South and Central America whose skin is used for leather." Originally the manuscript read at this point, "before you could say Jack Robinson" (UBC 10-25, p. 15), and the reference to the *Coclogenus paca Mexico* (the error persists throughout all the notes and manuscripts) came a few pages later; the Consul, looking at his neighbour's Scotty dog, Angus, who is in turn looking adoringly at Yvonne, remarks, "We could go to the zoo and see the tepezcuintle." Hugh asks in return, "What's a tepezcuintal?" (Lowry uses both spellings), to which the Consul mutters, "A dog. . . . Coclogenus paca Mexico. Well, a sort of high class scavenger, a groomed hyaena" (UBC 8-7, p. 16). In another version (UBC 10-25, p. 17), he adds, "A pariah with a university education." In the earlier drafts the Consul was considerably more bloody-minded towards Yvonne and Hugh, originally his daughter and her boyfriend, and his remarks were more obviously directed at them, but as the relationship between the three characters changed, the tepez-cuintle episode became increasingly redundant and was eliminated almost completely.

188.3 [184]   *Der englishe Dampfer tragt Schutzfarben gegen deutsche U-boote.* Ger. "The English steamer carries camouflage against German U-boats."

188.4 [184]   *the Emden.* The role played by the *Emden* was not unlike that played by the *Samaritan.* The *Emden,* named after the Westphalian seaport, was the flagship of the German naval forces in the Southern Hemisphere in World War I. She was a light cruiser, equipped with light armour and light guns and under the command of Karl von Müller. When the rest of the German navy left the Pacific early in the war, the *Emden* was left behind as the sole residual naval force against British, Australian, and Japanese shipping. She wrought havoc in the Indian Ocean during the first few months of the war, capturing some twenty-two merchantmen, sixteen of which were sunk. She became especially renowned for daring attacks in enemy harbours, once sailing under false colours and a false funnel into Penang. She was engaged by the Australian cruiser *Sydney* off the Cocos Islands in November 1914, and her loss effectively ended the German threat in the Antipodes.

188.5 [184]   *So verliess ich der Weltteil unserer Antipoden.* Ger. "Thus I abandoned the world of our Antipodes" (*Weltteil* having the sense of "continent" or "quarter of the globe"; verlies in the Penguin edition should read verliess). Before World War I, the Germans laid claim to Samoa, part of New Guinea, and island groups such as the Marianas and Carolines. They lost these during the war. As he repeats "Our Antipodes," the Consul gives Hugh a sharp glance to see if he is aware of the esoteric significance of the phrase: *Antipodes,* a Greek word meaning "having the feet apposite," originally referred to those dwelling directly opposite to each other on the globe, their feet as it were planted against each other; but it also meant (as in Sir Thomas Browne's *Religio Medici* #26: "the case of *Antipodes*"; or Thomas Burnet's preface to his *Sacred Theory of the Earth:* "there are Antipodes" believing in the existence of "another world." (Virgilius, bishop of Salzburg, was condemned in 780 for proclaiming the existence of the Antipodes") believing in the existence of "another world." (Virgilius, bishop of worlds.) To the Consul the word means, quite simply, the coexistence of the world of spirits with his own, a doctrine of opposites that leads him, inevitably, to thoughts of Boehme.

188.6 [184]   *Boehme.* Jakob Boehme (1575–1624), German shoemaker and mystical philosopher who was greatly influenced by Paracelsus. Claiming divine revelation and convinced that he had been allowed to see into the heart of things, he produced between 1612 and 1624 a number of treatises concerning the central mystical experience, the best known of which are *De tribus principiis* (1619); the *Mysterium Magnum* (1621) and, above all, *De signatura rerum* (1621), which asserts both the doctrine of opposites (see note **134.4**) and the belief that all nature manifests or is a signature of God, by the proper reading of which man draws closer to the Godhead. Boehme died in 1624, having foretold, it is said, the exact hour of his death.

188.7 [183]   *A Treatise of Sulphur.* Originally published (about 1610) in a volume entitled: "Nouum lumen chymicum. E naturae fonte manuali experienta depromptum. Cui accessit Tractatus de sulphure. Authoris anagramma Diui Leschi genus amo." ("A New Light of Alchymie: taken out of the fountain of Nature, and manual experience. To which is added a Treatise of Sulphur. Anagram of the author *Divi Leschi genus amo.*")

Michael Sendivogius (1566–1646) was a Moravian chemist who worked as a pupil and assistant to the famous alchemist Alexander Seton, one of the few who reportedly succeeded in transmuting metals into gold. Since the anagram (meaning "I love the Divine Race of Leschi") is a fair approximation of his name, the work was generally assumed to be that of Sendivogius, but it was in fact Seton's, whose widow Sendivogius had married. The *Treatise of Sulphur,* generally agreed to be his own, was published separately in 1616 under the anagram *Angelus doce mihi jus* ("Angel, Teach Me Right"); it was translated into English by John French as part of the *New Light* (London, 1650); and included in the *Musaeum Hermeticum* of 1678 (see note **188.10**), where it may be found in A. E. Waite's translation, pp. 127–58. The treatise is basically a defence of the value of sulphur to the alchemist, asking first, "Friend, why dost thou curse Sulphur," and answering in part that "A Prince without a people is unhappy; so is an Alchymist without Sulphur and Mercury."

188.8 [185]   *The Hermetical Triumph.* The full title reads:

> The Hermetical Triumph: or, The Victorious Philosophical Stone. A Treatise more compleat and more intelligible than any that has been yet, concerning The Hermetical Magistery. Translated from the French. To which is added, The Ancient War of the Knights. Translated from the German Original. As Also, Some Annotations upon the most material Points, where the two Translations differ. Done from a German Edition.

The English edition (London, P. Hanet, 1723) was translated from the 1689 French version by Alexander Toussaint Limojon de Saint-Didier, who used as his anagram "Dives sicut Ardens S." The basis of the work is in fact the short treatise, *The Ancient War of the Knights,* by an unknown German, concerning a discourse between the stone of the philosophers, and gold and mercury, cast as a dispute between these elements and ending with the triumph of the stone. This is followed by a longer discourse between *Pyrophilus* and *Eudoxus,* concerning the implications of the treatise, to which is appended another version of *The Ancient War* and a discursive comparison of the French and German versions. The whole may be compleat, but it is not particularly intelligible.

188.9 [185]   *The Secrets Revealed.* The full title reads:

> Secrets Reveal'd: or, An Open Entrance to the Shut-Palace of the King:

Containing, The greatest Treasure in Chymistry, Never yet so plainly Discovered. Composed By a most famous English-man, Styling himself Anonymus, or Eyraeneus Philaletha Cosmopolita: Who, by Inspiration and Reading, attained to the Philosopher's Stone at his Age of Twenty three Years, *Anno Domini,* 1645. Published for the Benefit of all *English-men,* by W. C. Esq; a true lover of Art and Nature.

The book was printed in London in 1669, as a translation of a Latin original of uncertain date. Described by its author as "a small but worthy Treatise of great Learning," the *Secrets Reveal'd* recounts the various operations by which the sophic mercury and the stone itself may be prepared. The title refers to the legend that King Solomon was an adept in alchemy and other occult arts, and that his palace contained much secret knowledge. The treatise was included in the *Musaeum Hermeticum* of 1678 and in Waite's *Hermetic Museum* (see note **188.10**), pp. 159–98, under the title *An Open Entrance to the Closed Palace of the King.* The anonymous alchemist, "Truth-loving Citizen of the World," has sometimes been identified as Thomas Vaughan, brother of the poet Henry, because the claim that by inspiration and reading he attained the philosopher's stone at the age of twenty-three, in 1645, suits Vaughan's birthdate and because Thomas Vaughan sometimes wrote under the pseudonym Eugenius Philalethes. A. E. Waite, in *The Holy Kabbalah,* X.xi, p. 473, distinguishes the two (as far as it is possible to do so), as the Consul was about to do to Hugh, p. 193 [189], before being so rudely interrupted by Laruelle (UBC 10–27, p. 42):

'Who were all these fogies anyway, you may ask? Who was that Eirenaeus Philalethes you were looking at, for example? Certainly I can tell you this Hugh,' the Consul staggered almost imperceptibly, 'He was not Eugenius Philalethes, who was Thomas Vaughan.'

188.10 [185] *The Musaeum Hermeticum.* The *Musaeum Hermeticum* was originally published (Lucan Jennis, Frankfurt, 1625) in nine tracts of 483 pages, then reissued in 1678 in a restored and enlarged form of twenty-one tracts and 867 pages. This version, with almost exactly the title Lowry cites, was edited and translated into English by A. E. Waite in 1839, under the title:

The Hermetic Museum Restored and Enlarged: Most faithfully instructing all Disciples of the Sopho-Spagyric Art how that Greatest and Truest Medicine of The Philosopher's Stone may be found and held. Now first done into English from the Latin Original published at

Frankfurt in the year 1678. Containing Twenty-two most celebrated Chemical Tracts.

Lowry's Latin citation includes a sentence Waite omits: "by means of which all things suffering any sort of defect may be restored, is to be found and possessed, containing 21 Chemical Tractati, at Frankfurt at the house of Hermann à Sande." The tracts include *A Treatise of Sulphur* and *An Open Entrance to the Closed Palace of the King* (see notes **188.7** and **188.9**), as well as other treatises upon the *Stone,* the *Golden Age Restored,* the *Sophic Hydrolith,* the *Janitor Pansophus,* and other medico-chemical matters. The "Sopho-Spagyricae" arts mentioned in the title refer to those practiced by the followers of Paracelsus. The "CIↃ" is 1000; the "IↃC" is 600. Hence: 1678.

189.1 [185]   *Sub-Mundanes.* The full title reads:

Sub-Mundanes; or, The Elementaries of the Cabala: being The History of Spirits Reprinted from the Text of the Abbot de Villars, Physio-Astro-Mystic, wherein is asserted that there are in existance on earth rational creatures besides man. With an illustrative Appendix from the Work "Demoniality," or "Incubi and Succubi," by the Rev. Father Sinistrati of Ameno. *"Honi soit qui mal y pense"* Privately Printed only for Subscribers. Bath. 1886

As the inner title page explains, the edition (of a 1680 version) was "Done into English" by one P.A., Gent. of London; and printed for "B.M., Printer to the Royal Society of the Sage, at the Signe of the Rosy-Crusian." It takes the form of "Five Pleasant Discourses as the Secret Sciences," cast as a dialogue between Count Gabalis and one of his neophytes, somewhat reluctant and sceptical, who is to be made worthy of receiving the Cabbalistical illuminations and of forming an alliance with the elementary powers. Its chief concern is to demonstrate the existence and nature of elementary spirits (sylphs, nymphs, gnomes, and salamanders) and to dispel the vulgar opinion that such beings are legions of devils. The Abbé Nicholas de Montfaucon de Villars (1635?–73?) was a French mystic, also known as the Comte de Gabalis, who was rumoured to have died of apoplexy for having betrayed the secret sciences. Notwithstanding, his discussion of elementary spirits became a widely read text of occult and Rosicrucian thought and was the source of Alexander Pope's "machinery" in *The Rape of the Lock.*

189.2 [185]   *Erekia . . . Illirikim; Apelki . . . Dresop . . . Arekesoli . . . Burasin . . . Glesi . . . Effrigis . . . the Mames . . . Ramisen.* As Epstein first noted,

p. 127, Lowry took this list directly from MacGregor-Mathers's *The Book of the Sacred Magic of Abra-Melin the Mage,* published in London, 1898. They are to be found on p. 122 of *The Sacred Magic,* listed among the servitors of Amaymon (Lowry cites about half the list):

> *Ramison:* Hebrew. The movers with a particular creeping motion.
> *Burasen:* Hebrew. Destroyers by stifling smoky breath.
> *Akesoli:* Greek? The distressful or pain-bringing ones.
> *Erekia:* Greek probably. One who tears asunder.
> *Illirikim:* Hebrew. They who shriek with a long drawn cry.
> *Mames:* Hebrew. They who move by backward motion.
> *Glesi:* Hebrew. One who glistens horribly, like an insect.
> *Effrigis:* Greek. One who quivers in a horrible manner.
> *Apelki:* Greek. The misleaders or turners aside.
> *Dresop:* Hebrew. They who attack their prey by tremulous motion.

The Consul's phrases, "the flesh inclothed" and "the evil questioners" are descriptions of *Labisi* and *Nilima* respectively, two others from the list, while his comment, "Perhaps you would not call them precisely rational," goes back to MacGregor-Mathers's preface, p. xxxiii, where he describes such elementals as not so much acting *irrationally* but with *intent.*

189.3 [186] *Hitler... wished to annihilate the Jews in order to obtain just such arcana.* Lowry "clarifies" this statement, "LJC," p. 76:

> And Hitler was another pseudo black magician out of the same drawer as Amorfas in the *Parsifal* he so much admired, and who has had the same inevitable fate. And if you don't believe that a British general actually told me that the real reason why Hitler destroyed the Polish Jews was to prevent their cabbalistic knowledge being used against him you can let me have my point on poetical grounds.

It has been claimed by some occultists that Hitler too was an adept, a black magician, even a front man for an occult group controlling the Nazi Party and that his otherwise inexplicable power over the German people was owing to his command of dark powers. Links between the Nazis and some occult groups have been affirmed, and it can be shown that the swastika, traditionally an emblem of light, when reversed like the Nazi one has been an emblem of the powers of darkness. For more details, see Trevor Ravenscroft, *The Spear of Destiny* (1973).

190.1 [186] *the telephone rang.* A last warning from the benevolent powers, perhaps, but deliberately rejected by the Consul.

190.2 [186] *why don't we go to the zoo.* Yvonne presumably means the tiny zoo in Cuernavaca's Chapultepec Park, the only one that could possibly be closer than the fictional Tomalín (there is a hint here of the original destination of Chapultepec, on the outskirts of Cuernavaca, described in *DATG* p. 164). In the manuscripts, the suggestion was originally the Consul's, leading up to the deleted tepezcuintle episode (see note **188.2**), here retained to lead up to Moctezuma's infernal regions, p. 191 [187].

190.3 [187] *like a detail in a Rousseau.* The paintings of Henri Rousseau (see note **136.1**) have a childlike simplicity, and often contain one strikingly incongruous detail, such as a fly in a fruit bowl (Andersen, p. 359) or a kitten with a ball of wool in a portrait.

191.1 [187] *her red shoes.* In the Consul's mind, though not Hugh's, the association between the clicking red heels and the scarlet woman of Revelation 17:4 is very much to the fore (see note **51.4**).

191.2 [187] *slim brown hands that do not rock the cradle.* A reference to the line "The hand that rocks the cradle rules the world" in the popular verse "The Hand that Rules the World" by William Ross Wallace (1819–81). The comment conveys something of the Consul's bitterness (though the thought is Hugh's) about Yvonne's remaining childless.

191.3 [187] *Job's warhorse.* The reference is to Job 39:19–25, where the horse, hearing the sound of trumpets and smelling the battle far-off, rejoices in its strength and mocks at fear. These verses are preceded by two which show the inability of the woman to understand the impulse or to admire the horse, thus neatly combining Hugh's anxiety about the Battle of the Ebro with Yvonne's unconcern.

191.4 [187] *They always had zoos in Mexico. . . . The poor chap thought he was in the infernal regions.* Prescott's *Conquest of Mexico* relates in detail the splendours of Tenochtitlán revealed to the astounded Spaniards shortly after their arrival in Moctezuma's capital, including the Aztec emperor's immense aviary and his menagerie of wild animals. The Spaniards were impressed, above all, by the reptiles and serpents (Prescott, IV.i, p. 320): "They gazed on the spectacle with a vague curiosity not unmixed with awe; and, as they listened to the wild cries of the ferocious animals and the hissing of the serpents, they almost fancied themselves in the infernal regions."

191.5 [187]   *stout Cortez.* An oblique reference to Keats's poem, "On First Looking into Chapman's Homer" (see note **275.2**).

191.6 [187]   *A curious bird is the scorpion.* A reference to the popular limerick (described in Baring-Gould's *Lure of the Limerick* as one of the few good clean ones), originally written by Dixon Lanier Merritt, a Florida newspaperman:

> A rare old bird is the pelican;
> His beak holds more than his belican.
>   He can take in his beak
>   Enough food for a week;
> I'm darned if I know how the helican!

The Consul, who is throughout identified with the scorpion, may be hinting at his own indifference to organized religions (priest) and to the cause of humanity (peon).

191.7 [198]   *He'll only sting himself to death anyway.* A reference to the popular belief that the scorpion ringed with fire will sting itself to death (see note **339.7**).

192.1 [188]   *666.* The Consul's "quiet delight" stems from his recognition that "666" is the number of the Beast in Revelation 13:18: "Here is wisdom. Let him that hath understanding count the number of the beast: for it is the number of a man; and his number is Six hundred threescore and six." The number 666, adopted by Aleister Crowley as his personal occult signature, was (by gematria) also the number of l'Empereur Napoléon in Tolstoy's *War and Peace,* IX.xix (see note **87.3**). The "obscure yellow plates" can still be found on ancient walls in Cuernavaca; however, they advertise not an insecticide but a medicinal cure-all (still obtainable), effective against coughs, colds, flu, and nasal congestion.

192.2 [188]   *had worked wonders.* An evocation of the novel's first epitaph: "Wonders are many, and none is more wonderful than man"; but with still the unspoken implication "only against Death shall he call for aid in vain." The Consul's "air of infallibility" will be as unavailing as the pope's.

192.3 [188]   *old Chagfordian tie.* Chagford, in south Devon, is a small market town on the edge of Dartmoor. Lowry's Cambridge friend, James Travers, had a silver-fox farm nearby, and Lowry visited him upon one disastrous occasion (Day, p. 181). There is no public school in the town, but many years previously a Mrs. Watkinson, whose husband had been killed in a submarine disaster, ran a small private institution for the sons of naval officers.

192.4 [188]   *A slight nutation.* A slight nodding. The Penguin "mutation" is a distinct error (one made by Reynal and Hitchcock in the original American setting, but firmly and clearly corrected by Lowry on the galley proofs). Nutation is the "wobbling" of the earth's axis owing to the gravitational attraction of the moon. Once in 18.61 years the celestial pole completes a small ellipse about its average position, and the irregular wavy motion tracing this path is called nutation. A further reference to Nut, the mother goddess of Ancient Egypt who was unfaithful to her husband, Ra, would seem rather remote.

192.5 [188]   *an old brush with Pathans.* Magnificently Anglo-Indian. The Pathans are a Moslem People of the Afghanistan-Pakistan borderland, fiercely independent, who gave the British rulers of the Raj considerable trouble on the northwest frontier, not far from Kashmir. If, however, the limp is "of nautical origin," it would suggest Captain Ahab's loss of his leg in his previous brush with Moby Dick.

192.6 [189]   *Plingen, plangen, aufgefangen.* An unknown rhyme, which flicks out only fragments of sense, but nevertheless hints at the Samaritan affair. Ger. *aufgefangen,* "captured"; *Bootle,* a dockside district in the north of Liverpool; *Nemesis,* the abstract force of retributive justice among the Greeks. The Consul's day does not promise to be an extraordinarily nice one.

193.1 [189]   *no se permite fijar anuncios.* Sp. "It is not permitted to post advertisements"; a slightly politer version of the more usual *No anunciar* ("Post No Bills").

193.2 [189]   *as in a dream of a dying Hindu.* The precise reference is obscure: the words may refer simply to the Brahman doctrine that the destiny of the soul in the afterlife depends on the mental attitude of the dying person, particularly the last thing that he thinks of. If he thinks of God, he enters a state of eternal bliss. If, however, he thinks of an animal or a human friend, he will be reborn as a cow, a horse, a dog, or may even enter the body of a newly born child and thus be condemned to the same cycle of pain endured in this world. The suggestion, here, may be that on the very brink of his own death, the Consul sees, or observes, or identifies with a very lowly person and that he may be condemned to a life of ignominy hereafter.

193.3 [189]   *Father is waiting for you. . . . Father has not forgotten.* On one level, the voice of Geoffrey's father, calling as in a dream from beyond Himavat; on another, that of Geoffrey (Papa), earlier seen as the billy-goat (see note **103.8**) and now threatening retribution for the violated past.

193.4 [189]   *Guelphs.* In the politics of the Italian city states, one of the two great parties, supporting the authority of the pope in opposition to the aristocratic party of the Ghibellines, who supported the emperor. Dante was a member of a Guelph family and fought for Florence against the Ghibellines of Arezzo in 1289.

193.5 [189]   *that no angel with six wings is ever transformed.* Presumably because this is a characteristic of the seraphim, the highest order of angel. This is No. XXX of the cabbalistic conclusions (*Conclusiones Philosophicae, Cabalisticae et Theologicae*) of Picus de Mirandula, originally published in Rome in 1486 (also noted by Jakobsen, p. 84). The conclusion is cited in Éliphas Lévi's *La Science des Esprits* (1865), and in A. E. Waite's *The Holy Kabbalah,* X.iii, p. 449. Waite dismisses as "mere ingenuity" Lévi's contention that it means "there is no change for the mind which is equilibrated perfectly," but though Lowry's direct source is undoubtedly Waite, it is significant that the phrase immediately precedes a violent change in the Consul's psychic equilibrium.

193.6 [189]   *no bird ever flew with one—.* Lowry's short story "June the 30th, 1934" offers a pertinent context: two men (one named Firmin) meet on a train, talk, and have one drink before deciding to have another on the grounds that "No bird ever flew with one wing" (*P & S,* p. 42).

193.7 [189]   *Thomas Burnet, author of the Telluris Theoria Sacra.* Thomas Burnet (1635?–1715), theologian and philosopher, student and fellow of Christ's College, Cambridge, took his M.A. in 1658, was procter, 1667, and later became clerk of the closet to William III, but had to resign the post in 1692 because of controversy caused by his *Archaeologiae Philosophicae,* which treated the Mosaic account of the Fall as allegory. Burnet's own account of the creation is expressed in his *Telluris Theoria Sacra* (Pt. I, 1680; Pt. II, 1689; translated from the original Latin into English 1684 and 1690):

> The Theory of the Earth: Containing an Account of the Original of the Earth, and of all the General Changes Which it hath already undergone, or is to undergo, Till the Consummation of all Things, by Thomas Burnet, D.D. The Two First Books Concerning The Deluge,

and Concerning Paradise.... The Two Last Books Concerning the Burning of the World, and Concerning the New Heavens and New Earth.

Burnet maintained that the earth resembled a gigantic egg, its face being smooth and uniform, without mountains and without a sea, but the action of the sun stirring and making volatile the waters of the deep within the shell, caused the shell to be crushed, and the internal waters to burst forth in a deluge, fragments of shell forming the mountains; while at the same time and as a result of the catastrophe the equator was diverted from its original coincidence with the ecliptic. Burnet's notions, if not accepted literally by Lowry, gave him a cosmology to frame his tragic action: an original paradise, the abyss, the deluge, and the vain attempt in a world heading towards its final conflagration to put together the broken materials of that first world.

193.8 [189]   *entered Christs in —*. The Consul is about to say 1654, as he had in an earlier draft (UBC 10–27, p. 42): "Thomas Burnet, author of the *Telluris Theoria Sacra*, entered Christ's in 1654, when Ralph Cudworth was master. Henry More must have been about my age then. Who were all these fogies anyway." He is quoting almost directly from A. E. Waite's *The Holy Kabbalah,* X.xiv, p. 485, where this information is given (see note **188.9**), based in turn on Waite's reading of Burnet's *Archaeologiae Philosophicae.* The Cambridge records, however, show that Burnet entered Christ's on 28 September 1655.

193.9 [189]   *Cáscaras! Caracoles! Virgen Santísima! Ave María! Fuego, fuego! Ay, qué me matan.... Acabóse.* Sp. "Great Heavens! Hey! Virgin most Holy! Hail Mary! Well, I'll be damned.... That's the limit." More literally, *cáscaras* are "shells" or "husks" or "peelings" (a touch of the Qliphoth); *caracoles* are "snails" (the word being used like its cognate, *caramba*); *fuego* is short for "fuego de Díos," "fire of God"; *qué me matan* is short for "Qué me maten si no es verdad!," "May I die if it's not true!"; and *acabóse,* "finished," has the sense of "the last straw." The unearthly screeching heralds the arrival of a malignant force (perhaps another emissary of Lucifer), and the Consul's equilibrium (see note **43.3.b**) is violently upset.

193.10 [190]   *Acabóse.* Although acabóse means "finished" in the sense of "that's the limit," Lowry may be intending a reference to Christ's last words, *consummatum est,* "it is finished" (John 19:30).

193.11 [190]   *the sideroad Yvonne had seemed anxious they should take.*

Yvonne is anxious to avoid Laruelle's house, just as Jacques is himself, p. 29 [23], but by a "favourite trick of the gods," her very efforts to avoid him contribute to their meeting. The infernal machine is relentless: Jacques comes forward, "as it were impelled by clockwork." The sideroad, if it ever existed, is not to be found in present-day Cuernavaca.

194.1 [191] *my "madhouse".* In an earlier manuscript (UBC 10-8, p. 10.B), Jacques's house was described as being like "a still from the Cabinet of Dr Caligari and the frontspiece to a cheap edition of Omar Khyyām." The revealing comparison is that with the celebrated German expressionist film *Das Cabinett der Dr. Caligari* (1919), based on screenplay by Hans Janowitz and Carl Mayer, directed by Robert Wiene, and starring Werner Krauss as the mad doctor and Conrad Veidt as Cesare, his somnambulist. The supposedly rational narrator of the film is telling someone of the beautiful woman just consigned to a lunatic asylum because of an attempted rape by a somnambulist, who has just murdered her lover. Yet, at the end of the film it appears that the whole thing has been a figment of the imagination of the narrator. Dr. Caligari, seen previously as the mad magician who controls the somnambulist, turns out to be the doctor in charge of the asylum; thus, he who was shown to be mad and to need restraining is the restrainer of the mad. To the Consul, feeling like the somnambulist, the figure of Jacques assumes all the features of the mad doctor, and the changing levels of perspective and reality leave his mind confused. In this state, then, he enters the madhouse and fairground of Chapter 7.

194.2 [191] *Hugues.* "Hugh" as a Frenchman might pronounce the word, the "g" presumably hard. The Penguin "Hughes" is an error.

195.1 [191] *It was a great coincidence our meeting here.* The words could refer to the Consul meeting Jacques in Quauhnahuac, the apparent chance meeting in the lane, or the meeting of Hugh and Jacques who "have something in common," that is, a past affair with Yvonne (according to Conrad Aiken, *Selected Letters,* p. 208, Lowry had himself used this phrase to one of Jan's lovers). Either way, the Consul's "changed even tone" suggests that it is not so much "an unusual bloody miracle" as part of an inexorable force of destiny closing around him.

195.2 [191] *the cartero.* Sp. "the postman." Lowry mentions in *DATG,* p. 142, that the very same postman was still at work in 1945.

196.1 [192] *Señor Calígula.* Caius Caesar (12–41 A.D.), Roman emperor from 37 to 41 A.D., whose reign was marked by excesses of cruelties and vice which were largely the product of his growing madness. He considered himself a god and proposed raising his horse Incitatus (already a senator) to the rank of consul (a fact Lowry could have found in Aiken's *Blue Voyage,* p. 49).

196.2 [192]   *Badrona, Diosdado. Diosdado,* the "God-given," appears behind the bar of the Farolito in Ch. 12; the Jefe de Jardineros, who appears in the same chapter, was originally named Fructuosa Badrona (Day, p. 268).

196.3 [192]   *Bright stamps of archers.* Those affixed to the previous express delivery from Juan Cerillo (see note **111.8**). The place names stamped on the card are all significant in the life of Geoffrey and Yvonne.

197.1 [193]   *the leonine Signal Peak on El Paso with Carlsbad Cavern Highway.* El Paso is the border city in the extreme western corner of Texas, linked to the Mexican Ciudad Juárez by the International Bridge, which is the most frequently used route in and out of Mexico. The name "El Paso" is also that of the pass through the mountains north of the city (El Paso del Norte). Signal Peak, also known as El Capitán (8,750 feet), is in the Guadalupe Mountains, just off Rt. 62 (the Carlsbad Highway), a few miles northeast of the city and pass. It is distinctly leonine in appearance and derives its name from the fact that Indians (and later U.S. cavalrymen) used it as a signalling point. The Carlsbad Caverns, across the state line in New Mexico, some miles east and slightly north of El Paso, are perhaps the largest complex of underground caverns in the world, famous for the immensity of their "rooms" and "corridors," and still largely unexplored.

Lowry's phrase "on El Paso" is confusing, since Signal Peak is some miles from the pass. Perhaps the card, which Yvonne must have bought when she entered the United States in December 1937, is of the kind in which a small photo, perhaps in a circle, is superimposed upon a larger picture of the more general area.

197.2 [193]   *The road turned a little corner in the distance and vanished.* Lowry deliberately contrived that the chapter should end "with a dying fall" and with the theme of Dante's path through the dark wood struck out by the vanishing road ("LJC," p. 76); the suggestion being that from this point on the Consul's path will become increasingly obscure as he enters the dark caverns within himself.

CHAPTER SEVEN

198.1 [194] *7.* Described by Lowry as "the fateful, the magic, the lucky good-bad number" ("LJC," p. 77; Lowry would have approved the pagination). Lowry goes on to speak of "the passion for order even in the smallest things that exist in the universe: 7 too is the number on the horse that will kill Yvonne and 7 the hour when the Consul will die." The significance of the number is discussed in Ch. 7 of Éliphas Lévi's *Transcendental Magic*, p. 80:

> The septenary is the sacred number in all theogonies and in all symbols, because it is composed of the triad and the tetrad. The number seven represents magical power in all its fulness; it is the mind reinforced by all elementary potencies; it is the soul served by Nature.

Lévi cites the seven deadly sins, the seven virtues, the seven planets, the seven seals of the Apocalypse, the seven genii of ancient mythologies, the seventh day of rest, the seven sacraments, the seven musical notes, the seven magical animals, the seven great archangels, concluding, p. 82, that "The virtue of the septenary is absolute in Magic, for this number is decisive in all things." Lowry's novel, which begins and ends at seven, accepts this judgment, and the number seven appears throughout: the tennis rackets, p. 10 [4], the Pleiades, p. 35 [29], the white horse at box seven, p. 185 [181], the Consul's reflections, p. 205 [202], Eriksen 43 and 34, pp. 81 and 212 [76 and 208]. It is in this chapter above all (as a similar list in *Blue Voyage* puts it, p. 51) that the Consul, his equilibrium upset, finds everything "at sixes and sevens."

198.2 [194] *Hercules's Butterfly.* Hercules is a summer constellation of the northern hemisphere, the brightest star of which is Ras Algethi (see note **55.1**). Although none of the stars is outstandingly brilliant, the pattern outlined by six of the brightest makes a figure something like a great butterfly flying westward. Lowry's sense is explained in *Lunar Caustic,* pp. 20–21:

> The constellations might have been monstrosities in the delirium of

God. Disaster seemed smeared over the whole universe. It was as if he were living in the pre-existence of some unimaginable catastrophe, and he steadied himself a moment against the sill, feeling the doomed earth itself stagger in its heaving spastic flight towards the Hercules Butterfly.

198.3 [194] *zacualis. . . . crenellated miradors . . . a bartizan. . . . merlons. . . . degenerate machicolations . . . a chevron. . . . the flying balcony.* The description is deliberately reminiscent of *Das Cabinett der Dr. Caligari* (see note **194.1**), which abounded in jagged gothic forms, oblique chimneys and pell-mell roofs, and windows in the form of arrows and kites, the painted shadows and zig-zag delineations designed to efface all rules of perspective (Kracauer, p. 69). The "madhouse" is described by Sigbjørn, *DATG* p. 153, when he returns to Cuernavaca in 1945:

> there were two towers with a sort of catwalk between, joining them on the roof, and on the one that seemed to be used as a mirador, there were all kinds of angels, and other round objects, carved out of red standstone. The funny chevron-shaped windows are still there, but there used to be some writing in gold leaf below them that you read from the road. And they seem to have knocked down one of the towers.

(a) *zacualis.* The two towers, Jacques's inadequate refuge against the coming of the second flood (see note **35.2**).

(b) *crenellated miradors.* A mirador (from Sp. *mirar,* "to behold") is a roof-top look-out (a common feature of many Cuernavaca houses); crenellated (from L. *crena,* "a notch") describes a series of regular tooth-like identations (crenels) on top of a battlement or wall.

(c) *a bartizan.* Sir Walter Scott's erroneous rendition of O.Fr. *bretesche,* "a battlement parapet"; specifically, an overhanging turret projecting from the top of a tower.

(d) *merlons.* From L. *mergae,* "a pitch-fork"; the solid "teeth" of a battlement or parapet lying between the crenels.

(e) *machicolations.* From M.L. *machiocolare,* "to crush"; openings in a gallery floor or parapet through which hot liquids and heavy stones could be dropped upon attackers.

(f) *a chevron.* From L. *capra,* a "she-goat," and O.Fr. *chevre;* in heraldry and the military, a design in the shape of an inverted V. Old photographs of Jacques's house confirm Lowry's description of the windows.

(g) *the flying balcony.* (p. 199 [196].) Here, the catwalk connecting the two towers; apparently modelled on "flying bridge," a term used by Caxton to render the Fr. *pont-levis* or fastened drawbridge; hence, a temporary bridge (*OED*).

198.4 [194]   *marzipan.* A confection made of ground almonds, sugar, and whites of eggs; the suggestion here is that Jacques's tower is a confection as unreal and fantastical as a wedding cake.

199.1 [194]   *bas relief.* Literally, low relief. A sculpturing of little depth into a flat surface; the best example of such low-relief work being the frieze on the Parthenon in Athens.

199.2 [195]   *that phrase of Frey Luis de León's.* The words are "No se puede vivir sin amar" ("one cannot live without loving"), put there by the Consul some time after having discovered Yvonne's adultery with Laruelle (see note **11.12**). As Lowry noted explicitly in an early draft (UBC 7-3, p. 9), the words are from Fray Luis de León (1527-91), Spanish friar and writer, who is discussed by Somerset Maugham in *Don Fernando; or, Variations on Some Spanish Themes* (1935), p. 246, in terms (also cited by Kilgallin, pp. 151-52) that suggest a close affinity with the Consul:

> He sought for happiness and tranquillity of spirit, but his temperament made it impossible for him to achieve them. They count him among the mystics. He never experienced the supernatural blessings which solace those who pursue the mystic way. He never acquired that aloofness from the things of the world that characterises them. He had an anxious longing for a rapture his uneasy nature prevented him from ever enjoying. He was a mystic only in so far as he was a poet. He looked at those snowcapped mountains and yearned to explore their mysteries, but he was held back by the busy affairs of the city. I always think that the phrase of his, no se puede vivir sin amar, one cannot live without loving, had for him an intimate, tragic meaning. It was not just a commonplace.

Fray Luis Ponce de León (1528?-91) was an Augustinian monk, mystic, poet, humanist, and theologian. He represented a traditional scholasticism and was tormented and imprisoned by his Dominican opponents, who advocated a Hebraic tradition. His works include *La perfecta casada* (1583), *Vita retirado* (1557), *Noche serena* (1571), and *De los nombres de Cristo* (1583), from which the words "no se puede vivir sin amar" are taken. The phrase appears in a chapter entitled "Principe de Paz" ("The Prince of Peace"), and reads in full:

Dos cosas infiero: la una, que todos aman, los buenos y los malos, los felices y los infelices, y que no se puede bivir [*sic*] sin amar; la otra, que como el amor en los unos es causa des su buena andanca, assi en los otros es la fuente de su miseria, y siendo en todos amor, háze en los unos y en los otros effectos muy differentes.

("Two things may be inferred: the first, that all men love, both the good and the bad, the happy and the unhappy, and that one cannot live without loving; the other, that just as love for some men is the cause of their good fortune, so for others it is the fountain of their misery, and accordingly love has very different effects in one group as opposed to the other.")

200.1 [196]   *the clubs of flying machines. . . . Golfing scorpions.* The Consul, who has already "overshot" the drinks, p. 199 [195], translates what he sees into golfing terms: the limbs and baskets of the ferris wheel and octopus of the fairground turn into the clubs which belabour him, p. 201 [196], and the little figures of players become scorpions of his mind. As the eagle flies, the Las Palmas Golf Club in Cuernavaca would be in sight from a mirador in the Calle Humboldt, but across the town, on the far bank of the Tlaltenango barranca, which flanks the other side of the city.

200.2 [196]   *unknown moons hurtling backwards.* Epstein, p. 133, suggests a debt to Ouspensky's *A New Model of the Universe,* the chapter (Ch. 7) dealing with sleep and dreams, where, she claims, the sensation of hurling or flying backwards is regarded by occultists as a phenomenon of black magic (Ouspensky also adds, p. 280, that the sensation is actually caused by an inconvenient position of the head or slightly deranged circulation of the blood). Havelock Ellis, in his *The World of Dreams* (1911), Ch. 6, also discusses such phenomena. The Consul's dream is similar to Hugh's, p. 179 [176], "the world hurling from all havens astern," which in turn seems like that of Demarest in *Blue Voyage,* p. 139, who feels under the ship and under the sea "the half-cold planet, which rushes through freezing space to destruction, carrying with it continents of worthless history, the sea, this ship."

202.1 [198]   *Only my heart—.* Given the immediate context of the counterpoised drawbridge, the unspoken words are probably "can't stretch" (see note **179.5**).

202.2 [198]   *poltergeist.* Ger. "a noise-ghost"; a spirit which haunts houses and plays annoying tricks on humans visiting or living there.

202.3 [198]   *Tarquin's ravishing strides.* The reference is to *Macbeth,* II.i. 49-56, where Macbeth steels himself to murder Duncan:

> Now o'er the one half-world
> Nature seems dead, and wicked dreams abuse
> The curtain'd sleep; now witchcraft celebrates
> Pale Hecate's offerings; and wither'd murder
> Alarum'd by his sentinel, the wolf,
> Whose howl's his watch, thus with his stealthy pace,
> With Tarquin's ravishing strides, toward his design
> Moves like a ghost.

Shakespeare's reference is to his own poem, "The Rape of Lucrece," which tells how Sextus Tarquinius, son of Tarquin, king of Rome, becomes inflamed with the beauty of Lucretia, the faithful wife of Collinatus, steals into her chamber at night, rapes her, and flees. Lucretia sends for her father and husband, dresses in mourning, tells her story, and stabs herself. The resulting outcry moves the populace to rise up against the Tarquins and overthrow their rule. Lines 365-66 of the poem seem equally pertinent to the Consul's darker meaning: "Into the chamber wickedly he stalks, / And gazeth on her yet unstainèd bed."

202.4 [198]   *Orozco charcoal drawings.* José Clemente Orozco (1883-1949), one of the greatest Mexican painters and muralists, whose deep sympathy for the poor and oppressed manifested itself in an expressionist form of protest. Criticism of his anticlerical and political caricatures and cartoons forced him to leave the country in 1916, but he returned to paint murals and a famous series of ink and wash drawings known as "Mexico in Revolution." His work is characterized by a strong element of caricature and exaggeration and by an explicit concern for social justice and revolution.

202.5 [198]   *two ruddy Riveras.* Diego Rivera (1886-1957), born in Guanajuato, is the most celebrated of all the Mexican muralists. His work is concerned above all with the political implications of the Mexican Revolution. His style was formed in Mexico and Europe under the influence of Cézanne, Renoir, and the cubists, but he was directed consistently towards transforming art in Mexico into a popular national movement. At times his work demonstrates greater concern with political message than aesthetic quality (hence the Consul's implicit reservations: people with ideas), but his bold use of colour and contrast has created some enduring if controversial masterpieces—above all, the murals on the wall of the Cortés Palace in Cuernavaca (1927), depicting a series of incidents from the Conquest through to the Revolution (see note **215.4**), and the vast murals in the National Palace (begun in 1929), depicting the history of Mexico from pre-Columbian times to the Revolution. The Consul's uncomplimentary "Amazons with legs like mutton" is not, however, an altogether unfair description of many of Rivera's stolid figures.

202.6 [199] *Los Borrachones.* The picture is called *Los Borrachones* rather than *Los Borrachos* because a *borrachón* is one who is like a drunk, as opposed to a *borracho,* a total drunk. The magnificent picture, which depicts so perfectly the vital conflict within the Consul's mind, probably owes more to Lowry's imagination than to any painter, but in the manuscript of *DATG* (UBC 14–22, p. 232) there is a line not to be found in the published version: "Los Borrachones of course could not be there [that is, in Cuernavaca], because it was in Taxco." Given this hint, one can clearly see in two separate paintings in the splendidly churrigueresque cathedral of Santa Prisca at Taxco (in part the model for Lowry's style—"LJC," p. 85), elements which have contributed to *Los Borrachones:* in the side chapel to the left, one painting shows demons pushing lost souls down to hell, while opposite it, on the right of the church, is a rather lacklustre picture of souls ascending, two of which (male sheltering female) look back with exactly the sublime selfless expression that Lowry indicates here.

202.7 [199] *hades.* The kingdom of Pluto, in Greek mythology God of the nether world; a gloomy sunless abode where, according to Homer, the ghosts of the dead flit about like bats.

203.1 [199] *Medusae.* Medusa was one of the three Gorgons, the only one who was mortal. By granting her favours to Poseidon she incurred the wrath of Athena, who changed her locks into serpents. She had the power of turning into stone all on whom she fixed her eyes, but Perseus, using his buckler as a mirror, escaped her glance and was able to cut off her head.

203.2 [199] *abnegating.* Refusing or renouncing. The angels have rejected the pleasures of alcohol and the company of drunkards. Ironically, Goethe's Mephistopheles is called "Der Geist, der stets verneint" ("the spirit of negation").

203.3 [199] *cuneiform stone idols squatted like bulbous infants.* Although the idols were described on p. 16 [10] as Mayan, their appearance and significance otherwise exactly suggests the stone Aztec images of *Las Cihua-*

teteo (a row of which can be seen in the National Museum of Anthropology). These are squat bulbous figures representing mothers who died in childbirth and who cry and call out into the night, turning themselves into frightful beings of ill-omen. The association, if it exists, gives added horror to the Consul's vision of "a whole row of fettered babies," the children Yvonne will never give him. A series of superficially similar idols, including some chained together, were previously to be found on the balcony of the Cortés Palace in front of the Rivera murals; they have since been removed, but they may well have been the immediate source of Lowry's inspiration.

203.4 [199] *lost wild talents.* An allusion to Charles Fort (1874–1932), American writer and eccentric, whom Lowry discovered and admired because he made "the inexplicable seem more dramatic" (*SL,* p. 26). His specialty was "the analysis of peculiar coincidences for which there exists no scientific explanation" (*SL,* p. 26): frogs and fishes falling from the skies, strange lights on the moon and in the air, reports of strange animals, inexplicable disappearances of men, spontaneous combustion, stones and meteors falling from space. He spent much of his life collecting and collating such reports, with the idea of generalizing from them "something of cosmic order or law" (Fort, p. xviii), and his findings were published in *The Book of the Damned* (1919), *New Lands* (1923), *Lo!* (1931) and *Wild Talents* (1932). By "wild talents" Fort meant the gift, uncontrolled in many but harnessed by adepts and magicians, of spiritual and psychic powers affecting material phenomena but not subject to rational explanation; the power, for instance, to cause cars to crash, to divine water, to make things explode, or to make fires burst forth spontaneously. This last talent Lowry believed he possessed in a self-destructive way (he lost his home and manuscripts through fire), and the power to induce fire, taken directly from *Wild Talents,* is the basis of Lowry's short story, "The Element Follows You Around, Sir," later used as Ch. 18 of *October Ferry.*

203.5 [199] *he was in hell himself.* An echo of Marlowe's *Doctor Faustus,* iii:

Faust: Where are you damned?
Mephistopheles: In hell.
Faust: How comes it then that thou are out of hell?
Mephistopheles: Why this is hell, nor am I out of it.

Marlowe's lines are echoed in Milton's *Paradise Lost,* I.254–55: "The mind is its own place, and in it self, / Can make a Heav'n of Hell, a Hell of Heav'n."

203.6 [199]   *The Farolito*. Sp. "the little lighthouse" (or, pedantically, since it is a diminutive of *farol* rather than *faro,* "the little lantern"). Originally a cantina in Oaxaca, within stumbling distance of the Hotel Francia, it became for Lowry a symbol of the lighthouse that invites the storm, the sanctuary and paradise of his despair. The Consul's problem is clearly stated, p. 205 [201]: "Could one be faithful to Yvonne and the Farolito both?" The "other terrible cantina in Oaxaca," p. 204 [200], is El Infierno, described on p. 350 [349], and clearly based on the same original.

203.7 [200]   *the lighthouse that invites the storm*. Lowry used this as the title of one of his poems, and also proposed using it for an unpublished collection of poetry (Day, p. 282). The image sums up perfectly the Consul's self-destructive qualities.

204.1 [200]   *when Saturn was in Capricorn*. A heavenly body is said to be "in" a zodiacal sign when it appears between the viewer and that part of the sky in which the particular constellation is to be found. Saturn has distinct connotations of evil: in traditional astrology it is the planet farthest from the sun and is the figure of time, the devourer of life, under whose patronage occur "works of malediction and death" (Éliphas Lévi, *Transcendental Magic,* p. 252). Capricorn, the Goat, suggests the cabrón with whom the Consul has frequently identified himself (see note **70.1**). Lowry's image seems to have been derived from Frater Achad's *The Egyptian Revival,* p. 34, where the path from Binah to Tiphereth is said to be "represented by 'The Devil' and the sign of Capricorn which is Ruled by Saturn from whose Sphere it springs." As Andersen says, p. 33, "The exact significance of Saturn in Capricorn may not be clear, but it is certain that this situation promises no good."

204.2 [200]   *Kubla Khan*. Alluding, not at all appropriately, to Coleridge's "Kubla Khan," ll. 12–16:

> But oh! that deep romantic chasm which slanted
> Down the green hill athwart a cedarn cover!
> A savage place! as holy and enchanted
> As e'er beneath a waning moon was haunted
> By woman wailing for her demon-lover!
> And from this chasm, with ceaseless turmoil seething.
> As if this earth in fast thick pants were breathing,
> A mighty fountain momently was forced.

The parallels between Coleridge's poem and *UTV* are far-reaching: the chasm and the fountain are important symbols, while the woman "wailing for her demon-lover" forms an obvious archetype of Yvonne.

204.3 [200] *neurasthenia.* From Gk. *astheneia,* "weakness"; weakness or exhaustion of the nervous system, with symptoms of fatigue, depression, and pains without apparent physical cause.

204.4 [200] *the Virgin of Guadalupe.* In 1531, on the hill of Tepeyac just north of Mexico City, a newly converted Indian named Juan Diego beheld a vision of a dark-skinned Virgin, who commanded him to have a shrine built in her honour. When the bishops refused to do so without proof of the visitation, the Virgin again appeared before Juan Diego and told him to gather roses from the previously barren hill. He did so, returned to the bishops, and on opening his cloak found that the roses had gone, but a painting of the Virgin covered the garment. The shrine was built, and during the wars of Independence, 1810, Hidalgo's forces carried the banner of the Virgin as the emblem of their crusade. As Patroness of Mexico, she has her special day, 12 December, on which her shrine becomes an object of pilgrimage. Because of her symbolic importance, the Consul's encounter with the beggar has greater significance than might first appear.

204.5 [200] *Sonnenaufgang!* Ger. "Sunrise!"; the title of the 1927 movie by Friedrich Wilhelm Murnau (1888–1931), Ufa director celebrated for his masterly innovative use of cinematic resources and best known for *Der Januskopf* (1920), *Der letzte Mann* (1924), *Tartüff* (1925), and *Faust* (1926), before he left Germany in 1926 for Hollywood where, apart from *Sunrise* (1927) and *Tabu* (1931), his success was limited. His career in many ways forms the model for that of Jacques Laruelle. *Sunrise,* Murnau's first Hollywood film, was a striking combination of German and Hollywood styles. Based on Hermann Sudermann's *Die Reise nach Tilsit,* produced by Fox, with screenplay by Carl Mayer, it starred George O'Brien as the man and Janet Gaynor as the wife. Murnau tried to create a poetic tragedy from the archetypal theme of infidelity, attempted murder, and remorse: the man, attempting to kill his unwanted wife, fails (much to his relief), and the couple are reconciled. The film is justly famous for its visual qualities: not only the close-ups showing the forces battling for possession of the man's soul, but also long, fluid landscape scenes and a celebrated sequence on a trolley car. A title of the film read that it was:

the song of two humans: This story of a man and his wife is of nowhere and everywhere. You might hear it anywhere and at any time. For everywhere the sun rises and sets—in the city's turmoil or under the open sky on the farm, life is much the same, sometimes bitter, sometimes sweet, tears and laughter, sin and forgiveness.

In a letter to Clemens ten Holder, his German translator (*SL,* p. 239), Lowry wrote:

> It was in Bonn I saw Murnau's *Sonnenaufgang;* 70 minutes of this wonderful film — though it falls to pieces later, doubtless due to the exigencies of Hollywood — have influenced me almost as much as any book I ever read.

204.6 [201]   *Start Point.* Known to sailors as "the Start"; a headland on the coast of Devon, described in *Ships and the Sea,* p. 57, as: "Start Point. White tower. 1 flash every 20 seconds. Visible 20 miles. Also low fixed light visible 20 miles. 274,000 C.P."

205.1 [201]   *Sutherland... gaunt lowland uncles chumbling shortbread.* Sutherland is a mountainous and sparsely populated country in the northern highlands of Scotland. To chumble is to nibble, to gnaw, or to chew into little pieces; the word is usually spelt chimble, but Lowry appears to be following John Clare's "Solitude," ll. 33–34: "And the little chumbling mouse / Gnarls the dead weed for her house."

205.2 [201]   *the Café Chagrin.* The Consul's regrets are cast in terms of a Bunyan-like allegory, but his use of French suggests Paris, "before Hugh came."

205.3 [201]   *Christ, oh pharos of the world.* An image which is not so much traditional Christian iconography as Lowry's own emblem of the Biblical conception of Christ as the light of the world (although Lowry may have met the image in Bishop Montgomery's *Visions,* 1909, pp. 99–103). The lighthouse of Alexandria, on the island of Pharos just outside the harbour of Alexandria, dates from about 270 A.D., and is one of the seven wonders of the ancient world.

205.4 [201]   *one of the little Mayan idols seemed to be weeping.* As Markson suggests, p. 103, the idol is a reminder of Niobe, who was turned to stone, yet weeps for the loss of her children (see note **203.3**).

205.5 [201]   *cocktails, despicable repast.* The custom of cocktails, invented in the 1920's, was taken up only slowly by the English, many of whom continued to abominate them as offences to the palate and a breach of social decorum. The canapés mentioned below are appetizers, such as crackers with cheese, paté, or other delicacies which accompany the serving of cocktails.

205.6 [201] *he took the postcard . . . and slipped it under Jacques's pillow.* To be discovered (see p. 19 [13]) at the precise moment that Hugh will call from Parián with the news of the deaths of the Consul and Yvonne.

206.1 [202] *the dream of dark magician in his visioned cave.* From Shelley's "Alastor," ll. 681–88 (see note **151.4**); this time with the significant change from "lovely" to "lousy."

206.2 [202] *spoon shot.* A "spoon" is a golf club used for the middle game, that is, somewhere between driving and putting on the green. It is typically used in situations where the ball is in a bad spot, such as in a bunker, and needs to be lofted out sharply.

206.3 [202] *the Golgotha Hole.* Golgotha, from Heb. *gulgoleth,* "a skull," is the hill of Calvary, the scene of Christ's crucifixion, as described in Matthew 27:33–34:

> And when they were come unto a place called Golgotha,
> that is to say, a place of a skull,
>   They gave him vinegar to drink mingled with gall: and
> when he had tasted thereof, he would not drink.

206.4 [202] *an eagle.* In golf, a score on a hole two strokes better than par; here anticipating the fanciful notion of Prometheus as saviour, retrieving lost balls.

206.5 [202] *Golf = gouffre = gulf.* As Kilgallin notes, p. 186, the Consul's reasoning is based on Gerard Manley Hopkins's *Early Diaries* (1864), p. 25:

> *Gulf, golf.* If this game has its name from the holes into which the ball is put, they may be connected, both being from the root meaning hollow. *Gulp, gula, hollow, hilt, koiλós, caelare* (to make hollow, to make grooves in, to grave) *caelum,* which is therefore same as though it were what it were once supposed to be a translation of *koiλóv, hole, hell,* ('The hollow hell') *skull, shell, hull* (of ships and beans).

The etymology is faulty, since "golf" probably derives from D. *kolf,* "a club," which has nothing to do with Fr. *gouffre,* "gulf," but Hopkins's note suggests why Geoffrey should connect golf and Golgotha, "the place of a skull." Gouffre is probably taken from Baudelaire's *Les Fleurs du Mal,* in which it is a key word; it is frequently aligned with *souffre,* "suffer," as in "L'Aube Spirituelle," ll. 5–7:

> Des Cieux Spirituels l'inaccessible azur,
> Pour l'homme terrassé qui rêve encore et souffre,
> S'ouvre et s'enfonce avec l'attirance du gouffre.

("From the Spiritual Heavens the inaccessible blue / reveals itself and mingles with the attraction of the gulf / for the earth-bound man who still dreams and suffers.")

206.6 [202]   *the Farolito, the nineteenth hole... The Case is Altered.* The "nineteenth hole" is the bar or tavern retired to at the end of the round. The Consul's fancy, perhaps playing with Frank Crumit's popular song of 1922 "Oh, How I Love the 19th Hole When the 18th Hole is Over," links the cosmic course laid out before him with his youthful experience in the Hell Bunker: the Farolito, like *The Case is Altered,* will signify a permanent transformation (see note **27.3**).

206.7 [202]   *the film he made out of Alastor.* Jacques's film, made before he went to Hollywood, seems very much "hoiked out of" (borrowed from, cut out of) the Ufa tradition of German expressionism, and in the Consul's description is a total burlesque of some of the more exciting advances taking place in film during the 1920's. In an earlier draft (UBC 7-7, p. 12) it was described as "a sort of avant-garde picture, a forerunner to Cocteau's *Sang d'un poete*": it featured a poet standing on the shore, a sequence of ruins, gargoyles, gothic subtitles, "inevitable" scenes of Indus and Oxus, the sea again, a swan flying into the sunset, the poet still on the shore, the swan still flying over an ever rougher sea, the moon rising upon the Caucasus, the boat rushing into a whirlpool and tossing in the sea, an orchestra playing the *Sacre du Printemps,* the poet escaping through a jungle taken from *In Darkest Africa,* the effect somehow conveyed of his being carried back through his life to the same starting place, "also the end of the world": all in all, fragments unlikely to shore up any ruin.

Many of the above details, only slightly modified, can be recognized in Shelley's "Alastor" (see note **151.4**): the poet's "wandering step" takes him not only to "awful ruins of the days of old" (l. 108), but also past Indus and

Oxus to wild exotic places such as Persia and Cashmire, and to the "lone Chorasmian shore" (l. 272), where, his soul elevated by the flight of a swan, he embarks upon the sea to meet Death, passes the ethereal cliffs of Caucasus (ll. 353–54), is driven into whirlpool and cavern, finally to rest his languid head and die in that obscurest chasm (l. 637), the vision fled.

206.8 [203] *In dunkelste Afrika.* More accurately, *Im dunkelsten Afrika,* German for *In darkest Africa.* Although Henry Stanley (of Livingstone fame) had written a popular book of that name about his 1890 expedition into the heart of the Congo to rescue the Emir Pasha, the reference here is probably to the 1927 film *Through Darkest Africa: In Search of White Rhinoceros.* It was a travelogue photographed by Harry K. Eustace, featuring himself and his wife. A film catalogue describes it as follows: "A typical animal hunt film in which are seen groups of animals grazing, playing, and resting — interspersed with frequent titles and candid shots of the hunters in pursuit of one exotic beast or another. Highlights include an animal burial ground, some native comic relief, hippopotami, and, of course, the white rhinoceros."

206.9 [203] *a swan out of the end of some old Corinne Griffith.* Corinne Griffith (1899?–1979), popularly known as "the Orchid Lady," was first a professional dancer, then an American leading lady in the 1920's. Her films include *Divorce Coupons* (1922), *Lilies of the Field* (1924), *Love's Wilderness* (1924), and *The Garden of Eden* (1928). Corinne Griffith productions are invariably love-romances, with entanglements and happy endings. The film with a swan in it has not been identified, but the swan itself is taken from Shelley's "Alastor," ll. 272–95, where the poet, "upon the lone Chorasmian shore," sees the swan rise high at his approach and, watching it fly, sees its flight home as an emblem of his soul's desire for its true rest.

206.10 [203] *Sarah Bernhardt.* Sarah Bernhardt (1845–1923), French actress and the most celebrated tragedienne of her time, was a member of the *Comédie Française* before turning to England and the London stage in 1879. She took part in a number of early films: *Hamlet,* (1900), *La Dame aux Camelias* (1912), *La Reine Elisabeth* (1912), *Jeanne Dore* (1915), and *Mothers of France* (1917). Her performances in these pieces do scant justice to her reputation as an actress.

206.11 [203] *the Sacre du Printemps.* The *Rite of Spring,* a revolutionary ballet written for Diaghilev by Igor Stravinsky (1882–1971), the first production of which caused a furore in Paris in 1913 (the narrator's father in "Forest Path," p. 270, played the French horn in that performance). It evokes a primeval account of the death and rebirth of nature in a tremendously immediate and emphatic manner and is marked by rhythmical energy, strikingly fierce thematic material, and sheer virtuosity of orchestration. Ironically, its best-known use in the movies is in Walt Disney's *Fantasia*.

207.1 [203]   *Silver king. . . . Zodiac Zone.* Brand names of golf balls: the Zodiac Zone, described in *October Ferry*, p. 115, as "an antique long-lost golf ball of forgotten make," was one of the first rubber-cored balls to become available in 1902; the Silver King, used in *The Clicking of Cuthbert* (see note **178.17**), was a popular make between the wars. A blind hole in golf is one that cannot be seen from the place where a ball is lying.

207.2 [203]   *Ozone.* From Gk. *ozein,* "to smell"; literally, a blue gas, O_3, formed by a silent electrical discharge in the air; more commonly used, as here, in the metaphorical sense of "pure air," which Lowry attributes to Gide (*SL,* p. 190).

207.3 [203]   *a sort of Donne of the fairways.* An imitation of John Donne's "A Hymn to God the Father":

> Wilt thou forgive that sinne where I begunne,
> Which was my sin, though it were done before?
> Wilt thou forgive that sinne; through which I runne,
> And do run still: though still I do deplore?
> And when thou hast done, thou has not done,
>   For, I have more.

> Wilt thou forgive that sinne which I have wonne
> Others to sinne? and, made my sinne their doore?
> Wilt thou forgive that sinne which I did shunne
> A year, or two; but wallowed in, a score?
> When thou has done, thou hast not done,
>   For I have more.

> I have a sinne of feare, that when I have spunne
> My last thred, I shall perish on the shore;
> But sweare by thy selfe, that at my death thy sonne
> Shall shine as he shines now, and heretofore;
> And, having done that, Thou hast done,
>   I fear no more.

207.4 [204]   *Percy Bysshe Shelley.* Percy Bysshe Shelley (1792–1822), poet and composer of numerous lyrics, odes, and poetic dramas, among which the Consul refers to "Alastor" (see notes **151.4** and **206.7**); *The Cenci* (see note **339.9**); *Julian and Maddalo* (see note **220.1**); and whose *Prometheus Unbound* (1820) constantly represents for the Consul an image of his own great battle. The story of Shelley's attempt to swim is perhaps apocryphal, but it is told in Edward Trelawney's *Records of Shelley, Byron, and the Author,* Ch. 7:

> I was bathing one day in a deep pool in the Arno, and astonished the Poet by performing a series of aquatic gymnastics, which I had learnt from the natives of the South Seas. On my coming out, while dressing, Shelley said mournfully,
> "Why can't I swim? It seems so very easy."
> I answered, "Because you think you can't. If you determine, you will; take a header off this bank, and when you rise turn on your back, you will float like a duck; but you must reverse the arch in your spine, for it's now bent the wrong way."
> He doffed his jacket and trousers, kicked off his shoes and socks, and plunged in; and there he lay stretched out on the bottom like a conger eel, not making the least effort or struggle to save himself. He would have been drowned if I had not instantly fished him out. When he recovered his breath, he said,
> "I always find the bottom of the well, and they say Truth lies there. In another minute I should have found it, and you would have found an empty shell. It is an easy way of getting rid of the body."

This episode took place not in the sea but in a pool of the river Arno, and there is no mention of the books. The Consul has associated the scene (which, as Trelawney points out, reflects Shelley's strong death-wish) with Shelley's actual death by drowning a little later. After Shelley's boat, the *Don Juan,* was swamped (perhaps rammed) in a storm after leaving Leghorn, 8 July 1822, Trelawney identified Shelley's corpse by the volumes of *Aeschylus* (some say *Sophocles*) in one pocket and Keats's poems in the other.

208.1 [205]   *Like the truth, it was well-nigh impossible to face.* Behind the Swedenborgian image of God as truth and sun lies an allusion to Shelley's perverse pride in sinking to the bottom: immediately following Trelawney's rescue of Shelley (see note **207.4**), the two enter into a detailed philosophical speculation about the nature of Truth:

Shelley: If we had known the great truths, they would have laid bare the great lies.
Tre: What do they mean by the great truths?
Shelley: They cannot calculate time, measure distance and say what is above or what is below us.

209.1 [205]   *the will of man is unconquerable.* A phrase already associated with Milton's Satan and total self-delusion (see note **97.4**); the Consul will no more be able to resist the drinks than he was earlier able to refrain from falling asleep.

209.2 [205]   *when we went to Cholula.* Laruelle recalls the trip to the pyramid, p. 17 [11]. What is unstated here is the awareness both men now share of Yvonne's presence between them at the time. It seems likely that the Consul, now so conscious of the truth, did not then know he had been deceived; hence his reference to the dust.

209.3 [205]   *this unanswerable and staggering injustice.* In the drafts (UBC 11–1, p. 14), Lowry showed the Consul drinking everything in sight (as he does on p. 212 [208]) *before* Jacques's return. In the final version, in the Consul's mind at least, the injustice of Jacques's remark is therefore heavily accentuated. Hill, p. 133, offers an excellent analysis of the state of mind which senses such "injustice" in what is fairly patently the direct and brutal truth:

> For it is one more affliction of the alcoholic that he is always ashamed of his drinking. This is why, drunk or sober, he maintains the fiction that he could drink moderately, and surely will next time. . . . Drinks are poured. He does not touch his, but instead scans the countryside through binoculars from a balcony, commenting lightly on random topics. The implication is plain: he is so indifferent to liquor that he has forgotten the drink is there. He has not forgotten.

As Hill says, the Consul is playing the "game" to the limit, and hence Laruelle's attack is unfair because, as the Consul understands the rules, he has been holding off the drink, winning the game — and to be accused like this, so unjustly, will give him precisely the excuse he is seeking to drink everything in sight.

209.4 [206]   *a hawser did not give.* That is, the Consul resists the temptation to drink. A hawser is a cable fastening a ship to a pier.

210.1 [206] *Médico. Cirujano.* Sp. "Doctor. Surgeon" (the words of the notice in Dr. Vigil's windows, p. 29 [23]). The Consul replies "guardedly" because of his fears of being followed around; a moment later he is shaken by the revelation that Vigil knows he is with Laruelle: it all seems part of the "plot."

210.2 [206] *cucumiform.* As Jakobsen notes, p. 87, *cucumiform,* "cucumber-shaped" has probably been suggested by *cuneiform,* "wedge-shaped" (from L. *cuneus,* "a wedge," the ancestor of the other four-letter word which underlies the Consul's association of the two terms). The Consul's sudden insight into "unaccommodated man" is crucially important to his final choice of hell.

211.1 [207] *Les Joyeuses Bourgeoises de Windsor.* A play in verse by the French dramatist Ernest Prarond (1821–1909), based on Shakespeare's *Merry Wives of Windsor.* The play deals with the amorous flirtations of the wives of Windsor, but the Consul's present mood is scarcely in keeping with its light-hearted tone.

211.2 [207] *Agrippa d'Aubigné.* Theodore Agrippa d'Aubigné (1552–1630), French Huguenot fighter, historian, poet, and tragedian, whose vigorous Calvinism made him at times the object of considerable persecution. After the death of Henry IV, he settled in Geneva where he wrote most of his works, the best known of which are his *Histoire universelle* of the period 1550–1601, centring on Henry IV and the Huguenots, and his long poem, "Les Tragiques" (1616), a strongly anti-papal epic about the religious wars of his day.

211.3 [207] *Collin d'Harleville.* Jean François Collin d'Harleville (1755–1806), a minor French dramatist and writer of light comedies in verse; notably *Le vieux Celibataire* (produced during the Revolution in 1792), but also *L'Inconstant* (1786), *L'Optimiste* (1788), *Les Châteaux en Espagne* (1788), and *Malice pour Malice* (1803).

211.4 [207] *Touchard — Lafosse.* Georges Touchard-Lafosse (1780–1847), French writer of the histories of Louis XIV, XV, and XVI, and of Charles XIV, king of Sweden; but who is best known for his *Chroniques de l'Oeil de Boeuf,* published in 1830 under the pseudonym of Madame la Comtesse Douairiere de B——. This was a witty and irreverent look through the keyholes at the court and society gossip and scandal of the age of Louis XIV to Louis XVI, the author's intention being to present a tableau at once historically accurate and of literary value, sparing nobody or anything, but always scrupulously true; the result is a delightful insight into the foibles and intrigues of another age.

211.5 [207]   *Tristan l'Hermite.* The pseudonym of François l'Hermite (1602–55), French poet and dramatist, who was at one time a member of the retinue of the Duke of Orléans. He is the author of four notable tragedies: *La Mariane* (1636), about the jealous love of Herod for Marianne, whom he puts to death; *La mort de Senèque* (1644), *La mort de Crispe* (1645), and *Osman* (1656). He also wrote a tragi-comedy called *La folie du sage* (1745) and a comedy called *Le Parasite* (1654) as well as a number of poems.

211.6 [207]   *Beaucoup de bruit pour rien.* Fr. "Much Ado About Nothing"; the title of another Shakespearean play, presumably suggested to the Consul by *Les Joyeuses Bourgeoises de Windsor,* dismissing Laruelle's intellectually light-weight volumes as offering nothing that will relieve his suffering.

211.7 [207]   *how to look at an ox-eye daisy.* The ox-eye daisy, *Chrysanthemum Leucanthemum,* is a common flower of the meadows, resembling the common daisy but much larger. The Consul's odd reflection, so very like his reaction to the sunflower (see note **148.1**) reflects his sense of being watched constantly. The daisy (the "eye of day") is a popular symbol of fidelity ("she loves me, she loves me not"), and the question of Yvonne's loyalty is very much to the fore.

211.8 [207]   *Medullary compression of the gibbus.* The gibbus (or gibbous) is a hump; usually the dorsal convexity seen in tuberculosis of the spine (Pott's disease) or caused by fracture. Medullary means pertaining to the *medulla oblongata,* the caudal part of the brain contiguous with the upper part of the spinal cord; the Consul's pun, "Our agreements were more or less bilateral," takes its point from the *medulla oblongata* being the point of crossing of the neural "eclectic systemës" to the opposite hemispheres of the brain.

212.1 [208]   *Erikson 34.* Dr. Guzmán's number, on the Erikson exchange, is the reverse of the Consul's (see note **81.2**). Guzmán, like Beckett's Godot, never appears, but he is mentioned frequently as a kind of medical saviour whom the Consul has wilfully ignored and who has perhaps given up on the Consul. The breakdown of communication between the Consul and Guzmán is thus a kind of primordial sin. Ironically, in trying to find this saviour, the Consul while flicking through the phone-book (A. B. C. G.), comes across the advertisements for Cafeaspirina and 666 and the names of his eventual destroyers, Zuzugoitea and Sanabria.

212.2 [208] *¿Qué quieres?* Sp. "What do you want?"; misunderstood by the Consul as *"Who* do you want?," to which he answers "God!"

212.3 [209] *Jean Cocteau's La Machine infernale.* Jean Cocteau (1891–1963), French playwright and film-maker, who was involved with the artistic avant-garde from an early age (collaborating with Satie on a ballet by Diaghilev with sets by Picasso). He was widely acclaimed for his *Orphée* (1926), *Sang d'un poete* (1930), and *La machine infernale,* written in 1932 and produced in Paris in 1934. Lowry saw the latter twice (he claimed that Cocteau had given him the ticket), and it made an indelible impression upon him. Cocteau's play is a retelling of Sophocles's *Oedipus Tyrranus* (see note **168.4**), keeping closely to the story-line but imbuing it with a marked cynicism and a strongly deterministic philosophy. Day, p. 323, outlines the play's relevance to *Under the Volcano:*

> This was Cocteau's version of the Oedipus tragedy. Before the play itself begins, a "Fantome" speaks to the audience of what is about to take place. At the conclusion of this preamble, the Fantome says:
>> Spectator, this machine you see here wound up to the full in such a way that the spring will slowly unwind the whole length of human life, is one of the most perfect constructed by the infernal gods for the mathematical destruction of a human life.
> This infernal machine is the universe itself: an ingeniously contrived clock-like mechanism in which every part, every minute, has its function in the machine's diabolical purpose—"the mathematical destruction of a human life." When Lowry wrote to Cape that *Under the Volcano* "can even be regarded as a sort of machine: it works, too, believe me, as I have found out," it was surely of Cocteau's clockwork instrument of execution that he was thinking: which means, among other things, that his novel would be the representation of the destruction, beautifully and horribly worked out, of a human life—that of Geoffrey Firmin, His Majesty's Consul in Quauhnahuac, Mexico. The spring of the machine has been unwinding the whole length of the Consul's life, bringing him inexorably to the morning of November 1, 1938: The Day of the Dead, when the living visit the cemeteries to commune with their departed loved ones.
> The spring of the Infernal Machine is, of course, Time. It has taken the Consul forty-two years to prepare himself for his last twelve hours.

212.4 [209] *Oui, mon enfant, mon petit enfant... les choses qui paraissent abominable aux humains, si tu savais, de l'endroit où j'habite, elles ont peu d'importance.* Fr. "Yes, my child, my little child ... things that appear abominable to humans, if you but knew, from the place where I dwell, they have little importance." From Cocteau's *La machine infernale:* the words, not quite accurately quoted, are from near the end of the play when the ghost of Jocasta returns as the mother of Oedipus to help him on his way to Colonus. The context is ominous: Oedipus says, "Je suis encore sur la terre" ("I am still on earth"), to which his mother replies "à peine" ("only just").

212.5 [209]   *sortes Shakespeareanae.* Divination by chance selection from Shakespeare's works; the Consul's action is duplicated by Laruelle one year later (see note **40.5**).

212.6 [209]   *The gods exist, they are the devil.* This quotation prefaces Cocteau's *La machine infernale:* "Les dieux existent: c'est le diable" (which should be translated: "The gods exist, that is the devil of it"). The erroneous attribution to Baudelaire arises because Baudelaire is the author of the two other quotations above this one in Cocteau's play. That the mistake is the Consul's rather than Lowry's is suggested by an earlier draft which read "it informed him" rather than "Baudelaire informed him" (UBC 7-7, p. 17), but the error supports other references to *Les Fleurs du Mal* worked into the final drafts.

213.1 [209]   *Runcible spoon.* From Edward Lear's nonsense poem, "The Owl and the Pussycat":

> They dined on mince and slices of quince,
> Which they ate with a runcible spoon,
> And hand in hand on the edge of the sand
> They danced by the light of the moon.

Although the word does not appear in the *OED,* there is such a thing as a runcible spoon (presumably named for the poem); it is a spoon with broad tines and a sharp edge for cutting which is used like a fork for the serving of hors d'oeuvres.

213.2 [210]   *white trousers of twenty-one inches breadth.* White flannel trousers were fashionable throughout the 1920's and 1930's, the "slim silhouette" persisting until the "Oxford bags" came into vogue. They were sometimes as wide as 24 inches at the bottom. Laruelle, an incurable Anglophile, not only adopts the current English fashion, but also, for "obscure purposes" of Lowry's own, is depicted as assuming increasingly the Consul's own character.

213.3 [210]   *a half-blue at the Sorbonne.* In Oxbridge parlance, a "blue" (from the light and dark blue of Oxford and Cambridge) is an award given to one chosen to represent his university in a major sport or activity such as cricket, rugby, or rowing; a "half-blue" for lesser sports such as archery. Such awards are not given by the Sorbonne.

213.4 [210]   *on just such afternoons as this.* An echo of Shakespeare's "In such a night as this," from *The Merchant of Venice,* V.i.1, where Lorenzo and Jessica are delighting in the memories of their love; like "The Owl and the Pussycat," above, it celebrates a relationship which is the direct antithesis of the Consul's.

214.1 [210]   *a scarab, of simple design, cut into a chalcedony.* A chalcedony is a semi-precious stone, a variety of quartz, usually translucent, and commonly used in jewellery; it was called by Pliny the Arabian stone (XXXVII. liv) and is sometimes considered the gemstone of Capricorn. A scarab is a beetle sacred to the ancient Egyptians. The male scarab was believed to be without a female counterpart and to lay eggs in a ball of dung or mud which it then rolled to the fertile waters of the Nile for hatching. The scarab is thus an emblem of a self-engendering deity and a symbol of the paradox of regeneration through the contamination of dung and death.

215.1 [211]   *Eggs.... Mescalito.* As the Consul walks down the street he earlier walked up, he hears in his mind, in reversed order, the insults directed at him that morning (see notes **61.2** and **58.1**). In like manner, Raskolnikov in *Crime and Punishment,* Pt. 3, Ch. 6, is accused of his crime by an unknown figure in the street.

215.2 [211]   *an improvised whirligig... the Great Carrousel.* A whirligig is a pole with a seat on the end which revolves round an axis — a crude, one-seat merry-go-round. A carrousel (the spelling is French rather than Spanish) is a much larger merry-go-round.

215.3 [211]   *the ayuntamiento.* In Mexico, the ayuntamiento is the usual word for the city chambers, the municipal offices, or the town hall. In 1938 the Cortés Palace was the centre of civic administration in Cuernavaca, containing offices for police, traffic, ambulance and library services, which since 1965 have been relocated in the Palacio Municipal.

215.4 [211]   *the Rivera frescoes.* A celebrated set of murals painted in 1927 by Diego Rivera (1886–1957) on the upper balcony at the back of the Cortés

Palace in Cuernavaca. The murals depict the history of Mexico from conquest to Revolution, with particular emphasis upon the history of Morelos.
The smaller north wall depicts the life of the Indians at the time of the conquest, then merges with battle-scenes between Indians and Spaniards on the
longer west wall. These in turn lead to the Spaniard's tree-crossing of the
Amanalco barranca to capture Quauhnahuac (see note **104.4**); and then to a
series of scenes depicting life for the Indians under Spanish rule: the brand-
ing of slaves; women at a native *tianguis,* or market, and men forced into
heavy labour; life on the sugar haciendas, with cruelty, abuse, and whip-
ping. On the south wall, directly opposite the Aztec sacrifice, is the Inquisi-
tion and a conflagration (Rivera believed that the Catholic church had
equally oppressed the Indians), and in the lower left corner a picture of
Emiliano Zapata, the revolutionary hero of Morelos, upon his white horse.
As Laruelle says, looked at from the north to south there is a slow darkening which indeed symbolizes the gradual imposition of the Spaniard's
conquering will upon the Indians, before the striking relief of Zapata's
horse; for Rivera the political message was always paramount.

215.5 [212] *the gradual imposition of the Americans' conquering friendship.* The Rivera murals on the Cortés Palace were commissioned and paid
for by Dwight Morrow, American ambassador to Mexico, who made his
home for many years in Cuernavaca. They were presented by him as a gift
to the people and city of Cuernavaca. Diego Rivera says in his autobiography, *My Art and My Life,* that he was called on in 1930 by Dwight W.
Morrow to paint a wall of the Cortés Palace in Cuernavaca: "I was given
complete freedom of choice as to subject matter and a fee of 30,000 pesos
[about $12,000] from which, however, I had to pay my assistants and buy
my own materials and equipment." He states that he spent $8,000 of his
own money on the restoration of the outer colonnade, whose walls he
decorated, and that he ended up flat broke. There is no suggestion that
Morrow attempted to dictate to the strong-willed artist how the murals
should be painted.

215.6 [212] *the Tlahuicans.* One of the seven Nahuatl tribes who, according to legend, originally set out from the fabled Chicomostoc in 830 A.D.,
and settled in the valley of Cuernavaca, which they soon dominated. They
established the state of Tlalnáhuac, whose borders were roughly those of
Morelos, and founded their capital at Quauhnahuac in 1197 (Aguirre,
p. 75; Díez, p. 48). Although their civilization rose to no great heights, the
Tlahuicans retained their independence until 1436, when they were brought
under Aztec sway by the angry lord, Moctezuma Ilhuicamina. They were
obliged to pay tribute, but retained some autonomy, and it was a combined

force of Aztecs and Tlahuicans who resisted Cortés when he attacked Quauhnahuac in 1521 (see note **104.4**). The battledress of these warriors consisted of padded and quilted cotton, topped by head-dresses or helmets, usually in the form of grotesque animal heads.

Lowry's source for this passage may have been Rosa E. King's *Tempest Over Mexico,* p. 319: "On the stone walls of Cortez's palace are painted now the heroic dark-skinned Tlahuicas in their war masks of wolves and *tigres,* who died defending this valley." The Consul's guilt was originally related to the themes of conquest and exploitation; in an earlier draft (UBC 7–13, p. 2) he had imagined himself hunted down by the Tlahuicans disguised as animals, and as pursued by a torrent of blood:

> the blood of Zapata, sweeping down on him, the landed proprietor, who had amassed half a million pesos out of Mexican oil, out of Mexican silver, the gringo, who, for his own ends had tapped Mexico's very veins . . . there was going to be a reckoning or two.

216.1 [212] *the Banco de Crédito y Ejidal.* The Bank of Ejidal Credit, set up to finance the ejidos or communal lands of the villages (see note **111.4**). The fine-featured Indian, like Juan Cerillo in Oaxaca, is obviously one who delivers money to the villages, and the risks involved in this undertaking are clearly demonstrated when he is next seen dying on the roadside in Ch. 8. The Banco de Crédito y Ejidal, no longer operative, was in the Calle Leyva directly behind the Cortés Palace.

216.2 [213] *surcingle.* From L. *cingulum,* "a girdle"; a wide belt passing beneath the belly of the horse to keep its load in place; the Consul's jingle drawing attention to the contents of the bags.

216.3 [213] *What is it Goethe says about the horse?* The Consul's reference is to Goethe's *Die Leiden des jungen Werthers* (*The Sorrows of Young Werther*), a novel in two parts, published in 1774. In the form of letters written by Werther to his friend Wilhelm, it tells of the hopeless passion Werther has conceived for Lotte, who is, alas, promised to another. At this point in the novel, near the end of Part I, Werther is miserable, his active powers are dulled, and, citing La Fontaine's fable about the horse (which, to avenge itself upon a stag, surrendered itself to man, but was not restored its liberty), he expresses his longing for a change of state, a desire for freedom:

> hernach, wenn ich so wieder dran denke, und mir die Fabel vom Pferde

einfällt, das seiner Freiheit ungedultig, sich Sattel und Zeug auflegen lässt, und zu Schanden geritten wird. Ich weiss nicht, was ich soll —

("After that, when I again think of it, there comes to me the fable of the horse that, weary of its liberty, allows itself to be saddled and bridled, and is ridden to death [literally, "in disgrace"]. I don't know what I shall do.")

Werther finally tears himself away, but unable to resist his passion, he returns to Lotte's town, takes a final farewell, and shoots himself. The intense sensibility and passion of the poetry made Goethe famous overnight, and the book generated a tide of feeling throughout Europe, young men adopting Werther's blue coat and yellow breeches to indulge their hopeless passions, some even to the point of suicide.

217.1 [213] *Sangriento Combate en Mora de Ebro. Los Aviones de los Rebeldes Bombardean Barcelona. Es inevitable la muerte del Papa.* Sp. "Bloody combat at Mora del Ebro. Rebel planes bombard Barcelona. The death of the Pope is inevitable." Mora del Ebro was a small village involved in the heavy fighting between 1 and 8 November which resulted in some ten thousand casualties. For "the death of the Pope" see note **233.4**.

217.2 [213] *a man was climbing a slippery flagpole.* The Consul has now entered a world which is in part Hades, a madhouse, and the fairground of Dr. Caligari (see note **194.1**). As Lowry points out, "LJC," p. 78, this man, like the one with the bicycle tire, p. 227 [224], is a projection of the Consul and of the futility of his life.

217.3 [213] *'Barcelona' and 'Valencia'.* Well-known Spanish lovesongs, telling of roses and moonlight and nights of romance in the cities of their names, which became ("Valencia" especially) very popular in England during the 1920's:
(a) *Barcelona.* The Catalán capital and Republican stronghold; the song is particularly incongruous given that rebel planes have just bombed the city. A popular English version ran:

> Back in Barcelona, dreamy Barcelona,
> Memories will come of one who bid you adieu.
> Spanish music playing, senoritas swaying,
> Flashing eyes that stare, are there, just daring you.
> Tender lips will kiss your cares away,
> Tender lips you'll miss will make you stay.

Back in Barcelona, dreamy Barcelona,
Paradise that lies 'neath skies of mystery.

(b) *Valencia*. The Mediterranean province and city, south of Barcelona; also the scene of heavy fighting during the war, the dream of "Valencia mía, jardín de España" and "las aromas de tus jazmineros" ("my garden of Spain" and "the smell of your jasmins") being now totally incongruous. A popular English version began:

Valencia . . . land of orange grove and sweet content,
   you called me from afar.
Valencia . . . where a lover croons his sentiment
   upon a light guitar.
Valencia . . . let me hold a rose between my lips
   while romance croons a lay.
Valencia . . . where a troubadour beneath the moon
   once stole my heart away.

217.4 [214] *Medea sacrificing her children*. Medea, daughter of Aeētes, king of Colchis, was (in the tragedy by Euripides) a magician whose art helped Jason obtain the golden fleece. She returned with Jason to Iolcus and thence to Corinth, where Jason deserted her for Glaucē, daughter of the king. Medea avenged herself terribly by destroying Glaucē and killing the two children she had had by Jason. The Consul may see the daub as yet another reminder of Yvonne's denying him children.

217.5 [214] *Pancho Villa*. Francisco Villa (1877–1923), Mexican revolutionary leader known as "the Centaur of the North." In 1913 he assumed leadership of the anti-Huerta movement in Chihuahua, and by a series of dashing raids he was in large measure responsible for Huerta's overthrow in 1914. His attack on Ciudad Juárez (watched from the rooftops by bemused Americans in neighbouring El Paso) was one of the first great triumphs of the revolutionary forces. Villa gained notoriety by crossing the U.S. border in 1916 in a series of raids, at least once inviting punitive retaliation from the U.S.A. In 1917 he was given a hacienda on condition that he would not again break the peace, but he was assassinated for complex political reasons in 1923. In appearance, Pancho Villa was tall and dark, with an impressive, bristling dark moustache. His name here evokes not only that moustache, but a sense of brainless dashing impulsiveness, "more a force of nature than of politics" (Womack, p. 192).

218.1 [215] *Una tequila y una gaseosa.* Sp. "A tequila and a mineral water"; almost exactly the order given one year later by Laruelle and Sr. Bustamente, but with Laruelle then ordering the stronger drink (see note **32.1**).

218.2 [215] *El Nilo.* Sp. "The Nile"; obviously a brand of mineral water, but a mystery surrounds this apparently simple name for there is no such gaseosa in Mexico, and the words were a very late addition to the manuscripts. There is, it seems, a private allusion here to a book in Lowry's own library, *The Nile: The Life Story of a River,* by Emil Ludwig, translated into English in 1937 (Lowry's copy is dated 1943). The opening paragraph of the foreword, p. vii, seems most pertinent:

> Every time I have written the life of a man, there has moved before my eyes the image, physical and spiritual, of a river, but only once have I beheld in a river the image of man and his fate. . . . The thought of the end of *Faust* as it stood embodied before my eyes in Aswân, fired me with the thought of writing the epic of the Nile as I had written the story of great men — as a parable.

The allusion seems to be deliberate, though not of great thematic importance unless to add to the Egyptian mysteries already suggested by Laruelle's scarab ring (see note **214.1**).

219.1 [215] *like lightning striking a tree which thereupon, miraculously, blossoms.* In microcosmic man, the spine is equivalent to the tree of life, and, as the Consul is undoubtedly aware, his image is a deliberate inversion of "the all-but-unretraceable path of God's lightning" (see note **44.3.c**), which, in Cabbalistic thought, represents the emanation of the Sephiroth, from Kether to Malkuth.

219.2 [216] *Oxygénée. Eau oxygénée,* that is, hydrogen peroxide (widely used as a bleach).

219.3 [216] *mescal . . . Tequila.* Within the novel, a contrast between tequila and mescal is maintained, with a strong imputation that mescal is the more fatal drink: "if I ever start to drink mescal again, I'm afraid, yes, that would be the end." In actual fact, however, tequila is simply a special variant of mescal: it derives its name from one of the towns of its manufacture, Tequila, in Jalisco, and is more properly known as mezcal de Tequila (de Barrios, p. 7). Only one species of the maguey cactus, the agave tequilana (also known as the mezcal azul), will produce tequila, and though the plant will grow elsewhere, true tequila with its distinctive flavour can be produced only in the vicinity of Guadalajara, Jalisco. Tequila is derived from the *piña* or heart of the tequila maguey. The piña, which weighs about 80 pounds, is cooked then shredded and the juice pressed out. Sugars are added to the juice, and fermentation takes place before distillation. After a second distillation the colourless liquid is aged in wooden casks for a period of between a few months and seven years, the quality and colour by and large dependent on the length of aging (de Barrios, p. 47).

Mescals (from Nah. *metl,* "maguey"), are produced more widely than tequila throughout Mexico, the major areas being the central highlands from Durango to San Luis Potosí, Chiapas, and Oaxaca, the latter being the best known. They too are made from argave piñas, quite a variety of which will yield different high-proof mescals. The process is essentially similar to that of distilling tequila (note: mescal is *not* distilled from pulque), but the liquor is usually made in small distilleries and consumed locally. In "LJC," p. 71, Lowry erroneously associates mescal with mescaline, the hallucinatory drug obtained from the buttons of mescal cactus. The confusion is of some importance to *UTV,* because the Consul frequently associates drunkenness with the abuse of his transcendent powers as a white magician.

219.4 [216] *Name of a name of God.* A direct transliteration of the common and mild French oath, "Nom d'un nom de Dieu," but Lowry would have doubtless seen in the invisible battle of demonic powers taking place in the background Laruelle calling for protection from the forces of darkness that have besieged the Consul's soul.

220.1 [216] *as Shelley says, the cold world shall not know.* The final line of Shelley's "Julian and Maddalo," written on the occasion of his visit to Venice in 1818. The poem is cast as a conversation between Julian (the author) and Maddalo (Lord Byron) about the power of man over his mind. Much of the poem is taken up with a philosophical discussion about whether man can achieve the ideal in this world through his own efforts, or whether one must accept the depravity of mankind and the hopelessness of life in this world, with perhaps some reward or vision of the ideal in an afterlife. The argument is unresolved.

The two poets then go to meet a maniac, a man driven to madness by unrequited love, and he too is unable to resolve their question. Years later Julian returns alone and meets Maddalo's daughter, who reveals that the maniac's fickle lady had returned but abandoned him once again. She says (ll. 613–17):

> 'Ask me no more but let the silent years
> Be closed and cered over their memory
> As yon mute marble where their corpses lie.'
>
> I urged and questioned still, she told me how
> All happened, but the cold world shall not know.

   The partial quotation from Shelley is germane to the situation of the Consul in several ways. Like the Consul, the maniac has been deserted by his mistress, who returns only to hurt him again. The debate between Julian and Maddalo is something like the on-going argument between Hugh, who represents an optimistic, activist position, and the Consul, who is the quietist, the pessimist. Finally, the Consul warns Laruelle—and the reader—that he can never know all that there is to know of the Consul, his personality, and the causes of his problems.

220.2 [217]   *camarones. . . . Cabrones. . . . Venus is a horned star.* By wilfully confusing shrimps (camarones) with goats and cuckolds (cabrones) and by alluding to the infidelity of Venus with Mars, the Consul is making a definite allusion to Laruelle's affair with Yvonne and to the fact that Laruelle, too, has been cuckolded.

221.1 [217]   *Ben Jonson.* Ben Jonson (1572–1637), poet and playwright, known (among many other works) for *The Alchemist* and *The Case Is Altered.* In 1619, the Scottish writer William Drummond of Hawthornden (1585–1649) entertained Jonson during the latter's tour of the north and made a record of his table-talk, entitled *Conversations with Ben Jonson,* in which (section xiii) he records that Jonson: "hath consumed a whole night in lying looking to his great toe, about which he hath seen tartars & turks Romans and Carthaginians, feight in his imagination." The point of Laruelle's analogy was clearer in an earlier draft (UBC 7–8, n.p.), when the nail was the thumbnail: "And it gets clearer and clearer. A universe perhaps. Precisely. But the point is, you forget what you've excluded. The whole hand, shall we say." The Consul, concentrating upon his own private battle, does not indulge in "clear seeing" and excludes too much of the universe. "In Terms of the Toenail" is the title of a very fine essay on Lowry by William Gass (*F & FL,* pp. 55–76), which nevertheless misses this point.

221.2 [218]   *Meccano.* A toy building set, sold mainly in England, and similar to the "Erector" sets in the United States.

221.3 [218]   *the wheel of the law.* In an earlier draft (UBC 10–29, p. 26)

Lowry made explicit the connection between the ferris wheel and the Buddhist wheel of the law, which he also mentioned in his "Letter to Jonathan Cape," p. 70. Originally this image of the universal law was derived from the sun, which moves inevitably each day in its progess across the sky. The sun image gradually evolved into the more complex figure of a wheel, which in Buddhism is called "the Dharma-chakra," the chain of cause and effect. So important is the concept that it is the subject of Buddha's first discourse, "The setting in Motion Onwards of the Wheel of the Law." The concept is also reflected in the image of the irresistible movement of the chariot of Juggernaut, the wheeled chariot in which Krishna rides, scouring the world of evil (see note **9.4.d**). For the Consul, the inevitable working out of cause and effect, of his own fate or doom, is observable in a number of images in the novel, including such circular movements as the passage of the sun overhead, the ferris wheel, and the movement of the stars in the night sky.

According to Joseph Campbell, the movements of the wheel of the law are not to be considered either bad or good. The wheel is both bad and good, positive or negative, is and not-is. From an Oriental or Hindu viewpoint (one with which the Consul is partially attuned to), his personal doom simply does not matter, and there are many moments in the book when he seems to realize, indeed welcome, such indifference in the universe.

221.4 [218] *Samaritana mía, alma pía, bebe en tu boca linda.* Sp. "My Samaritan woman, pious soul, drink in your beautiful mouth." The song is typical of the roundels taught by the nuns to small children in the Catholic schools of Mexico as a way of imparting Biblical teaching. The reference here is to John 4:6–42, where Christ comes to the well and asks the lowly Samaritan woman for a drink, offering in return the living water of God. The Consul, however, hears only the echo of the S.S. *Samaritan,* with no suggestion of forgiveness.

222.1 [218] *meteora.* The Consul's expression refers, in a general kind of way, to the translucent spots before the eyes which may occur under many conditions. The word (from Gk. *meta* plus *eoros* "lifted into the air") also applies to such various atmospheric phenomena as falling stars, bolidos, parhelia, and St. Elmo's fire. The Consul, with the full support of Charles Fort, senses in such effects the presence of malignant agencies.

222.2 [218] *the Qliphoth.* The world of matter, said to be the abode of evil spirits called shells (see note **44.3.d**).

222.3 [218] *the God of Flies.* Beelzebub: in Milton's *Paradise Lost,* the demon second only to Satan; in occult tradition, one of the eight sub-princes of darkness, whose name is described in MacGregor-Mathers's *The Sacred Magic,* p. 110:

> *Belzebud:* — Also written frequently "Beezebub," "Baalzebub," "Beelze-buth," and "Beelzeboul." From Hebrew, BOL, = Lord, and ZBVB, = Fly or Flies; Lord of Flies. Some derive the name from the Syriac "Beel d'Bobo," = Master of Calumny, or nearly the same signification as the Greek word Diabolos, whence are derived the modern French "Diable" and "Devil."

222.4 [218]   *why do people see rats. . . . all those rodents in the etymology.* The words cited by the Consul all possess the common sense of "biting":
(a) *Remors.* This O.Fr. word, "remorse," itself deriving from L. *remor-dere,* "to vex," "to torment," is the direct ancestor of the English word "remorse."
(b) *Mordeo.* L. "I bite," from *mordere,* "to bite."
(c) *La Mordida.* Sp. "the bite"; in particular, the sum of money paid under the table to the autoridades to facilitate getting things done or to keep out of trouble; Lowry's failure to recognize this need caused him great problems on his return visit to Mexico in 1946 (Day, p. 359). *La Mordida* is the name of Lowry's unfinished manuscript based upon the above episode.
(d) *Agenbite. The Agenbite of Inwit,* or *Prick of Conscience* (1340), is the title of Michael of Northgate's prose translation of a French moral treatise, *Le somme des vices et des virtues,* by Friar Lorens, dealing with the seven deadly sins. Lowry probably picked up the word from Joyce's *Ulysses,* Ch. 1, where Stephen Dedalus feels the bite of con-science because of his failure to heed his mother's dying wish.
(e) *rongeur.* Fr. "rodent"; from *ronger,* "to gnaw," "to eat into" (the verb is also used with the sense of feeling remorse).

The Consul's question, "Why do people see rats?," may be answered, ob-scurely, by Éliphas Lévi, *Transcendental Magic* Ch. 12, p. 114:

> The word ART when reversed, or read after the manner of sacred and primitive characters from right to left, gives three initials which express the different grades of the Great Work. T signifies triad, theory and travail; R, realisation; A, adaptation.

The Consul's imperfect Themurah (the transposition of letters in a word) constitutes or reflects his consistent abuse of the powers Lévi describes.

222.5 [219] *Facilis est descensus Averno.* L. "easy is the descent to Avernus"; From Virgil's *Aeneid,* VI.126–29:

> facilis descensus Averno:
> noctes atque dies patet atri ianua Ditis;
> sed revocare gradum superasque evadere ad auras,
> hoc opus, hic labor est.

("The descent to Avernus is easy: / night and day the door of gloomy Dis stands open; / but to recall the step and go forth upwards to the light of day, / this is the task, this the toil.")

The *Aeneid* recounts the adventures of Aeneas, son of Anchises, from the fall of Troy to the founding of Rome, Bk. VI describing a visit to the underworld, under the guidance of the Sibyl and the protection of the Golden Bough, where Aeneas discovers the fate of his posterity. Avernus, a lake in northern Italy, was reputed to be an entrance to the underworld because of its great depth and the gloomy woods about it; its vapours were believed to kill any birds that flew over it. The passage is cited in Thomas Taylor's "Eleusinian and Bacchic Mysteries" as a neo-Platonic image of the descent of the soul into the world of matter and of the difficulty of reuniting with its true nature. Laruelle's challenge to the Consul is unequivocal: he may be able to enter hell, but is he, like Aeneas, man enough to return.

222.6 [219] *Je crois que le vautour est doux à Promethée et que les Ixion se plaisent en Enfer.* Fr. "I believe that the vulture is gentle to Prometheus, and that the Ixions enjoy themselves in Hell." The sentence reads like a quotation, but it has not been identified, and it seems likely that Lowry has made it up. For Prometheus, see note **134.9**; Ixion (the plural form is strange), as a punishment for murdering his kin and attempting the chastity of Hera, was bound in Hades upon a wheel of fire which turned perpetually. The Consul's answer to Laruelle is implicit in these words: he chooses hell because he likes it.

223.1 [219] *the little dark cantina.* El Bosque, "the wood," which the Consul does not reach until p. 228 [225]. His steps here teeter ominously to the left; he walks the "wibberley wobberley" walk rather than with the erect manly Taskerson carriage, p. 26 [20], and, like the S.S. *Samaritan,* p. 38 [32], he cannot steer a straight course.

223.2 [220] *Dies Faustus.* L. "happy day"; with the pun on "Faustus dies" accentuated by the Consul's looking at his watch. There may also be a hint of *Dies Irae,* the medieval Latin hymn about the Day of Judgment attributed to Thomas de Celano (c. 1225) and often included in the requiem mass for the repose of the souls of the dead.

224.1 [220] *Dieu et mon droit.* Fr. "God and my right"; the motto of the British crown (originally "God and my right shall me defend"), set beneath the coat of arms held between the heraldic animals, the lion and the unicorn.

224.2 [221] *¡BRAVO ATRACCIÓN! 10 c. MÁQUINA INFERNAL.* Sp. "Great attraction! 10 centavos. Infernal Machine." The "coincidence" which strikes the Consul is the echo of Cocteau's *La machine infernale* on Laruelle's table (see note **212.3**). The machine is not the ferris wheel, but the kind of machine sometimes known as an octopus, with its "little confession box" at the end of each long tentacle. As Sherrill Grace notes, the fairground scene here, like that in *Das Cabinett der Dr. Caligari,* "symbolizes not only a madly revolving world perceived by the protagonist, but the helplessness of the individual soul caught up in superior whirling forces" ("Expressionist Vision," p. 103). The presence of the Chinese hunchback with his retiform, or net-like cap, adds to the horror with its suggestion of inscrutable demonic forces.

225.1 [222] *The Consul, like that poor fool who was bringing light to the world, was hung upside down over it.* The "poor fool bringing light to the world" is Christ, **205.3 [201],** and Prometheus, whose punishment was to be chained to a rock in the Caucasus, where an eagle continually tore at his liver; the reference to the one "hung upside down" is to Tarot card 12, the Hanged Man (the man who has seen the truth and must therefore suffer), usually depicted as hanging by his feet from a pi-shaped bar. The link between the two is found in Éliphas Lévi's *Transcendental Magic,* p. 116, where the Hanged Man is likened explicitly not only to the adept but also to Prometheus, "expiating by everlasting torture the penalty of his glorious theft."

225.2 [222] *999.* The Consul, inverted, sees the advertisement for the insecticide (see note **192.1**), but this number in England is that to be phoned in emergencies requiring police, fire brigade, or ambulance. But since 666 is the mark of the beast, 999 may well be the number of good and beneficent forces, 9 perhaps symbolizing a state of inner awareness and spiritual purification (an idea not incompatible with that of the Hanged Man). The implications are thus twofold: the Consul has reached a position of enlightenment, a point where he must "let everything go" (his stick, his passport, his pipe, his notecase) before breaking from the wheel of the law and reaching nirvana; on the other hand, his abuse of his mystical powers precludes his attaining such enlightenment — the wheel of fortune will turn, and the tree of life will be inverted to plunge him into the abyss.

226.1 [223] *the Luxembourg Gardens.* The gardens of the Luxembourg Palace in Paris, once the prerogative of the royal family, now the house of the senate. The gardens, dating from the early seventeenth century, are of a formal design, with beautiful flowerbeds and many statues depicting both mythological themes and famous women. Lowry claimed to have once encountered James Joyce there (*SL,* p. 250).

227.1 [223] *Scrooge.* Ebenezer Scrooge, tight-fisted old miser of Charles Dickens's *A Christmas Carol* (1843), who is visited by the ghost of his former partner Marley and beholds a series of visions, including one of his own death, as a result of which he wakes up next morning a changed man.

227.2 [224] *the Avenida Guerrero.* The street in Cuernavaca leading directly north from the zócalo, in 1938 going past the Piggly Wiggly store and the old market. Lowry says in *DATG,* p. 208, that this is the route taken by the Tomalín bus in Ch. 8 of his book, but in *UTV* the road is called the Avenida de la Revolución (see note **29.2**).

227.3 [224] *an old bicycle tyre.* The madman, eternally committed to a process of irreducible logic, is like Sisyphus, once king of Corinth, whose avarice and deceit condemned him to roll forever a heavy stone to the top of a hill, on reaching which it always rolled back again. The Consul seems now to have entered a shadowy world, which is largely a projection of his own mental hell, expressed in terms of the fairground setting in *Das Cabinett der Dr. Caligari* (see note **194.1**).

228.1 [225] *the Terminal Cantina El Bosque.* "El Bosque" means "the wood," and hence echoes the dark wood theme sounded on the first page of the novel (the Consul's confusion of Sp. *bosca* and It. *selva* drawing attention to Dante's *Inferno*). In an earlier draft (UBC 11-2, p. 279) Lowry had noted that "the terminal cantina was so dark etc" was out of Julian Green; the reference appears to be to the opening of Green's *Leviathan* (1925), translated into English as *The Dark Journey* (1929). At the beginning of the novel Paul Guéret enters a little deserted café and notes that a heavy curtain screens off the interior of the shop. The Terminal is literally the bus stop, in 1938 on the Avenida Juárez just south of the Cortés Palace, but the pun is a reminder that the Consul's dark journey is also one to death. When Lowry returned to Cuernavaca in 1945 (taking Green's novel with him), the bus stop had been moved to behind the palace and the Terminal Cantina was no more (*DATG,* p. 121).

228.2 [225] *'The Boskage'.* A boskage is a thicket, grove, or cluster of trees. The word appears in Rupert Brooke's "The Old Vicarage, Grantchester," which Lowry alludes to on p. 235 [232].

229.1 [225] *the English 'Jug and Bottle.'* The bar of a public house at which alcoholic drinks are sold for consumption off the premises.

229.2 [226] *big green barrels.* Señora Gregorio has a large variety of cheap potent drinks:
(a) *jerez.* Sherry, originally named from the town of Jerez (or Xeres) in Andalusia, Spain.
(b) *habanero.* From *Habanero,* "Havana"; a strong rum-like liquor originating from Cuba, but now produced in Tabasco; usually prepared from grape wines and Mexican brandy.
(c) *catalán.* From Catalonia, a province of northern Spain. Not one of the celebrated wines from that area, but rather a strong liquor distilled from sugar and imported from Spain.
(d) *parras.* A strong alcohol produced from grapes and associated with the Parras area of Coahuila, the best wine-producing area in Mexico. The vineyard at Parras de la Fuente was the earliest winery in Mexico.
(e) *zarzamora.* From Sp. *zarza,* "brambleberry"; a fortified blackberry wine.
(f) *málaga.* From Málaga, a province of southern Spain. Again, a fortified fruit liquor rather than the quality wines for which the region is renowned.
(g) *durazno.* A *durazno* (named after the town in Jalisco) is like a peach (Sp. *melocotón*), but slightly smaller; hence, a peach brandy.
(h) *membrillo.* Either the fortified wine produced in Andalusia or, more probably, a local aguardiente made from quinces (Sp. *membrillo,* "a quince").
(i) *rumpope.* A yellow drink, very like Advocaat, made from milk, sugar, alcohol, almond essence, vanilla, and egg-yolk.

229.3 [226] *a Psyche knot.* A hair style in which the hair is brushed back and twisted into a conical coil just above the nape; named for Psyche, who is traditionally depicted this way, and hence a reminder that Señora Gregorio too has lost her husband. Señora Gregorio, once English, may be loosely modelled on Rosa E. King, author of *Tempest over Mexico* (1935), for many years owner of the Bella Vista Hotel, who was also English and widowed.

230.1 [226] *No, tequila, por favor.... Un obsequio.* Sp. "No, tequila, please.... A gift." The Consul's concern to repay Señora Gregorio her 50 centavos and the free drink given him are in marked contrast with his devious scheming to get his change and outwit the barboy in Ch. 12. The immediate reference to *cincuenta dos,* "fifty-two" (his number on the Calle Humboldt), should remind the Consul that Yvonne had earlier given a tostón to the dark god who took her bags.

230.2 [227] *Lo mismo.* Sp. "the same." However, in Ch. 12 the Consul gravely replies to the similar question, "What's your names?" with the words "Blackstone... William Blackstone," p. 358 [358].

231.1 [228] *noseless.* One symptom of advanced syphilis, a disease which haunted Lowry's imagination.

232.1 [228] *Dispense usted, por Díos.* Sp. "Go away, for God's sake." The words (literally, "excuse yourself") are not noticeably harsh in tone.

232.2 [228] *thoughts of hope that go with you like little white birds.* The phrase "read or heard in youth or childhood" suggests a distant recollection of J. M. Barrie's *The Little White Bird* (1902) throughout which the souls of children are likened to birds, and in Ch. 20 of which the souls of a child and a dog are compared. There is a general neo-Platonic sense of the journey of the soul represented as the flight of a bird, but Lowry's poem, "Thunder Beyond Popocatepetl," suggests a specific awareness of Chekhov's *The Seagull.* The poem concludes:

> Reason remains although your mind forsakes
> It; and white birds fly higher against the thunder
> Than ever flew yours; where Chekov said was peace,
> When the heart changes and the thunder breaks.

The desire for such peace is also expressed in Yeats's "The White Birds," but it is the willed destruction of a living creature that makes the Chekovian reference seem more fitting.

232.3 [229] *Yet this day, pichicho, shalt thou be with me in —.* The essential reference here is to Luke 23:43, where Jesus says to one of the thieves crucified beside him: "Verily, I say unto thee, Today shalt thou be with me in paradise" (the unfinished nature of the Consul's quotation leaving *his* designation more ambiguous). Kilgallin, p. 186, has noted the direct allusion to Nordahl Grieg's *The Ship Sails On,* p. 217: as Benjamin Hall is contemplating suicide, he picks up the diseased ship's dog, Santos, and says before slowly climbing over the rail with the dog in his arms, "Santos . . . this day shalt thou be with me in paradise." Benjamin, unlike the Consul, changes his mind, and climbs back onto the deck.

The word "pichicho" was added to the manuscripts some time after the rest of the paragraph had been composed. It is a common enough term of endearment, but Lowry derived it from W. H. Hudson's *Far Away and Long Ago,* Ch. 1, where a strange-looking lame dog suddenly appeared:

> One of his hind legs had been broken or otherwise injured so that he limped and shuffled along in a peculiar lop-sided fashion; he had no tail, and his ears had been cropped close to his head. . . .
>
> No name to fit this singular canine visitor could be found, although he responded readily enough to the word *pichicho,* which is used to call any unnamed pup by, like pussy for cat. So it came to pass that the word *pichicho* — equivalent to "doggie" in English — stuck to him for only name until the end of the chapter, and the end was that, after spending some years with us, he mysteriously disappeared.

232.4 [229] *To what red tartar, oh mysterious beast?* An echo of John Keats's "Ode on a Grecian Urn," ll. 31–34:

> Who are these coming to the sacrifice?
>   To what green altar, O mysterious priest
> Lead'st thou that heifer lowing at the skies,
>   And all her silken flanks with garlands drest?

Keats's poem, a profound and moving meditation upon the power of art to transfix time, is neatly parodied by the Consul as he sees the pictures of wolves and sleigh caught forever in a frozen moment of eternity. The original line from Keats is quoted in *Blue Voyage,* p. 82, but in a context emphasizing slaughter rather than transcendence.

232.5 [229] *Rostov's wolf hunt in War and Peace.* In Bk. VII of Tolstoy's *War and Peace,* Nicholas Rostóv returns home on leave to settle the family's financial affairs, but finding them too confused he goes wolf-hunting instead. Chs. 3 to 5 tell of the preparations for the hunt, the pursuit of the wolf by the dogs, and its eventual capture, alive. As the word "incongruously" implies, there are no direct parallels between the two scenes (there is no sleigh in Tolstoy's account, for instance). After the hunt, Ch. 7, the party accepts the invitation of "Uncle" (in fact, a distant relative and neighbour of the Rostóvs) to spend the evening at his house. They are offered warm hospitality, food, and music, and almost spontaneously a night of happiness and cheer unfolds.

232.6 [229] *wolves never hunted in packs at all.* A perennial question with hunters and zoologists. At this time, there seems to be some agreement that wolves do occasionally hunt in packs, collaborating in the bringing down of the weak animals in herds of elk and reindeer.

232.7 [229] *while our real enemies go in sheepskin by.* An image based on Matthew 7:15, at the conclusion of Christ's Sermon on the Mount: "Beware of false prophets, which come to you in sheep's clothing; but inwardly they are ravening wolves."

233.1 [229] *Adiós.* Sp. "Goodbye," but with a suggestion of finality. Jakobsen, p. 43, senses some irony here since, instead of going to God ("a Díos") the Consul is now beginning his journey to hell (the accents, however, make this somewhat less likely).

233.2 [229] *In some kernice place where all those troubles you har now will har—.* The Consul starts, for he hears an echo of "Yet this day, *pichicho,* shalt thou be with me in—" (see note **232.3**). Señora Gregorio's words seem to combine two popular songs: "All My Trials Lord, Soon be Over," and "Some Place Green," which has the refrain:

> To some place green,
> To some place nice,
> Some place that men
> Call Paradise.

233.3 [230] *I have no house only a shadow. But whenever you are in need of a shadow my shadow is yours.* Based on the Mexican expression of hospitality, "a donde cae mi sombra, alla se encuentra tu casa" ("wherever my shadow falls, there will be found your house").

233.4 [230] *Es inevitable la muerte del Papa.* Sp. "The death of the Pope is inevitable"; the headline which the Consul had read on p. 217 [213] and thought referred to himself. The pope's illness stemmed from a variety of causes: arterio-sclerosis in 1936 had led to gangrene, cardiac asthma, and high blood pressure. He finally succumbed to influenza and a third heart attack. Lowry suggested that this reference was "quite possibly just an anachronism" ("LJC," p. 78), but that it had to stand since it was such a fine ending: he is probably drawing indirect attention to his own cleverness, because although Pius XI died on 10 February 1939, the Mexican papers throughout 1937 and 1938 had been full of reports of his likely death and his frequent relapses and recoveries.

CHAPTER EIGHT

234.1 [231] *Downhill.* The implications are legion: the word asserts the Samaritan theme of Luke 10:30 ("A certain man went *down* from Jerusalem to Jericho"); it echoes line 15 of Baudelaire's "Au lecteur" ("Chaque jour vers l'Enfer nous descendons d'un pas"); and it recalls Laruelle's "Facilis est descendus Averno" (see note **222.5**). From this point on, the Consul's descent towards the abyss is irresistible.

234.2 [231] *a 1918 Chevrolet.* The Chevrolet company was bought by General Motors in May 1918, and a new plant opened immediately in St. Louis, where the first Chevrolet trucks were produced. Although camión is the usual word in Mexico for bus, it literally means truck, and it seems likely that the camión consists of a bus-like top built on the frame of one of these early trucks.

234.3 [231] *the Baños de la Libertad, the Casa Brandes (La Primera en el Ramo de Electricidad).* For the Liberty Baths, see note **58.5**. The Casa Brandes, whose slogan means "The First in the Field of Electricity," is modelled on the Casa Broker, a pre-war firm of German origin which was reputedly the best in Mexico City for electrical equipment and tools. The name "Brandes" is in stark contrast to "Libertad" and forms one more reminder of the ubiquitous German presence.

234.4 [231] *At the market.* The old market in Cuernavaca was a few blocks up the Avenida Guerrero, directly north from the zócalo; it has since been relocated on the Acapantzingo side of the Amanalco barranca.

235.1 [232] *Modesto.* Juan Modesto Guilloto (1906–69), ex-woodcutter and former sergeant of the Spanish Foreign Legion under Franco, but later trained in Russia. In 1938, the communist general in charge of the Fifth Army Corps (the Army of the Ebro) and leader of the Republican forces as they retreated during the Battle of the Ebro (see note **99.3**); eventually (February 1939), he led his army into internment in France.

235.2 [232] *The clock over the market arch, like the one in Rupert Brooke.*
A reference to the concluding lines of Rupert Brooke's "The Old Vicarage,
Grantchester": "Stands the Church clock at ten to three? / And is there
honey still for tea?" The poem, written while Brooke was in Berlin in 1912,
celebrates the quietness and beauty of the small English village of Grantchester, near Cambridge, where Brooke had taken rooms while studying at
King's College. In his biography of Rupert Brooke, Christopher Hassal
states that the clock's erratic performance was a local joke, and notes, p.
342, that in 1911, "the church clock *had* stuck, but at half-past three."

235.3 [232] *the Avenida de la Revolución.* Although there are two streets
of this name in Cuernavaca, neither is the main highway out of town;
Lowry has combined Cuernavaca's Avenida Guerrero, which runs north
from the zócalo, with the main street, Morelos, which does not (see note
29.2).

235.4 [232] *the rajah shakes.* The d.t.'s; *rajah* having in Anglo-Indian
parlance the sense of "mighty" or "impressive."

235.5 [232] *a parrot, head cocked, looked down from its perch.* In Ch. 5
of the 1940 version of the novel (UBC 7-6, pp. 29–30) there was a long
shaggy-dog story about a parrot at sea who challenged the magician at the
ship's concert to make something disappear. At the crucial moment the ship
hit an iceberg and sank without trace, leaving the parrot on a little spar in an
empty ocean: "Marvellous!" said the parrot. In the same version,
immediately after the words "Quo Vadis?," the Consul, in reply to Hugh's
question about the rajah shakes, had said "Marvellous." Subsequent drafts
show Lowry working to fit the anecdote into Ch. 8 at this point before
deciding to omit it altogether. The parrot was originally intended to
anticipate another parrot in Ch. 12, but Lowry changed this latter bird to a
cock, p. 372 [372]. The story was then dropped, presumably because the
symbolic associations of the cock (see note **372.1**) were unsuited to the
parrot, but the latter persisted right up to the galleys before being finally
struck out: "The cock — or was it a parrot — flapped before his eyes" (UBC
9-24, n.p.), leaving only the parrot in Ch. 8, without even a "Marvellous!"
to mark the place of what had once been.

235.6 [232] *Inhumaciones.* Sp. "Burials." In his *A Heart for the Gods of
Mexico,* p. 464, Conrad Aiken verifies the existence of this undertaker's
shop with the Quo Vadis? sign and tells how, curious to find out its
meaning, he entered the shop and found himself amongst a tasteful display
of coffins of all sizes and colours, a young man tacking grey satin to a small

kite-shaped lid, "And the cynical question, 'Quo Vadis?'." The funeral parlour, now the Funeraria Herrera, still exists at Matamoros 32, but the sign (and the parrot) have long gone.

235.7 [232] *Quo Vadis?* L. "Where are you going?"; the words of Simon Peter to Christ (John 13:36) after the Last Supper:

> Simon Peter said unto him, Lord, whither goest thou? Jesus answered him, Whither I go, thou canst not follow me now; but thou shalt follow me afterwards.
> Peter said unto him, Lord, why can I not follow thee now? I will lay down my life for thy sake.
> Jesus answered him, Wilt thou lay down thy life for my sake? Verily, verily, I say unto thee, The cock shall not crow, till thou hast denied me thrice.

Despite Lowry's marginal instruction (UBC 11-2, n.p.) to retype and make it look less like the name of the book, the reference to the Polish novelist Henryk Sienkiewicz (1848-1916) stands out: *Quo Vadis?* (1896) is an historical romance set in Nero's Rome, showing against a background of Petronius and Nero the love of the young pagan Vincinius for the Christian girl Ligia (a Samaritan), the young man's eventual conversion to Christianity, and his consequent martyrdom. The title of the novel, reflecting the necessity of choosing for or against the Christian faith, implies the impossibility of the Consul's being faithful to both the Farolito and Yvonne.

235.8 [232] *a secluded square with great old trees.* Before the Leandro Valle road in Cuernavaca crosses the barranca, it goes past a tiny attractive park extending to the left along the ravine; de Davila, p. 70, identifies this as the Emilio Carranza Park, named in honour of a valiant aviator who lost his life in Jersey.

235.9 [232] *¿Le gusta este jardín, que es suyo? ¡Evite que sus hijos lo destruyan!* Sp. "Do you like this garden that is yours? See to it that your children do not destroy it!" This time the sign is correctly punctuated and translated (see note **132.3**). In his drafts (UBC 10-1, n.p.) Lowry had written of his worries about the sign (thereby disproving the apocryphal legend that he was not aware of the correct version himself until the book was virtually finished):

> Whether later on the Consul should see it (in VII) in its correct form is what perplexes me—it stretches the imagination a bit that both signs

should be wrong. On the other hand, if it is correct the second time he sees it, will he continue to translate it wrongly to himself? I feel it is important that he should always apply it to himself & see his own eviction in it for obvious reasons. Also, somewhere in the book, possibly in VIII, Hugh should see it, in its correct form, & translate it correctly. In any case I think the Spanish should be correct at the very end.

236.1 [233]   *Quod semper, quod ubique, quod ab omnibus.* This phrase, which should be completed by "creditum est," is a theological maxim meaning "what has always, everywhere, and by all (been believed)." It is known as the Rule of Vincent, after St. Vincent of Lérins, a fifth-century theologian whose *Commonitoria* tried to establish a definite criterion of orthodoxy (in part, an attack upon the more extreme implications of St. Augustine's doctrine of predestination). The rule asserts, in effect, that orthodox believers and the church must hold onto what has been implicitly believed from the start. The quotation had become somewhat of a catchphrase among the Oxbridge shining university wits and was often applied to buses (*omnibus* = "vehicle for all") in this way.

236.2 [233]   *Yvonne looked happy when Popocatepetl sprang into view.* In the original short story version (UBC 7-1, p. 2) Yvonne's happiness was at odds with the Consul's reaction: "To the Consul the volcano had taken on a sinister aspect: like a sort of Moby Dick, it had the air of beckoning them on, as it swung from one side of the horizon to the other, to some disaster, unique and immedicable."

236.3 [233]   *El Amor de los Amores.* Sp. "The love of [all] loves"; the picturesque beauty of the name belied (as the Consul's "Viva Franco" indicates) by the fact of its being a fascist joint.

236.4 [234]   *He's not an aerial pigeon.* That is, rather than a little secret ambassador of peace (see p. 234 [232]), he is a stool pigeon, in cahoots with those "birds" the Consul mentions on p. 250 [247].

237.1 [234]   *Hands of the Conquistador.* The *conquistadores* (Sp. "conquerors") were the Spanish adventurers and soldiers, particularly those led by Cortés in Mexico and Pizarro in Peru, who in the early decades of the sixteenth century conquered the Aztec, Inca, and other Indian civilizations of the New World to carve out the huge territories of New Spain and Spanish South America. Capable but rapacious, they lived by the sword, and were guilty of many cruelties to those they subdued. They are summed up in the pelado, p. 253 [250], whose bloody hands, like those of Orlac, symbolize not only the collective guilt of all mankind ("LJC," p. 69) but the personal guilt felt by the Consul over his own position in Mexico (see note **215.6**) and his inability to help the dying Indian.

237.2 [234]   *a kind of cheap Homburg.* A man's felt hat, with a curled brim and length-wise crease. It is not unusual in Mexico to see men wearing more than one hat.

237.3 [234]   *the Moroccan War.* Although Spain had tried to intervene in Morocco during the nineteenth century, she did not do so successfully until the twentieth, and then only at great cost, in a war that was protracted and messy. In 1906 Spanish troops landed and occupied some of the northern territories, and in November 1912 a Spanish protectorate in the north of Morocco was recognized by the other European powers. However, rebel troops under the able leadership of Abd-al-Krim exploited Spanish inefficiency in a long guerrilla war. A heavy defeat of the Spanish army in July 1921 and a series of setbacks in 1924, when the Spaniards were forced out of a large area of territory, caused great political reverberations in Spain. Although the pacification of the 7,500-square-mile territory was completed in 1934 (with the aid of French troops), Spain emerged with little glory, and the war did much to fuel the home fires of dissent before the outbreak of the Civil War. The Consul held a posting in nearby Rabat (French Morocco) at a key time during this war (see p. 162 [158]).

237.4 [234]   *A pelado.* From the verb *pelar,* "to pull out the hair" or "to peel" (in the sense of divesting the shell or husk); hence one that is discarded, a nobody, or in Hugh's words, a shoeless illiterate. The Consul's explanation of the word is an excellent one: thief, exploiter, a term of abuse by which the aggressor discredits the one ravaged. The word assumes a variety of meanings, none of them complimentary, and is used in conscious opposition to "compañero" (see note **250.1**).

238.1 [235]   *Here the American highway really began.* The American-style highway, leading in from the north but coming out as a goat-track, is described on p. 9 [3], but there is a slight contradiction within the novel at this point: the camión has taken a route twisting north and east through Quauhnahuac, but is now heading out of town in an easterly direction (following the present-day Plan de Ayala, a fine broad highway). In fact, the highway from Mexico to Acapulco, passing through the northeast of

Cuernavaca, had been opened by President Plutarco Calles on 11 November 1927, and the description here, rather than that on p. 9 [3], tallies more closely with the actual geography of Cuernavaca.

238.2 [235]   *Pearce oiltanks.* Presumably those previously belonging to the Pierce Oil Company, a subsidary of Standard Oil, and one of the American firms whose holdings had been expropriated by the Cárdenas government some months earlier (see note **36.1**). The present Pearce industries did not operate in Mexico during the 1930's.

238.3 [235]   *his pilgrim's bundle.* Hugh sees himself as travelling that night, like a medieval pilgrim or Bunyan's Christian, in the direction of Vera Cruz, the "True Cross."

238.4 [236]   *a school fifteen.* A rugby team (comprising fifteen players). The "foreign twenty-five line" is that drawn twenty-five yards out from the opposing team's goal-line.

239.1 [236]   *convolvulus.* A kind of bindweed, profusive in growth, with long twining tendrils which thread themselves about other plants. Convolvulus is used consistently throughout *Under the Volcano* (for example, pp. 102 and 127 [98 and 123]) as an emblem of something which strangles any blossoming hope.

239.2 [236]   *though there were twenty-one other paths they might have taken!* As Epstein has noted, p. 153, the twenty-two paths in Cabbalistic usage correspond to the twenty-two letters of the Hebrew alphabet, and, as the branches of the tree of life, constitute the paths that must be retraced towards Kether (see notes **44.3** and **89**.1). They are described in "Forest Path," p. 272, as "the twenty-one paths that lead back to Eden." The "final curve to the left" has the sinister implications of a deviation from the right and proper path, the left leading to the realm of the demonic powers.

240.1 [237]   *God bless us.* As Hugh is wryly aware, his thoughts echo Tiny Tim's "God bless Us, Every One," in Charles Dickens's *A Christmas Carol* (see note **156.3**).

240.2 [238]   *they had signed their Munich agreement.* That is, their death warrant, for their fate is as inevitable as that of Czechoslovakia (or the Spanish Republicans) once Chamberlain had signed the Munich Agreement with Hitler, 30 September 1938 (see note **103.2**).

240.3 [238]   *Su salud estará a salvo no escupiendo en el interior de este* *vehículo.* Sp. "For your health's sake, no spitting inside this vehicle."

241.1 [238]   *Cooperación de la Cruz Roja.* Sp. "[With the] help of the Red Cross"; somewhat ironically, since the services appear to be on strike when they are most needed. Pictures of the Virgin Mary, the Virgin of Guadalupe, or various saints are commonly found near the driver's seat in buses in Mexico.

241.2 [238]   *marguerites.* The ox-eye daisy, of the family *Compositas,* with white petals and a yellow eye, which, like a miniature sunflower, keeps following the Consul around.

241.3 [238]   *gangrened.* The extinguisher has turned green ("decomposed") because its copper metal has reacted with air; like the regular police and medical services, it is out of commission.

241.4 [238]   *quite as Prescott informed one.* Although Prescott's *Conquest of Mexico* describes the approaches to Popocatepetl in similar fashion (III.viii, p. 284), Hugh appears to be recalling Prescott's description of another volcano, Cofre de Perote, also known as Nauhcampatepetl (III.i., p. 214):

> It exhibits now, indeed, no vestige of a crater on its top, but abundant traces of volcanic action at its base, where acres of lava, blackened scoriae, and cinders, proclaim the convulsions of nature, while numerous shrubs and mouldering trunks of enormous trees, among the crevices, attest the antiquity of these events.

242.1 [239]   *a feeling, almost, of the fiesta.* The description is very similar to that on p. 57 [52], where Lowry in his manuscripts acknowledged a debt to Eisenstein (see note **77.1**). The suggestion of *Que Viva Mexico!* and the sense of tragic gaiety is again to the fore.

242.2 [239]   *candelabra cactus.* Large cacti which are branched like a candelabra (see note **332.1**), their "brutal" appearance symbolizing for Hugh so much of Mexico's history.

242.3 [239]   *Burned, perhaps, in the revolution.* The scene, so like the empty chapel in Pt. V of *The Waste Land,* is the visible result of the conflict of church and state that has long been part of Mexico's history: churches were the natural targets of the anti-clerical, pro-liberal forces during the Revolution of 1910–20, just as schools were for the militant Cristeros.

242.4 [239]   *the star of Lenin . . . Hero of the Soviet Republic.* There is, strictly speaking, no Order of the U.S.S.R. called the Star of Lenin, but there are the Order of Lenin and the Order of the Red Star, both of which were instituted 6 April 1930. The title Hero of the Soviet Union is the highest official recognition for services to the state and is awarded for the performance of some heroic deed. A Hero of the Soviet Union receives the highest order of the U.S.S.R., the Order of Lenin, and a Gold Star award and is entitled to special rewards and privileges.

243.1 [240]   *buses to Tetecala, to Jujuta, to Xuitepec: buses to Xochitepec, to Xoxitepec. . . . Xiutepecanochtitlantehuantepec, Quintanarooroo, Tlacolula, Moctezuma, Juarez, Puebla, Tlampam.* In the original version of this chapter (UBC 7-1), Lowry was much more restrained: there were buses to "Tocula, to Jujuta, buses to Xiutepec, to Xochitepec" (all reasonable destinations from Morelos), but in subsequent drafts he could not resist some of the odd names, and the result is a confusion of likely and impossible destinations:

(a) *Tetecala.* A small town in the southwest of Morelos, some twenty-five miles from Cuernavaca; the site of the pyramid of Xochicaloo. Buses going there would not be on this route.

(b) *Jujuta. Either* Jojutla, a barrio or suburb of Jiutepec, now on the outskirts of Cuernavaca (the location is right, but it is unlikely to be labelled as a distinct destination); *or* Jojutla de Juárez, a reasonably large town in the south of Morelos, some thirty miles south of Cuernavaca (the direction is correct).

(c) *Xuitepec.* More usually, Jiutepec: in 1938, a small town just off the Cuernavaca-Cuautla road a few miles from the centre of Cuernavaca (now an outer suburb).

(d) *Xochitepec.* A small town, about fifteen miles south of Cuernavaca on the Mexico-Acapulco highway. A large Aztec pyramid there was dedicated to the flower-goddess, Xochiquetzal.

(e) *Xoxitepec.* A variant spelling of the same place.

(f) *Xiutepecanochtitlantehuantepec.* A composite (or the impressions of three buses fused) of Xiutepec, Anochtitlán (see note **320.3**), and Tehuantepec (see note **12.4**). These last two destinations are likely only from Oaxaca and perhaps represent Lowry's efforts to create his fictional state of Parián from elements of both Morelos and Oaxaca; in "real" Mexico, however, they are impossible.

(g) *Quintanarooroo.* The territory of Quintana Roo, then administered by the State of Yucatán. There is no town of this name, and this fact, as well as the impossible distance, makes the labelling most unlikely.

(h) *Tlacolula.* The town of Tlacolula de Matamoros, some twenty-five miles from Oaxaca on the road to Mitla; it is significant as a rail terminus.

(i) *Moctezuma.* The tiny village of Moctezuma, on the Cuernavaca-Cuautla road some eight miles from Cuernavaca; far too small to be a terminal destination.

(j) *Juarez.* Again, Jojutla de Juárez, some thirty miles south of Cuernavaca (such alternative names are not unusual in Mexico).

(k) *Puebla.* The capital of the state of the same name and a large important city which is, however, not served directly by buses from Cuernavaca.

(l) *Tlampam.* More usually, Tlalpan, south of Mexico City; in 1938, the last distinctive suburb before the open road to Cuernavaca (a bus going there would not be on this road).

243.2 [240]   *an Indian screening sand.* Probably for the making of bricks.

243.3 [240]   *a bald boy, with ear-rings.* One of the "spiders" who haunts the Consul's waking hours (see p. 36 [30]).

243.4 [240]   *¡Atchis! ¡Instante! Resfriados, Dolores, Cafeasperina. Rechace Imitaciones. Las Manos de Orlac. Con Peter Lorre.* The advertisements read: "Atishoo! Instant Relief! Colds, Pains, Cafeasperina. Avoid other brands. The Hands of Orlac, with Peter Lorre." Once again, Cafeasperina (promising relief from dolores) is juxtaposed with *The Hands of Orlac* (see note **51.3**).

243.5 [240]   *Lostwithiel.* "Lost within the hills": a small Cornish market town on the Fowey river, surrounded (like Guanajuato) by steep hills. Small green signs of this kind are to be seen everywhere in the English countryside.

243.6 [240]   *¡Desviación! ¡Hombres Trabajando!* Sp. "Detour! Men Working!"

244.1 [241]   *hot tar smell.* Another odour of hell (see note **132.4**).

244.2 [241]   *a stone wayside cross.* Such wayside crosses are frequent in Mexico: some mark the place of burial of those who have died along the way; others afford a stopping place to pray for the continuing safety of the journey. The dying Indian, arms outstretched, is a figure of the crucified Christ.

245.1 [242]   *You can't touch him—it's the law.* Mexican law is based upon the Code Napoléon, which means, broadly speaking, that one is guilty until proved innocent. One ramification of this, which all tourists to Mexico are warned about, is that witnesses to an accident must not stop to help but must summon official aid. To become involved, even for charitable reasons, is to lay oneself open to charges of *mal medicina,* or aggravation. Both Geoffrey and Hugh appreciate the political necessity of non-intervention, especially with the police approaching, but the failure to be a good Samaritan intensifies the Consul's already anguished feelings of guilt about his failure to extend pity and charity to others. The incident as a whole is a crucial moment of truth which forms very much the emotional core of the novel and is closely linked to the mysterious Samaritan incident in the Consul's past (see note **38.1**), and to the moment of his death, p. 374 [374], when belatedly the Consul recognizes in the figure of the old fiddler the humanity and charity he has denied to the dying Indian.

246.1 [243] *A single bird flew, high.* A neo-Platonic image of the flight of the soul (see note **337.2**).

246.2 [243] *¡Diantre! ¿Dónde buscamos un médico?* Sp. "Devil take it! Where can we find a doctor?"

247.1 [244] *Pobrecito. . . . Chingar.* Sp. "Poor little thing . . . disgusting." The word pobrecito, though widely used, was especially associated in Morelos with the death of Zapata, 10 April 1919 (Womack, p. 7). *Chingar* literally means "to fuck," "to rape," but can be used in a variety of ways; Lowry's emphasis was revealed in the short story version of this chapter (UBC 7-1, p. 16): "these two words, the one of tender compassion, the other of fiendish contempt . . . were taken up as a kind of refrain"; that is, while some of the passengers show genuine compassion, others merely express their unfeeling contempt.

247.2 [245] *the chingados.* Sp. "the bastards" (literally, "the rapists"); an expression of the feelings of the common people towards the vigilante rurales and special police.

247.3 [245] *the rumour that the Servicio de Ambulancia had been suspended.* It had earlier been hinted (p. 49 [44]) that the ambulance service may be on strike, and the Consul's awareness of this can only intensify his feelings of guilt, since the chances of the Indian receiving aid from the police are even further reduced.

248.1 [245] *a green cross.* The Green Cross is an international organization, with its headquarters in France but also active in the Third World. It provides an ambulance service and other medical aids.

248.2 [245] *Dr Figueroa. Un hombre noble.* Although Dr. Figueroa is described as "a good man" (as is the Consul, p. 37 [31], "with all his faults"), the name of Ambrosío Figueroa stands out in Morelos as that of one of the most oppressive and reactionary political appointees in Cuernavaca during the early years of the Revolution (Womack, pp. 121–22).

248.3 [245] *there was a phone once . . . but it had discomposed.* Like the wires of the ciné, p. 31 [25], and the Consul's eclectic systemë, p. 148 [144], the phone is *descompuesto,* "out of order" (though the pun is much uglier now).

248.4 [245] *Vincente González.* Gral. Vincente González Fernandez, military chief of operations in Guerrero and Puebla before becoming chief of police in Mexico City under Cárdenas in 1934. He was responsible for carrying out the eviction from Mexico of Plutarco Calles and his henchmen (see note **111.7**), and in 1940 he was appointed governor of his native state, Oaxaca.

248.5 [246] *had Joshua appeared . . . to make the sun stand still.* A reference to Joshua 10:12–13, where the Israelites are attacking the city of Gibeon, and Joshua calls upon the sun to stand still:

> Then spake Joshua to the Lord in the day when the Lord delivered up the Amorites before the children of Israel, and he said in the sight of Israel, Sun, stand thou still upon Gibeon; and thou, Moon, in the valley of Ajalon.
> And the sun stood still, and the moon stayed, until the people had avenged themselves upon their enemies.

249.1 [247] *a Scotch terrier barked at them merrily.* With the help of the manuscripts identifying Angus as the neighbour's dog (see note **188.2**), and the reference to the Argentinian ambassador next door, p. 80 [76], it may be deduced that it is this dog who half-recognizes the Consul but "diplomatically" surges on past.

250.1 [247] *Compañero.* Sp. "companion," "comrade"; perhaps the most important word in the novel, its etymology ("one who shares bread") testifying to both its human and religious significance. As Spender has noted, p. xxii, compañero was the word of address used by the Reds during the Spanish civil war (like most of the Civil War references, it did not appear in the early drafts of the novel); it appeals both to Hugh's sense of brotherhood and to the Consul's sense of isolation. Though there is an obvious touch of Whitman implicit in the word, Kilgallin has suggested, p. 190, that Lowry's general debt is to Ralph Bates's Spanish novel, *The Olive Field* (1936) and his particular debt to Bates's Mexican novel, *The Fields of Paradise* (1941), a tale of love and violence and of the making of an ejido; the reference (Ch. 8, p. 111) is, however, very ambiguous:

> *Compañero!* We are never truly *compañeros* until we are dead and there is no more thought and no more need of companionship. Then we can lie still and not trouble one another, for not troubling one another is the kindest love. Only the dead are true *compañeros*.

250.2 [247] *They're not the pukka police.* The "three smiling vigilantes" are either members of the Unión Militar or the rurales (see notes **187.3** and **112.5**), and the Consul has no delusions about the probable fate of the Indian if left to their tender mercies. His use of "pukka" wryly reflects the sense of British justice and fair play that Laruelle suspects the Consul so passionately believes in (see p. 37 [31]).

250.3 [248] *the windmills.* The Consul is referring to Ch. 8 of *Don Quixote,* the famous scene in which the Knight of Sorry Aspect tilts at the windmills believing them to be giants; he means that they could have made, at best, only a quixotic gesture. The original short story version (UBC 7-1, p. 21) made the point more clearly: "'What windmills?' Hugh looked about him, startled. 'No, no,' the Consul said, 'I meant something else, only that Don Quixote wouldn't have hesitated that long.'"

250.4 [248] *war's senseless Titus Andronicus. Titus Andronicus,* printed in 1594, is generally attributed to Shakespeare and is the bard's goriest play. It deals with the revenge exacted by Titus Andronicus, a Roman general, for the atrocities committed against his daughter Lavinia, himself, and his sons and for the murder of his daughter's lover by Tamara, queen of the Goths, and Aaron the Moor, her paramour, who were in turn avenging the execution by Titus of Tamara's first-born son. As the above twisted syntax suggests, the play as a whole is full of horrors and senseless murders that do not even faintly add up to a "good story." Hugh's vision, "painted with expressionist violence" (Monbet, p. 31), was soon to find its equivalent in the nightmare of Picasso's *Guernica.*

251.1 [248] *the days of revolution in the valley.* Hugh's vision of "the stupid props of war's senseless Titus Andronicus" merges with the words shouted by Weber that morning, p. 103 [99], about the atrocities that had taken place during the Mexican Revolution. The women remain "frozen" because, unlike Hugh, they sense the futility of a revolution that gets back "just where you'd begun" (see note **105.9**).

251.2 [248]   *pity, the impulse to approach, and terror, the impulse to escape.* As Muriel Bradbrook first noted, pp. 131–32, these lines constitute a reference to I. A. Richards, *The Principles of Literary Criticism* (1924), Ch. 32, p. 245:

> What clearer instance of the "balance or reconciliation of opposite and discordant qualities" can be found than Tragedy. Pity, the impulse to approach, and Terror, the impulse to retreat, are brought in Tragedy to a reconciliation which they find nowhere else.... Their union in an ordered single response is the *catharsis* by which Tragedy is recognised.

As a Cambridge man, Hugh could well have heard I. A. Richards utter these very words. Less relevantly, perhaps, Conrad Aiken mentions in *Ushant*, p. 358, that he and Lowry took a copy of *Principles of Literary Criticism* with them to a bullfight in Granada, where a tragic drama was enacted before their eyes; Clarissa Lorenz, in "Call it Misadventure," confirms that they were in fact accompanied by Richards and his wife.

251.3 [249]   *Tierra, Libertad, Justicia y Ley.* Sp. "Land, Liberty, Justice and Law." The Zapatista slogan, "Tierra y Libertad" was a summation of their revolutionary Plan de Ayala, the basis of which was agrarian reform and the restoration of ancient rights, individual and communal, to the people. Originally promulgated in November 1911, the plan was the basis of the agrarian law passed on 26 October 1915, which formed one of the lasting ideals of the Revolution. The law concluded: "Reforma, Libertad, Justicia, y Ley" (Womack, p. 411); Hugh's addition of *frijoles* ("beans") casts cynical doubt upon the real substance of such ideals.

252.1 [249]   *the wet blue bag, the lunar caustic, the camel's-hair brush.* Medical aids of limited and superficial worth; Hugh is recalling his boy scout training:
(a) *the wet blue bag.* A small bag containing an alkaline blue powder used by laundresses; commonly used as an antidote to bee-stings.
(b) *the lunar caustic.* Fused silver nitrate used for cauterizing and the treatment of warts. Lowry would have intended a cross-reference to the numbered emotions of his protagonist in *Lunar Caustic* (see note **179.4**).
(c) *the camel's-hair brush.* A small fine brush (usually made from the tail hairs of a squirrel) used by artists for delicate lines and retouches.

253.1 [250]   *a sad bloodstained pile of silver pesos and centavos.* The reference to silver associates the pelado's guilt with that of the conquistadores and Judas.

254.1 [251]   *the shadow of the Sierra Madre.* The phrase is an echo of *The Treasure of the Sierra Madre* (1935) by the mysterious B. Traven (1890?–1969); a tale of gold and blood and treachery, in which the unheroic hero, Dobbs, betrays or murders his partners for all their gold and is himself murdered by some mestizos, who, thinking it is sand, scatter the gold to the winds. The relationship between Dobbs and his "companions" is the antithesis of any kind of human fellow-feeling.

254.2 [252]   *a recognized thing, like Abyssinia.* Italian intervention in Abyssinia, 1934–36, constitutes one of the most shameful episodes in modern history: for some years Abyssinia had retained a precarious independence, but it was generally recognized by the European powers as an Italian "sphere of interest." When relations between Haile Selassie and Mussolini became strained in 1934, the Ethiopian emperor appealed in vain to the League of Nations for protection against Italian aggression. None was forthcoming, Italian guns and tanks crushed Abyssinian spears, and the sanctions subsequently applied by the League against Italy were a hollow mockery. Equally shameful, in Hugh's opinion, was the willingness of the European powers, particularly England, to accept the one-sided and barbarous invasion as a *fait accompli,* and, indeed, to ratify by the Anglo-Italian agreement of April 1938 the establishment of an Italian protectorate in Abyssinia.

255.1 [252]   *a pulquería.* A cantina where pulque is sold (see note **113.3**); the incidents of the chapter now giving particular point to Lowry's suggestions of *Crime and Punishment.*

255.2 [253]   *Todos Contentos y Yo También.* Sp. "Everybody happy, including me." In the original drafts (UBC 7–1, pp. 23–24), the reasons for the Consul's happiness were explicit: "the certainty that he would drink a million tequilas between now and the end of his life stealing over him like a benison and postponing for the moment the necessity for the first one." Earlier in the same version (UBC 7–1, p. 19) he "was going to have fifty-seven drinks at the earliest opportunity"; that is, one for each of the cantinas mentioned on the first page of the novel. The drinks are thus the "ratification of death" that the vultures (the *xopilotes*) await.

CHAPTER NINE

256.1 [254] *Arena Tomalín. . . . What a wonderful time everybody was having.* The overblown, transparently jaunty prose seems to be in direct imitation of D. H. Lawrence at such moments (as in *St. Mawr* and *The Plumed Serpent*) that his heroines castigate and reject the meaningless "let's be happy" world and try to come to grips with their own experience; in particular, *The Plumed Serpent* opens with a scene in a bull-ring.

256.2 [254] *the 'Rocket.'* The celebrated steam engine built by George Stephenson (1781–1848), which in October 1829 won a £500 prize for its design and was subsequently employed on the Liverpool & Manchester Railway. It was not the first steam engine, Stephenson himself having built and run others previously, but the superiority of its design inaugurated, beyond all doubt, the age of steam.

256.3 [254] *donkey engine.* A small portable steam engine, commonly used on ships to lift cargo.

256.4 [254] *the brilliantly coloured serape of existence.* A direct echo of Eisenstein's *The Film Sense,* p. 197.

> Do you know what a "Serape" is? A Serape is the striped blanket that the Mexican indio, the Mexican charro—every Mexican wears. And the Serape could be the symbol of Mexico. So striped and violently contrasting are the cultures in Mexico running next to each other and at the same time being centuries away.

257.1 [255] *the bull must be caught in a special way.* One of the rules of the bull-throwing (see note **151.2**). In some cases the bull is thrown off balance with a pole. In another Mexican version the cowboys perform a "tailing," which means riding after the cow or calf, grasping its tail, and with a sudden twist upsetting it and throwing it to the ground.

257.2 [255] *always gay.* Given the "tragic history" of Mexico, p. 256 [254], there may be an echo of Yeats's "Lapus Lazuli," in which the word gay is used several times with the sense of "tragic joy." On the other hand *toujours gai* was a cliché of French music-hall and variety shows. The emotional tension of the chapter falls somewhere between the two.

258.1 [256] *Las Novedades.* "The Novelties"; a common title (especially in Oaxaca) for the kind of little kiosk that sells cigarettes, sweets, lottery tickets and soft drinks. The failure to ring Dr. Figueroa gives particular emphasis to the Consul's "Forward to the bloody arena then" and becomes yet one more item added to his burden of guilt.

258.2 [256] *Xiutepec.* Jiutepec, a small town about six miles south of Cuernavaca.

258.3 [256] *before the mirror.* Yvonne's vision of the old woman from Tarasco (see note **55.3**) is an intimation of death, also suggested by the Biblical image of "through a glass, darkly" (I Corinthians 13:12). Yet Yvonne's spiritual blindness may be suggested in that she fails to see that the old woman is also sympathetic (see note **368.2**).

258.4 [257] *olés.* Cries of applause and appreciation given at bullfights for feats of particular daring; half-hearted olés are a contradiction in terms.

259.1 [257] *Just like Ferdinand.* Yvonne is referring to the well-known children's book, *The Story of Ferdinand,* by Munro Leaf, first published in 1937 and almost immediately made into a film by Walt Disney. Unlike other bulls, Ferdinand preferred to sit and smell flowers, but on the day that five men came from Madrid to pick out the biggest, fastest, roughest bull, he inadvertently sat on a bee. Brought into the bull-ring, Ferdinand saw all the flowers in the señoritas' hair, sat down to smell them, refused to fight, and had to be taken home, where he happily sits beneath his favourite cork tree smelling the flowers. Yvonne's "hopefully" looks forward to such a happy ending, but unrealistically; at real bullfights, bulls that refuse to fight are butchered in the corrals.

259.2 [257] *Nandi... vehicle of Síva... Vindra... Huracán.* Síva is the Hindu god of destruction, the personification of the disintegrative forces of the cosmos, with whose worship many bloody rites are associated, but he is also the god of regeneration and sexuality, and the sacred Ganges which issues from Vishnu's foot gets its fertilizing power as it descends to earth through Síva's thick and luxuriant locks (*Hindu World,* II, p. 407). The *vāhana* or vehicle of Śiva is the bull Nandi, son of Kaśyapa and Surabhī, a sacred snow-white bull upon which the god is often depicted riding.

The name Vindra does not appear in Hindu mythology. Lowry may be associating Vrinda (a beautiful and saintly woman seduced by Śiva) with Indra, god of the storms, of lightning and thunder, whose weapon is the thunderbolt and who is the god celebrated above all in the *Rig-veda* as conqueror of Vritra, the dragon of chaos, and the one who brought cosmic order into being. The identification of Indra with the ancient Mexican god Huracán represents the Consul's "sensational" advance on Donnelly (see note **22.1**), though even this has been anticipated by Lewis Spence's suggestion of resemblances between Indra and the Mexican rain-god Tlaloc (*G of M,* p. 15).

259.3 [257]   *Charros.* The Mexican equivalent of a cowboy, but usually a weekend cowboy; groups of charros meet at *charreadas,* or rodeos, to practise feats of horsemanship, lassoing, bull-throwing, riding wild horses, and so forth. The charro costume, originally a practical working outfit, is often splendidly ornate; tight trousers with silver buttons and seams, a bolero jacket, and a wide-brimmed hat inlaid with silver thread.

260.1 [258]   *the Spanish–American war.* A brief war waged between Spain and the United States in 1898, the consequences of which were the loss by Spain of the last remnants of her four hundred-year empire in the Americas and the loss of the Philippines and Marianas in the Pacific. The United States gained Cuba, Guam, the Philippines, Hawaii, and a sense of its "manifest destiny" as a great nation. The immediate cause of the war was the sinking of the U.S.S. *Maine* in Havana harbour, 15 February 1898, an act which led to the outbreak of war in April. United States forces saw action in Manila and Cuba in a series of brief skirmishes which brought little honour to either side. Yvonne's earlier reference to the "new message from Garcia" (see note **100.1**) refers to one of the most publicized events of this war.

260.2 [258]   *synthetic hemp from the pineapple tops.* Hemp is a hard fibre derived from the leaves of various tropical plants, of which manila hemp is the most satisfactory because of its durability. Pina is the fibre obtained from the large leaves of the pineapple plant, and it is indeed used for making such things as mats, bags, and clothing. However, it is doubtful that pina could ever be used for making a really durable material like hemp.

260.3 [258]   *He sat on the lanai sipping okoolihao. Lanai* is a Hawaiian word meaning a "porch" or "verandah"; a living room area opening in part to the outdoors. *Okoolihao* (more commonly, *okelehao*) derives from a Hawaiian word meaning "iron buttocks," applied to an iron try-pot still; hence the alcoholic liquor, made from ti or taro roots, koji rice lees, and molasses, distilled therein.

260.4 [258]   *The World War.* If the year is 1914, and Yvonne is then six, she must have been born in 1908, the same year as Hugh.

260.5 [259]   *Consul to Iquique.* A consular appointment to Iquique, in the Atacama desert of northern Chile, is of about the same standing as one to Quauhnahuac, both at the end of long, dry, and spiritually desolate roads. The State Department records show that there had been an American consul in Iquique since February 1877, but that the consulate closed on 31 March 1915, reopening with the end of the war in January 1920. It finally closed in October 1931. Whatever else, then, Captain Constable could not have been an American consul during "those long war years in Chile."

261.1 [259]   *that republic of stupendous coastline yet narrow girth.* Chile has a coastline of 2,653 miles; but at its widest point the country is only 221 miles wide, and at its narrowest, only 31 miles wide.

261.2 [259]   *at Cape Horn, or in the nitrate country.* The southernmost and northernmost parts of Chile. The nitrate country is in the northern part of Chile, particularly in the Atacama desert. In this narrow strip, 450 miles long, is mined almost the entire world's supply of natural sodium nitrate, a mineral used in the production of both fertilizer and explosives.

261.3 [259]   *Bernado O'Higgins.* Bernado Riquelme O'Higgins (1778–1842), the liberator of Chile, was the illegitimate son of an Irish father and Spanish mother. Born in Chillán, Chile, he was educated in Peru, Spain, and England. He returned to Chile in 1802 and joined the revolutionists in 1810. By 1813 he was in command of the army, and though his first battles against the Spaniards were unsuccessful, in 1817 a spectacular cavalry charge under his leadership resulted in a decisive Chilean victory at the battle of Chacabuco. He was made dictator of Chile in 1818 and declared the independence of Chile from Spain, but his democratic sentiments and proposed reforms aroused opposition, and in 1823 he was deposed and exiled to Peru.

261.4 [259]   *Robinson Crusoe.* The figure of Robinson Crusoe, in the novel of that name by Daniel Defoe (1660?–1731), is usually taken as an image of self-reliance and self-sufficiency. Crusoe, shipwrecked upon an uninhabited Pacific island, saved tools and stores from the wreck, built a house, and a boat, domesticated goats, rescued Man Friday from cannibals, and was finally rescued by the coming of an English ship. Defoe's novel, written in 1719, was based upon the real-life adventures of one Alexander Selkirk, who in 1704 was marooned upon the island of Juan Fernandez, a few hundred miles off the coast of Chile, and was not rescued until 1709.

261.5 [259] *the Tropic of Capricorn.* The imaginary line which runs 23° 30′ south of the Equator. It passes slightly to the south of Iquique, where Consul Constable was stationed. The reference balances that to the location of Cuernavaca, which is almost directly on the Tropic of Cancer (see note 9.3).

261.6 [259] *the Armistice.* The cease-fire, beginning 11 November 1918, which marked the effective end of World War I.

261.7 [259] *Hilo.* The largest town (now a big city) on the island of Hawaii, close to Mauna Loa, the largest active volcano in the world.

261.8 [259] *a wire-fence company.* Several companies in Ohio continue to manufacture wire fences for use around farms. This detail, like many others concerning Yvonne's father, is based upon Margerie Lowry's father, John Stuart Bonner, who at one point was foreign manager of the Page Woven Wire Fence Company, in Adrian, Michigan (Day, p. 251).

262.1 [260] *cashiered from the army.* To be cashiered (from Du. *casseeren,* "to break") means to be given a dishonourable discharge for misconduct. The incident, illusionary or not, seems to have rankled with Captain Constable in much the same way that the *Samaritan* affair has with the Consul, and it is yet another incident (the drinking, the consular appointment, and the insanely complicated pipe are others) which suggests that Yvonne's emotional bondage to the older Geoffrey reduplicates her earlier ties to her father.

262.2 [260] *five years.* From approximately 1921 to 1926.

262.3 [260] *'serials.'* The serial adventures were shown each week in episodes, each of which ended at some suspenseful crisis. Adventurous, mysterious, often exotic, they were part of the regular fare of movie-goers during this period. The "queen" of the serials was Pearl White, famous for her appearances in such serials as *The Perils of Pauline.* Lowry's second wife had a brief career in serials.

263.1 [261]   *Bill Hodson, the cowboy star.* A fictitious figure, probably based on the popular cowboy star, William S. Hart (see note **65.3**).

263.2 [261]   *a little secret amusement.* Yvonne is amused, not simply because she knows more about horses than Hugh, but because she is aware that her Geoffrey (see note **113.5**) wants nothing else but to drink.

263.3 [261]   *that day in Robinson.* The day of Hugh and Yvonne's presumed "betrayal" of the Consul in Paris (see note **102.2**).

263.4 [261]   *Yvonne the Terrible.* A completely inappropriate reference to Ivan the Terrible, the powerful and brutal Russian tsar.

263.5 [261]   *the 'Boomp Girl. . . . 'double pick-offs'. . . . a 'flying mount'. . . . 'Oomph Girl.'* Hollywood slang:
(a)   *the 'Boomp Girl.'* A publicity name given to Yvonne and similar to such absurdities as the "It girl" (Clara Bow), the "Oomph Girl" (Anne Sheridan), and "The Body" (Marie McDonald).
(b)   *'double pick-offs.'* A Hollywood stunt whereby a rider on horseback goes between two other riders and pulls them to the ground.
(c)   *a 'flying mount.'* A western movie stunt where the actor or actress jumps or vaults into the saddle either from the side or from the rear by leap-frogging onto the horse's back.
(d)   *an 'Oomph Girl.'* The title eventually assigned to Anne Sheridan in a publicity stunt in the 1940's.

263.6 [262]   *Venus just emerging from the surf.* The columnist is probably just aware that Venus (Aphrodite), goddess of love, rose naked from the surf to become the wife of the lame smith, Vulcan (Hephaestus), to whom she was unfaithful with Mars (Ares), the god of war. The blurb unwittingly intimates Yvonne's future, and duplicates the image of herself that Yvonne sees in the printer's window, p. 59 [54].

264.1 [262]   *the University of Hawaii.* At first the College of Hawaii, it became the University of Hawaii in 1920. The main campus was at Honolulu, but Yvonne could have attended a branch campus at Hilo.

264.2 [262]   *the 'Madame Curie' of astronomy.* Nothing could less resemble Yvonne's dilettantish approach to her studies than the dedicated life of Madame Marie Curie (1867–1934), Polish-born chemist and physicist and, with her French husband Pierre, winner of the Nobel Prize for Physics in 1903 for the discovery of radium. Yvonne's wish to become "a star" is more appropriately achieved at the end of Ch. 11.

266.1 [264]   *Virgil Avenue or Mariposa.* Two streets about eight blocks from each other and running north and south off Wilshire Boulevard in central Los Angeles ("The City of the Angels"), in an area of large, grand homes and good hotels, where young promising actresses such as Yvonne might stay. The names also possess clear intimations of the *Divine Comedy* and the myth of Psyche (Sp. *mariposa,* "a butterfly").

266.2 [264]   *the Town House ... The Zebra Room.* The Town House, located at 52 Windward Avenue, Venice, Los Angeles, dates from 1906 and has been in its time a cathouse and a speak-easy during Prohibition. There was once, apparently, a cocktail bar called the Zebra Room within it, but the name is no longer used.

266.3 [264]   *'Man's public inquiry of the hour'.* An unidentified billboard which Yvonne also recalls, p. 331 [331], and which accentuates the sense of time running out. Her use of "hoarding" is unusual, since the word is specifically British.

267.1 [265]   *Times Square.* The area in New York City, at Broadway and 42nd, in the heart of the entertainment area. The district was formerly known as Longacre Square, but the name was changed in 1904 when the *New York Times* built a skyscraper there, well-known for its then innovative flashing illuminated news, which, as Yvonne says, travelled round the top of the building. The Astor Hotel was a part of the complex.

267.2 [265]   *the best for less.* Identified by Andersen, p. 46, as the slogan of Rudley's Food Stores, a New York Company, and seen by Bill Plantagenet in the opening pages of *Lunar Caustic;* a phrase that seems to underline the spiritual bankruptcy of a materialistic society (it is the conscious antithesis of "less is more" in *October Ferry,* p. 166).

267.3 [265]   *Dead End.* A 1937 American movie, directed by William Wyler, produced by Samuel Goldwyn, and starring Humphrey Bogart; from the stage play by Lillian Hellman and Sydney Kingsley. It was intended to be an examination of the urban slums as a breeding place for vice, but though the intended message was a humanitarian protest against slums, the Dead End Kids seemed so attractive that the message was lost and the potential delinquents ended up as heroes.

267.4 [265]   *Romeo and Juliet.* The 1936 version of Shakespeare's play, directed by George Cukor, with Leslie Howard and Norma Shearer "in a lavish studio-bound semi-pop version for MGM" (Halliwell, p. 620). The juxtaposition with *Dead End* is deliberately incongruous.

267.5 [266] *a mechanical crane.* A siphon or crooked pipe for drawing liquor out of a cask.

267.6 [266] *Le Destin de Yvonne Griffaton.* Fr. "The Destiny of Yvonne Griffaton"; a fictitious film, attributed in the novel to Jacques Laruelle in his pre-Hollywood days, the heroine of which Yvonne Constable closely identifies herself with. The name "Griffaton" suggests griffin, a fabulous monster with the head and wings of an eagle and the body of a lion.

267.7 [266] *the little cinema in Fourteenth Street.* The moviehouse, otherwise unidentified, is somewhere in Greenwich Village. The stills, or photographs displayed outside the cinema, display to Yvonne images of her own loneliness.

267.8 [266] *Dubonnet, Amer Picon, Les 10 Frattelinis, Moulin Rouge.* Advertising signs in Paris:
(a) *Dubonnet.* A dark red proprietary French apéritif made of a sweetened wine base, with bitter bark and quinine added to impart its characteristic taste.
(b) *Amer Picon.* A proprietary French bitters, first made in Algeria, used as an apéritif and made with a wine and brandy base to which has been added quinine (to impart a bitter taste), orange peel, and innumerable herbs. It is usually sweetened with grenadine or cassis and drunk with ice.
(c) *Les 10 Frattelinis.* The Fratellinis were a family of clowns of Italian origin, whose reputation was unsurpassed in Europe. There were originally ten children in the family, of whom only four survived.
(d) *Moulin Rouge.* Fr. "the Red Mill"; the celebrated night-spot in Montmartre, Paris, renowned for its dancing girls, the can-can, and the paintings of Toulouse-Lautrec. It epitomized more than anything else the daring permissiveness of Paris in the gay nineties and 1900's, but after a fire in 1915 it was converted first into a music hall and then a theatre.

268.1 [266] *a shadowy horse, gigantic.* As the word "statue" implies, this horse becomes associated in Yvonne's mind with the equestrian statue of the turbulent Huerta, p. 49 [44], and anticipates the horse that will trample her to death in Ch. 11.

268.2 [267] *the Folies Bergères.* The Folies-Bergères, a Parisian music hall in the Rue Richer, which opened in 1869 with programmes of light opera and pantomime but increasingly gained itself a reputation for shows featuring lavish decor and spectacular nudity. Its name in the early years of the century was almost synonymous with "gai Paris."

268.3 [267]   *the Opéra.* More fully, the Théâtre Nationale de l'Opéra, the Paris Opera House, designed by Charles Garnier and celebrated as one of the finest buildings of the Second Empire, with a striking, ornate front, beautiful marble columns, magnificent foyers and halls, and a huge concert chamber. The building was begun in 1861, and the first concert took place in 1875. The Opera also houses a rich library, the National Academy of Music, and a museum of musical mementos.

268.4 [267]   *Leoncavallo's Zaza.* Ruggero Leoncavallo (1858–1919) was an Italian composer of light opera, who wrote in conscious opposition to Wagner and Verdi. His fame rests mainly on *I Pagliacci* (1892), but his *Zazà* (1900) was a moderate success. This four-act opera, an adaptation of the play by Pierre Berton and Charles Simon, tells how Zazà, a young singer, falls in love with the wealthy Parisian Milio Dufresne, not knowing that he is married. She finds out and tells him untruthfully that she has revealed their intimacy to his wife, but finding that his love for his wife is real and his attraction to her merely a passing fancy, she relents, tells him the truth, and sends him back to his family, while she remains (like Yvonne) alone and desolate.

268.5 [267]   *in tumbrils. . . . shot by the Commune, shot by the Prussians.* Three phrases which summarize three phases of French history:
(a) *in tumbrils.* The French Revolution, which began in 1789, saw many aristocrats being taken to the guillotine in tumbrils, or open, horse-drawn carts.
(b) *shot by the Commune.* In 1871 there took place in Paris an insurrection against the government as a reaction to France's defeat in the Franco-Prussian War of 1876 and the collapse of Napoleon III's Second Empire (1852–70). The Republicans of Paris, rejecting the peace which the National Assembly had concluded with Germany and afraid that the assembly would restore the monarchy, formed a commune government and held out for some time against the military forces ordered to suppress them. They shot a number of liberals and monarchists, but the harsh repressive action following the "bloody week" in May 1871 did much to alienate French workers permanently from the government, and the episode remained for the left the first definite symbol of worker solidarity.
(c) *shot by the Prussians.* The Franco-Prussian War, from July 1870 to May 1871, resulted in a total victory for the newly unified Germany

under the able leadership of Bismarck, the payment of heavy indemnities by the French, the loss of Alsace and Lorraine to Germany, and a lasting bitterness between the two nations.

268.6 [267] *standing upright in death.* The opening chapter of P. C. Wren's *Beau Geste* (1924) tells of "the strange events at Zinderneuf," an outpost in the French Sahara. Major Henri de Beaujolais arrives at the apparently deserted fortress, which has been attacked by Arabs, and finds it "defended" by corpses, each proppped up in a life-like position. The explanation given later in the novel is that the bodies of dead men were placed at their posts to create the illusion of a fortress still manned.

268.7 [267] *the Dreyfus Case.* Alfred Dreyfus (1859–1935), a French officer of Jewish descent, unwittingly became the centre of a famous miscarriage of justice which led first to his imprisonment and then to a fierce controversy preceding his rehabilitation. Because of the alleged similarity of his handwriting and that upon an incriminating letter addressed to a German military attaché, he was arrested in 1894 and sent to the notorious Devil's Island. Despite evidence strongly suggesting his innocence, a violently anti-Semitic press campaign and military cover-up prevented the immediate re-opening of his case. In the ensuing controversy, which saw liberals and intellectuals arraigned against conservatives, royalists, the military, and the clergy, Émile Zola published his famous letter, "J'accuse!" ("I accuse"), in consequence of which he was sentenced to a year's imprisonment. It was not until 1906 that the sentence condemning Dreyfus was finally quashed.

268.8 [267] *mow.* To mouth or make grimaces.

269.1 [267] *The Life of the African Lungfish.* The lungfish, as its name implies, is a dipnoan or kind of fish that has lungs as well as gills. The film appears to be *Lungfisken,* a 1934 study of the lungfish by the Svensk Filmindustri (B.F.I., vol.I, 9061).

269.2 [267] *Scarface.* A 1932 film directed by Howard Hawks and produced by Howard Hughes, with a cast headed by Paul Muni and George Raft. The plot, based loosely on the career of Al Capone (whose nickname was "Scarface") tells of a gangster's rise from bodyguard to boss until he is eventually cornered and shot. The film depicts such scenes as the killing of Jim Colisimo and the St. Valentine's Day Massacre at greater length and in more cruelly realistic detail than previous gangster movies. Because of the violence and because it made crime seem so attractive, the film ran into censorship problems, and it was not allowed to circulate until the sub-title "The Shame of the Nation" was added.

269.3 [267] *this old man of the sea.* The story of Sinbad the Sailor is included in *The Thousand and One Nights,* or *Arabian Nights.* On his fifth voyage Sinbad is wrecked upon an island and meets an old man whom he offers to carry across a river, but no sooner is the Old Man of the Sea mounted upon Sinbad's back than his legs lock round Sinbad's neck so tightly that he is almost choked. Sinbad is forced to carry the old man night and day until at last he tricks him into getting drunk, dislodges him, and kills him. The story is often used as a metaphor for the weight of the past, an image not unlike that of the two Indians at the end of the chapter.

269.4 [268] *the music of Ravel. . . . Bolero.* Maurice Ravel (1875–1937), French composer best known for his ballet *Daphnis et Cloé* (1912), his *Concerto for the Left Hand* (1931), and the orchestral pieces *Shéhérazade* (1903), *Rhapsodie Espagnole* (1907), and *Boléro* (1928). A bolero is a Spanish dance, characterized by sharp turns of the body and a syncopated rhythm. Ravel's, originally intended to be a ballet, displays great virtuosity in its orchestration, and the music, representing a woman dancing on a table in a cafe full of men, has an almost hypnotic effect as it repeats itself and rises to a magnificent crescendo when passion breaks out, chairs are thrown, and knives are drawn. The date of its composition is not easy to reconcile with what is known of Laruelle's past as a filmmaker.

270.1 [268] *the Sphinx.* In Greek mythology, a winged creature with a human head and a lion's body; specifically, the huge statue at Giza depicting such a figure. There may also be a suggestion of the sphinx who appears in Cocteau's *La machine infernale* (see note **212.3**) and whose riddle Oedipus must solve to rid Thebes of its plague.

270.2 [268] *the Grand Tour.* In the eighteenth and nineteenth centuries, the essential completion of his formal education for the son of an English aristocrat. Tended by a servant or two and guided by a tutor, the young man would spend a year or so touring the capitals of Western Europe, perfecting his knowledge of other languages and social customs.

270.3 [268] *the Tour Eiffel.* The Eiffel Tower, a famous Parisian landmark, built by the French engineer Gustave Eiffel (1832–1923) for the Paris Exhibition of 1889. Its radically innovative design (a construction in three stages, utilizing thousands of prefabricated metal strips) presaged a new era in civil engineering and architectural design, and its height of almost 1000 feet made it the highest man-made structure of its day.

270.4 [269] *huaraches.* A kind of cheap leather sandal, worn everywhere in Mexico.

271.1 [269] *salmonberries and thimbleberries*. Small berries, commonly growing wild in British Columbia: salmonberries, (*Rubus parviflorus*) are sometimes distinguished from thimbleberries (*Rubus occidentalis*), but Armstrong's *Western Wild Flowers* (a copy of which Lowry owned) says the two are identical, p. 238. The fruit is like a small raspberry, but disappointing to the taste, for it is mostly seeds.

271.2 [269] *a pier*. Lowry's pier at Dollarton was an intensely personal symbol, and the news of its collapse in 1955 left him almost literally heartbroken (Day, p. 35). Even here there is a strong sense of identification of the frail structure with the rebuilding of their lives.

271.3 [270] *chenille*. A fabric with a deep pile. The image is of the green pine trees outlined against the sky, like a design in a deep-piled rug.

271.4 [270] *Scorpio and Triangulum, Bootes and the Great Bear*. Four constellations:
(a) *Scorpio*. The Scorpion, the eighth sign of the zodiac; a constellation in the southern hemisphere, lying partly in the milky way, the brightest star of which is Antares.
(b) *Triangulum*. *Triangulum Australe* (the "Southern Triangle"), a constellation of the southern hemisphere (on astrological charts, not far from the tail of Scorpio).
(c) *Bootes*. The herdsman (that is, of the Pleiades), a large constellation in the northern hemisphere near Ursa Major, the brightest star of which is Arcturus (mentioned frequently by Conrad Aiken).
(d) *Great Bear*. The constellation of Ursa Major, an extensive and conspicuous constellation in the northern hemisphere, whose position is often used to pinpoint others around it.

273.1 [272] *Guadalajara*. A stirring but sentimental song from Jalisco, Mexico, words and music by Pepe Guizar:

> Guadalajara, Guadalajara,
> Guadalajara, Guadalajara,
> tienes el alma de provinciana
> hueles a limpio a rosa temprana
> a verde jara fresca del río
> son mil palomas tu caserío
> Guadalajara, Guadalajara,
> sabes a pura tierra mojada.

("Guadalajara... / you hold the soul of the province, / you bring purity to the early rose, / the coolness of the river to the green thicket, / your country-dwelling the sound of a thousand doves. / Guadalajara, Guadalajara, / you form the pure moist earth.")

Hugh, repeating the title of the song, thinks immediately of the part he should have played at the Battle of Guadalajara (see note **106.2**) and is shortly after galvanized into action.

274.1 [272] *Indian summer.* In North America, a period of warm, mild weather following the first autumn frosts.

274.2 [273] *bracken.* Bushes or ferns. The word, common in England, is slightly unusual in Yvonne's mind.

275.1 [273] *See the old unhappy bull.* A reference to the opening lines of "The Bull," by Ralph Hodgson (1871-1962), a long miserable poem about a bull on its last legs, dreaming of the days when it had strength and vigour and turning to see the carrion birds and flies waiting for it to die:

> See an old unhappy bull,
> Sick in soul and body both,
> Slouching in the undergrowth
> Of the forest beautiful,
> Banished from the herd he led,
> Bulls and cows a thousand head.

The debt to Ralph Hodgson was explicitly acknowledged in the manuscripts (UBC 7-7, p. 7), as was the parallel between the Consul and John Bull. Hugh, overhearing an argument between the Consul and Yvonne, thinks of John Bull (the epitome of stolid British stupidity) and then of England's failure to intervene in Spain (see note **102.1**). The Consul has already identified himself with the bull in the ring, p. 261 [259], futilely trying to break out from the circle of necessity in which it is trapped.

275.2 [273] *wild surmises . . . Stout Cortéz. . . . Silent on a peak in Quauhnahuac.* The Consul repeats his pun from p. 191, making explicit his reference to Keats's "On First Looking into Chapman's Homer," ll. 11-14:

> Or like stout Cortez when with eagle eyes
> He star'd at the Pacific — and all his men
> Look'd at each other with a wild surmise —
> Silent, upon a peak in Darien.

P. G. Wodehouse, in *The Clicking of Cuthbert,* Ch. 2, had alluded to "stout Cortez staring at the Pacific"; as he notes in the second edition:

> Shortly after the appearance of this narrative in serial form in America, I received an anonymous letter containing the words, "You big stiff, it wasn't Cortez, it was Balboa." This, I believe, is historically accurate. On the other hand, if Cortez was good enough for Keats, he is good enough for me.

275.3 [273]   *the man in dark glasses.* The "reality" of the Consul's "spiders" is apparently substantiated by the fact of Yvonne's noticing them and the Consul's evasive response.

275.4 [274]   *Es ist vielleicht an ox.* Ger. (and English) "It is perhaps an ox," a construction modelled on the idiom "Das ist vielleicht 'n Kaffer," "he is an awful fool." Unlike a fighting bull, the castrated ox lacks all potency or fighting spirit. There may have been in Lowry's mind an echo of Tom Harrisson's "Letter to Oxford" (see note **329.2**), where the metaphor is used incessantly to describe the Oxbridge mentality.

275.5 [274]   *an oxymoron... Wisely foolish.* From Gk. *oxy,* "sharp" and *moros,* "foolish," a figure of rhetoric in which two contradictory notions are combined (the word itself being an example of such).

276.1 [275]   *cake-walking.* The cakewalk is a strutting dance or set of elaborate steps, originally performed by blacks in the American South for the prize of a cake.

277.1 [275]   *the poxbox.* One who carries syphilis; a strong obscenity, revealing a lot about the Consul's resentment of Hugh.

277.2 [275]   *galvanized itself like a frog.* To galvanize is to stimulate by the application of an electrical current. The word derives from Luigi Galvani (1737–98), professor of anatomy at Bologna, whose investigations into the nature of current electricity brought him fame. His experiments on frogs, 1774–80, were particularly significant in leading to the understanding of neural transmission of electrical currents in animal tissue. Lowry's simile may derive from Charles Fort's *Wild Talents,* where "The twitch of the legs of a frog" is associated with Galvani (Fort, p. 1028).

279.1 [277]   *They sat closely, hands clasped.* An echo of the Strauss song they used to sing (see note **45.2**):

Gib mir die Hand, dass ich sie heimlich drücke,
und wenn man's sieht, mir ist es einerlei,
gib mir nur einen deiner süssen Blicke,
wie einst im Mai.

("Give me your hand, so I may secretly press it, / and if anybody sees,
it's all one to me; / give me just one of your sweet glances, / as once in
May.")

This is the closest that Geoffrey and Yvonne will approach each other this
day, the last act symbolizing love and hope for the future. Lowry was
speaking of this scene when he said that "the real point of this chapter is
Hope, with a capital H, for this note must be struck in order to stress the
later downfall" ("LJC," p. 80).

280.1 [278]   *He left a little for Hugh, however.* Hill, p. 135, points out the
almost automatic defensive thinking of the alcoholic behind this small
detail, leaving a small swallow for Hugh so that nobody can accuse him of
finishing it off. The action itself constitutes an almost wilful renunciation of
Yvonne's vision the moment her attention is distracted.

280.2 [279]   *The Bishop of Tasmania.* The Consul's vision seems to combine a number of allusions with his own favourite image of broken bottles.
In an earlier draft (UBC 7–10, p. 3) he had simply said:

I once read of something of this kind happening to some explorers in
Tasmania. They were dying of thirst in the desert and then they saw this
lake and ran toward it. And it wasn't a mirage, although of course it
wasn't a lake either. What they saw were just acres and acres of broken
glass.

The vision may reflect T. S. Eliot's "Sunlight on a broken column," from
"The Hollow Men," l. 23, or Ouspensky's description of one who has lost
his way in the midst of the deceptions and illusions of the *reflected* phenom-
enal world, which he has mistaken for the noumenal world (*Tertium
Organum,* Ch. 16, p. 162). There is no desert in Tasmania, but the reference
to the bishop of Tasmania (see note **91.2**) suggests that Lowry may have in
mind Ch. 27 of Bishop Montgomery's *Visions* (1909), entitled "Uphill,"
which tells of an old missionary in "Regions Beyond" who sits alone on a
mountainside, sees the vision of a faint light eastward, but as he heads
towards it runs into dangerous rocks, falls, and hits his head. The details are
by no means exact, but the tone is remarkably similar, and the old man

concludes as he goes down to the valley, having received the vision of a life
of mystery:

> Again, look at the snow peak I cannot reach; thank God, it is a peak,
> not a volcano. It is nearer God, not nearer molten lava bursting from
> earth's fires. It is God I have approached. I shall not be swept down-
> ward as a cinder, but led upward by those hands I have felt.

280.3 [279] *Cradle Mountain.* A 5,069 foot mountain in northwestern
Tasmania which gives its name to the Cradle Mountain Scenic Reserve.

281.1 [279] *El Jardín Xicotancatl: only weeds lived in the greenhouse.* A
reminder of the earlier hint of conflict (see note **57.3**), and of Mariana's
deserted garden (see note **78.6**).

281.2 [279] *the little boat.* In Lowry's short story, "The Bravest Boat," a
small wooden boat, set adrift years before, has brought two lovers together
and has become an image of love which, against almost impossible odds,
has survived life's storms.

281.3 [280] *wild tripthongs.* More accurately, triphthongs. In linguistics,
the combining of three vowels in a single syllable; here, presumably, three
different notes of a bell combining in one wild peal.

281.4 [280] *Their shadows crawled before them in the dust.* A hint of
T. S. Eliot's *The Waste Land,* ll. 27–30:

> And I will show you something different from either
> Your shadow at morning striding behind you
> Or your shadow at evening rising to meet you;
> I will show you fear in a handful of dust.

The insolent shadow of the bicycle wheel sweeping past is a further assertion
of the wheel of the law and inevitable necessity (see note **221.3**).

281.5 [280] *an old lame Indian was carrying on his back . . . another poor
Indian.* The Consul, weighed down by his own burden of guilt (as Aeneas
beneath Anchises or Sinbad beneath the old man of the sea), experiences at
this moment an epiphany of hopelessness as he gazes on the old Indians.
Lowry comments, "LJC," p. 81:

The close of the chapter, with the Indian carrying his father, is a restatement and universalizing of the theme of humanity struggling on under the eternal tragic weight of the past. But it is also Freudian (man eternally carrying the psychological burden of his father), Sophoclean, Oedipean, what have you, which relates the Indian to the Consul again.

CHAPTER TEN

283.1 [281] *Mescal. . . . What had he said? . . . No, Señor Cervantes . . . mescal, poquito.* On p. 219 [216], the Consul had said to Laruelle that if ever he were to start to drink mescal again, that would be the end; his choice now signals the beginning of that end. As Hill says, p. 135, he orders mescal: "quite by accident, it seems. Well, now it's done, he might as well take it. Probably just what he needs—" (just as Don Birnam, in Charles Jackson's *The Lost Weekend* reasons, p. 11: "Oh well, I suppose I might as well drink it, now that I've ordered it"). The Consul evades responsibility by asking for mescal poquito, a little one; Yvonne had agreed, p. 275 [273], to his having a "poquitín," and the onus is now on Cervantes to keep it small. Hill continues: "he tells the bartender "poquito"—just a little one. Needless to say, the drink will be regulation size. . . . But the concept of the "little" drink is cherished by those for whom every drink is too big."

283.2 [281] *the Salón Ofélia.* The name of the restaurant-cantina reflects the tragic fate of the heroine of *Hamlet*. In Act IV.vii, the queen reports to Laertes that his sister, despairing of her love for Hamlet, has cast herself into the brook and drowned. See also note **42.3** for details of the salón in Oaxaca run by one José Cervantes (mentioned by Day, p. 243).

283.3 [281] *Lee Maitland.* The "shadowy Lee Maitland" (Kilgallin, p. 124) has not been identified with any certainty and is probably intended to remain a mystery. In an early short story, "In Le Havre," Lowry tells of a woman named Lee who abandons her husband after five months of marriage and returns to the United States; it is partly based on events in Lowry's first marriage. The woman seems to epitomize the Angel of Death (the Remington Lee and Lee Enfield are types of rifle), but also a failed sexuality (she is a Virginian, her name sounds like "mate-land," but the Consul's bouquet of flowers is a failure, their sap sticky, the flowers on the wrong end of the stalks); both these aspects having been anticipated in the Consul's "the erections of guns, disseminating death," p. 211 [207]. For the close identification of this "fair-haired angel from Virginia" and Baudelaire's angel, see note **283.4**.

283.4 [281]   *Baudelaire's angel.* The figure of the angel is used throughout Baudelaire's *Les Fleurs du Mal* (1861), sometimes as the incarnation of a feminine ideal, more often as representing the aspirations within debased man for something higher and more spiritual, as in "Bénédiction," ll. 21–24:

> Pourtant, sous la tutelle invisible d'un Ange,
> L'Enfant désherité s'enivre de soleil.
> Et dans tout ce qu'il boit et dans tout ce qu'il mange
> Retrouve l'ambroisie ct le nectar vermeil

("Nevertheless, under the invisibile tutelage of an Angel, / the disinherited child becomes drunk with the sun, / and in all he drinks and in all he eats / finds again ambrosia and rosy nectar.")

The angel also appears in "L'irremediable," the poem by Baudelaire which perhaps contains more images directly pertinent to *UTV* than any other.

Like Geoffrey, Baudelaire often hears his angels speaking to him and addresses to the angel his cries of anguish, as in "Réversibilité," ll. 1–5:

> Ange plein de gaité, connaissez-vous l'angoisse,
> La honte, les remords, les sanglots, les ennuis,
> Et les vagues terreurs de ces affreuses nuits
> Qui compriment le coeur comme un papier qu'on froisse?
> Ange plein de gaieté, connaissez-vous l'angoisse?

("Angel full of gaiety, do you know the anguish? / The shame, the remorse, the tears, the desolations, / and the vague terrors of these frightful nights / which compress the heart like a paper which one scribbles on? / Angel full of gaiety, do you know the anguish?")

A hint to Lowry's specific reference (anticipating "Un voyage à Cythère," p. 295 [293], but not directly alluding to it) is found in the earlier manuscripts (UBC 8–22, p. 1 and 11–14, p. 42), which differ significantly from the final version: "in that state of being where Baudelaire's angel indeed awakes ~~in the debauchee but~~ desiring ~~only continuity,~~ eternity, to meet trains perhaps" [Lowry's cross-outs]. The only poem among *Les Fleurs du Mal* which has this immediate conjunction of debauchée and angel is "L'Aube spirituelle" ("The Spiritual Dawn"), the theme of which is precisely that discussed by Baudelaire in his *Paradis artificiels:* the exceptional state of spirit and sensuality that may occur under the influence of wine and hashish (Baudelaire in fact calls it "paradisiaque") where one feels the presence of superior powers and a sense of spiritual elevation and grace, "une espèce d'excitation angélique." The poem begins:

> Quand chez les débauchés l'aube blanche et vermeille
> Entre en société de l'Idéal rongeur,
> Par l'opération d'un mystère vengeur
> Dans la brute assoupie un ange se réveille.

("When within the debauchees the white and rosy dawn, / in company with the gnawing Ideal, / with the action of a mysterious avenger, / enters into the drowsy brute, an angel awakes.")

The Consul's desire to meet the train is therefore to meet this fair-haired angel, the Ideal, and to experience the sense of spiritual awakening; his failure to do so plunges the incipient dawn into greater darkness.

283.5 [281] *to meet trains.* Lowry comments, "LJC," p. 81: "The opening train theme is related to Freudian death dreams." His reference is to Freud's *The Interpretation of Dreams* (Standard Edition, vol.5, p. 385): "Dreams of missing a train ... are dreams of consolation for another kind of anxiety felt in sleep—the fear of dying. 'Departing' on a journey is one of the commonest and best authenticated symbols of death." The Consul's desire to meet trains and his recurrent thoughts of the corpse that will be transported by express are powerful symbols of his urgent death-wish. The entire dream sequence (absent from most of the early drafts) may have been initiated not only by Lowry's reading of Freud but also by his recollection of Dunne, Ch. 5, p. 30. In a section called "The Memory-Train" Dunne puts forth the idea that when the mind wanders without knowingly aiming at any goal, "the set of images which is then observed appears to be arranged in a sequence which has little correspondence with any previously observed succession of events." The opening of Ch. 10 is a perfect example of what Dunne means by images building up other images.

283.6 [281] *Suspension Bridge.* The name "Suspension Bridge" was formerly that of two small towns on either side of the Niagara River, now incorporated respectively into the American and Canadian cities of Niagara Falls. It is also the name of a railway bridge over the Niagara River (near the Whirlpool Rapids). The first railway suspension bridge of its kind, it was built by John A. Roebling in 1855, measured 821 feet, and carried trains on an upper deck and other traffic below. This bridge was replaced in 1896 by another better capable of bearing heavier trains. The Consul's repeated "Suspension!" (here and on p. 316 [314]) seems to underline the apparent precariousness of both the bridge's and his own equilibrium.

283.7 [282] *the dehydrated onion factory.* The only such factories in North America at this time were in California; Lowry seems to have created the detail to facilitate the transition to Paris and "the delicious smell of onion soup."

283.8 [282] *Daemon's Coal.* The brand-name accentuates the infernal aspects of the Hell-Railway (see note **284.3**). The sweeps, or sweepers, are labourers who sweep up dust and small pieces of coal; the braziers are fires in oil drums, lit to keep railroad workers warm. The scene as a whole closely resembles the opening of Joyce's Night-town episode in *Ulysses.*

283.9 [282] *Vavin.* A metro stop and square in the Montparnasse area of Paris at the intersection of the Boulevards Montparnasse and Raspail, then in the heart of the artisitic and bohemian area. In an earlier draft (UBC 11–15, p. C) Lowry had accentuated the contrast with the present horror: "the Avenue d'Orléans, the Arrondissement 14er . . . oh Vavin, oh Montparnasse."

284.1 [282] *a banshee playing a shrieking nose-organ in D minor.* A banshee (from O.Ir. *Ben Sidhe,* "a woman of the fairies") in Irish or Scots folklore is a supernatural being said to take the shape of an old woman (not unlike the old woman from Tarasco, p. 55 [51]), and to foretell death by mournful wailing outside the dwelling of one fated to die. Pagnoulle, p. 152, notes the combination of banshee and shrieking train at the beginning of Faulkner's *Light in August;* both trains pass through the town without stopping. The nose-organ is presumably a demonic mixture of mouth-organ and a nose-flute (a small flute played by blowing through the nostrils), and the key of D-minor is that of Mozart's quartet, K 421, the finale of which is heard in the Consul's dying imagination, p. 374 [374].

284.2 [282] *cornflowers . . . meadowsweet . . . queen's lace.* Common meadow flowers; for the sexual implications of the failed bouquet, see note **283.3**:
(a) *cornflowers.* A small blue flower, *Centaurea cyanus,* of the daisy family, once commonly found in corn-fields.
(b) *meadowsweet.* Described by Armstrong, p. 278, as:

A charming plant, often covering the meadows with drifts of creamy bloom. The stars are smooth, succulent, brittle and branching, from six to twelve inches tall; the delicate flowers over an inch across, the petals hairy at base, but usually white and yellow.

(c) *Queen's lace.* More properly, Queen Anne's Lace, a wild plant of the carrot family, with fine leaves and clutches of tiny delicate white flowers.

284.3 [283]   *Hamilton, Ontario.* An industrial city at the head of Lake Ontario, some forty miles from Toronto on the route to Buffalo. D. C. Nimmo comments, *N & Q,* July 1969, p. 265:

> The Toronto, Hamilton and Buffalo Railway (T.H. & B.) is popularly known as the "To Hell and Back Railway," with Hamilton being Hell. Thus the placename plays a role in establishing the hellish landscape of the Consul's mental inferno.

285.1 [283]   *each wailing for its demon lover.* An infernal parody of Coleridge's "Kubla Khan," ll. 12–16, the deep romantic chasm now a horrific abyss (see notes **204.2** and **339.8**).

285.2 [283]   *If you only kept quiet, Claus, no one'd know you were crazy.* A general reference to the story of "Little Claus and Big Claus," by Hans Christian Andersen (1805–75); a fable which tells how Little Claus gets the better of Big Claus by tricking him several times. At one point, when Big Claus kills his grandmother to get a bushel of money, the doctor tells him to stop babbling on, but thinking him crazy the townspeople let him do what he likes.

285.3 [283]   *the storm country.* A general term for the Great Lakes Basin, particularly the area near Niagara on the Lake. Lowry apparently heard the sentence "the lightning is peeling the poles... and biting the wires" while living in Ontario in 1944; the references are repeated several times in *October Ferry.*

285.4 [283]   *Mr Quattras.* In Lowry's short story, "Elephant and Colosseum," pp. 144–45, a Mr. Quattras is a quartermaster who saves a fat Japanese woman; here, he is rescued by the Consul who, ironically, will be unable to save himself.

285.5 [283]   *Codrington.* A town on the eastern shore of Barbados in the Lesser Antilles.

285.6 [284]   *portents of doom, of the heart failing.* Lowry seems to have in mind not only the strange happenings of the dark night before the murder of Duncan (*Macbeth,* II.iv.1–19), but also De Quincey's "the retiring of the human heart" in the "deep syncope of earthly passion," in his essay on the knocking on the gate in *Macbeth* (see note **140.1**).

286.1 [284]   *C'était pendant l'horreur d'une profonde nuit.* Fr. "It was during the horror of a dark night." From Racine's *Athalie,* II.v (l. 490). *Athalie* (1691), Racine's last drama, is based upon the story of Athaliah and Joash in II Kings 11 and II Chronicles 22–23 and tells how the impious Athalie, queen of Judah and destroyer of the seed of the House of David, is troubled by a bad dream (both points pertinent to the line quoted by the Consul), which leads her to profane the temple by her presence. There she recognizes in Joas the youth who in her dream had theatened her life and realizes that he has somehow escaped her slaughter. Despite her endeavours, Joas is acclaimed king, and Athalie is hauled off to her death.

286.2 [284]   *Jull.* The "towering obelisk" is a monument to the Jull family in St. Jude's cemetery, Oakville. The monument itself is of white marble or high-quality stone and rises in a slim four-sided tapering column to a height of some forty feet. The earliest name recorded on it is that of Ellen Hagaman Jull who died 3 April 1878, aged five; her parents, Bennett Jull and Mary Hagaman are also listed there, as well as a number of their descendants. The word JULL in block capitals is inscribed on one face of the lower part of the monument.

286.3 [284]   *Mais tout dort, et l'armée, et les vents, et Neptune.* Fr. "But everything sleeps, the army, and the winds, and Neptune." From the opening scene of Racine's *Iphigénie* (1674), a play based on that of Euripides. The silence of the sea and winds is ominous for the Greek army gathered at Aulis preparing to go to Troy, since the oracle has demanded as the price of favourable winds the sacrifice of Iphigénie, daughter of Agamemnon. Torn between love for his daughter and obedience to the gods, Agamemnon finally gives in to Calchas and Ulysses and leads his daughter to the altar, where she believes she is to be given in marriage to Achilles. Although Iphigénie is prepared to accept her fate (and in Euripides's version does so), Racine depicts the outbreak of a struggle within the Greek camp, culminating in the alternative sacrifice of Ériphile (a character invented by Racine), also obscurely named Iphigénie. Again, the theme of sacrificed children emerges.

286.4 [284]   *Oakville.* An affluent suburb of Toronto, on the shores of Lake Ontario between Toronto and Hamilton, and associated in the Consul's mind (because of the similarity of spelling rather than sound) with his personal hell of Oaxaca. Lowry spent some months at Oakville in 1944 at the home of his friend Gerald Noxon after his shack at Dollarton had been burned, and while he was there, he completed the final manuscript of *Under the Volcano* (Day, pp. 301-3).

286.5 [284]   *I ain't telling you the word of a lie.* The grave-digger's words about the vault being dug up immediately remind the Consul of the corpse transported by express (see note **48.1**).

286.6 [284]   *a natural waterfall. . . . cascada.* The "natural" waterfall is based upon the artificial one (the flow-over from an aqueduct) that previously existed in Chapultepec Park, Cuernavaca (de Davila, p. 77), but which is now no more. The description may have been suggested in part by the "cascada bellisima de San Antón," the most beautiful waterfall of San Antón, a mile or so west of Cuernavaca.

287.1 [285]   *in hacienda days.* Since the colonial period, and up to the Revolution of 1910-20, life in rural Mexico had been dominated by the hacienda system, under which most of the best land had passed into the hands of a few wealthy families in the form of haciendas, or huge estates. Most of the arable land in Morelos was divided into thirty properties belonging to eighteen families, the greed for more land increasingly leading to the disappearance of villages and small holdings (pleasant days for the few, but at the expense of the many).

Morelos was the centre of sugar cultivation. Sugar cane was first planted in 1531, the first mill was operative in 1535, and production reached a high in 1910 (52 million kilograms), before a world glut brought lower prices and discontent to Morelos. The plantations functioned virtually as company towns with their own medical and social services, company stores, and police forces, and the lot of the peasants working for their absentee landlords was little short of slavery. The sugar mills and the plantations were obvious targets for the Zapatistas to attack, since they represented Porfirismo at its worst, even though the burning of plantations and the destruction of machinery caused greater hardship to the peasants who worked the land than to the landlords, most of whom discreetly disappeared for a few years before returning to a system that was to remain little different in substance until Cárdenas began to institute his land reforms (see note **111.4**).

287.2 [285]   *Originally settled by a scattering of those fierce forebears of Cervantes.* About 1116, a group of Toltec Indians escaping the destruction of Tula fled south and occupied the northern part of Morelos, from the volcanoes to Tepotzlán and Oaxtepec; they were immediately followed by a tribe of Chichimecas, a fierce and warlike people, other branches of whom set up the independent republics of Tlaxcala (see note **297.1**). The two groups were quickly integrated (Aguirre, p. 73; Díez, p. 47).

287.3 [285] *the traitorous Tlaxcalans.* Even today the Tlaxcalans are sometimes considered by other Mexicans as "traitors" because in 1519 they sided with Cortés and the conquistadors to bring about the destruction of Tenochtitlán and Aztec civilization (see note **33.1**). As Lowry noted, "LJC," p. 82:

> the whole Tlaxcala business *does* have an underlying deep seriousness. Tlaxcala, of course, just like Parián, is death: but the Tlaxcalans were Mexico's traitors—here the Consul is giving way to the forces within him that are betraying himself, that indeed have now finally betrayed him.

287.4 [285] *the nominal capital of the state.* See note **119.2.b:** insofar as Parián assumes some of the attributes of Cuautla, this reference is probably to the brief period between 11 May 1874 and 1 January 1876 when Cuautla was the seat of government for Morelos (de Davila, p. 141).

287.5 [285] *a weeping pepper tree.* Sp. "El árbol de piemiento que llora," a small ornamental green-pepper tree, growing to between four and six feet (scarcely adequate to support a springboard); the name is derived from the secretion of small drops of water when the peppers are ready for plucking.

287.6 [286] *the Horseshoe Falls in Wales. . . . Or Niagara.* The Horseshoe Falls in Wales are near Llangollen and are so called on early ordinance survey maps, though they are more usually referred to as the Horseshoe Weir. Like the falls in Chapultepec Park, Cuernavaca (see note **286.6**), they are artificial (this may account for the association), having been built by Thomas Telford as part of the system of supply and control for the Llangollen Canal. The weir takes water from the River Dee and eventually returns it into the Shropshire Union Canal. The shape is a perfect horseshoe, but the "falls" are only about three feet high; hence the irony of their juxtaposition against the Horseshoe Falls, Niagara, on the Canadian side of the Niagara River. These falls are much more impressive and larger than the American Falls on the other side of Goat Island and derive their name from the large horseshoe-shaped indentation at their centre, the result of rapid erosion which is progressively deepening the effect. Behind the Consul's casual observation lies the image of "whore's shoes" (see note **144.2**).

287.7 [286]   *the Maid of the Mist.* The small boats (there are usually two in operation) which carry tourists to the foot of the Niagara Falls. The service was begun in 1867, and a new boat with the same name replaced the original one in 1900.

288.1 [286]   *The Cave of the Winds. The Cascada Sagrada.* The Cave of the Winds is a popular tourist spot on Goat Island between the Horseshoe and American Falls. The "Cascada Sagrada" (Sp. "sacred waterfall") seems not to be a place but a variant of "cascara sagrada," a dried bark sometimes used as a laxative. The obscenity, used of the treacherous Boldini in P.C. Wren's *Beau Geste,* anticipates the Consul's later comments on the seat of all decisions, p. 295 [293].

288.2 [286]   *There were, in fact, rainbows.* An ironic detail because the rainbow has been, since the times of Noah, a sign of hope and a token of God's covenant to mankind.

288.3 [286]   *a dance of the seeker and his goal.* The dance, symbolically, is an act which has as its goal the transformation of the seeker of wisdom into that which he is seeking, but the Yeats-like vision of transcendent unity is abruptly shattered by the apparition of Cervantes's cock. Markson suggests, p. 139, that the Consul's vision perhaps owes something to Havelock Ellis: in a description of the effects of mescal (the drug), Ellis writes ("Mescal," pp. 135–36):

> the early visions consisted mostly of a furious succession of coloured arabesques, arising and descending or sliding at every possible angle into the field of view. It would be as difficult to give a description of the whirl of water at the bottom of a waterfall as to describe the chaos of colour and design which marked this period.

288.4 [286]   *Otro mescalito. Un poquito.* Sp. "Another mescal. A small one." The Consul may be asking for mescalito rather than mescal (see note **45.6**), but the diminutive plus the qualification "poquito" maintains his pretence of having had only a few tiny drinks (see note **283.1**).

288.5 [286]   *Muy fuerte, muy terreebly.* In garbled Spanish and English, "very strong, very terrible." Cervantes is telling the Consul about the powers of his fighting cock, but the words apply equally to the sexual impulse and to the powers of mescal.

288.6 [286]   *Was this the face that launched five hundred ships, and betrayed Christ into being in the Western Hemisphere.* The Consul is alluding to Marlowe's *Doctor Faustus,* sc. xiii, where Mephistophilis has evoked for Faustus the vision of Helen of Troy:

> Was this the face that launched a thousand ships
> And burnt the topless towers of Ilium?
> Sweet Helen, make me immortal with a kiss.

He is drawing a parallel between Helen, who betrayed her country by going with Paris to Troy, and Doña Marina, or Malinche, the Indian maiden who became the mistress of Cortés and who betrayed her people by revealing to Cortés Moctezuma's plans for murdering the Spaniards in Cholula before he had even reached Tenochtitlán (see note **17.4**). Malinche's treacherous beauty, the Consul is implying, like Helen's, was responsible for launching the ships of the Spanish conquistadors, and by her act of betrayal to her people she brought into being the worship of Christ in the New World. Cervantes, being Tlaxcalan, is likewise a betrayer of his people.

288.7 [287]   *Half past tree by the cock, the other fellow had said.* The "other fellow" is the proprietor of Las Novedades, p. 258 [256], who had told them the time when they had tried to get a doctor for the dying Indian. The phrase thus looks back to the Consul's past betrayal of humanity and forward to "half past sick by the cock," when he will perform his hideously mismanaged act of intercourse with María in Ch. 12. The overtures of Peter's betrayal of Christ ("before the cock shall crow thrice") are also present (see note **235.7**).

288.8 [287]   *Cuautla.* The second largest town of Morelos, some thirty miles southeast of Cuernavaca (along the road taken by the camión in Ch. 8). Once the old state capital, it contributes to the town of Parián (see note **119.2.b**) and is the setting of one of Lowry's better poems, "Thirty-five Mescals in Cuautla."

289.1 [287]   *to drink or not to drink.* As the Consul is surely aware, Hamlet's famous "To be or not to be" soliloquy (III.i.56–90) is a meditation upon the pros and cons of suicide.

289.2 [287]   *the earth was a ship, lashed by the Horn's tail, doomed never to make her Valparaiso.* The contrast is between the hell of Cape Horn, described, p. 52 [47], as a scorpion's tail, and Valparaiso, the Chilean city whose name means "Valley of Paradise." In *Blue Voyage,* p. 151, Conrad Aiken describes the doomed ship *Silvia Lee,* wrecked on her way round the Horn to Valparaiso.

289.3 [287] *flaming swords.* After the eviction of Adam and Eve from Paradise, God placed at the gates of Eden angels and a flaming sword to prohibit re-entry, as described in Genesis 3:24: "So he drove out the man; and he placed at the east of the garden of Eden Cherubims, and a flaming sword which turned every way, to keep the way of the tree of life." In occult and Cabbalistic thought, the flaming sword is often used to represent "the Law of Mystery which watches at the door of initiation to warn away the profane" (Éliphas Lévi, *Transcendental Magic,* p. 82).

289.4 [287] *the American Express.* The American Express Company has often been called on to handle such matters as the transportation of corpses. The *American Mercury* magazine (July 1956) reported that "Their well-organized shipping department does everything, from witnessing the funeral service, obtaining the undertaker's and doctor's certificates, to seeing that the American Embassy seals the coffin."

289.5 [287] *What is man but a little soul holding up a corpse?* A reference to Marcus Aurelius, *Meditations,* IV.41: "Thou art a little soul bearing up a corpse, as Epictetus said." Epictetus (50?–120 A.D.), for many years a slave, was a Roman stoic philosopher of Greek origin, whose works (including this fragment) are mostly lost; he is cited approvingly by the Roman emperor as one who expresses a common stoic ideal (see notes **112.9** and **306.2**), and the fragment stands for Lowry in conscious opposition to the psalmist's "What is man, that thou art mindful of him?" (see note **35.4**).

289.6 [287] *The soul! Ah, and did she not too have her savage and traitorous Tlaxcalans, her Cortés and her noches tristes... her pale Moctezuma.* The Consul had earlier said to Mr. Quincey, p. 139 [135]: "'Not real Indians... And I didn't mean in the garden; but in *here.*' He tapped his chest again. 'Yes, just the final frontier of consciousness, that's all.'"
(a) *Her savage and traitorous Tlaxcalans.* See note **287.3**: because of the aid they afforded Cortés against Moctezuma, the Tlaxcalans are commonly regarded as the betrayers of Mexico; the Consul is here clearly giving way to the forces within him that are betraying himself ("LJC," p. 82).
(b) *Cortés.* Hernán Cortés, Spanish conquistador (see note **33.1.a**); here evoked as one who batters and destroys the citadel of the soul.
(c) *her noches tristes.* The *Noche Triste,* or Sad Night, was the early morn-

ing of 1 July 1520, when Cortés and his men, trapped in Tenochtitlán, tried to make a break along the Tacuba causeway separating the Aztec city from the mainland. The Aztecs attacked, and the Spaniards fell into confusion as each man tried to save himself. Though Cortés escaped, some 450 Spaniards were killed or drowned, as well as some 4,000 of his Indian allies. According to tradition, once he had reached the mainland Cortés sat exhausted beneath a hugh ahuehuetl tree, the trunk of which is still preserved, and wept.

(d) *her pale Moctezuma.* To forestall sudden attacks by the Aztecs upon his men, Cortés had taken the Aztec emperor hostage, and although Moctezuma was treated with some kindness, he was at least once put in iron fetters (Prescott, IV.iii, p. 347). Prescott notes that Moctezuma's complexion was "somewhat paler than is often found in his dusky, or rather copper-colored race" (III.ix, p. 298), and describes the emperor's exceeding fondness for chocolate, "flavored with vanilla and other spices . . . no less than fifty jars or pitchers being prepared for his own daily consumption!" (IV.i, p. 323). Moctezuma remained a prisoner, but the Aztecs eventually attacked the Spaniards, and when Cortés ordered him to the rooftops to urge the Aztecs to desist, Moctezuma was struck by a stone and died (he may have been murdered by the Spaniards) three days later.

289.7 [288] *the maelstrom.* The maelström is a famous whirlpool in the Arctic Ocean off the coast of Norway, popularly supposed to suck in and destroy all vessels within a long radius and to be the entrance to the abyss beneath. It is described in Erich Pontoppidan's *Natural History of Norway* (see note **178.9**) as a stream whose "violence and roarings exceed those of a cataract" (I.iii, p. 77), and is the destroyer of the *Nautilus* at the end of Jules Verne's *Twenty Thousand Leagues under the Sea.* The Consul probably has in mind Edgar Allan Poe's short story, "A Descent into the Maelström," in which an old man tells of his inadvertent descent into the whirlpool. The maelström is at one point likened to the mighty cataract of Niagara, and at the moment the fisherman is trapped in the vortex, "the roaring noise of the water was completely drowned in a kind of shrill shriek."

290.1 [289] *the Virgin for those who have nobody with. . . . And for mariners on the sea.* One year later, Vigil will recall this visit to the Church of La Soledad, though he will not relish, as the Consul does, the magnificent irony of taking a revolver to a Red Cross ball and a church. The reference to "mariners on the sea" seems to be from Graham Greene's *The Lawless Roads,* pp. 252-53, where Greene describes both the loneliness of heartsick men and the Virgin's role as patroness of all sailors (see note **12.5**).

290.2 [289]   *Nothing is altered... I am still alone.* The Consul's inability to love ("No se puede vivir sin amar") increases his loneliness, despite the apparent answer to his prayers. The case has not been altered.

291.1 [289]   *the knowledge of the Mysteries.* The Mysteries (Orphic, Eleusinian, Bacchic, Osirian, Cabbalistic, and so forth) are the esoteric knowledge and secret rites and rituals known only to adepts and initiates, through which transcendent spiritual enlightenment may be obtained. An excellent statement of them is offered in Ouspensky's *A New Model of the Universe,* p. 26:

> In historical Greece the Mysteries appertained to secret societies of a special kind. These secret societies of priests and initiates arranged every year, or at definite intervals, special festivals, which were accompanied by allegorical theatrical performances. These theatrical performances, to which in particular the name of Mysteries was given, were held in different places—the best known were held at Delphi and Eleusis in Greece and on the island of Philae in Egypt.... Both in Greece and in Egypt the idea was always one and the same, namely, the death of the god and his resurrection. The theory of this ran through all the Mysteries. Its meaning may be interpreted in several ways. Probably the most correct is to think that the Mysteries represented the journey of the soul, the birth of the soul in matter, its death and resurrection, that is, its return into the former life.

Ouspensky also notes, p. 13, that "The idea of hidden knowledge and the possibility of finding it after a long and arduous search is the content of the legend of the Holy Grail"; the Consul's long and arduous search (particularly in Ch. 5) seems rather to have degenerated into a Rabelasian quest for the holy bottle.

291.2 [289]   *Destroy the world.* In Joseph Conrad's *Heart of Darkness* (1902), Kurtz, his mind subject to the powers of evil, nevertheless is entrusted by the International Society for the Suppression of Savage Customs with the making of a report. He begins with an eloquent, beautiful piece of writing, burning noble words, then, like a flash of lightning in the serene sky: "Exterminate all the brutes." The Consul's final cry, like that of Kurtz, expresses his wish not to be saved from the abominations he really desires.

291.3 [289]   *the History of Tlaxcala, in ten volumes.* This set does not exist. Its closest parallel before 1938 is Diego Muños Camargo's *Historia de Tlascala.* Camargo was a well-born and educated Tlascalan of the mid-sixteenth century, baptized and instructed in the Christian faith, who wrote in Castilian Spanish a remarkable history of his nation, its chief deficiency being an overzealous attempt to prove how readily the Tlascalans were converted to Christianity (the basis of similar errors in the travel folder later in the chapter). The *History* is not, however, in ten volumes. Lowry's early drafts refer at this point to "The *History of Oaxaca* in 10 volumes" (UBC 7-11, p. 4). Again, there is no likely candidate: the only real possibility is the *Historia de Oaxaca,* by Prbo. José Antonio Gay, first published in four volumes in 1882, dealing with the story of Oaxaca from its prehistory up to the revolution of 1814.

291.4 [289] *I call my wife my mother.* The Spanish term "Mamacita," "little mother," is a common endearment from a husband to his wife. Cervantes's somewhat rueful admission hints obliquely at the Oedipal theme.

291.5 [290] *this plan to climb Popo.* Since Popocatepetl has for the Consul an intensely personal private symbolism, Hugh's frivolous ambition to climb the mountain (especially with Yvonne) has for Geoffrey something of the sense of a deliberate trampling over sacred mysteries. In his *Autohagiography,* vol.2, p. 32, Aleister Crowley gives an account of his chamois-like ascent of the volcano.

292.1 [290] *Amecameca.... Tlamancas.... the Hotel Fausto.* Areas close to the volcanoes:
(a) *Amecameca.* In the state of Mexico, directly at the foot of Ixtaccihuatl but also close to Popocatepetl; the largest town in the immediate vicinity of the volcanoes and to that extent a model for Parián. It was once an Aztec holy city, and in his drafts (UBC 7-11, p. 15) Lowry toyed with the idea of spelling it "Ameccamecca."
(b) *Tlamancas.* More usually, Tlamacas; three miles from the Paseo de Cortés, between the two volcanoes; the route taken by Cortés from Cholula to the Valley of Mexico and the traditional starting place for expeditions (including Aleister Crowley's) that set off to climb Popocatepetl.
(c) *the Hotel Fausto.* A small lodge (described in Crowley's *Autohagiography,* Pt. 2, p. 32, as "the sulphur ranch") once ot be found near Tlamacas; used by Lowry with an awareness of the Faustian theme of aspiration, and with the sense of the irony of L. *faustus,* "lucky."

292.2 [290] *the supper at Emmaus.* In Luke 24:13-53, after the Crucifixion, two of the disciples on their way to the village of Emmaus are joined by a third who walks beside them and whom they fail to recognize. The stranger berates them for lack of faith and at supper in Emmaus reveals himself as the risen Saviour. The Consul's reference is somewhat inappropriate, since he does not want to be found out.

292.3 [290] *the bill of fare.* Cervantes's menu is a veritable hot-pot of howlers and obscenities, relished by the Consul and Hugh though most of the "incredible chrestomathy" (UBC 11–13, p. 6) escapes Yvonne:

(a) *Cauliflowers or pootootsies.* Cauliflowers (with perhaps a pun on "caul") and potatoes (Sp. *papizzas*), though Lowry toyed in the manuscripts with "poot tootsies... pig's feet" (UBC 7–11, p. 7).

(b) *extramapee syrup.* Uncertain. "Maple Syrup" makes little sense, and a more likely suggestion is Ham and Pea soup, extra thick. There may be a pun on Sp. *extremado,* a term applied to animals in heat.

(c) *Onans in garlic soup on egg.* Sp. "Sopa de ajo con huevo"; a dish made from garlic, paprika, and bread fried in olive oil, water added, and beaten eggs stirred in (here, with onions added). Onan in Genesis 38:9, unenthusiastic about his Levirate marriage, spilled his seed upon the ground.

(d) *Pep with milk.* Sp. "Chile con leche" (Fr. "poivrons au lait"), a dish made from peppers and milk. The pun on "lechery," p. 60 [55], remains unexploited in English but "el chile" is a common metaphor in Mexican Spanish for "el miembro viril."

(e) *Filete de Huachinango rebozado tartar con German friends.* Fillet of Red Snapper, dipped in flour and seasoning (before frying), with Tartar sauce and fried clams. The final pun (German friends = "almejas fritas," "fried clams"; hence, "alemanes fritos") contains ominous suggestions of the German officers burned alive in the furnaces of the *Samaritan,* p. 38 [32]. The pun may be upon Sp. *almendras,* "almonds," rather than *almejas,* "clams," but it is equally horrific either way.

(f) *Dr Moise von Schmidthaus's special soup.* Yvonne would not pronounce the words with such gusto if she knew the sanatario in which the doctor's soup had been prepared. One is reminded of the German Santa Claus, surveying his mangled sleigh: "Nein, nein, Donner and Blitzen, I said 'land on das Schmidthaus!'" One of Lowry's German teachers in Bonn was a Karlheinz Schmidhus (*SL,* p. 236).

(g) *a pepped petroot.* The underlying Spanish form is lost completely. It sounds like beetroot, spiced and peppered ("remolacha enchilada"), but the translation does not work. The Spanish edition of *UTV* offers "pitobel enchilado," apparently a kind of spiced gherkin, but the real reason for the dish is the Consul's rueful reflection, p. 353 [352], upon his pickled peter.

(h) *German friends. . . . tartar. . . . Tlaxcala.* Cervantes mishears "tartar" as "Tlaxcala," thereby linking burned Germans, red Tartars, and traitorous Tlaxcalans.

(i) *Stepped on eggs.* In Spanish, "huevos pisados," a deviation from "huevos pasados por agua," "soft-boiled eggs"; the pun arising from the expression "andar pisando huevos," "to walk gingerly," that is, on eggs (Jakobsen, p. 96).

(j) *Muy sabrosos.* Sp. "very tasty."

(k) *Divorced eggs.* Probably Lowry's invention: the French and Spanish editions of *UTV* simply translate the pun, without clarifying it, while Jakobsen suggests, p. 96, "huevos diversos." Perhaps a dish in which whites and yolks are separated or else "huevos revueltos," "scrambled eggs" (as in the common expression of human relationships, "juntos pero non revueltos," "together but not scrambled").

(l) *For fish, sliced of filet with peas.* A filet of fish with peas. In English and Spanish, innocent of innuendo, but the French translation plays with "poisson" and "pois."

(m) *Vol-au-vent à la reine: Somersaults for the queen.* Vol-au-vent ("a flight in the wind"; hence "somersaults") is a light puff-pastry shell filled with morsels of game, fish, or poultry in a white sauce; "à la reine" means filled with chicken.

(n) *poxy eggs.* Poached eggs, "huevos escalfados," occasionally semi-anglicized as "huevos poches."

(o) *veal liver tavernman.* "Foie de veau à l'aubergine purée," or veal pate with eggplant purée. The confusion arises because of the similarity of *aubergine,* "eggplant," and *aubergiste,* "tavernkeeper."

(p) *Pimesan chike chup.* Uncertain, perhaps diced chicken with Parmesan cheese or simply chicken soup with cheese.

(q) *spectral chicken of the house.* Special chicken of the house.

(r) *Youn' pigeon.* Sp. *pichoncito,* a plump young pigeon (the Spanish *joven,* "young," can be applied to a variety of fresh foods).

(s) *Red snappers with a fried tartar.* A repeat order of "Filete de Hauchinango rebozada tartar," but with the tartar (like the German friends) fried instead of the fish. The eighteenth-century expression, "to catch a tartar" (that is, to contract V.D.) turns the edible into the unspeakable.

(t) *served in its own ectoplasm.* Ectoplasm is the fluid secreted from the ectoderm or outer layer of cells in an animal embryo or an egg in its early stages, but the word also means, in spiritualism, the vaporous luminous substance supposedly emanating from the medium's body during a trance (hence the "apparition" of the "spectral chicken," p. 296 [240]).

(u)   *sea-sleeves in his ink.* Sp. "calamares en su tinta" or (more commonly in Mexico) "pulpos en su tinta," pieces of squid sautéed in olive oil, wine, spices, and the fluid from the ink-sac.

(v)   *tunny-fish.* Tuna, in Spanish *atún* (tuna being a variety of *nopáli* cactus).

(w)   *an exquisite mole.* Sp. "exquisito mole." The only thing in common with the animal is the colour: *mole* (two syllables) is a rich, black, chocolate-based sauce with spices, nuts, and chiles, which is served on top of tacos, enchiladas, and other dishes. Opinions on it vary from "Mexico's finest contribution to international cuisine" (Fodor, p. 288), to the Consul's more dubious opinion, voiced in an early draft (UBC 7-11, p. 9): "a black glutinous substance hotter than curry, delicious, but setting up a draft in the system."

(x)   *fashion melon.* Melon à la mode, that is, cantaloupe melons, chilled and served with ice-cream.

(y)   *Fig mermelade.* Sp. "mermalada de higo," but mermelada means "jam" as well as "marmalade," and hence is innocent of the over-ripe Lawrentian connotations.

(z)   *Brambleberry con crappe Gran Duc.* Pancakes ("crêpes"), Grand Duke style. Here, served with blackberry syrup or jelly.

(aa)   *omele he sourpusse.* Presumably "omelette surprise": eggs first hard-boiled, then mixed with butter, cream sauce, herbs and minced ham, dipped into breadcrumbs, and cooked in hot fat.

(bb)   *gin fish.* A gin fizz, a long, cool, effervescent drink made of gin, lemon juice, a little sugar, ice, and soda water.

(cc)   *silver fish.* Identified by Pagnoulle, p. 139, as "Poisson d'argent," a variety of apéritif.

(dd)   *Sparkenwein.* Sparkling wine.

(ee)   *Madre. . . . Badre.* More correctly, *vadre,* a small sea-fish of the Gulf of Mexico (not likely to be found in the river at Yautepec, the town halfway between Cuernavaca and Cuautla). The authority for this (a Vera Cruz waiter) remains unsubstantiated. Another possibility is *bagre,* a fresh-water fish.

(ff)   *the fish that dies.* Uncertain, perhaps a brand of gin (listed in *Harper's Trade Directory*) named "Green-Fish Dry." The "fish that dies" is in one sense Christ; in another, the Consul.

293.1 [291]   *Cerveca, sí, Moctezuma? Dos Equis? Carta Blanca?* There is not a specific brand of beer called "Moctezuma," but the Moctezuma breweries of Orizaba produce the dark beer called Dos Equis (XX). Carta

Blanca, the most widely drunk beer in Mexico, is a light clear beer brewed by the Cervecería Cuauhtémoc in Monterrey.

293.2 [291] *The Consul at first had ordered only shrimps and a hamburger sandwich.* Behind the innocuous choice lay, in the manuscripts, the Consul's conscious intent to underline his cuckoldom (UBC 7-11, p. 8): "The Consul ordered some camarones [see p. 220] and a 'hambuggeress' sandwich, 'that ought to be complicated enough for me,' he said."

293.3 [292] *Granada.* Granada, the romantic city of orange groves and summer nights in Andalusia, shapes itself in the Consul's mind to the city of his dreams, the city where he and Yvonne had plighted their troth. He imagines arriving from Algeciras (the southern seaport near Gibraltar), at the station (in the southwest of the town), and then moving in his mind onwards and upwards to the centre of the town, the Alhambra, and the hills beyond. The bull-ring still exists in the southwest of the city, near the Paseo de Triunfo and between the station and the Moorish cemetery, but the Hollywood Bar and British Consulate are no longer identifiable (though the former is described by Clarissa Lorenz in her article, "Call it Misadventure"). There is not in Granada a Convento de los Angeles as such, but the Ermita de San Sebastián (near the Alhambra) has a capillary dedicated to Nuestra Señora de los Angeles. The Washington Irving Hotel is a quality hotel near the Moorish palace on the Paseo de la Alhambra; it is also near the Pensión Carmona (the original of the Pensión America here), and the Pensión Mexico, p. 45 [40], where Lowry stayed when he was in Granada in 1933 (Day, p. 175). The Alhambra Palace (see note **45.3**) rises above and dominates the town, and the Generalife Gardens are beyond and above it. The Moorish tomb is a mystery: Lowry probably means the "Silla del Moro," or Seat of the Moor — some shapeless ruins on the summit of the hill behind the Generalife, where the last Moorish king Boabdil sat and gazed mournfully upon his city during an insurrection.

293.4 [292] *The Washington Irving Hotel.* The hotel is named for the American writer, Washington Irving (1783-1839), who was attached to the American legation in Spain in 1826 and over the next three years spent much time in Granada. He is best known for his *Rip van Winkle* and *Legend of Sleepy Hollow* (1820), and his *Life of George Washington* (1855-59), but he also wrote *A Chronicle of the Conquest of Granada* (1829) and *Tales of the Alhambra* (1832).

294.1 [292] *how many bottles since then.*
(a) *aguardiente.* a general name for brandies and rums of various kinds,

distilled from cane sugar (see note **339.1**).

(b) *anís.* a clear liquor distilled from alcohol and essence of aniseed (see note **10.1**).

(c) *jerez.* sherry (from Jerez, or Xeres, in Andalusia).

(d) *Highland Queen.* A brand of Scotch Whisky (Macdonald & Muir, Leith).

(e) *Oporto.* Port (from Oporto, in Portugal).

(f) *tinto.* Sp. "red wine."

(g) *blanco.* Sp. "white wine."

(h) *Pernod.* An apéritif with a taste like anisette.

(i) *Oxygénée.* Hydrogen peroxide (the Consul is recalling Jacques's words, p. 219 [216]).

(j) *absinthe.* A green bitter liquor, formerly (and still in Spain) flavoured with wormwood.

(k) *Calvados.* An apple brandy (from Calvados, Normandy).

(l) *bitter.* Bitter beer; a dry, heavily hopped draft brew.

(m) *Dubonnet.* A fortified red wine; a popular apéritif.

(n) *Falstaff.* Presumably a variety of sack, the dry white Spanish wine which was the favourite drink of Shakespeare's Sir John Falstaff.

(o) *Rye.* North American whiskey, distilled from rye rather than barley.

(p) *Johnny Walker.* The most celebrated of all Scotch whiskies (see note **95.6**).

(q) *Vieux whisky, blanc Canadien.* Aged, light Canadian whisky. No special brand name appears to be indicated.

(r) *apéritifs.* Drinks (such as martinis) to stimulate the appetite, cocktails.

(s) *digestifs.* Drinks, such as liqueurs and cordials, taken as an aid to digestion.

(t) *demis.* Half drinks, or half-shots.

(u) *dobles.* Sp. "Doubles"; that is, two measures of liquor in the one glass.

(v) *noch ein Herr Obers.* Ger. "one more, waiter."

(w) *et glas Araks.* Nor. "One glass of Arak"; Arak, or arrack, is a potent liquor derived from the juice of the coconut palm or from a fermented mash of rice and molasses.

(x) *tusen taks.* Nor. "A thousand thanks."

(y) *tequila.* Distilled juice of the cactus *agave tequiliana* (see note **219.3**).

(z) *gourds of beautiful mescal.* Mescal, the distilled juice of the maguey cactus (see note **219.3**), is frequently stored in gourds ("mescal en olla").

294.2 [292]   *dead Scotchmen on the Atlantic highlands.* Empty bottles of whisky, flung overboard and come to rest on the Atlantic Ridge, a massive submarine range of volcanic origin running the length of the mid-Atlantic, described by Donnelly, p. 49, as "the backbone of the ancient continent which once accompanied the whole of the Atlantic Ocean, and from whose washings Europe and America were constructed." Lowry uses the word "highlands" to emphasize the connection with Scotland.

295.1 [293] *there was an Indian.* Over the next four pages, fragments of the discussion between Yvonne and Hugh about the man by the roadside and the thief will continue to enter the Consul's consciousness, but in no logical order. The confusion of phrases reflects the uncontrollable mystery of time within the Consul's mind rather than any repetition of the actual words (it is possible to piece the conversation together in more or less sequential order by reading backwards and forwards over the pages).

295.2 [293] *Cave of the Winds, seat of all great decisions.* The pun, anticipated on p. 288 [286], has come to pass. There may also be an oblique reference to the Island of Aeolus, in Bk. 10 of Homer's *Odyssey,* where the winds were kept. Just as Joyce used this episode in *Ulysses,* Ch. 7, to show Bloom and Stephen in close proximity but not touching, so too may Lowry be using the allusion to hint at how close to yet how far from Yvonne the Consul is.

295.3 [293] *little Cythère of childhood.* Cythera is an island, some eight miles from Cape Malea, the southernmost promontory of Greece. It is known for its two great caves, and as the island of Venus it was a centre for the rites of Love. Lowry's use of the Fr. Cythère rather than the more usual Cythera links his Cave of the Winds to Baudelaire's poem, "Un Voyage a Cythère": Baudelaire imagines his soul, "Comme un ange enivré d'un soleil radieux" voyaging to Cythère, only to find an island "triste et noire," a desert with ferocious birds and ugly beasts, a tomb of sins and infamous cults. The poem concludes:

> Dans ton île, ô Venus! je n'ai trouvé debout
> Qu'un gibet symbolique où pendait mon image...
> -Ah! Seigneur! donnez-moi la force et le courage
> De contempler mon coeur et mon corps sans dégoût!

("In your isle, O Venus, I have found upright / only a symbolic gibbet where my image hangs. / Ah, Lord! give me the strength and the courage / to contemplate my heart and my body without disgust.")

The reference to childhood perhaps suggests that the Consul is contemplating the fact that in his youth he retreated to the toilet for his own private rituals in the worship of Venus.

295.4 [294] *A stone*. Literally, to scrape himself with (though Cervantes relents and brings the travel folder instead). The word, however, has a number of connotations which are pertinent to the novel:
(a) *the Philosopher's Stone*. The crude physical reality of the Consul's situation makes a total mockery of his spiritual and alchemical aspirations.
(b) *a tomb*. The toilet resembles a tomb, and hence is a reminder of the sepulchre in which the body of Christ was laid and the stone that was rolled across its door.
(c) *Sisyphus*. See note **227.3**: Sisyphus was condemned to roll forever a stone to the top of a hill, on reaching which it would roll back down again.
(d) *the Cyclops*. In the *Odyssey,* Bk. 9, Odysseus escapes from the cavern of the one-eyed Cyclops (Cervantes has an eye-patch), but as he shouts defiance, he is nearly destroyed by a huge stone the giant heaves at his departing ship.
(e) *Aztec sacrifice*. The cold grey stone hints at the irrevocable fate of the victims of Huitzilopotchli, stretched out on sacrificial altars, hearts for the gods of Mexico.
(f) *the Abyss*. The stone which served Jacob for a pillow (Genesis 28:18), which, refused by the builders of the temple (Psalm 118:22), was inscribed with the divine name and cast into the abyss to hold down the waters of the deep (A. E. Waite, *The Holy Kabbalah,* V.v, pp. 228–29).
(g) *Saturn*. Éliphas Lévi, in his *Transcendental Magic,* pp. 80–81, notes the occult implications of Saturn being given a stone instead of his children to devour; for the Consul, when Saturn is in Capricorn, life reaches bottom, p. 204 [200].
All these implications seem to be summed up in a manuscript variant (UBC 10–18, p. 11) finally deleted: the Consul reflects that there can be no peace "but must pay full toll to hell. For even were the stone of my own guilt rolled away there would still remain the guilt of the human race."

296.1 [294] *Dangerous Clam Magoo*. The Consul alludes to Robert Service's poem, "The Shooting of Dan McGrew," published in *The Spell of the Yukon and Other Verses* (1907). Dan dies, "pumped full of lead" in a saloon battle involving a struggle between two men over a worthless woman.

296.2 [294] *our poor spoiling brains and eggs at home*. Although this is a fair description of the Consul's present state of mind, the reference is to the meal that Concepta was to have prepared for them that night.

296.3 [294] *the apparition . . . of the spectral chicken*. The pun on spiritualism (emanating from the reference to ectoplasm, p. 293 [291]), is intentional.

296.4 [294] *Franklin Island.* An isolated and desolate island in the Ross Sea, Antarctica. It is some sixty miles north of Ross Island and was discovered in 1841 by Sir James Ross. There is also a small island of that name in Georgian Bay, in southeastern Ontario, Canada.

296.5 [294] *excusado.* In Mexico, the usual euphemism for the toilet.

296.6 [294] *Svidrigailov.* A character in Dostoievsky's *Crime and Punishment* (1866), the famous novel of guilt and expiation, in which Raskolnikov, having murdered a repellent old woman, finds himself psychologically incapable of supporting the burden of his guilt. He confesses, first to Sonia, then to the authorities, but accepts his seven-year exile to Siberia with joy, for it will mark a new beginning. Svidrigailov, who earlier had tried to seduce Rasknolnikov's sister Dunya, visits Raskolnikov in Part 4 of the novel, to try to get Raskolnikov to put in a good word for him with Dunya, whom he now wishes to marry. Svidrigailov talks of his past life in the country, and in reply to Raskolnikov's "I do not believe in a future life," comments (Pt. 4, Ch. 1):

> And what . . . if there were only spiders there, or something of the sort . . . . We're always thinking of eternity as an idea that cannot be understood, something immense. But why must it be? What if, instead of all this, you suddenly find just a little room there, something like a village bath-house, grimy, and spiders in every corner, and that's all eternity is. Sometimes, you know, I can't help feeling that that's probably what it is.

The passage was originally (UBC 7–6, p. 32) part of the Consul's horrific vision of insects on his own bathroom floor, at the end of Ch. 5, but the immediate reference to "Pulquería" (Raskolnikov's mother) is now made pertinent (see note **113.3**).

296.7 [295] *¡VISITE VD. TLAXCALA! Sus Monumentos, Sitios Históricos y De Bellezas Naturales. Lugar De Descanso, El Mejor Clima. El Aire Más Puro. El Cielo Más Azul.* Sp. "Visit Tlaxcala! Its Monuments, Historical Sites and Natural Beauties. Place of Tranquillity, The Best Climate. The Purest Air. The Bluest Sky." This, and the other Tlaxcaltecan passages, were taken almost verbatim from a travel folder which, according to Margerie Lowry, Malcolm had with him in Dollarton (Pottinger, p. 169). The folder is not to be found among Lowry's papers in the UBC Special Collections, nor in the records of the Tlaxcala Tourist Office, but (to judge by manuscript variants) changes from the original can have been only minimal, mainly deletions. Lowry's claim ("LJC," p. 82) that the folder described

Tlaxcala as a centre of black magic should probably be taken with a grain of salt, however. The idea of incorporating a tourist guide in this way might have been suggested by Melville's *Redburn:* the young hero arrives in Liverpool and uses an antiquated guide book to find his way around; Melville cites great chunks of it, but tongue in cheek reflects, Ch. 30:

> I will *not* quote thee, old Morocco, before the cold face of the marble-hearted world; for your antiquities would only be skipped and dishonoured by shallowminded readers; and for me, I should be charged with swelling-out my value by plagiarizing from a guidebook — the most vulgar and ignominious of thefts!

297.1 [295] *¡TLAXCALA! SEDE DE LA HISTORIA DE LA CONQUISTA.* The Tlaxcalans were a people of Chichimec origin, closely related linguistically to the Mexica or Azteca tribe, who forcibly established the independent state of Tlaxcala in the thirteenth century. They were never dominated by the Aztecs, but were constantly at war with their neighbours, since their strategic geographic position blocked Aztec control of the gulf coast and since their fiercely defended independence gave hope to other tribes who resented Aztec rule (facts that were to be of considerable importance to Cortés).

Although romantic historians have likened Tlaxcala to Republican Rome, in contrast with Imperial Tenochtitlán, the comparison is not altogether just. The Republic consisted of the four separate states or *señoríos* of Tepictipac, Ocotelolco, Tizatlán, and Quiahuiztlán, "bound together by a sort of federal compact" (Prescott, III.ii, p. 221), and by a common defensive policy. Each señorío was ruled by a senator, whose powers were both hereditary and absolute, from among whom, in times of war, a commander was chosen.

In 1519, when Cortés decided to approach Tenochtitlán by way of Tlaxcala, the senators disagreed about what action to take. Maxixcatzín, lord of Ocotelolco, wanted to comply with the conquerors' wishes, but Xicotencatl, lord of Tizatlán, urged resistance. Fighting began on 31 August 1519 and lasted for three weeks, at the end of which time the Tlaxcalans, having suffered great losses, sued for peace, and joined forces with the Spaniards in common cause against the Aztecs.

297.2 [295] *GEOGRAPHIC SITUATION.... CLIMATE.... HYDROGRAPHY.* Tlaxcala, to the east of Mexico and north of Puebla States, is the smallest state in the Mexican federation. The high surrounding mountains on every side, a natural defensive barrier against the Aztecs, mark off the state's natural boundaries. The valley is drained by the Rio Zahuapan, flowing northeast to southwest through the city of Tlaxcala and eventually linking up with (not "from") the Río Atoyac to form part of Mexico's most extensive waterway. The Zahuapan supplies very little power to very few factories (in the dry season it is little more than a dirty trickle, and Tlaxcaltecan industry, until very recently, was conspicuously absent). The laguna de Acuitlapilco, virtually bereft of web-footed fowl, is one of many such lagoons in the state; it does not drain directly into the Zahuapan system. Tlaxcala is primarily an agricultural area (the name meaning "land of bread"), its temperate climate favouring wheat, sheep, and cattle as well as the ever-present maguey. The standard of living among the "inhibitants" (the error is intentional) is, nevertheless, almost the lowest in Mexico.

298.1 [297] *CITY OF TLAXCALA*. Tlaxcala, capital city of the state, is a pleasant and attractive town of some twenty-five thousand inhabitants, which makes some effort to keep alive the sense of its historical importance. The comparison with Granada was made by Cortés in his second letter to Charles V, trying to impress his royal majesty with the importance of the new conquest by "affirming, that it was larger, stronger, and more populous than the Moorish capital, at the time of the conquest, and quite as well built" (Prescott, III.v, p. 253). The "Hotel for tourists" is the Hotel Tlaxcala (on the Calle Morelos, just off the zócalo), mentioned on p. 304 [302]. The "beautiful Central Park" is the zócalo, now called the Plaza de la Constitución, an attractive park, bounded by "four lateral avenues," with fresno trees (ashes), fountains, and "seats all over"; the park was previously named for Francisco I. Madero (1873–1913), the president who replaced Díaz in 1910, but whose liberal reforms failed to unite the country behind him (he was deposed and murdered by Victoriano Huerta in 1913– see note **49.3**). There is a causeway across the Zahuapan River at the point where the river divides to form an island, but any trace of a wood or senadores (from Sp. *sentar,* "to seat") has long gone, and thanks to increased air pollution, only on clear days can the "suggestive sceneries" of the volcanoes be admired.

299.1 [298] *SAN FRANCISCO CONVENT*. The Church of San Francisco and the Convent of the same name are the oldest upon the American mainland, dating from 1521. Despite their present air of neglect and decay they capture, as no others can, the scene of the early years of the conquest:
(a) *the first Apostolical See*. The first bishopric in Mexico was created in 1519 for Cozumel and Yucatán, but its location was later changed to Tlaxcala. The Dominican Julián Garcés, appointed 1526, arrived in

Tlaxcala in 1527 to assume his duties, and in that latter year another bishopric was created for the city of Mexico. The bishopric of Tlaxcala was later translated to Puebla.

(b) *were baptized the four Senators of the Tlaxcaltecan Republic.* The baptismal font is still to be found in the small side chapel to the right of the church (the original chapel), with the following inscription carved in stone above it:

> En esta fuente recibieron la fe catolica los cuatros senadores de la antigua república de Tlaxcala. El acto religioso huve lugar el ano de 1520, siendo ministro Dn. Juan Díaz Capellan del ejercito conquistador y padrinos el capitan Dn. Hernando Cortés y sus distinguidos officials Dn. Pedro de Alvarado, Dn. Andres de Tapia, Dn. Gonzalo de Sandoval y Dn. Cristobal de Olio. A Maxixcatzín se le dio el nombre de Lorenso, a Xicohtencatl de Vincente, a Tlahuexolotzín el de Gonzálo y a Zitlapopocatl el de Bartolmé. Asi lo refieren las historias escritas por Camargo, Torquemada y Betancourt.

> ("In this font the four Senators of the ancient Republic of Tlaxcala first received the Catholic faith. The religious ceremony took place in the year 1520, the minister being Don Juan Díaz, chaplain of the conquistador army, and godfathers Captain Don Hernando Cortés and his distinguished officers Don Pedro de Alvarado, Don Andres de Tapia, Don Gonzalo de Sandoval and Don Cristobal de Olio. To Maxixcatzín was given the name Lorenso, to Xicohtencatl Vincent, to Tlahuexolotzín that of Gonzalo, and to Zitlapopocatl that of Bartolomé. Thus say the histories written by Camargo, Torquemada and Betancourt.")

That the baptism took place there is little doubt, but the evidence is against its being as early as 1520; the main source of the story is Diego Muños Camargo's *Historia de Tlaxcala,* but as Prescott notes, Camargo was a Christianized Indian, living in the generation after the conquest, who "may very likely have felt as much desire to relieve his nation from the reproach of infidelity" (Prescott, III.v, p. 256).

(c) *a secret passage.* As the repetition indicates, the Consul's attention is caught by these words, with their suggestions of demonic winzes and dramatic escape (see note **351.5**). There is in fact a secret passage running from the church to the hospital of the convent, no longer accessible, but originally built to allow the priests and nuns to escape in times of sudden danger.

(d) *a majestic tower... the only one through America.* The brochure presumably means the only tower in the Americas which is separated (by some forty yards) from its church.

(e) *churrigueresque.* After the style of José Churriguera (1650–1723), native of Salamanca, Spain, whose name is associated with the gilded, ornate, and overloaded style ("muy complicado") so characteristic of many Mexican churches. Lowry described his own novel as churrigueresque ("LJC," p. 61).

(f) *the most celebrated artists.* The Church of San Francisco is full of paintings, large and small, many of which are suffering from irreversible deterioration. The names mentioned here are among those most celebrated in Mexican religious art:

(i) *Cabrera.* Miguel Cabrera (1695–1768), native of Oaxaca; one of the best known of Mexico's painters and sculptors, renowned for both the quantity and quality of his output. He is particularly celebrated for his depictions of the Virgin of Guadalupe, one of which is to be found to the left immediately inside the main doors.

(ii) *Echave.* There are three generations of painter by this name, but the likely one is Baltasar Echave Ibia (1580–1660), Mexican-born painter who worked in the baroque style.

(iii) *Juárez.* Luis Juárez, who flourished in the early seventeenth century. A disciple of the elder Echave (father of the above), his work abounds in angels and ecstasies and is remarkable for its striking light effects and colour contrasts. His son José achieved equal renown.

(g) *the famous pulpit.* The pulpit is to be found in the same side chapel as the baptismal font. It is carved from soft stone, and on it a deteriorating inscription can be read: "Aqui tuvo principio el Sto Evangelio en este Nuevo Mundo. Primer púlpito de Nueva España." ("Here for the first time the Holy Gospel was preached in this New World. The first pulpit of New Spain.").

(h) *The ceiling is the only one in the whole Spanish America.* The brochure is trying to point out a unique feature of the Iglesia de San Francisco, its wooden ceiling. Almost every church in Mexico has a Gothic, rib-vaulted ceiling, but this church has an exquisitely beautiful cedar ceiling, with panels and ribbed beams, and patterns of golden stars (not in the least "overloaded").

300.1 [298] *THE CITY PARISH.* The Iglesia San José, the unusual feature of which is its location off the main plaza instead of on the zócalo. The church was originally intended as a private sanctuary, the gift of Charles V of Spain to the town and people of Tlaxcala. The words "consecrated to Virgin Mary" remind the Consul of his own sorrows and his visit last night to La Soledad.

300.2 [299]   *TLAXCALA ROYAL CHAPEL.* The "Capilla real," or "Royal Chapel" was rebuilt to become the Palacio de Justicia, and only the portico, an archway, remains of the original building. The coats of arms displayed are in recognition of Tlaxcala's outstanding contribution to the expansion of New Spain and the Catholic faith. Tlaxcala was the first city in New Spain to be granted its own coat of arms. This was decreed by Charles V in 1535, and in 1563 the city was granted the appelation of "Leale e insinge Ciudad" ("Loyal and distinguished city"), both the coat of arms and the title engraved in the centre of the arch where they may still be seen today (an early draft, UBC 11–14, p. 20, indicates that this information was in the brochure but that Lowry chose to omit it).

300.3 [299]   *the Pilsener Kindl.* In *UTV,* identified simply as a pub in Mexico City which acts as a fascist meeting-place; in *DATG,* p. 99, it is called the "Münchener Kindl," an old German restaurant in the Gante which by 1945 had been changed into a cantina. During the war, many Germans were forced from their businesses and made to leave Mexico City, and, coincidentally, a large number were resettled near Amecameca, right under the volcanoes.

300.4 [299]   *a humming-bird.* Lowry would have read in Lewis Spence (*G of M,* p. 61) of the Aztec belief that the souls of dead warriors were transformed into hummingbirds, to sip forever honey from the flowers of paradise. An early draft (UBC 11–13, p. 15) read: "the humming-bird returned, a minute kingfisher, *nonpasserine autogiro:* no paserán," but the pun was dropped since the Spanish Civil War references (see note **303.3**) are more properly Hugh's.

301.1 [299]   *SANTUARIO OCOTLÁN IN TLAXCALA.* The *Santuario y Colegiata de Ocotlán* is a mile or so east of Tlaxcala, on a hill overlooking the town. It is an attractive church in the churrigueresque ("overloaded") style, decorated with ornate gold and stonework. The vestry, in particular, has many fine pictures, ornate woodwork, and a magnificent carved table. Although the present church was consecrated only in 1854 and dedicated in 1907, the legend it commemorates goes back to 1541. This is the story of Juan Diego and the Virgin of Ocotlán, an account similar to, but predating, the more famous apparition of the Virgin of Guadalupe (see note **204.4**), also to an Indian named Juan Diego. The story of the Virgin of the Burning Pine (the "ocete ardiente") is told in pictures and inscriptions inside the church. One fine day in the spring of 1541 Juan Diego, on his way to get some water for the sick, met the Virgin in a pine forest; she promised him the next time they met to give him some water that would better "samarián" the sick. When Juan Diego next met the Virgin, on the edge of a barranca, he asked for the water, and she created a fountain of pure water from the rocks. Juan Diego's story was examined by the Franciscans, who went to the pinewood that night. There they saw a large pine burning without being consumed and, opening it, found inside a beautiful image of Mary, which was taken to the nearby Capilla de San Lorenzo. The next night, miraculously, the image of the Virgin had mysteriously assumed the place of the saint.

301.2 [299] *The Miztecs.* The Mixtecs inhabited the mountainous sierra of Oaxaca before and during the rise of the Aztec civilization. Following the decline of the Zapotecs, the Mixtecs dominated the Valley of Oaxaca. The height of their civilization was reached in the thirteenth century, manifesting itself not only in the celebrated ruins of Monte Alban and Mitla but also in artistic carvings, codices, historical records, and delicate metalwork. The Mixtecs resisted the Aztecs in the fifteenth century, but they were subdued and forced to pay tribute. Their king Atonaltzín was murdered by his own subjects, who blamed disastrous alliances with the Tlaxcalans as one reason for their defeat. The name Atonalzin is that given by Lowry to Juan Fernando Márquez (Juan Cerillo) in his essay "Garden of Etla," probably as a private allusion to his friend's murder (described in *DATG,* pp. 249ff.).

301.3 [299] *the Toltecs.* A mysterious civilization, of which little is known. Apparently of Nahuatl origin, the Toltecs dominated Central America after the mysterious collapse of Teotihuacán and before the rise of Aztecs. Militaristic and efficient, they created an extensive empire, with its capital at Tula (a hundred miles north of Mexico City) and its religion centred about the worship of Quetzalcóatl and Tezcatlipoca (see note **301.4**). Their sway was broken in the mid-twelfth century by a series of disasters: famine and drought, civil war, and invasions from the north. Tula was eventually destroyed by invading barbarians, and the Toltec peoples scattered for all time.

301.4 [299] *Quetzelcoatl.* The plumed serpent, the most powerful of the gods in the pantheon of Teotihuacán, the city which dominated the central highlands in the Classic period, 200 B.C. to 1000 A.D. After the inexplicable decline of Teotihuacán, the Toltec warrior Ce Acatl Tolpiltzin became a devotee of the ancient god and assumed the name of his deity. Incredible benefactions were attributed to Tolpiltzin-Quetzalcóatl: infinite knowledge, the planting of corn, the invention of writing, the cultivated arts, the architecture of Tula, and so forth. The god was content with sacrifice of flowers and snakes and butterflies, unlike his bloodthirsty rival, the black magician Tezcatlipoca (identified by Spence, *M & M of M* p. 274, with Hurakán), who tricked Quetzalcóatl into drunkenness and the violation of his priestly vows of chastity. Quetzalcóatl with his followers left Tula for Cholula, where they stayed some time, before the god went east, coasting out to sea on a raft of serpents and then flashing into the heavens as the morning star. His way was marked by arrows shot through saplings, leaving cross-like signs, and he sent word that he would come again in the year Ce Acatl. By tradition, he was fair and bearded (like Cortés and the Consul), and when, five centuries later in the year Ce Acatl (1519), the Spaniards appeared from the east, white and bearded, with crosses and strange powers, fears were aroused (even in Tenochtitlán, the city of the god Huitzilopochtli) that this meant the return of Quetzalcóatl—fears which Cortés did nothing to allay and which contributed in no small manner to his initial success.

301.5 [299]   *the criollo... the mestizo.* The *criollo,* or *creole,* is the pure-blooded Mexican-born Spaniard, who, not having been born in Spain, was socially inferior to the Spaniard, but in turn superior to the *mestizo,* or half-breed, the offspring of mixed Spanish and Indian descent (who form more than 80 per cent of the present population). In early colonial days, social ranking by and large approximated to one's proportion of European blood, and even today, despite a conscious adulation of all things Indian, traces of this hierarchy persist.

301.6 [300]   *SAN BUENAVENTURA ATEMPAN.* After the disastrous Noche Triste and the retreat from Tenochtitlán (see note **289.6.c**), Cortés resolved to assault the Aztec city by water as well as by land, and, from the safety of Tlaxcala, he had his carpenters build thirteen brigantines, fitted out with both sails and oars. These were to be built in sections, transported manually to Texcoco, and assembled on the lake shore. The bold strategy worked, and in the final attack upon Tenochtitlán, May 1521, the ships gave the conquerors a necessary edge.

The ships were built at Atempa, a small town close to present-day Tlaxcala, and tested on the Río Zahuapan. As Prescott notes (V.vi, p. 487), quoting the Tlaxcaltecan historian Camargo: "Ansi se hicieron trece bergantines en el barrio de Atempa, junto a una hermita que se llama San Buenaventura." ("Thus thirteen brigantines were built in the suburb of Atempa, near a hermitage called San Buenaventura.")

301.7 [300]   *Mar Cantábrico.* Sp. "Singing Sea" (the name of the Bay of Biscay). The *Mar Cantábrico* (a modern equivalent of Cortés's brigantines) was a Spanish ship which took arms for the Republicans from the U.S.A. to Spain. In January 1938, just one day before a law was passed forbidding such shipments, the *Mar Cantábrico* set sail for Vera Cruz, where it picked up a further cargo, and thence to Spain. The ship was captured by the Nationalists, the Spaniards in her crew executed, and the arms used against the Republicans (Thomas, p. 576). Since Hugh's venture is so much like that of the ill-fated *Mar Cantábrico* (Lowry undoubtedly is using it as a model), the question immediately arises as to the likelihood of his success.

301.8 [300]   *a civilization which was as good if not better than that of the conquerors.* Despite its militaristic basis and its emphasis upon human sacrifice, the Aztecs in amazingly short time had created a civilization that was not only "deep-rooted," but which was also in many ways far ahead of its European counterparts: in terms of civic organization, plumbing, sewerage, cleanliness, education, and quality of life, Tenochtitlán had achieved standards unmatched by any European city of the day. Rivera's mural on the Cortés Palace (see note **215.4**), where an Inquisitional burning is set directly opposite the Aztec sacrifice, confirms Hugh's point graphically.

301.9 [300]   *had they been... there would never have been any exploitation.* A thesis derived from Claude Houghton's *Julian Grant Loses His Way* (1933). In an earlier draft (UBC 7-11, pp. 9-10), Hugh had said that communism "only came about when there was no more loot and I merely remarked that that wasn't original, that I had read exactly the same statement in a peculiar and lousy book called, I think, Julian Grant Loses His Way." Houghton's novel is the story of a man whose life has been one of emotional suicide, who has missed his opportunity to love, and whose afterlife materializes as an endless arid plain. At one point, p. 246, an ex-actor named Clarence Harlowe comments: "'We've reached the final stage of consciousness. Our civilisation has entered its Babel phase. No man understands the words of another. What is Order to one man is Chaos to the next.'" The explanation offered is an economic one: "The age of expansion is ended, and so there's no longer any loot. That's the point—just that— there's no loot. We're gangsters without victims."

302.1 [300]   *Moctezuma... Montezuma.* There is a discussion in Prescott, II.v, p. 164, about the spelling of the name. Montezuma is the usual English spelling, but the name is consistently Moctezuma in Mexico. The Moctezuma breweries in Orizaba produce Dos Equis beer, on the label of which (as the Consul said in an early draft, UBC 7-11, p. 12) there is "a feather-plumed impression of the glum chocolate-drinking washout." The Consul also stated, "That's all he is now, the name on a bottle of beer. And without the terrible and dangerous Tlaxcalans his descendants might still be rulers of Mexico." Lowry leaves unstated any suggestion that the Consul, in his Cave of the Winds, may well be suffering from Montezuma's Revenge.

302.2 [300]   *TIZATLÁN*. From Nah. "on top of the clay"; the first of the four señorios of the federation of Tlaxcala (see note **297.1**). A very populous town in ancient times, it was ruled by the elderly blind Xiocohtencatl. This señorio, more than the others, urged resistance to the invading Spaniards, and although the elder Xicohtencatl became reconciled to Spanish sovereignty and was baptized, his younger warrior son was not (see note **303.2**). The ruins of the palace, just north of Tlaxcala, are still to be seen, "also the genuine decorations carved on the sides showing their own hieroglyphs" (UBC 11–14, p. 24). The passage triggers off in the Consul's mind the image of his own father watching him; a like sense of inevitable destiny pressing upon him; the demands Yvonne is making upon him; and the need to escape.

302.3 [301]   *OCOTELULCO*. From Nah. "hill of pines"; the second of the four señorios of the federation of Tlaxcala (see note **297.1**), ruled over by Maxixcatzín who from the beginning had argued that the Spaniards be received cordially into Tlaxcala and who, according to tradition, willingly embraced the Christian faith himself. The reference to baptism triggers off in the Consul's mind images of rebirth, which linked together like one of Dunne's memory-trains (see note **283.5**), lead to thoughts of William Blackstone running, Napoleon's leg twitching, of being almost run over by the Englishman going to Guatemala, and the life-giving vision of Guanajuato.

303.1 [301]   *MATLALCUEYATL*. From Nah. *matatl,* "net," and *cueyatl,* "frogs"; the Nahuatl name for the volcano also known as Malinche (see note **375.1**) and popularly described as "La he enaguas azules" ("She of the blue skirts"). The volcano is on the border of Tlaxcala and Puebla states and was revered as a sanctuary to the mother of the gods. Donnelly, p. 100, discusses a picture in the Aztec codices representing "Matlalcueye, goddess of waters and consort of Tlaloc, god of rain"—the latter being a fearsome deity to whom children were sacrificed (suffocated in the water rather than drowned) to ensure the life of the waters and in the belief that life-giving rains would be in proportion to the sacrifices made.

303.2 [301]   *Xicohtencatl*. Xicohtencatl Axayacatzin, the son of the senator (see note **302.2**), who led the initial opposition of the Tlaxcalans against Cortés, and even after peace had been made, never really accepted the alliance. Although he helped Cortés against the Aztecs, he felt (with some justification) that the Spaniards were the greater threat, and during the final attack withdrew his aid, for which Cortés had him hanged. The harangue by Xicohtencatl to his soldiers before the first battle with the Spaniards is a celebrated piece of rhetoric recorded in the *Conquista de Méjico* (1684) by Don Antonio de Solís, but as Prescott sardonically notes, III.ii, p. 226: "Solis, who confounds [the] veteran with his son, has put a flourishing harangue in the mouth of the latter, which would be a rare gem of Indian eloquence, — were it not Castilian."

303.3 [301] *no pasarán*. Sp. "they shall not pass"; the Republican cry of defiance in the Spanish Civil War as they blocked Franco's advance towards Madrid. One of the leaders of the Spanish communist party (then represented in the legitimate government) was Dolores Ibarruri ("La Pasionaria"), who spoke heatedly over the radio on 19 July 1936 urging resistance against the fascists. She ended her speech with the words: "It is better to die on your feet than to live on your knees. *No pasarán!*" Like Xicotencatl's harangue to his warriors, the cry of defiance was a brave but ultimately futile gesture. The parallel between the two events in the Consul's mind sets off another train of images: "no pasarán" suggesting the Battle of Madrid; the Mexican Revolution; shooting on sight; his father watching him; other desperate attempts to escape; they have got his number; and the corpse transported by express.

303.4 [301] *RAILROAD AND BUS SERVICE*. The Consul forms a complex plan by which he and Yvonne can accompany Hugh part of the way to Vera Cruz, as far as Tlaxcala. Since Tlaxcala is not served directly by rail, and since the Mexico City–Vera Cruz line Hugh will be taking goes far to the north of Tlaxcala and the nearby city of Santa Ana Chiautempan, the timing is quite tricky and the Consul is proud at having worked it out. There are two ways of getting to Tlaxcala by train from Mexico City:
(a) By the Mexico–Vera Cruz line, as far as Apizaco (in the north of Tlaxcala State); then branching off to Santa Ana; and finally taking the "Flecha Roja" ("Red Arrow") buses at Santa Ana for the ten-minute ride to Tlaxcala.
(b) By the Mexico–Puebla line, running south of Tlaxcala State; getting off at San Martín Texmelucán (an important rail and road junction near the Puebla–Mexico border), and transferring to the "Estrella de Oro" ("Golden Arrow") buses for the fifteen-mile journey to Tlaxcala.
For the Consul, the journey is one to a whited city of death. Granada and Tlaxcala merge in his mind with the most beautiful white city at all, Tortu, where there is nobody to interfere with the business of drinking. The vision which unfolds of the white cities, the white sanctuary of Ocotlán, the white hotel, the cold white sheets, white bottles, and white cantinas may appear beautiful without, but within is full of all manner of corruption.

304.1 [302]   *happy as toads in the thunderstorm.* A delightful image, were it not for the quotation from Bunyan's *Grace Abounding* at the beginning of the book: "Now I blessed the condition of the dog and toad . . . for I knew they had no soul to perish under the everlasting weight of Hell or Sin, as mine was like to do."

304.2 [302]   *Something was wrong.* The effects of many drinks, to say nothing of the lemonade bottle of mescal in the excusado, are obviously showing, but the Consul will not admit this. Instead, he immediately notes that Hugh and Yvonne are themselves "quite surprisingly tight," and if they can see that he is also, just a little, then it must be because Cervantes has betrayed him. Hill, p. 136, offers a superb analysis of the Consul's state of mind:

> He has had, by alcoholic count, very little to drink — because the others did not see him drink the eight or nine secret mescals. He has sworn Cervantes, the bartender, to silence. Still, Hugh and Yvonne seem to suspect. Cervantes must have told on him. The bartender is a native of Tlaxcala; years ago the Tlaxcaltecans had betrayed Moctezuma to Cortez. With superb drunken logic, the Consul reasons that this Tlaxcaltecan has been "unable to resist" the equally grave crime of betraying him to his friends. How else could he justify Hugh's and Yvonne's attitude toward him? According to his double-entry drink-count system, he has been observing a code of conduct so nearly puritanical that he really ought to let down a bit and have a drink. He is probably surprised they don't suggest it. The fact that they can see he is drunk does not occur to him. By *his* count, he is obviously sober in *their* eyes.

305.1 [303]   *Et tu Bruto!* A variant of L. "And you, Brutus!" (the Penguin *Brute* is an error). From Shakespeare's *Julius Caesar,* III.i.77, where Caesar on the point of death sees among the conspirators his adopted son, Brutus; the Consul sees Hugh, to whom he has been as a father, in the act of betraying him. Since his scarcely cold chicken ("un bruto") has probably suggested the words, the Consul's rhetoric is somewhat undercut.

305.2 [303]   *the razor edge keen in sunlight.* The memory of Hugh shaving him and of Hugh in the bull-ring that afternoon fuse in the Consul's mind to form a composite image of death and supplantation. As A. E. Waite notes in his translation of Éliphas Lévi's *Transcendental Magic,* p. 14, it is a commonplace of occult thought that in the search for the greater mysteries the one initiated must slay his initiator. The Consul immediately thinks of *The Golden Bough,* Hugh's threat of decapitation, and the grim figure prowling around the grave of Nemi, awaiting the one who is to supplant him (see note **182.1**).

305.3 [304] *A Russian film about a revolt of some fishermen.* Hugh's story is set out in more detail in an earlier draft (UBC 7–11, p. 19): "'I once saw a Russian film' said Hugh, 'In Frisco. It was about fishermen. A shark was netted with a shoal of smaller fish and killed. But even after it was dead it continued to swallow the live fish.'" In like manner, Geoffrey's headlong rush to oblivion will swallow down anyone who happens to be near him, and his death will affect others even after he is gone. The later addition, "about a revolt," suggests Eisenstein's film *The Battleship Potemkin* (1925), which is about the uprising of some sailors in the 1905 Revolution, and features a remarkable massacre scene.

306.1 [304] *Actinium, Argon. . . . Columbium.* In a letter to Derek Pethick (*SL,* p. 200), Lowry admitted taking the elements out of the dictionary, but with the serious purpose of implying that the Consul feels that his battle against the very elements (a magician should control them) is a war that is bound to be lost. In an earlier short story, "June the 30th, 1934," (*P & S,* pp. 33–34) Lowry comments:

> Wasn't it a little ominous that Firmin, badly wounded in the war, should spend the rest of his life searching for the very metals with which Man *might* indeed construct a new world, a stellite paradise of inconceivable strength and delicacy that would enable him, through vast windows of new alloys, to let the light of the future pour in. . . . Man was doing nothing of the sort, but on the contrary, with diabolical genius, merely using them to prepare the subtler weapons of his own destruction.

The twenty-six elements listed may correspond to the number of letters in the alphabet, another potential source of power:
(a) *Actinium.* (Ac) A radio-active chemical found with uranium and radium in pitchblende. Wt. 227; no. 89.
(b) *Argon.* (A) An inert, colourless, odourless gas used in incandescent lightbulbs and radio-tubes. Wt. 39.944; no. 18.
(c) *Beryllium.* (Be) A hard rare metal found only in combination with other elements; it forms a tough light alloy with copper or nickel. Wt. 9.013; no. 4.
(d) *Dysprosium.* (Dy) A rare-earth; one of the most magnetic of all substances. Wt. 162.51; no. 66.
(e) *Niobium.* (Nb) A rare metal, discovered 1806. Wt. 92.91; no. 41.

Lowry comments (*SL,* p. 200) that he substituted this for *neptunium* since "it sounded sadder"; Niobe, daughter of Tantalus, so boasted of her children that they were slain by the gods, and she herself turned into stone, weeping for her loss.

(f) *Palladium.* (Pd) A rare silvery-white metal akin to platinum; used as a catalyst in alloys with gold and silver in jewellery. Wt. 106.4; no. 46. The palladium of Troy was the image of Pallas Athene, and the safety of the city depended upon that of the sacred object.

(g) *Praseodymium.* (Pr) A rare-earth whose salts are generally green. Wt. 140.92; no. 59.

(h) *Ruthenium.* (Ru) A hard brittle silver-grey metal akin to platinum. Wt. 101.1; no. 44.

(i) *Samarium.* (Sm) A metallic earth, with a lustrous pale-grey appearance; found in association with cerium, yttrium, and other elements. Wt. 150.35; no. 62. The suggestion of "Samaritan" cannot be missed.

(j) *Silicon.* (Si) A non-metallic element always found in combination and more abundant than any other element save oxygen, with which it combines to form silica. Wt. 29.09; no. 14.

(k) *Tantalum.* (Ta) A rare steel-blue, corrosion-resisting element used for electric filaments, grids and plates in radio tubes, and surgical instruments. Wt. 180.95; no. 73. The suggestion of Tantalus, denizen of Hades, is probably present.

(l) *Tellurium.* (Te) A rare non-metallic brittle element, usually found combined with gold and silver, and belonging to the same family as sulphur and selenium. Wt. 127.61; no. 52. There may be an echo of Thomas Burnet's *Telluris Theoria Sacra* (see note **193.7**).

(m) *Terbium.* (Tb) A metallic rare-earth. Wt. 158.93; no. 65.

(n) *Thorium.* (Th) A rare greyish radioactive element, occuring in monozite and thorite. Wt. 232.05; no. 90.

(o) *Thulium.* (Tm) A rare-earth. Wt. 168.94; no. 69.

(p) *Titanium.* (Ti) A dark-grey lustrous metallic chemical element, found in rutile and other minerals and used as a cleaning and deoxygenizing agent in molten steel. Wt. 47.90; no. 22.

(q) *Uranium.* (U) A hard heavy radioactive chemical element, found only in combination, chiefly in pitchblende, important (especially in the isotope of mass number 235) for atomic energy. Wt. 238.07; no. 92. Lowry noted (*SL,* p. 200) that this was listed in 1942, before the atomic bomb existed.

(r) *Vanadium.* (V) A rare silver-white metallic element, which can be alloyed to steel to give tensile strength. Wt. 50.95; no. 23.

(s) *Virginium.* (Vi) Now known as *Francium* (Fr), a radioactive element obtained artificially by the bombardment of thorium with protons. Wt. 223; no. 87.

(t) *Xenon*. (Xe) A heavy colourless inert gas, present in minute quantities in the air. Wt. 131.3; no. 54.

(u) *Ytterbium*. (Yb) A rare-earth resembling and found with yttrium. Wt. 173.04; no. 70.

(v) *Yttrium*. (Y) A rare metallic element found in gadolinite and samarskite. Wt. 88.92; no. 39.

(w) *Zirconium*. (Zr) A grey or black metal found with zircon and used in alloys and heat-resistent materials. Wt. 91.22; no. 40.

(x) *Europium*. (Eu) A chemical element of the rare-earth group. Wt. 152.0; no. 63.

(y) *Germanium*. (Ge) A rare greyish-white metallic element of the carbon family, discovered in 1886. Wt. 72.60; no. 32. A possible hint of "German friends" may be present.

(z) *Columbium*. The former name for niobium (see above). An earlier draft (UBC 11–13, pp. 17–18) suggested "British Columbium."

306.2 [305] *Matthew Arnold says, in his essay on Marcus Aurelius.* Matthew Arnold (1822–88), poet and critic, published his essay on Marcus Aurelius in 1865. In it he argued against John Stuart Mill's contention that Christianity is merely a protest against paganism which falls below the best morality of the ancients; instead, Arnold is concerned to show that Christian morality is equal to the best of Epictetus or Marcus Aurelius (hence the effrontery of Hugh quoting Arnold in defence of atheistic communism). Marcus Aurelius Antoninus (121–180 A.D.), Roman emperor and stoic philosopher, was the author of twelve books of *Meditations* (see note **112.9**) and to Arnold "perhaps the most beautiful figure in history . . . one of the best of men." Yet he persecuted the Christians, and Arnold seeks to explain why; not, he explains, because he and Antoninus Pius loved darkness rather than light:

> Far from this, the Christianity which these Emperors aimed at repressing was, in their conception of it, something philosophically contemptible, politically subversive, and morally abominable. As men, they sincerely regarded it much as well-conditioned people, with us, regard Mormonism; as rulers, they regarded it much as Liberal statesmen, with us, regard the Jesuits. A kind of Mormonism, constituted as a vast secret society, with obscure aims of political and social subversion, was what Antoninus Pius and Marcus Aurelius believed themselves to be repressing when they punished Christians. The early Christian apologists

again and again declare to us under what odious imputations the Christians lay, how general was the belief that these imputations were well-grounded, how sincere was the horror which the belief inspired. The multitude, convinced that the Christians were atheists who ate human flesh and thought incest no crime, displayed against them a fury so passionate as to embarrass and alarm their rulers. The severe expressions of Tacitus, *exitiabilis superstitio — odio humani generis convicti,* show how deeply the prejudices of the multitude imbued the educated class also. One asks oneself with astonishment how a doctrine so benign as that of Jesus Christ can have incurred misrepresentation so monstrous. The inner and moving cause of the misrepresentation lay, no doubt, in this, — that Christianity was a new spirit in the Roman world, like democracy in the modern world, like every new spirit with a similar mission assigned to it, should at its first appearance occasion an instinctive shrinking and repugnance in the world which it was to dissolve.

(a) *My notion of what we call.* The word "Communism" is blotted out by the Consul's shout, "Cervantes!"; a mocking comment upon the quixotic nature of Hugh's indoor marxmanship.

(b) *Mormonism.* The Mormons are a religious sect founded in the United States by Joseph Smith who claimed to have found, engraved on gold plates, an addition to the Bible which he translated as *The Book of Mormon.* After Smith's death, Brigham Young led the Mormons to Utah in 1847, where the Church of Jesus Christ of the Latter Day Saints was formally established. The Mormons believe, among other things, that Jesus Christ appeared in America after the ascension; that the American Indians can be identified with the Lost Tribes of Israel; and that at the millenium Christ will come again and rule for a thousand years.

(c) *the Jesuits.* The Society of Jesus, a Roman Catholic order founded in 1540 by St. Ignatius of Loyola and renowned for the severity of its self-discipline and the quality of its education. Members of the society were often employed by the pope on dangerous and delicate missions, and though the society was often suppressed, the total dedication of its members to their vocation made the order an object of special fear and suspicion among those who could not share its beliefs.

(d) *Antoninus Pius.* Antoninus Pius (86–161 A.D.), Roman emperor from 138 to 161 and uncle of Marcus Aurelius. He devoted himself to promoting the happiness of his people, and his reign was a happy and prosperous one. The hardback "Antonius Pius" is an error.

(e) *The inner and moving cause of the representation.* Arnold has "misrepresentation."

307.1 [306] *Black Flowers*. In Spanish, "Flores Negras," a sad love song by Sergio de Carlo (1937) about dark eyes, which, like black flowers, are untrue; a song disconcertingly appropriate to the Consul's present feelings about Yvonne:

> Me hacan daño tus ojos
> Me hacan daño tus manos
> Me hacan daño tus labios que saben fingir
> Y a mi sombra pregunto
> Si esos labios que adoro
> en un beso sagrado podrán mentir

("You have hurt me with your eyes, / you have hurt me with your hands, / you have hurt me with your lips which know how to pretend. / And I ask my shadow / if those lips I adore / in a sacred kiss can lie").

There may also be a suggestion of *Ixtlilxochitl* (Nah. "black flower"), lord of Texcoco, who had been deposed with the help of Moctezuma and was hence the Aztec ruler's sworn foe; in return for his throne, he offered his services to Cortés, serving the Spaniards so diligently that he achieved the unenviable reputation of having done more than any other Indian (except Malinche) to "rivet the chains of the white man round the necks of his countrymen" (Prescott, V.vii, p. 502).

307.2 [306] *cuántos trenes hay el día para Vera Cruz?* Sp. "How many trains are there a day for Vera Cruz?"; the Consul is still adamant that his is "a perfectly good idea." The town of Vera Cruz (originally, "La Villa Rica de la Vera Cruz") was founded a few miles from the present city by Cortés in 1519 before he set off into the interior towards the Aztec empire. It was thus the first Spanish settlement on the Mexican mainland. Tlaxcala is on the way to Vera Cruz, "the True Cross," but the way of the True Cross, the Via Dolorosa, was also the way to death.

308.1 [306] *La superstición dice... que cuando tres amigos prenden su cigarro con la misma cerilla, el último muere antes que los otros dos.* Sp. "Superstition says... that when three friends light their cigars with the same match, the last will die before the other two." Andersen notes, p. 412, that this superstition apparently grew out of a Russian belief that because three is a holy number only a priest could light three tapers; the belief apparently passed to the English in the Crimean War (1854–56) and received a new emphasis in the Boer War (1899–1902) when the Boers' marksmanship was so good that by the time a third cigarette was lit, they could take aim and fire.

308.2 [307]   *the Indo-Aryans, the Iranians.* The problem touched on here by the Consul concerns the disputed date of separation of the Iranians and the Hindus, who shared a common Indo-Aryan ancestry, and the consequences of that date for the development of their respective mythologies. Both groups, for instance, worshipped *Agni* and knew about Soma, but these and other similarities of ritual and worshop cannot always be placed indisputably into an historical context, nor can it be proven definitely, as tradition would have it, that the cause of the separation of the two groups was a spiritual conflict of some kind.

308.3 [307]   *the sacred fire, Agni.* As an object of worship, fire was deified by the ancient Hindus as *Agni,* giver of good things, opponent of darkness and evil, whose three heads personified three forms of fire: the sun, lightning, and the sacrificial fire. Agni, or fire, had first been brought down from heaven for the use of man by the Hindu Prometheus, *Mātarisvan,* at the command of Brighu, and the worship of Agni involved the ceremonial construction of the sacred fire altar and the ritual kindling (the *agnyādheya*) of the sacred flames. The fire-sticks (*aranī*) were ceremonial rubbing sticks, the friction of which generated the initial spark for the domestic hearth, which was lit before the flames were conveyed, with appropriate rituals and oblations, to other sacred sites (*Hindu World,* I, pp. 358–59).

308.4 [307]   *Soma, Amrita, the nectar of immortality.* Soma is a plant (today unidentifiable, but perhaps *Asclepias acida,* of the milkweed family) said to have been first cultivated in Indra's heaven and subsequently on Mount Mujavant. Indra performed all his heroic deeds under the influence of the juice extracted from the leaves and stem of the divine plant, which was said to confer vitality, transcendent vision, and inspiration upon those who drank it. Soma was raised to the position of a deity and praised as everlasting, omnipotent, all-healing, a bestower of riches and giver of immortality. The whole of the ninth book of the *Rig-Veda* is devoted to the praise of soma and tells of the extraction and preparation of the sacred juice, the libations to the gods, and the ritual drinking of *Amrita* (the celestial soma, the nectar of immortality; not always distinguished from soma itself). In an earlier draft (UBC 11–13, p. 16) the Consul commented:

> Yes, even the Indo-Aryans, before they separated from the Iranians, knew all about *soma.* The plant grew on the mountainsides they made it from, and what they made, of course, was Amrita, the nectar of immortality. One whole book of the Rig Veda praises it; one drink of it, *sine mora,* you were at the Gates of Heaven. Soma was the moon too, or

identified with it, bewitching them, and whose cup—Cervantes!—is even filling and emptying as he waxes and wanes.

308.5 [307] *bhang.* From Skr. *bhanga,* "hemp" or "hashish"; an Indian variety of common hemp, the leaves of which could be made into a drink with narcotic and intoxicating qualities (closely related to *gāñja,* a similar derivative which is dried and smoked). The Consul's contention that it is "much the same as *mescal*" seems to be based upon the mistaken belief that mescal is related to the hallucinatory drug, mescaline.

308.6 [307] *the Hamadan mosque.* The Khanaqah of Shah Hamadan in Srinagar, originally built in 1395 but twice destroyed by fire (1479, 1731), is an outstanding example of Kashmiri wooden architecture. Located on the right bank of the Jhelum River, it consists of a large hall, 63 by 43 feet, with some fourteen chambers on the north and south sides, delicately carved wooden panels and complex lattice work, and a pyramidical roof raised 125 feet from the ground (*History of Kashmir,* p. 583). The mosque is indeed similar to some of the Norwegian stave churches (such as that of Heddal), but the Consul's comparison is taken directly from Francis Younghusband's *Kashmir,* p. 67: "Near the third bridge is the fine Shah Hamadan mosque of an almost Norwegian type of architecture, built of wood with a tall taper spire and handsome ornaments hanging from the eaves."

308.7 [307] *The Borda gardens.* This is the sole reference to the Borda Gardens, one of the best known features of Cuernavaca, the reason being that Lowry has attributed so many of its qualities to Maximilian's ruined casa (see note **18.3**). The gardens, which are more or less opposite the Ciné Morelos, were built in the late eighteenth century by Manuel de la Borda, a son of José de la Borda, a Frenchman who had immigrated to Mexico as a young man in 1716 and made a fabulous fortune in silver from Taxco. The gardens, once a horticultural and architectural marvel, were let to run down badly, but they were restored under the brief and ill-fated monarchy of Maximilian and Carlota and today still possess much of their original enchantment.

309.1 [307] *the terrace of the Nishat Bagh.* The *Nishat Bagh,* the "Garden of Bliss," is, according to Francis Younghusband, "decidedly the favourite garden in Kashmir" (*Kashmir,* p. 82). Laid out about 1630 by Asaf Khan (some say Jehangir) on a site two miles south of the equally celebrated Shalimar Gardens (see note **82.8**), it commands a magnificent view of the

Dal Lake and the mountains to the west. The Nishat is arranged in ten terraces, three of which are much higher than the others. The stream feeding the gardens enters at the upper end and flows down the successive terraces in cascades formed by stone masonry in such a way as to vary the appearance of the waters. The gardens have pavilions at either end, many fountains and reservoirs, and beautiful walks shaded by giant chenars and cypresses. Its beauty is said to be greatest at dawn (*History of Kashmir,* pp. 592–94). One of the watercolours by Edward Molyneux in Younghusband's *Kashmir* (see note **87.6**), opposite p. 84, depicts "A Terrace of the Nishat Bagh."

309.2 [307] *the Vedic Gods.* The *Vedas* are the sacred texts of the Hindus, four in all, which celebrate numerous deities, of whom the most important are Vishnu, lord of the gods; Indra, god of the storm; Śiva, god of destruction and regeneration; Agni, the god of fire; Varuna, deity of the water; and Yama, god of death. The earlier Vedic religion was a form of nature worship, but though the Consul is making the point that the Vedic gods, unlike Popocatepetl and Ixtaccihuatl, were distinct personifications of abstract forces of nature, there were nevertheless countless myths and legends that accrued about their figures.

(a) *the sacred fire.* Deified as Agni (see note **308.3**) and kindled in a sacred ritual.

(b) *the sacrificial fire.* Over a score of different kinds of fires are described in the *Vedas,* each with its own purpose and ritual. The most important are the *gārhapatya,* or fire of the domestic hearth; the *āhavanīya,* or eastern fire, used for oblations to the gods; and the *dakshināgni,* or southern fire, which receives offerings for the demons (*Hindu World,* I, p. 359).

(c) *the stone soma press.* After the soma herbs have been rinsed and purified, they are crushed, with appropriate ceremony, between two stones (the *odri,* or upper stone, and the *grāvan,* or lower stone). There were pressings and libations morning, noon, and evening each day of the soma sacrifice.

(d) *the sacrifices of cakes and oxen and horses.* Descriptions of sacrificial rites constitute a substantial part of the *Vedas,* and sacrifice was seen as an essential condition of salvation, believed to provide strength and sustenance for the gods or carried out to achieve a specific purpose. The burnt offerings of ghee, grain, butter or cakes were known as *havis* and were an important accompaniment to other sacrifices. The description of the soma sacrifice in the *Rig-Veda* begins with the consecration and sacrifice of a cake to Agni and Vishnu, the cake being a symbolic representation of the sacrificial victim. The *sūlagava,* or sacrifice of the "impaled ox," took place in the spring and was to ensure an abundance of cattle, but the sacrifice of cattle was also an important part of the soma sacrifice. The most complex sacrificial ritual was the *aśvamedha*, or horse sacrifice (this did not form part of the soma sacrifice): a white horse was let loose and whatever country the animal entered, throughout the year, had to be conquered by the owner of the horse and the soldiers who followed. During this year, preparations for the main sacrifice were made, and elaborate attendant rituals were undertaken. At the end of the year the horse was led back and sacrificed with great ceremony. The first aśvamedha was said to have been performed by Brahma, to commemorate his recovery of the lost *Vedas,* and it was known that the performance of a hundred such aśvamedhas would give a mortal supremacy over Indra and the other gods. The last recorded aśvamedha was in 1750.

(e) *drinking rites.* The most important drinks, soma and amrita (see note **308.4**) were shared in libations by men and gods alike, the preparation and drinking attended throughout with elaborate ritual and ceremony and accompanied by appropriate verses from the *Vedas.* As the Consul points out, in both these and other rites, a meticulous care had to be taken at all times lest the sacrifice be rendered invalid, for the litany accompanying the ceremony was believed to directly influence the outcome of the sacrifice. The Brahman priest, however, had the power to expiate errors if they arose.

309.3 [307] *the immolation of wives. Suttee,* the Hindu practice of the voluntary (and often involuntary) self-immolation of widows on the funeral pyres of their husbands. The word is derived from Satī, the wife of Śiva, who committed suicide because of an insult to her husband. It seems not to have been a very ancient custom, since there is nothing about it in *Vedas,* but the Greeks recorded instances of the practice, and by the sixth and seventh centuries A.D. the life of a widow apart from her husband was unequivocally condemned. The practice of suttee reached fearful proportions and was not checked until long after the advent of British rule. A description of such an attempted immolation is given in Jules Verne's *Around the World in Eighty Days,* Ch. 13.

309.4 [307] *a Levirate marriage.* In Old Testament times among some of the Jewish tribes, the required marriage betwen a man and his brother's wife if the brother died without leaving a male heir, as decribed in Deuteronomy 25:5:

If brethen dwell together, and one of them die, and have no child, the wife of the dead shall not marry without unto a stranger: her husband's brother shall go in unto her, and take her to him to wife, and perform the duty of an husband's brother unto her.

Lowry would also have seen the reference to this in Donnelly, p. 207: "The same singular custom which is found among the Jews and the Hindoos, for 'a man to raise up seed for his deceased brother by marrying his widow,' was found among the Central American nations." The words set up ugly echoes as the Consul considers the relationship of Hugh and Yvonne.

309.5 [307] *an obscure relation... between Taxila and Tlaxcala.* The Consul's point, in brief, is that Alexander the Great would not have as readily conquered so much of India were it not for the aid of the king of Taxila, who gave him assistance against a neighbouring king, in much the same way that the Tlaxcalans had assisted Cortés against Moctezuma.

(a) *Taxila.* The ancient city of T'akhasila in the North Punjab, some seventeen miles northwest of Rawalpindi, celebrated before the arrival of Alexander as the foremost centre of learning in Ancient India and after the conquest important as a centre for the diffusion of Hellenistic values and art forms into the mainstream of Indian culture.

(b) *the Khyber Pass.* A famous defile through the Safed Koh range between Afghanistan and Pakistan, linking the Kabul Valley with Peshewar. The strategic heart of the North West Frontier, it was the centre of many skirmishes between British troops and rebel tribesmen in the nineteenth century.

(c) *the great pupil of Aristotle's.* Aristotle (384–322 B.C.), the great Greek philosopher, was appointed by Philip of Macedon as tutor to his son, Alexander, but he returned to Athens when the latter succeeded to the throne.

(d) *Alexander.* Alexander the Great (356–323 B.C.), son of Philip II of Macedon, who became king in 336 B.C. He led the Greek states in the war against Persia and in 334 crossed the Hellespont. He conquered Egypt, where he founded the great city of Alexandria, and having defeated the Persians at the battle of Arbeta in 331, he carried on to India, crossing the Indus in 326 B.C. He defeated the army of Porus and would have advanced much further into the interior, had not his soldiers, weary for home, mutinied and refused to go beyond the Hyphasis river. Alexander died of fever at Babylon in 323, aged only 32.

(e) *Ambhi.* Ambhi (or Omphis), king of Taxila, was ruler of the principality between the Indus and Hydaspes (Jhelum) rivers. As Alexander advanced upon his kingdom, he sent an embassy to meet the Greek con-

queror, offering to place his men at Alexander's services against his
enemy, the Paurave monarch.

(f) *the Paurave monarch.* Porus, ruler of the kingdom between the Jhelum
and Chenab rivers, decided to oppose the Macedonian king, and on the
banks of the Jhelum river put forward an army of 30,000 infantry,
4,000 cavalry, 300 chariots, and 200 elephants, only to be defeated by
Alexander's 11,000 men. Porus, severely wounded, was brought to
Alexander after the battle. Demanding to be treated like a king, he was
confirmed as governor over Alexander's newly conquered territories.

(g) *the Jhelma and the Chenab.* Alternately, the Hydaspes and the Ace-
sines; rivers which defined the boundaries of the Paurave monarch's
kingdom. The Jhelum flows through the Vale of Kashmir and past
Srinagar into the Punjab; the Chenab arises in Kashmir and flows
southwest into Pakistan.

309.6 [307]   *Sir Thomas Browne* (1605–82) was an English writer and physician who lived at Norwich. He is famous for his combination of wit and
curious learning, which, combined with a beautifully cadenced prose style,
expressed his sceptical yet devout inquiries into many matters concerning religion and science. He is best known for his *Religio Medici* (1642), a confession of Christian faith tempered by a profound scepticism, but he was also
the author of *Pseudodoxia Epidemica,* or *Vulgar Errors* (1646), the *Garden
of Cyrus* (1658) and *Hydriotaphia,* or *Urne Burial* (1658). The Consul's references are to Ch. 5 of this last work, which is a profound and moving
meditation upon the power of death and time to obliviate all fame.

(a) *Archimedes.* 287–212 B.C., the famous mathematician of Syracuse, inventor of the Archimedes screw and a lens to set ships on fire, but best
known for his cry of "Eureka" when he discovered the laws of specific
gravity. He is mentioned by Browne in relation to Methuselah (see
below).

(b) *Moses.* The Old Testament patriarch who led his people out of the
bondage of Egypt towards the Promised Land. He too is cited in relation to Methuselah (see below).

(c) *Achilles.* Son of Peleus and Thetis, the bravest of the Greeks during the
Trojan wars. In his infancy he had been dipped in the Styx and was
invulnerable except for his heel. To prevent his going to Troy, Thetis
disguised him in female dress, but Odysseus found him out and brought
him to Troy. Achilles, disputing with Agamemnon, retired to his tent,
and remained there until the death of his friend Patroclus recalled him
to action, whereupon he slew Hector. He was later wounded in the heel
by Paris and died. Browne comments, in context of "the necessity of

oblivion": "What Song the *Syrens* sang, or what name *Achilles* assumed when he hid himself among women, though puzling Questions, are not beyond all Conjecture."

(d) *Methuselah*. In Genesis 5:27, Methuselah is described as having lived in all "nine hundred sixty and nine years: and he died"; the longest lived of all Biblical patriarchs, but whose years still ended in death. Browne comments:

> If we begin to die when we live, and long life be but a prolongation of death, our life is a sad composition; we live with death, and die not in a moment. How many pulses made up the life of *Methuselah,* were work for *Archimedes:* Common Counters sum up the life of *Moses* his man.

(e) *Charles V*. King of Spain from 1516 until 1558 and Holy Roman Emperor from 1520, but one whose chances of immortality are dismissed by Browne with the words "and *Charles* the fift can never hope to live within two *Methuselas* of *Hector*"; for though some ancient heroes (such as Hector) have "outlasted their Monuments," long life and recent fame is no antidote against the opium of time.

(f) *Pontius Pilate*. Governor of Judea at the time of Jesus, who was forced to make the final decision about sentencing Christ to death. He is cited by Browne as an example of how it is better to live a good but anonymous life than to possess infamous renown of this kind: "And who had not rather have been the good theef, then *Pilate*?"

309.7 [308]   *Yus Asaf*. The Consul is talking about the legend (which he would have found in Younghusband's *Kashmir,* pp. 129–30) which claims that Jesus did not die upon the cross, but (with the connivance of Pontius Pilate and aid of Joseph of Arimathea) was taken down and later travelled eastward to Kashmir, under the name of Yus Asaf, to carry out the second part of his mission, that of finding the lost tribes of Israel, who had reputedly settled in Kashmir. There he preached, fathered children, and died a natural death at a ripe old age. His tomb, in a building called the Rozabal, is to be found in Srinagar. There may have been a holy man named Yus Asaf who came from the west to Kashmir about the time of Christ, but identification of him with Jesus depends upon accepting such matters as that Christ did not die upon the cross, that He went eastwards, that the name "Jesus" can be identified with "Yus Asaf," and that there can be some degree of compatibility between the teachings of Christ and those ascribed to Yus Asaf. The legend continues to thrive in Kashmir and elsewhere, even though evidence for all four points is extremely problematical.

309.8 [308]   *the lost tribes of Israel.* Behind the Consul's words lies the notion that Kashmir was settled by the lost tribes of Israel, finding whom was the second part of Christ's mission on earth. Originally there were twelve tribes of Israel, descendants of the twelve sons of Jacob (Genesis 35:22–26), but after reaching the Promised Land, the tribes of Judah and Benjamin occupied the south and the other ten the north. Eventually the kingdom split in two, and hostilities took place between Judah and Israel. When Ahaz of Judah called upon the Assyrians for help, the ten tribes of Israel fell under the Assyrian yoke, were taken east and resettled, so that "there was none left but the tribe of Judah only" (2 Kings 17:18). Scripture is thereafter reticent about the fate of the tribes, but on the strength of references in the *Apocrypha* about their going further east, the legend arose of their travelling to India and of the descent of the Kashmiris from them. Like the identification of Yus Asaf with Jesus, the evidence is questionable.

309.9 [308]   *The act of a madman or a drunkard, old bean.* What follows is an exact word-for-word quotation from Tolstoy's Second Epilogue to *War and Peace,* Modern Library Edition, p. 1126 (thus confirming the Consul's claim, p. 87 [82], that he had once known the philosophical section by heart). Tolstoy's point is that our wider understanding of the causes of such action, the *necessity* of such action, diminishes the concept of freedom involved: "the more necessity is seen in it, the less freedom." The words form a statement of the infernal machine and thus tend to undercut the validity of the Consul's "choice" of hell at the end of the chapter.

310.1 (308)   *that little bit in seven flats, on the black keys.* The "little bit in seven flats" is probably the piece known to small children as "Daddy's Shirt," in which one finger plays the note of D-flat on every second beat, while another runs thrice down the black keys. Of Beethoven's (and his own) tendency to "overspread" himself, Lowry wrote: "most of his themes are so simple they could be played by just rolling an orange down the black keys" ("LJC," p. 79). In Jules Verne's *Twenty Thousand Leagues under the Sea,* Pt. I, Ch. 21, Captain Nemo is observed playing his organ: "The captain's fingers were then running over the keys of the instrument, and I remarked that he touched only the black keys, which gave to his melodies an essentially Scottish character."

310.2 [308]   *When we have absolutely no understanding of the causes of an action . . . we ascribe, according to Tolstoy, a greater element of free will to it.* Tolstoy's *War and Peace* concludes with a long philosophical epilogue called "The Forces that Move Nations," which concludes that we must renounce a freedom that does not exist and recognize a dependence of which we are not conscious (see note **87.1**).

Tolstoy's actual words are (*War and Peace,* p. 1128):

> When we have absolutely no understanding of the causes of an action — whether vicious or virtuous or simply non-moral — we ascribe a greater element of free will to it. In the case of a crime, we are more urgent in demanding punishment for the act; in the case of a virtuous act, we are warmer in our appreciation of its merits. In cases of no moral bearing, we recognize more individuality, originality, and independence in it.

Tolstoy's "three considerations" on which our conception of freedom and necessity depend are, p. 1127:

1. The relation of the man committing the act to the external world.
2. His relation to time.
3. His relation to the causes leading to the act.

As Tolstoy says (*War and Peace,* p. 1129):

> In all legislative codes the exoneration of crime or admission of mitigating circumstances rests only on those three classes of consideration. The guilt is conceived as greater or less according to the greater or lesser knowledge of the conditions in which the man judged is to be placed, the greater or less interval of time between the perpetration of the crime and the judgment of it, and the greater or less comprehension of the causes that led to the act.

310.3 [309] *Moreover, according to Tolstoy.* The Consul is in fact condensing Tolstoy's words (*War and Peace,* p. 1127) which follow immediately after his "three considerations." The argument continues for some three pages, but Tolstoy's essential point is that the more we perceive of such influences as the Consul cites, the smaller must be the idea we form of a man's freedom, and the greater our conception of the necessity to which he is subject. Among the examples of "dishonest conduct" cited by Tolstoy is "the relapse of the reformed drunkard into drunkenness" (p. 1129).

311.1 [309] *no, parras, por favor.* Sp. "No, *parras,* please." *Parras* is a strong, wine-based *aguardiente* (see note **229.2.d**).

311.2 [309] *ignoratio elenchi.* L. "ignorance of the point in question"; the logical fallacy of arguing to the wrong point.

311.3 [309]   *poor little defenceless China.* At that moment in the process of being brutally overrun by the Japanese, "astride all roads from Shanghai" (p. 184 [180]), and, like Spain, torn apart by a cruel civil war.

311.4 [309]   *there's a sort of determinism about the fate of nations.* The Consul's insight is "not exactly original" for at least six reasons:

(a)   It forms a succinct summary of Spengler's *The Decline of the West* (see note **104.5**); in an early draft (UBC 11–14, p. 37), Hugh accuses the Consul of "quoting Spengler" at him.

(b)   It epitomizes the thought of the philosophical epilogue of Tolstoy's *War and Peace* (see note **310.2**).

(c)   It reflects the message of the long Tolstoy-like epilogue, "Disintegration of Values" at the end of Hermann Broch's *The Sleepwalkers: A Trilogy* (1928–31), which concludes, p. 628, that "the final indivisible unit in the disintegration of values is the human individual." In an early draft (UBC 7–11, p. 17) Hugh had studied Tolstoy and Broch at Stanford and compared *War and Peace* with *Die Schlafwandler,* "a sort of contemporary record of decay."

(d)   It derives directly (as manuscript notes acknowledge) from Claude Houghton's *Julian Grant Loses His Way* (see note **301.9**).

(e)   It expresses an argument between Conrad Aiken and Malcolm Lowry in Cuernavaca, as Aiken pointed out in a letter to the *TLS,* 16 February 1967, p. 127:

And I might add, for those who are interested, that the entire argument, between the Consul and the other, about Marxism in *Under the Volcano,* was a verbatim report of an argument between Malcolm and myself, with the positions reversed. What the Consul says, I said.

(f)   Lowry had already posed the question in his then unpublished short story "June the 30th, 1934" (*P & S,* p. 43): "Was there really a sort of determination about the fate of nations? Could it be true that, in the end, they got what too they deserved?"

311.5 [310]   *Poor little defenceless Ethiopia.* Recently overrun by vastly superior Italian forces (tanks against spears), with England acquiescing in the despoliation as being "a recognized thing" (see note **254.2**). The subsequent failure of the League of Nations to support that African country's sovereignty was an international disgrace.

311.6 [310]   *poor little defenceless Flanders.* In 1914, Belgium, which had tried to remain neutral, was overrun by German armies to facilitate their attack upon France. The uproar about the "rape of Belgium" was an important element in Allied propaganda.

311.7 [310]   *poor little defenceless Belgian Congo.* As Joseph Conrad's *Heart of Darkness* makes clear, the exploitation by Belgium of its territories in the Congo was an example of the evils of colonialism at their most rapacious. Brave little Belgium, soon to be a victim (see note **311.6**), had in her turn been a conqueror.

311.8 [310]   *poor little defenceless Latvia.* An independent republic from 1918, after centuries of having been part of Poland or Russia, in 1938 about to be forcibly incorporated (as Lowry would have known when writing) into the Soviet Union.

311.9 [310]   *or Finland.* At the time of Lowry's writing, Finland was fighting to retain its precarious independence from Russia, and although, unlike Latvia, it succeeded, success was bought at the cost of economic domination by the Soviet Union and the loss of territories in the Murmansk and Karelia regions.

311.10 [310]   *or even Russia.* Possibly a reference to Russia's humiliating defeat at the hands of Germany in World War I; the Consul may also be anticipating (since the event was a few years in the future) the invasion of Russia by Hitler's Legions in 1941.

312.1 [310]   *Countries, civilizations, empires, great hordes perish for no reason at all.* A philosophy movingly expressed in Yeats's "Lapis Lazuli," where the survival of the human spirit is epitomized by the glittering gay eyes of the Chinamen who stare upon the tragic scene of old civilizations put to the sword.

312.2 [310]   *Timbuctoo.* A town in Mali, in the central Saharan desert; again used as equivalent to "the middle of nowhere." The Penguin "Timbuktu" is an accepted variant.

312.3 [310]   *poor little defenceless Montenegro.* The principality of Montenegro had alone of all the Balkan states managed to retain its independence from Turkey, and at the Congress of Berlin (1878) its independence and territories were recognized by the European powers. However, with the growing power of Austria in the Balkans, Montenegran autonomy became increasingly dependent upon Austrian control, and although independence was maintained during "Tolstoy's day," the state was absorbed by Serbia at the end of World War I.

312.4 [310] *poor little defenceless Serbia.* Serbia had for centuries suffered from Turkish domination, and nationalistic uprisings in the early years of the nineteenth century, though supported by Russia, met with irregular success and invited cruel repression. In 1830 it became an autonomous principality under Turkish suzerainty, and in 1833 it achieved a precarious independence, sandwiched between the Turkish and Austrian empires, until incorporated in 1918 within the kingdom of the Serbs, Croats, and Slovenes.

312.5 [310] *poor little defenceless Greece.* Throughout the 1820's the Greek struggle for independence from Turkey was a rallying call to English liberals, and poets like Shelley and Byron took up the cause (Byron in fact died at Missolonghi in 1824). In an effort to crush the rising, the Ottoman government called upon the Egyptians for aid, and although Greek independence became a fact in 1830 with the Treaty of London, it was possible only because of the "interference" of the European powers. Shelley wrote a long poem, *Hellas* (1821), in defence of Greece and Panhellenism. "As it will be again, of course" refers to the coming World War II, when Greece was cruelly invaded by German troops.

312.6 [310] *Boswell's—poor little defenceless Corsica.* James Boswell (1740–95), the Scottish writer best known for his *Life of Johnson* (1791) and his *Journal of a Tour to the Hebrides* (1785), in his earlier days had much travelled upon the Continent, including Corsica, where he had become absorbed in the cause of Corsican independence. As a result, he published *An Account of Corsica* (1768) and *Essays in Favour of the Brave Corsicans* (1769), and in his *Life of Johnson* (26 April 1768) he replies plaintively to Johnson's advice to empty his head of Corsica:

> But how can you bid me "empty my head of Corsica?" My noble-minded friend, do you not feel for an oppressed nation bravely struggling to be free.... Empty my head of Corsica! Empty it of honour, empty it of humanity, empty it of piety. No! while I live, Corsica and the cause of the brave islanders shall ever employ much of my attention.

Corsica had been under the domination of France or Genoa for centuries, but some years after the successful revolt against the Genoese in 1529, Paoli (see note **312.7**) set up an independent state in 1755. Genoa sold its "rights" in the island to France in 1768, and in 1769 Paoli's troops were defeated by the French, Corsica becoming part of France.

312.7 [310]   *Paoli.* Pasquale Paoli (1726–1807), Corsican patriot and general who had resisted mightily the sell-out and intervention by France in the affairs of his country, but who fled to England when the French took over the island in 1769. Boswell, who had called upon Chatham in Corsican dress to plead Paoli's cause and whose *An Account of Corsica* was dedicated to the general, hastened down from Scotland to meet him. Boswell stayed in London with Paoli, who tried unsuccessfully to break him of his drinking habits. On the outbreak of Revolution in 1789, Paoli returned to France and was appointed lieutenant-general of Corsica, but disgusted by the excesses of the Revolution, he returned to England in 1794.

312.8 [310]   *Monboddo.* James Burnett, Lord Monboddo (1714–99), a Scottish judge with impassioned enthusiasms for Greek philosophy and natural history. He combined a brilliant legal career with an eccentric philosophy of language and nature. He is cited by the Consul, not for his views on Corsica, but for his primitivist way of life upon his small estate in Scotland where he delighted in living as a peasant-farmer. At Boswell's insistence, Johnson visited him there on their tour to the Hebrides in 1773, and the two men, despite a marked difference in their outspoken views, got on tolerably well.

312.9 [310]   *Applesquires and fairies.* Idyllic innocence is undercut by the common eighteenth century meaning of "applesquires" as "catamites"; hence the rather ambiguous fairies. There is no basis for this particular eccentricity in Monboddo's life.

312.10 [310]   *Rousseau—not douanier—knew he was talking nonsense.* Not Henri Rousseau, "the customs officer" and painter of jungle scenes (see note **136.1**), but Jean Jacques Rousseau (1712–78), French philosopher and political writer, whose wretched life was sadly at odds with the ideals he professed. He is best known for his *Confessions* (published posthumously), but also for *La Nouvelle Héloise* (1761), *Émile* (1762), *Du Contrat Social* (1762), each of which expresses the essential ethic that sin is owing not to nature but to society and that man has fallen away from the natural primitive state where he was once both good and happy. The Consul's specific reference (as Jakobsen notes, p. 99) is to Boswell's *Life of Johnson,* 30 September 1769, where Johnson dismisses Boswell's arguments for the "superior happiness of savage life" by replying that whereas Monboddo talked insufferable nonsense about such matters, Rousseau talked nonsense so well that he must have known it was nonsense.

313.1 [311] *that conversation with the volunteers in the train.* As Hugh tries to point out, this is not in Tolstoy's *War and Peace,* but rather in his *Anna Karenina* (1875–76), the story of the adulterous love between Anna Karenina, wife of a wealthy Russian administrator, and Vronsky, a cavalry officer, for whom she leaves her husband and child. She is ostracized by society, the love affair dwindles, and in total isolation and despair she throws herself beneath a train. The episode which the Consul refers to is in Pt. 8, Ch. 3, near the end of the novel, and the Consul's description is a fair report of what Katavasov sees and hears.

313.2 [311] *Katamasov or whoever he was.* From *Anna Karenina,* actually, Fyodor Vassilievitch Katavasov, a professor of philosophy and minor character in the novel. The manuscript originally read Katavasov (UBC 7–11, p. 25), so the error is Hugh's rather than Lowry's, but in *Anna Karenina* Pt. 8, Ch. 15 the sentiment is actually uttered by Sergey Ivanovitch Koznishev, brother of Levin (though in the presence of Katavasov), and is followed up further by Katavasov and Koznishev in Ch. 16. Hugh thus aligns himself with Sergey Ivanovitch, but Katavasov (and Tolstoy) have by now a more pessimistic view of the truth.

313.3 [311] *a diplomatic corps which merely remains in San Sebastian.* San Sebastián, on the French border with Spain, was a popular resort town and acted as the seat of government during the hot summer months. In 1930–31 it had been the centre of the left-wing revolutionary activity that had eventually ousted the monarchy. The town was surrendered by the Basques to Nationalists in September 1936, by which time the British embassy, having earlier moved from Madrid to San Sebastián, had set itself up in St. Jean de Luz, on the French side of the International Bridge (Thomas, p. 346), where it remained for the duration of hostilities.

313.4 [312] *War and Peace. . . . able to distinguish it from Anna Karenina.* Hugh is correct in so far as the conversation about the volunteers in the train is from *Anna Karenina,* but the Consul's real point is Tolstoy's epilogue on historical determinism at the end of *War and Peace* (see note **310.2**).

314.1 [313] *oratio obliqua.* L. "indirect speech." A formal rhetorical term found in Quintilian's study of oratory. Another possible translation would be "indoor marksmanship" (see note **14.2**).

314.2 [313] *the children I might have wanted.* Although the Consul's desire is a perfectly natural one (and one that appears to have been frustrated in Lowry's life with Jan), its occult implictions are stated firmly by A. E. Waite, *The Holy Kabbalah,* VIII.ii, p. 378, in a section subtitled "The Mystery of Sex":

> Now, the Sacred Name is never attached to an incomplete man, being one who is unmarried, or one who dies without issue. Such a person does not penetrate after death into the vestibule of Paradise on account of his incompleteness.

315.1 [313]   *ninney-hammers.* Elizabethan slang, meaning "simpletons" (a contraction of "an innocent"). The force of "hammer" is uncertain, but the Consul gives it a markedly sexual emphasis. If "gills like codfish and veins like racehorses" is a quotation, it has not been traced.

315.2 [313]   *prime as goats... hot as monkeys... salt as wolves.* From *Othello,* III.iii.402-5, where Iago is trying to convince an all-too-willing Othello that he has been cuckolded:

> It is impossible you should see this,
> Were they as prime as goats, as hot as monkeys,
> As salt as wolves in pride, and fools as gross
> As ignorance made drunk.

315.3 [313]   *As if he plucked up kisses.* From *Othello,* III.iii 426-27: Iago, asked to give proof of Desdemona's infidelity, reports that he has heard Cassio say in his sleep:

> "Sweet Desdemona,
> Let us be wary, let us hide our loves!"
> And then, sir, would he gripe and wring my hand,
> Cry "O, sweet creature!" and then kiss me hard,
> As if he pluck'd my kisses by the roots,
> That grew upon my lips; then laid his leg
> Over my thigh, and sigh'd, and kiss'd; and then
> Cried, "Cursed fate, that gave thee to the Moor!"

315.4 [313]   *paddling palms.* From *The Winters Tale,* I.ii.115, where Leontes, king of Sicilia, is (like Othello) only too ready to detect in the willingness of his queen Hermione to give her hand to Polixenes signs of his imminent betrayal:

But to be paddling palms and pinching fingers,
As now they are, and making practis'd smiles,
As in a looking-glass; and then to sigh, as 'twere
The mort o' the deer; O! that is entertainment
My bosom likes not, nor my brows.

315.5 [313] *Poor little defenceless me.* The phrase echoes the list of bullied nations, p. 311 [310], who, according to the Consul, get what they deserve. The Consul's sudden realization of its implications turns his great battle for the survival of the human consciousness, p. 221 [217], into a piddling little fight for freedom.

315.6 [313] *triskeles. Triskeles,* more commonly *triskelions,* are symbolic devices depicting three bent legs radiating from a centre, as in the emblem of the Isle of Man. The third leg is sometimes said to have sexual implications. The reference to "strumming" (triskeles/ukuleles) mocks traditional pictures of Hawaii and Hugh playing hot music on his guitar.

315.7 [313] *the infinite trismus. Trismus,* from Gk. trizein, "to grind the teeth," is a grinding or rasping, but in medical terms refers to tetanus or lockjaw. The Consul's image appears to be one of bodies locked together in an eternal brothel.

315.8 [314] *Lee Maitland . . . Baudelaire's angel.* In his failure to experience the sense of spiritual awakening, the Consul does not realize that, after drinking all night at the Red Cross ball he had been greeted that morning by Yvonne, who could have been the angel to waken the soul "Dans la brute assoupie" (see note **283.4**).

316.1 [313] *I choose. . . . Tlax. . . . Hell. . . . Because. . . . I like it.* Tlaxcala throughout the book has been a metaphor for dishonour, betrayal, and death. At this moment, the Consul, "suspended" between the choice of Yvonne or the Farolito, life and death, makes his existential decision. Given the power of the infernal machine and the preceding discussion of historical determinism, the "freedom" of his choice is very much the point at issue.

316.2 [314] *In fact I'm running.* In one sense, like Faustus, "headlong into the earth"; but also like the hapless hero of *Julian Grant Loses His Way,* who near the end of the novel rushes from the Metropolitan Café only to wake up in hell, in a world (like the Farolito of Ch. 12) which is virtually the projection of his own interior state.

CHAPTER ELEVEN

317.1 [316] *Sunset.* As Sherrill Grace suggests ("Experimental Vision," p. 106), this cryptic direction forms a conscious inversion of Murnau's *Sunrise* (see note **204.5**), with the unstated implication that no reconciliation will take place between the Consul and Yvonne.

317.2 [316] *with the grace of a Rebecca.* Rebekah, daughter of Bethuel, "very fair to look upon," was chosen to be the wife of Isaac as she drew water in the evening from the well outside the city of Nahor (Genesis 24).

317.3 [316] *The storm, that had already dispatched its outriders.* "Outriders" are armed attendants on horseback accompanying a carriage or stage-coach. In Hindu mythology these clouds are the *Maruts,* the storm winds, companions in battle with Indra. The storm on p. 16 [10] is described as "dark swift horses surging up the sky" and that in the Consul's mind, p. 149 [145], as a darkness "that will come galloping out of nowhere across the fields of the mind." The reference thus anticipates the sudden violence that will strike Yvonne down at the end of the chapter.

317.4 [317] *white handbells, tongue downwards.* The detail acts as a reminder of Goethe's church–bell with its giant protruding tongue (see note **79.2**). The themes of abnegated responsibility and consequent retribution are very much to the fore in this chapter.

318.1 [317] *worn-out ploughshares... abandoned American cars.* One year from now Jacques Laruelle will see an abandoned plough, its arms raised to heaven in mute supplication, p. 15 [9], and the total wreck of a faded blue Ford, an emblem of the Consul (see note **19.2**).

318.2 [317] *Infernal bird of Prometheus!* The vulture, which every day would tear at the liver of Prometheus as he lay chained upon the Caucasus (see note **134.9**). The vultures, vile and ugly, nevertheless symbolize for Lowry the human spirit which blossoms in the shadow of the abbatoir.

318.3 [317] *the condor.* A large vulture (*Cathartes gryphus*) found in the highest parts of the South American Andes and capable of ascending to great heights. Thomas Nuttall's *Ornithology* comments, p. 104: "Indeed the Condor frequents and nests upon the summit of the Andes, above which they are seen to soar in the boundless ocean of space, enjoying the invigorating and rarified atmosphere."

318.4 [317]   *low hills... purple and sad.* A last reminder of the earthly paradise about to be lost (see note **20.8**).

318.5 [318]   *Chimborazo, Popocatepetl.* A reference to W. J. Turner's "Romance" (see note **69.1**); Popocatepetl has indeed stolen the Consul's soul away. Chimborazo is an extinct volcano in Ecuador; at 20,660 feet one of the highest peaks of the Andes (in the eighteenth century it was believed to be the highest mountain on earth).

318.6 [318]   *the tragic Indian legend.* Yvonne is alluding to the story of the love of Popocatepetl, prince of the lowly Chichimecas, for Ixtaccihuatl, princess of the great Toltecs. The father of Ixtaccihuatl forbade the match, but seeing his daughter's grief he relented and imposed upon the prince a number of duties to perform. Before they could be carried out, Ixtaccihuatl died, but holding in his heart the hope that she might come back to life, the prince took her body up into the hills, where he built a fire at sunset and knelt beside her to watch for signs of life. At last Quetzalcóatl took pity on them and changed them into volcanoes, the princess sleeping but the prince glowing as he maintains eternal vigilance over his beloved.

319.1 [318]   *the two paths... like the arms... of a man being crucified.* The paths stretch out like the arms of the dying Indian, p. 244 [241], but Lowry's sense, which he hints at, "LJC," p. 83, is more esoteric: "On the surface Hugh and Yvonne are simply searching for the Consul, but such a search would have added meaning to anyone who knows anything of the Eleusinian mysteries." The Eleusinian mysteries, which date back to the nineteenth century B.C., are among the most ancient of the Greek rites and festivals which originally associated the seasonal cycle of crops and vegetation and the cycle of the sun with human death and resurrection. The myths and legends associated with the mysteries are complex, and according to Thomas Taylor's "Eleusinian and Bacchic Mysteries" (1790), they symbolize the descent of the soul into the world of matter (represented by the dark wood) and the search for spiritual enlightenment. In many treatments of the rites there is a ritual bathing (as in Ch. 10), followed by a long wandering search through a labyrinth or dark wood in search of truth, or the lost word, or a lost child. This forms an enactment of the torchlight search of the grief–stricken Demeter (or Ceres, or the earth) for Persephone (or Prosperine, or the sun), snatched away to the underworld by gloomy Dis (or Pluto, or the darkness). The search often has overtones of fertility, the blessings withheld until the lost one is restored; and initiation into the higher mysteries.

Lowry continues, "LJC," p. 83: "the same esoteric idea of this kind of search also appears in Shakespeare's *Tempest*" (he repeats the idea in *October Ferry*, p. 137). As Andersen suggests, p. 144, Lowry is probably referring to Colin Still's books on the subject of *The Tempest* and the Eleusinian mysteries (*Shakespeare's Mystery Play*, 1921, and *The Timeless Theme*, 1936). In the latter, p. 135, Still argues that *The Tempest* must be seen "as a dramatic representation of the Mystery of Redemption, conceived as a psychological experience and expressed in mythological form." Lowry's depiction of Yvonne's last hour has the same intention. In the dark wood, as things shimmer between their realistic and symbolic meanings, the choice of paths revealed in the form of the crucified Christ and the Hanged Man (the soul asleep, awaiting its awakening) becomes the first decision that must be confronted, the first step that must be taken upon the next stage of the soul's journey.

319.2 [318] *leguminous.* Lowry is using the word to evoke the dank smell of the jungle, which he likens to the distinctive protein-like smell of legumes; but he may also be implying a pun on vegetation/vegetable.

319.3 [318] *the Rum–Popo.* A Freudian slip: the restaurant-cantina is El Popo, named for the volcano, and rumpope is a yellowish, egg-based alcoholic drink (see note **229.2.i**).

319.4 [318] *five thousand bobolinks.* The bobolink, so-called from its rollicking musical song, is a common black and white North American songbird which migrates in huge flocks each winter to South America. It is described in *October Ferry*, p. 115, as: "the blithe bobolink, friend of hay and clover: the merry bobolink that was also called (ex post facto knowledge too) skunk blackbird, *le goglu,* Dolichonyz oryzivorus, the bobolink that said clink." Nuttall states in his *Ornithology,* p. 198, that bobolinks fix their abode "in the savannahs of Ohio and Michigan" and describes, p. 201, "their awakening and faultering voices" as being "like the noise of a distant torrent."

319.5 [319] *El Petate.* Sp. "the mat." The word also has connotations of a liar and of one who is tired of living (it is unlikely that Lowry was aware of either). In *DATG,* p. 101, Lowry acknowledges that the original of El Petate was in Mexico City, where he had once written a poem on the menu (as the Consul has in El Popo, p. 331).

320.1 [319]   *Their mouths opened and shut soundlessly, their brown hands traced patterns in the air, courteously.* Lowry may have read Albert Camus's *The Myth of Sisyphus* (1942) in which the famous passage occurs (Gallimard edition, p. 29):

> Men also secrete something inhuman. In certain lucid hours, the mechanical aspect of their gestures, their dumb show deprived of meaning makes all that surrounds them foolish. A man speaks on the telephone behind a glass partition; one does not hear him, but one sees his mime without hearing or understanding why he lives. This uneasiness in front of the inhumanity of man himself, this incalculable fall before the image of what we are, this "nausea" as it is called by a contemporary author [Jean Paul Sartre], this is also absurdity. Likewise the stranger who, in certain seconds, meets us in the mirror, the familiar and yet disturbing brother whom we find in our own photographs, this also is absurdity.

320.2 [319]   *Moctezuma, Criollo, Cafeaspirina, Mentholatum—no se rasque las picaduras de los insectos!* Advertisements for beer, a brand of cigar, aspirin, and a menthol-based ointment—"Don't scratch insect bites!"

320.3 [319]   *the formerly prosperous village of Anochtitlán, which had burned.* The model for this village is the town of Nochixtlán, more properly Asunción Nochixtlán, some eighty miles northwest of Oaxaca on the road to Cuernavaca. The largest town of its district, it was of considerable strategic importance during the Revolution of 1910-20, and in December 1916 it was captured and pillaged by the forces of General Cordova. As punishment for its "disaffection" (Iturribarria, p. 381), the suburb of Chocuno was put to the torch and burnt to the ground. Lowry calls the town *A*noch*t*itlán partly because his friend Juan Fernando Márquez always pronounced the "a" (*DATG*, p.220), presumably as an abbreviation of Asunción, and also because the extra "a" and "t" extends the name Nochixtlán to rhyme with Tenochtitlán, the Aztec city destroyed and pillaged by Cortés (see note **33.1**).

320.4 [319]   *a small eagle.* The eagle was originally a hawk (UBC 11-18, p. 6), and Lowry was concerned lest his debt to Yeats ("The Second Coming" and *A Vision*) be too obvious. He also refers (in various drafts and letters) to parallels between this bird and others: to hawks and eagles described in Nuttall's *Ornithology,* which he used as a source; to Walter van Tilburg Clark's "Hook," the story of a hawk, once magnificently supreme, wounded by a shotgun blast and unable to fly; to Chaucer's *The Maunciple's Tale*

("Taak any byrd and put it in a cage"), which he had used to preface *Ultramarine;* and to James Stephens's poem, "The Lark," about a small bird cowering in the dark, its wing broken, its song gone, its mate far away. None of these references is at all obvious, but the eagle symbolizes perfectly the neo-Platonic notion of the soul escaping from the dark wood.

320.5 [320] *an amate and a sabina.* The amate (from Nah. *amatl,* "paper," so called because its bark was used by the Indians for this purpose) is a kind of fig-tree which abounds in the warmer areas of Mexico; the sabina (from L. *sapinus,* "a sabine") is a tree of the cypress family, evergreen with extended branches (also known as the *ahuehuetl*). The two trees are often found together, and a celebrated pair, undoubtedly those that Lowry has in mind, was to be found at Chapultepec park in Cuernavaca, as described in de Davila, p. 77:

> Along this path you will encounter some interesting specimens of Amates and Sabinos. The amate is a persistent and tenacious tree. Its roots will break huge rocks in order to find their way to moisture, and the strangest freak of all is that the roots do not mind crawling great distances over or around obstacles in their downward course.
>
> Do not fail to see the amate, the roots of which form the shape of an octopus and a giraffe over the gigantic boulders of which it grows. Then note the strange embracing of a sabino and an amate. I have seen other examples of the amate and the sabino intertwined, but this is by far the best example which I have seen.

In an earlier draft (UBC 7-2, p. 24) the amate and the sabino formed part of Laruelle's jungle-scene, p. 206 [203], and Lowry noted distinctly how the roots of the sabino "broke the rocks to get near the life–giving water."

320.6 [320] *extravagant fructification.* The embracing trees and fecundity of nature may bring home to Yvonne a sense of her fruitless relation with Geoffrey.

321.1 [320] *cordage.* Here used in the sense of a ship's rigging. Booms are the wooden spars to which a ship's sails are attached.

321.2 [320] *it was free . . . at that moment appeared one star.* Yvonne's freeing of the eagle anticipates the release of her own soul at the end of the chapter when she is taken up into the heavens. The star that suddenly appears is Venus, with which Yvonne has already been identified (see note **49.8**), and into which Quetzalcóatl was transformed (see note **301.4**). Her

act of releasing the eagle corresponds to the Consul's first attempt to free
the horse in Ch. 12.

322.1 [321] *whip-poor-will, whip-peri-will.* The whip-poor-will, so
named for its haunting plaintive cry, is a nocturnal bird of the *caprimul-
gidae* (goatsucker) family, described by Peterson, p. 93, as: "ample-tailed
nocturnal birds with small bills and weak, tiny feet. During the day they rest
horizontally on some limb, or on the ground, where their mottled brown
pattern blends with the surroundings." Lewis Spence comments that the
"mournful chant" of this bird relayed to the Aztec priests messages from the
dead (*M of M & P,* pp. 97–98). The word "peri" in the second part of the cry
is taken directly from Thomas Nuttall's *Ornithology,* p. 743, but also suggests a reference to Thomas Moore's *Lalla Rookh,* the second part of which
is called "Paradise and the Peri." A peri, in Persian mythology, is a being like an elf or genie, but formed of fire and descended from fallen
angels, and hence excluded from Paradise until its penance is complete.
Moore's poem begins:

> One morn a Peri at the gate
> Of Eden stood, disconsolate;
> And as she listen'd to the Springs
>   Of life within, like music flowing,
> And caught the light upon her wings
>   Through the half-open portal glowing
> She wept to think her recreant race
> Should e'er have lost that glorious place.

322.2 [321] *Cayenne.* A city, river and island in French Guiana; mentioned in Nuttall's *Ornithology,* p. 746, as a wintering place of the whip-
poor-will from September to March. Nuttall also comments, p. 745, that
the bird has no nest, and, p. 743, that it is sometimes dreaded as an omen of
misfortune.

322.3 [321] *Scorpio, setting.* As Lowry noted, *SL* p. 188, the novel's action takes place in Scorpio. The Consul has by now thoroughly identified
himself with the scorpion (see note **339.7**), and the setting of the constellation is clearly emblematic of his own fall. The relations between Yvonne,
the Consul, and Hugh are neatly defined in MacGregor-Mathers's *The Kabbalah Unveiled,* p. 24: "Scorpio, as a good emblem, being symbolized by the
eagle, as an evil emblem by the scorpion, and as of a mixed nature by the
snake."

322.4 [322] *they would rise and set.*

(a) *Fomalhaut.* From Ar. *Fum al Hut,* "the mouth of the fish"; a star of the first magnitude in the constellation of Piscis Australis, the Southern Fish. It has been called "lonely" because it occupies a position in the sky otherwise barren of large-magnitude stars.

(b) *Aldebaran.* From Ar. *Al Dabaran,* "the follower" (that is, of the Pleiades); a star of the first magnitude in the constellation of Taurus, forming the bull's eye.

(c) *the Pleiades.* A group of stars in the constellation of Taurus, six of which are readily visible, while a seventh, Merope (perhaps to be linked with Yvonne), shines less brightly, since in legend she fell in love with the mortal Sisyphus. The sentence "As Scorpio sets in the southwest, the Pleiades are rising in the northeast" reads as if from an introductory astronomy text and underlines the opposition of the Consul and Yvonne.

(d) *Orion.* An equatorial constellation near Taurus, containing the first-magnitude stars Rigel and Betelgeuse. In legend, the huntsman Orion loved Diana, and on his death he was placed in the heavens near her as a constellation. Kilgallin, p. 198, suggests that the figure of Orion, who died of the sting of Scorpio, is an emblem of the Consul.

(e) *Cetus.* The Whale, an equatorial constellation south of Pisces and Aries; in legend sometimes identified with the fabled creature sent to devour Andromeda and turned to stone by the Medusa's head.

(f) *Mira.* A star, *Omicron Ceti,* in the constellation Cetis; remarkable for its varying brightness.

323.1 [322] *careen.* In nautical usage, the sudden sideways movement of a ship. Lowry intends a pun upon the constellation Carina, "the Keel," often considered part of the constellation Argo, "the Ship."

323.2 [322] *giant Antares ranging to its end.* Antares, "the scorpion's heart" (see note **55.2**); a star of the first magnitude in the constellation Scorpio. In an early draft (UBC 7–12, p. 17), Yvonne underlined the implications: "'That's Antares,' Yvonne said, 'It's nearly five hundred times as big as our sun. And it's dying. A dying sun, just an ember.'"

323.3 [322] *Aries, Taurus, Gemini, the Crab, Leo, Virgo, the Scales and the Scorpion, Capricorn the Sea–goat and Aquarius the Water Bearer, Pisces, and once more, triumphantly, Aries.* The signs of the Zodiac, named in their traditional order eastward from the vernal equinox. The Zodiac itself is the zone centred on the ecliptic and extending for 8° on either side of it, the zone in which the moon and all the planets are always found, whatever their orbital position may be. The "Zodiac Zone" (this understanding underlies the Consul's pun, p. 207 [203]) is divided into twelve equal sections, and the signs are named for the constellations that were in them at the time of Hipparchus of Nicaea (190–120 B.C.), the greatest astronomer of ancient Greece.

(a) *Aries.* The Ram; the first constellation in the Zodiac, representing the ram on which Phrixus and Helle rode through the air to escape their stepmother Ino. Helle fell off and drowned in the Hellespont, but Phrixus rode to Colchis where he sacrificed the ram and hung its golden fleece upon a tree, from whence Jason captured it. Aries is still considered the first sign even though the vernal equinox is now in Pisces.

(b) *Taurus.* The Bull; A V-shaped figure of five stars marks the face of the bull and represents the animal into which Jupiter changed himself when he carried the princess Europa across the Mediterranean. The eye of the bull is the giant red star, Aldebaran, and the Pleiades form its shoulder.

(c) *Gemini.* The Twins; a large bright group of stars northeast of Orion, representing the Greek twins Castor and Pollux, sons of Leda and Zeus, who act as the tutelary deities of soldiers and sailors.

(d) *the Crab.* Cancer; the least conspicuous constellation of the Zodiac, containing no bright stars. It represents the giant crab that seized the foot of Hercules when he was fighting the Hydra and gives its name to the Tropic of Cancer since the sun is in this sign at the summer solstice, when it begins to move backwards.

(e) *Leo.* The Lion; a large constellation in the spring evening sky representing the Nemean Lion slain by Hercules as the first of his twelve labours.

(f) *Virgo.* The Virgin; a large group of stars representing Ceres, goddess of the harvest, with a few heads of wheat in her hand (the sun is in this sign in August, the time of the harvest).

(g) *the Scales.* Libra; representing the balancing of night and day because the autumn equinox was in this sign when it was first described in ancient Mesopotamia. Lowry links it with Scorpio, reflecting the opinion among the ancient Greeks that these stars were the claws of the Scorpion, which in their early Zodiac covered the space of two signs.

(h) *Scorpio.* The Scorpion; a large conspicuous constellation representing the scorpion that killed Orion when he boasted that no living creature could harm him and placed by Zeus on the opposite side of the sky so it could not do so again (as it rises Orion sets, as if in fear). It is the most brilliant of the constellations and contains the giant red star Antares.

(i) *Sagittarius.* The Archer; inexplicably missing from Lowry's list. It represents the centaur Chiron, aiming an arrow at the Scorpion, and was also known as the "Bull-killer," since Taurus sets when it rises.

(j) *Capricorn the sea-goat.* An inconspicuous constellation, south of the equator, containing no bright stars. It represents the god Pan, who, frightened by the monster Typhon, plunged into the Nile; the part of him under water was changed into a fish and that above into a goat. The constellation gave its name to the Tropic of Capricorn because the sun at the winter solstice was formerly in the sign.

(k) *Aquarius the Water Bearer.* A large but inconspicuous constellation south of Pegasus, representing Zeus pouring rain upon the earth.

(l) *Pisces.* The Fish; a long irregular group of stars representing Venus and Cupid, who, frightened by the giant Typhon, jumped into the Euphrates and changed themselves into fishes.

(m) *and once more, triumphantly, Aries.* The reappearance of the sun in Aries is a triumphant attestation of continuity and renewed life, as spring takes over from winter, and the Voyage That Never Ends continues its pattern of death and rebirth.

323.4 [323] *the beneficent Pleiades.* A cluster of stars in Taurus and one of the most important constellations in the northern heavens. The daughters of Atlas, they grieved at the burden heaven imposed on their father who had to support the weight of the firmament on his shoulders; because of their sympathy, they were rewarded with a place in heaven. In another version of the myth, Orion saw them in the forest and pursued them; they appealed to Zeus, who turned them into doves, whereupon they flew up into the sky. Orion and his dogs followed them in the heavens, continuing the passionate chase. Still another myth says that they killed themselves out of grief for the accidental death of their brother Hyas.

The Pleiades have been frequently associated with unpleasant omens, prophecies, or events on earth. Because they are an autumn sign, they are in many cultures considered the bringers of death. They reach their zenith on November the first; hence they are "high overhead" here, on the evening of 2 November. In some cultures, prayers of the dead were recited on this day. The Aztecs believed that the end of the world would occur in the month of the Pleiades, our November, when the Pleiades were considered to be the guiding spirits (see note **35.3**).

The Pleiades thus have a dual role in *Under the Volcano.* On the one hand they stand for death and doom, and they dominate the events of Chapters 11 and 12. However, Yvonne considers them beneficent, as standing, somehow, for rebirth and regeneration. Her mood of calm acceptance at the end of this chapter may reflect the older tradition of the interceding influence of the Pleiades.

325.5 [323] *the dead child of the earth.* Yvonne is alluding to the theory that the moon was once part of the earth, but as a result of cataclysmic gravitational pulls it was torn from its parent to become a dead, barren satellite. She probably has in mind her own dead child, p. 76 [72], and perhaps those she has never had with the Consul.

(a) *The Sea of Fecundity.* The Mare Foecunditatis, a large dark area near the western limits of the moon, covering more than 150,000 square miles. It is roughly diamond-shaped, but its boundaries are irregular and not well-defined.

(b) *the sea of Nectar.* The Mare Nectaris, a circular (rather than pentagonal) plain in the southwest quadrant of the moon, adjoining the southern end of the Mare Tranquillitatus.

(c) *Frascatorius.* Fracastorius, formerly a huge ring plain some sixty miles in diameter, but its wall at the southern end broken down by an overflow of the Mare Nectaris. The north wall is not observable.

(d) *Endymion.* A great crater, seventy-eight miles in diameter, near the northwest limb between the Mare Humboldtianum and Mare Frigoris. Its dark floor makes it particularly prominent, and its broken walls rise some 10,000 to 15,000 feet above the surface of the moon.

(e) *the Leibnitz mountains.* A range of mountains near the south lunar pole; named for the German mathematician Gottfried Wilhelm Leibnitz (1646–1716), logician and inventor of the calculus.

(f) *Proclus.* A crater, some eighteen miles in diameter, about fifty miles east of the Mare Crisium with very steep walls rising to 8,000 feet.

(g) *the Marsh of a Dream.* The Palus Somnii, the Marsh of Sleep, in the northwest quadrant of the moon, adjoining the Mare Tranquillitatus.

(h) *Hercules and Atlas.* Two large craters, each about fifty miles in diameter, in the northwest limb near Endymion, forming a double crater whose walls rise to 11,000 feet in the north.

324.1 [323] *in the midst of cataclysm.* In part, a reference to the violent crashes of meteorites and space debris on the surface of the moon and modern notions of entropy; also, however, suggesting the disturbance caused to the planetary system by the Fall of Man.

324.2 [323] *The cemetery was swarming with people.* The celebrations of the Day of the Dead (see note **9.8)** include all-night vigils at the gravesides of the departed.

324.3 [323] *a heliograph of lightning.* A heliograph is a device for sending messages by flashing the rays of the sun from a mirror; the light captures in a tiny frozen moment of time a scene not unlike that at the end of Ch. 1 when Laruelle burns the letter.

324.4 [324] *A sound like windbells.* Windbells are clusters of small bells or chimes hung so as to strike each other when blown by the wind; the "ghostly tintinnabulation" (with its echo of Poe's "The Bells") will be heard by Vigil and Laruelle a year later, p. 10 [4].

325.1 [324]   *Euzkadi.* In Mexico, the common brand name of a make of automobile tire (an affiliate of Goodrich); also, as Hugh is only too well aware, the name of the short-lived Republic of the free Basque provinces, which under the leadership of José Antonio Aguirre declared a provisional government on 7 October 1936 but which shortly afterwards came under attack from the Nationalist forces. The Republicans could not or would not come to the aid of this separatist movement, and on 26 April 1937 Guernica was bombed and strafed. On 19 June 1937, after much shelling and bombing, Bilbao was taken; subsequently every effort was made to extinguish Basque separatist feeling. In an early version of the novel, in Chapter 2, Yvonne and Hugh flew with Weber into Quauhnahuac (UBC 7-3, p. 20):

> They made a neat three-point landing in a field, coming to rest under an enormous advertisement for motor tires: *Euzkadi.*
> "Isn't that the old name of the Basque country?" inquired Hugh, as he picked up the two little bags. "It confuses me why it should be the name of a make of motor tires. Damn it, you can't get away from the thought of Spain at all."

Lowry may also have had in mind a couple of private allusions: in *DATG,* p. 111, Sigbjørn drives past "the familiar sign, Euzkadi, another Vulcanización," hence a reminder of the Volcanoes; while in an early draft (UBC 7-11, p. 12) he had the Consul reflect: "Euzkadi . . . was the country of the Atlanteans" (a detail derived from Donnelly, pp. 172-73). Neither detail is made anything of in the final version, but the sign makes an unspoken criticism of Hugh's dallying.

325.2 [324]   *the state line.* The town of Amecameca, in part the model for Parián, is at the foot of Ixtaccihuatl, in Mexico State but near the Morelos-Mexico State boundaries.

325.3 [324]   *But only Yvonne had seen him.* As Éliphas Lévi points out, in relation to the existence of the sidereal body: "Apparitions of persons dear to us coincidentally with the moment of their death are phenomena of the same order and attributable to the same cause" (*Transcendental Magic,* p. 127).

326.1 [325]   *macaws.* Large brightly coloured and harsh-voiced parrots found throughout Central and South America. The question "Quo Vadis?," p. 235 [232], goes unheard.

326.2 [325] *crepitated.* From L. *crepitare,* "to crackle"; rattled, crackled.

326.3 [326] *Comment? . . . Mescal, por favor. . . . ¿Como no?* Fr. and Sp. "What? . . . Mescal, please. . . . Why not?" The delay for drinks now constitutes an alcohol-related abnegation of responsibility; in earlier drafts it was a deliberate (if misguided) decision to pause and give the Consul time to calm down and get over his rage.

327.1 [326] *La Paloma.* A traditional Mexican love song, very popular, in which a love-lorn sailor envies the dove its wings, that he may fly to his beloved. The best-known version is that by Sebastian Yradier (1809–65), the chorus of which goes:

> Sí a tu ventana llega una paloma
> tra-la-la con cariño que es mi persona
> cuenta-la tus amores bien de mi vida
> corona-la de flores que es cosa mia.

("If a dove, which is me in disguise, / comes to your window singing with affection, / tell her how much you love me, / and crown my little bird with flowers.")

As the manuscripts indicate (UBC 11-7, p. 12), this was the version Lowry had in mind, but another version, popular in Mexico, begins:

> Paloma blanca, blanca paloma
> quién tuviera tus alas, tus alas quién tuviera,
> para volar y volar para
> donde están mis amores, mis amores donde están.

("White dove, white dove / . . . who would have your wings . . . / to fly . . . / to where my love is.")

The song hints at the Consul's white birds of p. 232 [228] and anticipates Yvonne's transformation at the end of the chapter. There is a legend that Maximilian, facing the firing squad, asked as his final request for a band to play "La Paloma."

327.2 [326] *It was the house of her spirit.* Yvonne's dream is both created and dissolved by the mescal she is drinking, as was the Consul's "phantom dance of souls" (see note **288.3**).

328.1 [327] *ocho pesos cincuenta.* Sp. "Eight pesos fifty (centavos)" (about \$1.90). If Hugh was serious about the implications of his guitar-playing, and of Phillipson's picture, p. 181 [178], then his purchase of the guitar clearly represents a regression to the infantile.

328.2 [327]   *the Internationale.* The revolutionary socialist hymn, written in 1871 by Eugène Pottier (1816–87), with music by Pierre Degeyter (with a deplorable lack of solidarity, this was disputed by his brother Adolphe). It was first performed in 1888 in Lille, and after the First Congress of the Second International in Paris (1889), it was accepted as the international hymn for the revolutionary struggle of the proletariat and was adopted in 1918 as the state anthem of the Soviet Union.

328.3 [327]   *Como tu quieras.* Sp. "As you wish."

328.4 [328]   *The kind of lie Sir Walter Raleigh meditates.* Sir Walter Raleigh (1552?–1618), Elizabethan poet, historian, statesman, and courtier, whose glittering career at court ended in his long confinement in the Tower, a final disastrous voyage to South America, and his execution. The reference here, as Hugh explains, is to Raleigh's poem, "The Lie," printed in 1611, in which the poet addresses his soul and tells of the falsity of worldly institutions and fortune. The poem begins:

> Go, soul, the body's guest,
>   Upon a thankless arrant.
> Fear not to touch the best;
>   The truth shall be thy warrant.
> Go, since I needs must die,
>   And give the world the lie.
>
> Say to the Court, it glows
>   And shines like rotten wood;
> Say to the Church, it shows
>   What's good, and doth no good:
> If Church and Court reply,
>   Then give them both the lie.

Hugh, in picking up the guitar again, wants to prove to himself and others that he is capable of "showing the world"; as Yvonne immediately points out, he is simply dramatizing himself again.

328.5 [328]   *Salud y pesetas.* Sp. "Health and wealth." This time, unlike the salutation between Laruelle and Vigil, p. 12 [6], the stock reply from

Hugh to Yvonne is not forthcoming: "y tiempo para gastarlas" ("and time to enjoy them").

329.1 [328] *men like Gandhi, or Nehru.* Mahatma Gandhi and Jawaharlal Nehru, architects of Indian independence, are mentioned by Hugh on p. 157 [153] as being among the few public figures he secretly respects.

329.2 [328] *Throw the bloody little man in the river.* In a letter to Albert Erskine ("Correspondance," pp. 184–85), Lowry attributes his remark to Tom Harrisson's "Letter to Oxford" and suggests that it makes reference to what the world does to "poetic" young men. Tom Harrisson's [sic] "Letter" (1933) is a belligerent attack upon the Oxbridge bovine mentality. Lowry has taken and compressed two phrases from it: on p. 47, Harrisson talks of the "bloody people" who think one is (at 21) too young to write; and on pp. 67–68, describing the physical oxes who beat up anyone different from themselves, he writes:

> But I am for intolerance. I am for beat-ups. I am for good red hate. Put the miserable little man in the river. Put everyone in the river. . . . No cause is destroyed by intolerance or violent persecution. Lenin, Socrates, Lawrence, Darwin, Jesus Christ — every great movement of to-day started from one man who was crucified, in body or mind, to save the whole world.

Hugh, pp. 180 and 182 [176 and 179], has earlier used the phrases "Genius thrown into the river" and "Bloody little man."

329.3 [328] *set Barabbas free.* The cry of the multitude before Pontius Pilate when, having found no fault in Christ, he offered in accordance with the customs of the Passover to set one prisoner free; offered the choice of Christ or Barabbas, the crowd cried for the man who was guilty of both sedition and murder, and Pilate washed his hands of the affair. In a letter to Albert Erskine ("Correspondance," p. 185), Lowry claims that his phrase is based on "Gi os Barrabas frei" (more correctly, "Gi os Barrabas fri"), the final words of Nordahl Grieg's play *Barrabas* (1927), performed (Lowry says) for one night only in the National Theatre of Oslo, in 1929.

329.4 [328] *O'Dwyer for ever.* In 1919 there occurred an atrocity in the Punjab area of India that is still called "the Amritsar massacre." When the Indians rebelled against the imprisonment of two nationalist leaders and rioted in the streets, the military, under the leadership of Brigadier-General Dyer rode into a densely packed crowd and began firing. There were 379 dead and 1,200 wounded in the incident. The lieutenant–governor of the Punjab was Sir Michael O'Dwyer, and the similarity of the last names has plagued historians ever since, as it does here.

The specific point that Hugh seems to be referring to is the hearing and trial which followed the massacre. General Dyer defended himself with the aplomb of a seasoned colonialist, admitting that he had attempted to set a "ferocious" example for the rest of India. The government condemned his action with the phrases "unfortunate" and "injudicious," and he was removed from his position. A large part of Parliament, the press, and the public continued to support Dyer, however, and a testimonial sum of £26,000 was collected in his honour. The event was important historically since it convinced Gandhi and other leaders of India that negotiation with Great Britain was impossible.

329.5 [328]   *And if Russia should prove.* False: an ironic echo of Othello's "If she be false, O! then heaven mocks itself" (III.iii.278). Hugh is already uncomfortably aware that Russia had withdrawn the International Brigades (see note **157.1**) and seems to have a foreboding of the infamous Nazi–Soviet pact of August 1939, personally initiated by his hero, Stalin, by which Poland was divided between the two great powers and each recognized the other's "legitimate" sphere of influence in Eastern Europe. This agreement, a total betrayal of all that international socialism stood for, proved to be the final blow to the already shattered faith of many intellectuals and liberals who had fought for the party throughout the 1930's.

329.6 [329]   *'El Popo': Servicio a la carte.* Sp. "El Popo: à la carte service" (that is, items chosen and paid for separately, rather than the equally common "comida corrida," or fixed price meal). The El Popo offers:
(a) *Sopa de ajo.* Garlic soup.
(b) *Enchiladas de salsa verde.* Large maize–meal tortas wrapped about a filling of chicken, meat, or vegetable, in green sauce (a hot chile sauce made with Mexican green tomatoes).
(c) *Chiles rellenos.* Large poblana chiles stuffed with cheese, chopped meat, vegetables, and so forth, and dipped in flour and egg before being fried in deep fat.
(d) *Rajas a la 'Popo.'* Sliced peppers, Popo style.
(e) *Machitos en salsa verde.* Fried morsels of tripe or offal (especially pork), with green sauce (though *machitos* may also mean "ducklings").
(f) *Menudo estilo soñora.* Giblets, sonora style (Lowry probably means "Sonora," a northern state of Mexico; *soñar* means "to dream").
(g) *Pierna de ternera al horno.* Leg of roast veal.
(h) *Cabrito al horno.* Roast kid.

(i)   *Asado de Pollo.* Roast chicken.
(j)   *Chuletas de cerdo.* Port cutlets.
(k)   *Filete con papas o al gusto.* Steak with potatoes, or as you like it.
(l)   *Sandwiches.* Sandwiches, usually with hot sauce or pepper added to the filling.
(m) *Frijoles refritos.* Re-fried beans; that is, boiled beans (*frijoles*) placed in a vessel of very hot fat and mashed; often served with cream and tacos.
(n)   *Chocolate a la española.* Spanish chocolate: hot, sweet, drinking chocolate, made with milk and spices, with a lot of chocolate.
(o)   *Chocolate a la francesa.* French chocolate: hot, sweet, drinking chocolate, made with milk, but not as thick as the Spanish.
(p)   *Café solo o con leche.* Coffee, black or with milk.

330.1 [329]   *Lotería Nacional Para La Beneficencia Pública.* Sp. "National Lottery for the Public Benefit." The National Lottery of Mexico was inaugurated several centuries ago by Spanish noblemen wishing to establish a charitable foundation. Draws are frequent, tickets cheap, possible returns high, and the state-regulated lottery is completely honest, its net profit going to support public hospitals and other charitable institutions. Some draws are to aid specific charities or cultural organizations; others are simply for the public benefit or assistance. Lowry notes (*DATG,* p. 101) that he had this particular menu with him in Niagara when he completed the manuscript of *UTV*; it has subsequently turned up in the William Temple collection at the University of British Columbia.

330.2 [329]   *Hotel Restaurant El Popo se observa la más estricta moralidad, siendo esta disposición de su proprietario una garantía para el pasajero, que llegue en compañía.* Sp. "The Hotel Restaurant El Popo observes the highest standards, this on the part of its proprietor being a guarantee for the visitor who arrives accompanied (by a lady)."

330.3 [330]   *Recknung.* More accurately, *Rechnung;* Ger. "bill." The Consul consumes one rum and anís, one Salon Brasse rum, and a double tequila. The incredible cheapness of the drinks (about $0.46 for the total), even by 1938 standards, shows why Mexico was a drinker's paradise. The word Rechnung has ominous suggestions of the "reckoning" due from the earlier incident involving the German officers (see note **38.1**). In Robert Service's "The Reckoning," in *The Spell of the Yukon* (to which the Consul has alluded, p. 296 [294]), the same pun is made, and the word "reckless," p. 317 [316], seems equally loaded.

330.4 [330] *dearth ... filth. ... rope ... cope ... grope ... of a cold cell.*
Although the Consul's method of composition resembles that of G. M.
Hopkins (see note **206.5**), the poem itself seems very like Francis Thompson's "The Hound of Heaven" (1893), a poem describing the poet's flight
from God, the pursuit, and the overtaking. The poem begins:

> I fled Him, down the nights and down the days;
>   I fled Him, down the arches of the years;
> I fled Him, down the labyrinthine ways
>   Of my own mind; and in the midst of tears
> I hid from Him, and under running laughter.
>   Up vistaed hopes I sped;
>   And shot, precipitated,
> Adown Titanic glooms of chasmed fears,
> From those strong Feet that followed, followed after.

The Consul's use of "preterite," in its theological sense of "those passed
over," the non-elect, accentuates this sense of one who is running from the
light.

331.1 [331] *man's public inquiry of the hour!* The hoarding, with the giant
blue clock and great pendulum, which Yvonne had earlier recalled seeing in
Los Angeles, p. 266 [264].

331.2 [331] *the stars to the north and east.*
(a) *Pegasus.* A northern constellation; named after the winged horse of
    Greek mythology who sprung from the blood of Medusa slain by
    Perseus, whose hooves struck out the spring of poetic inspiration on
    Mount Helicon, and who was ridden by Bellerophon when he slew the
    Chimera. When Bellerophon tried to fly to heaven, Pegasus was stung
    by a fly sent by Jupiter; he threw off his rider and took his place in the
    skies alone.
(b) *Vega.* The Harp-Star; a blue-white star of the first magnitude in the
    northern constellation of Lyra.
(c) *Deneb.* From Ar. "Al Dhanab al Dajājah, " "the hen's tail"; an apparently fixed star of the first magnitude in the constellation of Cygnus,
    the Swan.
(d) *Altair.* A pale-yellow star of the first magnitude in the constellation of
    Aquila, the Eagle (at the junction of the right wing with the body).
(e) *Hercules.* Also called "The Kneeler"; a northern constellation, near
    Lyra, named after the greatest hero of Greek mythology (see note
    163.5).

331.3 [331] *a ruined Grecian temple.* In the Eleusinian mysteries (see note **319.1**), the candidate making the ritual search for the lost Persephone would pass from the darkness of the wood or labyrinth into the vestibule of a temple, where further tests and initiations would take place before he or she proceeded to the final transmission (Colin Still, *The Timeless Theme,* p. 79).

332.1 [331] *the candelabras.* In Spanish, *candelabros,* giant organ cacti (*cereus marginatus* and related varieties), whose spreading barrel-like stems here suggest the torches of the Eleusinian searches (see note **319.1**).

332.2 [332] *En los talleres y arsenales / a guerra! todos, tocan ya; . . . todas, tocan ya; / morir ¿quién quiere por la gloria / o por vendedores de cañones?* Sp. "In the workshops and the arsenals, to war, everybody, move now, / everybody, move now. Who would want to die for glory, / or for the sellers of guns?" The song has not been identified for certain, but it may well be a verse from Luis de Tapia's "En el crisol del Acero" ("In the crucible of steel"), the song of the Fifth Regiment of the International Brigade at the defence of Madrid, which begins:

> En el crisol del Acero
> se funden en un afán,
> el campesino, el obrero,
> el arisco guerrillero
> y el invicto capitán.

"In the crucible of steel, / forged by a single passion, / are the peasant, the worker, / the fierce guerrilla fighter / and the invincible captain.")

333.1 [333] *Adelante, la juventud, / al asalto, vamos ya, / y contra los imperialismos, / para un nuevo mundo hacer.* Sp. "Forward, youth, to the assault, let's go. And against the imperialists create a new world." The song is unidentified, but seems to be one associated with the FIJL, the Federación Ibérica de Juventudes, an anarchist youth party, whose slogan was "Adelante por la nueva sociedad."

333.2 [333] *More target practice.* Hugh is wrong again, for the last time on a day marked by a long string of errors.

334.1 [334] *Hijos del pueblo que oprimen cadenas / esa injusticia no debe existir / si tu existencia es un mundo de penas / antes que esclavo, prefiere* *morir prefiere morir.* Sp. "Sons of the people whom chains oppress, this injustice must not exist. If your existence is a world of grief, rather than be a slave, choose to die, choose to die." This is an anarchist song, "Hijos del Pueblo," described by Thomas, p. 196, as: "A song in can-can rhythm, despite its words, which was selected as the anthem of the anarchist movement at the Second Literary Competition, in the Palacio de Bellas Artes, Barcelona (1890)." The irony, at this particular moment, could not be more devastating.

334.2 [334]   *a wind like an express train.* An explicit suggestion of the Freudian death-train (see note **283.5**).

335.1 [334]   *doors open for Jesus to walk in.* Also used of a thunderstorm in *October Ferry,* p. 121; though the words are not exact, the phrasing suggests an echo of Oscar Wilde's "The Ballad of Reading Gaol" (1898), Pt. 5:

> Ah! happy they whose hearts can break
>   And peace of pardon win!
> How else may man make straight his plan
>   And cleanse his soul from Sin?
> How else but through a broken heart
>   May Lord Christ enter in?

Lowry may also have had in mind Holman Hunt's painting, *The Light of the World* (1854), which depicts Christ holding a lantern and waiting outside a door.

335.2 [335]   *the riderless horse.* According to Lowry, "LJC," p. 84, the horse is the evil force which the Consul has released; he has in mind Éliphas Lévi's image of the devil as "an unbridled horse which overthrows its rider and precipitates him into the abyss" (see note **28.1**). Yvonne's dying vision integrates the riderless horse with the statue of Huerta, p. 49 [44], and her memories of being trapped in the ravine, p. 262 [260]. Her fall is in one sense from the tree of life, which, according to A. E. Waite, is capable of "preserving all who are attached to it from death forever" (*The Holy Kabbalah,* VII.i, p. 269).

335.3 [335]   *constellations, in the hub of which ... burned Polaris.* As the planets, in concentric order from the sun, whirl about, they transform themselves into a cosmic carousel swinging around the axle-tree of the universe:
(a) *Polaris.* The North Star is a star of second magnitude standing alone at

the extremity of Ursa Minor; it marks almost exactly the position of the north celestial pole, and hence of the world's imagined axle-tree.

(b) *Cassiopeia*. The constellation between Andromeda and Orpheus; in Greek legend, Cassiopeia was the wife of Orpheus and mother of Andromeda.

(c) *Cepheus*. The constellation surrounded by Cassiopeia, Ursa Major, Draco, and Cygnus; in Greek legend, Cepheus was the husband of Cassiopeia.

(d) *the Lynx*. The northern constellation between Auriga and Ursa Major covering a large area of the sky but with few bright stars.

(e) *Ursa Major*. The Great Bear, the most conspicuous of northern constellations, near the pole and containing fifty-three visible stars, seven of which form the Big Dipper.

(f) *Ursa Minor*. The Little Bear; the northernmost constellation; containing twenty-three visible stars, including those which form the Little Dipper, the most important of which is Polaris.

(g) *the Dragon*. The constellation Draco, lying partially between the Big Dipper and Little Dipper; said to be the snake snatched by Minerva from the giants and whirled into the sky.

336.1 [336] *the house was on fire.* Lowry's personal recollections of the destruction by fire of his house at Dollarton, and the loss of his own manuscripts (Day, p. 300), becomes a cosmic image of a world heading towards its final conflagration (see note **193.7**). The passage deliberately re-enacts the burning of the Consul's letter by Laruelle at the end of Ch. 1.

337.1 [336] *the dark waters of Eridanus.* Eridanus is a southern constellation, the River, described by Lowry in "The Forest Path to the Spring," p. 227:

the starry constellation Eridanus, known both as the River of Death and the River of Life, and placed there by Jupiter in remembrance of Phaethon, who once had the splendid illusion that he could guide the fiery steeds of the sun as well as his father Phoebus.

Legend merely states that Jupiter, sensing the danger to the world, shot a thunderbolt which, striking Phaethon, hurled him, his hair on fire, into the River Po.

In the same story, Lowry tells how Eridanus, his name for the small community in which he lived, "perpetually under the shadow of eviction" (p. 226), had taken its name from a wrecked steamer of the defunct Astra line, which had been driven ashore and on whose stern could be made out the words: "*Eridanus,* Liverpool." It was beside the Eridanus, or Po, that Dante supposedly began composing the *Paradiso.*

337.2 [336]   *borne towards the stars.* After their deaths, the daughters of Atlas were transformed, first into doves, then into the Pleiades (see note **323.4**). Lowry was concerned that this chapter, in contrast with the final one, should end with an upward movement and with a sense of cosmic purpose. He comments, "LJC," p. 84: "a not dissimilar idea appears at the end of one of Julian Green's books, but my notion came obviously from *Faust,* where Marguerite is hauled up to heaven on pulleys, while the devil hauls Faust down to hell." The reference to Julian Green (despite Lowry's reference to Green's *Journal,* "Correspondance" p. 185) appears to be to the end of *Mont-Cinere* (1924; published in English as *Avarice House*), Lowry having in mind the parallel between his burning house and Green's burning mansion rather than any ascent towards the stars. The reference to *Faust* is (somewhat vaguely) to the end of Gounod's opera (1859) rather than to Goethe's dramatic poem. The ending of the chapter transforms elements from its beginning: the "diamond brightness" of the volcano, p. 323 [322], shapes itself into diamond birds (an Australian species with sparkling plumage); the "eddies of green and orange birds," p. 317 [316], become eddies of stars; and the Pleiades rise as Scorpio sets, p. 322 [322]. In a pun which is not altogether flippant, Yvonne (Merope) has at last become a star.

CHAPTER TWELVE

338.1 [337] *'Mescal,' said the Consul.* A deliberate echo of the beginning of Ch. 10 and a further confirmation of the words on p. 219 [216]: "if I ever start to drink mescal again, I'm afraid, yes, that would be the end." This time, there is no afterthought or qualification of "mescal poquito," or "mescalito": in fact, in an earlier draft (UBC 11-20, p. 1) the Consul had demanded: "Mescal . . . si, mescal doble, por buen favor, señorita. Si, mescal grande."

338.2 [337] *the ticking of his watch, his heart, his conscience.* The ticking was last heard at the end of Chapter 10. As Markson notes, p. 189, this same ticking (of a soul awaiting death) is the theme of Lowry's poem, "Thirty-five Mescals in Cuautla":

> This ticking is most terrible of all —
> You hear the sound I mean on ships and trains,
> You hear it everywhere, for it is doom;
> The tick of real death, not the tick of time;
> The termite at the rotten wainscot of the world —
> And it is death to you, though well you know
> The heart's silent tick, the tick of real death,
> Only the tick of time — still only the heart's chime
> When body's alarm wakes whirring to terror.

A similar image is to be found in Conrad Aiken's *Three Preludes,* I.18-19 (a poem chosen, presumably by Lowry, for the sixth issue of *Experiment,* the Cambridge University literary magazine): "The alarm-clock ticks, the pulse keeps time with it, / Night and the mind are full of sound." The poem concludes, ll. 71-73:

> These things are only the uprush from the void,
> The wings angelic and demonic, the sound of the abyss
> Dedicated to death. And this is you.

In both poems, and in the novel, the image of time running out is immediately reinforced by that of "subterranean collapse" as the foundations of the deep seem about to open.

338.3 [337]   *a white rabbit.* Among the Aztecs the rabbit was an emblem of drunkenness, a crime punishable by death. Lewis Spence comments (*M of M & P,* p. 104):

> When a man was intoxicated with the native Mexican drink of *pulque,* a liquor made from the juice of the *Argave Americana,* he was believed to be under the influence of a god or spirit. The commonest form under which the drink-god was worshipped was the rabbit, that animal being considered to be utterly devoid of sense. This particular divinity was known as Ome-tochtli. The scale of debauchery which it was desired to reach was indicated by the number of rabbits worshipped, the highest number, four hundred [see note **9.4.f.**], representing the most extreme degree of intoxication.

Spence also comments (*M & M of M,* p. 84) that a rabbit in the house was regarded among the Aztecs as a sign of bad luck, a portent borne out in the year of One-Rabbit in the cycle preceding the coming of the Spaniards, when there were ominous lights in the sky and other harbingers of disaster.

338.4 [337]   *Indian corn.* Corn which has kernels of various colours, such as the purple and black here. The rabbit, nibbling at the "stops," is likened to someone playing a mouth organ.

338.5 [337]   *a beautiful Oaxaqueñan gourd of mescal de olla.* The phrase "de olla" simply means "from the pot" (urn, gourd); mescal from Oaxaca, particularly in the cantinas, is often kept in gourds, some of which are large and intricately decorated.

338.6 [338]   *Bottles of Tenampa, Berreteaga, Tequila Añejo, Anís doble de Mallorca . . . Henry Mallet's 'delicioso licor'. . . . Anís del Mono.*
(a)   *Tenampa.* A raw, rum-based liquor, originally from Tenampa in the east of the state of Vera Cruz.
(b)   *Berreteaga.* A kind of habanero from Tabasco, now produced more widely; its name derives from the original makers, "Berreteaga (Don Martín) y compañia."
(c)   *Tequila Añejo.* "Old Tequila," half a bottle of which is still in the bottom of the Consul's garden (see note **131.2**).
(d)   *Anís doble de Mallorca.* A high-proof anisette from Majorca.
(e)   *Henry Mallet's 'delicioso liquor.'* One of the many "deliciosos liquores"

made since 1891 by the firm of Henri Vallet, Mexico City.

(f) *Anís del Mono.* Sp. "Anisette of the Monkey"; that drunk on the ter-race of the Casino de la Selva by Vigil and Laruelle, who also notice the demon on the label (see note **10.1**). The voluted or spiral shape may form an unobtrusive reference to the shape of Dante's hell.

338.7 [338] *crossed long spoons.* The proximity of the bottle depicting the devil brandishing a pitchfork gives particular emphasis to the proverbial ex-pression, "he who sups with the devil needs a long spoon."

339.1 [338] *aguardiente.* From Sp. *agua,* "water," and *ardiente,* "burning"; a word meaning brandy or liquor generally, but having in Mexican usage the specific sense of a liquor distilled from cane sugar by the action of adding an already fermented wine or fruit stock to a liquid sugar base. The state of Morelos, particularly in the last years of the Porfiriato, was the leading Mexican producer of aguardientes. The bulbous jars containing the aguardientes have the same shape as Jacques's cuneiform stone idols, p. 203 [199].

339.2 [338] *Hotel Bella Vista Gran Baile a Beneficio de la Crux Roja. Los Mejores Artistas del radio en acción. No falte Vd.* Sp. "Hotel Bella Vista Grand Ball for the benefit of the Red Cross. The best radio stars in action. Don't miss it." As on p. 49 [45], the advertisement makes an oblique com-mentary upon the Consul's inability to render the dying Indian first aid.

339.3 [338] *A Few Fleas.* With an almost Beckett-like irony, the son of Diosdado, "God-given," is named "A Few Fleas"; a reference to the com-mon expression "ser uno de pocas pulgas," or "de malas pulgas," that is, one who is easily irritated, quarrelsome (literally, "to be one of a few fleas," or "of bad fleas").

339.4 [338] *El Hijo del Diablo. . . . Ti-to.* Neither the magazine, *Ti-to,* nor the title, "The Son of the Devil," has been identified, but comic books of this kind are read by both adults and children throughout Mexico. The word Ti-to is probably a meaningless diminutive (it can mean "cham-ber-pot"), but Lowry may possibly have recalled A. E. Waite's description of Thomas Burnet's dismissal of much of the worthless literature on the Cabbala (*The Holy Kabbalah,* X.xiv p. 484):

Its devices, he says, are the diversions of our children, and in truth it would seem hard to decide whether intellectual superiority and philos-ophical seriousness should be ascribed to rabbinical anagrams or to the apparatus of "Tit: Tat: To." In any case, "they do not belong to sane literature, much less to wisdom."

339.5 [338] *chocolate skulls... chocolate skeletons... funeral wagons.* Items of confectionery, often very intricate and beautifully made, produced for the Day of the Dead. As Eisenstein comments (*The Film Sense,* pp. 197–98):

> Deathday in Mexico. Day of the greatest fun and merriment. The day when Mexico provokes death and makes fun of it — death is but a step to another cycle of life — why then fear it! Hat stores display skulls wearing top and straw hats. Candy takes the shape of skulls in sugar and coffins of confectionery. Parties go to the cemetery, taking food to the dead. Parties play and sing on the graves. And the food of the dead is eaten by the living.

As the word "yes" implies, the Consul recalls Mr. Quincey's testy reply to his "I'm on the wagon," p. 137 [133]: "The funeral wagon, I'd say, Firmin."

339.6 [338] *De pronto, Dalia vuelve en Sigrita llamando la atención de un guardia que pasea. ¡Suélteme! ¡Suélteme!* Sp. "Suddenly Dalia turns from Sigrita, calling the attention of a guard who is passing. Save me! Save me!" (literally, "release me").

339.7 [338] *maybe the scorpion, not wanting to be saved, had stung itself to death.* Lowry comments, *SL* p. 198: "The scorpion is an image of suicide (scorpions sting themselves to death, so they say — Dr. Johnson called this a lie, but there is in fact some scientific evidence for it)." As manuscript variants make clear (UBC 7-3, p. 6, and 10-25, p. 18), the Consul's source for this story, so emblematic of his own fate, is Boswell's *Life of Johnson,* at the beginning of 1768:

> I told him that I had several times, when in Italy, seen the experiment of placing a scorpion within a circle of burning coals; that it ran round and round in extreme pain; and finding no way to escape, retired to the centre, and like a true Stoick philosopher, darted its sting into its head, and thus at once freed itself from its woes.... Johnson would not admit the fact.

339.8 [338] *In Parián did Kubla Khan.* An echo of the opening lines of Coleridge's "Kubla Khan":

> In Xanadu did Kubla Khan
> A stately pleasure dome decree:
> Where Alph, the sacred river, ran
> Through caverns measureless to man
> Down to a sunless sea.

The implied reference, however, is to the "deep romantic chasm" of l. 12 (see note **204.2**).

339.9 [338] *Shelley*. Although there are craggy precipices in "Alastor," the Consul's specific reference is to Shelley's *The Cenci*, III.i.243–65:

> *Beatrice:*   But I remember
> Two miles on this side of the fort, the road
> Crosses a deep ravine; 'tis rough and narrow,
> And winds with short turns down the precipice;
> And in its depth there is a mighty rock,
> Which has, from unimaginable years,
> Sustained itself with terror and with toil
> Over a gulf, and with the agony
> With which it clings seems slowly coming down;
> Even as a wretched soul hour after hour,
> Clings to the mass of life; yet clinging, leans;
> And leaning, makes more dark the dread abyss
> In which it fears to fall; beneath this crag
> Huge as despair, as if in weariness,
> The melancholy mountain yawns... below,
> You hear but see not an impetuous torrent
> Ranging among the caverns, and a bridge
> Crosses the chasm; and high above there grow,
> With intersecting trunks, from crag to crag,
> Cedars, and yews, and pines; whose tangled hair
> Is matted in one solid roof of shade
> By the dark ivy's twine. At noonday here
> 'Tis twilight, and at sunset blackest night.

The Cenci (1819) is a poetic tragedy by Shelley about Count Francesco Cenci, who after a life of wickedness and debauchery conceives an implacable hatred, in the form of an incestuous passion, against his daughter Beatrice. To end her miseries, Beatrice plots with her stepmother and brother to murder the tyrant. The passage referred to by the Consul comes at the moment of plotting the count's death. Though the plot is successful, suspicions are aroused, and the three conspirators are executed.

339.10 [338]   *Calderón.* Pedro Calderón de la Barca (1600–81), Spanish poet and official dramatist at the court of Philip IV, and a prolific writer of plays upon historical and religious themes. His *El Mágico Prodigioso* (*The Marvellous Magician*) was translated in part by Shelley; since there are references in it to falling headlong down a dark abyss, it may have been what the Consul has in mind. The more probable allusion, however, is to *La Vida es Sueño* (*Life Is a Dream*), 1636, the central theme of which is the tragic realization by Segismund, "an imprisoned titan," that all who live are only dreaming. The play was edited in 1923 by H. J. Chaytor (fellow of St. Catharine's), and later translated by Roy Campbell. The opening act describes the towering crags, and the funereal gap, l. 54, "yawning wide, out of which night itself seems born."

340.1 [339]   *La Despedida.* Sp. "The Parting"; the picture of the great rock torn apart by superlapidary forces (see note **59.5**), seen then by Yvonne and now by the Consul as symbolic of the impossibility of their reunion. The "spinning flywheel," already in motion that morning, has brought nearer the implacable machinery which is to crush the Consul.

340.2 [339]   *Tartarus under Mt Aetna . . . the monster Typhoeus.* Tartarus is the lower region of Hades, bound by a triple wall and surrounded by the waters of Phlegethon; the place to which the rebel Titans had been consigned (see note **134.7**). It also formed the home of Typhoeus, a monster with a hundred heads and fearful eyes and voices (Lowry is quoting *Webster's*), conquered by Zeus and buried under Mt. Etna, where he breathes out smoke and flames. Typhoeus is usually identified with another monster, Typhon, who was, strictly speaking, his son.

340.3 [339]   *A mercurochrome agony down the west.* Mercurochrome is a crystalline dye, used in solution as an antiseptic for cuts and grazes and remarkable for its brilliant redness. The sky evokes the agony of Faustus, who sees Christ's blood stream in the firmament; the agony of Christ's passion; and the unbandaging of great giants in agony, p. 41 [35]. There is also a conscious echoing, both here and at the end of the paragraph, of the end of *Lord Jim:* "The sky over Patusan was blood-red, immense, streaming like an open vein. An enormous sun had nested crimson amongst the tree-tops, and the forest below had a black and forbidding face." The moment of Jim's death resembles the Consul's in a number of obvious ways: it takes place at sunset; both men are shot by thugs and with a pistol; and both deaths are almost self-willed acts of contrition for past failures of nerve.

340.4 [339] *a soldier slept under a tree.* The same soldier ("or wasn't it a soldier, but something else?") is seen on p. 347 [347], the hint being (as Markson has noted, p. 193) that the shape is that of the dead dog which will be tossed into the barranca after the Consul.

340.5 [339] *The building . . . glowered at him with one eye.* An ominous suggestion of the Cyclops, who wrought such destruction among the men of Odysseus. Although there is by no means a conscious attempt to sustain parallels with the *Odyssey,* allusions such as this, of dungeons like pig-pens, p. 341 [340], and the men transformed into animals, p. 342 [341], show that Homer's poem has contributed to the Consul's nightmare world.

340.6 [339] *a clock pointing to six.* The barracks' clock still points to six on p. 348 [347], which has led Markson, p. 184, to suggest parallels with the Mad Hatter's Tea Party in *Alice in Wonderland.* More to the point is a re- minder of *Doctor Faustus,* sc.xiv, as Faustus realizes that time is running out: "Now hast thou but one bare hour to live, / And then thou must be damned perpetually." Even more ominous is the suggestion of Rimbaud's "Un Saison en Enfer":

> Ah ça! l'horloge de la vie s'est arrêtée tout a l'heure. Je ne suis plus au monde. — La théologie est sérieuse, l'enfer est certainement en bas — et le ciel en haut. — Extase, cauchemar, sommeil dans un nid de flammes.

> ("Ah, that! the clock of life has just stopped. I am no longer of the world. Theology is no joke, hell is certainly below, and heaven above. Ecstasy, nightmare, sleep in a nest of flames.")

340.7 [340] *puttees.* Strips of cloth wound round the legs from ankle to knee, usually a part of military uniforms. They were originally of Anglo– Indian origin. The fact that the sentries wear puttees which are flapping is a comment on their level of military efficiency and legitimacy (the same slop- piness and flapping puttees can be seen in Graham Greene's *The Power and the Glory*).

340.8 [340] *He was inscribing something in copperplate handwriting.* Like the public scribe, p. 58 [53], the corporal is an embodiment of Thoth, scribe of the gods, and though the Consul will feel "oddly reassured" when the soldier is still there, p. 342 [341], the implication is nevertheless that a final "reckoning" is being made before the sudden change of worlds.

341.1 [340]   *the fifty centavos.* With drunken logic, the Consul goes to ridiculous lengths to regain the fifty centavos that he was only too willing to give Sra. Gregorio that afternoon.

342.1 [341]   *his swagger stick.* A short cane carried by army officers, here connoting the military or paramilitary insolence so much at odds with the quality of *simpatico,* or quiet pride and dignity, of the two beggars.

342.2 [341]   *Con German friends.* The Consul's earlier grisly pun on fried clams (see note **292.3.e**) is here made explicit. The Consul's suspicions of Nazi influence will soon be verified.

343.1 [342]   *the dreadful night.* An echo of "The City of Dreadful Night" (1874) by James Thomson (1834–82), a Victorian poet from a poverty-stricken background, whose misery was aggravated by insomnia and alcoholic addiction. His poem is prefaced with Dante's "Per me si va nella città dolente" (see note **47.3**), and Thomson describes the agonies of the night, ll. 71–77:

> The City is of Night, but not of Sleep;
>   There sweet sleep is not for the weary brain;
> The pitiless hours like years and ages creep,
>   A night seems termless hell. This dreadful strain
> Of thought and consciousness which never ceases,
> Or which some moments' stupor but increases,
>   This, worse than woe, makes wretches there insane.

The dreadful strains of demonic orchestras, the snatches of fearful sleep, imaginary parties arriving, and the dark's spinets are all evoked in the Consul's letter, p. 41 [35], likewise composed in the Farolito of the mind.

343.2 [342]   *Monterey peeper.* A Monterey pipe (from Monterey, California, rather than Monterrey, Mexico) has, like its "high class" tobacco, connotations of the good life totally incongruous here. There was, however, an "El Buen Tono" brand of tobacco in Mexico.

343.3 [342]   *¿ — es suyo? . . . Si, señor, muchas gracias. . . . De nada, señor.* Sp. "Is this yours? . . . Yes, many thanks, señor. . . . Not at all." The Consul's immediate "where are the letters" echoes his guilty thoughts of the morning (see note **96.1**).

343.4 [343]   *La rame inutile fatigua vainement une mer immobile.* Fr. "The useless oar vainly stirs a motionless sea." From Racine's *Iphigénie,* I.i.49–50, said by Agamemnon, king of the Greeks, as he waits in vain for the winds that will take them to Troy (see note **286.3**).

344.1 [343] *In Spain.... Andalusia.... Granada.* Andalusia is the region of southern Spain, drained by the Guadalquivir and bounded to the north by the Sierra Morena (the "Dark Mountains"). The region consists of eight provinces, including Granada and Almería, between which is found the Sierra Nevada (the "Snowy Mountains"), with the highest peaks in Spain: "the pride and delight of Granada; the source of her cooling breezes and perpetual verdure; of her gushing fountains and perennial streams" (*Tales of the Alhambra,* p. 69). In a letter to James Stern (*SL,* p. 29), Lowry describes a similar incident as having happened to him in Oaxaca (see note **41.8**). The basis of the confusion here is the reference to Granada; though the Consul has in mind the place he met Yvonne, the romantic city of the popular song (paradise... sunshine and orange groves... the whispering breeze telling tales of love), Diosdado hears the word as *grenadas,* "grenades" (Jakobsen, p. 103), and immediately associates it with gun-running. Grenada was captured by the Nationalists in July 1936, but as a city with strong Republican sympathies, it was a point of unrest throughout the war.

344.2 [343] *one of the boxes in the Chinese puzzle.* The Farolito was described, p. 204 [200], as "composed of numerous little rooms, each smaller and darker than the last, opening one into another, the last and darkest of all being no bigger than a cell." As W. H. New points out ("Lowry's Reading," Woodcock p. 126), "Lowry envisioned the universe as a series of Chinese boxes, with man in one of them, controlling some and controlled by others." In John Dunne's *An Experiment with Time,* p. 158, time is described as akin to a universe of Chinese boxes; and the attendant of the infernal machine (which is in one sense time), p. 225 [221], is a Chinese hunchback.

344.3 [343] *the old Tarascan woman of the Bella Vista.* The presentiment of death which Yvonne earlier experienced (see note **55.3**) is now made manifest, but the Consul still does not heed it.

344.4 [344] *from one somnambulism into another.* The word "tomorrow" evokes *Macbeth,* V.v.17–23, where Macbeth hears of the death of his sleepwalking queen:

> She should have died hereafter.
> There would have been a time for such a word.

> To-morrow, and to-morrow and to-morrow,
> Creeps in this petty pace from day to day,
> To the last syllable of recorded time;
> And all our yesterdays have lighted fools
> The way to dusty death.

There may also be a reference to Bellini's opera, *La sonnambula* (1831), outlined in Oscar Thompson's *Plots of the Operas* (which Lowry owned), and of Hermann Broch's *Die Schlafwandler* (1928–31), a study of social decline which is much obsessed with death and sees every system of values as having sprung from irrational impulses (see also note **311.4.c**). The main allusion, however, is to *Das Cabinett der Dr. Caligari* (see note **194.1**), in which the somnambulist, Cesare, completely under the power of the mad doctor's mind, attempts to rape and murder. In both Robert Wiene's film and Lowry's novel, sleepwalking has the meaning of being under the hypnotic control of an alien, even deranged consciousness (a meaning also stated in Éliphas Lévi's *Transcendental Magic,* p. 67).

345.1 [344]   *in another country.* A reference to Marlowe's *The Jew of Malta,* IV.i.40–41, where Barabas the Jew is fencing accusations that he sent the poisoned broth which killed an entire nunnery:

> *Fr. Barn.* Thou hast committed—
> *Bar.*   Fornication—but that was in another country;
>   And besides, the wench is dead.

The phrase was used to preface T. S. Eliot's "Portrait of a Lady," which deals with emotional failure, and in the title of Ernest Hemingway's short story "In Another Country" (published in *Men without Women,* 1928), set in a military hospital and describing the fear of dying.

345.2 [344]   *why is the barman's name Sherlock?* The name is "unforgettable" because it is that of Sherlock Holmes, the famous detective created by Sir Arthur Conan Doyle (1859–1930). To the Consul's suspicious mind, the barman seems to be in cahoots with the police, apparently investigating the circumstances of a suspicious fire. The private reference is to the proprietor of the Riverside Inn, Oakville, where the Lowrys had gone after their shack had burned down (*DATG,* p. 181). There may even be a further personal reference to the suicide of Lowry's college friend, Paul Fitte (an incident at the heart of *October Ferry*), Sherlock Court being part of St. Catharine's College.

345.3 [344]   *Coriolanus is dead. Coriolanus* is a Roman historical play, written by Shakespeare about 1608 and telling the story of Caius Marcius, otherwise Coriolanus. It is proposed that he be made Consul, but his arrogant contempt of the Roman crowd makes him unpopular, and he is banished. In revenge, he gathers forces to attack Rome, but he spares the city when beseeched to do so by his wife, mother, and son. His supporters turn against him, and Coriolanus, "an eagle in a dovecote," is slain by the conspirators in a public place in Antium.

345.4 [345] *it is this silence that frightens me.* Yvonne, probably unwittingly, is echoing Pascal's *Pensees* #91 (in some editions #206): "Le silence éternel de ces espaces infinis m'effraie" ("the eternal silence of these infinite spaces frightens me"). Pascal has just been considering, frightened and astonished, the insignificant span of a man's life and the tiny space he occupies, "abîmé dans l'infinie immensité des espaces que j'ignore et qui m'ignorant" ("abyssed in the infinite immensity of space, which I do not know and which does not know me").

346.1 [346] *Days filled with cheap and tarnished moments... restless and haunted nights.* Both the sentiment and imagery are akin to T. S. Eliot's "The Love Song of J. Alfred Prufrock," ll. 4–6:

> Let us go, through certain half–deserted streets,
> The muttering retreats
> Of restless nights in one–night cheap hotels.

Other echoes from the poem are to be discerned in the Consul's letter from the Farolito (see note **42.1**).

346.2 [346] *The darkness of remembered ways.* Perhaps an echo of Shelley's "Julian and Maddalo," l. 31: "charged with light memories of remembered hours," where the poet remembers the exhilaration of evening rides before the advent of sorrow and madness (see note **220.1**).

347.1 [346] *the letters of Heloise and Abelard.* A celebrated correspondence between Pierre Abélard (1079–1142), brilliant disputant and teacher at the schools of Ste. Geneviève and Notre Dame in Paris; and Héloise (1101–64), his pupil, niece of Canon Fulbert of Notre Dame. The love affair, both intense and moving, ended in tragedy when Fulbert's men broke into Abélard's room one night and castrated him; Héloise retired to a convent, and the correspondence arose from the tragic separation. As the Consul observes, somewhat cynically, Yvonne's empassioned and rhetorically heightened prose bears a distinct resemblance to that of Héloise to Abélard.

347.2 [346] *mescal Xicotancatl.* The Tlaxcalan mescal accentuates the theme of betrayal as the Consul, once again, turns from Yvonne towards his drink.

348.1 [347] *her rebozo.* A rebozo is a hand-woven woollen shawl invariably worn by the women of Mexico.

348.2 [347] *bumblepuppy.* An outdoor game similar to modern tetherball. A ball is tied to a post by a long cord, and two players bat the ball back and forth, attempting to wind the cord and ball completely around the post. Ch. 3 of Aldous Huxley's *Brave New World* depicts a centrifugal version of the game, updated for Utopian consumption.

348.3 [347] *¿Quiere María?* Sp. "Do you want María?" The Spanish is rather garbled (one might expect "¿Quiere usted a María?"), and the expression here suggests "María wants...," that is, that she is asking the Consul to come with her. He acquiesces without a struggle. The prostitute's name is, ironically, that of the Virgin whom the Consul is also seeking. The episode is a direct analogue of that in Marlowe's *Doctor Faustus,* sc. xiii, when Mephistophilis, to keep Faustus's thoughts from salvation, offers him the vision of Helen of Troy:

> Was this the face that launched a thousand ships
> And burnt the topless towers of Ilium?
> Sweet Helen, make me immortal with a kiss.
> Her lips suck forth my soul; see where it flies!
> Come, Helen, come, give me my soul again.
> Here will I dwell, for heaven be in these lips,
> And all is dross that is not Helena.

This moment seals the doom of Faustus, not simply because it represents intercourse with a demon, but because it convinces Faustus that he cannot be saved. In like manner, having made love to María, the Consul is only too willing to consider this "stupid unprophylactic rejection" of Yvonne as final and to use the fear of venereal disease as an excuse for not seeking further contact with his wife.

As Cross points out, p. 129, Lowry had also tried in earlier drafts to stress a connection between the Consul's assignation and Goethe's *Faust* 2 at the moment Faust wishes that his striving would cease (the moment before his death, immediately preceding the lines Lowry uses to preface his novel):

As with a shamed grimace he gave María... her few pesos, a knowledge of what hell really was blazed on his soul. "Verweile doch, du bist so schön," he said, and laughed self-accusingly.

348.4 [347] *the mingitorio.* Sp. "the urinal": somewhat flattered by the title "Señores," "gentlemen." The proximity of the sexual act to the excretory functions (St. Augustine's "inter urinas et faeces nasquimur") is a familiar source of psychosexual repulsion in some men and hints strongly at the Consul's sexual inadequacies.

349.1 [348] *the final stupid unprophylactic rejection.* Unprophylactic has the sense of "incapable of protecting against disease"; the Consul's failure to use a prophylactic, or condom, convincing him "for brutal hygenic reasons alone" of the impossibility of approaching Yvonne again. The completion of this "hideously mismanaged act of intercourse," p. 288 [287], is in marked contrast with his impotence of the morning, p. 95 [90].

349.2 [348] *erectis whoribus.* A mock-Latin pun upon "erection" and "whore" which forms a total perversion of the earlier "copula maritalis" (see note **91.10**), though, ironically, this grimoire achieves the successful act of intercourse. Jakobsen, p. 9, points out the underlying L. "erectis auribus," "with attentive (or pricked) ears," and notes the reference to Virgil's *Aeneid,* I.151-52: "tum pietate gravem ac meritis si forte virum quem / conspexere, silent arrectisque auribus adstant"; ("then, if haply they set eyes on a man honoured for noble character and service, / they are silent and stand by with attentive ears"). The lines form part of an extended simile used by mighty Neptune as he calms the waves which Juno has raised to smash Aeneas's ships and which threaten the sailors with instant death. As Jakobsen notes, p. 10, no voice comes for the Consul, as it did for Aeneas, to silence the storm.

349.3 [348] *Zapotecan.* The language of the Zapotec Indians of the Oaxaca region; a tongue generically distinct from *Nahua,* the lingua franca of most of pre-Columbian Mexico. The language is still spoken today in the Oaxaca area by a few thousand native speakers; insofar as Lowry has located Parián near the volcanoes, María seems somewhat out of place.

349.4 [349] *the nightly escape from the sleeping Hotel Francia.* The Hotel Francia, Calle 20 de Noviembre, Oaxaca, is only a block or two from the Farolito, which also serves as a model for El Infierno, "the other Farolito." Lowry tells the story of the vulture in the washbasin and the slaughtered fawns in *DATG* (see note **41.8**); the latter, however, attributed to a restaurant in Mexico City. The references to "the cold shower-bath... used only once before" and "the dark open sewers" are probably Lowry's chagrined recollections of an incident described in Conrad Aiken's *Ushant,* p. 356, which tells how Lowry, disastrously drunk, had stumbled into "the Bilbo Canal," or sewage ditch, at the bottom of his garden in Cuernavaca.

350.1 [349]   *how alike are the groans of love to those of the dying.* The phrase, repeated on p. 351 [351], was originally intended to afford a contrast with Ch. 11, which, in the early drafts, was to conclude with Hugh and Yvonne (then the Consul's daughter) making love beneath the stars as the Consul was pitched into the abyss.

351.1 [350]   *too heavy, like his burden of sorrow.* An explicit parallel between Geoffrey's sorrows and those of Christ on his way to Calvary, unable to shoulder the heavy burden of the cross.

351.2 [350]   *you cannot drink of it.* The words of Señora Gregorio, p. 231 [228], this time uncorrected; a reference to Mark 14:25, and the wine of the Last Supper: "Verily I say unto you, I will drink no more of the fruit of the vine, until the day that I drink it new in the Kingdom of God."

351.3 [350]   *Salina Cruz.* The town on the Gulf of Tehuantepec which is the main port of Oaxaca State. Wine from the area is not distinguished for its quality; hence the hyperbole of ichor, in Greek mythology the ethereal fluid flowing instead of blood in the veins of the gods (the word ichor is used metaphorically for a divine drink, but it also means the watery discharge from a wound or ulcer).

351.4 [350]   *not daring to look for mail.* The Consul's fear of receiving (or not receiving) a letter from Yvonne are conveyed by his ironically appropriate use of her words (see note **345.4**).

351.5 [351]   *through the secret passage.* The idea of a secret passage seems to have special meaning for the Consul, who had earlier picked out the same words from the Tlaxcala travel folder, p. 299 [298]. He may be thinking of Swedenborg's *Heaven and Hell,* throughout which secret passages form "gates" to the underworld; or he may be thinking of Erich Pontoppidan's *Natural History of Norway* (see note **178.9**), in Pt. 2, Ch. 2 of which the significance of strange fissures among the mountains is discussed. In Jules Verne's *Twenty Thousand Leagues under the Sea,* Pt. 2, Ch. 5, the *Nautilus* makes her way from the Red Sea to the Mediterranean by means of a secret passage known only to Captain Nemo. The idea of a secret passage is thus an intrinsic part of the antediluvian cosmology which so intrigues the Consul.

352.1 [351]   *a picture of Canada.* An immediate reminder of the northern paradise from which the Consul has now excluded himself; he will not be there, nor among the company of saints, in a month's time. Lowry's poem, "Thirty-Five Mescals in Cuautla," about the horrors of passing time, concludes with the lines:

> On the pictured calendar, set to the future,
> The two reindeer battle to death, while man,
> The tick of real death, not the tick of time,
> Hearing, thrusts his canoe into a moon,
> Risen to bring us madness none too soon.

352.2 [351]   *the Saints for each December day.* The Saints listed are those who have as their feast the first seven days of December (with the omission of Saint Barbara, whose feast is 4 December). Manuscript instructions (UBC 7–13, p. 16) stated "copy from original," but the "original" has not been found:
(a) *Santa Natalia.* 1 December. The wife of Adrian, who was martyred at Nicomedia in 304; she instructed him in the Christian faith, visited him in prison, and took away his relics after the execution.
(b) *Santa Bibiana.* 2 December. More commonly, Viviana, to whom a church was dedicated in Rome in the fifth century; she is the patron saint of the insane and epileptics.
(c) *S. Franciso Xavier.* 3 December. Francis Xavier (1506–52), missionary to India, the East Indies, and Japan, who baptized numerous converts and did much to relieve the sufferings of oppressed native peoples. He died while secretly visiting China, but his body was taken back to Goa, where it is enshrined. He is patron saint of missionaries in foreign parts.
(d) *Santa Sabas.* 5 December. Saint Sabas (439–532), abbot, whose example and teaching influenced the development of eastern monasticism. After living for years in solitude, he founded a community near Jerusalem, and his monastery, Mar Saba, still exists, occupied by monks of the Eastern Orthodox Church.
(e) *S. Nicolas de Bari.* 6 December. A fourth-century bishop and one of the most popular saints of Christendom; the saint of sailors, children, merchants, and pawnbrokers. Little is known of his actual life, but legend about him has been extensive, for example, the story of how he saved three girls from prostitution by throwing bags of gold into their win-

dows at night. As patron saint of children, he is in part the origin of
Father Christmas.

(f) *S. Ambrosio.* 7 December. Ambrose (334–97), bishop and doctor of the
church was chosen by popular acclaim to be bishop of Milan in 374. He
baptized Augustine in 386 and is numbered among the great thinkers of
the early church.

352.3 [351]   *mercapatan.* From Fr. *mercure,* "mercury," and *capter,* "to
capture." The mercaptans are various chemical substances (sometimes
known as thiols) closely related to alcohols but whose oxygen molecules
have been replaced by sulfur and which adhere to mercury. They are characterized by their penetrating and disagreeable sulfuric smell, about which
Lowry comments in a marginal note to an earlier draft (UBC 11–21, p. 14);
"mercapatan is the vilest smelling compound man has ever invented."

352.4 [352]   *Clinica Dr Vigil, Enfermedades Secretas de Ambos Sexos,
Vías Urinarias, Trastornos Sexuales, Debilidad Sexual, Derrames Noc-
turnos, Emisiones Prematuras, Espermatorrea, Impotencia. 666.* Sp. "Dr.
Vigil's Clinic, Intimate Complaints of Both Sexes, Urinary Passages, Sexual
Disturbances, Sexual Debility, Nocturnal Emissions, Premature Ejacu-
lations, Spermatorrhea, Impotence. 666." The last detail, from the insecticide advertisement (see note **192.1**) is effectively illustrated by the dead
scorpion (the Consul?) in the runnel. The slashed advertisements are very
different from those in Dr. Vigil's window, p. 29 [23].

353.1 [352]   *606 — The pricked peetroot, pickled betroot.* 606 (the Penguin
666 is an error) is the number of the compound which, before the days of
penicillin, proved to be the most successful in the treatment of syphilis. The
"magic bullet," as the capsule of the drug was called, is usually associated
with the name of Paul Ehrlich, but the compound was in fact discovered by
his collaborator, Sahachiro Hata, with Ehrlich handling the early testing
and reluctantly agreeing to its release for general use in 1910. The drug was
patented under the name of *Salvarsan* and marketed in the United States as
Arsphenamine. The Consul, terrified by thoughts of V.D., plays graphically with the phrases "half past sick by the cock" and the "pepped petroot"
of the menu, p. 292 [290].

353.2 [352]   *some sort of stool pigeon.* Lowry's "strictest sense of the term"
is explained in his letter to James Stern (*SL,* p. 29), where he tells of his
experiences in an Oaxaqueñan prison (see note **41.8**):

it was an improving experience. For instance I learned the true derivation of the word *stool pigeon*. A stool pigeon is one who sits at stool all day in prison and inveigles political prisoners into conversations, then conveys messages about them. If he's lucky, he gets a bit of buggery thrown in on the side.

353.3 [353] *the corporal was no longer writing.* The "reckoning" is complete (see note **340.8**).

353.4 [353] *Pineaus Lake.* Pinaus Lake, near Vernon, British Columbia (see note **124.1**).

353.5 [353] *Indian Pipe.* Described by Armstrong, p. 358, as:

an odd plant, all translucent, white, beautiful but unnatural, glimmering in the dark heart of the forest like a pallid ghost, mournfully changing to grey and black as it fades... bearing a single flower, beautiful but scentless... also called ghost-flower and corpse-plant.

353.6 [353] *acting Lithuanian Consul to Vernon.* Vernon, British Columbia, a small town about 190 miles northeast of Vancouver, would be too small for a permanent consular posting, but the Consul would be acting from a larger centre (perhaps Kamloops, probably Vancouver). The Baltic state of Lithuania, independent between the two world wars, would not have had representatives in such a place, but this kind of delegated acting authority is a common enough practice. The reference to the drowned Lithuanian (a kind of "other") is the only remaining trace of the Consul's previous career as a lecturer in Lithuania (see note **61.3**).

354.1 [353] *My little grey home in the west.* A song made popular in 1911 by Hermann Löhr (1876–1943), composer of romantic and sentimental themes, to words by D. Eardley-Wilmot:

When the golden sun sinks in the hills,
    And the toil of a long day is o'er —
Though the road may be long, in the lilt of a song
    I forget I was weary before.
Far ahead, where the blue shadows fall,
    I shall come to contentment and rest;
And the toils of the day will be all charmed away
    In my little grey home of the west.

> There are hands that will welcome me in,
>   There are lips I am burning to kiss—
> There are two eyes that shine just because they are mine,
>   And a thousand things other men miss.
> It's a corner of heaven itself
>   Though it's only a tumble-down nest—
> But with love brooding there, why, no place can compare
>   With my little grey home in the west.

The connotations of death are more explicit in Conrad Aiken's *Blue Voyage,* p. 28, where Demarest envisions his own death while listening to the song; his mind creates the image of:

> A brick vault in the cemetery, overgrown, oversnarled with gaudy trumpet vine, steaming in the tropic sun. Bones in the tropic dust. My little red home in the south. Bees and bones and trumpet flowers: nostalgia, Gauguin, heart of darkness.

354.2 [354] *their great Chinese wall.* An appropriate metaphor: the Great Wall of China, 2,400 miles long, was built in the third century B.C. to protect civilized China from the rampant Mongolian hordes. Again, the Consul uses his fears of venereal disease to evade the promise of a loving relation with Yvonne, but as he himself admits, "those reasons were without quite secure basis as yet."

355.1 [354] *at the bottom.* The repetition of the phrase suggests not only the barranca, but Gorki's *The Lower Depths;* "at the bottom" being a literal translation of the Russian *Na D'ne.*

355.2 [355] *some correspondence between the subnormal world itself and the abnormally suspicious delirious one within him.* Words echoed a year later by Laruelle, as he too recognizes the rhyming of the natural and spiritual universes (see note **40.4**). In *October Ferry,* p. 146, Ethan Llewelyn describes the feeling as an "image or state of being that finally appeared to imply, represent, an unreality, a desolation, disorder, falsity that was beyond evil."

355.3 [355] *¿Qué hacéis aquí?... Nada.* Sp. "What are you doing here. ... Nothing" (the familiar "tu" form being used in contempt). In "The Consul's Murder," p. 55, Andrew Pottinger shows clearly *why* Geoffrey Firmin should look so suspicious in the eyes of the police and how in the final version of the novel Lowry had made several changes in order to build up that culpability: his failure to pay for the drinks and María, the loss of his passport, the incriminating telegraph, and the map of Spain were all later additions, and the final scene of the novel has been carefully constructed from two disturbed perspectives (the Consul's is equally as distorted as that of the police), this underlining the tragic misunderstanding that leads to the shooting.

355.4 [355] *Veo que la tierra anda; estoy esperando que pase mi casa por acquí para meterme en ella.* The Consul translates his joke below; the Spanish means literally: "I see that the world is turning; I am hoping that my house will pass by here to put myself into it."

355.5 [355] *sam browne.* A military belt with one or two diagonal shoulder straps, designed to carry weight of a pistol or sword; named after General Sir Samuel J. Browne (1824–1901), British army officer.

356.1 [356] *otiose.* From L. *otium,* "leisure"; the usual sense is "idle" or "indolent," but Lowry seems to be using it almost as a synonym for "obtuse."

356.2 [356] *Zicker.* Ger. *sicher,* "certainly"; the Consul's German, as well as his Spanish, letting him down. The Re*ck*nung is closer.

357.1 [356] *Castilian.* From Castile, considered the traditional, aristocratic area of Spain; the connotations are of well-bred superiority.

357.2 [357] *Comment non.... Oui. Es muy asombrosa.... Jawohl. Correcto, señor.* A linguistic pot-pourri of French, Spanish, German, and English. "Comment non," Fr. "how no" (a meaningless variation of Sp. ¿como no?, "and why not?"); "Oui. Es muy asombrosa": Fr. "yes," plus Sp. "It is very wonderful"; "Jawohl. Correcto, señor": Ger. "yes, indeed"; plus pseudo–Sp. "correct, señor." There is not, however, any Portuguese, despite the reference to Pernambuco, a state (and formerly the city now called Recife) of northeast Brazil.

357.3 [357] *You make a map of the Spain.* In his letter to James Stern (*SL,* p. 29), Lowry tells of a similar incident in which he got into trouble with the police for drawing a map of the Sierra Madre mountains in tequila on a bar (see note **41.8**).

358.1 [357] *You have murdered a man and escaped through seven states.*

This passage, now almost totally obscure, was partially clarified in the various drafts (UBC 9–24) where the Consul hears talk "going over his head" about a sailor who had deserted ship at Belize, British Honduras, and who had walked there through Yucatán; he is presumably to be identified with the sailor who accosts the Consul, p. 363 [363]. The misidentification is one more "justification" for the police hostility.

358.2 [357]   *¿Inglés? ¿Español? ¿Americano? ¿Alemán? ¿Russish? You come a from the you-are-essy-essy?* After his "What are you for?", the policeman asks in Spanish: "English? Spanish? American? German? Russian?" (U.R.S.S. = la Unión de Repúblicas Socialistas Soviéticas; ruso is the usual adjective).

358.3 [359]   *Progresión al culo.* Sp. "Progress to the bottom"; that is, implying that the Consul is on his way down. The pun on "arse" also works in Spanish, as the chief of municipality's "obscene circular movement of the hips," p. 369 [369], later implies. The phrase is the antithesis of Vigil's more sympathetic "progresión a ratos," p. 142 [138].

358.4 [358]   *¿Como se llama?* Sp. "What's your name?" The Consul flushes at the gibe of "Trotsky," the exiled Bolshevik revolutionary then living in Mexico City and soon to be assassinated (see note **33.7**). Trotsky's short goatee beard made him instantly recognizable anywhere in Mexico.

358.5 [358]   *Zuzugoitea.* A strange name (perhaps with connotations of Sp. *zuzo,* "mutt"), which has already caught the Consul's eye as he flicked through Laruelle's phonebook, p. 212 [208]. Epstein, p. 204, suggests a pun on *Goetia,* "a Catalog listing demons."

359.1 [358]   *Juden.* Ger. "Jewish"; the use of the German rather than the Spanish judío being an ominous reflection of the atrocities already beginning in Europe and the anti–Semitic campaign in Mexico City.

359.2 [358]   *Chief of Gardens. . . . Chief of Rostrums. . . . Chief of . . . Municipality.* The word *jefe* mean, roughly, "chief" or boss," and the titles, odd as they sound, are not untypical of the names of offices that might be delegated by those in power to their political underlings (each title being in effect a licence for corruption and graft). The jefe de jardineros, however, remains distinct from the others: a figure of God, of Mr. McGregor, of inflexible authority; of whom Lowry commented (UBC 11–20, p.H.20) in a marginal note, "The Chief of Gardens — the fair man — just stands there, he is the *deus ex machina.*" As Markson suggests, p. 200, among all these "chiefs," the Consul himself must be seen as Bunyan's "Chief of Sinners."

359.3 [359] *at the crossroads of his career.* Although the phrase is common enough, it suggests the story of Oedipus, fated to meet and kill his father "at a place where three highways meet." There is also a suggestion of Ibsen's *Peer Gynt* (mentioned by Hugh, p. 167 [163]). Peer, returning home from his wanderings, is greeted at the crossroads by the mysterious figure of the button-moulder who wishes to melt him down for having led a worthless existence, for having never been himself, and for having denied his love to Solveig, who has waited for him. Like Peer, the Consul is at this moment faced with a destiny that is inexorable; unlike Peer, he will not be redeemed by love.

360.1 [359] *Fructuoso Sanabria.* The name of the jefe de jardineros is not as improbable as might appear, since Sanabria is a reasonably common surname; the connotation, nevertheless, is one of "fruitful health" and hence of the Garden of Eden from which the Consul is excluded.

360.2 [360] *Someone was sitting next to him.* The fair young man is an embodiment of the Consul himself as he once had been, his future all before him and at that stage rightly contemptuous of his later image. The scene is a perfect example of what Dunne describes as an image displaced in time (*An Experiment with Time,* p. 50).

360.3 [360] *this telephone... seemed to be working properly.* Although Edmonds insists, p. 83, that the phone call has confirmed that the Consul is an enemy of the fascists and should be destroyed, the sense of supernatural intercourse with the spiritual world is nonetheless intimated.

361.1 [360] *no sail was in sight.* At the beginning of Act III of Wagner's *Tristan and Isolde,* Tristan lies sick of a deadly wound, awaiting Isolde's ship, but the shepherd sent out to look for her sail reports (in the words used by Eliot in *The Waste Land,* l. 42), "Oed' und leer das Meer" ("Waste and void the sea").

361.2 [360] *if Yvonne, if only as a daughter.* The image here is of Antigone, daughter of Oedipus, leading her blind father to Colonus, comforting him in his afflictions and acting as his guide. In the earliest versions of the novel, Yvonne had been intended as the Consul's daughter rather than his wife.

361.3 [361] *When he had striven upwards.* Recollecting Laruelle's picture of Los Borrachones (see note **202.6**), the Consul relates its meaning to the message of eternal striving so central to Goethe's *Faust,* a crucial line of which forms one of the three epigraphs to the novel.

362.1 [362] *did not each correspond... to some fraction of his being.* In one sense, all the figures around the Consul now, and the various familiars seen throughout the day, exist as projections of his spiritual being; having willed even this final nightmare (Jakobsen, p. 55), he must accept responsibility for it. In like manner, Ethan Llewelyn in *October Ferry,* p. 145, suddenly sees the hotel beer parlour as "the exact outward representation of his inner state of mind." Lowry perhaps derived the idea from the final chapters of Claude Houghton's *Julian Grant Loses His Way* (a novel contemptuously dismissed by the Consul, UBC 11–13, p. 11, as a book about hell by a man who had obviously not been there), in which the central figure, Julian Grant, finds himself in a hell which is entirely the projection of his own interior state and of his failure (at the crossroads of his life) to have loved.

362.2 [362] *a black dog.* The black dog (the constant follower of Cornelius Agrippa) embodies the demonic powers which prevent the Consul from flying up to heaven; in particular, it constitutes a reference to Goethe's Mephistopheles, who first appeared to Faust in the guise of a black poodle.

363.1 [362] *One for the road.* Just as on p. 361 [360], the Consul makes "no move" though his way is apparently clear. Hill, p. 140, analyses his motivation:

> A moment comes when they neglect to keep watch on him. He can walk out, and save his life. But he needs one more drink — "one for the road." He has, in fact, chosen to die. And it is not only for symbolic reasons that Lowry has him prefer that last drink to a run for survival. It is the choice an alcoholic might well make in such a situation. Accustomed to reaching for a drink whenever a difficult decision must be made, he finds it perfectly natural to do the same when faced with the most awesome decision of all.

363.2 [363] *limey.* American slang for an English sailor; either from the lime juice originally served on British ships to prevent scurvy or from Limehouse, a section of London close to the docks.

363.3 [363] *the county of Pope.* The "county of Pope" seems to combine the duchy of Popocatepetl ("Popo"); with England, birthplace of Alexander Pope (1688–1744); and Geoffrey Firmin ("Papa"). The cross-eyed sailor is thus assuming a shared identity which the Consul would wish to deny, yet in one sense (see note **358.1**) the Consul will die in his place.

363.4 [363] *Mozart was the man what writ the Bible.* Mozart, composer of the D-minor quartet (see note **374.4**), is confused with Moses, Old Testament prophet and giver of the law. At the moment of the Consul's death, p. 374 [374], the D-minor quartet is attributed to Moses.

364.1 [363] *The Black Swan is in Winchester.* The word "Winchester" acts as a reminder that Weber is now smuggling arms, but the reference is to the city in the south of England. The Black Swan was a well-known pub and landmark in Winchester until it was demolished shortly before World War II. During World War I, there had been a large military camp on the outskirts of the city, which was used in the later days of the war to house P.O.W.'s. There is in fact a girls' boarding school directly opposite the site of the camp, but Weber seems to be living out a fantasy since it was not built until 1932–34.

364.2 [364] *Time was circumfluent.* The Consul's mescal-drugged consciousness of the circular flowing of time and his heightened awareness of images from his past are almost a parody of Ouspensky's notion of time, *A New Model of the Universe,* p. 238 (in relation to Tarot card 14, Temperance):

> Men think that everything is flowing in one direction. They do not see that everything eternally meets, that one thing comes from the past and another from the future, and that time is a multitude of circles turning in different directions.

364.3 [364] *I am an outcast from myself, a shadow.* A deliberate echoing of Señora Gregorio's "I have no house only a shadow. But whenever you are in need of a shadow, my shadow is yours" (see note **233.3**). Such fragments of Yvonne's letters alternate with the confused babel of voices over the next few pages.

364.4 [364] *They captured me in Flanders.* Weber, either a German or Austrian, had been captured at Flanders, a region straddling parts of France and Belgium, where several crucial battles had been fought in World War I.

364.5 [364] *I'm just a country b-hoy.* Either the country and western song published in 1954 by Fred Brooks and Marshall Barer (the date of composition cannot be ascertained), which begins:

> I'm just a country boy,
>   Money have I none,
> But I have silver in the moon,
>   And gold in the noonday sun.

Or "I'm just a country boy at heart," by "Pinky" Tomlin, Connie Lee, and Paul Parks, featured in the 1937 Melody Pictures musical film, *Sing While You're Able.* A typical verse runs:

> I've seen the moon rise over Broadway,
> I've felt enchantment from the start,
> Yet I keep thinking of a harvest moon:
> I guess I'm just a Country Boy at heart.

365.1 [364]   *—de la Légion Etrangère. Vous n'avez pas de nation. La France est votre mère.* A marching song of the French Foreign Legion, "Soldats de la Légion":

> Soldats de la Légion,
> De la Légion Étrangère,
> N'ayant pas de nation,
> La France est votre mère.

("Soldiers of the Legion, / of the Foreign Legion, / having no nation, / France is your mother.")

365.2 [364] *¡Mar Cantábrico!* The ill-fated ship that tried to take arms to the Spanish Republicans (see note **301.7**).

365.3 [364]   *to walk in the light.* In alchemy, to have achieved the state of a perfect man, when the conscious will and intellect are flooded with the super-personal *lumen naturae,* or light of nature. In terms of the *Cabbala,* to have reached Kether, "Light," and to stand directly facing the godhead ("Ain Soph"). Yvonne has obviously been reading something.

365.4 [365]   *the spreadeagle.* A horrific torture, with such possible refinements as cutting off the eyelids, the basic idea of which was to have the victim staked out, legs and arms spread, in the hot sun.

366.1 [365]   *¿Quiere usted la salvación de México? . . . ¿Quiere usted que Cristo sea nuestro Rey?* Sp. "Do you want the salvation of Mexico? . . . Do you want Christ to be our King?" Politically, the message has overtones of the Cristeros (see note **111.6**), whose religious fanaticism was allied with right-wing politics; personally, there is a suggestion of Faustus-like intercession, which the Consul, like Peter denying Christ, wilfully rejects three times.

367.1 [366]   *hand in hand.* Yvonne's sentiment falls somewhere between the ending of Edward Lear's "The Owl and the Pussy-Cat", "And hand in hand on the edge of the sand, / They danced by the light of the moon," and the tragic conclusion of Milton's *Paradise Lost:* "They, hand in hand with wand'ring steps and slow, / Through Eden took their solitary way."

367.2 [366]   *the Babel... the trip to Cholula.* Although the Consul seems to be recalling the associations between the Tower of Babel and the pyramid at Cholula (see note **17.3**), his deeper awareness of the betrayal associated with that trip (see notes **17.4** and **209.2**) destroys any chance of Yvonne's prayers being heard. As Frater Achad points out (*The Egyptian Revival,* p. 41), "The fall of the Tower of Babel has resulted in the loss of the Universal Language, since when confusion has prevailed."

367.3 [366]   *Japan no good for U. S., for America.* Japanese influence in Mexico was increasing throughout the 1930's, and though never as strong as that of Germany, gave the United States reason to be nervous. In the summer of 1938, Cárdenas announced that exports of oil to Japan would be stepped up, which made the United States all the more apprehensive.

367.4 [366]   *No bueno. Mehican, diez y ocho.* Sp. "No good. Mexican, eighteen." The confused words nevertheless reflect the limited Mexican enthusiasm for entering the war (as Mexico was to do, 24 May 1942) on the side of the United States, her traditional enemy. The words "diez y ocho" are probably a reminder of American intervention in Mexico during the Revolution, when American troops landed at Vera Cruz (though strictly speaking the American presence on Mexican soil was between 1914–16).

367.5 [367]   *the Star Spangled Banner.* A patriotic song, composed by Francis Scott Key in 1814, as the British fleet attacked Fort McHenry, Baltimore. (Contrary to popular legend, Key was not a prisoner of the British at the time he wrote the ballad.) The song achieved instant popularity, but it was not officially adopted by the United States as its national anthem until 1931. It begins:

> O say can you see by the dawn's early light
> What so proudly we hail'd at the twilight's last gleaming,

Whose broad stripes and bright stars through the perilous fight
　O'er the ramparts we watched, were so gallantly streaming?
　　And the rocket's red glare, the bomb bursting in air,
　　　Gave proof through the night that our flag was still there,
　O say does that star spangled banner yet wave
　O'er the land of the free and the home of the brave?

368.1 [367] *hombres, malos, Cacos.... Brutos. No bueno.... Comprendo.* Sp. "(these) men, bad, thieves.... Brutes. No good.... Understand." Like the legless beggars, the potter had been noticed on the Consul's previous visit to the Farolito (see p. 41 [35]). Lowry seems to be using the form of the verb ending in "o" (such as chingao, p. 369 [369]) as an ungrammatical imperative.

368.2 [368] *Muy malo.... no policía.... diablos.... Vámonos.* Sp. "Very bad.... not police.... devils.... Let's go." The old woman's statement that they have killed twenty *viejos* ("old men") is borne out by the chief of rostrums, p. 373 [372]: "I shoot de twenty people." The Consul's reply, "Gracias buena amiga" ("Thank you, good friend") is given even less expression by the Penguin misprint. The old woman with the dominoes, previously a figure of death, now has an important role as a mother figure, protecting the Consul from his fate, but (like Yvonne on p. 55 [50]) the Consul wilfully fails to acknowledge the hope and sanctuary that she (like Sra. Gregorio earlier) is offering.

368.3 [368] *me gusta gusta gusta.... no savee nada.* Corrupt Spanish: "me gusta," "I like"; "no sabe nada," "he knows nothing."

368.4 [368] *Life for your pipe.* In *Moby Dick,* Ch. 30, Captain Ahab equates his pipe with his life and throws it, smouldering, into the sea.

369.1 [368] *it's a long, longy, longy, longy — way to Tipperaire.* A somewhat stretched out version of the well-known British marching song of World War I:

　　It's a long way to Tipperary, it's a long way to go.
　　It's a long way to Tipperary, to the sweetest girl I know.
　　Goodbye Picadilly, farewell Leicester Square,
　　It's a long long way to Tipperary, but my heart's right there.

369.2 [368] *Noch ein habanero.... Bolshevisten.* Ger. "Another habanero. . . . Bolshevists"; the language being a clear indication of the presence of German friends.

369.3 [368] *Buenas tardes, señores.* This time, consciously or not, the Consul is behind the clock (see note **57.1**); the correct greeting for this time of the evening is "Buenas noches."

369.4 [369] *la comida.* Sp. "the meal"; though hints of "the comedy," divine or otherwise, are unavoidable.

369.5 [369] *¿Donde están vuestras palomas?* Sp. "Where are your doves?" The use of vuestras, the familiar plural form of the second person possessive, conforms to Castilian rather than Latin American usage and may confirm to those nearby hints of the Consul's involvement with Spain.

369.6 [369] *Chingao, cabrón.* Sp. "Screw you, cuckold."

370.1 [370] *Federación Anarquista Ibérica.* Sp. "Iberian Anarchist Federation," or FAI. The anarchists were a communist movement espousing Bakunian rather than Marxist principles (that is, self-governing communes rather than the communist state) and dedicated to the overthrowing of monarchy and central government. Though banned since 1872, the movement continued underground, occasionally emerging to "hasten the millenium" (Thomas, p. 62) with unexpected acts of violence. The FAI itself was formed in Valencia in 1927 and became particularly strong in Barcelona. Though Republican in sympathy and commanding wide general support, the movement's inefficient internal organization and its dedication to goals sometimes different from those of the Republicans made it a force not always to be relied upon. Hugh's affiliation with the group is somewhat unlikely, and it is probably there for the sake of the pun on "Anti–Christ."

371.1 [370] *the uncontrollable face on the bar-room floor.* An echo of Yeats's "uncontrollable mystery on the bestial floor" (see note **150.2**); also a reference to the song "The Face on the Barroom Floor," by the popular vaudeville entertainer Taylor Holmes (1878–1959), recorded in October 1923 along with "The Shooting of Dan McGrew" (Rust, p. 359).

371.2 [371] *Al Capón.* Al Capone (1897–1947), nicknamed "Scarface" (see note **269.2**); the most notorious gangster of the Prohibition period in Chicago, who was finally imprisoned on a charge of tax evasion. The Spanish "el capón" also means "capon," a castrated fowl.

371.3 [371] *Incalculable are the benefits civilization has brought us.* The source of this paragraph, if any, remains obscure, but the words are deliberately designed to echo the speech from *Antigone* which prefaces the novel and to testify, even if ironically, to the survival of the human spirit.

372.1 [371]   *an enormous rooster.* The cock had once been a parrot (see note **235.5**), but as symbolic meanings accrued around "cock," the parrot was dropped. Such meanings include:

(a) "Half past sick by the cock," p. 353 [352], and the encounter with María; both surprisingly late additions to the manuscripts but crucial to both the Faustian theme and the various meanings of the Consul's impotence.

(b) Cervantes's "bruto," which materialized in Ch. 10 in much this way. In the earlier drafts a major force driving the Consul to his chosen death was the thought of atoning for the afflictions wrought by the Europeans upon the Tlahuicans of the valley (see note **215.6**). This was replaced with a more complex sense of betrayal, in part echoing Peter's betrayal of Christ, but associated above all with the "traitorous Tlaxcalans" who had "betrayed Christ into being in the Western Hemisphere" (see note **288.6**).

(c) The hint of Laruelle, Gallic cock and sexual betrayer (the emblem of France is the cockerel), whom the Consul sees and strikes at in the expression of the chief of rostrums; the word "merded" adds force to this suggestion.

372.2 [371]   *You poxboxes. You coxcoxes.* The 1940 version of this chapter (UBC 7–13, p. 28) gave the Consul's accusations about killing the Indian in much greater detail and made this the basic reason for his being shot (there was even an affirmation of Cárdenas and *La Vida Impersonal*); the final shooting is deliberately more gratuitous. The word "coxcox" seems meaningless, (it can mean "hop-scotch"), but the Consul may be echoing Lewis Spence's coxcoxtli, a bird with the comb of a cock (*G of M,* p. 177), with the imputation of coxcomb; or there may be an obscure reference to the story of Coxcox (see note **91.3**), with intimations of the deluge. (Noah, the Hebrew Coxcox, commonly portrayed as a drunk in the Middle Ages.)

372.3 [372]   *Only the poor, only through God. . . . Don Quixote.* This forms the Consul's personal version of Christ's Sermon on the Mount (Matthew 5–7), which begins: "Blessed are the poor in spirit: for theirs is the kingdom of heaven." The allusion to "old men carrying their fathers" is to the end of Ch. 9, while the reference to Don Quixote takes up that to the windmills, p. 250 [248]. In an early version of that passage (UBC 11–14, p. 9) the Consul had added: "Perhaps Don Quixote wouldn't have hesitated so long. . . . A character for whom I've the greatest respect by the way."

373.1 [373]   *glittering like a topaz.* A topaz is a semi-precious stone, a fluo-silicate of aluminum, usually yellow in colour and often perfectly clear. Webb, p. 314, cites A. E. Waite's "Grand Orient" (in *The Complete Manual of Occult Divination,* p. 195) upon the occult significance of this jewel: "those who desire to regain lost perilous positions should not fail to carry [a topaz] about their persons."

373.2 [373]   *A Colt .17.* A revolver purchased by the United States Army from the Colt Company during the First World War, and designated .17 for the year. It came in several large calibres, including .38 and .357, and had a double action. The supply was exhausted in the early 1930's, but by that time Latin American military or police could have picked these revolvers up as surplus military equipment or through the illegal gun trade.

373.3 [373]   *Lightning flashed.* The "all-but-unretraceable path of God's lightning" (see note **44.3.c**) is the flaming sword which descends from Kether to Malkuth and connects the ten Sephiroth. The Consul at the moment of his death has a vision of the path his soul should have taken towards the light.

373.4 [373]   *Released, the horse reared.* Lowry comments, "LJC," p. 85: "The slightly ridiculous horse that the Consul releases and which kills Yvonne is of course the destructive force . . . which his own final absorption by the powers of evil releases."

374.1 [373]   *Christ . . . this is a dingy way to die.* The word "dingy" appears in the letter to Yvonne, p. 45 [40]: "Oh Yvonne, we cannot allow what we created to sink down to oblivion in this dingy fashion—." The paradox here, like that of the Crucifixion of Christ, is that the dinginess embraces humanity and God. Following the Consul's evocation of Christ are seven words which correspond to the seven last words from the cross.

374.2 [373]   *A bell spoke out: Dolente . . . dolore.* See note **47.3**: the passing bell, ringing out both damnation and compassion, tolls for all mankind. The Consul belatedly recognizes, in the charity of the old fiddler, the love he had earlier withheld from the dying Indian. This recognition may be a love that comes too late, but at the same time it is one that affords a saving grace. As Lowry noted, "LJC," p. 85:

I don't think the chapter's final effect should be depressing: I feel you should most definitely get your katharsis, while there is even a hint of redemption for the poor old Consul at the end, who realises that he is after all part of humanity: and indeed, as I have said before, what profundity and final meaning there is in his fate should be seen also in its universal relationship to the ultimate fate of mankind.

The compañero reference was not originally present here; instead, in terms explicitly Christian (and thus somewhat alien from the Consul's consciousness), the beggar offered the dying man a drink from his bowl, and the Consul murmured in reply something about the water of everlasting life (UBC 7-13, p. 31). In the final version, the word compañero fulfils the pattern of guilt, penance, and forgiveness (exemplified by the Samaritan affair, the dying Indian, and the dying Consul) in a way that if not outwardly Christian is nevertheless emotionally, morally, and aesthetically complete.

374.3 [374] *little bowler hats.* Bowler hats, part of the dress of British diplomats, are intimately associated with Charlie Chaplin, the figure of the little man beset by authority, yet ultimately triumphing over it.

374.4 [374] *The Siciliana. Finale of the D minor quartet by Moses.* A Siciliana is a dance of Sicilian origin, with a swaying rhythm; it is usually in a minor key and is often pastoral in character. Mozart's quartet in D-minor, K 421 (June 1783) is one of a set of six dedicated to Haydn, and its finale, modelled on Haydn's Op.33, no. 5, is a siciliano (Allegretto ma non troppo), in the form of a theme, four variations, and an extended return to the theme, the air having a plaintively melancholy quality about it.

374.5 [374] *Alcestis.* An opera in three acts by Christoph Willibald Gluck (1714-87), first performed in 1767. In classical mythology Alcestis was the wife of Admetus. She agrees to die in place of her husband, but because of the great love and sorrow shown by Admetus, she is rescued at the gates of the underworld by Hercules, and the opera ends in general rejoicing, the couple restored. Lowry's evocation of the opera may have been in response to his reading of Julian Green's *Journal,* 16 January 1933, where Green discusses the "belle musique funèbre" ("the beautiful funereal music") of *Alcestis* and concludes: "Le vrai sujet de cet opéra c'est la mort" ("the true subject of this opera is death").

374.6 [374] *The chords of a guitar.* An intimation at the moment of the Consul's death of Hugh and Yvonne in Ch. 11. The cross-reference was originally intended to be cynical, the Consul hearing their cries of love as he died (see note **350.1**), but humanity triumphed in the final version, the Consul dying partly in place of Hugh and with the awareness, if too late, of Yvonne's love.

374.7 [374] *He was in Kashmir.* The description could be right out of the opening chapters of Francis Younghusband's *Kashmir,* in which the beauty of the mountains, meadows, and flowers (trefoil is clover) is given at length. The memory of the Consul's childhood and the mountains into which his father disappeared blends with his sacred Popocatepetl into an image of his life's journey, only to open out into the horrors of hell.

375.1 [375] *the heights.*
(a) *Pico de Orizabe.* Otherwise *Citlatepetl,* from Nah. *citla,* "star," and *tepetl,* "mountain"; the mountain that touches the stars. On the Vera Cruz-Puebla border is Pico de Orizabe, at 18,700 feet, the highest peak in Mexico, with a well-shaped, snow-covered cone.
(b) *Malinche.* Otherwise *Matlalcueyatl,* "she of the blue skirts" (see note **303.1**). A dormant volcano, 14,636 feet, on the Puebla-Tlaxcala border, whose several craters are snow-covered in the winter. Malinche was also the Mexican name for Doña Marina, mistress of Cortés and betrayer of her people.
(c) *Cofre de Perote.* Otherwise *Naucampatepetl,* from Nah. *nauhcampa,* "of four sides," and *tepetl,* "mountain." An extinct volcano, 14,048 feet, in the state of Vera Cruz not far from Pico de Orizabe. It takes its name (as Prescott notes, III.i, p. 214) from the huge coffer-like rock on its summit.

376.1 [375] *pandemonium.* Gr. *pan,* "all," plus *daimon,* "demon," the abode of all devils. In Milton's *Paradise Lost,* I.756 it is described as "the high Capital" of Satan and his peers and is the venue of their council.

376.2 [375] *somebody threw a dead dog after him down the ravine.* As Kilgallin has noted, p. 201, John Sommerfield's *Volunteer in Spain* ends with a grotesque scene of a corpse in a gutter, its blood and brains mingling with those of a dead dog. This act is likewise one of total contempt, yet it shows that Geoffrey's familiar (like Yudhishthira's companion, p. 129) will accompany him even in death. In *The Egyptian Book of the Dead,* the dog-headed Anubis is the conductor of souls to the underworld, and his role of guide is assumed in *The Mexican Book of the Dead* by the shade of a dead dog that assists its master across the final river (Lewis Spence, *G of M,* p. 64). In *DATG,* p. 239, Lowry outlines the myth, which he there claims (somewhat dubiously, but for dramatic purposes) to have heard only after *Under the Volcano* was written:

The Mexicans believed that in the journey taken by the spirit in the realm of the dead there came a time when a wide river, difficult to cross, was reached. For this reason they killed a dog to accompany his master on the last journey. The spirit of the dog was supposed to reach the far side of the river in advance of the man, and upon seeing his master would jump into the water and help him across.

377.1 [377] *¿LE GUSTA ESTE JARDÍN QUE ES SUYO? ¡EVITE QUE SUS HIJOS LO DESTRUYAN!* Sp. "Do you like this garden that is yours? See to it that your children do not destroy it." These last words are very much part of the novel, and in his manuscript notes (see note **235.9**), Lowry was most concerned that the Spanish at the very end should be in the correct form (the Penguin error is explained by the fact that, despite this concern, the wrong version somehow persisted right into the galleys, and in the British Cape edition of 1947 remained there). The sign gives a last and terrible warning of Eden, the garden from which the Consul, drunk on guilt and terrified of the forces within him, has wilfully evicted himself.

Appendix 1. References

This is not a bibliography, but a short-title list of books and articles referred to repeatedly in the commentary (those mentioned only once are generally noted in the body of the text). The list includes Lowry's sources (wherever possible in the editions he used); many of the standard critical works on Lowry; and a number of works that have proved useful in explicating Lowry's text. It does not include references to dramatists, poets, and novelists unless they are particularly significant, and it may be assumed that references to well-known authors (to scene, line, and chapter rather than page) will be found in any standard edition. Classical references, unless otherwise specified, are to the Loeb editions; other translations are our own. References to Shakespeare are to the Oxford edition, and those to the Bible are to the Authorized King James version. The listing is in two parts: (a) Specific texts referred to in the commentary (b) General sources used throughout the commentary, but in such a way as to make specific acknowledgement impossible.

Specific Texts

Aguirre. José Urbán Aguirre. *Geografía e historia del estado de Morelos.* 2d ed. Cuernavaca, 1963.

The Anatomy of the Body of God. Frater Achad (Charles Stansfeld-Jones). *The Anatomy of the Body of God.* Chicago: Collegium ad Spiritum Sanctum, 1925.

Andersen. Gladys M. Andersen. "A Guide to *Under the Volcano.*" Ph.D. diss., University of the Pacific, Stockton, 1970.

Armstrong. Margaret Armstrong. *Field Book of Western Wild Flowers.* New York: Putnam's, 1915.

Ashby. Joe C. Ashby. *Organized Labor and the Mexican Revolution under Lázaro Cárdenas.* Chapel Hill: University of North Carolina Press, 1963.

Barbarous Mexico. John Kenneth Turner, *Barbarous Mexico.* 1910; reprint, Austin: University of Texas Press, 1969.

Baxter. Edith Lorraine Baxter. "The Mexican Setting in *Under the Volcano.*" M. A. thesis, University of Alberta, 1973.

Beau Geste. P. C. Wren. *Beau Geste.* London: John Murray, 1924.

Benítez. Fernando Benítez. *Lázaro Cárdenas y la Revolución Mexicana.* Mexico: Fundo de Cultura Economica, 1978.

B.F.I. The various catalogues of the British Film Institute, London.

Blue Voyage. Conrad Aiken, *Blue Voyage.* In *The Collected Novels of Conrad Aiken,* pp. 15–166. New York: Holt, Rinehart & Winston, 1964.

Bonnefoi. Genviève Bonnefoi. "Souvenir de Quauhnahuac." *Les lettres nouvelles* 5 (1960): 94–108.

Bradbrook. Muriel C. Bradbrook. *Malcolm Lowry: His Art and Early Life.* Cambridge: Cambridge University Press, 1974.

"Call It Misadventure." Clarissa Lorenz. "Call It Misadventure." *Atlantic* 225 (June 1970): 106–12.

"The Consul's Murder." Andrew Pottinger, "The Consul's Murder." *Canadian Literature* 67 (Winter 1976): 53–63.

"Correspondance." Letters by Lowry, published in *Les lettres nouvelles* 5 (1960): 184–205.

Costa. Richard Hauer Costa. *Malcolm Lowry.* New York: Twayne, 1972.

Cross. Richard K. Cross. *Malcolm Lowry: A Preface to His Fiction.* London: Athlone Press, 1980.

DATG. Malcolm Lowry. *Dark as the Grave Wherein My Friend Is Laid.* 1969; reprint, Harmondsworth: Penguin, 1972.

Day. Douglas Day. *Malcolm Lowry: A Biography.* London: Oxford University Press, 1974.

de Barrios. Virginia B. de Barrios. *A Guide to Tequila, Mezcal and Pulque.* 1970; 2d ed. Mexico: Editorial minutiae Mexicana, 1980.

de Davila. Esta O. de Davila. *Paradise in Mexico: Morelos and Its Capital Cuernavaca.* Mexico: Editorial Cultural, 1937.

Díez. Domingo Díez, *Summa Morelense: bosquejo histórico geográfico de Morelos.* 1934?; reprint, Cuernavaca: Imprenta Tlahuica, 1967.

Doctor Faustus. Christopher Marlowe. *The Tragical History of Doctor Faustus.* In *Eight Famous Elizabethan Plays,* ed. E. C. Dunn. New York: Random House, 1932.

Dodson. Daniel B. Dodson. *Malcolm Lowry.* New York: Columbia University Press, 1970.

Donnelly. Ignatius Donnelly. *Atlantis: The Antediluvian World.* New York: Harper Brothers, 1882.

Doyen. Victor Doyen, "Fighting the Albatross of Self." Ph.D. diss., University of Louvain, 1973.

Edmonds. Dale Edmonds, *"Under the Volcano:* A Reading of the 'Immediate Level'." *Tulane Studies in English* 16 (1968): 63–105; reprinted in Wood, pp. 57–100.

The Egyptian Revival. Frater Achad (Charles Stansfeld-Jones). *The Egyptian Revival.* Chicago: Collegium ad Spiritum Sanctum, 1923.

Epstein. Perle S. Epstein. *The Private Labyrinth of Malcolm Lowry.* New York: Holt, Rinehart & Winston, 1969.

An Experiment with Time. J. W. Dunne, *An Experiment with Time.* 1927; 5th ed. London: Faber & Faber, 1939.

"Expressionist Vision." Sherrill E. Grace. "Malcolm Lowry and the Expressionist Vision." In *The Art of Malcolm Lowry,* ed. Anne Smith. London: Vision Press, 1978, pp. 93–111.

F & FL. William H. Gass. "In Terms of the Toenail." In *Fiction and the Figures of Life.* New York: Knopf, 1970, pp. 55–76.

Fantasia of the Unconscious. D. H. Lawrence. *Fantasia of the Unconscious, and Psychoanalysis and the Unconscious.* 1923; reprint, London: Heinemann, 1961.

The Film Sense. Sergei Eisenstein. *The Film Sense.* Trans. and ed. by Jay Leyda. 1943; reprint, London: Faber & Faber, 1948.

Fischer. Louis Fischer. *Men and Politics.* New York: Harper & Row, 1941.

Fodor. *Fodor's Mexico, 1979.* Ed. Margerie Lockett. New York: David McKay, 1979.

"Forest Path." Malcolm Lowry. "A Forest Path to the Spring." In *Hear Us O Lord from Heaven Thy Dwelling Place.* 1961; reprint, Harmondsworth: Penguin, 1969, pp. 216-87.

Fort. Charles Fort. *The Books of Charles Fort.* Ed. Tiffany Thayer. New York: Henry Holt & Co., 1941.

G of M. Lewis Spence. *The Gods of Mexico.* London: Fisher Unwin, 1923.

The Golden Bough. Sir James Frazer. *The Golden Bough.* 1912; reprinted and condensed. New York: Macmillan, 1942.

Grace. Sherrill E. Grace. "The Voyage That Never Ends." Ph.D. diss., McGill University, 1974. Published under same title, 1982.

Great Circle. Conrad Aiken. *Great Circle.* In *The Collected Novels of Conrad Aiken,* pp. 167-296. New York: Holt, Rinehart & Winston, 1964.

Halliwell. Leslie Halliwell. *The Filmgoer's Companion.* 6th ed. New York: Avon, 1978.

A Heart for the Gods of Mexico. Conrad Aiken. *A Heart for the Gods of Mexico.* In *The Collected Novels of Conrad Aiken,* pp. 417-72. New York: Holt, Rinehart & Winston, 1964.

Hear Us O Lord. Malcolm Lowry. *Hear Us O Lord from Heaven Thy Dwelling Place.* 1961; reprint, Harmondsworth: Penguin, 1969.

Heaven and Hell. Emanuel Swedenborg. *Heaven and Hell: Things Heard and Seen.* Trans. James Hyde. London: Frederick Warne & Co., 1904.

Hill. Art Hill. "The Alcoholic on Alcoholism." *Canadian Literature* 62 (Autumn 1974): 33-48; reprinted in Wood, pp. 126-42.

Hindu World. Benjamin Walker. *Hindu World: An Encyclopedic Survey of Hinduism.* 2 vols. London: Allen & Unwin, 1968.

History of Kashmir. Prithivi Nath Kaul Bamzai. *A History of Kashmir.* 1962; 2d ed. New Delhi: Metropolitan Book Co., 1973.

Holmyard. E. J. Holmyard. *Alchemy.* Harmondsworth: Penguin, 1957.

The Holy Kabbalah. A. E. Waite. *The Holy Kabbalah.* London: Williams & Norgate, 1929.

The Infernal Machine. Jean Cocteau. *La machine infernale.* Paris: Livre de Poche, 1934.

Iturribarria. Jorge Fernando Iturribarria. *Oaxaca en la historia.* Mexico: Editorio stylo, 1955.

Jakobsen. Arnt Lykke Jakobsen. *Introduction and Notes to "Under the Volcano."* Copenhagen: B. Stougaard Jensen, 1980.

James. William James, *The Varieties of Religious Experience.* New York: Modern Library, 1902.

Journal. Julian Green. *Les années faciles: Journal (1928-1934).* Paris: Librairie Plon, 1938.

Julian Grant Loses His Way. Claude Houghton (Claude Houghton Oldfield). *Julian*

Grant Loses His Way. London: Heinemann, 1933.

The Kabbalah Unveiled. S. L. MacGregor-Mathers. *The Kabbalah Unveiled.* 1888; reprint, London: Routledge & Kegan Paul, 1970.

Kashmir. Sir Francis Younghusband. *Kashmir* (with watercolours by Major Edward Molyneux). London: Adam & Charles Black, 1911.

Kilgallin. Tony Kilgallin. *Lowry.* Erin, Ont.: Press Porcepic, 1973.

Kilgallin, 1965. Antony R. Kilgallin. "The Use of Literary Sources for Theme and Style in *Under the Volcano.*" M. A. thesis, University of Toronto, 1965.

Kilgallin, "Faust." Antony R. Kilgallin, "Faust and *Under the Volcano.*" In Woodcock, pp. 26–37.

Kracauer. Siegfried Kracauer. *A Psychological History of the German Film from Caligari to Hitler.* Princeton: Princeton University Press, 1947.

The Last Great Cause. Stanley Weintraub. *The Last Great Cause: The Intellectuals and the Spanish Civil War.* New York: Weybright & Tolley, 1968.

The Lawless Roads. Graham Greene. *The Lawless Roads.* London: Heinemann, 1939.

Letters. D. H. Lawrence. *The Letters of D. H. Lawrence.* Ed. Aldous Huxley. London: Heinemann, 1932.

"Letter to Oxford." Tom Harrisson. "Letter to Oxford." Wyck: Reynold Bray, 1934.

Life of Johnson. James Boswell. *Life of Johnson.* London: Oxford University Press, 1961.

"LJC." Malcolm Lowry. "A Letter to Jonathan Cape." In *Selected Letters,* pp. 57–88.

Lunar Caustic. Malcolm Lowry. *Lunar Caustic.* 1963; reprint, London: Cape, 1968.

M & M of M. Lewis Spence. *The Magic and Mysteries of Mexico.* London: Rider & Co., [1930].

Markson. David Markson. *Malcolm Lowry's Volcano: Myth Symbol Meaning.* New York: Time Books, 1978.

"Mescal." Havelock Ellis. "Mescal: A New Artificial Paradise." *Contemporary Review* 73 (January 1898): 130–41.

MLN. Malcolm Lowry Newsletter. Ed. Paul Tiessen. Wilfrid Laurier University, Ontario, Canada.

M of M & P. Lewis Spence. *The Myths of Mexico and Peru.* London: Harrop & Co., 1919.

Monbet. Josine Monbet. "Malcolm Lowry's *Under the Volcano.*" Diplome d'Etudes Superieures, Université de Bordeaux, 1967–68.

Natural History of Norway. Erich Pontoppidan. *The Natural History of Norway,* Trans. from the Danish (anon). London: A. Linde, 1775.

A New Model of the Universe. P. D. Ouspensky. *A New Model of the Universe.* 1931, 3d ed. London: Routledge & Kegan Paul, 1938.

OCEL. The Oxford Companion to English Literature. Ed. Sir Paul Harvey. 4th ed., rev. Oxford: Clarendon Press, 1967.

October Ferry. Malcolm Lowry. *October Ferry to Gabriola.* 1971; reprint, Harmondsworth: Penguin, 1979.

Ornithology. Thomas Nuttall. *A Manual of Ornithology of the United States and Canada.* Boston: Hilliard, Gray & Co., 1840.

P & S. Malcolm Lowry. *Psalms and Songs*. Ed. Margerie Lowry. New York: New American Library, 1975.

Pernety. Dom. A. J. Pernety. *Dictionnaire Mytho-Hermétique*. Paris: Chez Baude, 1758.

Peterson. Roger T. Peterson. *A Field Guide to Western Birds*. Boston: Houghton Mifflin Co., 1941.

Pliny. *Pliny's Natural History*. Ed. H. Rackham. 10 vols. (Loeb). London: Heinemann, 1958.

Pottinger. Andrew Pottinger. "The Revising of *Under the Volcano*." Ph.D. diss., University of British Columbia, 1978.

"Preface to a Novel." Lowry's introduction to the French translation of *Under the Volcano*. In Woodcock, pp. 9–15.

Prescott. W. H. Prescott. *History of the Conquest of Mexico*. 1842; reprint, New York: Modern Library, n.d.

QBL. Frater Achad (Charles Stansfeld-Jones). *QBL or the Bride's Reception*. Chicago: Collegium ad Spiritum Sanctum, 1922.

Ramsey. Robin H. Ramsey. "The Impact of Time and Memory on Malcolm Lowry's Fiction." M. A. thesis, University of British Columbia, 1970.

Rust. Brian Rust. *The Complete Entertainment Discography*. New Rochelle: Arlington House, 1973.

The Sacred Magic. S. L. MacGregor-Mathers. *The Book of the Sacred Magic of Abra-Melin, the Mage*. London: J. M. Watkins, 1898.

Sacred Theory of the Earth. Thomas Burnet. *The Theory of the Earth*. 2 vols. London: R. Norton for Walter Kettilby, 1684–90.

Selected Letters. Conrad Aiken. *Selected Letters of Conrad Aiken*. Ed. Joseph Killorin. New Haven: Yale University Press, 1978.

The Ship Sails On. Nordahl Grieg. *The Ship Sails On* (1924). Trans. A. G. Chater. New York: Knopf, 1927.

Ships and the Sea. R. D. Talbot-Booth. *Ships and the Sea*. 1936; 7th ed. London: Sampson Low, Marston & Co., 1942.

SL. Malcolm Lowry. *The Selected Letters of Malcolm Lowry*. Ed. Harvey Breit and Margerie Bonner Lowry. London: Cape, 1967.

SP. Malcolm Lowry. *Selected Poems*. Ed. Earle Birney and Margerie Bonner Lowry. San Francisco: City Lights Books, 1962.

Spender. Stephen Spender's introduction to the 1965 Lippincott edition of *Under the Volcano*, pp. vii-xxvi.

Spengler. Oswald Spengler. *The Decline of the West*. Trans. C. F. Atkinson. London: Allen & Unwin, 1926–29.

Tales of the Alhambra. Washington Irving. *Tales of the Alhambra*. 1832; reprint, Barcelona: Editorial escudo de oro, 1981.

Tempest over Mexico. Rosa E. King. *Tempest Over Mexico*. Boston: Little, Brown & Co., 1935.

Tertium Organum. P. D. Ouspensky. *Tertium Organum*. Trans. Nicholas Bessaraboff & Claude Bragdon. 2d ed. London: Kegan Paul, Trench, Trubner & Co., 1923.

Thomas. Hugh Thomas. *The Spanish Civil War*. 1961; 3d ed., rev. Harmondsworth:

Penguin, 1977.

TM. Texas Manuscript: the final draft of *Under the Volcano,* given by Lowry to Gerald Noxon, and now at the University of Texas at Austin.

Transcendental Magic. Éliphas Lévi (Alphonse Louis Constant). *Transcendental Magic: Its Doctrine and Ritual* (1855–56). Trans. A. E. Waite. 1896; reprint, London: Rider & Co., 1968.

UBC. The Lowry manuscripts in Special Collections at the University of British Columbia Library, as itemized by Judith Combs, 1973. A typical entry (UBC 7–2, p. 4) means box 7, file 2, page 4.

Ultramarine. Malcolm Lowry. *Ultramarine.* 1933; rev. ed. Harmondsworth: Penguin, 1974.

Ushant. Conrad Aiken. *Ushant: An Essay.* 1952; reprint, London: W. H. Allen, 1963.

UTV. Malcolm Lowry. *Under the Volcano.* 1947; reprint, Harmondsworth: Penguin, 1962. In the commentary, direct references to *UTV* are to the Penguin edition, but cross-referenced to the 1947 Reynal & Hitchcock edition, the pagination of which is identical to the Cape and Lippincott editions of 1965 (though not to the 1947 Cape edition).

Volunteer in Spain. John Sommerfield. *Volunteer in Spain.* London: Lawrence & Wishart, 1937.

Walker. Ronald G. Walker. *Infernal Paradise: Mexico and the Modern English Novel.* Berkeley and Los Angeles: University of California Press, 1978.

Webb. Jennifer Webb. "The Quest for Unity in Malcolm Lowry." Ph.D. diss., Macquarie University, 1979.

Womack. John J. Womack. *Zapata and the Mexican Revolution.* London: Thames & Hudson, 1969.

Wood. Barry Wood, ed. *Malcolm Lowry: The Writer and His Critics.* Ottawa: Tecumsah Press, 1980.

Woodcock. George Woodcock, ed. *Malcolm Lowry: The Man and His Work.* Vancouver: University of British Columbia Press, 1971.

General Sources

The *Encyclopaedia Britannica* (various editions); the *Encyclopedia Americana;* the *Great Soviet Encyclopedia;* the *Encyclopedia Judaica;* the *Grand Larousse; Brockhaus Enzyklopädie; Meyer's Enzyklopädisches Lexikon; Chamber's Encyclopedia;* the *Enciclopedia de México;* and, above all, the *Encyclopedia universal ilustrada Europea-Americana.*

The *Oxford English Dictionary; Webster's Third New International Dictionary;* the *English Dialect Dictionary;* Eric Partridge's *Origins* and *Dictionary of Slang and Unconventional English;* F. J. Santamaría;s *Diccionaire de Méjicanismos;* the *Diccionario Porrua;* C. M. Ordoño's *Diccionario de la lengua Nahuatl;* Cirlot's *Dictionary of Symbols;* Wilfrid Granville's *A Dictionary of Sailors' Slang.*

Lippincott's Gazetteer; Webster's Geographical Dictionary; The Times Atlas of the World; The Times Atlas of the Moon; the Admiralty Pilots and Sailing Instructions (various editions) for the Red Sea and waters south of Japan; R. H. Allen's *Stars and Their Names;* G. E. Satterthwaite's *Encyclopedia of Astronomy;* the Shell Guides to England and Wales; J. W. Clark's *A Concise Guide to the Town and University of Cambridge.*

Fodor's *Mexico;* Loraine Carlson's *Traveleer Guide to Mexico City;* S. G. Morley's *The Ancient Maya;* Alice Howe's *Cuernavaca;* Miguel Salinas's *Historias y paisajes morelenses;* de Davila's *Paradise in Mexico;* Bernal Díez's *Historia verdadera;* W. H. Prescott's *Conquest of Mexico;* Camargo's *Historia de Tlaxcala;* Gay's *Historia de Oaxaca;* Gary Jenning's *Aztec.*

The *Larousse Mythology;* the series *Man, Myth and Magic,* ed. Richard Cavendish; *Everyman's Dictionary of Non-Classical Mythology;* Sir James Frazer's *The Golden Bough;* Benjamin Walker's *Hindu World;* John Read's *Prelude to Chemistry;* Holmyard's *Alchemy;* Éliphas Lévi's *Transcendental Magic;* Frater Achad's *QBL;* A. E. Waite's *Alchemist through the Ages, The Hermetic Museum, The Holy Kabbalah, The Secret Tradition of Alchemy.*

Halliwell's *The Filmgoer's Companion;* the *Oxford Companion to Film;* Dimmitt's *A Title Guide to the Talkies;* Grove's *Dictionary of Music and Musicians;* the *Oxford Companion to Music;* Brian Rust's *The Complete Entertainment Discography;* Oscar Thompson's *Plots of the Operas;* the W. B. Yeats edition of the *Oxford Book of Modern Verse;* Stevenson's *Quotations;* the *Oxford Dictionary of Classical Literature;* the Oxford companions to English, French, and German Literature; the Penguin *Dictionary of Saints;* the *Dictionary of National Biography.*

Appendix 2. Glossary

The following list includes common words and phrases repeated in the text. Expressions not listed will be found at the appropriate place in the commentary.

Abarrotes, Sp. grocery store, liquor store
abbatoir, Fr. slaughterhouse
adiós, Sp. goodbye
aguardiente, any kind of raw brandy
alacrán, Sp. scorpion
a la Cascada, Sp. to the waterfall
alas, Sp. wings
alemán, Sp. German
allons-nous-en, Fr. let's go
Americano, Sp. American
amigo, Sp. friend
amour propre, Fr. self-esteem
anís, an aniseed-based liquor
aquí, Sp. here
autoridades, Sp. officials
avenida, Sp. avenue; street
ayuntamiento, Sp. town hall, municipal offices

barranca, Sp. ravine
borracho, Sp. drunk, drunkard
botica, Sp. pharmacy
boudin, Fr. black pudding
bruto, Sp. brute
bueno, Sp. good
buenas noches, Sp. good evening
buenas tardes, Sp. good afternoon
buenas días, Sp. good morning

caballo, Sp. horse
cabrón, Sp. billy goat; cuckold
cacos, Sp. bad
calle, Sp. street

camión, Sp. truck, bus
cantina, Sp. bar
cartero, Sp. postman
cassis, Fr. black currant
cerveza, Sp. beer
cervecería, Sp. brewery
charros, Sp. cowboys
chingar, Sp. to fuck, to rape
ciné, Sp. cinema
cinquenta centavos, Sp. fifty cents
cinquenta dos, Sp. fifty-two
claro, Sp. clearly, you understand
comida, Sp. meal
comisaría de Policia, Sp. commissioner of police
comment?, Fr. how?, what?
¿como no?, Sp. and why not?
¿como se llama?, Sp. what's your name?
como tu quieras, Sp. as you wish
compañero, Sp. comrade
comprenez?, Fr. do you understand?
con permiso, Sp. with your permission
¿cuanto?, Sp. how much?
¿cui bono?, L. to whom the good?, what's the good?

de nada, Sp. not at all
descompuesto, Sp. broken down, out of order
despedida, Sp. parting, separation
diablo, Sp. devil; what the devil
dolente... dolore, It. sorrow, grief
dos, Sp. two

escritor, Sp. writer
es inevitable, Sp. it is inevitable
españa, Sp. Spain
español, Sp. Spanish
esposa, Sp. wife

¿es suyo?, Sp. Is this yours?
estupido, Sp. fool
evite que sus hijos lo destruyan, Sp.
    See that your children don't destroy
    it
exactemente, Sp. exactly
excusado, Sp. toilet

feuerstick, Nor. match
fiesta, Sp. festival
frijoles, Sp. beans

gaseosa, Sp. mineral water
gracias, Sp. thank you
guapa, Sp. dashing

habanero, a rum-like aguardiente
hacienda, Sp. ranch
hasta la vista, Sp. farewell
hombre, Sp. man; my friend
hombre noble, Sp. a good man

Il vient d'arriver, Fr. he has just arrived
infierno, Sp. inferno
inglese, Sp. English

jefe, Sp. chief, boss
Juden, Ger. Jew

la légion étrangère, Fr. the Foreign
    Legion
¿le gusta este jardin?, Sp. Do you like
    this garden?

madrugada, Sp. dawn
malos, Sp. evil
manos de Orlac (Las), Sp. The Hands
    of Orlac
mère, Fr. mother
mescal de ollo, Sp. mescal from the
    gourd
mescalito, Sp. a little mescal
mingitorio, Sp. urinal
mismo, Sp. same
momentito, Sp. a little moment; just a
    moment

muchacha, Sp. a little girl
muchas gracias, Sp. many thanks
mucho dinero, Sp. a lot of money
muy borracho, Sp. very drunk
muy complicado, Sp. very complicated
muy correcto, Sp. very proper; most
    fitting
muy fuerte, Sp. very strong
muy hermosa, Sp. very pretty
muy sabroso, Sp. very tasty

nada, Sp. nothing
naturalamente, Sp. naturally
noch ein, Ger. one more
no pasarán, Sp. they shall not pass
norteamericano, Sp. North American
no se permite fijar anuncios, Sp. post
    no bills
no se puede vivir sin amar, Sp. one
    cannot live without loving

ochas, a hot drink, infused with raw
    spirits
ocho pesos cincuenta, Sp. eight pesos
    fifty centavos
oiga, Sp. listen
otro mescalito, Sp. another small
    mescal
otro tequila, Sp. another tequila

paraiso, Sp. paradise
pasaporte, Sp. passport
peluquería, Sp. hairdresser's
peon, Sp. peasant
perfectamente borracho, Sp. totally
    drunk
perro, Sp. dog
persona non grata, L. unwanted, not
    welcome
pobrecito, Sp. poor little thing
poco, Sp. little
poco a poco, Sp. little by little
policía, Sp. police, policeman
policía de Seguridad, Sp. Security
    police
poquito, Sp. small, tiny

por favor, Sp. please
¿por que?, Sp. why?
¿por que no?, Sp. And why not?
positivamente, Sp. positively, absolutely
precisamente, Sp. precisely
préservatifs, Fr. condoms
progresión al culo, Sp. progression to the bottom
progresión a ratos, Sp. gradual progression
pulque, an alcoholic beer, made from the maguey cactus
pulquería, a cantina selling pulque
pulques finos, Sp. fine pulques

que es suyo, Sp. which is yours
¿que haceis aquí?, Sp. What are you doing here?
¡Que hombre!, Sp. What a man!
¿que hora?, Sp. What is the time?
Qué tal, Sp. hello
¿quien sabe?, Sp. who knows?
¿quiere usted la salvación de Mexico?, Sp. Do you want the salvation of Mexico?
¿quiere usted que Cristo sea nuestro Rey?, Sp. Do you want Christ to be our King?

rebozo, Sp. a shawl
rurales, Sp. vigilante police

salida, Sp. exit
salud y pesetas, Sp. health and wealth
serape, a large shawl

simpatico, Sp. sympathetic
sinarquistas, a fascist military organization

también, Sp. also
tequila anejo, Sp. old tequila
todes contentos y yo también, Sp. Everybody happy, including me
tostón, a coin worth 50 centavos

unión militar, Sp. military union

vámonos, Sp. let's go
verdad, Sp. true; is that so?
vero, Sp. true
via Dolorosa, It. Street of Sorrows
vida impersonal, Sp. the impersonal life
videre, L. to see
viejos, Sp. old men
vino, Sp. wine
viva el Cristo Rey, Sp. Long live Christ the King

y tiempo para gastarlas, Sp. and time to enjoy them

xopilotes, Sp. vultures

zacuali, the tower on Jacques's house
zócalo, the central plaza of a town

Note. The unit of Mexican currency is the peso. 1 peso = 100 centavos. In 1938, the peso was worth $0.22 U.S.

Appendix 3.

The Cabbala: This diagram, taken from Frater Achad's *QBL,* illustrates the thirty-two "paths and spheres of the Holy Cabbala," relates each to its respective Tarot card, and gives each the numerological and astrological significance that Lowry sometimes makes use of.

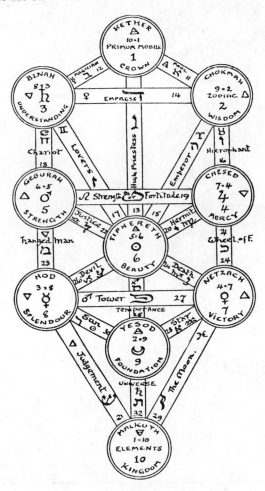

Tree of Life with Correspondences.

Appendix 4. Maps

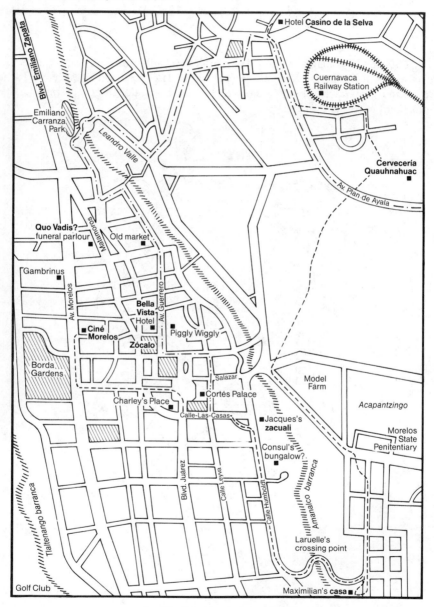

1. The Town of Cuernavaca.

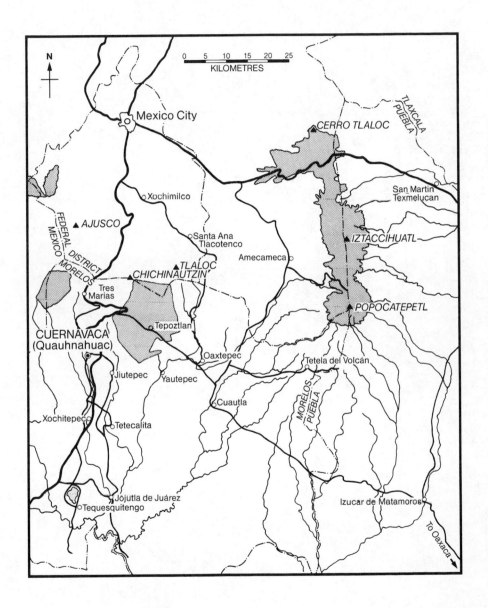

2. The Valley of Morelos.

INDEX

(Compiled by Chris Ackerley)

This index has been designed as a complement to the rest of the text. While it lists recurrent words, references, and motifs in *Under the Volcano,* it also tries to suggest further correspondences that were inappropriate within the commentary. Thus, under the heading of *Paris* will be found an entry 288.6 (Paris, the abductor of Helen), and 347.1 (Abélard and Héloise): such entries should not be taken immediately as evidence of a *Pale Fire* mentality in the compositor, but are intended to suggest that the theme of *betrayal* associated with *Paris* and *Robinson* has further manifestations and correspondences latent in the text or sub-text. Entries in italics are of greater significance. I have tried to list all recurrent motifs and references of a literary nature; references to people, places, facts and things appear only if they can be construed as somehow "thematic," that is, if their significance within the text is such as to exert an influence over parts and details to which they do not explicitly refer. Lowry's method was essentially "poetic" in this respect, and the use of the Index may help find the way through his forest of symbols.